Geert Mak

IN EUROPE

Geert Mak is among the most popular writers in the Netherlands, the author of numerous best-selling books of nonfiction. He lives in Amsterdam.

ALSO BY

Geert Mak

Jorwerd: The Death of the Village in Late Twentieth-Century Europe

Amsterdam: A Brief Life of the City

Geert Mak

In Europe

Travels Through the Twentieth Century

TRANSLATED
FROM THE DUTCH
BY

Sam Garrett

VINTAGE BOOKS
A Division of Random House, Inc.
New York

For Mietsie

FIRST VINTAGE BOOKS EDITION, JUNE 2008

Translation copyright © 2007, 2008 by Sam Garrett

All rights reserved. Published in the United States by Vintage Books, a division of Random House, Inc., New York, and in Canada by Random House of Canada Limited, Toronto. Originally published in the Netherlands as In Europa by Uitgeverij Atlas, Amsterdam. Copyright © 2004 by Geert Mak. First published in translation in Great Britain by Harvill Secker, an imprint of Random House Group Ltd., London, and subsequently published in hardcover in the United States by Pantheon Books, a division of Random House, Inc., New York, in 2007. This edition includes a translation of an unpublished epilogue by Geert Mak, copyright © by Geert Mak.

Vintage and colophon are registered trademarks of Random House, Inc.

The Library of Congress has cataloged the Pantheon edition as follows:
Mak, Geert.
[In Europa. English]
In Europe : travels through the twentieth century /
Geert Mak.
p. cm.
Includes bibliographical references and index.
1. Europe—History—20th century. 2. Europe—
Description and travel. 3. Mak, Geert—Travel—Europe. 4. Journalists—Netherlands—
Diaries. 5. Historians—Netherlands—Diaries. I. Title.
D424M3513 2007
940.5—dc22
2007009260

Vintage ISBN: 978-0-307-28057-2

Author photograph © Bob Bronshof/Hollandse Hoogte
Maps by Peter Palm, Berlin, Germany

www.vintagebooks.com

Printed in the United States of America
10 9 8 7 6 5 4 3 2

Contents

CONTENTS

A man sets out to chart the world. Through the years, he peoples a space with images of provinces, kingdoms, mountains, bays, ships, islands, fishes, rooms, tools, stars, horses and people. Shortly before his death he discovers that the patient labyrinth of lines traces the images of his own face.

Jorge Luis Borges

Prologue

NO ONE IN THE VILLAGE HAD EVER SEEN THE SEA — EXCEPT FOR THE DUTCH PEOPLE, the mayor and Jósef Puszka, who had been there during the war. The houses were built along a little brook; a handful of yellowed, crumbling farms, green gardens, bright apple trees, two little churches, old willows and oaks, wooden fences, chickens, dogs, children, Hungarians, Swabians, Gypsies.

The storks had left by now. Their nests lay silent and empty atop the chimneys. The summer was in afterglow, the mayor sweated as he cut back the municipal grass. There was not a mechanical sound to be heard: only voices, a dog, a rooster, a gaggle of geese overhead, a wooden wagon creaking down the road, the mayor's scythe. Later in the afternoon the ovens were lit; a thin blue veil of smoke floated across the rooftops. Now and then a pig squealed.

These were the final months of the millennium, and I was travelling back and forth through Europe for one year. The paper I worked for, the NRC Handelsblad, had commissioned me to do so, and my pieces appeared each day in the bottom right-hand corner of the front page. It was to be a sort of final inspection: what shape was the continent in, here at the conclusion of the twentieth century? At the same time, it was to be a historical journey: I would follow, as far as possible, the course of history, in search of the traces it had left behind. I did indeed find the silent witnesses, dozens of them: an overgrown crater on the Somme, a machine-gunned doorpost in Berlin's Oranienburger Strasse, a snowy forest outside Vilnius, a newspaper archive in Munich, a hillside near Barcelona, a small red and white sandal at Auschwitz. This journey also had something to do with me. I needed to get out, to cross borders, to find out what it meant, that misty term 'Europe'.

Europe, as I saw in the course of that year, is a continent in which one can easily travel back and forth through time. All the different stages of the twentieth century are being lived, or relived, somewhere. Aboard Istanbul's ferries it is always 1948. In Lisbon it is forever 1956. At the Gare de Lyon in Paris, the year is 2020. In Budapest, the young men wear our fathers' faces.

In this southern Hungarian village of Vásárosbéc, time had stopped in 1925. Around two hundred people lived there in 1999. A quarter of them or more were Gypsies. They lived off their meagre unemployment benefits – about sixty euros a month – and the women went door to door selling baskets and nondescript wares. Their homes were falling apart, the doors were lengths of cloth, and sometimes even the frames had disappeared, stoked for warmth during a cold winter.

Even poorer were the Rumanian Gypsies, who showed up in the village occasionally in their wooden caravans. And poorer than poor were the wandering Albanian Gypsies. They were, in fact, the pariahs among the community of the poor, the absolute rock bottom of the European barrel.

I was staying with friends. They had moved into the house of the village barber, Jósef Puszka, after he died. In the attic they had found a little notebook full of pencil scratches from spring 1945, and the names of places like Ålborg, Lübeck, Stuttgart and Berlin. Someone had deciphered a few lines of it for my friends:

In the prisoner of war camp, Hagenau. Oh, my God, I have no one in this world. When I get back, there may not even be a girl left for me in the village. I'm like a little bird chirping far away. No dear mother to look after that little bird. Oh, my God, please help me get home, to my father and mother. So far from my country, such a long walk away from everyone.

In the middle of the village, along a muddy path, I stumbled upon a weathered block of concrete, a humble monument, decorated with the figure of something like a knight, and two dates – 1914 and 1918 – at the top. Below that, thirty-six names, thirty-six boys, enough to fill the village café.

1999 was the year of the euro, of the general proliferation of the mobile phone, of Internet for all and sundry, of bridges bombed at Novi Sad, of jubilant stock markets in Amsterdam and London, of the hottest September in living memory, of the fear that the millennium bug would drive all computers crazy on 1 January.

In Vásárosbéc, 1999 was the last year the ragman made his rounds with horse and cart. I had the good fortune of being there on that historic day: he had bought himself a truck. That same spring, four unemployed Gypsies had begun work paving yet another stretch of the sandy road, perhaps even with a layer of tarmac this time. And the bell-ringer was sacked; he had stolen a pension cheque that belonged to the mayor's mother. That, too, was 1999.

In the café I met them all: the mayor, Crazy Maria, the toothless man (also known as 'the Spy'), the village lush, the Gypsies, the postman's wife who lived with her cow. There was no getting around being introduced to the veteran, a big friendly man in a camouflage outfit who kept his nightmares at bay with alcohol and dubious toadstools. He spoke French, everyone said, but the only word of it I ever heard him utter was 'Marseille'.

Later that same evening, the new bell-ringer and the man who collected the rubbish sang songs from long ago, and everyone beat out the rhythm on the tables:

> We laboured in the forest,
> High upon the crack of dawn
> With the day still full of foggy dew
> We worked among the fallen trunks,
> High on the slopes, the horses strained

and:

> We worked on the railroad from Budapest to Pécs
> The bright new blinking railroad
> Blasted through rock, the tunnel at Pécs

Travelling across Europe, all those months, had been like peeling off layers of old paint. More than ever I realised how, generation upon generation, a shell of distance and alienation had developed between Eastern and Western Europeans.

Do we Europeans have a common history? Of course, everyone can rattle their way down the list: Roman Empire, Renaissance, Reformation, Enlightenment, 1914, 1945, 1989. But then one need only look at the enormous differences in the way that history has been experienced by individual Europeans: the older Polish truck driver I spoke to, who had been forced four times in his life to learn a new language; the German couple, bombed out of their home and then endlessly driven from place to place throughout Eastern Europe; the Basque family that fell apart one Christmas Eve arguing about the Spanish Civil War, and never spoke to each other again; the serene satisfaction of the Dutch, the Danes and the Swedes, who have usually avoided catching the full brunt of History. Put a group of Russians, Germans, Britons, Czechs and Spaniards at one table and have them recite their family histories: they are worlds unto themselves. Yet, even so, it is all Europe.

The history of the twentieth century, after all, was not a play performed before their eyes, but a major or minor part of their – and our – own lives. 'We are a part of this century. This century is a part of us,' Eric Hobsbawm wrote at the outset of his magisterial history of the twentieth century. To him, for example, 30 January, 1933 was not only the day Hitler became chancellor, but also the wintry afternoon in Berlin when a fifteen-year-old boy walked home from school with his sister and, somewhere along the way, saw a newspaper billboard. 'I still see it before me, as in a dream.'

For my own elderly Aunt Maart in Schiedam, who was seven at the time, 3 August, 1914 – the day the First World War broke out – was a warm Monday that suddenly took on something oppressive. Workers stood around in little groups in front of their houses, women wiped their eyes with a corner of their aprons, and a man shouted to a friend: 'Hey, it's war!'

For Winrich Behr, one of those whose story is included in this book, the fall of Stalingrad was the telegram he received as a German liaison officer: '31.01.07.45 Uhr Russe vor der Tür. Wir bereiten Zerstörung vor/ APL 6. Oa/ 31.1.07.45 Uhr Wir Zerstören. AOK6.'

For twelve-year-old Ira Klejner of St Petersburg (Leningrad then), 6 March, 1953, the day Stalin's death was announced, meant a kitchen in a communal household, her fear that she would not be able to weep, and her relief when a tear at last rolled down her cheek, into the yolk of the fried egg she was eating.

For me, a nine-year-old, November 1956 smelled of red peppers, strange dishes brought to our sedate, canal-side home in Leeuwaarden by Hungarian refugees, quiet, shy people who learned Dutch by reading Donald Duck comics.

Now the twentieth century has itself become history, our personal history and that of the films, books and museums. As I write, the backdrops to the stage of international affairs are changing quickly. Seats of power shift, alliances break down, fresh coalitions arise, new priorities take pride of place.

Vásárosbéc is preparing for its country's entry into the European Union. Within the space of three years, six more Dutch people have arrived and bought at least a dozen houses. Most of them are attracted by the low prices in Eastern Europe, several of them probably prompted in their exodus by a problem, the sort of people with a past one runs into everywhere at the continent's edge: back taxes, a disastrous divorce, a bankrupt business, trouble with the law.

In one of the Dutch people's gardens stands a huge German eagle made of plaster, on a wall at one side of the house the owner has had his portrait painted, on horseback, waving a cowboy hat, ready to tame the Wild East. Another Dutchman spent more than 100,000 euros to have his home transformed into a little mansion, where he spends three weeks each year. The rest of the time the house stands empty. He has made one minor miscalculation, though: his nearest neighbour is the village's robber headman, who lives with his eight children in what is more or less a pigsty. This neighbour has carefully begun testing the locked shutters of the Dutchman's El Dorado. His children already cavort in the man's pool.

In the café they asked my friend what it means, this 'new Europe'. After the Gypsy on the shrieking accordion had been silenced, he explained that, in the course of history, this part of Europe had become increasingly poor, that everyone looked up to wealthy and powerful Western Europe, and that it was only natural that they should now want to be a part of it.

But first, my wise friend told them, you will have to go through a deep valley of even greater poverty, so that in the ten years that follow you may perhaps be able to climb up to the subsistence level of the West. 'And what's more, you're going to lose some very precious things: friendship, the ability to get by without a lot of money, the skills to repair things that are broken, the freedom to raise your own pigs and slaughter them as you see fit, the freedom to burn as much timber as you like . . . any number of other things.'

'What?' they asked him. 'No more slaughtering our own pigs? No more burning wood?' They looked at him in disbelief. At that time they did not know that, before long, they wouldn't be allowed to smoke in the café either. 'The bell-ringer walked out during my story,' my friend wrote to us. 'I can hear him ringing the church bell right now, to mark the setting sun. There are some things that go on unchanged.'

The world order of the twentieth century – in so far as one can speak of 'order' at all – seems to be gone for good. Save that: Berlin can never be understood without Versailles, nor London without Munich, Vichy without Verdun, Moscow without Stalingrad, Bonn without Dresden, Vásárosbéc without Yalta, Amsterdam without Auschwitz.

The bell-ringer, Crazy Maria, Winrich Behr, Ira Klejner, the mayor, the toothless man, my old Aunt Maart, my wise friend – every one of us, whether we like it or not, carries with us the amazing twentieth century. The stories will continue to make the rounds in whispers, generation after generation, the countless experiences and dreams, the moments of courage and betrayal, the memories full of fear and pain, the images of joy.

In Europe

I January 1900–14

Finland
Helsinki
St Petersburg

Riga

Moscow

Witebsk

Kaunas

Königsberg
Minsk

RUSSIA

Bug

Brest-Litovsk

Warsaw

Kiev

Rowno

Dniepr

Don

Volga

Chernowitz

Dniestr

Bug

Sea
of Azov

udapest

Crimea
Kertch

Sukhumi

UNGARY

RUMANIA

Black
Sea

Batoum

Danube

Bucharest

Kars

Belgrade

SERBIA

BULGARIA

Trabzon

Erzurum

Sofia
Eastern-
Rumelia

ONTE-
EGRO

Constantinople

OTTOMAN EMPIRE

Euphrates

Tigris

Saloniki

Gallipoli

Athens

GREECE

Cyprus

Crete

Mediterranean

⟵ Geert Mak's Route

0   100   200   300 km

Chapter One

Amsterdam

WHEN I LEFT AMSTERDAM ON MONDAY MORNING, 4 JANUARY, 1999, a storm was rampaging through the town. The wind made ripples on the watery cobblestones, white horses on the River IJ, and whistled beneath the high iron roof of Central Station. For a moment I thought that God's hand had momentarily tilted up all that iron, then set it back in place.

I was dragging my big, black suitcase. In it was a laptop, a mobile phone I could use to dispatch my daily columns, a few shirts, a sponge bag, a CD-ROM of the *Encyclopaedia Britannica*, and at least fifteen books to soothe my nerves. My plan was to begin with the baroque cities of 1900, with the lightness of the Paris World's Fair, with Queen Victoria's reign over an empire of certainties, with the upsurge of Berlin.

The air was full of noises: the slapping of the waves, the crying of gulls on the wind, the roaring of the storm through the bare treetops, the trams, the traffic. There was very little light. The clouds chased across the sky from west to east, like dark-grey riders. For a moment they wafted a few notes along with them, the floating single strokes of a carillon. The newspapers reported that Morse code had now been phased out completely, and that the slipstreams of low-flying Ilyushins at Oostend airbase regularly sucked tiles off the neighbouring roofs. On the financial markets, the euro had made a brilliant debut. 'Euro kicks off with challenge to dollar's hegemony' was *Le Monde*'s headline, and that morning the currency had briefly risen as high as $1.19. But Holland that day was ruled by the wind, the last, untamed force that left its mark in all directions, north-east, south-west, a persistent slamming that had shaped the lakes and polders, the course of canals, the dykes, the roads and even the railway track along which I rode south, into the wet polder landscape.

The boy with the blue tie and the pleasant face sitting beside me snapped open his computer right away, conjured up a whole series of spreadsheets and began phoning his colleagues. His name was Peter Smithuis. 'The Germans want a hundred per cent solution, the other Europeans only need seventy-five,' he spoke into the void. 'What we can do now is look for something like a seventy-five-plus option, and neutralise the Germans by putting them back at a hundred per cent anyway . . . Oh, mmm. Off stream since July? Be careful, you know how it goes, if we let them decide too fast, everything will grind to a halt.'

The rain clattered against the windows of the compartment, under the Moerdijk Bridge the ships danced on the waves, at Zevenbergen a tree was in very early blossom, a thousand red dots in the water. Beyond Roosendaal the pylons became rusty, the only trace of a border between prim Holland and the rest of Europe.

Before I had left I had a long talk with the oldest Dutchman I knew. Of all the people I spoke to that year, he was the only one who had lived through the entire century (with the exception of Alexandra Vasilyeva, that is, who was born in 1897 and had actually seen the czar and made her glorious stage debut at the Mariinsky theatre).

His name was Marinus van der Goes van Naters, but people called him 'the Red nobleman'. He was born in 1900 and had once played a prominent role in the Dutch Social Democratic Party.

He told me about Nijmegen, where, when he was growing up, a total of two cars cruised the streets: one De Dion-Bouton and one Spijker, both handcrafted down to the last detail. 'My brother and I would run to the window whenever one of them came by.' He had never been particularly fond of those first car owners. 'They were the same people you see these days talking into portable telephones.'

On class relations: 'At a certain point we became completely enraptured by the new social order that was on its way. We wanted to talk to a worker, but we didn't know any. Through acquaintances of an acquaintance we finally met a worker's wife, who read something aloud to us from a newspaper. I still wonder why, if we wanted to meet one so badly, we didn't just go up to a worker on the street and talk to him!'

On technology: 'My friend and I were always fascinated by the phenomenon of electricity. We had read an adventure novel that talked about a machine you could use to talk to people without wires, no matter how far away they were. That seemed unbelievable to us. We installed lights, built telephones we could use to talk to each other two rooms away, we made sparks fly, we invented things, real inventions!'

My host took a book down from the shelf, its pages loose with age and use. Edward Bellamy, *In het jaar 2000*, Amsterdam 1890. 'This is what we talked about, things like this.' The story is a simple one: a nineteenth-century man falls into a deep sleep after being hypnotised and does not wake up until the year 2000. He finds himself in a city full of statues, fountains, covered walkways, gentlemen in top hats, ladies in evening dress. Thanks to electrical light, there is no more darkness. Night has been banished. Every home has a listening device, connected by an open telephone line to one of the municipal concert halls.

'Here, read what one of those twentieth-century creatures says here: "At home we have comfort, but we seek the glory of life within society itself." That was the kind of world we were looking for, in the year 2000. Money would no longer play any role. Every citizen would be safeguarded against "hunger, cold and nakedness", products and services would be exchanged by means of an ingenious credit system, food prepared in huge, communal restaurants and delivered, if need be, by tube mail. The boys would be "sturdy", the girls "fresh and strong", the sexes would be free and informal in their dealings with each other, private shops would disappear, there would be no more advertising, publishing houses would be collectivised, newspaper editors would be elected by their readers, criminality and greed abolished, and – read for yourself – even the "crudest of individuals" would adopt "the comportment of the civilised classes". Here, this passage: "Kneeling, my countenance bowed to the earth, I confessed in tears my unworthiness to breathe the air of this golden age. The long and sorrowful winter of mankind has come to an end. The heavens have opened to us." What a book!'

The wintry light fell on the yellowed wallpaper of the study, the faded books on the shelf, the standing lamp with its cloth shade and tassels, my host's strong hands, slightly spotted skin, his clear eyes.

'What do I think about this century, now that it's over? Ah, a century is only a mathematical construct, a human fantasy, isn't it? Back then I thought in terms of months, a year at the most. Now I think in twenty-year spans, that seems like nothing to me any more. Growing so immoderately old spoils one. Time no longer fazes you . . .'

Chapter Two

Paris

THE NEW CENTURY WAS A WOMAN, THEY WERE ALL IN AGREEMENT on that back in 1900. Take, for example, the drawing on the cover of the piano music for the English song 'Dawn of the Century', a 'march & two step' by one E. M. Paul. Amid golden clouds a woman balances on a winged wheel, around her float a tram, a typewriter, a telephone, a sewing machine, a camera, a harvester, a railway engine and, at the bottom of the picture, there is even a car turning the corner.

The European metropolises were feminine as well, if only in the lavish shapes of the thousands of little palaces of the bourgeoisie along the new boulevards and residential streets, with their curlicues and garlands in every 'neo' style imaginable, a ruttish profusion still found from Berlin to Barcelona.

So too the cover of the catalogue for the 1900 Paris World's Fair: a woman, of course, a rather hefty one this time, her hair blowing in the wind, a banner in her hand. Above the gate to the fairgrounds, a plaster woman six metres tall, in a wide cloak and evening dress by the couturier Paquin. At the official opening, Émile Loubet, the French president, spoke of the virtues of the new century: justice and human kindness. His minister of employment expected even more good things: gentleness and solidarity.

The fifty million visitors traipsed from one miracle to the next. There were X-ray machines with which you could look right through men and women, there was an automobile exhibition, there was equipment for wireless telegraphy, and from outside the gates one could catch the first underground line of Le Métro, built in less than eighteen months from Porte de Vincennes to Porte Maillot. Forty countries took part. California had dug an imitation gold mine, Egypt came with a temple and an antique tomb, Great Britain showed off all the colonies of its empire, Germany had a steam locomotive that could travel at 120 kph. France exhibited a model of Clément Ader's motorised flying machine, a gigantic bat with a thirty-metre wingspan; humans, after all, were destined to leave the earth one day.

There was a Dance Palace where a wide variety of ballets were performed, a Grand Palais full of French paintings and sculpture, and a building where the visitor could 'travel' around the entire world on a special ceiling for two francs, from the blossoming orchards of Japan by way of the Acropolis to the coasts of Spain, all depicted with extreme skill by the painter Dumoulin and his team. There was a cineorama, a variation on the panorama, where one could revel in the view from an airship or a compartment aboard the Trans-Siberian Express. The military section displayed the newest technologies in warfare: the machine gun, the torpedo, the gun turret, wireless telegraphy equipment, the personnel carrier. And completely new were the shows at the phono-cinema theatre, with newsreels accompanied by a phonograph recording. Among other things, the shaky images filmed by the Pathé Brothers showed – extra! – the Rostand family in their box at the premiere of *L'Aiglon*, and other sensations of the day: the test flight of Graf Zeppelin's first airship, the opening of a railway line through Africa, new cotton mills in Manchester, victorious Englishmen in the course of the Boer War, a speech by the kaiser, the launching of a battle cruiser.

The map in the catalogue provides a bird's-eye view of the impressive fair grounds: from the Grand Palais, along the lanes of pavilions on both banks of the Seine, to the Eiffel Tower and the great exhibition halls on the Champ de Mars. The World's Fair was a part of the city as a whole. Or, put differently, Paris with its boulevards laid out from 1853 under the prefecture of Georges Haussmann blended seamlessly with the fair, because Paris had become a permanent exhibition in itself, the grand display window of France, the city state of the new century. And both – as the photographs in the catalogue also show – were created for the new urbanite par excellence, the boulevardier, the actor/viewer of the theatre of the street, the young people on an allowance, the noble property owner, the wealthy officer, the youthful bourgeois relieved of all financial concerns.

'The weather is so warm, so lovely, that I go outside again after dinner, even though I feel fatigue coming on,' noted the young writer André Gide in the summer of 1905. 'First along the Champs-Élysées, strutting past the *cafés-concerts*, I bustle through to the rotunda, then turn back along the Élysées again; the crowd is partying, in greater numbers and with greater cheer, all the way to the rue Royale.'

On other days he rides the roof rack of an omnibus, walks in the Bois de Boulogne, visits the opera, then heads back to a new exhibition featuring Gauguin, Van Gogh and Cézanne, 'impossible not to visit the Louvre these days'.

The boulevardier's haven was the café, the marble table with kirsch and hot chocolate and friends all around, the democratic successor to the aristocratic salon. His prime trait was an infallible sense of timing: to be found in the best establishment at the best moment. The urban stroller moved between the old age and the new, plunging into the anonymity of the crowd, then falling back into the old security of one's own class. It was a way of life that showed up everywhere in the literature of the day, a modern courtliness that conquered every major European city.

André Gide, 1 September, 1905: 'I am swept off my feet, I let myself be carried along by this monotone flow, dragged along by the course of the days. A great lethargy overtakes me, from the moment I arise to the evening hour; the game saves me at times, but gradually I lose my normal life.'

I stroll from the Champ de Mars along the Seine and the roaring traffic on both banks to the boarded-up entrance of the Grand Palais, which is now being restored. Big neon letters on the Eiffel Tower read '347 days till the year 2000'. Of the old World's Fair, the Grand Palais and the Petit Palais are still standing, and of course the Pont Alexandre III, with its four pillars at the corners, gigantic golden horses atop those, and along the edges a lacework of bronze lanterns with glass like cut diamonds.

In that same April in which the Pont Alexandre III and the 1900 World's Fair were opened, the anti-Semitic daily *La Libre Parole* took up a collection to present a pair of rapiers to the Jew-hater Raphaël Viau, to commemorate his twelfth duel 'for the good cause'. Viau expressed his hope that the blades 'would not long remain unsullied'.

Around the turn of the century, three major scandals rocked Europe's capitals. They were cracks in the façade, the first fissures in that steadfast world of rank and class. In London, in 1895, there was the conviction of the brilliant writer Oscar Wilde for perversity. In Berlin, a similar scandal took place in the period 1907–9 concerning Prince Philipp zu Eulenburg, former ambassador to Vienna and one of the German emperor's intimate friends. But the scandal with the greatest impact was the Dreyfus affair.

No other issue occupied the French more intensely between 1897–9 than the possible rehabilitation of the unjustly accused Alfred Dreyfus. This Jewish army captain had been banished to Devil's Island for allegedly having spied for the Germans. Gradually, however, it became increasingly clear that officers of the war council had tampered with his dossier and then, to refute the rising groundswell of suspicion, had continued to pile forgery upon forgery. The nation's military command knew about it, but refused to budge. To admit to such fraud would be tantamount to blasphemy, and would cast a taint on the *gloire militaire*.

Before long the affair was being monitored breathlessly all over Europe. After Émile Zola forced a reopening of the case on 13 January, 1898 – his fiery 'J'Accuse!' in L'Aurore was intended primarily to provoke charges of libel – scores of other European writers and intellectuals became involved. What was more important? The rights of the individual, or the prestige of the army and the nation? The progressive principles of the Enlightenment, or the old values of the counter-revolution, of the days of glory from before 1789?

The Dreyfus affair, as historian Barbara Tuchman put it, was 'the death-struggle of the old world'. 'In those years, life seemed to have been temporarily suspended,' wrote the future prime minister, Léon Blum. It was 'a human crisis, not as far-reaching or long-lasting as the French Revolution, but no less violent for that ... It was as though the whole world revolved around one affair, and in the most intimate feelings and personal relationships all was interrupted, all was disrupted, all was seen through different eyes.'

Friends stopped seeing each other: Dreyfus lay between them like a live grenade. Family members avoided each other. Famous salons fell asunder. A certain M. Pistoul, manufacturer of wooden crates, was taken to court by his mother-in-law after a family row over Dreyfus. He had called her an '*intellectuelle*'; she had accused him of being a 'monster' and a 'traitor'; he had struck her; her daughter had filed for divorce. During Dreyfus' retrial, Marcel Proust sat in the public gallery each day with coffee and sandwiches, so as not to miss a moment. He and his brother Robert helped to circulate a petition, 'The Intellectuals' Protest', and collected 3,000 signatures, including those of that notable arbiter of good taste Anatole France, and of André Gide and Claude Monet. For Monet, the petition meant the end of his friendship with his colleague Edgar Degas, and an enraged M. Proust Sr refused to speak to either of his sons for a week.

The Dreyfus scandal, like those surrounding Oscar Wilde and Philipp zu Eulenburg, had been drawn to the public's attention by a newspaper. And it was, above all, a clash of the papers. The affair's unprecedented vitality was due to the phenomenon of the 'high-circulation daily' appearing all over Europe, sensation-hungry papers with hundreds of thousands of readers and a distribution network that stretched to the remotest corners of the country. Around the turn of the century, Paris alone had between twenty-five and thirty-five dailies reporting and creating a wide variety of news. Berlin had sixty papers, twelve of which appeared twice a day. In London, the *Daily Mail* cost twopence, and had a circulation of 500,000: eleven times that of the staid and respectable *Times*. There arose in this way a new force, the force of 'public opinion', and it did not take the newspaper magnates long to learn to play on popular sentiment like a church organ. They inflated rumours and glossed over facts, everything was allowable for the purposes of higher sales, political gain or the pure adrenaline of making the news.

Yet the question remains: why was French public opinion so susceptible to this particular affair? Anti-Semitism definitely played a part. The anti-Dreyfus papers ran columns every day about the perfidious role of the 'syndicate', a burgeoning conspiracy of Jews, Freemasons, socialists and foreigners who were out to tear France apart with their deception, lies, bribery and forgeries. When Dreyfus was first court-martialled, the crowd at the courthouse gates shouted '*À mort! À mort les juifs!*' The Viennese *Neue Freie Presse*'s Jewish correspondent in Paris was so shocked that he went home and penned the first sentences of his tract *Der Judenstaat*: the Jews had to be given a country of their own. The correspondent's name was Theodor Herzl. And so the first seed of what was to become the state of Israel sprouted here, at the Dreyfus trial.

But that was not all. What was really taking place, in fact, was a collision between two Frances: the old, static France of the status quo, and the modern, dynamic France of the press, public debate, justice and truth. Between the France of the palaces, in other words, and the France of the boulevards.

Strangely enough, the affair also blew over almost as quickly as it had arisen. On 9 September, 1899 Dreyfus was convicted once more, despite obvious tampering with the evidence. Europe was stunned to discover that such things were possible in an enlightened France. 'Scandalous, cynical, disgusting and barbaric,' the correspondent for *The Times* wrote. The French began to realise that the affair was damaging their country in the eyes of international opinion – and on the eve of a world's fair that was to be the biggest ever held. Dreyfus was offered a pardon and accepted it, too tired to fight on.

In 1906 the army rehabilitated him. He was promoted to the rank of major and received the *Légion d'honneur*. Zola died in 1902; in 1908 his ashes were interred at the Panthéon. Once free, Dreyfus himself proved less idealistic than those who had fought for him. 'We were prepared to die for Dreyfus,' one of his most avid supporters later said. 'But Dreyfus himself was not.' Years later, when a group of intellectuals asked him to sign a petition to save the lives of Sacco and Vanzetti – two American victims of a political process – he flew into a rage: he wanted nothing more to do with such affairs.

During my first few days in Paris, I take as my guide a copy of the 1896 Baedeker. In it, the avenue Jean-Jaurès is still the rue d'Allemagne, the Sacré-Coeur is still under construction, the most important painter of the day is Louis Meissonier, and the vanes of the Moulin de Galette have only recently stopped turning. I hail one of the 13,000 *fiacres*, or hop aboard one of the forty omnibus lines crossing the city. Everything works and moves by horse-power, tens of thousands of horses for the cabs, omnibuses, carts and coaches, my entire city guide smells of horse. And all those horses must be stabled and fed – hence the hay and oats markets – and watered – there are 2,000 city fountains – to say nothing of disposing of all that manure.

The days have been sunny and mild. From my hotel window I look out over the roofs of Montmartre, the ruins of an old windmill, the misty hills in the distance. Beneath my window are a few old gardens with tall trees, a house with a sun porch, the early spring sounds of the black-birds, sparrows and starlings. Darkness falls gradually. Between the roofs and the grey of the evening sky, more and more yellow lights appear. The city hums quietly.

> The waters are blue and the plants are pink; the evening is sweet
> to behold;
> People go walking.
> The big ladies go walking; behind them, the little ladies.

It was with this ode to Paris, written by the Vietnamese Nguyen Trong Hiep in 1897, that the wandering European writer Walter Benjamin begins his essay 'The Capital of the Nineteenth Century'. Why did he – and so many with him – choose to grant the title to Paris? Why was the name Paris still on everyone's lips around 1900, when global power had long been focused in London, industry in Berlin, the future of good and evil in Vienna? Why was nineteenth-century Paris seen so widely as the spring-board to the modern age?

That overwhelming unanimity had to do, first of all, with the new building materials and construction techniques, the iron and glass used here so much more freely and artfully than anywhere else. Take, for example, the palaces, the Eiffel Tower, the metro tunnels under the Seine with their immense iron stairways and lifts half the size of a railway car. And everywhere the famous galleries, the 'indoor boulevards' that formed the motif for Benjamin's most important work.

The lush interiors of the bourgeoisie – 'the purses of the private man', as Benjamin called them – became safe havens for the arts. The rise of photography – Paris led the way in that as well – forced painters to find totally new forms. It was now the splendour of a movement that made its way onto canvas, or the impression of a late afternoon. In this way the Impressionists blazed trails for painters like Pablo Picasso, who later pulled scenes and objects apart in search of structure.

The ties between the artists were intense, the market eager. Claude Monet immediately sold his first paintings for 300 francs, twice the monthly salary of a teacher. Week after week in his diary, André Gide speaks of new exhibitions. Those were the places to which 'the whole world' went, the things 'the whole world' talked about.

Paris overwhelmed the senses as well with its boulevards, with that stunning order imposed on the city by prefect Haussmann. In that order, Benjamin said, 'the institutions of the worldly and spiritual dominion of the citizenry found their apotheosis'. Of course, Haussmann's *grands travaux* were based on the necessities of law and order – from that point on, military units could operate much more easily in the event of a rebellion – but that was not their most important objective. The boulevards were primarily designed to be modern transport corridors between the various terminals; nineteenth-century Paris, like London and Brussels, was a complete chaos of horses, carts, carriages, coaches and omnibuses. They also served as visual corridors between monuments and major government buildings, national symbols to be viewed in awe by Parisians and visitors alike and therefore requiring a great deal of space. The boulevards served as dividing lines between the city's bourgeoisie and the common workfolk, between the wealthy arrondissements and dirty, smoky suburbs. But at the same time Haussmann's plan generated unprecedented dynamism, because it was based, for the first time, on an all-inclusive view of the phenomenon of the 'city'.

'Modern Paris could not exist within the boundaries of the Paris of the past,' enthused the poet and journalist Théophile Gautier. 'Civilisation blazes broad trails through the old town's dark maze of little streets, crossings and dead-end alleys: she brings down houses the way the pioneers in America bring down trees.' In this way Paris was to become the outpost of the modern age, a beacon for the modern spirit, a light in the provincial darkness, France's song of glory, the city state of the new Europe.

No other metropolis is so much a city and, at the same time, so infused with the countryside as Paris. In the three-minute walk from my hotel to the nearest boulevard I pass six greengrocers, five bakeries, five butchers, three fishmongers. Shop after shop, the crates are displayed on the pavement: apples, oranges, lettuce, cabbage, leeks, radiant in the winter sun.

The butcher shops are hung with sausages and hams, the fish lie in trays along the pavement, from the bakeries wafts the scent of hundreds of varieties of crisp and gleaming bread.

It has always been a complicated relationship, that of the Parisians with their mysterious rural roots, 'la France profonde', and an intense one as well. Many Parisians, or their parents, or otherwise their grand-parents, originally come from the countryside. These days the French are not ashamed of that, they actually cultivate and flaunt it with holiday houses and products from 'home' on the table. It's all a part of 'l'excep-tion Française', even though one third of France's urban population today consists of foreigners.

Around the turn of the century, however, they seemingly wanted to shake off the dust of the countryside as soon as they arrived in Paris. In that sense, too, one could speak of two French nations. The more the big cities grew to be machines full of light and movement, the darker and sleepier the provinces seemed.

Generally speaking, the Parisians saw farm folk as savages or barbar-ians. One could pick them out in a crowd by the sound of their clumping, clattering clogs, and even when they wore shoes in the city, their strange, waddling gait immediately gave them away. This social rift was found everywhere in Europe, but nowhere as emphatically as in France.

Around 1880, there were still many people in the Pyrenees, the Alps and the Massif Central, in all those villages and river valleys where Europe today spends its holidays, who had never seen a cart or a wagon. Everything went by horse or mule. Local dialects predominated; according to official figures from 1863, one quarter of all French citizens barely spoke a word of French. Many regions were still using units of measure and weight, and some of them even currencies, that had been officially done away with a hundred years earlier. Anyone who had visited Paris, even if only for a day, bore the honorary title 'Parisian' for the rest of their lives.

There was nothing very romantic about 'pure' French country life. The provincial court records bear constant witness to inhuman poverty and harshness. A daughter-in-law murdered 'because she was sickly and no good to us'; a mother-in-law thrown down a well to avoid paying a yearly annuity of twenty francs and three sacks of grain. One old man's wife and daughter beat him severely with a pestle, a hammer and a rake, because they had grown tired of feeding him. Little Rémi from Malot's Sans Famille could be found everywhere: in 1905, there were some 400,000 beggars wandering the French countryside.

While enormous facilities for the supply and drainage of water were being built in Paris – small underground lakes can still be found there today – the gutters of provincial French towns like Rouen and Bordeaux were still open sewers. Rennes, a city of 70,000 inhabitants at the turn of the century, could claim precisely thirty bathtubs and two houses with a bathroom. In the literature of the day one finds an increasing number of complaints about the stench of domestic staff, for example, or of fellow passengers.

But here, too, began a period of rapid and radical change. Starting in the 1880s, the French state allocated tens of millions of francs to the development plan advanced by the ambitious Charles de Saulces de Freycinet. By building roads and schools, this minister of public works hoped quickly to narrow the gap between Paris and the provinces, while at the same time giving the stagnating French economy a badly needed boost.

The measures soon bore fruit. By 1900, the infamous black bread, symbol of grinding poverty and backwardness, was almost nowhere to be found. Within two decades, stiff traditional costume was replaced by supple, ready-made clothing; around 1909, a farm girl at the fair was almost indistinguishable from a dressed-up factory maid from the city. The market stands run by public scribes also began to disappear: from 1880, every farm child learned to read and write, effectively putting an end to a brand of dependency we can scarcely fathom today.

The regionalist writer Émile Guillaumin described the lives of five hired men hoeing a field of beets near Moulins on a hot summer's day in 1902. Eight years later, in 1910, the first of these farm workers had become a hotel doorman, the second lived in the city of Vichy, the third worked in a furniture factory, the fourth was a domestic servant. Only the fifth man still worked the land. Today, in 1999, I dare assert, no more than two of their one hundred great-grandchildren still work the soil. At least thirty of them will have ended up in Paris, and the Parisians – more than the residents of any other metropolis – seemed to realise that they are all the great-grandchildren of beet-weeders, and that they must grant due respect to both beets and their hoers.

At Opéra metro station I start a conversation with Pierre Maillot. With his grey beard and plain spectacles, he is standing in one of the corridors holding a tin can and a cardboard sign: 'I beg your forgiveness. But I am hungry.' This is how he earns about a hundred francs (roughly fifteen euros) a day, enough for a bed and a lonely meal with a quarter-litre of wine. The older people are generous, but the young ones tease him. 'I have my only friend right here with me,' he says, reaching into his inside pocket and pulling out a bible with a red plastic cover. Then he tells me a complicated story about prisons, a divorce, problems inside his head, vanished unemployment benefits and the other vagaries of a man's life.

Up at street level, there's a demonstration going on. To my knowledge there is no other city in Europe where the papers each day print maps, as nonchalantly as they do the weather report, showing the anticipated routes of popular assemblies: illegal aliens, dentistry students, royalists, telecommunications workers, it goes on day after day. I come across a group of students. They are angry because their teachers have been laid off in mid-term. Philippine Didier explains to me that she will not now be able to complete her Greek exams. Like her fellow students, she plans to attend the École Nationale d'Administration, the ENA, the breeding ground for France's top politicians and administrators. 'The minister hates us,' Philippine says with great conviction. 'It seems he once failed his exams himself.' I begin seeing all these sloppy pea jackets, bent spectacles, velour caps and backpacks through different eyes: standing here before me, I realise, is the French elite of the year 2030, the cabinet ministers, the top officials, the iron rails on which France rolls along, the Establishment of the future.

In Paris, even the ordinary is often impressive. That applies particularly to the city's public transport system. Paris and its environs have a network the likes of which cities such as London, Amsterdam and Berlin will only be implementing thirty or forty years from now. Every detail speaks of an unparalleled feeling for quality: the automatic ticket system, the uniform prices, the clear signposting, the high frequency of departures, the seeming effortlessness with which the trains rocket all these thousands of people through the city.

You rarely see anyone running for a train: the next one will be coming in two to four minutes. One seldom feels unsafe: there are always people around, every corner is put to good use. And only very rarely is one ever tempted to go by car: nothing can equal the speed, for example, of the RER connection between the Eiffel Tower and Versailles. And most amazing of all is that the system has been running exactly this way for many years, as though it is the most normal thing in the world. If you want to catch a glimpse of the future, you need only travel around Paris for an afternoon.

Meanwhile, my antiquated Baedeker has started baulking. The outskirts of Paris today comprise a jungle of factories, warehouses and tower blocks, but the foldable map at the guide's centre shows light-green fields and woods, with villages such as Neuilly, Pantin and Montreuil. Le Bourget is a market town along a tributary of the Seine. Later it housed the most famous airport in Paris; today that airport is a museum.

Originally, my expedition to Le Bourget was dedicated to the airplane in which Louis Blériot became the first man to fly across the Channel on 25 July, 1909, but in the end I spend the entire morning ogling the machines built by his predecessors, the bunglers and the bluffers. See here the building blocks of progress: intelligence, nonconformity and, above all, chutzpah. Take Félix du Temple's steam-powered airplane, for example, built in 1857; I know nothing about the man himself, but I can see him before me in his workshop: his plane is of the flapping-swallow variety, atop it a ship's rudder, beside that a burnished copper kettle complete with steam whistle. Or Traia Vuia's square cart, a fixed wing attached to the top of something that looks like the undercarriage of a pram, in which the first manned flight was made in France on 18 March, 1906, over a distance of twelve metres, at a height of fifty centimetres.

Then there is the machine that belonged to Louis Blériot himself. I found an old newspaper article by the Dutch correspondent Alexander Cohen, dealing with a series of aviation experiments at the parade grounds in Issy-les-Moulineaux late on a dusky Friday afternoon, 22 November, 1907. Cohen watched M. Farman leave the ground in a 'giant insect' of canvas, bamboo and aluminium, and fly for several hundred metres. Which was more than could be said of Blériot's 'flying beast'.

The Libellule, as Blériot's juggernaut was called, put-putted across the parade grounds at breakneck speed, made several impressive pirouettes, but never left the ground.

A little more than eighteen months later, however, Blériot climbed aboard this construct of filament and canvas and flew to England. Just before the flight, his machine seemed on the point of falling apart: the fish glue holding it together had started to rot. Just before departure, he casually asked someone which direction it was to Dover.

And then there are the photographs of the airmen. Melvin Vaniman (with cap) stares straight ahead, behind him an engine that looks as if it belongs in an ocean-going freighter. Coudron (1910, Breton beret) has something casual about him, he looks as though he stands a chance. Gilbert (1910, suit and tie), looking like a respectable family man, is lying in a sort of hammock beneath his bamboo aircraft. The entire plane is hung with tassels. I look Octave Gilbert right in the eye. His fatherly hands nervously grip the little reins attached to the two bicycle wheels that comprise his landing gear. Fear, dignity: for him, all that is subordinate to progress. His face, full of courage and despair.

Chapter Three

London

'I STILL RELISH YOUNG PEOPLE'S AMAZEMENT WHEN I TELL THEM THAT, before 1915, I travelled to India and America without possessing a passport, without actually ever having seen one,' Stefan Zweig wrote in 1941.

My Baedeker guide, too, considers a passport superfluous, 'but they often prove useful in establishing the traveller's identity when one wishes to gain admission to museums on days when they are closed to the general public.'

The passport was part of life in Western Europe for less than a century, and today I once again go zipping across borders unhindered in the high-speed Eurostar. (Not that the state is unaware of my whereabouts; I am scrutinised and shadowed electronically in dozens of different ways, but that is another story.) Only here in Great Britain do they still do things the old way. My papers are inspected earnestly by conscientious, solid citizens in Her Majesty's service.

For Britain, the century began with a funeral; the morning after my arrival, therefore, I dive immediately into the newspaper archives of the new British Library, that gigantic red-brick warehouse of thought.

Queen Victoria's funeral was held on Friday, 1 February, 1901, I read in the special commemorative edition (price: twopence) of the *Yorkshire Post*. Hundreds of thousands looked on as the procession trundled through London, with the bagpipes of the Scots and Irish Guards leading the way. The *Post*'s correspondent John Foster Fraser goes to great lengths to reproduce the sound of the muffled drums: 'Rumble – rattle rumble – rattle.' The rest of his report deals mainly with the family following after the bier: the new king, Edward – 'his cheeks ashen, his eyes dull and tired'; his cousin, Wilhelm II, kaiser of Germany – 'moustaches drooping'; his second cousin Leopold II, king of Belgium; his brother-in-law, the Greek king George I; 'blond and blue-eyed' nephew Heinrich of Prussia; the 'manly-built' Grand Duke of Hesse 'with his firm chin'; and so the entire House of Hanover and its entourage shuffled through London, with Kaiser Wilhelm out in front.

This was the European summit of 1901. Foreign affairs was still largely a matter for royal households, and for decades short, resolute Victoria in her perpetual black satin dresses had been almost literally the 'grandmother of Europe', or at least of the clan network of European rulers. Those rulers all had their quarrels, large and small. But at the same time there were countless family weddings, parties and funerals, photograph sessions during which they switched uniforms: the future King George V in Prussian pomp, Kaiser Wilhelm in British uniform. Kaiser 'Willy' in Russian braid, Czar 'Nicky' in Prussian gear. When the queen died on 22 January, 1901, it was as a kind of primal mother (according to an eyewitness report from Lord Reginald Esher): 'The queen occasionally recognised those around her and spoke their names. Reid, the physician, put his arm around her and supported her. The Prince of Wales knelt beside her bed. The German kaiser stood silently at the head, beside the queen. The other children and grandchildren were there as well, all their names were spoken from time to time. She died peacefully. After the king left for London, the German kaiser arranged the rest.'

In the end it was Kaiser Wilhelm, along with his uncle, King George, who lifted his grandmother Victoria into her coffin. That was how things went among the eternal kin, within the European family.

And there was yet another bedrock certainty: the British Empire. In Southwark, on Walworth Road, one finds the Cuming Museum. This 'British Museum in miniature', as it is sometimes called, is in fact more like an incredible collection of curiosities, piled high in the upper room of a library. Over the span of 120 years, father and son Richard (1777–1870) and Henry Cuming (1807–1902) dragged everything they could lay their hands on back to this plush lair; they were true nineteenth-century gentlemen. Father Richard's passion was born in 1782, when an aunt gave him three fossils and an old Indian coin for his fifth birthday. When Henry Cuming died in 1902, he left behind more than 100,000 objects, plus enough money to run a museum that would preserve the results of their collectors' frenzy for all eternity. Consequently, we can still today wander about in the dream world of two Victorians.

The museum's cabinets and showcases contain, among other things: a length of Roman sewer pipe, an apple corer made from a sheep's bone, a phial containing crumbs from the wedding cake of Edward VIII, a stuffed chimpanzee – originally sold as 'the mummy of a two-hundred-year-old man' – an orange tooter from the 1864 races at Epsom, a piece of plaster from the room in which Napoleon died, every programme from every play the Cumings ever attended, a pair of Etruscan vases, a cigarette butt thrown away by a member of the royal family, a Roman child's toy, a medieval flute found in the Thames, a piece of the vest of Charles 1 and six 'figurines from a lost civilisation', kilned and aged in 1857 by two dredgers who turned a profit on the Cumings' collectors' mania.

A walk through this museum inevitably leaves one with the image of a huge pyramid of bones, knick-knacks, cake crumbs and slices of mummy, and atop it all two neatly dressed London gentlemen. With their museum they hoped to 'create a storehouse of knowledge' for 'the merchant and the manufacturer, the archaeologist and the historian, the painter and the playwright, the military man and the naval strategist, the philanthropist and the philosopher, for the lover of culture in general'. The more they collected, the Cumings believed, the more people would know. And the more people knew about other cultures, past and present, the better they would realise that Britain under Queen Victoria formed the apotheosis of human civilisation, and that the Briton was the pinnacle of creation.

The Cumings were eccentric, of course, even in their own day. But they did reflect the mentality of the times, and they said openly what many Britons thought. What's more, they had the wherewithal to draw their personal conclusions. As the current curator has rightly noted, it is a collection that flies in the face of all known international agreements. The Cumings could never have hauled in their Indian masks, Roman toy sheep, Egyptian falcon mummies, Pacific scalps and Chinese inkpots so easily had their country not grown during that same period into the mightiest power on earth. Around 1900, the British Empire stretched from North to South Pole: Canada, Egypt, the Cape colonies, India, Burma, Malacca, Singapore, Australia and so on. The British Navy was strong enough to fight two wars at the same time, its fleet could – theoretically, at least – take on the combined navies of Germany, Russia and the United States. The British aristocracy was imitated all over Europe, not only by the German kaiser and the Russian czar, but also by the German nobility, who preferred to marry English girls, the German upper classes, who liked to stroll through town in English coats and trousers, and by the French *haut monde* who organised *le Derby* at Chantilly, *le Steeplechase* at Auteuil and who met at *le Jockey Club*.

Only in the distance was there the faint rumble of new powers to come: Germany, the United States, Japan. The British coal and iron industries were the factory of the world, the City of London its financial core. The major European bankers had all moved to London after the currency market in Paris collapsed in 1870, and that was where the big money continued to circulate.

The City was a world unto itself, with its own codes and its own honour system. To a certain extent, the entrepreneurial and the personal mingled there in much the same way as within the royal houses of Europe. The City, wrote Jean Monnet, the son of a French cognac manufacturer and a trainee there in the year 1904, 'is more than a neighbourhood of offices and banks: it is also a gathering, socially most exclusive, but professionally open to the world at large.' Lines ran from the City to Shanghai, Tokyo and New Delhi, to New York and Chicago and back again, and at the same time everyone knew each other personally; from their games of golf, or the hours they spent together, regardless of rank or position, in London's commuter trains. Monnet: 'It is a closely woven community in which business rivalry is mitigated by personal relationships. Everyone sees to his own affairs, but at the same time to the affairs of the City. An Englishman will therefore not say: "I am sending my son to such-and-such a company or bank." Instead, he says: "I am sending him to the City."'

Outside the City as well, the empire lent British society a certain standing. It imposed a lifestyle in which a number of traits were highly valued: militarism, a pronounced awareness of rank and class, a sort of frontier mentality, a typically British, undercooled machismo. A great deal of travelling was done, all over the world, and at the same time as British cosmopolitism upheld a strong sense of its own superiority. A great deal was learned about plants, animals and human cultures, but at the centre of the world stood Britannia. And at the summit of creation stood the Cumings, striving diligently for immortality, at the top of the heap for all time.

In 1862, the city chronicler Henry Mayhew wrote: 'Because London is the largest of all cities, it is also home to the largest number of human wrecks. Wrecks, too, because their misery seems all the more miserable by reason of its juxtaposition with the wealthiest, most comfortable life in the world.'

From 2.6 million in 1850, London's population grew to 5.5 million by 1891, and 7.1 million by 1911. A hundred years after the start of the Industrial Revolution, Great Britain was still a rural society in 1870. Two thirds of all Britons lived in the countryside or in small towns. By 1914, it was only a quarter.

Between 1850–6, Karl Marx lived with his five children, his wife and a servant girl in two rooms at 28 Dean Street. Marx was and remained a burgher, unlike most of his contemporaries on Dean Street. When thinking of those times, there is always one photograph that comes to mind: the dilapidated shoes of three street urchins, the holes in their soles showing the bottoms of their bare feet, covered by a thick layer of dirt and calluses; six times an engrossing jumble of leather, iron and human skin.

In 1885, the socialists claimed, one out of every four Londoners was living in dire poverty. The shipping magnate Charles Booth wanted to find out for himself, so he organised the world's first large scale sociological study, based on figures from the Poor Act, police reports and a massive door-to-door survey. Between 1891–1903 he published seventeen volumes of *Life and Labour of the People of London*, complete with maps and large black and dark-blue sectors. Booth divided the poverty he found into neat categories: 'Lowest class, vicious, semi-criminal.' And, beside that: 'Very poor, casual. Chronic want.' The situation was actually worse than the publication made out: one third of London's population, Booth found, fell under the latter two headings.

28 Dean Street. I can't help myself, I have to take a look. The house is still there, but the ground floor is now a trendy restaurant. The waitresses

don't mind my going upstairs for a look. The one-time Marx residence, it seems, has been converted into a modern meeting place for young urban professionals, with halogen lighting, anonymous pastel-blue walls, a table with a dozen chairs and a big white poster with 'Karl Marx' written on it in little black letters. That's it. 'Sorry,' one of the girls says. 'I don't know anything about Mr Marx either.'

What would Karl Marx himself have seen along the way as he fled from overcrowded Dean Street to his table in the Reading Room of the British Library? Foreign visitors of the day spoke of 'paths by Oxford Street, thick with human excrement, gangs of pale children loitering on filthy steps; the embankment by London Bridge where whole families huddle together through the night, heads bowed, shivering from the cold.'

Booth's surveyors found thousands of sweatshops for women in London's back rooms. There they made brushes, glued matchboxes, folded decorations, filled mattresses.

London's poverty never let up. In the summer, half the city stank of excrement. There were more than a hundred different sewer systems, run by eight different boards. During times of heavy rainfall, all the systems overflowed. Most of the faeces of the millions of inhabitants ended up in the Thames. To ward off the stench, sheets drenched in chloride were hung before the windows of the Houses of Parliament. The nuisance reached its peak in 1858, the year of the 'Great Stink'. Only after the government intervened was a modern sewage system built.

All this filth, stench, humidity and darkness was aggravated even further on the days of smog, the notorious London fog, an extreme form of air pollution that regularly blanketed the city up to the 1960s. The fog would come up suddenly, and throughout the years dozens of varieties of smog were noted: black as night, bottlefly green, pea soup, brown, plain grey, orange. On such days the city floated in a cloud of yellow, brown or green, with here and there a feeble dot of light from a gas lamp.

London was the capital of a worldwide empire, but you couldn't tell that by looking at the city itself. Paris, well, now – *there* was a capital. A number of other European cities had modernised themselves in similar fashion. But London was an affront to the self-esteem of many Britons. Their capital was almost devoid of beautiful squares or elegant boulevards, the traffic snarled, the streets were split by puffing steam trains on viaducts, one neighbourhood after another was destroyed for the construction of railway stations and Underground lines, the city's centre was encircled by endless slums.

All this was largely due to the medieval manner in which the city was run. Strictly speaking, London itself consisted of only one little town, the City of London, with around it a series of 'parishes' responsible for running the metropolis at large. Government after government ran into a brick wall of fiercely defended parish rights. Central planning, indispensable for any metropolis for the construction of roads, water systems, sewage and rail connections, was almost impossible in London.

For some, however, the chaos of London, this piling up of wayward building styles without much in the way of planning, constituted a political statement: an act of defiance against the absolute power of a ruler, against a bureaucracy, against a Haussmann. Many British subjects – then and now – attached great importance to their own domain. They were willing to conform to the rigours of a tightly run public life, but as compensation they demanded great freedom in their own, private realm. Within those private boundaries they could behave as eccentrically as they liked. 'My home is my castle': the government was expected to rein itself in, the planners could only go so far, chaos was simply the price one paid. According to the urban historian Michiel Wagenaar, it was in this way that there arose 'the urban landscape of the free market'.

And that was not all. Filthy nineteenth-century London virtually forced its own inhabitants to get out, and before long that exodus was actually made possible by the construction of a rail network. It was around London, therefore, before anywhere else in Europe, that there arose a new phenomenon: the rural estate, the anti-city of the stately suburb, home front for a new generation of comfortable merchants, a place in which they could foster their own norms and values, their own forms of leisure and, ultimately, their own ideas about nation, religion and politics.

I have been invited to tea at the home of Nigel Nicolson, eighty-two years old, publisher, diarist and former Member of Parliament. He is the grandson of the third Lord Sackville, and the son of diplomat and MP

Harold Nicolson and the writer Vita Sackville-West – also known as the protagonist of Virginia Woolf's *Orlando*. It is late afternoon, the sky is beginning to change colour, and among the rolling hills around Sissinghurst Castle one occasionally hears the report of the pheasant-shooters' guns.

We are sitting in the kitchen, where it is almost cold enough to see our own breath. Most of the castle has now been surrendered to the National Trust – money! – and the day trippers. Nicolson lives alone. He is wearing an unusual quilted robe.

The afternoon is destined to be a memorable one. He tells me about the lives of his parents – one of the most oft-described of English marriages – but most of our time is spent trying out the brand new microwave oven he has recently received as a gift. 'A miracle, a miracle,' he keeps shouting. 'But how on earth does one go about heating up a mince pie?'

I teach him how to boil a cup of milk using the microwave, and he tells me about his years growing up at Knole – hundreds of rooms and chimneys – and at Sissinghurst. 'We didn't have a normal mother-son relationship,' he says matter-of-factly. 'My mother spent all day working in her room in the tower here. In the space of thirty years, I may have gone in there three times. The one who always busied herself with my younger brother and I was Virginia Woolf. Some funny woman once said to me: "You do know, I suppose, that Virginia loves your mother?" To which I replied: "Of course she does! Don't we all?"'

Virginia was the ideal 'auntie'. 'She taught us to look at things through the eyes of a true writer. She always wanted to know more. 'What colour coat was that teacher wearing?' she would ask. 'How did his voice sound? How did he smell? Details, details!' One time, when we were catching butterflies, she asked us: 'Tell me, what is it like to be a child?' I still remember my reply: 'You know very well what it's like, Virginia, because you were a child once yourself. But I have no idea what it's like to be you, because I've never been big.'

I asked him whether having such celebrated parents was ever a burden to him. 'A film was made about their lives, even a television series. But they weren't like that at all. Harold, my father, was portrayed as a wet, while in fact he was a very astute man. With such parents, a certain undeserved fame rubs off on one. But at the same time, it has also worked very much to my advantage. My inheritance was not extensive in the financial sense, but rich in contacts and influence. And it lent me a natural self-confidence, a background against which I could place myself. My father put it this way: "I detested the rich, but I was wild about learning, science, intellect, the mind. I have always taken the side of the underdog, but I have also adhered to the principal of the aristocracy."'

The next day, at a café. We snow is falling outside the window. A couple of tired-looking men are drinking coffee. One of them is picking languidly at a steak and kidney pie. Between the mirrors on the walls are colourful pictures of blossoming balconies in summer, and of a pavement café in a warm, sunny village.

The tabloid paper the Sun has been busy for days demolishing the reputation of an adulterous cabinet minister. The facts have long been known to all and thoroughly hashed over, and now the man is being slowly, bone by bone, broken on the wheel. Finally, it's off with his head. 'WOULD YOU SLEEP WITH THIS MAN?' yesterday's headline read; below it an unflattering portrait of the victim and two phone numbers, one for 'YES', the other for 'NO'. 'Some call him a dwarf, others compare him to a shrimp, yet still he continues to attract women. Why?'

The next day the tabloid opens with: '966 BRITONS WANT TO SLEEP WITH ROBIN COOK, BUT WE'RE NOT GIVING THE MINISTER THEIR PHONE NUMBERS.' A 'leading' psychologist is called in to explain the phenomenon. The inside page contains a cut-out mask of the unfortunate minister's face.

Today Sun journalists donned Robin Cook masks and went into town to note the public's reaction. 'In Soho, a café emptied out in a panic.'

Nowhere but in England are the papers so full of fascinating misbehaviour. There is always a scandal brewing, there is always a politician, village vicar or bank manager being pilloried, yet at the same time the country breathes a remarkable sense of order. When I first travelled to England – I was around twenty at the time – I was looking only for the castles, boarding schools, neat lawns, red double-decker buses and businessmen in black bowlers. Clichés, I thought. But from the train between Harwich and London, I actually saw castles in the evening light, and lawns and schoolboys playing cricket, and London was full of bowler hats. The country seemed so predictable, so neat, that during those first few days

I had the feeling nothing could ever go wrong here, that even the most minor of traffic accidents was simply out of the question.

That orderliness and those newspapers have everything to do with each other. There is no order without tar and feathers. In part, that civic duty is the product of something else: the remarkable discipline to which the lion's share of the populace has subjected itself since the late nineteenth century.

The worst of the poverty gradually dwindled after 1870, and from 1900 one could speak of something like a state of general welfare. The clothing worn by young workers, especially the women among them, began to look more and more like that of the staid classes: unthinkable only a generation earlier. Around the same time, British political thinking, from left to right, began extracting itself, to a certain extent, from the straightjacket of the class system. London, of course, was still subject to crippling strikes and demonstrations – the entire dockside was paralysed in the summer of 1911 by a strike involving 20,000 workers, until at last the army was called in. But meanwhile the ideal of the 'organic' society, the shared citizenry of workers, the middle class and perhaps even the aristocracy was gradually catching on with broad sections of the public.

Did everyone, though, believe in that 'shared citizenry'? A brief section of newsreel has been preserved of the Derby held in June 1913. We see the horses hurtling around the bend at high speed, neck and neck. In the background we catch a glimpse of the crowd, men in straw hats, here and there a woman. Then something happens, so quickly as to be almost imperceptible: a woman runs onto the track, there is a whirl of bodies, then the horses are past and spectators rush towards a pile of clothing. That is how she entered history. Waving two flags, the narrator says, Emily Davison threw herself in front of the king's horse for the cause of female suffrage. She died four days later.

I wanted to find out more about her. The British Library, though, contained only a short commemorative volume published shortly after her death, a bijou in a finely tooled case. The frontispiece shows a proud woman in a gown, diploma in hand. She is frowning gravely for the photographer, but obviously capable of breaking into a smile at any moment. That impression is confirmed only a few pages later: Emily loved life, she was generous, enthusiastic and exceptionally cheerful.

Her story reads like a classic account of radicalisation. And, at the same time, as a nineteenth-century story, a story about the place where two eras clashed.

Emily Davison came from a good family, but even in early childhood there was something wayward about her. 'I don't want to be good!' she often shouted at her nanny. When her parents died she had to leave school. Like many women in her situation she became a governess, but she spent her evening hours studying and so finally left school with exceptional grades. She was at one with the dreams and ambitions of the nineteenth century, but was also brutally confronted with the dark side of that same century: the social pressures, the curtailment of the individual, the double standards, the never-ending conflict between desire and possibility.

Shortly before Emily was born, John Stuart Mill – prompted by his blue-stocking spouse Harriet Taylor – published The Subjection of Women in 1869. The title speaks for itself. The country may have been ruled by a queen, but women in other walks of life had no say whatsoever. A man held absolute sway over his wife's person and her possessions. University degrees were off-limits to women, a situation that continued at Cambridge until 1948. Women frequently earned less than half a man's salary for the same work. Many professions actually barred women from their ranks. Many poor girls turned to whoring to survive.

But, after 1870, there came a change. Women began making themselves heard on subjects such as education, charity work, health care, mandatory vaccination and prostitution. Starting in 1880, the major political parties established women's organisations, and demonstrations for female suffrage began in 1900. In 1908 a window was shattered at 10 Downing Street; in 1913, one wing of Liberal leader David Lloyd George's mansion was blown up in order to 'rouse his conscience'. With remarkable speed, women who had been brought up as delicate Victorian china dolls were becoming modern physicians, bookkeepers, civil servants and teachers, and sometimes even dyed-in-the-wool feminists.

Simple curiosity was what brought Emily Davison into contact with these suffragettes: she had read strange newspaper reports about gatherings of radical women, and she wanted to see them with her own eyes. Before long she had joined their ranks. When a mass demonstration was held on 21 June, 1908, Emily was one of the most enthusiastic organisers.

It is not clear what drove her; we can only guess. What is clear is that she was drawn into a current of political action, demonstrations of solidarity and intense friendships. Rage was not her sole motive. She was deeply convinced, as her female biographer wrote, that 'she had been called by God not only to work, but also to fight for the cause she had embraced, like a Joan of Arc leading the French Army. Her prayers were always long, and the Bible always lay beside her bed.' Emily united in herself the contradictions of her day; a hotchpotch of modern militancy and religious romanticism.

She went further and further for the sake of the cause. On 20 March, 1909, a delegation of women who had demanded to speak to Prime Minister Herbert Asquith were arrested heavy-handedly. Emily was among them. She spent a month in jail. On 30 July she was arrested again for disrupting one of Lloyd George's political rallies. The suffragettes detested the Liberal leader, probably because he resembled them more closely than the rest. Lloyd George, who had started off as a poor laywer in Wales, was a reckless man and a skilled manipulator, a passionate opponent of the Conservatives, a man bound and determined to break England wide open with major social reforms. This time, Emily Davison was sentenced to two months.

She became one of the first to wield the new weapon of the powerless: the hunger strike. 'When they locked me in the cell, I smashed seventeen windows right away,' she wrote to a friend afterwards. 'Then they threw me into another cell, where everything was bolted down . . . Then the real gnawing began. I fasted for 124 hours, and they set me free. I lost nineteen pounds and a great deal of muscle. I suppose you're in Switzerland now? Send me some picture postcards.' On the wall of her cell she had scrawled the following text: 'Rebellion against tyranny is obedience to God. Emily.'

After that she was arrested again and again, went on hunger strike once more, was force-fed through a tube and finally attempted to throw herself down the prison stairwell. 'My idea was, one great tragedy can prevent many more. But the safety net prevented serious injury.'

Emily's story was not the only one of its kind. Although most of those in the women's movement did their best to remain calm and as rational as possible, in order to break through the image of the 'emotional' female who was unfit 'by nature' for business and politics, another part of that movement radicalised in a way that had never been seen before. In the *Suffragette* of 26 December, 1913, I stumbled upon a list of the major polit-actions of that year, 130 in total. The following is a random selection, taken from only a single month:

2 April: arson at a church in Hampstead Garden; 4 April: a house in Chorley Wood destroyed by fire, a bomb attack at Oxted station, an empty train destroyed by an explosion in Devonport, famous paintings damaged in Manchester; 8 April: an explosion in the grounds of Dudley Castle; a bomb found on the crowded Kingston train; 11 April: a cricket pavilion destroyed in Tunbridge Wells; 12 April: arson at public schools in Gateshead; 19 April: an attempt to sabotage the famous lighthouse at Eddystone; 20 April: an attempt to blow up the offices of the *York Herald*; 26 April: a rail carriage in Teddington destroyed by fire.

They were gradually becoming highly organised female guerrillas. But after the outbreak of the First World War, it suddenly stopped. The women ceased their attacks, and the government released all female militants. Had things gone differently, how would it have all turned out?

I was reminded of a doll's house I had seen at the Bethnal Green Museum of Childhood, showing the home of the Loebe family in Kilburn, the whole Edwardian female universe in a nutshell: the bedroom, the busy nursery, the bathroom, the parlour with its grand piano and conservatory, the full dining room with carpets, cupboards, mirrors and knick-knacks, the kitchen with a fish on the table and two cats prowling below, everything reduced to a scale of 1:10.

In that Edwardian world, a family dwelling of this type was the ultimate symbol of the sheltered environment, regularity and eternal routine. Emily and her companions in arms rejected that, and their behaviour may better reflect what was actually happening in the country than all the doll's houses put together. Around 1900, Great Britain was much more modern than the British people themselves wished to admit. All the traditions – the bowler hats, the gentlemen's clubs and burnished walnut institutions – could not hide the fact that the City was filling with female personnel, that women were at work everywhere in the field of education, that class distinctions were fading and that feudal gentility could not be combined with the equality of modern citizens. The empire's sober, macho values, in other words, collided head-on with the increasing priority given to care, consumption, democracy and women's rights.

Beneath the surface, from 1900–14, the England of the broad middle classes lacked the manifest cohesion of that doll's house, the inner calm of the cathedral. In the words of Jose Harris it was, in fact, 'a chaotic and amorphous society, characterised by countless contradictory trends and opinions, and well capable of flying completely off the handle.' It was, to put it differently, a society in which people at all stages of historical development lived side by side: modern commuters beside villagers who scraped together a living in exactly the same way that their grandparents and great-grandparents had done; Victorian patriarchs beside female academics; colonial conquistadors beside liberal ministers.

Within this field of contradictions, and driven by her own religious fervour, Emily Davison went further and further adrift. Slowly but surely, she began considering herself a martyr, a sacrificial lamb. On Tuesday 3 June, 1913 she was a free woman once more. She walked around at the 'All in a Garden' fair organised by the women's movement, and paused for a long time before the statue of Joan of Arc. She told her friends cheerfully that she would come back here every day, 'except for tomorrow. Tomorrow I'm going to the Derby.' She refused to elaborate. 'Read the papers, you'll see.' The next morning she rushed into the main office. 'I need to borrow two flags.' In everything now, she *was* Joan of Arc.

But dying was not a part of her plan. When she committed her ultimate act, the train ticket home, third class, was still in her pocket.

Chapter Four

Berlin

DOORN CASTLE, IN THE HILLS EAST OF THE DUTCH CITY OF UTRECHT, contains everything there is to say about Kaiser Wilhelm II. Five locomotives, pulling a total of ninety-five freight cars, had carried the last of the imperial attributes to the Netherlands in winter 1919, and there they remain to this day, huddled together in less than two dozen medium-sized rooms and a large attic.

Wilhelm's world contained, among other things, paintings of Frederick the Great, portraits of himself, walls full of battles and parades, tapestries that had belonged to Marie-Antoinette, 600 uniforms – most of which he had designed himself – the special fork which allowed the kaiser, lame in one arm, to cut his own food, a '*Garven Laufgewichtswaage 200kg*', two reinforced dining-room chairs guaranteed not to collapse under the weight of the emperor or his spouse, cabinets full of cigarette cases and snuffboxes, a heavy leather chair with built-in lectern for ease of discourse, a gold-embossed 'Patent Water Flush Chamber' toilet pot, twelve special hot-chocolate cups, an *Unser Kaiserpaar* album with a decorative silver binding, a drawing of the 1913 wedding banquet of the emperor's daughter, Victoria Louise, in which all of Europe's major sovereigns are seen sitting merrily together at the table and, lest we forget, a conjugal bed four metres square.

In addition to his palace at Potsdam and his immense yacht the *Hohenzollern*, the kaiser possessed at the height of his power some thirty castles and estates all over Germany. He visited a third of them each year, sometimes for no more than a weekend. There was nothing he loved more than to speed through the countryside at night in his own creamy-white train with gold trimmings. During the hunting season he would sometimes kill more than a thousand animals in a single week. Whenever he graced a military manoeuvre with his imperial presence, every unit of his own army had to win – which did not always suit the purpose of the manoeuvre. The *Hohenzollern* – with 350 crew members and space for 80 guests – was kept in readiness for him to board at any moment. In Europe he was known as the 'showman of the continent', the 'crown megalomaniac', the man who 'wanted every day to be his birthday'.

After his fall, and Germany's defeat in 1918, all he had left was this park estate at Doorn with the stiff, white villa at its heart. He ruled over his own life with military precision: prayers at 9.00, newspapers at 9.15, chopping wood at 10.30, correspondence at 12.00, lunch at 1.00, nap from 2.00 to 4.00, working and reading from 4.00 to 8.00, then dinner. In the grass near the villa I happened upon the graves of his three dogs: Arno, Topsy and 'the faithful Santos, 1907–27. *Begleitete Seine Majestät im Weltkriege 1914–18*'.

His grandson told me that, after the German defeat and his abdication, Wilhelm was a mental wreck. But he was also furious. He lectured endlessly to his visitors, and in 1919 was even heard to say: 'God's wrath will be terrible. Such general treason on the part of a people against its ruler has no precedent in world history.' The dream of seizing the throne once more continued to prowl the house, usually set in motion by Wilhelm's new wife, the young Princess Hermine, a stalwart lady who had moved in at Doorn soon after the death of the old empress. On Christmas Day 1931, Sigurd von Illsemann, an aides-de-camp, wrote in his diary: 'All one has heard here at Doorn for months is the story of how the National Socialists will restore the kaiser to the throne; all hope, all thought, every utterance and all writing stems from this conviction.'

During his exile, Wilhelm stopped throwing parties. Queen Wilhelmina of the Netherlands never once deigned to meet him. She had, people said, no desire to consort with rulers who abandoned land and army after hitting upon hard times. But Wilhelm's memoirs betray no shred of guilt. He still saw himself as the German emperor. He read everything he could about politics and psychology, and preached to his visitors, but he himself was incapable of extracting any learning from the knowledge and experience of others. He would simply change the facts to make them fit the world of his imagination.

Yet he was not the ogre people for so long supposed him to be, the man who had purposely paved the way for a pan-European war. He had been more of a magician's apprentice, haplessly unable to get the genie back in the bottle. Or, in the words of Winston Churchill, a 'careless tourist [who] had flung down his burning cigarette in the ante-room of the magazine Europe had become', then went sailing on his yacht, and upon his return found 'the building impenetrable with smoke . . . His undeniable cleverness and versatility, his personal grace and vivacity, only aggravated his dangers by concealing his inadequacy,' Churchill wrote. 'But underneath all this posing and its trappings, was a very ordinary, vain, but on the whole well-meaning man, hoping to pass himself off as a second Frederick the Great.'

Doorn and Berlin lay a universe apart, yet turn-of-the-century Berlin was nonetheless a reflection of that attitude towards life expressed in the packed salons at Doorn.

According to *Berlin für Kenner*, a German Baedeker published in 1900, Berlin was 'the most glorious city in the world . . . the seat of the German kaiser and the king of Prussia', with a 'garrison of 23,000 men', 'as numerous as the railway ties between Frankfurt and Berlin', while the population had a combined balance of '362 million in savings in the bank'.

At the same time, Berlin was and is a city that lurches back and forth as it moves through time, like a runaway train compartment on the Ringbahn. Midway through the twentieth century, in the 1950s, an elderly citizen of Berlin could have told you about the sleepy nineteenth century provincial city of his childhood, the imperial Berlin of his youth, the starving Berlin of 1915, the wild and roaring Berlin of the mid-1920s, the Nazi Berlin of his children, the ravaged Berlin of 1945 and the reconstructed, divided Berlin of his grandchildren. All one and the same city, all within the space of one lifetime.

Within that period, there was half a century, from 1871 to 1918, during which Berlin bore the title of 'imperial capital'. Standing on the banks of the Oder, fifty kilometres outside Berlin, one found oneself at the geographic centre of the German Empire, 600 kilometres from Aken and

800 kilometres from Königsberg, the present-day Kaliningrad. Today that spot is marked by a Polish border post.

Berlin was the parvenu of Europe, but the city – with the frenetic energy of all newcomers – did everything it could to make up for its lagging behind London, Paris and Rome. Even today some of the neighbourhoods resemble a febrile European dream: a Jugendstil villa here, something a bit Venetian there, beside it a bit of Paris or Munich, with styles and shapes filched from all over the continent. The myth of Berlin was fabricated as well: supposedly, the city had started out as a Germanic settlement, with the bear as its symbol and eponym. In actual fact, however, for the first 600 years of its existence Berlin was a purely Slavic village. Its name has nothing to do with bears, but with the Slavic word brl, meaning 'swamp'. The actual connotation is something along the lines of 'Swampy Place', in Old Polish. Yet that, of course, is hardly the stuff of which a Great German historical tradition can be made.

I had come to Berlin aboard the TGV and the ICE, travelling at 300kph past the villages of northern France, past cows with dungy backsides, a woman hanging the laundry, a pensive hare in a bare field.

Next came the broad, stern German lowlands. We were cruising at 200 kph now. The passengers in the first-class compartment spoke only to their mobiles: 'Yeah, put my name on that EP.' 'Take a look at whether that Fassinger order is already on the net.'

After Wuppertal, a group of skinheads settled in on the platform between compartments. They sat there smoking and drinking beer, occasionally breaking into raucous laughter and loud belching. Beans, goulash soup and potatoes with sausage were being served in the club car. The first-class passengers ate in silence. The skinheads and the restaurant personnel were the only ones who spoke. 'Shit!' the boys kept yelling at each other, 'Shit! Shit!' It was a grey day, an unremitting greyish-green, all the way from Paris to Berlin.

Now, from my room, I look out on a courtyard full of brown leaves, a part of the earth where no one ever walks, sits or plays, occupied only by a large tree grasping for light. Darkness is falling. There is snow in the air. The windows across the way are dark, except for one warm, yellow rectangle, behind which someone is writing at a table.

These are lovely, private surroundings, excellent for getting some work done on my dispatches or doing a little background reading. For days I have been immersed in the diary of Käthe Kollwitz: sculptress and cartoonist for the satirical weekly *Simplicissimus*; wife of the social democrat general practitioner Karl Kollwitz; mother of two sons, Hans and Peter. A vivacious woman who was gradually tethered to earth by life at respectable Weissenburger Strasse 25. Here, to quote a few of her entries, is how she saw Berlin at the time:

8 September, 1909
Went with Peter to Tempelhof airfield yesterday. Wright flew for fifty-two minutes. He looked handsome, and seemed sure of himself. Once Wright had flown by, a little boy asked: 'Is he real? I thought he was glued to it.' The North Pole was discovered by both Cook and Peary.

30 November, 1909
With Karl and Hans to the third Sombart reading, which was about whether there was such a thing as a Jewish essence, and if so what that might be . . . He talked about ghetto Jews and non-ghetto Jews. Why are the Spanish Jews, who are of pure Semitic origin, not ghetto Jews? Can't they be forced into that? In any case, they are more handsome and walk more erectly than ghetto Jews.

5 February, 1911
At [SDP leader Paul] Singer's funeral, the entire fourth borough walked in front of the coffin. The procession lasted more than an hour before the hearses passed. After a while, the appearance of the crowd made me sad. So many undereducated people. So many mean, stupid faces. So many ill and malformed. Yet still, as social democrats, they represented a favourable cross section of the population.

16 April, 1912
The British steamer *Titanic* has sunk, with more than a thousand people on board. Soost, the workman, earns twenty-eight marks a week, six of which go to pay the rent, twenty-two he hands over

to his wife. She has to pay for beds and sleeping space, leaving fourteen or fifteen marks for Soost, his wife and their six children to live on.

Their youngest is one month old . . . One of the older children is mentally retarded. Soost's wife is thirty-five, and she's already borne nine children, three of whom died. But all of them, she says, were as sturdy as this little boy at birth, they only weakened and died because she couldn't breastfeed them; she had no milk because she had to perform hard labour and couldn't care for herself.

October 1912

A Polygamy Bond has been set up in Jena. A hundred superior specimens of manhood desire intercourse with 1,000 superior specimens of womanhood, for the purposes of propagation. As soon as the woman becomes pregnant, the conjugal bonds are dissolved. All this with a view to racial advancement.

New Year's Eve, 1913

Last New Year's Eve, with all the rumours of war, was a hard one for me to bear. Now the year is over and nothing much in particular has happened . . . Mother is still alive. I asked her whether she wouldn't like to start all over again. She shook her head slowly and said: 'It's enough.' So she slowly fades, a languid, dusky sinking.

The name of the hotel where I am staying is the Imperator. It's actually more like a boarding house, an enormous apartment building built around two courtyards, with high-ceilinged hallways and rooms en suite. In imperial times it housed the families of citizens of substance, but since the 1920s it has served as a boarding house. Miraculously enough, the building survived the war. Here is Berlin at its best: cozy, the walls covered in art, the sheets and napkins snowy white, the crispiest *Brötchen* in town. The entrance to all this solid living, a lovely oak staircase, always smells of beeswax. The hall is covered in golden curlicues, forms in stucco and plaster. The balcony is held on high by two nymphs. The portico to the neighbour's house, with its profusion of marble, borders on the royal. Above the landing are two blank coats of arms. The façade is punctuated by half-pillars. The copper nameplates beside the massive front door blare the message; this is a house for dentists, doctors, insurance agents and a respectable widow, who takes in boarders.

This street is one great cultural derivation: Berlin's nouveau riche copied their emperor's style in the same way that their emperor copied his from the capitals of a more ancient Europe. They were built this way everywhere in the better neighbourhoods, the apartment buildings with a gateway for carriages – used, in actual fact, only by the coal merchant or milkman – the impressive vestibules and palatial stairways, the divided stateliness of a façade, the cut-rate grandeur.

In this campaign for glory, Kaiser Wilhelm himself set the tone. The whole city was permeated with his romanticised view of history. Wilhelm's hand could be seen everywhere: in the countless statues of winged deities, in the many museums, in the thirty-five neo-Gothic churches – one of the empress' hobbies – in the thousands of oak leaves, laurel wreaths and other 'national' symbols, in the copper statue of the city's pudgy pseudo-goddess, Berolina, at Alexanderplatz, in the Siegfrieds with their imperial swords, in the Germanias with their triumphal chariots. London and Paris had long histories, but Berlin lacked continuity; these instant monuments served to fill the historical vacuum.

Wilhelm was deeply impressed by his arch rival England and copied whatever he could: Kew Gardens at Lichterfelde, Oxford at Dahlem, the famous Round Reading Room of the British Museum in his own Kaiserliche Bibliothek. But everything, of course, had to be bigger than its counterpart in England. At the Tiergarten, as an eternal tribute to his ancestors – but above all to himself – he had built the 700-metre-long Siegesallee, lined with marble statuary. That eternity, by the way, did not last long: the marble statues of the Electors (which Wilhelm felt looked 'as though made by Michelangelo') were tossed into the Landwehrkanal not long after the Second World War; today, a few of them have been dredged up and brought back to the Siegesallee and the Tiergarten.

Wilhelm had a specific objective in all this, of course. As Germany made its ascent it was not only faced with the same conflicts seen in Great Britain and France, but it was also one of Europe's youngest nations. When Wilhelm II took the throne in 1888, the country was less than twenty years old. Most of its inhabitants did not even consider themselves Germans;

they were Saxons, Prussians or Württembergers. Every town, every valley had its own dialect. Only the upper class spoke High German; when travelling, middle-class Germans had trouble understanding each other. The local courts at Munich, Dresden and Weimar still maintained their royal status, with jealously guarded ranks and privileges. Bavaria, Württemberg, Saxony and Baden had their own armies, their own currencies and postage stamps, and even their own diplomatic services.

At the same time, young Germany had major ambitions in the field of international politics. Europe had been living in relative peace for decades, a situation often summarised by the phrase 'inside Europe, balance rules; outside Europe, Britain rules'. The great Prussian chancellor Bismarck's sole objective was to make a united Germany's new-found power a part of that system, and at first he succeeded wonderfully well. With patience and wisdom he had allowed Europe to grow accustomed to the new configuration. He had circumvented the major risks: an alliance between Russia and France which would have locked Germany in from both sides, and the disruptive potential of the perpetual issue of the Balkans, to say nothing of the danger of Germany being dragged into a possible war between Russia and Austria. Bismarck's Germany was, as the diplomat and author Sebastian Haffner put it, a contented nation.

In 1890, Bismarck was bumped aside by the young Wilhelm, effectively putting an end to the politics of patience and caution. The kaiser and his new ministers represented a discontented, restless, misunderstood Germany. Just as the eighteenth century had been the century of the French, and the nineteenth the century of the British, in their eyes the twentieth century was to be German. And, in a certain sense, it was. Around the turn of the century they began assembling a gigantic fleet, as a retort to British naval power. They cultivated the old enmities with Russia and France, thereby driving those countries into each other's arms. They began an arms race. Their thinking and behaviour focused increasingly on an altered version of stability: outside Europe, balance rules; inside Europe, Germany rules.

Yet despite its appropriation of power, the new German nation lacked the natural status of older countries such as France and Great Britain. On the one hand, a modern civil society was developing, with prospering trade and industry; on the other, however, real power was still in the hands of a few hundred aristocratic families and an associate caste of top officials and officers who danced to the kaiser's tunes. On the one hand, the Germans' self-awareness was growing with each passing year; on the other, Germany continued to live in a state of uncertainty about its national character and even its national boundaries, beyond which there were Germans living as well. The German state, in short, was much smaller than the German nation.

Wilhelm II's task, therefore, was somehow to provide emotional cohesion for this disconnected land. As in every brand-new nation, the new subjects had to be given the feeling 'this is something to which I want to belong, this is a great thing, this will lift us out of the mire of our existence'. That is why young nations build monuments, grand government buildings and sometimes even whole capitals. But Kaiser Wilhelm took things a step further. He adopted a quasi-national style of government as well, a brand of theatre that fit his own person to a tee. The result, in the words of the German historian Michael Stürmer, was a ruling style consisting of 'a great deal of propaganda, sweeping gestures and alluring prospects, a pinch of the very old and a pinch of the very new, and none of it real: pure bread and games.'

Wilhelm's theatricality lacked conviction in other ways too. Germany had long ceased to be the country of regimental colours, laurel wreaths and Electors chiselled in marble. Beneath the great display of tradition, it had, like Britain, become a modern and pluriform nation with countless intellectual, economic and cultural ties with the rest of the world. In Britain, many of the traditions still had a certain historical basis, and enjoyed broad popular support. The superficial forms created by Wilhelm, however, were empty and came far too late.

The remarkable thing was that these same contradictions were a part of Wilhelm himself. His manner was nostalgic, but at the same time his interests enthusiastically embraced all things new. When he heard about the incredible speed at which the American Barnum & Bailey's circus, which was touring Germany at the time, could load and unload its circus trains, he immediately sent a few officers to take a look. The Germany Army then actually adopted several of the circus' techniques. Many such modernisations were spurred on by Wilhelm's enthusiasm. During his reign, Berlin, alongside New York, became the world's major centre for the chemical industry and electrical engineering. The mega-concern Siemens, for example, owed its success primarily to the enormous sums spent by the German imperial army on the development of telegraph, telephone, radio and other modern communications systems. With more than half a million employees, the Prussian rail network was the largest and best-organised enterprise in Europe. Contemporaries described the hustle and bustle of the Potsdamer Platz as 'deafening': in 1896, the square was crossed each day by 6,000 freight cars, 1,500 private coaches, 7,000 hansom cabs, 2,000 omnibuses and 4,000 trams.

Under Wilhelm, therefore, Germany was more than a relic of a mystical, nonexistent past. It was, as the British urban historian Peter Hall correctly describes it, the world's first modern military-industrial state. It was a meeting place of extremes, a disconcerting clash between old dreams and the modern age.

Much of that Berlin has since been obliterated, but Wilhelm's cathedral, the Dom (1905), survives. Here the kaiser's voice can still be heard. In his younger years he believed that he was God's instrument on earth, and that any criticism of his policies was an act of blasphemy. Churches were named after the Hohenzollerns, and for good reason.

This Dom is a combination of St Peter's, St Paul's and Notre Dame. It is a brash attempt to catch up on the entire Renaissance and the eighteenth century in one fell swoop. All gold and marble, no expense or hardship was too great, yet the building still reminds one vaguely of a fake cathedral in the Arizona desert. Wilhelm had an enormous box built for himself, the size of a classroom, with a red marble staircase broad enough for a horse. To the left and right of the imperial box, apostles and Electors look down on us as one; in God's eyes, all men are equal, and the emperor is more equal than all.

As I pass by the imperial crypt, I notice that there is a celebration in progress: Elector Johan Cicero (1455–99) has been dead for precisely 500 years, and atop his spick-and-span sarcophagus – the crypt's *mise en scène* resembles nothing so much as a garage – is a fresh wreath with a lovely black ribbon. At the solemn consecration ceremony, Wilhelm promised the church leaders that he would make Berlin a second Vatican. So much has happened in this church since then – the benediction for the armies of 1914, the weekly prayers for Hitler, Göring's wedding – that it is a miracle the building itself did not go completely – despite the heavy damage it incurred during the Second World War – by the sword.

Then, of course, there was that other Berlin, the Berlin of the gigantic housing projects, the massive blocks of flats built around one, two or sometimes even three courtyards, hundreds of dank little apartments, beehives that stank all day of nappies and sauerkraut. Like London and Paris, Berlin experienced a population explosion: from one million inhabitants in 1870 to almost four million in 1914. In the end, almost every square metre had been built upon. The regulations handed down by the city administration were limited almost entirely to the minimum size of the courtyards: 5.34 metres square, the minimum turning circle of a horse-drawn fire engine. The term 'housing blocks' says it all: red and ochre piles of shoeboxes that overran the city, inhabited not by individual families, but by 'the masses'.

Hobrecht's vision of the integrated city had come to naught: the 1912 edition of the *Bärenführer* advised 'adventuresome' visitors to take a ride on the Ringbahn, to catch a glimpse of 'that other Berlin', where 'hoi polloi' lived. In my research, I came across a written complaint filed by residents of the Prenzlauer Berg neighbourhood concerning the lack of toilets. The reply from the Prussian civil servant stated that 'an average bowel movement takes three to four minutes, including the time needed to arrange one's clothing' and that 'even if the bowel movement were to take ten minutes, the twelve hours in a day leave sufficient time for seventy-two persons to make use of the toilet.'

Berlin had a reputation as one of the cleanest, most efficient and best-maintained cities in Europe, but the city also had something chilly about it. The Polish writer Jósef Kraszewski saw streets full of soldiers walking along 'like machines', with measured tread, but what was more: 'their demeanour was mimicked by the corner merchant, the coachman, the doorman, even the beggar.' It was a city, he wrote, that was orderly, obedient and disciplined, 'as in an ongoing state of siege'.

Today, in early 1999, all that has changed. West and East Berlin are now doing their cautious best to become reacquainted, like a couple following a long separation. In clothing and lifestyle the citizens of Berlin are heading inch by inch towards rapprochement, but chaos still reigns in the shared household. Drivers from West Berlin keep colliding with the trams of the East, a phenomenon they forgot about long ago. The sewers of East Berlin regularly produce huge potholes in the streets; amid the victorious class struggle, the communist authorities of the last half-century forgot that the city's subterranean pipes and tunnels needed some occasional maintenance. Sometimes a water main will burst, and huge geysers will blow in the midst of traffic.

Just outside the door of the Dom stands a weathered chunk of concrete. Once it was a monument to commemorate anti-fascist resistance by the city's young communists: 'United always in friendship with the Soviet Union.' Now it has been put up on four wooden chocks, ready to be hoisted away. This, too, has passed.

Meanwhile, on the Kurfürstendamm, just around the corner from my lodgings, the matchbox game provides a glimmer of hope. Around noon each day the partners in the little gambling operation report for work. It is always a telling moment. The team consists of five men. There is one 'pitcher', a skinny man who skilfully conceals a little ball under one of three matchboxes, and four 'players'. The men wear leather coats of clearly Eastern European origin; all but one, that is, a grey-haired fellow in a long camel-hair overcoat, clearly a man of substance. The pitcher rolls out his rug, squats down and starts performing his prestidigitation with the matchboxes. The players begin drawing in the guileless. One of them 'wins', ups the ante and does a stiff little dance of joy. The 'man of substance' nods approvingly, and places the occasional bet as well. The most fascinating element is the laughter: every three minutes, the black-leather group begins laughing wildly and pounding each other on the back in affected joy and comradeship. Berlin, as Oswald Spengler once wrote, is Europe's 'whore of Babylon'. This is where it's all happening, the guileless think, this is the place for me to be.

The Berlin phone book is still rife with Polish, Czech and Russian names. Around 1900, more than sixty per cent of the city's population consisted of immigrants or the children of immigrants. To many visitors, Berlin seemed to have something American about it, something reminiscent of Chicago. The bare squares and noisy houses reminded the artist/author Karl Scheffler of 'American or Australian towns that spring up deep in the wilderness'. He gave his 1910 depiction of the city the significant title *Berlin: Ein Stadtschicksal*, and felt that 'no trace of the born gentleman is to be found in the modern citizen of Berlin'. The dense colonial hordes, he said, had 'come pouring into the city from the Eastern plains, lured by the promise of Americanism'.

This is, of course, pure nonsense: it was not the promise of urban culture that attracted these penniless farmers; it was desperation, by and large, that drove them from their villages. But the sense of momentum and alienation did elicit a certain reaction within the city, a kind of pessimism of progress, a nostalgia for the traditional German community – whatever that may have been. Around 1910, large groups of young people marched out of town into the countryside each weekend under the rubric '*Los von Berlin*'. The leader of these *Wandervögel* had his followers greet him with a raised arm and a shout of '*Heil!*' Käthe Kollwitz complained in her diary that her younger son, Peter, was such a great fan that he wore the regulation 'natural' clothing and imitated the movement's leaders right down to the smallest gesture.

Of what were the people of Berlin afraid? Not of war, in any case. War in their eyes was almost a ritual, a courageous and glorious thing. Were they afraid of socialism, and the rise of the lower class? A bit. Of losing their hard-won, middle-class prosperity? Probably. Of their own decline, of the new, of the unknown? Certainly. And what about the 'Jewish syndicate'? Not everyone feared that, but some parts of the population assuredly did.

The roots of that anti-Semitism ran deep, even back into the Middle Ages. On 28 October, 1873, after a boom that lasted several years, the Berlin stock market collapsed. That crash was followed by a chain of bankruptcies – large factories, railway companies, brokerage firms – and within the space of a few days many citizens lost everything they possessed. The economy recovered quite quickly, but the psychological effect of the crash echoed on for a generation or more. In the first decade of the twentieth century, many of Berlin's fearful petits bourgeois felt envy and hatred when they saw wealthy Jews driving around the city. At the universities, a pseudo-scientific theory was developed to provide a basis for this mood of 'conspiracy', 'decay' and 'betrayal'; it spoke of parasitic Jews and

Germanic 'Lichtmenschen', of the depraved city and the pure German soil. Bismarck's banker, Gerson von Bleichröder, the first Jew to be admitted to the German nobility, was barely tolerated by the better families; at a *Hofball* no one would dance with his wife, until an officer was explicitly ordered to do so.

At the same time, Berlin's artistic and cultural climate was being shaped more and more by liberal middle-class families with a broad education, a world in which Jews played a central role. The same went for the socialist movement. Furthermore, around 1910 – in Berlin, as well as in other major European cities such as Warsaw, Krakow and Vienna – one could barely speak any longer of 'the' Jews. The group had become too diverse for that. You had orthodox believers and communists, atheists and racists, Zionists of all shapes and sizes, liberals and social democrats. Most of them no longer understood Yiddish, the immigrants spoke dozens of languages and dialects, and the Jews of Berlin considered themselves Germans, that above all. The great majority had become completely secularised. Of all the famous German Jews of the day, not one still had ties with the Jewish faith.

The success of that Jewish community can still be seen in the partially restored synagogue on Oranienburger Strasse, once the largest Jewish house of worship in Germany, with more than three thousand seats and an illuminated dome that was more than fifty metres high and stood out sharply against Berlin's skyline. It was a triumphal building: significant is the placement of the dome, which was built close to the street, not above the Torah as usual, to make the building stand out as much as possible. The photographs of the official opening show that everyone who was anyone in the Berlin of that day was in attendance.

Services and concerts went on in the grand synagogue without interruption, even after the Nazi takeover in 1933. The list still hangs there: on 9 February, 1935 the concert performance of *Joy in Winter*; on 11 November, 1935 a congregational meeting on the subject of emigration; on 20 November, 1935 a benefit concert for the Jewish Winter Aid programme, featuring Ferdinand Hiller's 'The Destruction of Jerusalem'; on 15 February, 1936 a meeting 'To Strengthen the Cohesion of the Congregation'; on 13 March, 1938 a memorial service for the victims of the Great War; on 24 April, 1938 a performance of Händel's oratorio *Saul*.

During the Kristallnacht in November 1938, the synagogue itself was saved by a brave policeman from the sixteenth precinct who, pistol in hand, chased the *Sturmabteilung* out of the already burning building. The final performance was held on 31 March, 1940: a closing concert for the Jewish Winter Aid programme.

I come across a photograph taken in 1933. The girls' section of the Auerbachische Orphanage, a couple of little girls playing in a children's kitchen, proudly pushing their doll around in a pram, their eyes gleaming.

'Peace, solidarity and cooperation are only conceivable among peoples and nations who know who they are,' Václav Havel, then president of Czechoslovakia, wrote a lifetime later. And here he touched upon a deep human truth. 'If I don't know who I am, who I want to be, what I want to achieve, where I begin and where I end, then my relations with the people around me and the world at large will inevitably be tense, suspicious and burdened by an inferiority complex that may go hidden behind puffed-up bravura.'

That applies to individuals, but also to the relations between nations, and it applies even more so to those situations in which the weaknesses of nations and of individuals more or less coincide.

On the south-eastern side of Berlin, behind the incineration plant and the cable factories, lies Köpenick. This suburb made world news in 1906 when the unemployed cobbler Wilhelm Voigt put on an old captain's uniform, ordered a group of soldiers to follow him, occupied the town hall 'on His Majesty's orders' and had them hand over the municipal cash box, containing 4,000 marks.

Later, I saw a photograph of this captain from Köpenick: an extraordinary hapless character with a cap three sizes too big for him. Köpenick tells the story of a society where the officer's cap was all-powerful, no matter who wore it. In 'his' city, the kaiser gave officers free rein. He insisted that his army remain free of all outside coercion. Wilhelm had increased the number of officers sevenfold, but the aristocracy remained in power. The military, in other words, did not become civilised: the civilians became militarised. The captain from Köpenick, it turned out later, had never served in the army, and had arranged the whole ruse more or less on instinct. Everyone fell for it. After centuries of humiliation, of

French and Austrian troops sacking and looting their way through a divided Germany, the military class had become Germany's most important mass symbol. The army represented the German nation, 'the marching forest' as Elias Canetti called it, the 'closed ranks'. All outsiders were no longer German.

None of this, however, meant that Wilhelm was out to start a war. For him, the military was largely a mannerism, a way to impose order on his young nation. War was something completely different; something courageous and romantic in the eyes of his generation, but not a reality. Yet in the end the adoration for Wagner, for the Romantic movement, for the Reinheitskultur, the nostalgia for the house in the woods, Wilhelm's fairytale world, would prevail over the logical reasoning of the strategists, managers, financiers and scientists.

'If one asks oneself today, with all due care, why Europe plunged itself into war in 1914, one cannot find a single sensible reason or even a cause,' Stefan Zweig wrote later. 'It was not about ideas, it was not even about those little areas along the border; I can find no explanation but a surplus of energy, a tragic consequence of the internal momentum that had been building up over the course of forty years.'

In the end, the captain from Köpenick was arrested. During his imprisonment he became so popular that, after two and half years, the kaiser granted him a pardon. His story was filmed, recorded on wax, made into a play by Carl Zuckmayer and told on countless occasions to the people of Berlin, who loved laughing at their own freak show. One of the wax records with the voice of cobbler Voigt has been preserved at the Heimatmuseum in Köpenick. I wanted to experience that magic for myself.

On my way there I found myself in a crowd of several dozen elderly people, who had gathered in a rainy park to commemorate Köpenick's 'Week of Blood'. The mayor read the names of the twenty-four Jews, socialists and communists who, in January 1933, had been kicked to death by the SA in this same, respectable Köpenick. Another eighty people were beaten until crippled.

After the ceremony was over, I spent a little time talking to an elderly lady who had been with the Dutch resistance as a girl, who had fallen in love with her liaison officer in the German communist underground and followed him here after the war was over. Together they had hoped to help build the new, promised non-fascist DDR. 'I spent my whole life here among the common people, sharing their lives,' she said. 'Because the fact of the matter is, the Devil cut us from the same piece of cloth, and it's cloth from the bargain basement at that.' Her name was An de Lange. In Köpenick she had become old and wrinkled. She told me her story, then disappeared.

By the time I got to the Heimatmuseum, it was closed. I never heard the captain's crackly voice.

Chapter Five

Vienna

outside it has started snowing. Dark grey clouds are hanging on the horizon. The Czech buffet car smells of soup and hot apple pie. For the first few hours, I am the only customer. The cook stands in the kitchen wearing his big white hat, doing nothing. As the waiter's attitude turns to one of melancholy devotion, we rumble alongside frozen rivers, past a world of rusty iron, road workers with noses reddened by the cold, past bonfires beside the tracks and villages where the blue smoke rolls sleepily from the chimneys, and everywhere the snow is falling.

We pass a river, an electrical plant with steaming stacks, an ochre-coloured station with a dirty banner and an old man pushing a pram full of oranges. The conductor has started looking like a wise, old professor.

After Prague the snowflakes begin to whip and drift, the wind howls, the locomotive hoots in the distance. We stop and wait at a nameless station. There is light coming from a kitchen window. A woman is standing at the counter. She is bathing a child, who is standing naked in the sink. Then both of them slip away. A little while later we are in Vienna.

'The merry apocalypse' was what they once called this city, this odd mixture of creativity, middle-class normality, human suffering, power, complicity and schizophrenia. Around 1914 it was the power base for a huge empire that suffered from one major flaw: it no longer had a function, other than to amplify its own hum.

In the centuries that went before, the dual Austro-Hungarian monarchy had played a crucial role in Central and Eastern Europe. The Habsburg emperors had brought the southern German peoples back into the fold. They had driven the Ottoman Turks from the gates of Vienna. They had made it possible for Germans, Hungarians, Rumanians, Italians, Rhaetians, Serbs, Croatians, Poles, Slovenes, Slovaks, Czechs, Jews and Gypsies to live together in peace. Furthermore, they had launched a cultural counter-offensive in the near-oriental regions of the Balkans. There too, a Western administration and a workable system of law was imposed.

After that the empire gradually creaked to a halt, it became a crazy quilt of nationalities bound together by an elderly emperor, Franz Josef I. 'The emperor was an old man. He was the oldest emperor in the world,' wrote Joseph Roth in The Radetzky March, his classic tale of that world's decline. 'Death walked around him, in a circle, in a circle, and mowed and mowed. The field was already empty, only the emperor still stood there, waiting, like a forgotten silver haulm.'

In the early twentieth century the empire was still seen as a super-power. With almost fifty million inhabitants in 1910, it was second in size only to Germany (sixty-five million). After that came Great Britain (forty-five million) and France (almost forty million). From just over 230,000 in 1801, the population of Vienna had increased to more than two million in 1910. Aristocrats from all over the empire gathered there with all the coachmen, maids, carpenters, whores and lackeys they needed for a comfortable life. Impoverished farmers also came pouring into the imperial capital, dreaming of a little prosperity and happiness. And to them were added tens of thousands of impoverished Jews, driven west by the pogroms in Russia, Poland and Galicia.

Vienna was considered the Arcadia of the middle class, and authors such as Roth and Zweig would write about it later with profound nostalgia. But for those who did not belong to the moneyed classes, life was hard there. The housing shortage in Vienna was worse than anywhere else in Europe. In 1910, barely one per cent of all Viennese families had their own home, only seven per cent of the houses had a bathroom, and fewer than twenty-five per cent of them a toilet. There were many Bettgeher, people who rented, not a room, but merely a bed to sleep in. Countless citizens of Vienna spent their days coughing and nauseous, with tuberculosis and intestinal ailments from the city's filthy drinking water.

'Today, long after the great storm has destroyed it, we know that that world of security was merely a castle in the air,' Stefan Zweig wrote many years later. 'Yet still, my parents inhabited it as though it were a house of stone.' For him, as for most of his contemporaries, the sudden collapse of the Habsburg Empire in 1918 was a disconcerting experience. Almost every Viennese writer has since puzzled over the question. How could it have been? How could the Germans have been so willing to bid farewell to the Hohenzollerns in 1918? How could life in Great Britain and France go on as usual? Why was it only in Austria that everything fell apart? And then Vienna: how could this symbol of the illustrious empire suddenly have become a monstrous fish floundering on a dry seabed?

Along the Ringbahn, the entire history of European architecture is tipped out over unsuspecting passers-by. This was the 'via triumphalis' of Emperor Franz Josef and the liberal moneyed classes, the eternal Ring along which every self-respecting flâneur took his daily steps between the Kärntnerstrasse and the Schwarzenbergplatz, and along which today old ladies show off their fur coats as the trams go crawling past.

The Ring was built around medieval Vienna in 1865, in the space freed when the city's old fortifications were torn down. A space 500 metres wide and 4 kilometres long was created and filled with hotels, the palaces of both old and new wealth, expensive apartments for the rich and huge public buildings: the parliament (neo-Hellenistic), the town hall (neo-Gothic) and the Burg theatre, the Royal Opera, the stock exchange and the university (neo-Renaissance).

Here the old city was not torn down, as it was in Paris and Brussels, but set like a gem in a broad corona of new construction. Musty medieval Vienna, long immured in its city walls, was suddenly thrown open. The Ring served as an area of transition to the suburbs and the working-class neighbourhoods that lay beyond. And, just as in Paris, the broad arterial had an important military function as well: in the event of rioting, troops could be brought in quickly everywhere. Barracks were built at strategic locations, as well as an impressive arsenal complex.

Alongside Berlin, Vienna was the fastest-growing metropolis on the continent. But at the same time it was a city stuck in the past. Telephones and elevators were a rarity, most clothing was still sewn by hand and, until 1918, typewriters were banned from government offices. Around the turn of the century more than half the population lived from the proceeds of their small businesses, which they bitterly defended against outside competition. Until 1900, department stores were banned in Vienna.

Unlike Berlin, Vienna had always been a city of conspicuous consumption, a hub where the aristocrats lived lavishly from the revenues of their estates and other holdings. Surrounding them was an enormous network of services: tailors, cobblers, doormen, architects, doctors, psychiatrists, artists and, lest we forget, musicians, actors and the *Süsse Madel*. But Vienna, unlike London or Berlin, never became a dynamic industrial or financial centre.

Here too arose a city with a great internal contradiction: due to the great dependency on the power of the emperor and the aristocracy, the atmosphere was, on the one hand, very conservative and formal; on the other hand, rationality and intellect reigned supreme, for this was also the locus of all the empire's talent.

The city's structure was just as ambiguous as all other facets of Viennese life. It did its utmost to generate awe for the emperor's power, and more than that: the layout of the city's streets actually formed a direct reflection of imperial order. At the same time, for many young Viennese, the Ring was the symbol of theatrical falsehood, a Potemkin project full of obscurantism and counterfeit history, the product of stage designers who wanted everyone to think that Vienna was populated only by nobility, and by no one else.

Somewhere I saw a group portrait by the painter Theo Zasche, painted in 1908 and showing all of Vienna's prominent citizens on the Sirk corner of the Ring, the haunt of the elite across from the Opera – what the pamphleteer Karl Kraus called the 'cosmic intersection' of Vienna. I see 'Direktor Gustav Mahler' walking along, 'Hofoper- und Kammersängerin Selma Kurtz' turning to look over her shoulder, 'Erherzog Eugen' being greeted by 'Fürst Max Egon Fürstenberg', 'Baron Oton Bourgoin' put-putting past in an automobile, and so 'all Vienna' passes before my eyes.

In one corner of the watercolour is a bright advertising pillar. It is one of the kiosks which, as people claimed later, camouflaged the entrances to underground Vienna, the secret network of tunnels beneath the houses, the murky world where dozens of *Kanalstrotter* made a living by collecting old buttons and dropped coins. In the city above, no one even knew it was there.

It is quiet in Vienna's U-Bahn. In early 1914, Robert Musil spoke of the Viennese tram as a 'shimmering, rattling box . . . a machine in which a few hundred kilos of human beings are shaken back and forth, to make of them a future . . . A hundred years ago they sat in the post-chaise with just such expressions on their faces, and a hundred years from now God only knows what they will be up to, but as new people in the new machines of the future they will sit there in just this way.'

I am in that future now, and I take a good look around me. To my right sits a chubby-cheeked lady wrapped in furs, wearing gold spectacles and a sort of brown turban by way of a hat. She looks to be in her fifties, but I can tell by her complexion that she's no older than thirty. Across from her sits her husband, grey coat, glum beard. In the seat in front of me is a man in a leather jacket and a thick woollen cap, his head bowed. This is how he averts his face to keep an eye on the world, for his twinkling eyes are sharp and observant, all the better to anticipate or ward off its blows.

I have gone walking, taken the tram, visited the home of artist-architect Friedensreich Hundertwasser. The Hundertwasser house looks like a brightly coloured Hobbit den, with bulging floors, trees growing out of the windows, naughty ornaments and a photograph of the architect himself in the 1960s, wild and completely naked, as befits an artist. The building is now one of the city's major tourist attractions, and the Viennese are so very proud of it: look at the things we dare!

Seldom have I seen an exception that so proves the rule. Modern-day Vienna is like a city of high officials with nothing more to be high about. The atmosphere is doting, the shops are stocked with perfume and cakes, every snowdrift is immediately made to toe the line. It is almost impossible to imagine that this city can still reproduce, that people still make love here, that beneath these endless hats and responsible suits there can still be bodies, pale and trembling. At least five times a day I walk up and down Kärntnerstrasse, the big shopping street between the Stephansdom and the Opera, the heart line of the city. The people walking there, young and old, nod to each other, and only two drunk tramps disturb the peace; but not really – just like Hundertwasser, they are a part of this closed system, the way a bakery drawn by Anton Pieck cannot exist without a pair of shivering waifs peering through the window.

There is only one place in which you can take shelter from this city: in a coffee house. Without coffee houses there is no Vienna; without Vienna, there are no coffee houses.

They still exist, these fantastic pleasure domes full of mirrors, leather sofas and brown marble walls, these roomy and intimate spaces where the glasses and cups tinkle festively all day long, where the evenings are warm as the wet snow blows against the windows, where poets, students and bookkeepers coexist, where it smells of coffee and *Apfelstrudel*, where you can look, talk, read or stare into your beloved's eyes.

Vienna around the turn of the century was a typical city of the senses, and the coffee house played a central role in that. 'Nowhere was it easier to be European,' Stefan Zweig suggested, and explained that the coffee houses had all the major European newspapers, 'as well as all the principal literary and cultural magazines from all over the world.' Nothing, he felt, contributed more to the intellectual versatility of Vienna than the coffee house. Politically, everything was locked down tight, so what could one do but flee into art, into one's own soul? 'We truly *did* know what was in the wind, for we lived continually with nostrils flared. We found what was new because we wanted the new, because we hungered after something that belonged to us and to us alone – and not to the world of our fathers.'

There was always some reason for excitement at those worn tables. The new play by a certain Oskar Kokoschka, for example, entitled *Mörder, Hoffnung der Frauen*. Or a stunningly bare building, designed by Adolf Loos in his quest for the new purity. Or the composer Arnold Schönberg, who had racked his audiences with tonalities never heard before and was booed out of the hall – people had even thrown chairs. Or the latest erotic novel by Leopold von Sacher-Masoch, in which male slaves were reduced to quivering heaps by robust ladies with whips. Or the 'secret nerves' of which psychiatrist Sigmund Freud spoke so compellingly. Or the cuts made in Mahler's rendition of Wagner's *Die Walküre*, a concession to the composer's many detractors. Or the most recent 'quarterly figures' published by Karl Kraus' anti-newspaper *Die Fackel*:

Anonymous diatribes: 236
Anonymous threats: 83
Molestations: 1

Now it is Friday evening, and the quiet of a village reigns over the echoing Kärntnerstrasse. A cold wind is blowing. The only sound is coming from a ghetto blaster in the middle of the street. A group of about ten young people are swaying to something that sounds like house music, two girls in checkered outfits up in front, a tawny man at the back, clearly the boss. All the dancers are wearing green jockey caps. Four pedestrians have stopped to watch. A woman hands out pamphlets. The pamphlets say that this is a new church, that Christ will be returning soon, and that no train derails unless it is God's will.

The snow falls softly between the big white buildings of the Hofburg, in the courtyards, on the roofs, the chimneys and the marble heroes.

These days everything revolves around the next ball, and inside the Hofburg the people of Vienna are dancing the gold leaf off the walls. On 22 January was the Officers' Ball, on 23 January the Pharmacists' Ball, on 25 January the Hunters' Ball, yesterday was the Technology Ball, tomorrow there will be the Doctors' Ball, on 6 February there will be a Hofburg Gala Ball, on 12 February the Scientists' Ball, and on 13 February the Jurists' Ball.

'Everyone knew everyone by name, as though they were all brothers, but they greeted each other as one ruler greets the other,' wrote Joseph Roth. 'They knew the young and the old, the good horsemen and the bad, the gallants and the players, the quick-witted, the ambitious, the favourite sons, the heirs to an ancient, time-honoured, proverbial and generally venerated stupidity, as well as the intelligent ones, who would be taking power tomorrow.'

The Austro-Hungarian Empire was a textbook example of what anthropologist Benedict Anderson called an 'imaginary community', a nation bound together by people who had never met, but who in their minds sensed each other to be family, brothers and sisters.

Emperor Franz Josef I took the throne in December 1848 and held it until November 1916, one of the longest recorded reigns. Throughout all those decades he remained a binding element, partly because he did not try to forge national unities where there were none to be forged. As king of Hungary he spent weeks each year in Budapest, dressed in Hungarian uniform, with Hungarian ministers and a Hungarian parliament. He always spoke of 'my peoples', and never of 'my people'.

He was the heart of this imaginary community. In the Hofburg I had felt the ambience that was still his: in the cabinet conference room with its white walls, right beside his dressing room; in his austere bedroom with the single iron bed; in the bedchamber that once belonged to him and his wife, with Empress Sisi's gymnastics equipment still against the wall; in his study, with the little desk, the portrait of Field Marshal Joseph von Radetzky and his telephone, number 61.

The significance of Franz Josef lay not in what he did, but in what he was. His was a symbolic role, and one he took very seriously. He adhered strictly to Spanish court etiquette, and the story goes that the royal physician who rushed to his deathbed was upbraided by the emperor for the way he was dressed. Unlike the German kaiser, Franz Josef had a sincere dislike of all innovation. Flush toilets were only installed at the Hofburg after persistent requests from the empress; he distrusted telephones and trains, and refused to tolerate electric light because it hurt his eyes.

He lived according to the Habsburg concept of *Hausmacht*, the unshakable conviction that the Habsburg dynasty was God's instrument on earth. As long as the aristocracy and the people remained true to God and the emperor, all would be well. Revolution and godlessness, on the other hand, could undermine the system swiftly and fatally. In the end, that was exactly what happened.

In addition to the *Hausmacht*, there was also a clear-cut hierarchy of high-born nobility and 'service nobility', the nobility appointed for reasons of merit. Only high-born nobility and officers were *hoffähig* and allowed to attend the court. Consisting of no more than eighty families, they spent from December to May attending each other's parties and funerals, and intermarried to such an extent that they were indeed one big family.

In France and England, the wealthier citizenry had broken the power of the aristocracy; in Vienna that had not happened, and the well-to-do never succeeded in merging with the aristocracy. Strictly speaking, the liberal citizenry ruled along with the emperor and his nobles, but they did not have the upper hand. In addition, an enormous chasm yawned between the sensual, loose culture of the aristocracy and the orderly, rational and puritanical culture of the bourgeoisie. The middle-class citizen of Vienna remained a desperate onlooker, a failed parvenu, a person dying to belong, who lived behind façades, staircases and vestibules full of aristocratic ornaments, but who, in the long run, lacked the means, the language and the culture.

But during the second half of the nineteenth century, something strange occurred: real life began slipping away from beneath the imaginary kingdom. The empire became an increasingly hollow shell, believed in by the nobility and citizenry only for lack of an alternative.

The rebel nationalists, however, had no part in the fantasy: in *The Radetzky March*, for example, Joseph Roth's Hungarian officers begin excitedly chattering away in their own language when they hear of the attempt on Crown Prince Franz Ferdinand's life in Sarajevo in 1914: 'We are in agreement, my compatriots and I, that we can only be pleased if the swine really is dead!'

Excluded from the fantasy, too, were the millions of farmers and poorer citizens, who led real lives and had real problems. From no other nation were the people so eager to emigrate: between 1900–19, 3.5 million Habsburg subjects left for America, more than from any other country. And in no other army – except for the Russian – was desertion as widespread in the First World War as from the Austro-Hungarian Army. The number of Habsburgers taken prisoner (2.2 million) was twelve times that of the British (170,000). At the end of *The Radetzky March*, the high-born protagonist, Lieutenant Trotta, plunges into the fray. Soldier Onufrij, his valet, simply goes into hiding in his village. 'The harvest was about to begin. In the imperial and royal army, there was nothing left for him to do.'

It is Sunday. I go to the Stephansdom for edification. The priest welcomes us with a hearty '*Grüss Gott*' and notes that last night at Klagenfurt the temperature plummeted to eighteen degrees below zero. The congregation sings hesitantly, the psalms rising up in clouds from their fur collars. The priest tells a story about the legendary mayor of New York, Fiorello Henry La Guardia. When still a judge, La Guardia once tried a poor man for stealing a loaf of bread. He sentenced him to a fine of ten dollars, then pulled out his own wallet and gave the man ten dollars with which to pay his fine. 'Justice,' the priest says, 'must always go hand in hand with compassion.' 'Amen,' everyone nods, and we all turn and shake each other's hands. Then a Japanese girl comes strolling up the aisle, looks around in surprise and starts taking pictures of the congregation.

Does anything ever really happen here? At Ottakring station, a woman in a fur coat is sitting on the lap of a man in a fur coat. A drunken man staggers down Kärntnerstrasse. At the central train station, a pretty woman walks by, the first one I've seen in Vienna. She has dark hair, light, almond-shaped eyes, but the most striking thing about her is the dignity in her movements. She is pushing a little cart; her job is to empty the rubbish bins and sweep the floor. That, apparently, is how she earns her living. These are the only things I have to report from this city.

Today, on this Sunday, I am on my way to put a rose on the grave of the unknown waif. Along the Danube, behind the neglected shipyards and the last dusty silos, lies the graveyard for bodies washed up from the river, the Friedhof der Namenlosen. Here lie all the unknown persons who jumped from bridges in desperation at the beginning of the twentieth century, a regular occurrence in the highly strung Vienna of that day.

The wind roars through the bare branches. My rose ends up beside a few faded plastic flowers, on the grave of someone who turns out to have a name after all, Aloisia Marscha (1877–1905).

All the city's bells are rung at eventide, the air is silver with their tolling. Stephansplatz is deserted, except for a few tourist carriages. The moon above the old houses is full and yellow. It is freezing hard. On the street the vendors are offering chestnuts and roast potatoes.

There is a peculiar drawing of the Michaelerplatz, made in 1911 or 1912. In it, the young artist A. Hitler depicts the square in its entirety, with the exception of one building. That building housed a haberdashery, and was put up by the modernist architect Adolf Loos in 1910. The artist has replaced that building with one copied from an eighteenth-century drawing. Loos' 'house without eyebrows' was already famous at the time, but Hitler would not allow it to exist.

These days the Loos building is home to a bank. At first glance, to our eyes, it blends in quite well with the surroundings. The portico is made of beautiful green marble, with two huge round pillars, and the interior is marked by warm wooden walls and ceilings. Beside Loos' quiet façade, the neighbouring house front is a potpourri of flowers, wreaths and other gaudy bits and pieces. From the square itself you can see how the portico of the Loos house recedes elegantly from the sweep of the Michaelerplatz, how it provides an ironic retort to the pomp of the Hofburg. This building plays with its surroundings, and that is an uncommon thing.

The Loos house, plain and without ornament, was a plea for candour in the arts, and an early example of modernist architecture. It was a reaction to all those 'neo' styles that dominated the major cities of Europe until 1914. But in the eyes of many Viennese citizens of the day, the house was a monstrosity. It was a textbook case of all of the dangerous modernity being dumped on the German race by the liberals and the *krumm-nasige Hebräer*. All things 'historically healthy' had to be protected against this 'corrupt art', and whether Adolf Loos was actually a Jew or not is of no real concern. For many German and Catholic citizens, 'Jewish' and 'modern' were synonyms. This was, however, not completely wide of the mark: without Mahler, Wittgenstein, Freud, Schnitzler, Zweig, Roth, Herzl, Kraus and all the rest of the city's Jewish talent, Vienna would never have been such an important cultural centre.

Almost everything that would prove formative to the twentieth century was already lying dormant within Vienna in 1900. That also went for the politicians. The street here was ruled by the same characters one came across later all over Europe: the ideologist, the populist, the pioneer and the social democrat, all of whom would, in time, set everything right.

Let us first consider the last of these. The founder of Austrian socialism, Victor Adler, was born a Jew and baptised a Christian, he was a humanist, a liberal and, in his younger years, even a German nationalist. He felt that a great working-class revolution was inevitable; in the meantime, it was up to the socialist movement to prepare to take over the country's reins. He devoted himself, therefore, to advocating all forms of adult education, public libraries, workers' groups and other social-democratic organisations. In 1905 he organised a general strike to force the introduction of universal suffrage. In 1907 he finally got his way: the social democrats won eighty-seven seats on the imperial council.

Adler in this way became the nexus of a parliamentary movement that was peppered with radical slogans, but which, in practice, focused less and less on the class struggle and more and more on the welfare of the community as a whole. His son, Friedrich Adler, had other ideas. He chose the path of violent revolution. In 1916, he assassinated the prime minister.

The second prototype that Europe would come to see often was that of the nationalist ideologue. Georg Ritter von Schönerer was short and stocky, and 'his fat, red, beery face did not make an unpleasant impression at first,' as a contemporary put it. 'But as soon as he opens his mouth, this man shows himself to be very different. Then the otherwise tired eyes begin to shine, the hands begin to move and the face takes on a lively expression, while the words that roll from his lips resonate loudly through the chamber.' Schönerer, however, lacked the charisma needed to mobilise a mass following. His influence was derived from street violence and heated rhetoric.

In his early years, Schönerer had been a progressive landowner, the founder of schools and libraries, a father to his subordinates. He had worked closely with Victor Adler and other progressive liberals. Later, however, like many liberals, he became obsessed with the idea that 'his' superior Germans were being besieged within the Habsburg Empire by a circle of Slavic peoples. The only real liberals, he felt, were German liberals; only they were the bearers of the true cultural heritage. He had the words *Heil, Bismarck!* chiselled in huge runes on boulders at his estate.

In anti-Semitism, too, he was exceptionally fanatical. He demanded that Jews be expelled from most professions, institutions of learning and the newspapers – yea, from the German people as a whole: '*Durch Reinheit zur Einheit*'. On 18 February, 1884, at a party meeting, he became the first political leader in Europe to have posted a sign saying '*JUDEN*

IST DER EINTRITT VERBOTEN'. Hundreds of clubs – gymnastics, music, mountaineering, cycling, student, walking and book clubs – followed his example.

In the long run, Schönerer's movement developed into a kind of pseudo-Germanic cult with symbols and rituals of its own: runes, 'heil' salutes, solstice celebrations, bonfires, battle songs, all under the leadership of a single führer. Before being allowed to marry, his followers first had to prove their Aryan descent and 'biological' health. Anyone not wishing to contribute to the 'Reinheit des deutschen Blutes' was a 'traitor to the German people' and a 'Judenknecht'.

In the end, Schönerer went too far in his singularly un-Viennese fervour. In 1888, he and a few political associates barged into the editorial offices of the Neue Wiener Tageblatt, destroyed the presses of 'this Jewish rag' and beat up the editors. In liberal Vienna this could not go unpunished. Schönerer was sentenced to prison and lost his right to vote or hold office for five years; after that, he spent his time primarily in agitating on the margins of political life. But his influence remained considerable: anti-Semitism as a political goal, mass nationalism, blood, soil and German mysticism, the concept of völkische art, even the Führerprinzip – Central Europe was infected for good.

The third Viennese figure to play a formative role in Europe was the Christian Democrat populist Karl Lüger, a caretaker's son. He had a perfect ear for the sentiments of the average German-Viennese citizen, the common man, the shopkeeper afraid of industrialisation and whatever else the modern age brought with it. As the city's mayor, he was also an early pioneer of urban socialism. He had a great many new schools built, he set up a municipal gas, water and electric company and an excellent tram network, he organised a food programme for undernourished children and was far ahead of his time when it came to public housing and urban renewal.

Karl Lüger was a master of public relations; a term which, had it only existed in that day, would have fit him to a tee. He kept himself unsullied by the corruption within Vienna's administrative machinery; even his most fervent opponents had to admit that his behaviour was unimpeachable. In everything he did it was clear that he loved the role of the good-hearted, jovial city father who showed up at countless birthday celebrations and jubilees wearing his chain of office, a mayor so concerned with 'the little man' that, in his own words, he wished he 'could place a hansom cab at the disposal of every citizen who has had a few drinks too many'.

In his populism, Lüger went further than most Christian Democrat politicians. After Schönerer's fall, he immediately adopted the slogans that had brought Schönerer such success: Aryan purity, the nationalisation of big companies that had 'fallen into Jewish hands', the struggle against capitalism, down with the 'Jewish press' and modern art. In this regard, Lüger's vitriol was legendary. In 1894 he shouted to the national assembly that 'anti-Semitism will only meet its demise when the last Jew has met his'. And when confronted with his own statement that he 'could not care less whether Jews were shot or hanged', Lüger corrected his critic immediately: 'Shot or beheaded! That's what I said!'

In part, such popular opinions shared common roots with those in Berlin: the stock market crash of 1873, jealousy of more successful Jewish rivals, the longing for a scapegoat, an aversion to the flood of immigrants, and a fear of the modern age, seemingly personified by the Jews. In conservative, Catholic Vienna, Jewishness was synonymous with a particular mindset: freethinking, internationally oriented, nonconformist, without ties to church or nation – everything, in other words, the Viennese lower-middle class despised.

The Jews' non-national character gave rise to bad blood as well. They took no part in the sophisticated power plays between nationalities; they were really the only ones who had no nationality at all. Nor were they anxious for such a status, for they had no need of it. As Hannah Arendt rightly noted, the Jews in Austria were the darlings of the state par excellence: 'Thus a perfect harmony of interests was established between the powerful Jews and the state.' And in his celebrated Fin-de-Siècle Vienna, Carl Schorske wrote: 'The emperor and the liberal system offered the Jews a status without desiring from them a nationality; they became the supranational people of a multinational state, the only ones to follow in the footsteps of the old aristocracy.' Nationalists such as Lüger and Schönerer wanted to see a 180-degree change: they hated the multinational state, and above all they hated the state's multinational darlings.

The undertone of Lüger's anti-Semitism, however, was different from Schönerer's. Despite its vociferous nature, it was more opportunistic than doctrinaire, more social than racial. Lüger remained the cordial Viennese who enjoyed sitting around the table with the same Jewish capitalists he hounded in the city council. 'I decide who's a Jew and who isn't.' That was Lüger.

In 1922, a decade after Lüger's death, the Viennese journalist Hugo Bettauer published *Die Stadt ohne Juden: ein Roman von Übermorgen* (The City Without Jews: a Novel for the Day After Tomorrow), a satire of anti-Semitism. Bettauer described a Vienna from which the Jews had suddenly disappeared. There would be no more bankers to advise non-Jews on their speculations, non-Jewish women would lose all interest in fashion because they no longer needed to compete with Jewish women, prostitutes with drunken pimps could no longer be comforted with presents from their soft-hearted Jewish admirers. Three years later, Bettauer, a friend of Karl Kraus, was shot and killed by a student, then forgotten.

The response to all this – Zionism – was, predictably enough, invented in Vienna as well. Why should the Jews continue to refuse national status? Would they not be much better off actually pursuing such a status? This was the theory developed by the liberal Jewish leader Theodor Herzl around the turn of the century: the time had come to set up a new Jewish state. At the same time, Herzl hoped this would be the salvation of liberalism: his new Jewish state would be, above all, a liberal one.

Herzl came from a wealthy, enlightened family in which religion amounted to little more than a 'pious family memory'. In his younger years he considered himself a citizen of Vienna like any other, and during his student days even joined an outspokenly nationalistic *Burschenschaft*. When his fraternity club began gravitating towards anti-Semitism, he offered his resignation on the basis of his Jewish background, and his 'love of freedom'. But he was deeply offended when his 'brothers' dropped him with no further ado. As a correspondent for the *Neue Freie Presse* in Paris, where he reported on the Dreyfus affair, he heard the modern, cultured French shouting '*À mort! À mort les juifs!*', and realised that assimilation itself could not safeguard Jewish dignity. Herzl decided to turn things around. In the past, the Jews had always sought solutions in the outside world. Now they had to understand that the promised land was in *them*, in their own minds, their own wills. 'The promised land lies there where we will bear it,' he wrote. 'The Jews who desire it will have their own state, and will deserve it as well.'

In 1896 he wrote his most important piece of work, *Der Judenstaat – An Attempt at a Modern Solution to the Jewish Question*. Support began pouring in from such major Jewish philanthropists as the German baron Maurice de Hirsch and the Rothschilds, while his speeches also drew an unparalleled enthusiastic response from the Jews in the ghettos. 'This is no longer the elegant Dr Herzl from Vienna, this is a royal heir to King David, risen from the grave,' crowed the writer Ben Ami after the first Zionist congress in 1897.

But what did Theodor Herzl really want? In the National Library I ploughed my way through a yellowed copy of *Der Judenstaat*, and several of his other writings. What strikes one is the way in which Herzl tried again and again to make this dream state attractive to poor Eastern European Jews as well. Just as Schönerer, through his stories about German tribes and rites, had used history to drum up a nation, just as Lüger had harkened back to the medieval Catholic order, so too Herzl repeatedly referred to the mighty Israel of King David. And, like his foes, he also linked that past to the modern age. The International Socialists dreamed of an eight hour working day, so Herzl's Jewish state would have a seven hour working day, reflected in the white national flag with its seven golden stars. 'Humane, well lighted and healthy schools' would be built everywhere. Much of the work would be done by 'workers' brigades' of young people. Hebrew would not be the main language, for there would be a great many languages. The rabbinate would be respected, but also expected to keep to the temples, as the army to its barracks. Although he recognised their propaganda value, Palestine and Jerusalem were not Herzl's first choice.

The conclusion I arrived at was strange, but almost inevitable: the Promised Land of which Israel's pioneers dreamed was, in its deepest sense, not so much a Jewish Palestine as a liberal Vienna. In Herzl's utopia, there was no Star of David.

And finally we arrive at the anonymous observer to all this: the daydreamer, the homeless pauper, the hopeless painter Adolf Hitler. He spent six years in Vienna, from September 1907 until May 1913, between the ages of eighteen and twenty-four. Without a doubt, the city made an enormous impression on him. According to his future assistant Albert Speer, decades later Hitler could still draw the Ring with all its great monuments, to scale, by heart.

'Adolf Hitler, as he was known [to friends and colleagues], did not particularly stand out amid the drab army of Viennese workers and the unemployed, neither by reason of any special talent, nor by reason of any lack of scruples, any criminality or demonic trait.' This is how the historian Brigitte Haman summarises the conclusions of her impressive search for traces of Adolf Hitler in Vienna. In those days, she says, he could not have been much more than yet another hot-tempered eccentric, talking everyone's ear off and idolising the German people. No one had yet noticed the 'compelling power' of his regard. In his Viennese days, little or nothing could be seen of anti-Semitism on his part. For in spite of his avid political interest, he had only one goal: to become an architect.

None of this, however, rules out the fact that many of Hitler's ideas were drawn from the Vienna of that day. In his later views, the fin de siècle politics of Vienna are found everywhere. Schönerer's ideology and the cult that surrounded him were transferred almost intact to Hitler's National Socialist movement, up to and including the Führerprinzip and the street violence. His histrionic style, too, was probably borrowed almost directly from Schönerer. Years later, he would tell his table companions that he was a true 'Schönererian', and that he had come to Vienna as an art student with a great antipathy for Lüger. Only later did that antipathy turn to admiration. The roots of Hitler's radical racism, therefore, are probably best attributed to Schönerer.

What Hitler learned from Lüger, however, was at least as important: the political theatrics, the key role of public relations, and above all the crucial importance of social policies and major public-works projects. Demagoguery alone was never enough: people had to be governed as well. Hitler learned from Lüger, as he admitted in a speech much later, that 'great works can secure the dominion' of a movement. 'If the words no longer reverberate, then the stones must speak.'

Is there anything left in Austria of this young Viennese eccentric? A few hours by train from Vienna lies Leonding, once a small village, now a suburb of Linz, with a village square and a bakery-cum-bistro where the local ladies spend their mornings in gossip. The American historian John Lukacs heard about the grave right after 1945 – friends of his who had recently been released from Mauthausen had picnicked near it – and he told me it was still there. But when I see the snowy churchyard I can barely imagine it. Almost all the graves are shiny and new, making it look as though an entire generation has died in this village in the last few years. The graves are usually emptied here after ten years, the poster with regulations says, and I almost abandon hope.

I search the graveyard systematically, scanning all the Fritzes, Franzes, Aloises and Theresas lying here. After forty-five minutes of ploughing through the snow, after I have covered almost the entire churchyard, I stumble upon it. The strange thing is that I feel no satisfaction, only a shock. The stone with the big black cross stands a little awry. An enormous pine tree is growing from the grave. The enamel portraits of the deceased are all too familiar. With half-frozen fingers I jot down: *Alois Hitler, k.-u.-k.k. Zollamts Oberoffizial i.P. und Hausbesitzer, gest. 3 Jänner 1903 im 65. Lebensjahr. Dessen Gattin Frau Klara Hitler, gest. Dez. 1907 i.47 Lebj. RIP.* The stone allows no further inscription for her.

The low yellow house behind the graveyard is still there as well, the house where their little boy devoured Karl May westerns, played Boer War and chased the rats in the churchyard.

The Hitlers have no living descendants, but their headstone is decorated with freshly cut pine boughs and violets. The letters have recently been gilded. There are three new candles on the grave. A new wreath hangs on the cross.

In the train on the way home I read in the *Wiener Zeitung* about the trial of the forty-nine-year-old Franz Fuchs, who carried out a one-man terror and bombing campaign for four years. Four Gypsy children were killed in one of his attacks. In the courtroom, all he did was shout slogans:

Up with the German folk! Foreign blood, no thank you! Minority privileges, no thank you! Squandering our *Lebensraum* on foreign

peoples, no thank you! International Socialism, no thank you!
Counter-German racism, no thank you! Zionistic anti-Teutonism,
no thank you!

It is Wednesday, 3 February, 1999.

II February 1914–18

Finland

Helsinki

St Petersburg/
Petrograd

Moscow

Riga

Witebsk

Kaunas

nigsberg   Minsk

nenberg   Front Line
Aug. 1917

RUSSIA

Brest-Litovsk

arsaw

Kiev

Rowno

Dnieper

Volga

Front Line
April 1915

Chernowitz

Don

apest

Sea
of Azov

Crimea   Kertch

Sukhumi

Front Line
June 1918

NGARY

RUMANIA

Black
Sea

Batoum

Front Line
Oct. 1915

Kars

Bucharest   Danube

Trabzon

Belgrade

Front Line
Aug. 1916

Erzurum

alevo

BULGARIA

SERBIA   Sofia

Tigris

BANIA   Saloniki

Adrianopolis   Constantinople

Skopje

Gallipoli

OTTOMAN EMPIRE

GREECE

Athens

Cyprus

Crete   Mediterranean

← Geert Mak's Route

0   100   200   300 km

Chapter Six

Vienna

THE DAYS AT HIS PARENTS' HOUSE WERE FILLED WITH THE MURMUR of the waves, birds were always singing in the gardens. Irfan Orga lived in Constantinople, which would later be called Istanbul. He was five, the son of a wealthy carpet merchant. He lived behind the Blue Mosque, the house looked over the Sea of Marmara.

Later, Irfan committed his memories to paper, and in them he describes the bedroom as he awoke, full of marine light, the morning kiss from his beaming mother, the games of 'lion' in his grandfather's big, soft bed, and later their walk together to the coffee house. There comes a day when his grandfather suddenly begins to stagger, together they limp home, the doctor arrives, there is excitement, sorrow, he is allowed to see his grandfather for a moment, and for the rest Irfan remembers mostly the wait in the sunny garden and the cooing of a wood pigeon.

That was in spring 1914. The Orga family spent their last summer together with Uncle Ahmet and Aunt Ayşe at the beach resort of Sariyer, in a house on the Bosphorus. Uncle Ahmet swam in the sea each morning, and in the cool of the evening he taught Irfan how to fish. 'One time I saw a school of dolphins, and watched breathlessly as they jumped through the air.' As they rowed home, Irfan's uncle told him stories. Aunt Ayşe and his mother drank coffee under the magnolia. 'They looked so flowery and elegant, sitting there on their chaises longues, chattering like sparrows while the sun washed their brightly coloured silk dresses back to pastel.' Later, lying in bed, Irfan could hear the adults talking quietly on the veranda.

Halfway through that summer he noticed the tone change. One evening the conversation was grimmer, the adults laughed less. Irfan heard his father say something about 'war' in Europe, and that he and Uncle Ahmet would have to 'go', and that he therefore wanted to sell his house and the business as soon as possible. 'I listened sleepily to what they were saying, and heard that strange, new word 'war' pop up again and again. That word seemed lately to rule everyone's thoughts, and resurfaced at regular intervals when the men were together. My father said: "The German officers aren't training the Turkish Army for their dark eyes." To which my uncle replied: "But if we enter this new war, we're done for as a nation."'

On the surface, it remained a holiday like all the others. Irfan's father relaxed in the garden, the children grew browner with each passing day, the ladies went for short rides and paid a few visits. They were happy days, and they were quickly over.

When they took the ferry back to Constantinople, the ship passed the garden with the magnolia tree one last time, the garden of the swimming parties and the stories. 'We waved bravely to my uncle and aunt, but none of us knew that we were saying farewell to a life that was going to disappear from the face of the earth.'

After the summer holidays, Irfan started at a new school. He overheard another sentence: 'The situation is serious.' The family business was sold. Everyone began squirrelling away goods. Shops closed, prices rose. Women were almost the only ones who ventured out onto the street. That fall, the Orgas moved to a smaller house.

Not long after, one evening in November, they heard the sound of drumbeats approaching. The family went to the door. Irfan's father put his arm around his shoulder, the boy leaned against him. Then a man appeared from around the corner, beating a big bass drum: 'All men born between 1880–5 are to report to the recruitment centre within forty-eight hours.'

The next day there was no bread to be had. Uncle Ahmet had been born in 1885. He came to say goodbye, and drank his coffee in silence. Then Irfan's mother began sewing a crude white duffel bag, with careful little stitches. A few weeks later, the drum came for his father.

'We didn't have the slightest expectation of war,' Joseph Roth wrote of spring 1914. 'That month of May in the city of Vienna floated in the little silver-edged cups of coffee, drifted over the table linen, the narrow staffs of chocolate crammed with filling, the red and green millefeuilles that looked like exquisite jewels, and suddenly chief councillor Sorgsam blurted out, right in the middle of the month of May: "Gentlemen, there will now be war!"'

The main storyline is well known: how the Austro-Hungarian crown prince and his wife pay a state visit to Sarajevo, on Vidov Dan of all days, the day the Serbs commemorate each year their defeat at Turkish hands in Kosovo in 1389; the fatal shooting; the arrest of the 'terrorist', the nineteen-year-old Bosnian-Serb nationalist Gavrilo Princip; Austria's list of humiliating demands to Serbia; Russia supporting 'brother nation' Serbia in its refusal; Germany siding automatically with Austria; France adhering to its alliance with Russia; Great Britain's fruitless attempts to mediate; the chain reaction of mobilisations which neither the czar nor the two emperors could bring to a halt; the fate that had an impact on the lives of almost all Europeans.

It was a war that started in the poor, peasant corner of south-eastern Europe, but took on its horror and vastness only with the participation of every major Western industrialised nation. It was a war that sloshed back and forth like waves in a basin: the trigger lay in the East, the escalation in the West, but the greatest destruction ultimately occurred, again, in the East.

Throughout almost all those years of war, the West was split by a long, stubborn front that stretched through Flanders and along the Franco-German border. In the East, the Germans were able to break through quite quickly; there, another front had been drawn through the middle of Poland. At first, that was the case in the Balkans as well: Austrian troops took Belgrade in late 1915. Then their advance ground to a halt, due in part to fierce Serb resistance in Macedonia. The Italians, too, put up a bitter struggle against the Austrians, their losses almost equalling those of the British. No less than eleven major battles were fought in the Alps, and Caporetto (present-day Kobarid in Slovenia) became a sort of Italian Verdun: there, between October 1915 and September 1917, more than 300,000 soldiers were killed or wounded. The Mediterranean was in the hands of the French and British navies, and in spring 1915 the British tried to invade Gallipoli in order to break through to Constantinople by way of the Dardanelles. Their plan was to create a single Allied-Russian front, but the attack on Austria and Germany's 'soft white underbelly' failed.

Irfan Orga's little world was demolished within the year. Uncle Ahmet went missing in the Syrian desert. Aunt Ayşe died of a broken heart. The family's house burned down, taking with it all the family's hoarded capital. Irfan's father died during the forced marches to the Dardanelles. The family sank into poverty. The children ended up at boarding schools, Irfan ate grass to still his hunger, his mother slipped into madness. Only Grandmother Orga remained on her feet, hardened, old, tough as nails.

Gavrilo Princip was too young to be executed. Instead, he wasted away after four years in a cell in the Little Fort at Theresienstadt, later used as a Nazi transit camp in the 1940s. In retrospect, his prison psychiatrist reported, he was stunned by what his action had precipitated. He had been furious about the boorish Austrian annexation of the former Turkish province of Bosnia-Herzegovina in 1908. He had been bitter about his country's backwardness and poverty. That was all that was on his mind; except, of course and above all, a glorious and heroic death for himself.

Europe seemed to tumble into this war almost accidentally. During summer 1914, in almost every country one noted a sort of blithe patriotism, a sense of 'stop and fix it', a minor blip in a glorious age of welfare and progress. 'Back for Christmas' was the British motto. In Berlin, the kaiser told his soldiers that they would be home again 'before the leaves have fallen'. The cafés were full of happy faces, and people stood up and clinked their glasses together whenever the national anthem, 'Heil dir im Siegerkranz', was played. Café Piccadilly was quickly rechristened the Vaterland Café, Hotel Westminster became the Lindenhof. Czar Nicholas II appeared on the balcony of the Winter Palace and was cheered by an enthusiastic crowd, which then sang the national anthem and kneeled before him in unison. Strikes were called off. The Duma held a recess 'in order not to hinder the government's work with undue politics'. The name St Petersburg, sounding overly Teutonic now, was changed to Petrograd. The French cooper Louis Barthas wrote in his diary: 'To my great amazement, the announcement [of the mobilisation] seemed to give rise to more enthusiasm than despair. In their innocence, people seem to love the idea of living in an age when something grand and compelling is about to happen.'

In Berlin, Käthe Kollwitz saw her sons leave for war. Hans was already in the army, Peter volunteered for duty after seeing a company march away while bystanders sang a 'rousing popular chorus' of 'Die Wacht am Rhein.' It was hard for her, but her husband Karl said: 'These wonderful children – we shall have to work hard to deserve them.' In the evening, after dinner, the family read aloud a war novella about a man who had been summoned to his dying friend. After that there was singing in the living room, 'old country ballads and war songs'. Käthe went to the barracks to visit her sons. 'In the courtyard, Hans. In uniform. His baby face.'

There were those, however, who sensed that this war would put an end to their old, familiar world. The writer Vera Brittain, studying at Oxford at the time, read the summons to mobilisation pasted up everywhere 'with the feeling that I had been transported back into an uglier century'. The German Jewish industrialist Walter Rathenau, son of the founder of AEG, sat quietly in his chair, tears running down his cheeks. Behind the scenes, he had done everything in his power to slow down the arms race and prevent this war. 'While the people were in the grip of wild enthusiasm, Rathenau was wringing his hands,' his friend, cosmopolite and diarist Harry Kessler wrote.

During the final week of peace, the newspapers of the European socialists were full of editorials against the war and against militarism. Mass meetings were held, demonstrations organised and plans forged for an international general strike to stop the war machinery in its tracks, but nothing came of it. On Wednesday, 29 July, the Socialist International Congress held an emergency meeting in Brussels, but with little result. That evening the socialist leaders stood on the stage before a cheering crowd, the French party leader Jean Jaurès put his arm around the German social democrat Hugo Haase, both men clearly moved, and then the workers marched en masse through Brussels, waving white signs with the slogan 'Guerre à la Guerre!' and singing the 'Internationale' over and over.

Two days later, on Friday, 31 July, Jaurès was shot and killed by a nation-alist in Paris. The German socialists were deeply shocked, and expressed their condolences to their French comrades at this great loss.

Four days later, on Tuesday, 4 August, Lenin's agent in Berlin, Alexandra Kollontai, saw with her own eyes how these same socialists – some of them having even come to the Reichstag in uniform – voted enthusias-tically in favour of Kaiser Wilhelm's war budget. 'I couldn't believe it,' she wrote in her diary. 'I was convinced that they had either gone mad or that I was the one who had lost my senses.' After that fateful vote, she went in a daze to the parliament and was stopped in a corridor by a social-democrat representative, who asked her angrily what a Russian was doing in the Reichstag.

The French socialists behaved no differently. Jaurès was honoured amid a groundswell of national unity. From now on, the fatherland would take precedence over all the rest. Within a week the 'Internationale' had been forgotten, but three months later all enthusiasm for the war was gone as well. When Louis Barthas marched off to war, people doffed their hats, 'as for a procession of condemned men.'

Why were people so keen to go to battle in 1914? The people's rage in Germany was directed principally against the British, the arrogant empire blocking the development of young, dynamic Germany: '*Gott strafe England!*' Furthermore, for Germany it was a pre-emptive war: the kaiser and his generals were deeply concerned about Russia's burgeoning military power. They feared that, within the next few years, Russia would have an exem-plary fleet in the Baltic, rail connections up to the German border and an army bigger than anything Germany could hope to equal. 'Every year we wait lessens our chances,' General Helmuth von Moltke announced in spring 1914, to anyone who cared to listen.

The motives of the French, however, had more to do with the past: revenge for the humiliations that had followed the Franco-Prussian War of 1870–1, and the reclamation of their former glory. The Austrians wanted, above all, to deal once and for all with rebel Serbia. '*Serbien muss sterben,*' the students shouted. And besides, a military injection could do their teetering monarchy no harm. For years the squares of Moscow and St Petersburg had been crowded with excited nationalists who wanted to protect their Serb brothers from Austria. What's more, Russia was feeling increasingly threatened by Germany. Turkey, on the other hand, took part because it was in desperate need of German support against its old enemy, Russia.

Great Britain was a special case. The British government hesitated for an unusually long time. There are those who say that this long hesitation was itself one of the causes of the war: had Wilhelm known beforehand that Britain would join the fray, he would never have started the conflict so lightly. As late as 1 August, it was still almost certain – according to notes made by the young naval minister, Winston Churchill – that the United Kingdom would remain neutral. More than three quarters of cabinet ministers were determined not to let the country be dragged into any European conflict. By 3 August, however, the majority of the cabinet considered war to be inevitable. The British had always seen Antwerp as 'the pistol aimed at Europe's heart', and as more and more reports came in about German ultimatums to neutral Belgium, the mood shifted with each passing hour. Now that Germany was pushing the fulcrum of war to the west, there was far more at stake than simply a few treaties. Now it was about the balance of power, about turning the tide of Wilhelm's imperial ambitions, and above all about maintaining the old division of power: balance within Europe, Britain outside Europe. In addition, there was also the momentum of the country's own military planning, a genie that could scarcely be put back into the bottle. During summer 1914, a mechanism had been set in motion among all the world's powers that, after only a few days, could no longer be brought to a halt: the network of war plans, the enormous maze of scenarios that had been developed decades earlier and which would ultimately act as gigantic flywheels, as prophesies bringing about their own fulfilment.

These war plans were a new phenomenon. As detailed as railway time-tables, they also had everything to do with the railways themselves. The capacity of the national rail networks had been calculated precisely: the number of foot soldiers a railway could accommodate each day, which trunk lines could be used in the case of an advance, and the number of days it would take to conquer a given stronghold.

This rigid military planning had catastrophic political effects. As soon as one of the powers mobilised, the others could only follow. An army that arrived at the front one week late would already have lost half the war. The French chief of staff Joseph Joffre warned in 1914 that, according to his calculations, every day the mobilisation was postponed equalled a twenty-five-kilometre-wide swathe of territory surrendered to the enemy. The German general staff made a similar claim. By early August 1914, the government leaders were the only ones who could stop the ticking clock. They realised too late what was happening, failed and panicked.

Most of my final day in Vienna is spent in the cellars of the Neue Hofburg, in the warm shelter of the National Library. In what state of mind did the common man in his Viennese café, drinking his coffee and reading his paper, view this oncoming world war? Did he, on 28 June, 1914, have any clue that Gavrilo Princip's potshots at Franz Ferdinand and his wife Sophie had signalled the onset of a series of catastrophic years?

Later it was suggested that he did, but the back editions of the *Neue Freie Presse* tell a different story. I read them one after the other, day by day, for the months of June, July and August 1914.

True destiny is often as trivial as the plot of a disaster movie. First there is normal Viennese life, with gossip, road accidents and the daily adverts: 'Feschoform. Poetry in motion! For her firm bust, the true Viennese beauty thanks only Feschoform bosom enhancer!' The clothing stores are competing with large advertisements, Germania offers a life insurance policy 'covering acts of war and trips around the world', and, to guard against the unmentionable, one is urged to use 'H. Ungers Frauenschutz'.

The monarchy is not altogether ignored. The foreign pages report a serious Greco-Turkish conflict, there are major problems with Serbia, the crown prince is leaving to inspect manoeuvres in a tense Bosnia. The editorial pages are full of reports on troop movements, ultimata and warships popping up here and there.

Then there is the extra edition, which hit the streets on Sunday evening, 28 June, with huge headlines and the facts of the assassinations. In the days that follow the paper reports endlessly on the culprit's origins, the correct text of the crown prince's final words – 'Soferl, bleibe leben für unsere Kinder' (Sophie, stay alive for our children's sake) – the state of siege in Sarajevo, the preparations for the state funeral. The prince's last telegram to his children: 'Grüsse und Küsse von Papi'. The report of student demonstrations in front of the Serbian embassy in Vienna. On the Vienna, London and Berlin stock exchanges, the killings are the talk of the day, but trading remains calm. 'The political consequences of this act are being greatly exaggerated,' the paper writes on Thursday, 2 July.

After that comes the arrival of the royal corpses and the state funeral. When it is all over, much of Vienna goes on wrangling for days about whether protocol was correctly observed with regard to the nobility and the military. The city sinks into a holiday torpor. Lessner's department store fills pages with the summer sales of foulard silk.

There is a little summertime news. Wilhelm will leave on 6 July for a holiday cruise on the *Hohenzollern*. He will be gone for three weeks, to the seclusion of the Norwegian fjords. His chief of staff and the state secretary of the navy will also be leaving Berlin. The Austrian cabinet does not convene until Tuesday, 7 July, ten days after the killings in Sarajevo.

On Monday, 13 July, more than two weeks after the attack, the *Neue Freie Presse* opens for the first time with the growing tension between Austria and Serbia. Princip and his cohorts, it seems, were aided by the Serb secret police. Austria demands redress. It continues to be a glorious summer, and everyone is confident that international diplomacy will succeed in extinguishing the fires of conflict. Meanwhile, envoys are sent back and forth and old alliances reconfirmed: Austria does not dare to act without Germany, and receives the assurance that Germany will help out; Russia supports Serbia, but has no real desire to go to war. The paper reports that the Russian ambassador in Belgrade has died of a heart attack. Otherwise everything remains still, for almost three weeks. On 16 July, French president Raymond Poincaré pays a state visit to St Petersburg. The stock exchange is caught in the summer doldrums. Even the keen-witted British minister of foreign affairs, Edward Grey, will be leaving for a weekend of fishing on 25 July.

It is only after 20 July that unrest truly arrives in the pages of the *Neue Freie Presse*. Russia is openly interfering in the affair, the paper hints at 'steps' and 'ultimatums', on Friday, 24 July we read that the German kaiser plans to come back early from his holidays, and two days later – along with the call to mobilisation – the word 'war' appears in the paper for the first time.

Even the Serbian chief of staff is caught unawares. That weekend he happens to be in Budapest, visiting his daughter, and he is promptly arrested by Austrian plainclothesmen. The *Neue*: 'Putnik jumped up, pushed one of the detectives away and pulled his pistol. The impression was that he planned to take his own life.' Meanwhile, his daughter started weeping and wailing. The next day the general has already been released and put on a train with due ceremony, 'on the grounds that the Austrian Army is possessed of too much chivalry to rob the enemy army of its highest commander'.

In the evening edition of that same Sunday I come across, for the first time as well, an editorial warning that a war between Austria and Serbia could become 'total', and stating the need to 'contain the conflict'.

On Monday, 27 July, the paper reports on British attempts to restore peace. The mutual alliances are not nearly as binding as was later suggested, and the diplomats still have plenty of room to manoeuvre. Germany, for example, is in no way obliged to come to Austria's assistance in this matter. Russia need not support Serbia through thick and thin. Britain was not at all bound to enter the war for the sake of Belgium.

The first map of a possible theatre of war is published on Tuesday, 28 July. Rumours are circulating about Russian mobilisation and a possible German counter-mobilisation.

The next day, the *Neue Freie Presse* prints the text of Emperor Franz Josef's declaration of war against Serbia: 'To my peoples'. Behind the scenes, the danger of this crisis has now fully sunk in. Among the French there is a growing fear that Germany will now march against them too. After all, an attack on Russia – according to the Franco-Russian convention of 1892 – also constitutes an attack on France.

Thursday, 30 July: Germany and Great Britain are still hoping to convince Austria and Russia to halt the mobilisation.

On Friday, 31 July, reports come in concerning a general mobilisation in Russia and German ultimata to France and Russia.

On Saturday, 1 August, the headline of the morning edition reads: '*Die Monarchie und das verbündete Deutschland in Waffen*'. Germany, along with Austria, is mobilising against the Russians. France receives a German ultimatum: the country must declare its neutrality within eighteen hours. A French mobilisation will mean 'immediate war'.

At the bottom of the same page, Stefan Zweig writes of his hurried return to Vienna from Ostend: 'The beach and the sea. People grabbing papers, tossing them open, the pages struggling in the wind, to find the reports. Only the reports! For the rest is impossible to read, in these French papers: it is too painful, it excites, it embitters ... French, the language people have used for years with love and loftiness, suddenly sounds belligerent.'

On Sunday, 2 August, the paper reports that there has been an exchange of telegrams between Kaiser Wilhelm and Czar Nicholas. The desperate texts would be made public only later: 'I understand fully how difficult it is for you and your government to defy the power of your public's opinion. That is why, because of the hearty and tender friendship that has bound us so strongly for so long, I am applying my greatest influence to compel the Austrians . . .' Signed: Cousin Willy.

'I can see that within a very short time I shall have to bow to the pressure that is being applied to me, and that I will be forced to take extreme measures that will lead to war. In an attempt to prevent the calamity of a European war, I therefore beg you, in the name of our old friendship, to do whatever you can to keep our allies from going too far . . .' Signed: Cousin Nicky.

On Monday, 3 August, the morning edition opens with Germany's declaration of war on Russia. France mobilises. The Russian diplomatic mission leaves Berlin. Along the Russian-German border, the first hostilities are reported. The first strange rumours start flowing in as well. 'A French airplane has dropped a bomb on Nuremberg. This is behaviour unworthy of a cultured nation. Even in war, there are limits to the decent use of force.'

Two days later, in the evening edition: the British Empire declares war on the German Empire. Diplomatic relations end.

Within a few days, all the switches have been thrown. Everything is ready for the Great European War, 1914–45.

Let us take one good, close look. On the right side of the uniform's collar, beside the general's star, we see a hole several millimetres in diameter. That is all. The rest of the uniform is covered in bloodstains. Rips in the front of the coat and the sleeves bear witness to the physicians' panic, to the attempts to save what can still be saved.

Franz Ferdinand's sky-blue uniform is still on display in a glass case in the Heeresgeschichtliches Museum in Vienna. The same hall contains the green and black open touring car in which the heir to the Habsburg throne and his wife Sophie were sitting as they made their tour of Sarajevo, a huge, tinny thing that resembles an old jalopy from a cartoon.

Gavrilo Princip and his five romantic school friends had spread out along the quay that morning, to murder the hated symbol of the nation. The first would-be assassin was afraid to open fire; the second decided that, on second thoughts, he had no desire to spatter Sophie's blindingly white dress with blood; the third was clever enough to take up a position right beside a policeman. He did, however, throw his hand grenade. Panic broke out, a few people were wounded, the crown prince and his wife remained unharmed. Princip, who was waiting a little further along, was disappointed and went to drink a cup of coffee.

At the town hall Franz Ferdinand flew into a rage, especially when he noticed that the text of his speech had been spattered with blood. A little later, at Sophie's suggestion, they decided to drive to the hospital to visit the wounded. But the chauffeur was not informed of the change of plans. The delegation drove back down the quay, and turned the corner onto Franz Josef Street. 'Wrong!' shouted the Bosnian governor, who was also in the car. The chauffeur tried to backup, the car stalled for a moment. Of all the infernal luck, precisely at the spot where Gavrilo Princip happened to be standing. He jumped onto the running board, shot Franz Ferdinand, then pointed his Browning at the governor, but the second bullet hit Sophie, who was bent over her husband.

'The crown prince was hit precisely in an artery,' I read in the coroner's report, printed in the *Neue Freie Presse* of 3 July, 1914. 'Had the bullet entered a little further to the left or to the right, the damage would never have been fatal. As a physician, I can only conclude that the bullet struck him there more or less by accident. There was no way Princip could have aimed so carefully. That is also to be seen from the fact that the first bullet went through the side of the automobile before striking the crown princess.'

'It was Sunday, I was a student,' Joseph Roth wrote. 'That afternoon a girl came by. They wore their hair in braids back then. She was carrying a big, yellow straw hat, it was imbued with summer and reminded me of hay, crickets and poppies. The hat contained a telegram, the first extra edition I had ever seen, crumpled, terrifying, a lightning bolt of paper. "You know," said the girl, "they've killed the crown prince. My father came home from the café. We're not staying here, are we?"

'Eighteen months later — how durable love was in times of peace! — she was standing there, she too, amid the clouds of smoke, along the rails at Freight Station 2, the music braying incessantly, train carriages grating, engines screaming, little shivering women hanging like wilted wreaths on the green men, the new uniforms still smelling of the tailors' blocks, we were a company on the march, destination secret, probably Serbia . . . Her father never went to the café again; he was already lying in a mass grave.'

Chapter Seven

Ypres

TUESDAY, 9 FEBRUARY, 1999. ACROSS THE FLATS BEHIND DIKSMUIDE, the sky is full of snow. The clouds do not come blowing in but rise up from the land, like a broad, black wall. Behind me the sun is still shining, bright light on the mud in the fields, on the snow in the furrows, the handful of red houses, the steeples in the distance. At the same time, the landscape has something austere about it. Take out a few electric pylons, a couple of pig farms, and you have a battlefield again.

Imagine, I'm a British soldier, we've crossed the Channel in rollicking good cheer, and now here we march: 'Let the war come, here we are, here we are, here we are at last!' One of our captains writes home: 'I love war. It's like a big picnic, but without the pointlessness of a picnic.' The Germans have moved through Belgium into northern France, but the French have cut them off at the Marne. Now we are going to do the same, in West Flanders.

How would I feel then?

In 1999, there were still some hundred and fifty very old Britons left to talk about it. In November 1998, at the eightieth anniversary of the war's end, I saw them march through London, using canes, sitting in wheelchairs, then came the veterans of Dunkirk, D-Day and the Falklands, then the nurses and the 'walking wounded', two, three generations went by, full of blood-soaked ideals and virtues.

A brittle Jack Rogers (b. 1895) told BBC television: 'We had no idea where we were going. But at a certain point we saw flashes in the distance. Then we began hearing noises: thunderclaps, heavier all the time. And then suddenly we realised: we are going into a war!' Dick Barron (b. 1896) talked about what happened soon afterwards: 'My own mate fell, shot through the head, I tried to push his brains back into the hole, ridiculous of course . . .' Tommy Gay (b. 1898): 'You heard the bullets flying past your ears, ping, ping, and all I could think was: what a miracle that they're not hitting me.'

In November 1914 alone, 100,000 men fell in the vicinity of Ypres. In the immediate vicinity, another 400,000 would follow. Norman Collins (b. 1898) had the job of burying the dead, who had sometimes been lying on the battlefield for weeks. 'The first one I saw like that, I touched him, and a rat came running out of his skull. Then you thought: all those ambitions and aspirations, all the things they hoped to change in the world, but in reality they all died within a few minutes.'

Jack Rogers agrees to sing a trench song for the camera, in a high, shaky voice:

> I want to go home,
> I want to go home,
> I don't want to go to the trenches no more
> The whiz-bangs and the shrapnel they whistle and roar
> I don't want to go over the top any more
> Take me over the sea
> Where the Allemands can't take me
> Oh my, I don't want to die
> I want to go home.

Now for the other side. Imagine I'm a boy from Munich. We've all been whipped up by German propaganda, our brief training camp was an exciting interlude in our staid lives, and here we come, 3,000 students strong. This band of soldiers even includes engineers and doctors. No one wants to miss this. 'Life was magnified a thousandfold in this grand struggle, everything that had once been fell into nothingness,' one of them wrote later. Thanks to the Big Berthas, our men have destroyed the fortifications at Liège, taken Antwerp, and now we are marching at night against the British at Ypres. I cite this same soldier: 'Then when the day begins to take shape out of the mist, an iron how-do-you-do suddenly comes whistling over our heads, and with a hard crack drives the little projectiles into our ranks, making the slimy earth spatter up all over; but before the cloud has had time to disperse, the first hurrah from 2,000 throats has already sounded in reply. The author of the letter, Adolf Hitler, writes that as the artillery started to crackle and thunder, all the men began singing. This is probably nonsense, although the students of Munich were crazy enough for it to have been true. Afterwards people would speak of the Murder of the Innocents at Ypres, and Langemark has been called 'the place the second World War was born'.

The British facing them had been through the Boer War, they were professional. The 3,000 German boys – only a few of them survived into manhood – now lie in a separate section of the war cemetery, surrounded by plaques bearing the names of their student fraternities. One half of Hitler's 16th Bavarian Reserve Infantry Regiment was killed, approximately 1,800 men. He himself came away unscathed. Later he was wounded, locals say in a wood not far from here, where the faint remains of trenches can still be seen.

Peter Kollwitz, too, fell that week, on the same front, close to Roggeveld-Esen. Käthe Kollwitz: 'I dreamed we were with a lot of people in a big hall. Someone shouted 'Where is Peter?' It was he himself who shouted it, I saw his dark silhouette standing against something light. I went to him, embraced him, but didn't dare to look at him, afraid it would turn out not to be him. I looked at his feet and they were his, at his arms, his hands, they were all his, but I knew that if I tried to look at his face, I would know again that he was dead.'

Approaching what was once the West Flanders front, you can tell by the buildings that you're getting close: suddenly, none of the houses and farms along the road date from before 1920.

Ypres is the heart of this rebuilt past. During the First World War, the fortified medieval town was a striking, vulnerable promontory along the front. If the Germans broke through, they could be in Calais and Dunkirk the next day. The British supply lines would be gravely endangered, and the Germans would have a new front that was much easier to defend, and several important harbours in addition.

The fighting at Ypres, in other words, served key military interests. Hundreds of thousands died on the enormous mud flats around the city and the neighbouring villages. At the local museum, In Flanders Fields, a scale model shows what Ypres looked like on 11 November,

1918: one huge grey plain full of knee-high rubble, with the charred ruins of the monumental Lakenhal sticking up like a broken molar. My hotel, Old Tom on the Great Market, has been wiped away as well, from the looks of it. In fact, the Great Market in its entirety has been reduced to dust.

Even today, Ypres has something unreal about it. It resembles a normal old town, but it is obvious: everything here has been reconstructed. Houses and buildings that were two, three, five hundred years old are all replicas built with the greatest care and attention. The crowning glory of this intense predilection for the past is the Lakenhal. The broken molar of 1918 is still in my mind's eye, but the huge hall is so beautiful, so unmistakably ancient, that I stop believing in anything else.

A friend of mine once found in a flea market a pastel drawing of a bare and blasted landscape, with a little steeple in the background and in the foreground a few half-frozen puddles and some barbed wire. There's not a living soul to be seen, but the drawing is covered with a sort of haze that suggests the passing of some huge catastrophe. At the same time the light is frozen, as though everything is in waiting. Beneath it: 'Février 1917, Pervijze, G. R.'

Where did G. R. stand to draw this? My friend comes down for a day and together we drive through the countryside around Ypres. We view the overfull German cemetery at Langemark: had fate not missed by a hair the addition of one other name to the list of the dead, between Hirsch, Erich von, and Hoch, Bruno, the history of Europe would have been very different indeed. At Zillebeke we visit the Museum Hooge Crater and the Hill 62 Museum, two private collections of the sort found everywhere along the front, full of photographs, rusty helmets, mortar shells, rifles, bayonets, old bottles, buckles, bones, pipes. Many of the finds are also for sale. In the garden of Hill 62 there are still a few of the original trenches, now filled with yellow meltwater.

At Houtem we watch a carnival pass by with about sixty children in it, dressed as devils, Chinamen, cats, witches and fairies, a flutter of bright little birds in a grey, quiet street with all the shutters closed.

And then suddenly we find the view from the pastel drawing, along the deserted railway tracks between Diksmuide and Nieuwpoort. It is the same spot, unmistakably, close to where two roads intersect. The scene

seems almost unchanged: fields, water, barbed wire, houses and barns
stuck loosely to the plain, as though they could be peeled off again at
any moment. That same haze is still hanging over the land.

'Everywhere mud and rats, rats, piles of them! In the winter the sentries
had to be carried off because their feet were frozen. And the shooting!
A friend of mine, he came from Lier as well. At one point he suddenly
said: "I never knew I had such beautiful flesh." And he grabbed his leg
like this. Calm as you please. Then he asked a buddy for a cigarette and
sat there smoking it. His leg had been shot off at the knee, it looked like
it had been sawed in two!'

Belgian veteran Arthur Wouters (b.1895) is telling his story, probably
for the umpteenth time, to a Belgian TV crew. When the war began, the
Belgian Army had 200,000 soldiers. A little more than two months later,
at the first battle on the Yser, only 75,000 of them were left. By Christmas
1914, 747,000 Germans and 854,000 French had already been killed or
wounded, and the original British Expeditionary Forces – 117,000 men
in total – had been almost completely decimated.

On 31 August, on the Eastern Front, the Germans had won a bloody
battle with 70,000 Russian casualties and 100,000 prisoners taken.
Afterwards, this battle at Tannenberg became enveloped in a mist of all
manner of Teutonic tales of heroism and whatever else the German Empire
had to offer in the way of mythology. The truth was that a high price had
to be paid for that victory: the Germans deployed dozens of regiments
there which were badly needed on the French front. That is one reason
why their western offensive became bogged down. In France, General
Alexander von Kluck's 1st Army had to advance an average of twenty
kilometres a day over a period of three weeks, with 84,000 horses which
required more than a million kilos of feed each day. It was madness to
suppose that one could work an army that way for weeks and still have
them fresh enough to defeat the French.

But the Allied forces were in bad shape as well. For centuries, the
British had been concentrating on the maintenance of their empire. They
were equipped for wars in Africa, Asia and the Middle East, but not in
Europe. In the years preceding the war their army had served largely as
a colonial police force, attuned more to brief skirmishes. In 1914 the

British Army had neither the experience nor the troops to fight a modern, large-scale war in Europe. All that still had to be mustered.

The French had suffered grave losses back in August and, to make things worse, the lion's share of their heavy industry had fallen into German hands. But they were fighting on their own soil, amid their own people, and that quickly proved to be a major advantage. On 23 August, 1914 there were twenty-four German divisions opposing seventeen Allied divisions. By 6 September that had changed to twenty-four against forty-one. The French brought everything they had into action, including the entire fleet of Parisian taxis, to get their troops to the Marne on time. The Germans were beaten back, lost a quarter of a million troops, and dug in.

After that the war froze. The soldiers began connecting their foxholes, and both sides of the front were soon marked by enormous networks of muddy hideaways and trenches. No one, no soldier, no strategist, was prepared for such a war. Except for a few minor oscillations, the war would barely move from these positions; it was not until 1918 that a German offensive once again turned things upside down.

For months in 1915, Lieutenant Ernst Jünger kept a diary of the events in the 'windy little segment of the long front that we have come to regard as home, where we have gradually come to know every overgrown hollow, every dilapidated earthen bunker.'

30 October

Last night, after a cloudburst, the breastworks collapsed and mixed with rainwater into a tough mush that turned the trenches into a quagmire. The only comfort was that the English were no better off, for we could see them energetically bailing water out of their trenches as well. Because we were on somewhat higher ground, we pumped our bilge water in their direction. We watched through our telescopic sights as well. When the walls of the trenches collapsed, it uncovered a row of corpses from last autumn's fighting.

9 November

Among the diversions offered by this post is the hunting of various animals, most particularly the partridges that live in huge numbers in these abandoned fields. Because we have no cartridges with shot, we have no choice but to creep up quietly on the relatively fearless 'dinner party candidates' and shoot their heads off, otherwise little of the meat would remain. While doing this, we must take care not to leave our trenches in the heat of the pursuit, for otherwise we would turn from hunters into prey.

28 December
My faithful man August Kettler was killed on the road to Monchy, where he was going to fetch my dinner. He was the first of my many stewards to be struck down by a mortar attack, which threw him to the ground with a piece of shrapnel through his windpipe. When he left with the pans, I said to him: 'August, don't let anything happen to you along the way.' 'Oh, Lieutenant, why should anything happen?!' Now I was summoned and found him gasping on the ground close to our shelter, every breath he took sucked air into his lungs through the wound in his throat. I had him carried back, he died a few days later in the field hospital. For him, as for many others, I found it particularly sad that the victim couldn't talk, only stare desperately at his helpers, like an animal in torment.'

The letter sent by the British government to the family of those who died in battle contained the following standard phrase: 'He was killed by a bullet, straight to the heart.' In reality, however, only very few were fortunate enough for that. Countless soldiers bled to death between the front lines, where no one could help them, amid the dying donkeys and whinnying horses. After the first day of the Battle of the Somme, as the British Lieutenant Hornshaw reported, an unearthly wailing and groaning rose up from no-man's-land, 'a sound like moist fingers being dragged down an enormous windowpane'.

After the first year of the war, Corporal Louis Barthas noted that only three of his 13th Group's old guard were left. The others had all been wounded or killed. In Berlin, Käthe Kollwitz saw a uniformed boy, no older than fifteen, wearing the Iron Cross. Boys of that age were apparently being sent to the front.

By late 1915 the number of Allied soldiers who had been killed or wounded on the Western Front amounted to more than two million. The Germans had lost 900,000. The field hospitals on both sides of the front resembled meat-processing plants. In Berlin I stumbled upon the story of the Jewish hospital train *Viktoria Louise*, dispatched by the Jüdisches Krankenhaus with the best surgeons on board. The train even had its own operating car. More than 100,000 of the country's 500,000 Jews fought in the war, proportionally more than of any other ethnic group. The war brought equality at last. That, however, is not how the German military staff saw it: in late 1916, orders were passed down that all Jews were to be registered separately. About 15,000 German Jews died in the war.

Everywhere the troops were weakened by malnutrition, shelling and the grim conditions in the trenches, but life was harder on the Allied side. The Germans, bent on defending their positions, dug in solidly. The French and British positions still to be seen today resemble little more than overgrown ditches. During the winter months they were mostly muddy, stinking, open sewers along which soldiers were shuttled back and forth, without much in the way of rest and with almost no protection. Corporal Barthas kept careful note of where he slept during those years: in a cellar, on the podium of a ballroom, in a pigsty, beneath a tarpaulin on a street, in a church, in a draughty attic, under a cart, in the ruins of a house and often simply in a hole in the ground. Notorious among the British was 'trench foot', a condition caused by weeks of walking around in wet footwear. The disease caused the feet to swell, after which the skin changed colour, the toes died and the feet had to be amputated.

The troops suffered from mental problems as well, something mentioned in every war diary. According to Ernst Jünger, the roar of a nonstop nocturnal artillery attack was so disturbing that soldiers would forget their own names or how to count to three. He likened the permanent fear of death to a sense of being tied up and having someone swing a sledgehammer past your head again and again, knowing that your skull could be smashed any moment. Towards the end of the war he lost almost half his company, more than sixty men, to one direct hit. The seasoned veteran Jünger broke down and cried in front of the survivors.

Barthas described a trench immediately after a direct hit: a decapitated soldier, a badly mutilated body, a pile of German corpses, the dead body of a young soldier who looked as though he were asleep, a few survivors staring apathetically into space. Then, suddenly another round came in: 'The trench was aflame . . . I heard whistling and cracking, but also terrible screams of pain. Sergeant Vergès' eyes were burned. Two poor bastards were rolling around on the ground at my feet . . . they had been turned into human torches.' He himself blacked out. 'They say I was staring vacantly and talking gibberish.'

Nervous collapses were so common that each army had its own term for them. The Belgians called it '*d'n klop*', the Germans spoke of '*Kriegsneurose*' or '*Granatfieber*', the French called it '*choque traumatique*', but in the end the English phrase 'shell shock' was adopted for the phenomenon. Whatever the language, the symptoms remained the same: uncontrollable weeping, extreme fatigue and panic attacks. Foot soldiers were also subject to a hysterical form of shell shock, accompanied by paralysis, muteness, deafness and facial tics.

At the town hall in Poperinge one can still view the cells reserved for soldiers charged with 'desertion' and 'cowardice'. According to a secret British Army directive, the only proper punishment for cowardice was death, and medical reasons were not considered extenuating. Later studies of court documents have shown that many of the 'pansies' were probably psychiatric patients. The French executed an estimated 1,600 of their own soldiers, the British 300, the Germans 50. Later, a new tactic was invented: jolts of electricity through the brain were used to get 'cowards' back on their feet, quickly and radically.

Amid these cruelties, soldiers and officers did all they could to preserve a few remnants of 'normal' existence. 'I often sat with a feeling of comfortable security at the table in my little bunker, the wooden walls of which were hung with weapons and reminded one of the Wild West,' Ernst Jünger wrote. 'I would drink a cup of tea, smoke and read, while my steward fussed with the little wood stove spreading the aroma of toast.'

Corporal Barthas reported that the French shelters close to Vermelles sometimes resembled little villas. Even along the front lines, 'sparks, flames and smoke' rose up day and night 'from the hundreds of little chimneys'. In the war museum at Péronne, one can see a British officer's complete set of 'field' tea-service accoutrements, pleasingly arranged in a wicker basket. Beside it lies a German accordion with a makeshift songbook written by one M. Erdmeier, *Allerhand Schützgrabengestanzl*. Other Germans planted garden plots with rhododendron, snowdrops and *Parole-uhren*, little windmills that milled away the hours. The Belgians formed 'families', with a 'father' who referred to his bunkmate as his *wuf*, wife.

In the British trenches a special newspaper was distributed, the blackly humorous *Wipers Times*, published by a writer and printer who had found an old printing press in a ruin. The 8 September, 1917 edition shows an elderly British soldier, still in the trenches. The caption reads: 'He stroked his hoary snow-white beard / And gazed with eyes now long since bleared . . .' Another sketch shows 'The Trenches, in the year 1950'. All this bears witness to the unbearable suspicion that was taking hold of more and more soldiers: that no solution would ever be found to this deadlock.

Perhaps it was courage born of desperation, the urge to move at any price, that led again and again to mass suicide attacks. Passchendaele, a wet and muddy hamlet not far from Ypres, was renamed Passion Dale by the British, because it had to be attacked again and again. Estimates are that some 60,000 men, a quarter of all those who died, drowned in the treacherous bogs around the handful of houses. They sank into the mud, disappeared into the thousands of holes and craters left by the artillery shells. 'See that little stream – we could walk to it in two minutes. It took the British a month to walk to it – a whole empire walking very slowly, dying in front and pushing forward behind. And another empire walked very slowly backwards a few inches a day, leaving the dead like a million bloody rugs.'

Meanwhile, the nineteenth century's final traces of innocence were disappearing fast. The Belgian Army had entered the war with uniforms that looked as though they came from a school play: shakos, clogs, capotes, felt caps, rucksacks made of dog skins, huge blue coats that absorbed all the water of Ypres. The Scottish Highland Regiment vehemently insisted on wearing their kilts, until it turned out that mustard gas could have a disastrous effect on intimate body parts. The German lancers wore huge, shiny eagles on their hats, and leather helmets you could push a bullet through with your thumb. The French proudly wore their red uniform

caps, blue coats and red trousers. No one had ever thought about camouflage or other practical matters: these were uniforms of honour and rank.
Early in 1915, steel helmets and grey and khaki uniforms began appearing
at the front, the pragmatic forms of the new century. The British toy
manufacturer Meccano followed the technical developments closely.
Examples can be seen today in London's Imperial War Museum: model
713, a machine gun mounted on a tripod; model 6.42, a complete battleship, and model 710: the Aeroscope, a kind of tall crane used to view the
front from on high.

But, as is usually the case, it took a long time for all these new technological developments to win a place in the imaginations of the generals,
politicians and others. The magnitude of the killing between 1914–18 was
due largely to the persistent combination of old strategies with ultramodern technologies. At first, almost no one understood that such modernities as the machine gun, poison gas, the airplane and later the tank called
for an entirely new way of waging war. The common foot soldier at the
front was often the first to become aware of this technical mismatch. He
found himself having been sent to war with antiquated equipment, he
found himself withstanding a mustard-gas attack with only a urine-
drenched rag held over his mouth and nose, he saw his comrades during
a bayonet attack being mowed down by newfangled machine guns, and
his bitterness grew.

A British officer, William Pressey, reported seeing 200 French cavalrymen advancing across a hilltop close to Amiens, a stirring sight with their
plumed helmets and gleaming lances. 'They laughed and waved their
lances at us, shouting "*Le Bosch fini*", "Death to the Kraut!"' Just after they
disappeared from sight he heard the dry rattle of machine guns. Only a
few stray horses came back.

At Houthulst, where these days St Christoffel Church organises weekend
masses and the blessing of automobiles, there is a huge Belgian war
cemetery. Schoolchildren have hung letters on the bluish slabs. To the
dead they have written: 'You were given only five bullets a day. Too bad
it happened. But you fought well.' And: 'If another war comes, you won't
be there to see it. But I hope a war never comes. See you in heaven.'

I hear a dull thud. A blue mist comes floating across the frosty fields.

In the field behind the cemetery, the DOVO, the Belgian War Munition Demolition Service, has blown up another heap of First World War ammunition. They do it twice a day, one and a half tons a day. And there is no end in sight. When the farmers find grenades they leave them at the base of the utility masts, and the miners collect them. And so it goes on here. Generation after generation, this soil continues to vomit up grenades, buttons, buckles, knives, skulls, bottles, rifles, sometimes even a whole tank. The Great War never ends.

Chapter Eight

Cassel

THIS PLACE SHOULD BE VISITED IN NOVEMBER, OR IN FEBRUARY, when no grass, wheat or barley is growing, when the ground has returned to earth again, damp, muddy, full of puddles and wet snow. Late in the afternoon I drive to Cassel, just across the French border. The sun is hanging low over rolling fields, a huge orange ball about to sink into the ground. After that the sky turns a very fragile light blue with little pink clouds. Then darkness falls.

Hôtel de Schoebeque has, they say, changed little since the French commander-in-chief, Ferdinand Foch, and King George V stayed here. Here sat the switchmen of fate, the chiefs of staff, the men who encountered the tens of thousands of dead only in statistics. The gate is locked. I hop over the fence and wander through the gardens, and in the last light of day I see what they saw: the plain stretching out past Ypres, with all the roads, fields and hedgerows like a chessboard at your feet.

The First World War already had a few of the characteristics that would make the next one so murderous: the massive scale, the technology, the alienation, the anonymity. The civilian, though, was still being spared: only five per cent of the victims of the First World War were civilians, compared with fifty per cent in the Second World War. The war, though not yet about race, was about origin, nationality and rank. And everywhere the governing classes willingly sacrificed hundreds of thousands of farm boys, workers and office clerks, without mercy, on behalf of a few vague moves on the chessboard.

From all those soldiers' humiliating experiences at the front there gradually rose new social and rebellious movements, each with its own tone and its own appearance in every country. The fronts became in this way

the breeding grounds for a series of mass movements that would dominate European politics for decades, varying from angry veterans in Italy
to frustrated officers in Germany to hard line pacifist-socialists in France
and Belgium.

An almost aristocratic distance was maintained between French officers and their men. Maréchal Joseph Joffre refused to be told how many
soldiers had been killed, for this would only 'distract' him. Corporal
Barthas regularly describes the comfort enjoyed by French officers, while
exhausted soldiers marched through the countryside like 'cattle', 'slaves'
or 'lepers', hacked away at trenches and slept among the rats. But the
British commander-in-chief, Earl Haig, was the most ruthless strategist.

Some later characterised Haig as 'the Scot who seized the opportunity
to liquidate more Englishmen than anyone before him'. But during the
war years he was idolised. No matter how you looked at it, within only
a few years he had succeeded in whipping the little British Army of regulars into an excellently trained military force with millions of troops, and
so saved the British Empire. Here too, the technological lag played a role.
The only wise place for a general to be in modern warfare is, in fact,
behind the lines, at the end of a bundle of telephone wires. Fighting
generals – fifty-six British generals were killed during the war – were
brave, they were good for morale, but otherwise they simply got in the
way. At the same time, the first telephones and other communications
systems were still too unreliable to allow generals to work in this way,
especially during combat.

Were there actually switchmen of fate, working behind the scenes? There
certainly were. First of all, one had the French brandy merchant Jean
Monnet, whom we met earlier in the City of London. As soon as he
heard that war had broken out, he asked for a meeting with the prime
minister, René Viviani, a friend of a friend. Monnet, twenty-six at the
time, raised a matter with Viviani which, as he wrote later, he would
probably not have mentioned had he been older and wiser. It was a new
kind of problem, a twentieth-century problem. For this mass war, Monnet
reasoned, all of the warring nations' resources had to be brought to bear,
and that required new forms of organisation and cooperation.

War was no longer simply a matter for the battlefield. Winning a

modern war involved less heroic things as well, such as supply chains
and shipping capacity. Germany, with its massive industrial base, seemed
significantly better prepared for such warfare than either Great Britain or
France. It was vitally important, therefore, that the two countries combine
their economies, 'as though forming a single nation'. Following on the
heels of decades of overblown nationalism, this was an outright revolutionary idea.

The French prime minister agreed with him. Monnet succeeded in
convincing the British as well – he had vast connections due to his business – and there arose an Allied Transport Pool and a Wheat Executive.
These bodies focused, for the first time in European history, on common
interests rather than on national ones.

Without the Wheat Executive, France would almost certainly have
starved. Without the Allied Transport Pool, the German submarines would
have been able to cut off all supply lines to the continent, as they almost
succeeded in doing in the spring of 1917. When faced with the same
problems in 1940, Great Britain and France established similar cooperative ties, but then in the service of a more ambitious ideal: their
possible continuation in times of peace as well. In a certain sense, the
Wheat Executive and the Allied Transport Pool were the kernel of what
would later develop into the European Union.

There were other switchmen of fate: Karel Cogge, a Belgian lock-
keeper, for example, along with a constantly inebriated ship's mate Hendrik
Geeraerd and a local historian, Emeric Feys. It was Feys who found, in
his archives, old plans for the inundation of the local marshlands. And it
was on his instructions, in late October 1914, that Cogge opened the
sluices at Veurne-Sas. When the water did not rise quickly enough, it was
Geeraerd who, under cover of night, succeeded in prying open the abandoned and overgrown sluice doors in the Noordvaart canal. In this way
they were able, at the very last moment, to flood the plain around the
Yser. To this trio belongs the credit for halting the German advance at
Nieuwpoort.

There are still two Cogges in the Nieuwpoort phone book: Kurt and
Georges. I call Georges. 'Yes, he was my great-uncle, my grandmother
told me about it once. No, no one knows any more about it, they're all
dead. Kurt? He's my son! And I have a grandson, too!'

And so the Cogges of Nieuwpoort live on, completely undaunted by history.

During the Great War, the town of Poperinge was the first relatively quiet spot behind the lines. Believe it or not, a sign still hangs in the square which reads SAFE or UNSAFE – depending on where the wind was coming from during a gas attack – but that didn't stop the fun. This was where one found the first glass, and the much-sung last woman:

> After the war fini
> English soldiers parti
> Mademoiselles de Poperinge vont pleurer
> Avec plenty bébé!

The stately Talbot House stood outside that whirl of activity. It was an Everyman's club, where soldiers from any rank and class could find rest for a while. That egalitarian atmosphere still prevails, around the stair-cases, the furniture, the candelabras, the books, the paintings, the water jugs, the piano the men sang at. Until the late 1980s, veterans still came to stay here. Even the tranquil garden has remained unchanged, including the sign inviting one to 'Come into the garden and forget about the war.'

I drink tea at the kitchen table, talk a little with a young Scotsman, look at all the empty chairs around us, muse over the boys from back then. In London I had met Lyn MacDonald, an expert on the First World War, a writer who traced and interviewed hundreds of veterans before it was too late, the mother confessor of the last survivors.

She told me how she had become intrigued by all those little clubs of old men who got together regularly in the 1960s and 1970s to raise a glass and sing a song. 'The mere fact that they were together, that was enough. No one who hadn't been through the war could really under-stand what that meant.'

MacDonald always spoke of them as 'the boys'. 'When I interviewed them, I quickly found myself talking, not to extremely old men, but to very young men from 1914. To them, that war was often more real than the rest of their lives. As one of them put it: "I lived my entire life between the ages of eighteen and twenty-one, the rest was only the credits."'

During our conversation, she warned me against judging too hastily: 'That generation wasn't mad, they were fantastic people. But they had very different ideals: patriotism, a sense of duty, service, self-sacrifice. They were typical Victorians, and after the war they came back to a world where they felt less and less at home.'

But still, what drove them? What drove all those men to take part in collective suicide? Lyn MacDonald told me about a man who was wounded, fell, and all he could think was: 'What a waste! All those months of expensive training, and I haven't even fired a shot!' Everything in him wanted to fight, to prove himself.

'Going over the top', the leap from the trenches, was the definitive experience of the First World War, and at the same time the most terrifying: endless waiting, the passing round of rum, vomiting from nerves, the count, the whistles, out of the trenches, towards the enemy, through the barbed wire, running for your life in an unimaginable pandemonium of bullets, mines and mortars, and then shooting, burning, stabbing, killing. 'Over the top, boys, come on, over the top.' And they went.

Friends, neighbours, fellow villagers all volunteered together, were trained together and went over the top together. 'You went, right, it was your duty, you'd signed up for it,' said Arthur Wagstaff (b. 1898) in the BBC documentary mentioned earlier. Tommy Gay: 'Me and my mate were always together, the first time we went over the top we went together, but I never saw him after that. There was nothing but bullets. But not one of them had my name on it!' Robbie Burns (b. 1897): 'Before every major attack you had the feeling this could be the very last time. You didn't let it show, you didn't talk about it, you kept it to yourself.'

At the start of the Battle of the Somme, even the most hardened soldiers fouled themselves when they realised that their commander had made a fatal mistake: ten minutes before the attack, he had stopped the shelling of the German positions. That gave the Germans, as they well knew, enough time to run from their bunkers, man their machine guns and slaughter the attackers. And that is exactly what happened. But they still went when the whistle blew.

All manner of explanations can of course be given for this phenomenon, varying from the patriotism on the home front to the strong sense of camaraderie and the tight discipline within the British and German armies. Barthas describes the start of an absurd attack in Northern France, in the early hours of 17 December, 1914, straight into the German machine guns with no cover. A major had given the order. At first the captain refused to pass it along, the two men fought, then the captain climbed out of the trench and was shot down after taking a few steps. Barthas: 'In the trenches the men were moaning and begging "But I have three children." Or they screamed "Mama, Mama." Another soldier begged for mercy. But the major, revolver in hand and beside himself with rage, threatened to shoot anyone who hesitated.' Finally, they went, just a little more afraid of their major than they were of the enemy.

There is also another side to the story. The soldiers had not, after all, gone to war to 'die for their fatherland', but to kill, to wound, to mutilate. In most of the letters and diaries from the front, however, this subject is carefully avoided. Emphasis is always placed on the suffering and the dying, but one reads little about the actual experience of killing.

What was the motive? After a year of war, Barthas said he never wanted to hear the word 'patriotic' again: 'It was very simple: we were forced to do it as victims of an unrelenting fate . . . We had lost our sense of values and our humanity. We were degraded to the status of pack animals: indifferent, unfeeling and deadened.' Barthas was a committed socialist and humanist, and found his own solution to the problem: he fired only in self-defence, never for any other reason.

The attitude adopted by the poet Robert Graves was the polar opposite of this, perhaps in part because Graves was an officer and wished to do all he could to renounce his German origins. He had no qualms about treating an unsuspecting German, whom he had heard humming a tune from Die lustige Witwe during a reconnaissance mission, to a mortar attack fifteen minutes later. He killed with calm pragmatism. He had come up with a sort of formula for taking risks: 'We would all take any risk, even the certainty of death, to save life or to maintain an important position. To take life we would run, say, a one-in-five risk.'

This same pragmatism also extended to the killing of prisoners. Although it was in violation of every military convention and code of honour, Barthas, Graves and other diarists mention it frequently. Prisoners on the way to the rear lines would have a live grenade stuffed into their pockets, or were simply shot down. When a German patrol found a wounded man in no-man's-land, there was every chance they would slit his throat. Graves: 'We ourselves preferred the mace.'

The most important thing in actual combat was the group, the soldiers with whom one interacted on a daily basis. 'Regimental pride', Graves called it. 'No one wanted to be a bigger coward than his neighbour,' Barthas observed. 'Besides that, the men, stubborn as they were, believed in their own good luck.' This same sense of solidarity was sometimes a powerful motive for killing: protecting the group, avenging a fallen comrade. Ernst Jünger describes how one of his men, the father of four children, was killed by a British sniper: 'His comrades hung around the foxholes for a long time, hoping to avenge him. They wept with rage. They seemed to consider the Englishman who had fired the deadly shot to be their personal enemy.' After the death of one of his best friends, the English poet Siegfried Sassoon volunteered for patrol duty every night 'looking for Germans to kill'.

'I think a curse should rest on me – because I love this war,' wrote Winston Churchill to Violet Asquith, the prime minister's daughter, in early 1915. 'I know it's smashing and shattering the lives of thousands every moment – & yet – I can't help it – I enjoy every second of it.'

Still, in most of the accounts of the Great War, one finds little or nothing of the individual passion for killing. On the contrary. Barthas relates how his men, while pursuing the enemy, were suddenly handed butchers' knives. Clearly, these were to be used to kill the German wounded or prisoners. Most of the soldiers threw them aside: 'These are weapons for murderers, not for soldiers.' During the Battle of the Somme, German machine-gunners – shocked by the slaughter – regularly stopped firing long enough to allow British soldiers to crawl back to their trenches. Some British officers even felt that the soldiers' greatest reservations about going over the top had to do not with their fear of dying, but their fear of killing.

The British machine-gunner Albert Depew was one of the few who wrote openly about how, in 1918, he had jumped a German in a trench and run his bayonet right through the man. 'He was as delicate as a pencil. When I returned to our trenches after my first charge, I could not sleep for a long time afterwards for remembering what that fellow looked like and how my bayonet slipped into him and how he screamed when he fell. He had his leg and his neck twisted under him after he got it. I thought about it a lot, and it grew to be almost a habit that whenever I was going to sleep I would think about him, and then all hope of sleeping was gone.'

Chapter Nine

Verdun

YPRES LIVES OFF THE PAST, OFF ITS STEP-GABLES, ITS NEWLY constructed Middle Ages, off the graves and the dead. Ever since 1927, two buglers from the local volunteer fire department meet each evening at eight to sound the last post. Riek van den Kerkhove has been doing it for nineteen years now, Antoon Verschoot for almost forty-six. They pull up on their bicycles, snap to attention, wait until two policemen have stopped traffic, then let the notes echo from the walls of the enormous Menenpoort with its plaques holding the names of 54,896 dead soldiers. A dozen or so people stand around, looking on. Within a matter of moments it is over, they shake hands with the policemen, the traffic races on across the cobblestones again.

Antoon's broad face shines with amiability. He's retired now, but he continues to do this. 'It's hard sometimes, in the winter, when you've been sitting nice and warm in front of the TV.' Riek says: 'It's an obligation of honour.' He missed the call only once, when he was busy pulling someone out of the water. But otherwise the last post is always sounded, even when a house is burning down at the same time. 'It goes before all the rest, you know,' Antoon says.

When will the emotion of the Great War fade? When will it finally become history? When will the Battle of the Somme become something like the Battle of Waterloo? Allow me to hazard a guess: within the next ten years. Somewhere between the third and fourth generation, somewhere between the grandchildren — who can scarcely remember anyone who was involved — and the great-grandchildren the feeling will change. In the great charnel house at Verdun, the daily Mass recently became monthly. To the south

of the Somme a huge airport is planned, to be built across two war cemeteries. See here the writing on the wall. The spectacle, not the memory,
gradually becomes the crux of the matter.

At the Queen Victoria's Rifles Café, the tables still bear long rows of
vues stéréoscopiques from the 1920s. For three quarters of a century the proprietor has been earning a handful of francs from his selection of the grisliest stereo photographs: corpses caught in the barbed wire, decapitated
Germans, part of a horse in a tree. Today, this has all been raised to perfection. In the Yser Tower at Diksmuide you can stick your nose in a machine
and smell the gas. Chlorine gas actually does smell a bit like bleach,
mustard gas a little like mustard. At the impressive In Flanders Field peace
museum at Ypres you can enter a darkened room for a trip through no-
man's-land, complete with snatches of dreams: what was going on in
the mind of a German or British soldier as he went over the top? The
room is full of noise and death rattles, full of images of running soldiers,
phantoms from a peaceful life before the war: 'Why me? Why us?' Using
a computer programme, you can pick out a soldier at will and trace the
course of his life. I adopt Charles Hamilton Sorley, reading Greats at
Oxford. He was killed at Loos, 'a bullet through the head'.

There are other approaches as well. At the new Historial de la Grande
Guerre in Péronne, all the glory and illusions have been stripped away.
The military uniforms and equipment are not displayed upright, but on
the floor, like fallen men. Of course, that's how it was, almost everything
here once belonged to the dead. But I am afraid the Historial will remain
the lone exception. Today little cars trundle on rails through the old citadel
of Verdun, like in an amusement park ride, and I am sure in twenty years'
time they will be trundling everywhere, through cunning replicas of the
trenches complete with rats, excrement and the smell of corpses, the
whinnying of dying horses and the cries of the mortally wounded. Slowly
the feeling shifts from one of solidarity to one of curiosity.

Along the autoroute from Lille to Paris, the Battle of the Somme is only
a tap of the accelerator. In late summer 1916, 1.2 million people died
here, between two exits. The motorway runs at a slight distance from the
eastern boundary of the battlefield. Drivers are kept informed of that as
well, on big brown signs along the road, LA GRANDE GUERRE, the way a

famous chateau or a pleasant vintage might be pointed out elsewhere. Then they flash by, back into the serenity of present-day Picardy.

Here the war has already entered the next phase, that of a popular tourist attraction, a mainstay of the region's commercial infrastructure. Everywhere one finds folders promoting these centres of infernal attraction; staying at my hotel – it is 15 February, the heart of winter – there are at least three couples touring the front lines. The museums compete by offering even more audio and visual effects. For the first time in ages, I can receive Dutch channels on the TV in my room. On the news they are interviewing tourists who were stranded for a few days in a snow-bound Swiss village. 'What we've been through!' one tanned woman says. 'We felt just like refugees.' Another one cries 'Everything, we've lost every-thing!' She's talking about a suitcase full of skiing outfits and make-up.

It is foggy outside, and as the day progresses the fog grows thicker. I drive carefully to the Somme. The blue contours of a ship are barely visible at the locks on the Canal du Nord. Close by is a stand of black willows, a few coots are swimming around, then all this dissolves again into silence and greyness. All the trenches, all the craters, all the forgotten remnants, all the lost bodies are covered in a white veil from sky to earth.

The Somme was the battle of total planning. On paper, there was no way this offensive could go wrong. The confrontation had been on the drawing boards for months on either side of the front, while at least a million soldiers and 200,000 horses, along with untold quantities of rifles, cannons and munitions, were being assembled. The countless tents, field kitchens, field hospitals, command posts and halting-places looked like little cities. 'It was one big anthill,' Louis Barthas wrote on 9 October, 1916, when he arrived at the Somme halfway through the battle. 'There were convoys driving back and forth along the roads that passed through the camp, heavy munitions trucks, ambulances and all manner of mili-tary vehicles. Railway tracks had also been built, along which massive convoys of supplies, ammunition and food were transported . . . The camp was too big to be taken in at a glance. All you could hear was the noisy hubbub, mixed with the thundering of cannons in the distance.'

The British had even built a special bunker along the front line for Geoffrey Malins, the man assigned to make their victory film. The Germans, supposedly wiped out by days of shelling, nevertheless proved to be alive and kicking at the start of the battle. Their barbed-wire barriers, their strong positions, their machine guns, all were still intact. It was the greatest slaughter in British military history. Of the 100,000 men who moved out that day, more than 19,000 had been killed by noon. Forty thousand were wounded. General Sir Beauvoir de Lisle reported: 'It was a remarkable display of training and discipline, and the attack failed only because dead men cannot move on.'

It took weeks before the British were able to recover the bodies of their comrades. 'Wounded, they had crawled into shell craters, wrapped themselves in their waterproof blankets, pulled out their bibles and died like that.'

Thanks to tips from Lyn MacDonald's veterans, I am able to find Malin's cinematic vantage point. It is, in all probability, this large hollow beside the Scottish monument at Beaumont Hamel, now covered in tall grass but an excellent place indeed for a camera. I squat down in it and see the images in my mind's eye. A group of soldiers has taken cover against the shoulder of the rutted road in front of me, ready for a renewed attack. They are young boys, half calm, half tense, one of them turns and looks boldly into the lens, another moves off camera, some are fussing with their equipment and take a swig from a canteen. One is casually smoking a cigarette, while another lies in the foreground, acting tough, showing off. One final draw on the cigarette, a signal sounds, the bayonets are mounted on the rifles, and then it all breaks loose.

What the film does not show is how it ended: less than two minutes later, all these men were dead.

I take the bus along the old infantry lines. The war cemeteries stand like orchards along the farmers' roads, stop by stop. I visit the field where almost the entire Royal Newfoundland Regiment was mown down during a senseless attack, a case of collective suicide that even today could serve as an example for Muslim fundamentalists. No fewer than 700 boys. Their desperate passage can still be precisely traced. Sheep graze around the bomb craters and trenches. The barbed wire is gone, the bodies have vanished, but the Canadian fir trees planted here make a fearsome noise: hear their branches talking in the wind.

I am reminded of a conversation that Vera Brittain, as an army nurse, overheard in a hospital ward. A sergeant told of a fantastic captain he had had, an officer who always got his boys out of a tight spot. He was killed at the Somme, and they had mourned him like a brother. 'But a while back, just before the Krauts came into Albert, we were in a bit of a fix and I was doing all I could to get us out of it, and suddenly I see him, with his clear eyes and his old grin, bringing up the rear. So, Will, he says, that was a close shave. And I go to answer him, and suddenly he's gone.' Then someone else in the ward began to talk about a couple of stretcher-bearers, a top crew. 'One day one of those coal bins comes whistling down and they're gone. But last week a few of our boys saw them again, carrying a couple of wounded fellows down the trench. And in the train I met a boy who swears they carried him out of it.'

Robert Graves mentions a similar experience. During a banquet held for his company, he wrote, he saw at the window one of his soldiers, a fellow by the name of Challonner. 'There was no mistaking him or the cap badge he was wearing. I jumped up and looked out of the window, but saw nothing except a fag end smoking on the pavement.' Challoner had been killed a month earlier.

Vera Brittain tended not to put much stock in it, but her men were adamant. 'That's right, Sister, they're dead. But they were our mates when they were killed at the Somme in '16, and it's a fact: they still fight along-side us.'

The next day I ride through gentle, rolling countryside, the weekend-house country of Paris, green and modest. In the fields ploughed red I can still see the vague, whitish traces of trenches. This is a region of grad-ualness. The towns and villages display no grand movements, they contain no huge monuments, no shocking modernities.

In the little roadside restaurants everyone is served the menu of the day, no option: soup, chicken, cheese, pudding, coffee. The men know each other well, they shake hands after their meal and then climb back into their trucks or vans. I find a hotel with a grandma knitting and a chambermaid with big eyes. Later, in the corridor, I see her again with a mobile phone, and all she says into it is 'Je t'aime . . . oui, je t'aime . . . merci . . . mais je t'aime . . .'

Verdun is a peaceful town, and contains the most horrible war memorial I have ever seen. It is a tower, atop which a knight glowers threateningly across the rooftops. If I were a three-year-old citizen of Verdun, I would be afraid to close my eyes at night. At the knight's feet lies a museum, marked by the usual pride and pomp, the same drive for glory that almost destroyed the French Army. The Battle of Verdun began on 21 February, 1916 and lasted ten months. It accounted for 260,000 lives, almost one a minute. In the long run no one got much further because of it, but that did not bother German chief of staff Erich von Falkenhayn. What he wanted, above all, was bodies. He knew that the fortifications of Verdun had long been the gateway to France, that the city had always had a special symbolic significance for the French, and he wanted them literally to 'bleed to death' here. The German code name for the attack on Verdun was 'Gericht', the place of execution.

Falkenhayn understood the mentality of the French generals very well. They threw everyone and everything they had into the fray, thinking only of glorious attacks, and were barely concerned with the lives of their troops. That is reflected in what remains of the French trenches: shallow and makeshift, in contrast to the German concrete. Verdun was a trap for the French Army, with pride and glory as its bait.

The only supply line, the legendary Voie Sacrée, remained intact, but that too was part of the German plan: to bleed to death, one needs an artery. The French foot soldiers called Verdun 'the big sausage machine', and as they came marching up they could see from afar the stinking hell of rumbling and flame, a gaping maw signifying the end of everything. For the German soldier, in fact, it was hardly different: 330,000 of them would be killed or wounded, compared to 360,000 Frenchmen. Verdun was much more traumatic for the average Frenchman, however, because the French Army worked by rotation. Most French soldiers, therefore, had a chance to become personally acquainted with 'the big sausage machine', even if only for a while, with all the accompanying physical and psychological consequences.

Corporal Barthas' company arrived at Verdun on 12 May, 1916. They were to relieve the troops of the 125th Regiment. When they entered the trenches, all they found was 'one huge pile of ripped-apart human flesh'. The day before, it seems, there had been a massive mortar attack.

'Everywhere lay wreckage, ruined rifles, torn knapsacks from which tender letters and carefully cherished memories had fallen and were scattered in the wind. There were also shattered canteens, shoulder bags torn to shreds, all bearing the insignia of the 125th Regiment.'

One day later they were allowed to leave again, in a terrible night-time journey on foot across the battlefield, 'across barbed wire, poles, split sandbags, corpses and assorted wreckage . . . After each lightning flash of mortar fire, the darkness seemed only blacker.'

Across those same fields today hangs a thick, cold layer of fog. The land-scape, in Barthas' day shelled into barrenness, is now covered with gaunt trees. Until not so very long ago, nothing would grow here at all, except the hardy Canadian firs. Trenches and shell craters are still visible every-where, filled with brown meltwater. All the war sights are indicated with large signs. I work my way quickly past all the highlights of this macabre Disneyland: the monument, the charnel house, the firebombed village, the fortress of glory, the sacred trench with the bayonets of seventeen stalwart soldiers who, according to legend, were buried alive in a mortar attack. (Sticking a bayonet into the ground was a quick way to mark the grave of a few poor sods, but of course no one here cares to hear about that.)

The Douaumount ossuary rises up from the mist. The enormous grey charnel house, the size of a large secondary school, contains the bones of more than 130,000 of the fallen. You can see them through the little half-misted windows at the back of the building; here and there some orderly soul has neatly piled them up: femurs with femurs, ribs with ribs, arms with arms, whole and half skulls, all with lovely young teeth.

The fog makes everything quiet and introverted. The snow melting off the roof drips on and on into the gutters, and that is the only sound.

Chapter Ten

Versailles

LOUIS BARTHAS, EARLY AUGUST 1916, AT THE FRONT IN CHAMPAGNE: 'Two days later, our 6th Group went to occupy Guard Post Number Ten. It was only a normal barricade in an old corridor connecting the German lines. Six metres from our barricade, the Germans had set up one of their own. Barbed wire had been scattered between the two, but only four leaps separated the two peoples, two races bent on exterminating each other. How amazed, how perturbed patriotic civilians would have been to see how calm and peaceful it was there. One soldier would be smoking, the other would be reading or writing. Some were arguing without lowering their voices. Their amazement would turn to dismay if they saw the French and German sentries sitting on their breastworks, calmly smoking a pipe and, from time to time, taking a breath of fresh air and sharing a little small talk, like good neighbours.'

What our corporal describes here is a situation that in no way fits the commonly accepted view of suffering and heroism. It does not correspond to the military historians' dissertations on strategy, or with the official accounts of battles and bloodshed. Little research has been done into such 'live and let live' situations. Still, they must have presented themselves rather often, between battles and along the endless stretches of front line where nothing ever happened.

There was always a certain sense of understanding between the enemies: foot soldiers, whether German, British, French or Belgian, all die in the same way, and they knew that. They had, after a certain fashion, respect for each other. And they came to their enemy's defence when the home front characterised them as 'cowardly' or 'stupid'.

In his autobiographical novel Le feu, Henri Barbusse speaks of two different worlds: the front, 'where there are too many of the unfortunate', and the hinterland, 'where too much good fortune exists'. In the former world, mutual understanding occasionally led to outbursts of fraternisation. At the spot where the Yser Tower now stands, at Diksmuide in Belgium, the Belgian and German soldiers famously celebrated Christmas Eve together in 1914. The Germans plied the Belgians with schnapps. A German officer returned a stolen monstrance. Elsewhere during those days there were also large-scale displays of brotherhood. In one sector, nine British divisions had organised a ceasefire along a front almost fifty kilometres in length. 'On New Year's Eve we counted off the minutes back and forth, and agreed to fire volleys at midnight,' a German student wrote to his parents. 'We sang, they applauded (we were sixty or seventy metres apart) . . . Then I shouted to ask them whether they had any musical instruments over there, upon which they produced a pair of bagpipes (it was a Scottish regiment, barelegged in short skirts). They played their poetic Scottish songs and sang.'

One German soldier was not at all amused: the enigmatic, fanatical corporal Adolf Hitler. 'This should not be allowed to happen during a war,' the *Gefreiter* fulminated.

One year later, in the soaking wet December of 1915, ad hoc ceasefires were once again held along the front in northern France. On the dreary morning of 12 December, with trenches on both sides filled with water, Ernst Jünger saw the dreary no-man's-land suddenly transformed into 'a county fair'. Between the rolls of barbed wire, 'lively bartering had begun for schnapps, cigarettes, uniform buttons and other things.' Jünger quickly put an end to it. After a brief gentlemen's consultation with a British officer on the other side, it was decided to resume the war in exactly three minutes.

In Barthas' sector, where the same thing happened, the fraternisation lasted for days: 'We smiled at each other, began talking, shaking hands, trading tobacco, coffee and wine. If only we had spoken the same language!' The Socialist International, betrayed and forgotten in 1914, seemed to have been revived by the war. Barthas: 'One day, a huge German fellow climbed up onto a hillock and delivered a speech, the words of which only the Germans understood, but the meaning of which we understood very well indeed, for he took his rifle and broke it in two against a tree trunk. Applause sounded from both sides, and both sides raised the Internationale.'

Such open signs of brotherly feeling were relatively rare, however, and each one can be offset by countless tales of atrocity. 'Mucking about with the enemy' was taboo. Yet these were no isolated incidents. Life in the trenches was for many soldiers only tolerable because of a number of tacit agreements with their partners in adversity on the other side of the line. Despite its enormity, the First World War was, in that sense, old-fashioned; it was a war of proximity, of looking the enemy in the eye, a war in which the specialist, modern technology and push-button killing were already making their appearance, but were not yet totally decisive.

In many areas along the front, for example, the rule was to leave each other alone as much as possible at meal times, during the retrieval of the wounded from no-man's-land, and during night patrols. Any number of diarists make mention of the 'immunity' of mobile field kitchens, in accordance with the same indisputable logic: if you blow up the enemy's kitchen, in five minutes' time you yourself will be without dinner. Interesting too was the tacit agreement between the opposing military engineers, as witnessed by Barthas: the enemy's tunnels were only to be blown up between two at night and six in the morning; during those hours, therefore, no one ever worked on the tunnels. This rule saved the lives of a great many military engineers.

Here and there, things were taken one step further. Vera Brittain relates the story of a Scottish sergeant who had been posted across from a Saxon regiment at Ypres. These two forces had agreed not to aim at each other when they fired. They made a great deal of noise, an outsider would have thought the men were fighting hard, but in practice no one was hit. The battle was reduced to a series of rituals, as with the Greeks and Trojans.

Other letters and diaries make mention of this system as well. 'They're quiet fellows, the Saxons, they don't want to fight any more than we do, so there is a kind of understanding between us,' wrote one British officer. Another said: 'On the front we were on, the Boche signals when the artillery is going to fire and shows us the no. of rounds by holding fingers up.' Robert Graves witnessed letters arriving from the Germans, rolled up in old mortar shells: 'Your little dog has run over to us and we are keeping it safe here.' Newspapers were fired back and forth in the same fashion.

Barthas spent some time in a sector where the Germans and the French fired only six mortar rounds a day, 'out of courtesy'. That was all. The makeshift bridges across a nearby river were held under fire by enemy machine-gunners. Shots were rarely ever fired though, except when Barthas ventured out onto one of the bridges carrying a cane and a pair of binoculars, and the Germans mistook him for an officer. Then the bullets flew past his ears.

This incident is indicative of the increasing social tension on both sides of the front. Almost everyone had abandoned the socialist class struggle back in 1914, but the frustration at the front gradually revived it with a vengeance. The British referred to their commander-in-chief, Haig, as 'the Butcher of the Somme'. The pacifist movement was growing. Lieutenant Siegfried Sassoon publicly announced that he no longer wished to serve in the army: 'I have seen and endured the suffering of the troops, and I can no longer be a party to prolong these sufferings for ends which I believe to be evil and unjust.' German graffiti on trains going to the front read: 'Wilhelm and Sons, Cannon Fodder'. In his diaries, Barthas reported an increasing number of incidents: German and French soldiers singing the 'Internationale' together from their respective trenches, orders being ignored, mutinous units which were then pounded to a pulp by their own artillery. Sometimes the men bleated like sheep as they marched to the slaughterhouse of the front lines.

For French soldiers at the front, Verdun was an emotional turning point. On a village square in May 1916, Barthas heard a soldier bark at a major: 'I'm telling you that we didn't see any of you on Hill 304 [during the battle]. There will be no more saluting here.' Shortly before this, medals had been passed out to the 'heroes of the fatherland', complete with a 'patriotic kiss' from the general. The poilus rolled on the ground in laughter. They had no more respect for anyone or anything.

One year later, within the space of several months in spring 1917, more than 100,000 soldiers were senselessly killed on the Chemin des Dames, but still the French generals wanted to push on. Furloughs promised were postponed again and again. During those same months, more and more rumours began filtering in about Russian mutinies. In late May 1917, Barthas was at a meeting of hundreds of soldiers in the courtyard of an inn. The soldiers were in their cups, and a corporal began singing a protest song about the dismal life in the trenches. The entire crowd joined in on the refrain, 'and when it was finished they applauded wildly, shouting slogans such as "Peace or Revolution!", "Down with the war!" and "Furlough, furlough!"' The next evening, 'the "Internationale" rose up like a hurricane'.

On the following Sunday, the soldiers decided to seize control of the regiment and set up a 'soviet'. Barthas was chosen to be its chairman. 'I refused of course, for I had no desire to become acquainted with the firing squad simply for the sake of some childish imitation of the Russians.' He agreed, however, to write a manifesto concerning the postponed leaves of absence. It never went any further than that.

In other regiments, however, the soldiers went much further than that. They stopped fighting, set up soldiers' councils, raised the red flag and even hijacked trains. Officers were intimidated, and when orders were disobeyed they looked the other way. At its peak the French mutiny involved 30–40,000 soldiers. The army was in a state of disorder for months, the British had to take over parts of the French front, and the French never completely recovered. The commanders no longer dared to issue orders for major attacks.

Barthas' regiment was placed under strict disciplinary constraint, but also received a breather. Some 350 mutineers were exiled to Devil's Island and 550 were condemned to death, of whom 49 were actually executed by order of the newly appointed commander-in-chief Philippe Pétain. On several occasions soldiers refused to take part in firing squads. In protest, they merely fired their shots over the condemned men's heads, leaving the commanding officer to perform the execution himself.

The French command did have one bit of good luck, though: the Germans never found out how extensive the mutiny really was. The French authorities never brought up the matter again.

In the long run, the war was decided not by events along the fronts, but by a slowly shifting balance of economic and technological power. What young Jean Monnet had predicted did indeed come to pass. All participants were weakened by the struggle. In France, infant mortality rose by one fifth. In England, cases of tuberculosis rose by twenty-five per cent. Yet Germany suffered even more.

Due to the Allied blockade of all German shipping, the country received far too few staples. The first food riots took place in Berlin in April 1917. In January 1918, a strike by half a million workers closed down the metal and munitions industry. Food rations – 2,000 calories under normal conditions – had been reduced to 1,000. The German arms industry began breaking down, particularly when it came to modern weaponry. In 1918 the Germans had only one quarter of the number of trucks available to the Allies. The 'land cruiser', of which Winston Churchill had already dreamed in 1914, a vehicle that could roll right over the trenches 'and everything in them', this monstrous 'tank', had meanwhile been developed by the Allies into a serious weapon. They had 800 of them. The Germans had ten.

Illustrative of the mood in Germany was the popular song by the young poet Bertolt Brecht about a soldier who had long since died 'a hero's death', but who was exhumed by the doctors and passed the physical 'because this soldier died before his time'. Then he was made to drink 'fiery schnapps', smothered in incense to mask the smell of decay, received a nurse on each arm and 'a half-naked dame', the music blared and there the soldier went marching off, 'with oompah-pah and hurrah', on his way to another 'hero's death'.

In summer 1918, Brecht's soldier also came down with Spanish flu. In early July, Käthe Kollwitz reported that her husband's practice in Berlin was suddenly swamped with more than a hundred cases of influenza. This unknown illness was particularly virulent, and the exhausted continent was struck hard. The outbreak of Spanish flu probably took place all over the world at the same time, but it was in neutral Spain that medical publications first mentioned it; hence its name.

Few events in the twentieth century were as disastrous for the people of Europe, and at the same time so quickly forgotten. Still, almost every village cemetery today contains the traces of this epidemic; my own father, as a student, caught Spanish flu and barely survived. It is estimated that between forty and a hundred million people died worldwide. It probably claimed more lives in Europe than the entire First World War. What is certain is that the wave of influenza was one of the factors that made the Germans break off their final offensive in July 1918, and then lose the war. It was against this background that the struggle took place during the last eighteen months of the conflict.

In the same month in which Louis Barthas narrowly missed being catapulted to chairman of a soviet of soldiers, the first American troops landed in France in May 1917. The American Congress had hesitated for a long time, but finally lost patience when the Germans torpedoed five American ships in March 1917; war was declared on Germany on 6 April. It remains unclear why President Woodrow Wilson abandoned his attempts to move the Allies and the Central Europeans towards a 'peace without victory'. The 'Zimmermann Telegram', however, may have played a major role. In that telegram, sent to the German ambassador in Mexico on 16 January, 1917, the German minister of foreign affairs, Arthur Zimmermann, announced the launch of a full scale submarine war against the United States. He also proposed the idea of joining with Mexico in a war against America, which would allow the Mexicans, with profuse German support, to retake the territories they had lost in Texas, Arizona and New Mexico. The telegram was intercepted by the British, decoded and sent to the Americans. After several weeks of hesitation, Zimmermann confessed to an American correspondent that the telegram was not a fake.

In the eyes of Vera Brittain, the American soldiers looked like 'Tommies in heaven . . . so godlike, so magnificent, so splendidly unimpaired in comparison with the tired, nerve-racked men of the British Army'. The military strategists were less euphoric. It would, they expected, take at least a year to mobilise the four million Americans promised and ship them to Europe.

At first, therefore, the German commanders were not too worried. They themselves had dragged America into the war with their 'unlimited submarine war', and they planned to apply those same submarines to make troop transports from the United States virtually impossible. In addition, the war on the Eastern Front was going swimmingly. From as early as autumn 1916, the Russian Army had been crippled by massive mutinies, the czar had abdicated in March 1917, and the soldiers remained restless. In November the revolutionaries had seized power, the Russian Front collapsed and, on 3 March, 1918, a peace treaty was signed at Brest-Livotsk. The Germans had achieved half of their original objectives, albeit three years later than planned.

By then Germany held almost half of all the Russian territory west of Moscow. In the months that followed, the remaining divisions would push back the borders even further, all the way to the Caucasus. Never had Germany controlled territories to the East as extensive as those they held in summer 1918. Its troops freed, Austria had delivered the Italians a crushing defeat at Caporetto in October 1917, a traumatic event that left a profound scar on Italian history. Germany and Austria were confident of their success. On 20 March, 1918, the Austro-Hungarian Army opened a regular air connection between Vienna and Kiev, the first of its kind in Europe. In that same week, three giant cannons specially designed and manufactured by Krupp fired their first rounds on Paris, from more than a hundred kilometres distant. More than 250 Parisians were killed. The kaiser gave German schoolchildren a 'victory day' off.

Then began a race against the clock: the Germans had to move as many units as possible from east to west before the Americans finished building up their intervention force. During the first weeks of 1918, General Erich Ludendorff promised the kaiser that Paris would lie at his feet by early April. And indeed, the great German spring offensive of 1918 broke straight through the French lines. The battlefield was covered in a thick fog of chlorine gas, phosgene and tear gas. Flame-throwers were used. Of the men directly in the path of the flames, an English eye-witness wrote 'nothing more was ever seen'.

'We lived in great fear, like a miserable little bird waiting beneath a leaf for a huge thunderstorm to break loose,' Barthas wrote of those days.

The Germans were finally halted less than sixty kilometres from Paris. On 2 June, a young fighter pilot by the name of Hermann Göring received a medal for having shot down eighteen Allied planes. The German aircraft industry was now producing 300 planes a month. On 8 July, Wilhelm II dismissed his minister of foreign affairs for having had the nerve to speak of a peace that would be achieved by means other than military alone.

Ludendorff launched his new offensive along the Marne on 14 July, using every division at his disposal. Berlin expected Paris to capitulate within days, and the Allies to sue for peace within months. But Ludendorff's attack was blocked by a French ruse: they had dug fake trenches, and lured the Germans into wasting munitions. What the Germans had failed to anticipate above all, however, was the fierceness of the newly arrived American troops. 'Retreat?' their legendary captain Lloyd Williams is reported to have said. 'Hell, we just got here!'

Each month now, a quarter of a million fresh, healthy and well-trained Americans arrived at the front. After four days, the Germans retreated. On 15 July, Berlin was still dreaming of Paris. 'By the 18th, even the greatest optimist among us knew that all was lost,' Georg van Herling wrote in his diary. 'The history of the world was played out in three days.'

After that began the Allied counteroffensive, aided with a new weapon that defied all trenches: the tank. German morale collapsed. The figures speak for themselves: until late July 1918, the monthly tally of German prisoners of war was less than 4,000, by August that had become 40,000, and by September 70,000.

In the Balkans, too, the tide had turned. As early as 1915, the dynamic British naval minister, Winston Churchill, had tried to open a new front along the Dardanelles and Gallipoli, a failure that claimed the lives of hundreds of thousands of men, including Irfan Orga's father. But in summer 1918 the Turkish and Bulgarian defences collapsed anyway. Central Europe was now open to the Allied armies from the south-east.

In short, the German generals simply could no longer fight on. The failure of the spring offensive, Spanish flu, fear of the dozens of new American divisions, the Balkans, the revolution that came sweeping in from the East: enough was enough. Supplies of food and munitions stagnated. Officers were increasingly forced to send their men into the fray at gunpoint. At railway stations, where it was more difficult to keep an eye on them, huge numbers of German soldiers regularly disappeared.

In the end, the war stopped as suddenly as it had started four years earlier. By late September 1918, Ludendorff realised that Germany was in dire straits. Within the space of a few days he 'arranged' a new, social-democrat government, thereby saving the army and his generals' honour.

On 29 September he reported to Kaiser Wilhelm that the war had been lost. In late October, during the Austro-German conference in Vienna, the 500-year-old Austro-Hungarian monarchy was disbanded. The new emperor, Karel I, promised autonomy to his realm's major national minorities – the Hungarians, the Czechs and the peoples of the Balkans. Shortly afterwards, he abdicated. But it was already too late. The nationals had seized power. Czech, Polish, Croatian, German and Hungarian regiments deserted. On 3 November, Austria announced a ceasefire. Germany followed suit just over a week later.

Driving north today from Compiègne one sees countryside flat as a prairie, with hills along the distant horizon. Behind those hills lies the famous forest where the armistice was signed in a railway carriage in November 1918. These days the spot is good for a Sunday afternoon walk, and nothing more, and the historic site is now a park. Then it was a dense and rugged forest with two sets of tracks running through it for the transport of heavy artillery, an ideal place for two trains to meet undisturbed.

Germany arrived flying the white flag of truce. Its raw materials were depleted, the national industry had now also been struck hard by Spanish flu, its soldiers were deserting by the thousand. A few days earlier, in Munich, the Free Bavarian People's Republic had been established after the king of Bavaria had fled. In Berlin, demonstrations were a daily occurrence. The red flag had been raised over Cologne after a group of sailors had seized power there. Kaiser Wilhelm stood shivering on a station platform at the border town of Eijsden, waiting to be admitted to the Netherlands.

Around the historic railway carriage – the same one in which Hitler, in turn, accepted France's capitulation on 20 June, 1940 – a museum has now been built. I see a half smoked, petrified cigar once puffed on by Marshal Foch. Visitors can peek through a window at the famous table where the gentlemen signed the agreement. Funny, though: this railway carriage looks awfully neat and new! Only then does it begin to dawn on me that this is all replicated history. Hitler took the original wagons-lit, number 2419D, to Berlin in June 1940, from where it was towed to the Black Forest at the end of the war. There, on the night of 2 April,

1945, that symbol of German humiliation was set ablaze by SS troops. There was not to be a third Compiègne.

Two trains, therefore, in a boring stand of trees on a drizzly November day. The German delegation requested the cessation of all military operations, because Germany was faced with a revolution. This was news to Foch, and it strengthened his resolve not to discuss any compromise whatsoever. The Germans had no choice but to accept the Allied conditions. When they heard those conditions they were deeply shocked and raised a futile plea for a joint European struggle against the revolution and Bolshevism, but Foch was having none of it: 'Your country is suffering from the malady of the vanquished; Western Europe can defend itself against the danger of which you speak.' Halfway through the morning of 11 November, 1918, the armistice was announced.

Louis Barthas heard the news in the barracks at Vitré. 'Not a single soldier remained in his room. They ran down the corridors like madmen, to the police post where a telegram had been hung up. In two laconic sentences, the telegram announced the liberation of millions of people, the end of their torment and their return to civilian life.' Vera Brittain wrote: 'When the sound of victorious guns burst over London at 11 a.m. on 11 November, 1918, the men and women who looked incredulously into each other's faces did not cry "We've won the war!" They only said "The war is over."'

In Berlin, Harry Kessler wandered through the empty rooms of the plundered imperial palace. He was amazed by the tasteless knick-knacks on the floor and the nationalistic kitsch still on the walls. 'So it was out of this ambience that the world war was born.' He was not angry at the looters, but above all amazed at the mediocrity of the rulers who had collected this rubbish and believed in it.

After hearing the news, Robert Graves walked alone along a peaceful Embankment, 'cursing and sobbing and thinking of the dead'.

In a little more than four years the First World War, which had begun so airily in the summer of 1914, had put an end to at least half a dozen monarchies and two empires: the Habsburg and the Ottoman. The optimism of the Enlightenment, the silent hope that everything would gradually become better, had been extinguished for good. The Western European democracies were put under heavy duress; totalitarian ideologies − communism, fascism and National Socialism − had free rein.

The First World War was the product of a disastrous chemical reaction: the combination of a young, unstable and ambitious German nation with the unheard-of power of modern weaponry. It was the first industrial war, a war of machine guns, grenades, mines and gas, a war that was no longer seen as a heroic struggle but as a machine that could be stopped by nothing and no one. It was also the first total war, a war involving not only armies, but entire societies. In this new century, the military system proved to be fully intertwined with industry and peoples. Armaments and supplies were refreshed on the production line, the wounded and dead replaced en masse by new troops. Winning battles had long ceased to be enough; the whole enemy society had to be brought to its knees by blockades, starvation and other means.

The enormous debts incurred in the war would sour international relations for decades. In France the war became a national obsession, a source of pessimism and insecurity. The British Empire, four years earlier the most secure and powerful realm in Western history, emerged from the war in financial ruins. As late as 1965, the British treasure was still reserving one per cent of tax revenues to repay the war loans it had received from America. Thanks to the war, however, a number of other countries saw their welfare and gold reserves significantly increase: America (by £278 million) and Japan (£183 million), in particular, but also Spain (£84 million), Argentina (£49 million) and the Netherlands (£41 million).

More than 70 million soldiers had fought on the Eastern and Western fronts, 9.4 million (or 13.5 per cent) of them were killed and 15.4 million were wounded. It was a truly world war: more Australians, and almost twice as many Canadians, fought in it than Belgians. About 3 million soldiers had been brought in from throughout the British Empire, and more than 4 million from the United States. The fighting in Africa had been bitter as well: all of the British, French, German and Belgian colonies, all over the continent, were involved. More than 2 million Africans took part in the conflict, mostly as bearers of weapons, food and the wounded.

In Europe, a whole generation was marked by the war: 13 million young Germans fought in it (of whom 2 million – or 15.4 per cent – were killed), 7.8 million Frenchmen (1.3 million, 16.7 per cent), 5.7 million Britons (0.7 million, 12.3 per cent), 350,000 Belgians (38,000, 10.8 per cent), 15.7 million Russians (1.8 million, 11.5 per cent), 9 million Austro-Hungarians (1.1 million, 12.2 per cent) and 750,000 Serbs (280,000, 37.3 per cent). Of the 3 million Turks who followed the drumbeat to war, 800,000 – more than a quarter – never returned.

In many European families, decades went by with no return to normal family life. Germany alone had more than half a million war widows, most of whom never remarried. In the average French village, one out of every five young men was killed in the war. For years, street life was characterised by what was referred to in those days as 'broken faces'. The homes themselves were ruled by 'destroyed men' and 'wounded patriarchs'. Only one out of every three soldiers returned more or less unharmed.

I am reminded of the scene sketched by Joseph Roth of a mass demonstration of war invalids in Lviv, Galicia, shortly after the war:

> An exodus of stumps, a procession of bodily remains . . . Behind the blind came the one-armed men, and behind them the men without arms, and behind the armless men the ones who had been wounded in the head . . . There were the invalids, their faces one great, gaping red hole wrapped in white bandages, with reddish wounded folds for ears. There stood the lumps of flesh and blood, soldiers without limbs, trunks in uniform, the empty sleeves pinned behind the back in a show of coquettish horror . . . Behind the car walked the shell-shocked. They still had everything, eyes, noses and ears, arms and legs, all they lacked was their senses, they had no idea why or for what they had been brought here, they all looked like brothers, all experiencing the same great annihilative nothingness.

Today there are Japanese tourists walking around in the Great Hall of Mirrors at Versailles, where the final peace treaty was signed on 28 June, 1919. The carpets and furnishing spread a faint, elderly odour of piss. The mood at the time, the youthful British diplomat Harold Nicolson wrote, was like that at a wedding: no applause, but no solemn silence either.

At the time, Nicolson was an advisor to the Big Three: Great Britain, France and America. Yet he considered the Treaty of Versailles unworthy of the paper on which it was written. At Sissinghurst that afternoon, his son, Nigel Nicolson, had told me that his father had immediately fore-seen the gravest trouble: the final negotiations had been raced through much too speedily, and the Germans, of course, had not been consulted at all. 'In one letter to my mother he wrote: "So I went in. There were Wilson and Lloyd George and Clemenceau with their armchairs drawn close over my map on the hearth rug . . . It is appalling that these igno-rant and irresponsible men should be cutting [Asia Minor] to bits as if they were dividing a cake. And with no one there except me . . ."'

At first, however, all those young diplomats had been full of high hopes. Their thinking was deeply influenced by the magazine New Europe, they dreamed of a 'new Greece' and a 'new Poland', they wanted to break with the old Europe. 'Bias there was, and prejudice,' Harold Nicolson wrote later. 'But they proceed, not from any revengeful desire to subju-gate and penalise our late enemies, but from a fervent aspiration to create and fortify the new nations whom we regarded, with maternal instinct, as the justification of our sufferings and of our victory.'

The Paris peace conference, held between January and June 1919, was a fascinating event for all concerned: three world leaders who gathered for six months, along with the representatives of almost thirty nations, to establish a new European order and new borders in Africa, the Middle East and the Balkans, who created a new Poland, who granted independ-ence to the Baltic States, who amputated whole sections of Germany and Hungary. One out of every eight Germans became the subject of a hither-to foreign power. With the Treaty of Trianon (1920), Hungary lost two thirds of its territory and a third of its population. For decades, the trauma of Trianon would dominate Hungarian politics.

The world leaders were aware, at least partly, of the problem they were creating: ethnic diversity, particularly in Central Europe, was so complex that every line they drew on the map produced a new national minority. 'People' and 'nation' were rarely one. That was why they stipulated that all new governments, if they wished to be recognised as such, were to sign a treaty committing themselves to guaranteeing their minorities certain rights. Those rights were to be confirmed in the newly established League of Nations, an organisation designed to permanently safeguard against the kind of escalation seen in 1914.

Those minorities accounted for thirty-five million Europeans in all. The decisions made at Versailles affected at least a quarter of the population of Central and Eastern Europe. Here was where the old scores were settled, boundaries drawn, nations moulded, minorities formed and the demons released which were to dominate Europe for the rest of the century:

A few excerpts from Nicolson's 1919 diary:

Friday, 7 February
Spent most of the day tracing Rumanian and Czech frontiers with Charles Seymour of the US delegation. There are only a few points at which we differ.

Sunday, 2 March
Dine with Princess Soutzo at the Ritz — a swell affair . . . . Marcel Proust and Abel Bonnard . . . there as well. Proust is white, unshaven, grubby, slip-faced. He puts his fur coat on afterwards and sits hunched there in white kid gloves. Two cups of black coffee he has, with chunks of sugar. Yet in his talk there is no affectation. He asks me questions. Will I please tell him how the committees work? I say: 'Well, we generally meet at 10.0, there are secretaries behind . . .' 'Mais non, mais non, you are going too fast. Start anew. You take a car to the delegation. You get out at the Quai d'Orsay. You walk up the steps. You enter the Great Hall. And then? With more precision, dear sir, more precision.' So I tell him everything. The sham cordiality of it all: the handshakes: the maps: the rustle of papers: the tea in the next room: the macaroons. He listens enthralled, interrupting from time to time: 'But with more precision, dear sir, do not go too fast.'

Saturday, 8 March
Very tired, dispirited and uneasy. *Are* we making a good peace? Are we? Are we? There was a very gloomy telegram in from [General]

Plumer. He begs us to feed Germany. Says our troops cannot stand spectacle of starving children.

Thursday, 3 April

Arrive Vienna at about 10.0 a.m.. Allen and I walk to the embassy, where our mission is in residence. The town has an unkempt appearance: paper lying about: the grass plots round the statues are strewn with litter: many windows broken and repaired by boards nailed up. The people in the streets are dejected and ill-dressed: they stare at us in astonishment. And indeed we are a funny sight, when viewed in a bunch like that . . . I feel that my plump pink face is an insult to these wretched people.

Tuesday, 13 May

To President Wilson's house . . . The door opens and Hankey tells me to come in. A heavily furnished study with my huge map on the carpet. Bending over it (bubble, bubble, toil and trouble) are Clemenceau, Lloyd George and President Wilson. They have pulled up armchairs and crouch low over the map. Lloyd George says – genial, always – 'Now, Nicolson, listen with all your ears.' He then proceeds to expound the agreement which they have reached. I make certain minor suggestions, plus a caveat that they are putting Konia in the Italian Zone. I also point out that they are cutting the Baghdad railway. This is brushed aside. President Wilson says: "And what about the Islands?' 'They are,' I answer firmly, 'Greek islands, Mr. President.' 'Then they should go to Greece?' Harold Nicolson: 'Rather!' President Wilson: 'RatHER!' . . .

It is immoral and impracticable. But I obey my orders . . . Nearly dead with fatigue and indignation.

Wednesday, 28 May

Have been working like a little beaver to prevent the Austrian peace treaty from being as rotten as the German. The more I read the latter, the sicker it makes me. The great crime is in the reparation clauses, which were drawn up solely to please the House of Commons, and which are quite impossible to execute. If I were the

Germans, I shouldn't sign for a moment. You see it gives them no hope whatsoever, either now or in the future.

Sunday, 8 June
There is not a single person among the younger people here who is not unhappy and disappointed at the terms. The only people who approve are the old fire-eaters.

Finally, the day of the signing at Versailles itself arrives: 28 June, 1919. Harold Nicolson described the genial conversation in the Hall of Mirrors. 'It is, as always on such occasions, like water running into a tin bath.'

The German delegation, consisting of two men, was announced. The silence was oppressive. Their footsteps creaked on the parquet. They were deathly pale. They entered with eyes fixed on the ceiling, but there too, I see now, they found only humiliation. The entire ceiling is covered with scenes of French victory, of routed Dutchmen and Prussians, of proud French kings, their enemies grovelling in the dust at their feet.

'It has all been terrible. To bed, sick of life.'

III March 1917–24

FINLAND
Helsinki
Kronstadt   Petrograd
Narva
Tallinn   Novgorod
ESTONIA
(1918/20)
Moscow
LATVIA
Riga   (1918/20)
LITHUANIA
(1918/20)   Witebsk
Königsberg   Wilna   Minsk
SOVIET UNION
Brest-Litovsk
Warsaw   Wolhynien
(1921)   Kiev
POLAND   Rowno
Dnepr
East
Galicia
(1919)
OVAKIA   Chernowitz   Sea
of Azov   Krasnodar
Budapest   Crimea
UNGARY   Georgian
SSR   Tiflis
(1920)   RUMANIA   Batoum   Armenia
SSR
Belgrade   Bucharest   Black Sea   Kars   Armenia
(1918 Independence,
1920 Turk./Sov. Occupat.)
SLAVIA   Trabzon
Sarajevo   BULGARIA   Sinop   Erzurum
Serbia
Montenegro
(1918)   Sofia
Skopje   Edirne   Istanbul
(1918-23 Allied Occupat.)   Ankara
Tirana   (1919/20)
ALBANIA   Salonika   Gallipoli
(1923)   TURKEY
(1922 Abolition of the
Sultanate/Ottoman Empire)
GREECE   Alexandrette
Athens
Latakia   Syria
(1920 French Mandate)
Cyprus   Tripoli
Crete   Lebanon
Mediterranean

0   100   200   300 km

Geert Mak's Route

Chapter Eleven

Doorn

'I WAS, UNTIL MY RETIREMENT, A MANUFACTURER OF COLOURINGS and flavourings. Queen Victoria was my great-great-grandmother, Kaiser Wilhelm II was my grandfather. We live here, close to Hanover, in a villa to which we gradually added more wings as the children came along. As you can see: a nice sitting room, a dining room, a fine house. Yes, those royal portraits came with the inheritance. The exact relation? I'm the fourth son of Prince Oscar. Oscar was the fifth son of Kaiser Wilhelm II. I'm a prince, yes, a Prussian prince.

'Did I notice the change? I had an absolutely wonderful childhood at Potsdam, I went to school there, and after that I joined the army, the cavalry, because I was crazy about horses. That was in December 1939. The war had already begun.

'My oldest brother Oscar was killed almost immediately. Shortly afterwards my cousin Wilhelm, the crown prince's eldest son, died as well. They organised a huge funeral for him at Potsdam, thousands of people attended. After that all of the kaiser's descendants were brought back from the front, including me. The Nazis did not want another demonstration of imperial loyalty like that. In 1943 we were all actually discharged from military service. The grounds given were: unsuited, due to international family ties. After the war I wanted to attend university, but the British were having none of it. Once again, it was those 'international family ties'.

'In the long run, through a friend, I found a position at a plant for colourings and flavourings, and together we were able to build that company into an international firm with twenty-two subsidiaries. Later on I'll be picking up my grandchildren at the station in Göttingen. No, I'm doing quite well, thank you.

'The last German emperor, in other words, was my grandfather. From the time I was very young we always spent a week or two each summer at Doorn. He was a true grandfather. He had the special gift of being able to make every grandchild feel that he or she was his favourite. Our life at home was quite spartan, so we hugely enjoyed all that lovely Dutch food he served us. He was the one who introduced us to art and literature. He was interested in everything. As children, we were amazed by that.

'I knew him, in other words, as a very different man from the one you read about in the history books. He probably mellowed as he grew older as well; in any case I never heard him speak an unfriendly word to anyone.

'At first, living at Doorn was extremely difficult for him. The Dutch sheltered and protected him quite chivalrously, but he had fallen from the highest heights to the lowest depths, psychologically as well. Sometime you should read what was written about him at his silver jubilee, and then what they all said about him after the war. When a system of government as huge as that collapses, with everything and everyone in it who bore any responsibility, then the first reaction is to put the blame on the person who was at the top. In this case, that was my grandfather.

'Back then there was also all that pomp and circumstance. They held that against him too. Every period, of course, has its own style – those long-winded communist diatribes from the days of the DDR wouldn't be tolerated any more either – so a lot of it had to do with the spirit of the times. At the same time, my grandfather was truly a man of broad interests. Technical things, scientific discoveries, educational reform, theatre, art, he was engrossed by all of that. Perhaps his interests were a bit too broad. Altogether, in my view, that gave him a certain ambivalence. He saw himself as an heir to the old Prussian rulers, but in actual fact he was much more a representative of the modern Germany, and naturally that created a certain tension.

'The way I see it, the course of events leading up to the First World War had something fateful to it. No single European at that time could have imagined that out of all those little German states, a modern superpower would emerge so quickly. That wasn't particularly pleasant for all the surrounding countries, especially when that new Germany began behaving like the nouveau riche. You're right, if Germany had shown a little more caution, it would all have turned out differently.

'I still feel quite a strong bond with my grandfather. These days I see many things differently, but I always try to place his actions in the context of the day in which he lived. You see, the German Empire created in 1871 still had to reach maturity, it still had to adopt a whole new form. Before that, Germany was a quilt of smaller and larger princedoms, and in fact they were not at all keen about becoming united. Furthermore, there was a deep, deep chasm between Protestants and Catholics, and you had the extremely repressive Socialist Act as well, with all the struggle associated with that. Still, that empire survived the First World War, the victors allowed it to go on existing, it survived the Second World War, and today that unity is recognised by virtually all Germans.

'The whole process took place in the space of only two or three generations, during the lifetimes of my grandfather, my father and I. So yes, I feel a part of it, just as I feel an affinity with those who live in what was once the DDR. I often think my generation, the generation which lived through and survived the Third Reich, we are probably the ones who understand best what the people in the DDR went through. We understand how a simple individual has to keep himself going under an authoritarian regime like that. I can understand them much better than my children's generation. They've never known anything but freedom.

'Once again, you can't judge people outside the context of the age in which they live. Someone in my mother's family, for example, was deeply involved in the plot against Hitler on 20 July, 1944. He was arrested and hanged. But still, in the late 1920s that same man had been such a wild-eyed Nazi that my father refused to allow him to enter our home. We found out much too late that he had changed from a fanatical supporter to a vehement opponent. And I myself, if I hadn't had my background at home, I wonder whether I would not have become a Nazi too, in 1933, during the so-called 'national rebirth'. All I can do is hope that, like that distant cousin of mine, I would have had the courage later to turn actively against that regime. But there weren't many like him.

'Within our family, there was much disagreement about the Nazis. I can still remember one Christmas Eve when we children were sent out of the room because my uncles – who were all rather temperamental –

had started a very loud argument about one of them having joined the National Socialist German Workers' Party, the NSDAP.

'My father and my uncle, Eitel Fritz, the second son, who never had children, were absolutely anti-Nazi. The crown prince, my uncle Wilhelm, believed at first that the Nazis could perhaps help him to retrieve the crown, which was utter nonsense. Later on he became a fell opponent as well.

'My uncle August, though, he was a real Nazi. He even became *Gruppenführer* in the stormtroopers, the SA. Strangely enough, he was the kind of man from whom you would never expect something like that. A real aesthete, most of his friends were Jewish artists. But he, of all people, climbed onto the bandwagon and never had the courage to hop off again. Whether he was that staunch in the war, I'm not sure. But it doesn't matter. In those days a great many simple people danced to his pipes and trusted him: oh, one of the kaiser's sons is a member as well. That is what you can blame him for most. A person in his position must be able to think ahead, more than most. But of course that's easy to say now.

'My grandfather was very critical of the Nazis. One evening after dinner in 1934, I remember him reading a newspaper report to us about the murder of Dolfuss, and how upset he was by that. The gangster mentality it showed, just like the killings of SA leader Röhm and his men, he despised that.

'Yes, of course, on the other hand there was that congratulatory telegram he sent to Hitler on 17 June, 1940, for his victory over France. "What a turn of events, led by the hand of God!" I've always wondered whether my grandfather wrote that himself, or whether it was his private advisor, General Dommes. He knew there were all kinds of problems between the kaiser and the Nazis. Perhaps he hoped in that way to improve relations with Berlin.

'But let me be frank: my grandfather was certainly enthusiastic about the successes of the *Wehrmacht*, in which he knew a great many people. In his own eyes he always remained a bit of an army man. There was also a certain amount of national pride, a feeling many Germans had at the time, even if they were not at all fond of National Socialism.

'But that feeling passed soon enough. Just after I returned from the

French campaign, in summer 1940, I spent a weekend with him at Doorn. He ranted against Hitler, against his strategy. The struggle for England was more or less over by that time, Churchill had refused all ceasefire proposals, and there were signs that Hitler was going to move against Russia. My grandfather saw the catastrophe coming: Germany would inevitably be caught waging a war on two fronts. That was the last time I saw him.

'These days, our family only gets together for funerals and on special occasions. My second cousins, the daughters of Crown Prince Wilhelm's son, Louis Ferdinand, organise a concert at Schloss Hohenzollern once a year, and we see each other then. My grandfather's body is kept in a mausoleum at Doorn, in a coffin on trestles, so that he can be repatriated right away if Germany should request that. But I believe Doorn is an excellent final resting place for him. He felt quite content there in later years, and to send him to Berlin and have him shoved in among those hundred and fifty other sarcophagi, in that terrible family tomb . . .

'My father moved to an estate near Göttingen after the war. My uncle August spent some time in a prisoner-of-war camp, and died soon after he was released. My other uncle, the crown prince, was taken prisoner by the French. Later he was sent back to the castle at Hohenzollern. But he was already a broken man. He had no more illusions that Germany would some day embrace the monarchy again. Louis Ferdinand still toyed with that idea, but he was the only one. Sometimes he would say: "If called, I am ready."

'But then, who would ever call him?'

Chapter Twelve

Stockholm

SUNDAY, 28 FEBRUARY. I LEAVE BERLIN AT 10.30, AND AT 2.30 I see the Baltic, at the end of a long, bare field of stubble running down to the shoreline. Not much of anything happens during this trip. At first we roll along in the sunshine for a bit, then the sky goes grey. The landscape spreads out flat as a tabletop. Spring is nowhere in sight, many of the fields are covered in water. We stop at an old-fashioned, staunch-looking station painted yellow, with decorative female breasts moulded beneath the eaves – Wittenberge – and then I fall asleep.

In the old days, during a trip like this, the saltwater would have been flying in all directions. At Puttgarden they slid the carriages one by one, puffing and steaming, onto the ferry to Rødbyhavn and fastened them down with chains, the ship's horn would scream, smoke would come pouring from the stacks and there it would go, creaking and swaying. These days the train rolls into a floating amusement park full of shops and cafés, with lots of chrome and marble, a magic kingdom in which everything happens automatically, right down to the sliding doors and flushing toilets.

After that there is the rolling countryside of Scandinavia, white houses, cows around a pond, a blonde girl on a bike at a crossing. In the late afternoon we roll across little inland seas and huge bridges. The sky clears, a very faint blue, a big white moon is suspended on the horizon, floating above the water. Then the world slowly empties out.

My route is following a strange detour now. I am trying to travel in the tracks of Vladimir Ilyich Ulyanov, Bolshevik leader and professional revolutionary, who returned in April 1917 from the dissident den of Zurich – by way of Germany, Sweden and Finland – to Petrograd, as St Petersburg was known then.

Russia at the time was in an uproar. Striking workers marched across Petrograd's Nevski Prospect, entire army units mutinied, Czar Nicholas II had stepped down, soldiers' and workers' soviets had seized power and a provisional government had been set up, the February Revolution was over. This was the moment for which Ulyanov, better known as Lenin, had been waiting the past thirty years, the culmination of a life full of theories, intrigues, exile, study and even more theories: the moment a young Pole burst into his sparsely furnished room at Spiegelgasse 14 or 15 March, 1917, and cried out 'Russia is in revolt!' That afternoon all of the city's Russian expatriates rushed the news-stands along Zurich's lake shore and gaped at a little article, squeezed between the reports run over from the front onto page two of the *Neue Zürcher Zeitung*: one week earlier, it said, on 23 February by the Russian calendar, the revolution had broken out in the Russian capital. The Duma had ordered the arrest of the czar's ministers. Nothing more was known.

Were these revolutionaries-at-arm's-length surprised by this turn of events? That would be putting it mildly. Lenin, as his wife Nadezhda Krupskaya later wrote, was shocked and silenced, 'stunned'. As the leader of the Bolsheviks he should, of course, have been informed of what was going on, but he was not. The Mensheviks, his opponents within the revolutionary movement, had taken things into their own hands. He must have been at his wit's end: he had missed the crucial moment around which his whole live had revolved. Now he saw that the long-awaited revolution could take place without him, the leader of the rigidly organised Bolsheviks, knowing a thing about it.

To many Russians, Vladimir Ulyanov was a living symbol. For seventeen years his life had consisted of poverty and exile, persecution by czarist agents, conflicts with the Mensheviks and his own comrades, and all of it at a far remove from the Russian proletariat: that, of course, never stopped him from developing one theory after another about them. His isolation increased even further after the outbreak of the First World War. In 1914, only twenty-six of the members on the roll of Lenin's secret political cell were not living in exile; by 1916, only ten of those were still active. The movement's already slender funding dried up. By early 1917, the Ulyanovs were having a hard time paying the rent for the house on the Spiegelgasse. In his desperation, Lenin quarrelled with almost all of his supporters: the brilliant Nikolai Bukarin, 'that pig Trotsky', the gifted German theoretician Rosa Luxemburg, and the charming Polish 'con man' Karl Radek.

Politically, too, he was at the end of his tether. The Swiss police were much more interested in the Cabaret Voltaire, opposite his house, where a group of artists had been giving unintelligible performances since 1916, reading manifestos, shrieking, sobbing, whistling and pounding out rhythms on the tables. That, too, was a form of protest: these poets and painters felt that it was futile to search for truth in bourgeois society, that the world was one big lie, and that only after casting off the ballast of the old culture could they arrive at anything new. Their movement was called Dada, and the impact they had on twentieth-century art was, in retrospect, almost as great as Lenin's on international politics.

As far as we know, no revolutionary communion was held between the neighbours. Lenin's biographers describe the group of Russian exiles as an unhappy, frustrated, homesick circle. 'The world in which they lived was small, incestuous in character, marked by fierce conflicts between opposing factions and rigid loyalties within them,' writes Michael Pearson. 'Outside these narrow limits of cafés and revolutionary journals, Lenin was virtually unknown.'

Eight months later, this same man would gain control over an empire of more than 150 million souls. But on 15 March, 1917, Lenin's most serious problem was how to cover the distance between Zurich and Russia, as well as between his theoretical revolution and actual events.

How was he to go about it? Lenin's first plan was to travel in the guise of a deaf-mute Swede, in order to move as quickly as possible through Germany and Scandinavia to Petrograd. After that he hit upon the idea of chartering a plane, until his comrades convinced him that airplanes and war made for an exceptionally risky combination. Finally, someone came up with the idea of asking the German government for a temporary transit visa.

Contact was established via the German consul in Bern, and Berlin agreed at once. The authorities were even willing, if necessary, to smuggle the revolutionaries through the front lines into Russia. This generosity was not wholly altruistic. As from 1914, ultra-conservative Germany had developed an intense interest in all revolutionaries who could make life difficult for their enemies. And the imperial intelligence service was well equipped to do so: it was already maintaining a measure of regular contact with almost all of the movements that would later play a role in Europe. For a long time, therefore, Germany had been familiar with Lenin's group of Bolsheviks. The Germans were anxious to put a speedy end to the war in the East – the more so after American troops began arriving on the Western Front – and so were willing to export these revolutionary bacilli to the Russian enemy as swiftly as possible.

For Lenin, the Germans' eagerness constituted a major political risk; his trip could now be seen as 'consorting with the enemy'. Especially since Lenin did not bother to wait for permission from the provisional government. It was his idea to have the train granted the same kind of extra-territorial status as a foreign embassy, a kind of political vacuum in which he could travel through Germany without, at least officially, being infected by the German foe. This request, too, was honoured by the German government.

And so it was that on 9 April, 1917, the Ulyanovs left the Zähringerhof hotel in Zurich to go home.

Many of their fellow travellers later wrote accounts of the trip in the 'sealed train', and their stories provide an interesting look at the clique that was soon to turn Europe upside down. There were more than thirty Russian exiles on board, as well as a child, the four-year-old Robert. During the farewell lunch, Lenin gave a speech, a pastoral letter 'to the Swiss workers' in which he stressed that the socialist revolution would be a long-term affair, particularly in backward Russia. Ulyanov and Nadezhda were the only ones who had a second-class compartment to themselves. The two German officers escorting the exiles remained at the back of the carriage, behind a line drawn in chalk on the floor to demarcate the 'Russian' and 'German' sections.

As soon as the train pulled out of Gottmadingen station on the German border, the atmosphere grew livelier. The compartments were filled with talk and laughter. A few of the Russians in the third-class carriage began singing the 'Marseillaise'. Robert's 'happy voice could be heard all over the train', Nadezhda wrote later. The little boy was particularly fond of Grigori Sokolnikov, and kept climbing onto his lap.

A conflict arose almost immediately between the smokers and the non-smokers. Lenin, who absolutely despised cigarette smoke, ruled that smoking was to be allowed only in the toilet. A line formed, and soon a second argument arose between the smokers and those who wished to use the toilet for its rightful purpose. Lenin solved the problem by drawing up toilet passes: smokers received a second-category pass, others a first-category pass.

Meanwhile, Nadezhda sat looking out at the bare German landscape, and was surprised to note the absence of adult males. 'Only women, teenagers and children could be seen at the wayside stations, on the fields, and in the streets of the towns,' she wrote. During a stop at a station, Sokolnikov wondered why people were looking so interestedly into his carriage, until he realised that there was a piece of white Swiss bread lying on the windowsill. Lenin spent hours staring out of the window, his thumbs hooked in the armholes of his vest, long after it had grown dark and the occasional light flashing by was all there was to be seen.

That evening brought a new crisis for the exasperated leader to solve. Karl Radek was in the compartment next to the Ulyanovs, along with Olga Ravich, Georgi Safarov and Lenin's great love, Inesa Armand. Radek was a jovial Polish Jew, a squat little pipe smoker with curly hair and thick glasses. He was an excellent organiser and a natural storyteller. Furthermore, he could do a perfect imitation of Lenin. The laughter cut straight through the thin carriage walls.

The party atmosphere was heightened yet further when Charitonov and the exuberant Grigori Usivitch came to visit the compartment. Lenin had already poked his head in a few times to quieten things down – and received a boisterous welcome from Radek – but when Olga Ravitch's screeches of laughter once again penetrated all the walls and beyond the borders of propriety, he yanked open the door of the compartment, grabbed Olga by the hand without saying a word, led her down the corridor and pushed her into a compartment far away from his own. In the end, Lenin had to order lights out, 'as a disciplinary party command'. But even that did not help.

The next morning, at Stuttgart station, the German social democrat Wilhelm Janson tried to make contact with the revolutionary travellers. The Bolsheviks played deaf: any contact, after all, would have ruined the

myth of the 'sealed train'. In addition, the Russian and German socialists had had a parting of the ways. During the war, the unions and the
social democrats had become respected negotiating partners for the
German government. The Russians had known only exile and a covert
existence. All their hopes were fixed on a revolution, in whatever form,
not on evolution or compromise. 'If Janson tries to enter our train, we'll
throw him out on his ear,' Lenin shouted in a rage. 'Tell him to go to
hell.'

As the train approached Mannheim, the Russians in the third-class
compartment began singing again. When French revolutionary songs also
began echoing through the train, the German officers at the back went
into action. They angrily approached the line of chalk: these French songs
were an insult to the German nation. The Russian merrymakers finally
desisted.

In Frankfurt the evening rush hour had just begun, and the station
was full of German troops. One of the men on the train, Fritz Platten,
was Swiss. As a citizen of a neutral country, he was free to leave the
train. In the station restaurant he ordered beer, sandwiches and newspapers for all his fellow passengers. While talking to some German
soldiers, he must have let slip that there were Russian revolutionaries in
the train who were determined to put an end to the war. Whatever the
case, soldiers suddenly began leaving their lines and rushing up to the
carriages. 'Each man had a jug of beer in his hand,' Radek wrote. 'They
ran up to us, asking whether peace was coming, and when.' It was more
than he could resist, of course: hanging out the window, he gave the
call to revolution, until the soldiers were pulled away by their startled
officers.

The next day, when the train rolled through the suburbs of Berlin,
Grigori Zinovyev said they were 'silent as the grave'. At Potsdamer the
train stopped for at least half a day. On Thursday, 12 April, the Russians
finally reached the Baltic coast. Here they took the Swedish ferry to
Trelleborg, and journeyed on from there to Stockholm.

As far as I know, there is only one photograph of the travellers. It was
taken in Stockholm, on Friday, 13 April, 1917. We see the group crossing
a street, Lenin out in front, carrying an umbrella and wearing a hat like

a businessman, gesturing extravagantly. Behind him, and wearing an enormous hat as well, is Nadezhda. In the middle we see the elegant outlines of Inessa Armand, in the background little Robert, hanging on Zinovyev's arm.

It was spring when the picture was taken, and the harbour was already free of ice floes. The city was all water and smoke, little steamboats were sailing everywhere, one could barely pick one's way through all the barrels and carts. The clear streets of the Söderholm neighbourhood, where the Swedish business classes now give their eye teeth to buy a house, in those days stank as badly as the alleys of London or the slums of Amsterdam.

Eighty years later, looking out of the train in the half-light of early morning, I see only the big, wet shape of the capital in the process of waking up, roads filled with cars, a frozen river, flats. In the afternoon a different Stockholm appears, a glorious city in alternating shades of ochre and red, its water sparkling in the low sun. At first glance, the city's pace is pleasantly calm. For both mothers and fathers, Sweden provides a generous maternity leave. On a Monday morning in the Drottninggatan one sees twice as many men as women pushing prams. These house husbands have nothing hurried about them, they stroll along as peacefully as young mothers, with all the time in the world.

Stockholm was and is a city of bureaucrats, calm regents who for centuries have managed an immense hinterland from behind their piles of paper. Here the smokestacks began to rise up only half a century after London and Berlin, but things went quickly after that. When Lenin was here, Sweden was already a spectacular case of the 'winning disadvantage': the poor, backward countryside turned out to contain staggering quantities of raw materials and fuels. In addition, for generations the isolation of their farms had forced Sweden's rural people to develop an amazing degree of versatility and inventiveness. In remote places they had to make and repair everything they needed, which turned them into an uncommonly energetic and versatile people. The Swedish farming class, in other words, formed the ideal army of labourers for a nascent industrial state.

In the course of the nineteenth century, therefore, Sweden went through a quiet revolution. Countless farmers had freed themselves from their villages and started anew in the city, the people's relationship to nature had changed, and traditions were severed. By 1917, in fact, a reaction to that could already be seen: the latent nostalgia for the old-fashioned farming life still present among modern-day Swedes. Stockholm's town hall, still under construction at the time of Lenin's visit, perfectly reflects the mixed feelings of that day: the woodworked windows speak of Sweden's history, its shadowy archways are decorated with trolls and other mystic rural motifs, and some of its courtyards are reminiscent of Venice, the Renaissance, of the North's eternal longing for the lightness of Italy.

I took a detour to Saltsjöbaden, a handful of red wooden houses and the huge Grand Hotel along the shores of a snowy lake, less than half an hour by train from Stockholm. Here, on a quiet December day in 1938, the famous Swedish 'consensus model' was born, a distant precursor of the Dutch polder model. Seated at the round dining table in the little room of the hotel tower, representatives of the government, employers and unions, under the motto 'No rich individuals, but rich concerns', laid the foundations for an impressive welfare state. The model meshed seamlessly with Swedish puritanical traditions, centralised government and 'flat' organisational structures.

For almost eighty years, therefore, cool reason has governed here, and that can be seen all over Stockholm. The outlying neighbourhoods with their broad lanes and large, leafy courtyards remind one of the Amsterdam of H. P. Berlage and Cornelis van Eesteren. Homeless people, prostitutes and drug addicts are skilfully kept under control and neatly filed away. Here the bicycle locks are flimsier than anywhere else in Europe. Everyone dresses almost alike, there is almost no sprucing up, but that is also char- acteristic of a rural society. A rare individual may stand out, but largely by reason of his or her bearing. These are the bosses; you sense it, but you scarcely notice.

In front of the Riksdaghuset I run into Magnus Lundquist. He has been standing here all day, holding a huge banner. Painted on the left of the banner is a crown of thorns, and below that a head covered in red blotches. In the middle is a large cross. To the right I see a detail of a hip bearing a deep wound. Near the top of the banner is a shining, kingly figure on a white horse, with a Star of David on his forehead. Beside him is a dove. Above that an angelic figure in a pose of beatification. The edges of the banner are lined with bible verses.

Magnus' big blue eyes look right through me. 'What are you doing?' I ask. 'This is the real Jesus,' he says. Tomorrow an exhibition will open here, on the theme of Jesus as homosexual.

At dinner that evening I exchange national excesses with Lars-Olof Franzén, the thinking heart of *Dagens Nyheter*. I tell him about tons of cocaine being smuggled into the Netherlands with the express permission of the ministry of justice, about expense-account falsification in the public sector and large-scale fraud in the construction industry. In Sweden, people are outraged by the sums paid to directors in the form of golden handshakes, they find it preposterous; after all, we built up those companies together!

A country can be known by its scandals. According to Franzén, issues like the ones we have mentioned are characteristic of a widening gap between common Europeans and the elite, here as well. 'The Swedes are introverts, seemingly shy, but actually they are quite proud,' Franzén says. 'They use their own efforts as a benchmark. That is where their values lie.'

While today's political leaders are concerned only with money and EU membership, old-fashioned equality and solidarity are still held dear by the common Swede. 'Generally, people here feel that the politicians are busy selling out democracy. Nationalism doesn't play a particularly big role in that, more like a deep concern about the future of our society as such. The Swedes already miss the quality our health system once offered. And they think that today's leaders have fallen under the spell of greed.'

He tells me that the first time he saw a beggar was in Paris in the 1960s. And he talks about how long ago he had heard people in New York talking only about money, about what everything cost, even down to a divorce. 'It was unbelievable to me. I could never have imagined that would be normal in Stockholm too, thirty years later.'

We talk about the influence Sweden had on the United States. During the famines in the nineteenth century, almost a quarter of all Swedes emigrated there. 'Every family has uncles or distant cousins living in America.' Roosevelt's New Deal was inspired by the example of the Swedish social democrats. 'But I believe the influence now runs only in the other direction,' Franzén says glumly.

*

Watching TV that evening, I feel like a refugee. I don't understand a word these Swedes say, but I stare in astonishment at their uniform clothing, their deliberate movements, their pious body language. The woman reading the news looks as though she might burst into tears at any moment. The commercials are of an unparalleled corniness. Everything drips with nostalgia. At least one out of every three programmes is dominated by old farms, rural families and other bygone delights. The evening news is followed by an unintelligible sitcom about a supermarket, a shop manager and a blonde woman with preposterous breasts. Then follows an episode from a *Heimat* series about a village, all rural and green. Nowhere else in the world can five actors stand still for so long on camera without speaking a word. And I believe that, at that moment, they were in the throes of a knock-down-drag-out argument.

How did Lenin and Stockholm get along in 1917? The mayor welcomed the foreign guest with due ceremony, the Swedish socialists threw a banquet in his honour, there were journalists present, photographers, and even a man with a film camera. For the first time in his life, Ulyanov was received as a prominent statesman. But his core ideas were not understood. The Swedes gave him money for the rest of his journey, and a little extra to buy a nice suit and a pair of decent shoes, even though, in his own words, he was 'not going to Russia to open a haberdashery'. Then they put him on the next train to his fatherland. Swedish socialism was clearly on a different track. Less than three years later, they would renounce the world revolution and form the world's first democratic socialist government.

One interesting character had travelled all the way from Germany to Stockholm just to see Lenin: the socialist multimillionaire Alexander Helphand, otherwise known as 'Parvoes'. Parvoes had known Lenin back in his days as a young Marxist journalist. Later, by obscure means, he acquired a fortune in Istanbul. His former comrades lost faith in him, especially after it became clear that his business contacts extended all the way to the Wilhelmstrasse in Berlin.

Parvoes had, however – in his own way – remained committed to the revolution, and particularly to the money/revolution combination. In late 1914 he began drawing the attention of his German diplomat friends to the overlapping interests of German and Russian Marxists. Both, after all, were battling the same enemy: the czar and his regime. The Germans were all ears. At the ministry of foreign affairs, officials were all too conscious of the fact that Germany had become trapped in an endless, exhausting war on two fronts. Military means alone could never break the impasse. And so a new idea was launched within the ministry: the 'revolutionisation' of Russia. Serious domestic upheaval would, after all, force the czar to sue for peace, and allow Germany to concentrate all its war efforts on the Western Front. Parvoes' plan was a godsend. Pumping money into it could clearly produce great results.

For the Germans, therefore, the February Revolution of 1917 came as a long-awaited blessing. Top priority was granted to transporting Lenin and his group to Russia: at Halle, the private train of Crown Prince Wilhelm was even shunted for two hours onto a side rail to allow the Russians to pass. Major operations on the Eastern Front were postponed so as not to stimulate Russian patriotism unduly. The German treasury immediately gave five million marks to Parvoes 'for political objectives within Russia'.

Lenin and Parvoes had last met in May 1915. Their long tête-à-tête at that time was later dismissed by both as a chat about how the revolution was going. Yet the conversation no doubt covered a great deal more than that. In Stockholm, however, Lenin categorically refused to see Parvoes. It seemed to him far too great a political risk. Parvoes met with Karl Radek instead. Radek almost certainly spoke on Lenin's behalf. Then Parvoes went straight back to Berlin, for a personal meeting with the deputy minister of foreign affairs, Arthur Zimmermann.

Probably – but one can only conjecture here, for nothing of what was discussed was ever committed to paper – both of these meetings dealt with the details of the German funding that ultimately helped the Russian Bolsheviks to seize power. That would allow a direct connection to be established between the Germans, Parvoes and a certain Jacob Hanecki (aka Fürstenburg), Lenin's representative in Stockholm and a man with whom the Bolshevik leader maintained almost daily contact.

On the evening of Monday, 2 April, 1917 – 20 March, by the old Russian calendar – the German emissary to Denmark, who was also one of Parvoes' close associates, sent the following telegram to his superiors in Berlin: 'We must now do everything in our power to create the greatest possible chaos in Russia. We must do all we can to exploit the differences between the moderates and the extremists, because it is in our supreme interest that the latter gain the upper hand.' Nothing in the archives, by the way, indicates any German interest in the actual substance of Lenin's revolutionary plans. Chaos in Russia and then a quick truce, that was all the Germans cared about.

Late that Friday, on 31 March by the Russian calendar, the group – with the exception of Radek, who was officially an Austrian national – left for Finland. On the platform, a Swedish socialist gave a farewell speech: 'Cherished leader, be careful that terrible things are not done in Petrograd.' After settling into his sleeping compartment, Lenin quickly crawled up onto the top berth. He took off his vest – despite Nadezhda's protests that he would catch a cold – and began reading the Russian papers he had rounded up in Stockholm. For the rest of the evening, his travelling companions heard only an occasional, disjointed cry: 'Oh, the swine! . . . Bastards! . . . Traitors!'

Chapter Thirteen

Helsinki

SWEDEN AND FINLAND ARE TWO SEPARATE WORLDS. IN THE OLD DAYS, the only way to travel between the two countries in winter was by sled, a long trek across the frozen Gulf of Bothnia.

Lenin's train skirted the gulf. I travel aboard the *Silja Serenade*, a twelve-storey *Titanic* with five restaurants, a theatre, a casino, a promenade deck as big as a medium-sized shopping centre, and 2,000 passengers who take it all in their stride. At 6.00 in the evening we shove off from the quay at Stockholm and watch the last apartment buildings gliding by. In the distant houses, dinner is on the table, the television is on, children are preparing for bed and we are sailing off into the night. Other palaces drift beside ours, on their way to Estonia, Latvia or one of the Swedish islands.

The ship shakes and cracks all night. At first light I go outside. On the upper deck I discover that an icy cold storm is blowing, but the ship glides forth like God's own steam iron. We plough our way through an endless whiteness, the ice floes smack against the hull with dull thuds, and on the snow-covered deck I have to steady myself against the howling wind. Meanwhile, down in the 'Maxim' and 'Le bon vivant' lounges, people are breakfasting quietly. The perfume shop is doing brisk business. Further down in the ship one hears a gentle thundering, but when the lift door opens on the lowest deck of all, one level below where the truck drivers sleep, the noise rolls in waves, pounding and roaring.

The sidewalks of Helsinki are covered in slippery brown sludge. Almost twenty inches of snow fell here last week, but now the thaw has set in. Huge chunks of ice regularly come sliding off the roofs. The Finns seem not to notice. They waddle like ducks down the slick streets. A kinder-garten class comes by. In their thick woollen caps, their colourful snow trousers and body warmers, the children look like little Martians. Along the shore of the Gulf of Finland, a few people are swimming in the icy water. They have chopped a hole in the ice and splash around in it, a terrible thing to behold, but the spectators are enthusiastic: 'The water here is always four degrees above zero, and even at twenty below it's an amazing feeling. All your rheumatism and head colds just vanish into the sea.'

A little further along is Café Ursula, a circular pavilion with a view of the frozen water and the snowy islands. In the misty distance, two fisher-men are sitting beside a hole in the ice. I have an appointment with the writer Claes Andersson, until recently Finland's minister of culture and an old acquaintance of Lars-Olof Franzén. 'We are eternally beholden to Lenin, because he was the first Russian leader to recognise our inde-pendence,' Andersson says. 'But we have never been interested in his Bolshevism.'

He talks about the Finns' own civil war, the bloody conflict of 1918 between the Red farmers and workers and the White conservatives. The Whites won, and countless Reds died. The Finns were reunified only by the Soviet invasion of November 1939. The Russians, who felt that the Finnish border was much too close (thirty kilometres) to the city that was now Leningrad, had demanded an exchange of territories. Although the Russian Army was many times greater, the invasion at first made little progress. In the vast woods and on the frozen lakes, no less than three Russian division were eliminated. The Finns, being expert skiers, were at home in the snow and the woods, but ultimately they lacked the force needed to repel the invaders. Reinforcement from the international community arrived too late, and the country capitulated in March 1940. Huge parts of Finland's territory had to be ceded, one in every eight Finns fell under Soviet rule. 'Despite all the promises, we were left to our own devices again and again,' Andersson says. 'For a long time after that, this country was very bitter.'

For years the Finns lived on the margin between the Soviet Union and the West. Today they embrace the euro, although that has yet to arrive in

Helsinki. 'We consciously dragged Finland into the European Union,' Andersson tells me. 'We had suffered for too long under the status of a small country, with a minor, defenceless currency, dependent on the whims of the superpowers.' Andersson had opposed EU membership at first. 'As a minister, I was personally involved in all those negotiations. They were even more boring and bureaucratic than I'd expected. But still, at one point I started to realise how useful it could be. If this is the price one pays to arrive at a compromise, and to avoid international conflicts in the future, then so be it, I reckoned. For me, Europe became more and more of a project for peace.'

But don't the introverted Finns have the same misgivings about Europe as the Swedes? 'The Swedes see themselves as a wealthy, healthy, independent state. They were always at the head of the class. We survived two violent wars, we know what it is to suffer, we were completely dependent on the Russians. We know that we have to act, that we have to make sacrifices. Nothing has ever happened to the Swedes. They've always had the feeling that they can do whatever they want. That feeling makes all the difference.'

Meanwhile, in these March days of 1999, the Finns are calmly and composedly manoeuvring their way towards their national elections; all is well, and everyone wants to keep it that way. Everywhere one sees posters showing serious-looking men and women, the same fresh faces you see on the city councils of provincial Dutch towns. The candidates are worried about day-care centres, health care, about Finland's young people and two per cent of the population that is not Finnish. 'Finland for the Finns', one sees that here as well. On 1 January, 1999, Finland had precisely 1,272 asylum seekers and almost no illegal immigrants – yet still the country is home to at least 80,000 non-Finns. That is a source of great concern for many political parties.

That evening I attend the jubilee concert of the Helsingen Sotainvalidirpiirin Vejeskuro, the Helsinki Veterans' Chorus, directed by Tapio Tiitu, Arvo Kuikka and Erik Ahonius. The auditorium is full of wives and widows, the members of the chorus wear an average of three medals, the members of the executive committee walk around in big sashes. For the rest, it could just as easily be a musical evening in the northern Dutch town of Dokkum . . . except for the language. Finnish is not just incomprehensible, it is a heavily encrypted version of at least three incomprehensible languages rolled into one: Swedish, Hungarian, Estonian, etc., incomprehensibility to the umpteenth degree. And, at the same time, it is a joy to listen to. Clearly, this must be a very lovely language.

The members of the chorus look to be retired teachers and attorneys, and probably are just that. But these are also the same men in white who courageously defied the Soviet Union in winter 1939–40. They provided a merciless demonstration of how ineffective the Red Army was: with their millions, the Soviets only barely succeeded in defeating 200,000 Finns. The Russian debacle in Finland made Hitler highly optimistic when he sent his troops to the East. That was a fatal mistake.

Now the veterans have started singing in dark, melancholy voices. The first song sounds like 'My Country 'tis of Thee'. The second one sounds like Verdi's 'Slave Chorus'. The third one seems to be a Finnish variation of 'Land of Hope and Glory'. And the next seven numbers are highly reminiscent of the old hymns of the Dutch Reformed Church.

During the interval, I exchange a few words with Colonel Milos Syltamaa (b. 1921). The oldest member of the chorus is ninety-two, the average age is seventy-nine. 'Every year our chorus shrinks a little, that's the way it goes. That's right, we all fought hard. Against the Germans, too, you bet. We did quite well. Our forests aren't at all like the parks they have down there!'

Our conversation is interrupted by a committee member in a sash. They are taking up the collection. And then comes a new song.

I want to hear an outsider's opinion, so I arrange to talk to the Palestinian Amayya Abu-Hanna. 'Let's meet under the clock at Stockmann's,' she said on the phone. 'You'll recognise me right away. I'll be the only person who isn't blonde.' Stockmann's department store is a household name here. It is more than just the Harrods of Helsinki. Stockmann's is a minia-ture Finland, and Finland is the 1950s, 1960s and 1990s in one.

At the moment, Stockmann's is changing fast, Amayya assures me. 'There's a café in the basement now; ten years ago that would have been unthinkable. Back then, there were only a couple of grindingly boring clubs in the whole city.' She takes me to the magazine section, which is largely reserved for publications about cooking and interior decorating. 'That's become all the rage. Finnish chairs used to come in only one or two colours, and the only thing the Finns ate were potatoes and sausage. Now we even have a Thai restaurant. Everyone talks about "the city". Young people are forever boasting about being true "Hessalinen", and not farmers from the countryside'. The lingerie department on another floor has quadrupled in size in the last year. 'Even sex is now seen as a source of pleasure, not just a way to make little Finns.'

Amayya Abu-Hanna is little and slender, she has short black hair and dark, lively eyes. She has lived in Finland for almost twenty years, and until recently she was one of the best known Finnish TV anchorwomen. It took her — 'Yes, of course, I fell in love with a Finn' — quite a while to acclimatise. 'It can be awfully grey and overcast here for months on end, with lots of rain and wet snow. You know the story of Jonah and the whale? Well, that's how I felt during those first winters. I even had to learn how to walk all over again, in the snow, bowlegged, bent over. What's more, everything I'd been taught at home about right and wrong turned out to be precisely the opposite here. Here, for example, "peace" means silence, quiet, no other people, deep in the woods. To me, peace is something that is actually all about other people, it's something social, the opposite of war. Curiosity and ambition were always seen at home as something good, but not for the Finns. In my view, a concept like "equality" had to do with honesty. But for them it's "not standing out". They even have a negative term for "colourful", something like "eye-bashing".'

She reads to me from Stockmann's spring catalogue. '"Dress like the rest; after all, don't you have better things to do?" Where else could you sell clothes with a slogan like that?' Amayya was in politics for a while as well. 'That's when I discovered the good sides of this country. People mean what they say, for example. That was refreshing to me. I expected a great deal of corruption. Not a bit of it. Everything was squeaky clean.'

For the moment, Amayya is unemployed. 'It all became too much. I had no problem working as a journalist, but as soon as my face appeared on TV, all hell broke loose. Threats, a letter bomb, I even had to move out of my house. No blacks, no Russians — in other words, no whores

– in our living rooms! I was replaced by a real blonde Finnish woman. And then everyone pretended as though it had never happened.'

Friday evenings are an ordeal for her. This highly disciplined country has one escape valve: alcohol. Screaming, urinating in the street: if a person is drunk, they can get away with all of that. 'When Friday evening comes they scream at everyone with dark skin, every drunk who comes along grabs at my hair and shouts: "What are you doing here, you're black!" Or: "Hey, *babushka!*" Or: "Hey, are you circumcised?"'

'Racism', however, is not a word Amayya uses lightly. 'I'm still quite proud of the producer who took a chance on me. Where else in Europe would you see a TV anchorwoman with dark skin *and* a foreign accent? This has always been a tight-knit, homogeneous society. But they still have someone here like Lola Odusoga, an eloquent Finnish girl whose father came from the Ivory Coast. In 1996 she was the most popular Miss Finland of all time, a calm, hardworking kid from the countryside close to Turku, very sweet, and black as ebony.

'The Finns actually remind me of the Bedouins, a people completely shaped by geographical extremes,' Amayya says. 'They consider themselves unique, more than unique. Women play a major role. A lot of them have children without getting married. You sense that Christianity is only a thin veneer here, it's clearly something that's been imposed. Their pride comes from knowing that they can survive under extreme conditions. And just like the Bedouins, they feel threatened when other people think they can do that as well. It's understandable, really: the greater the isolation people live in, the more afraid they are when the world opens up.'

The next day I take the Sibelius Express through the white coniferous forest to St Petersburg. We cross huge plains with no trace of human existence. Sometimes, after a few kilometres, there will be a wooden farmhouse with its windows lit up. After an hour, the gangways between the carriages are covered in powder snow, even the corridors are dusted white here and there. In the dining car they're serving salmon and mashed potatoes, twenty people at one big table, eating what the cook has to offer.

Between Finland and Russia is an old-fashioned border with watchtowers, passport stamps and serious men. After that comes a debatable zone: do the telegraph poles here actually look a bit shoddier, the wooden houses just a little less neat? The snow still masks the differences. But half an hour later the train slowly pulls into a grey city. Men are fishing on the frozen river; behind them are towers with golden domes; in front of the station dozens of old women all try to sell their one jar of pickles, or two bottles of vodka, or a knitted sweater. Now we really have crossed the border, the only border that counts.

'Everyone in our group sat glued to the windows,' Nadezhda Krupskaya recalled. A few soldiers had boarded the train. Little Robert was sitting on the lap of a Russian war veteran, his arms around the man's neck. The man shared his raisin bread with him. The soldiers gave Lenin a few back copies of *Pravda*, Zinovyev reported, 'he shook his head and threw up his hands in despair.'

The group got off the train in Petrograd, at Finland Station. By then, according to the Russian calendar, it was 3 April. Nadezhda had been worried: if they arrived so late, how would they ever find a hansom cab to take them to where they were staying? They had no idea what awaited them.

In those first weeks following the revolution it was customary to give all homecoming exiles a great welcome, and the Bolsheviks had gone all out for their leader. Even the Mensheviks took part in the celebration. Huge triumphal arches had been set up on the platforms. Banners bearing 'every revolutionary slogan one could imagine' hung above the honour guards from the various army units. 'The crowd in front of Finland Station blocked the entire square, you could barely move, and the trams were almost unable to get through,' recalled the journalist Nikolai Suchanov, editor of Gorky's *Letopis* (Chronicle). The Ulyanovs were led into what had once been the czar's private waiting room. Military bands played the 'Marsellaise'; the soldiers had not had enough time to practise the 'Internationale'. Lenin made a couple of short speeches. Suchanov was able to catch only a few words: 'Scandalous imperialistic massacre . . . lies and deception . . . capitalist pirates'. The crowd was ecstatic.

The Bolsheviks had set up their headquarters in Kshesinskaya Palace, the enormous villa Czar Nicholas II had built for his mistress, the ballerina Matilda Kshesinsky. ('I'm not a capitalist! I worked hard for this!' was what she shouted at the first Bolshevik intruders.) A banquet had been laid out in the huge halls and passageways, but Lenin hardly had a chance to eat. Everyone wanted to talk to him. Only past midnight did he begin his big speech.

For two full hours, he drilled his followers on the new party line. 'I'll never forget that harangue,' Suchanov wrote. 'It amazed and shocked not only me, an apostate who was there by chance, but also all the true believers.' Lenin launched a ferocious attack on the new leaders, calling them 'opportunists' and 'betrayers of the revolution', and that alone, Suchanov noted, 'caused the heads of his listeners to spin'. After all, these 'mouthpieces of the bourgeoisie' were former revolutionaries and had all, like Lenin, spent years in exile. Until Lenin's arrival, the Bolsheviks of Petrograd had enthusiastically supported the provisional government as well. For didn't the revolution belong to everyone?

Yet Lenin's opinions could not have come as a complete surprise. In the first telegrams and letters he sent after the revolution, he – unafflicted by any knowledge of the local situation – had already given strict instructions to the Bolsheviks in St Petersburg: give no support to the provisional government, arm the workers, all power to the soviets! His comrades had found these positions so unrealistic that only excerpts from those letters had been made public.

Suddenly, however, yet another wild idea had been added to the list; namely, that the transition from the 'bourgeois democracy' to the 'socialist revolution' had to take place within a few months. When he left Zurich, Lenin had said that Russia was a 'country of farmers', 'one of the most backward countries in Europe'. A place where socialism could not 'immediately triumph'. Somewhere along the way, he must have changed his mind.

As soon as he arrived in Petrograd, Lenin began talking about the need for a 'second revolution', in order not to 'become a slave to capitalism'. All power was 'immediately' to be placed in the hands of the soviets. This, less than one month after the fall of the czar, sounded the death knell for the provisional government. It also constituted a definitive break with the Mensheviks and the other revolutionary groups. Lenin's sudden change of course clashed with almost all the revolutionary theories, which assumed that a long period would be needed between the 'civil revolution' and the 'proletarian revolution'. That was held to be particularly

true of less developed countries such as Russia. The slogan 'all power to
the soviets' seemed less than practical too. Those councils, after all, had
always been little more than loose configurations of contentious committees for the organisation of workers' strikes, and could hardly be expected
to assume governmental power immediately.

The day after his arrival, Lenin launched the April Theses, the new
programme he had worked on during his train journey: no support for
the provisional government; withdrawal from the war; a complete break
with capitalism; the expropriation of all private lands; the nationalisation
of the banks; the dismantling of the army and the police corps and the
establishment of a republic of soviets, led by farmers and workers. His
vision clashed so dramatically with the prevailing mood in Petrograd that
even many Bolsheviks felt that Lenin had lost touch with reality. He had
been in exile too long. 'Life in all its complexity is unknown to Lenin,'
Gorky wrote at the time. 'He doesn't know the common people. He has
never lived among them.'

Lenin ultimately emerged as the winner of the revolution. But, as the
historian Richard Pipes rightly explains, that was not because of his huge
support or astute vision. The Bolshevik's success lay in their cocksure-
ness. They established bonds with precisely those groups from which the
socialist parties in Western Europe had alienated themselves: farmers and
soldiers. Against all the odds, they seized power at exactly the right
moment. And they had powerful allies: Berlin, gold German marks and
the hard winds of world war.

A number of mysteries still surround Lenin's return to Russia. What made
him change his mind during the train journey through Germany and
Sweden? Some historians point to the strikingly long stop – of at least
half a day – that Lenin's 'sealed train' made in Berlin. They suspect that,
in the course of that stop, Lenin was in contact with several top German
officials concerning the strategy to be pursued. It is a wild assumption,
for an escapade like that does not match up with Lenin's extreme caution
on precisely this point: in Stockholm, after all, he refused to meet with
or even see his old comrade Parvoes.

Far more likely is that something changed within Lenin himself during
that journey. After the meeting between Parvoes and Radek in Stockholm,

he may suddenly have realised that his penniless Bolsheviks could, within only a matter of weeks, have tens of millions of gold German marks at their disposal, providing unparalleled opportunities for organisation and propaganda.

About one fact, however, there is virtually no room for disagreement: after this train journey, the German millions came flowing in. In the communist history books, stories to this effect – which began to circulate within a few months – were always dismissed as 'foul slander and obscurantist rumours'. Today, however, no one can avoid the conclusion that the glorious October Revolution was actually financed by the German ministry of foreign affairs.

First of all, there are the German records themselves, made public after 1945. In them, one sees that the ministry had set up a special contact group for Parvoes and his people as early as 1916, under the code name 'Stockholm'. The following is taken directly from the confidential report submitted to the kaiser, and dated 3 December, 1917: 'It was not until the Bolsheviks began receiving a steady supply of funding from us, through diverse channels and under assorted headings, that they were able to transform their most important organ, *Pravda*, into an energetic propaganda vehicle and to broaden the narrow base of their party.' Calculations recorded by the Germany ministry of foreign affairs on 5 February, 1918 show that 40,580,997 gold marks had been allocated for 'propaganda and special objectives' in Russia, and that 26,566,122 of those marks had already been paid out as of 31 January. Such sums would today be equivalent to hundreds of millions of euros. All available information indicates that the lion's share of this funding went to the Bolsheviks.

The Russians, understandably enough, carefully eradicated all traces of this operation. In summer 1917, the provisional government – with the help of the French intelligence service – began a thorough investigation into alleged financial contacts between the Germans and the Bolsheviks. Yet Lenin and his companions were never taken to court. The dossier, all twenty-one volumes of it, was confiscated and destroyed right after the October Revolution, on the orders of Lev Trotsky.

The results, however, were plain to see. From spring 1917 the Bolsheviks' propaganda activities were so massive and widespread that they could not possibly have been funded from the party's own coffers. In February

1917 the Bolsheviks did not own a single printing press. In March, *Pravda* was in such dire straits that relief benefits had to be organised to keep it running. Four months later, the Bolshevik press had a combined daily circulation of 320,000 newspapers, as well as around 350,000 pamphlets and brochures. *Pravda* appeared in more than forty editions, including in Polish and Armenian. Some 100,000 newspapers were distributed daily among the armed forces: the *Soldatsja Pravda* for the infantry, the *Gols Pravdy* for the navy, the *Okopnaja Pravada* (Trench Truth) for the front. There was enough money to pay party officials a regular salary, a luxury unheard of in Bolshevik circles. Party membership swelled between April and August 1917 from 23,000 to 200,000. The Bolsheviks never deigned to explain this sudden and profuse wealth.

Does this mean that Lenin was actually nothing but a mere German agent? Not at all. Throughout his life his conduct shows that he was purely a revolutionary in heart and soul, a revolutionary who made all else secondary to that goal, and who was even prepared to make a pact with the Devil to achieve his objectives. His alliance with the Germans was purely a coalition of opportunity, one that served the interests of both parties at a given moment, but which could be tossed aside again at the next. Lenin, in fact, had only one goal: grand, worldwide revolution. Within that context, the Russian Revolution was but a start.

The travelling party fell apart. Karl Radek became editor of *Izvestia*, was one of the delegation that negotiated a peace with Germany, and then became Lenin's most important agent in Poland and Berlin. For all his lightheartedness, he loved being close to the centre of power; one day, it was too late for him to withdraw. During a Stalinist show trial in January 1937 he was convicted of 'sabotage, treason and terrorism'. He ended up in the Gulag and died there two years later: beaten to death, stabbed to death or thrown to his death on a concrete floor, the rumours disagree. Grigori Sokolnikov met a similar fate: he was murdered in 1939 in one of Stalin's prisons, apparently by his fellow prisoners.

For a time, Grigori Zinovyev was considered Lenin's natural successor, but lost out to Stalin. He was executed in August 1936. Olga Ravitsj, his wife, disappeared in the Gulag. In late 1918 Parvoes fled to Switzerland, where he had a bank account containing more than two million Swiss francs. Later he returned to Germany, for he had financial interests all over Europe. After his death in Berlin in December 1924, all his personal documents vanished into thin air.

Inessa Armand did not live long: she served, among other things, as head of the women's section of the central committee of the Bolshevik Party, but became overworked and died of cholera and a broken heart in September 1920. Nadezhda Krupskaya grew fat, interfering and querulous. In 1926 she succeeded in expanding the Soviet Union's list of banned literature by at least a hundred books, including the work of Dostoyevsky, the Koran and the Bible. She died in 1939.

Lenin survived Inessa Armand by no more than four years. An attempt was made on his life in 1918. He was deeply traumatised, his reign of terror became more intense, and he never completely recovered. After 1921 his health deteriorated. He died on 21 January, 1924, before reaching the age of fifty-four.

Chapter Fourteen

Petrograd

ST PETERSBURG, 15 MARCH, 1999. IT TAKES DAYS TO FALL IN LOVE
with the Hotel Neva, but then it is for ever. Who could help but fall for
its curlicue staircases and czarist corridors, its unrelenting Stalinist
mattresses, the central heating adjustable at all hours by simply opening
or closing the window just a crack, its gurgling showers, the yellowish-
brown moisture from its taps, the middle-aged *babushkas* who rule over
their floors like little empresses, the red beets and soggy eggs at breakfast? Your first instinct is to get away as quickly as possible, but then you
start developing a strange affection for all this, and after that you are lost.

Of course the hotel has its typical Russian quirks. In the canteen, for
example, you see a NO SMOKING sign, while everyone there is nonchalantly puffing away. The true Russia hand knows: that sign has nothing
to do with smoking, but everything to do with power. It allows the
canteen supervisor to ban or permit smoking as she sees fit, to hand out
favours and sanctions, to exercise sovereignty, in other words, over her
little fiefdom. Clean towels? That has to be discussed at length with two
other female supervisors. A table at which to write? But now I have gone
too far! 'You'll have to request permission from the superior!' our lady
of the corridor cries. The table eventually arrives, bringing with it the
next problem: what about a chair?

And so I while away my days here, chez Oblomov. At night the temper-
ature drops to around twelve below zero, during the day the sun shines.
From my room I have a view of the stone cannons adorning the front
of an old munitions plant, and of a brightly lit branch office of the former
KGB. The Neva is a wide, white expanse of ice. The sky is a brilliant blue.
Children are playing on the canals.

Everyone else is talking about what a rotten winter it has been. In August the city was still lively and bright, then the rouble turned into Monopoly money, after that the weather turned cold, companies went bankrupt, building projects came to a halt, and the birds haven't even started singing yet.

Candles and incense smoulder in the smudgy black vaults of the church nearby. It is full of people, young and old, wrapped up snugly in shawls. A little market has sprung up close to the tiled stove. At least a dozen women have set up a trade in vodka, leeks and assorted obscurities.

In one of the naves, a priest begins chanting. Leaning against a wall are four coffin lids, and now I see the four corpses as well: two emaciated old people and two somewhat younger souls, a man with a pointed face and a skinny woman with dark hair and bushy eyebrows. The women around the stove genuflect from behind their wares. And the winter holds on, it will never end, even though everyone is long exhausted.

My growing attachment to this city and the indolent life at the hotel, I reflect, may have something to do with a deep and fundamental sense of recognition. The last time I was here was about six years ago, and little has changed in the city since. The revolution of Sony, IBM and Head & Shoulders that has been sweeping the Poles, Czechs, Hungarians and East Germans along with it since 1989 seems to have got stranded here amid the drab houses and brownish snow. Moscow is where all the money is made on the black market. In St Petersburg the trams are the same weathered wrecks they were then, the potholes in the streets are as deep as ever, the rubbish lies around for a long, long time, and every couple of hundred metres along the street you see someone tinkering with his car. The city is still torn down the middle each evening when the bridges over the Neva are pulled up for a few hours, providing the perfect adulterer's excuse: 'Sorry, I had to wait for the bridge.'

What *has* disappeared in the last six years is the established order. The St Petersburg Times of 16 March, 1999 reports a bank robbery by the pensioner Dmitri Setrakov: during the rouble crisis of August 1998 he lost his entire life savings of $20,000; no one helped him; his last resort was a TOZ-106 hunting rifle. Another article: in the city of Prokopyevsk, three patients in an intensive care ward are in additional mortal danger because

the hospital cannot pay its electricity bill. A whole government apparatus has gone bust here. If my hotel pays any taxes at all, it is to the
boss of the shabby guards at the door, a mafia chieftain who runs a
little country of his own. Someone recounts the story of the local entrepreneur Sergei M. Like everyone, Sergei pays for protection, for a 'roof'
as they say here. One day an angry customer came into Sergei's place
of business, accompanied by an armed gangster, to demand his money
back. Sergei was given permission to call his 'roof'. Within a few minutes
his protector was there in the office, fully armed. The two gangsters
talked calmly for a few minutes; it soon turned out that Sergei's roof
belonged to a network of patronage within the St Petersburg mafia that
ranked higher than the customer's. The case was closed: Sergei was not
bothered again.

And so it goes everywhere in this stateless state, even unto the old
Singer factory that now houses Dom Knigi, the biggest bookshop in St
Petersburg. At Dom Knigi, every department – fiction, non-fiction, children's literature – is watched over by a heavily armed commando, the
guardian angel sent by yet another private state. A simple shopping trip
in this city leads you from one sovereignty to the next.

The old section of St Petersburg is essentially a frozen metropolis from
1917, with the same doors and decorated house fronts, the same street
lamps and the same graceful bridges. The only difference with 1917 is
that all of this is eighty years older now and a great deal more ramshackle,
for there has never been money for maintenance or restoration. But on
the other hand, where else does one find a city where money was no
object for two whole centuries, a city that was moulded by the best
European architects of the eighteenth and nineteenth centuries and then
more or less forgotten?

The communist leaders who came later focused all their razing and
renewal on Moscow. They did not like Leningrad, and that was the salvation of the beautiful banks of the Neva, the lovely, low ochre-yellow
buildings and Nevsky Prospect, which today looks much as it did in
Gogol's day, except that little is left of the 'carnivalesque atmosphere', the
'cheerful carriages' and the 'spotlessly clean sidewalks'.

The history of St Petersburg reflects the relationship between Russia
and Europe. And, by association, it also reflects the gulf between the

Russian state and the Russian people, which grew wider and went on growing until it finally became unbridgeable.

St Petersburg itself, like Vienna, like Berlin, reflects the dream of an old dynasty, with all the accompanying peculiarities. But St Petersburg has much more going for it. The city, after all, was designed and built as a grand attempt to force a change in the course and the thinking of a semi-medieval nation. That ambition, that evangelical message, can be seen on the streets and buildings everywhere, even today. The physical forms have something overly deliberate about them, like a caricature of nineteenth-century Europe. The palaces here are more exuberant than anywhere else, the boulevards wider than any I have seen, the opulence is that of the parvenu. Here reigns, as the Marquis de Custine once wrote, a typical 'façade culture', one 'without roots in history or in the Russian soil, an apparent order, like a veil thrown over the Asiatic barbarism'.

St Petersburg symbolises the continuing identity crisis of this huge empire to Europe's east: who are we really, where do we want to belong? 'Of course we're Europeans,' say the two schoolgirls I speak to briefly on Nevsky Prospect. But at the same time they talk excitedly about their upcoming holiday 'to Europe', as though that were some far-off and exotic world.

A friend of a friend grants me a taste of the atmosphere of the palace that once belonged to Felix Yusupov, the nobleman who later murdered the seer Grigori Rasputin. I am even allowed a peek at the room and the untidy garden where it all happened. Yusupov, an Oxford graduate, was 'merely' married to the czar's niece, yet the palace has the size and the allure of the residences of a Western European potentate. Aristocrats like Yusupov did absolutely nothing at all, but until 1914 were the reigning European champions at the noble art of wasting money. The notes I make during the visit are punctuated solely with exclamation marks. The Turkish bath! The Jugendstil dining room! The prince did not have much time to enjoy it, however: in 1917 he fled head over heels to Paris, where he died at a ripe old age in the 1960s. I take a peek at his private theatre: a complete miniature Bolshoi, a chocolate box lined with red velvet, with every last accoutrement, exclusively for the prince and his guests.

Like his cousin Wilhelm II, Czar Nicholas II felt a strong bond with his English kin. The czar was married to Queen Victoria's granddaughter, spoke English like a Cambridge don, cultivated public-school manners and was known as 'the most civil man in Europe'. At the same time, he aspired to the status of a true Russian czar, the absolute ruler over a vast, semi-Asiatic empire.

And just like Kaiser Wilhelm, Nicholas preferred living in a past of his own making. He intended his dynasty to remain a beacon in the uncertain days of modernisation and democratisation. Many of the glorious façades of St Petersburg's eighteenth-century palaces were replaced, with the czar's approval, with new ones in a hotchpotch of neo-Renaissance, neo-baroque or 'pre-modern Gothic' styles. In that way, too, the city resembled Berlin; the nouveau riche left their mark on both cities with identical conviction.

The reign of Nicholas II began under a bad sign. A few days after his coronation, during the traditional distribution of cake and beverages, he watched as 1,400 people were trampled to death in the crowd. In 1881 – Nicholas was thirteen at the time – his relatively liberal grandfather Alexander II was murdered in his carriage by 'nihilistic' revolutionaries. That was the first, and perhaps the seminal, turning point in modern Russian history. After that, moderate reformers could accomplish almost nothing. The second was the popular rebellion of 1905. The third and pivotal change was the Bolshevik coup of 1917.

Ten years after the death of Alexander II, the country was racked by unparalleled famine. The czarist regime could not do a thing. Countless well-to-do volunteers went to the countryside to help the suffering farmers, and for many of them the contrast between the grinding poverty of the farmers and the regime's shortsighted arrogance came as a shock. In 1894, Alexander III, a reactionary mogul, died unexpectedly of a kidney ailment. His son Nicholas had to assume power whether he liked it or not.

Kaiser Wilhelm, despite his conservatism, was thoroughly interested in all forms of modern technology, but Nicholas was obsessed with seventeenth-century fantasies. The role he wished to play fitted neither his age nor his person. He yearned for absolute power over an empire, but at the same time lacked the vision and skills needed for such a position. To make matters worse he did not even realise that he lacked those talents, or that Russia was actually in need of very different qualities indeed. His greatest achievement came in 1913: the pompous celebration of 300 years of the Romanov dynasty. It was one, great nostalgic cry for a non-existent past.

During those same years, Russian literacy rose from twenty per cent in 1897 to forty per cent in 1914. Between 1860 and 1914, the number of university students grew from 5,000 to nearly 70,000, and the number of Russian newspapers from 13 to more than 850. Even the Russian *miri*, the village communes of peasant farmers, were opening up to the real world. But Nicholas had no eye for any of that.

On Sunday, 9 January, 1905, his soldiers opened fire on a praying, kneeling crowd in St Petersburg. About 200 people were killed, hundreds more were wounded. The myth of 'Papa Czar' was shattered and the Russian people were furious, riots and disturbances broke out everywhere. Some 3,000 rural estates were looted. From the famous steps at the quayside in Odessa, soldiers fired on a crowd that was demonstrating in support of mutineers on the battleship *Potemkin*. More than 2,000 people were killed: shot, trampled or drowned. In late 1905, a revolt in Moscow was crushed at the last moment.

A czarist countermovement arose: anti-liberal, anti-socialist, and above all anti-Semitic. Some 700 pogroms took place across Russia in the fall of 1905. In Odessa 800 Jews were murdered, more than 100,000 lost their homes. And rightly so, according to the czar. 'Nine out of every ten of the troublemakers were Jews,' he wrote contentedly to his mother on 27 October, 1905. To him, the pogroms were a clear demonstration of what an enraged crowd of loyal subjects could do: 'They encircle the houses where the revolutionaries have sought refuge, set them on fire and kill everyone who tries to escape.'

In 1905, the Russian Army was called in to crush a total of 720 major and minor revolts. An estimated 15,000 'politicals' were executed, 45,000 sent into exile or to prison. Tens of thousands of farmers were flogged, hundreds of thousands of huts were put to the torch.

A Russian friend of mine knew a very old woman who spent time in prison in those days. Her family sent her books, wrapped in white bread. 'The guards brought them to her, watched as she unpacked the books – she pounced on them right away – and were all too happy to receive the bread in return.'

In due course the czar announced a few reforms, but retracted them just as quickly. A new sense of uncertainty took hold of the moneyed classes. For the first time, the bourgeoisie had witnessed the destructive rage of millions of poverty-stricken Russians. And, after the violent repression of the revolts, the bitterness only increased. More than ever the farmers became aware of their own utter powerlessness and poverty, the strikes in the cities grew in frequency and intensity, the intellectuals began taking part as well, and a growing number of key administrators became disgusted with the rigid czarist court.

Around the courtyards of the Peter and Paul Fortress, the citadel built by Peter the Great in 1703, one can still visit the dungeons in which revolutionaries were held in those days. A survey of those imprisoned here reads like a roll of honour: there were Decabrists, nihilists, populists, Marxists, socialist revolutionaries, Mensheviks, Bolsheviks and, later, more Menshevik prisoners of the Bolsheviks, along with priests and royalists. By 1917 the average Bolshevik activist had spent four years in prison, an active Menshevik five. The rest of Europe had long embraced the liberal motto of 'that which is not forbidden is allowed', but in Russia it was just the opposite: 'all that is not explicitly allowed is forbidden.'

For many years, the final souvenir of that famous April night in 1917 stood before the Lenin Musuem: the antique armoured car in which Lenin was driven from Finland Station to Kshesinskaya Palace. Today both museum and armoured car have disappeared. In their stead, pride of place has now been given to the old equestrian statue of Czar Alexander III, an implacable bronze giant on a horse with legs like pillars, a caricature of the ponderous rigour of the czarist autocracy. The statue was so preposterous that the Bolsheviks only bothered to have it removed in the 1930s. The saying had it that the sculptor, Pavel Trubetskov, was not at all interested in politics, but had merely wished to portray 'one animal atop another'. The citizens of Petrograd laughed about that.

St Petersburg was obviously not the ideal capital for the last of the Romanovs. Their hearts lay further to the east and south; Moscow was the city of the Russian past, of devout farmers who bowed to church and czar. The ministries and palaces of St Petersburg were reminiscent of

Paris or Rome, the city itself had European leanings, and no Orthodox Church could compete with that.

The two cities reacted quite differently to the czar's power base. Inspired by the West, the aristocracy of St Petersburg tried to limit the power of the regime with legislative rules and bureaucratic models. In this way, despite all obstructions, a number of aristocrats were able to play a major role in the initial modernisation of Russia.

And then one had the Muscovite model, based on the premise of a 'spiritual communion' between the czar and the common Russian folk. Power here was not an expression of law or popular will; it was, first and foremost, a matter of faith.

The last czar saw himself as God's representative on earth. 'I regard Russia as one big estate, with the czar as its owner, the nobility as overseers and the working people as its farmers,' he said in 1902. With the support of the common people – embodied by the farmyard stench of court clergy like Rasputin – he believed he could stand up to the power of the bureaucrats, the merchants, the intellectuals and revolutionaries. There was, in his eyes, no 'social question': peasants were no different from farmers.

In the longer term, this dream vision collided so forcefully with reality that what the czar achieved was the very opposite of what he was aiming for: no power, but a black hole at the centre of the ruling system, a vacuum that would one day be filled by whatever revolutionary movement came along.

The idea that Russia 'groaned eternally under the czarist yoke' is therefore incorrect. There was, of course, an active secret police and hundreds, sometimes thousands, of people were killed during the suppression of popular uprisings, but the prime characteristic of the czarist regime was its general want of sufficient administrative power to rule the Russian vastness effectively. Around the turn of the century there were only four civil servants to every thousand Russians. In Germany, it was one in twelve; in France, one in seventeen. A little over 8,000 policemen were employed for a total rural population of more than a hundred million souls. In other words, in addition to an enormous void at the centre of power, the Russian Empire in 1917 had almost no administrative infrastructure. Here too lay the fallow ground that the Bolsheviks would later cultivate in their own fashion.

The countryside was rife with backward potentates. The village hovels, the medieval customs, the superstition, the barbaric punishments, the low value attached to human life, all this was largely due to that same lack of effective administration. So too the poverty in the cities: living conditions in St Petersburg under the czars were even more deplorable than those in Berlin or London. Between 1860–1900, the population tripled. According to the 1904 census, an average of sixteen people lived in each apartment, at least six in each room, twice as many as in Paris or Vienna. The drinking water supply was so inadequate that a cholera epidemic in 1908 killed 30,000 city dwellers. By 1917, the planned improvements had still never made it past the drawing board.

Lured by government support, foreigners brought modern industry to St Petersburg. In Vyborg, Ludwig Nobel set up the giant Phoenix engineering works. The Russian-American 'Triangle' rubber firm had more than 11,000 employees. At least 5,000 workers were employed at the Nevsky docks. Vast, red-brick factory complexes were squeezed in everywhere amid the slums: no worker could permit himself the time or expense involved in moving to another neighbourhood. At the same time, this metropolis – just as in Moscow – retained something rural. The countryside was a palpable presence, on the markets, in the characters one saw on the street, in the way neighbours and colleagues interacted. It was something London and Paris had lost long before, the old mir, which was preserved even in St Petersburg.

My friend Yuri Klejner takes me to the Museum of the October Revolution, now rechristened the Museum for Political History. The museum is housed in the same Kshesinskaya Palace at which Lenin arrived that first evening before delivering his fire-and-brimstone speech. Here, too, is where the first offices of *Pravda* were located. The old newspaper-office atmosphere of the lovely art nouveau villa has been minutely reconstructed, right down to the desks, typewriters, oil lamps and antique telephones. In the middle of the hall is a huge model of the emblem of the former Soviet Union, in shiny red and gold plastic. On the wall is a big map of Russia as it was in the year 1912.

Yuri is a historian and a professor of English literature, and above all a fantastic storyteller. But here he is given no chance. The matron who suddenly appears before us is seething with rage: we are not even allowed to whisper as long as the official guide is speaking. She wears her grey hair pulled back in a bun, in accordance with former Party fashion. When we refuse to be silent, she all but throws us out of the building.

During those first few months, Lenin spoke to the masses from the balcony here on any number of occasions. His exact words are no longer known, but the scene itself was repeated later in countless Soviet films, played by actors who looked a little like Lenin. The action is always the same: Lenin walks out onto the balcony, and the crowd falls silent.

'I always thought that was the way it went, too,' Yuri whispers, 'until I ran into an old woman in Estonia who told me she had worked as a governess in Petrograd in 1917. "Where did you live?" I asked her. "Beside the palace," she said. "Did you see Lenin there?" "Of course I did." "Did you ever see him speak from the balcony?" "Oh yes, I was standing on the next balcony." This woman was in deadly earnest, the way all those Baltic people are. So I asked her: "How did that go?" "During those first few weeks there were usually a few hundred people in the crowd," she told me, "and they were all shouting. And Lenin would start to speak and they would just keep shouting. Angry, approving, everything at the same time." "Did they really shout that loudly?" "Oh yes, we were standing almost beside him and we could barely hear a word he said."'

On display here are the famous photographs of the massacre in front of the Winter Palace in January 1905, on Bloody Sunday. And the petition the crowd was trying to hand over: 'We, the workers and citizens of St Petersburg, of the various estates, our wives, our children and our old, helpless parents, we come to you, Sire, looking for assistance and protection . . .'

'1905 was a crucial year,' Yuri says. 'The Russians wanted to win a fast war in order to boost morale. They saw Japan as an odd little country they could knock over just like that. But the Japanese were definitely no backward orientals any more, and the Russians lost. Tens of thousands of soldiers were killed, famine swept the country. The movement that arose among the people then was, above all, a symbolic revolution. It was organised by a priest, Georgi Gapon, and meshed perfectly with the philosophy of the czar himself, of the father caring for his children. All the czar would have had to say was: "My children, I love you." But he had his soldiers fire on the praying crowd. No one forgave him for that. The czar himself laid the foundation for the communist revolution.'

In the museum, as one would expect, there are dozens of portraits of famous and less famous revolutionaries. The striking thing is almost all of them have a particular look in their eyes.

'Burning,' I say.

'Fiery,' Yuri says.

'Something mad,' I say.

Just as in Paris, London and Vienna, the cafés and salons of St Petersburg had witnessed one philosophical fashion after another. In 1840 it was Hegel, in 1860 it was Darwin, and in 1880 it was 'almost indecent' for a student not to be a Marxist. And the Russians dealt with the phenomenon of philosophy in an unusual way. Every doctrine was embraced as the absolute truth, a religion that allowed no room for even the slightest doubt. These religiously tinted feelings were, without exception, mingled with a sense of guilt. Almost all the radical intellectuals, after all, came from wealthy families; even Lenin lived for years from the proceeds from his grandfather's estate in Kazan, the whole time damning the practices of 'rural capitalism'.

The primal Russian revolutionary was more an anchorite than he was an intellectual, Yuri feels. Take Rakhmetov, the gruesome hero of Nikolai Chernyshevsky's 1863 novel What Is To Be Done?, which influenced whole generations. Rakhmetov allowed nothing to distract him from his political objectives, not even a beautiful widow who fell in love with him. He lived like a puritan, ate only raw beef and even slept on a bed of nails when his sexual urges threatened to get out of hand.

Yuri tells me about one of his grandmother's friends, another of these early revolutionaries. 'He was arrested, but refused to talk. Then the secret police played a nasty trick on him: they just let him go. His revolutionary comrades of course thought he had told them everything. They lured him to a remote place, had him sit down, poured a bottle of acid over his head and ran away. He was blinded, and wore a mask for the rest of his life. But the worst thing, he wrote later, was that his comrades never asked him a thing, they simply assumed that he had betrayed them, the truth did not interest them at all.'

On Sunday evening, 17 September, 1916, the French ambassador Maurice Paléologue was present, as was his custom, at the opening of Petrograd's new theatre season. In his journal he describes his impressions of that evening. In the Mariinsky theatre one saw the loveliest of jewels and gorgeous wardrobes, and everywhere there were young beauties, 'their bright eyes . . . sparkling with merriment'. The enormous hall with its blue and gold tapestries was filled to the rafters. 'From the stalls to the back row of the highest circle I could see nothing but a crowd of cheery, smiling faces.' Still, the ambassador also felt the approach of something ominous. 'There was something blithe and unreal to it all,' he wrote.

That applied to the whole city. Everyone was talking about the 'German' Czarina Alexandra – Alice of Hesse – and her protégé Rasputin, who had reportedly committed treason. A palace coup had failed – on 16 December, Rasputin was murdered (albeit with great difficulty) and his body thrown into the Neva by the clique surrounding Prince Yusopov. The czar only grew more recalcitrant. The town was buzzing with the word 'revolution'. The wealthy gambled away their fortunes, drank their cellars dry and threw one wild party after another. 'More and more people are behaving like animals and madmen,' Maxim Gorky wrote to a friend in November 1915. And, in that same month, to his wife: 'We will soon have a famine. I advise you to buy ten pounds of bread and hide it. In the suburbs of Petrograd you can see well-dressed women begging on the streets. It is very cold.'

The Great World Revolution finally began on Thursday morning, 23 February, 1917, in Petrograd's Vyborg district. A group of housewives had been waiting in vain to buy bread. It was the first mild day after three months of bitter cold. The women grew unruly. There were a few minor disturbances, and then the workers from the nearby factories joined in. That same afternoon, 100,000 workers, women and children marched on Nevsky Prospect, chanting slogans such as 'Bread!' and 'Down with the czar!' Two days later, on Saturday, 25 February, the city was shut down by a general strike.

The Cossacks were called in against the strikers. When the cavalrymen had assembled for the charge on Nevsky Prospect, a young girl left the crowd, walked up to the commanding officer and, amid a breathless silence, handed him a bouquet of red roses. The man smiled, accepted the roses and bowed. A thundering cheer went up from both demonstrators and soldiers. 'Our fathers, mothers, sisters and brothers are crying for bread,' a young sergeant shouted. 'Are we going to kill them?' This would not be another 1905. Czar Nicholas II's fate was sealed. On 2 March, he abdicated, leaving the throne to his younger brother, Grand Duke Michael. The next day, Michael decided not to accept. That was the end of the Romanov dynasty, which had been in power for more than three centuries.

Six months after the opening of the theatre season, on 7 April, 1917, Paléologue went to the Mariinsky again. 'All of the imperial coats of arms and the golden eagles have been removed. The box attendants have exchanged their sumptuous court liveries for miserable grey jackets. The theatre was filled with an audience of bourgeois, students and soldiers.' The stately dukes had been arrested, the aides-de-camp in their gaudy uniforms had been shot, the rest were fleeing for their lives. In the box formerly reserved for the czar there were now deportees, just back from exile in Siberia. They stared at the crowd in wonder and awe. That was the end of the 1916–17 season.

The Mariinsky still stands. The 'Mari', as the people call it, is a classic Eastern European theatre. One Saturday evening I go there and watch a performance of *Boris Gudonov*, from the gallery. In my row are two old ladies in floral dresses and five schoolgirls wearing starched white blouses, there are twenty sailors in the row in front of me. Nothing seems to have changed since the days of the czar. The Mariinsky is a temple; ballet and theatre are its perfectly performed rituals.

The next morning I leave for a day trip with Yuri's family, all packed into his long-suffering Lada. The stamina of this country, even of its objects of daily use, is impressive. The poor tyres bash constantly through holes in the asphalt, the shock absorbers, frame and differential groan, and it all keeps working.

First we stop in to see Grandma, Yuri's great-grandmother. Alexandra Vasilyeva, a retired theatre director, is lying under a red chequered blanket, her little face white amid the fluffy pillows. She is 102.

Alexandra was once one of those young beauties the French ambassador saw at the Mariinsky, 'sparkling with excitement'. 'Oh, were you there last night?' she warbles from her bed. 'I used to go there all the time, I got free tickets from a merchant friend.' She giggles. 'I would sit there in all my plainness, amid all that gold and jewellery. And then came the revolution. Those were exciting days! And dangerous! My husband was a very fussy dresser, and whenever we were stopped somewhere we always trembled in fear at the thought that we might look too neat and capitalist. He could have been shot right there on the spot, in those natty clothes of his! Fortunately he worked in the movies, and he always carried a letter from the film company. Those soldiers and bandits thought a film star was fantastic, they wouldn't shoot someone like that.'

Her voice trails off; she has fallen asleep again.

She went on directing plays all her life, Yuri whispers. Even now, she continues to do so. She talks in her sleep, giving instructions on the lighting, directing the actors. In her dreams she is always at work, in Moscow, Kiev, Odessa, St Petersburg, everywhere.

We drive down Ulitsa Sovyetskaya. The façades are a brownish-grey, just like the clumps of snow still lying in the street. The only colour comes from the red traffic light. This street was where the idealistic sisters Anna and Nadezhda Alliluyeva once lived. Their house was a major nest of revolutionaries in 1917. A stern-looking woman opens the door. The apartment has been maintained as a revolutionary relic, completely intact, spacious and bright with sunny rooms, a cupboard full of books, a samovar for tea, a piano to sing songs to. Sergei Alliluyev, the girls' father, was a worker who must have earned a decent salary: in the Soviet era he could never have afforded a house like this for his daughters.

The Alliluyevas, with their unadulterated working-class background, were an exception in the little world of the Bolsheviks. The interiors here speak of a desire for order and bourgeois comfort, something a 'damned' revolutionary did not strive for. Nevertheless, during the brief period he spent here hiding from the provisional government, Lenin was all too willing to put up with the girls' bourgeois respectability. I gaze in awe at the plain zinc bathtub in which the great leader once scrubbed his back.

Stalin was a frequent guest here as well. He had his eye on the younger sister, Nadezhda. She was seventeen, he was thirty-nine, and she fairly swooned at the sight of his revolutionary moustache. Rumour had it that

Nadezhda was in fact Stalin's daughter; as a young man, he'd had an affair with Mother Alliluyeva. Five months after they married she bore him a son, Vasil, followed in 1927 by a daughter, Svetlana. In November 1932, Nadezhda, who contradicted her husband too often, was apparently driven to suicide. Her sister Anna was sentenced to ten years in prison in 1948, her brother-in-law was shot in 1938, her daughter Svetlana fled to the United States, her son Vasili joined the air force, ended up in prison for corruption and died a lonely alcoholic in Kazan. But the stern-looking housekeeper tells us none of that.

As we drive out of town, the tyres of our Lada are put through a living hell: the worn and mangled road to the island fortress of Kronstadt. Until only four years ago this area was off-limits, but this Sunday afternoon we can drive right in. Here lay the heart of Petrograd's Bolshevik revolution. This was home base for the sailors of the *Aurora*. Here is where the new future began. And here too, in February 1921, arose the first opposition to the Bolsheviks.

The dam we drive across took years to build, and has created considerable problems for the Neva Delta ecosystem. Along the way we pass dozens of petrified projects: half-completed locks, bridges that end somewhere in mid-air, viaducts with neither entrance nor exit. Everything here is in one great state of incompletion. The island itself houses two centuries of military architecture: red arsenals, yellow barracks and elegant nineteenth-century officers' messes, bullet holes from the 1920s and the Second World War, stark, rectangular neighbourhoods full of living quarters from more recent decades. Beside the huge Seaman's Cathedral lies Anchor Square, now empty and bare, but once known as the 'Free University' because of the fiery speeches made there.

The sun is shining. Little groups of cadets stroll along the waterfront. With their black caps and gold clasps they look like fishermen from some Zuider Zee town. A little further along is a row of huge, grey warships, the remnants of a proud Soviet fleet. Encouraged by the sailors, I take a few pictures. Five years ago, that would have cost me a few months in jail. The rust and poverty aboard these ships are much greater enemies than any spy could ever be.

In the car, the talk turns to leaving and staying. Yuri and his wife Ira have always dreamed of escaping the flat tyres and flaking concrete. Their son Sasha, a twenty-two-year-old law student, definitely wants to stay, as do his friends. 'That's the striking thing about this generation,' Ira says. 'They love this city. They know that all kinds of things can happen, good and bad, from one day to the next, and they want to be around to see it.'

Sasha says his friends all have their own reasons for staying. 'A lot of people simply can't leave. Others stay for the scams. They see so much murky water to fish in, so many opportunities to make some fast money, you'd never find that in the neat, orderly West. And then there are the students, people like me. We think it's more exciting here. We don't feel like listening to the biased viewpoints of the Americans and the Europeans, the kind of people who think they know everything about Russian literature.'

'We never used to have the feeling that this country was our country,' Yuri says. 'But now we do, no matter how miserably things are going. Under Stalin, Khrushchev and Brezhnev, the general feeling was that it was "them against us". Now we know that we're ruled by a clique of bandits, but somehow it's still our regime.'

Ira believes it's a bit more complicated than that. 'Stalin and Brezhnev didn't cheat us. They didn't act as though they were anything but what they were. "Love us, or we'll have you shot," they said. So we pretended we loved them. Now we have the right to respond. They cheat everyone, they buy people's favours, but you can still say: don't let yourself be bought. Now we truly have the government we deserve.'

At that point, the Lada finally comes down with a puncture. Yuri stops in the middle of the road to change the back tyre, the traffic goes racing by on both sides.

At last we arrive in the little village of Razliv, a group of wooden houses where Lenin, disguised as a worker, hid in a barn in 1917. A series of demonstrations had got out of hand, and the Bolsheviks could not avoid taking the blame. Lenin himself was on holiday at the time, and the 'attempted revolution' degenerated into a looting party. To make matters worse, the public's opinion of Lenin and his crew took a huge swing when the provisional government published evidence of German aid to the Bolshevik cause.

Lenin had no intention of standing trial. His life and work were too important to him to risk playing the martyr, and he was less courageous in practice than he was in theory. So he took to his heels, along with his old friend Grigori Zinovyev. They spent four days in a barn, until a worker, Nikolai Yemelyanov, rowed them across the lake at Razliv and hid them for a while in a straw hut. After that the great leader went to Finland until the affair blew over. That's the whole story.

The Bolsheviks, though, did have an excellent feeling for theatre, and knew that their ideology could only be made palatable to the Russian people by turning it into a new religion. As far as that went, Lenin's early hardships came as a godsend. In the Museum of Political History I had seen a huge painting of a room full of workers, right before the start of a strike. Their pose was that of the disciples in *The Last Supper*. At the Smolny Institute, Lenin's shirts are cherished as relics. And Lenin's official life story was moulded in the same way by Soviet writers to resemble that of Christ. Just as in the Gospels, Lenin's destiny was established at birth, and from that moment on everything went as it had been appointed. Never did he doubt, never did he make a mistake.

Every religion, of course, contains the same particular episode: the prophet's flight from evil. Marxist-Leninism needed something of the sort too. The days at Razliv were made to fit the bill. Not long after Lenin's death, a monument was erected next to the little straw hut. A museum was built as well; it contained, among other things, Lenin's pillow and his feather bed (today there is a little sign beside those objects saying 'Replica'). And so Razliv became a prosperous place of pilgrimage to which crowds of visitors came each year, and where the legend was sold in the form of books and souvenirs.

Fifty years later, the original hut was absolutely rotten and worn out. In deepest secrecy, therefore, Lenin's hiding place was torn down in 1970. The whole thing was then rebuilt in the old style, but with new materials. In addition, a kind of glass box was erected around the hut, the kind one sees more often at sacred sites. Through it, we can view the interior: a table, a bed, a samovar, a chair at the window, a teacup with four dead flies in it, a stable with space for one cow. Lenin's stable at Bethlehem.

Yemelyanov, the only real worker in the whole story, came to rue the day he rowed Lenin to the other shore. He was dragged from one prison camp to the next. 'Stalin was in the rowing boat, too,' the party chieftains maintained for years, but Yemelyanov knew that it had actually been Stalin's great rival, Grigori Zinovyev. That was enough to ruin the rest of the man's life. He died in 1958. Even after his death, he was still harassed. The workers from the nearby factory wanted to bear him to the graveyard on their shoulders, but for some reason the local party committee had decided he was to be buried in secret. A tug of war ensued, the police trying to shove his coffin into a truck, the workers pulling it out again.

'Christ Almighty,' says the neighbour who tells us the story. 'It was no better than when Yemelyanov was still alive. Put him in prison, take him out again, put him back in. Good Lord, what a life!'

In the woods around the little hut in the glass box, children are playing in the snow. Smoke curls from the chimney. We take a short stroll. Yuri tells me of his discovery, when leafing through the latest edition of the *Great Encyclopaedia of Russian Philosophy* last week, that Karl Marx was no longer stuck between McLuhan and Marcuse. 'What, is Marx suddenly not a philosopher any more?' he said. 'I went back and took a good look at the list of editors who worked on the encyclopaedia. They're exactly the same ones who did it back in the days of communism. And they're still just as trigger-happy with the red pencil!'

The parking lot is crowded with the Mercedes and American jeeps of the modern-day residents of Razliv. Until the 1980s, the little straw hut was taken down in winter and then set up again each spring. But after perestroika it was burned down so often that they stopped trying. Unbelief had become the order of the day.

The heart of the *ancien régime* was the Winter Palace. With its 1,057 crystal rooms and 117 golden stairways, it was a gigantic beehive where some 4,000 courtiers lived and schemed as they swarmed around the absolute centre of power, the czar. It was the stage of Russian power, and in 1917 it was, of course, the stage for the revolution.

For one whole summer the palace housed the provisional government led by Prime Minister Alexander Kerensky. The gilded chambers were the scene of endless meetings. Kerensky's secretary at the time, Pitirim Sorokin, described the prime minister as a man with 'a terrible aversion to authority, force and cruelty ... He believes it is quite possible to govern by means of kind words and noble sentiment. A good man, but a weak leader. In essence, the very picture of the Russian intelligentsia.' For the Bolsheviks, the Winter Palace was the grand prize, the symbol of everything that was wrong with Russia.

Today, more than eighty years later, Yuri Klejner shows me around the palace. For decades, his father worked here as head of the technical service. To him, the Winter Palace is like a second home. He shows me the sunny winter solarium with its view of the Neva, the hanging gardens on the roof (complete with trees), the immense marble throne room, the floors inlaid with dozens of types of wood, and the most ornate golden coach I had ever seen. The imperial eagles on the chandeliers survived the revolution, as did the iron coat hooks in the quarters of the czar's palace guards. 'Very little has changed here since 1917,' Yuri tells me. 'The palace was made into a museum almost at once.' Picassos now hang in Nicholas II's private chambers. Some of the rooms have a splendid view of the square, the rest are low-ceilinged and plain.

In the hall is a huge block of marble bearing the text: 'In memory of the storming of this palace by the revolutionary workers, soldiers and seamen on the evening of 26 October ...'

Yuri takes me to a small set of stairs close to a side entrance. 'If fighting went on anywhere, it was here. In all the Soviet films you see the soldiers running up the central stairway with lots of shooting and people taking cover behind the pillars. Those are the images that are burned into our collective memory. But in reality, none of that took place. There was no real storming of the palace. It all went very quickly. All of the central points in the city, the train stations, the electricity plant, the telephone switchboard, were already in the hands of the Bolsheviks. In the street, life went on as usual, the trams were running, the restaurants remained open. And there was no mass uproar. In the old pictures of the October Revolution you can see how few people were really involved.'

Yuri stresses it over and over: the only real revolution in 1917 was the February Revolution, the revolt by the Mensheviks and the socialist revolutionaries, Western-oriented intellectuals who hoped gradually to mould Russia into a European democracy. The Bolsheviks' October Revolution (for Westerners it was actually in November, because of the different calendars used) was in every way a forced and unnatural happening. Their coup would ultimately clear the way for a brand of Eastern despotism of which Czar Nicholas II could only dream, but then behind a socialist façade.

'Look how easy it must have been: if there had been one man with a machine gun on those stairs, and another one on the landing, the Winter Palace could never have been stormed. But it was complete chaos. Kerensky had already fled the city. The rest of the provisional government was in the Winter Palace, without lights, without a telephone, with no idea what to do. The building was defended by a battalion of women and cadets. A couple of Bolshevik commissioners simply forced their way in through a side entrance, a few soldiers followed them, and the initial looting was stopped. Then the commissioners came back outside through the big front doors and told the crowd: "Go home, it's all over."'

But what about the world-famous cannonade from the cruiser *Aurora*, which supposedly signalled the start of the revolution? 'That was just a single blank shell, it didn't mean a thing. There's still a replica of the *Aurora* in the Neva, you can see it from here. All fake. The Bolsheviks never cared about the substance, it was always the theatrics.' Yuri Klejner tells me how, in recent years, guides at the palace tried to tell the real story. They had to stop, because they received too many complaints. 'These days they're back at the Jordanian Stairs again, up to their knees in blood.'

He shows me the Malachite Room with its enormous green pillars and its view of the river. 'This is where the provisional government met for the last time. The ministers were arrested afterwards in the private dining room next door. In the 1950s, an old man came to the palace and insisted on seeing this room. "You know, this is where they arrested me," he said. "When was that?" "In 1917." As it turned out, he had been the state secretary of railways in the provisional government, too insignificant a post to be killed.' The clock in the side room has been stopped at the time the arrests were made, 1.40 a.m.

The cabinet ministers of the provisional government were carried off, like so many others, to the Peter and Paul Fortress. 'The winter season at the Peter and Paul Fortress Health Spa got off to a roaring start,' the satirical magazine the *Devil's Peppermill* wrote in early 1918. 'Government ministers, statesmen, politicians, elected officials, writers and other prominent figures from the czarist regime and the provisional government, members of the soviets and the constitutional assembly, social democrats and social revolutionaries all arrived at this well known holiday resort with its illustrious therapies: cold, starvation and mandatory rest, punctuated on occasion by surgical procedures, bloodbaths and other exciting activities.'

In the meantime, the old Russia was falling apart. On 3 March, 1918, the Bolsheviks and the Germans signed the 'humiliating treaty' of Brest-Litovsk. The Russian Empire lost Finland, Russian Poland, the Baltic States and the Ukraine. Russia's 'warm' connections to Europe via the Caspian and the Black Sea were cut off. The country lost thirty-two per cent of its agricultural land, thirty-four per cent of its population, fifty-four per cent of its industry and eighty-nine per cent of its coal mines. The terms of the treaty were so humiliating that the party leadership almost decided to resume the war against Germany. Lenin was able to prevent that, but the motion was defeated by only a single vote. His German financiers had every reason to be satisfied. As a European power, Russia was finished.

A series of famines broke out, and at the same time two civil wars were fought: the first between the Reds and the Whites (the latter including countless social democrats), and the second between central Russia and the warlords of the Ukraine and Caucasus. In southern Russia and the Ukraine, the Whites murdered at least 100,000 Jews between 1918–19. Kiev changed regimes no fewer than sixteen times between the end of 1918 and summer 1920. By 1921, the entire Russian production of foodstuffs had shrunk to half the level of 1913. Between 1917–20, the population of Moscow decreased by a half, that of Petrograd by two thirds.

Lenin used the chaos to start immediately on a programme of agricultural reforms. 'Hang (and make sure that the hanging takes place in full view of the people) no fewer than a hundred known kulaks, rich men, bloodsuckers,' he directed in a letter to the Bolsheviks in a distant, troubled province. 'Do it in such a fashion that for hundreds of kilometres around the people might see, tremble, know, shout: They are strangling and will strangle to death the bloodsucking kulaks . . . Find some truly hard people.'

As early as August 1918 he ordered the first forced-labour camps to be built, to accommodate 'unreliable elements'. Four years later there were eighty-four of them, with more than 80,000 prisoners, more than had ever been arrested under the czar. During his time in power, Lenin's secret police, the Cheka, was probably responsible for some 200,000 executions. In 1922 the Cheka was renamed, but during that brief period 'those two syllables' – as Ilya Ehrenburg wrote – 'summoned up so much fear and emotion in every citizen who had lived through the revolution' that they were never forgotten. During the chaotic period between 1917–22, an estimated three to five million people were killed. This was how Russia separated itself from Europe.

'Now I'm going to tell you a story from my own life,' Yuri says once we are standing outside, in the square before the Winter Palace. 'In the early 1950s my father was responsible for all technical matters in the Hermitage. During popular demonstrations in this square, it was his job to make sure those statues up there did not fall off the roof. And that huge pillar was to remain standing as well, of course. An accident like that would have been an absurd coincidence, but whenever something like that did happen it was called "sabotage", and someone had to bear the blame. That person was my father, a scapegoat from the word go. That's the way the Soviet system worked.

'My father would therefore climb up onto this pillar and onto the roof with the other man responsible, the head municipal architect, they would look around, mumble to each other about what a load of nonsense it was, and have a little drink together. That's the way the Soviet system worked as well.

'Every year on 1 May and 7 November, a huge parade and demonstration was held here. There was no television at the time, so everyone wanted to be there. Thanks to his remarkable responsibility for roof and pillar, my father was on good terms with the security service at the Winter Palace, and one day we received permission to view the parade from the palace itself. I was even allowed to bring a friend.

'So there we stood on 7 November, 1952, at that window, with a few other families and the ever-present plainclothes policeman. I was six, my friend was seven. Below they were carrying around huge portraits. I loved Comrade Stalin, and that was the extent of my knowledge of politics. But my friend wanted to show how smart he was, and suddenly he asked my father: "Alexander Alexandrovitch, if Stalin dies, who will be his successor?" Well, the very idea that Stalin would ever die was taboo, and talking about his successor was nothing less than a deadly sin. My father turned white as a sheet. Later he told me that the plainclothesman had clearly heard the comment, and that a whole range of emotions had crossed the man's face. Starting with: Should I arrest this man? Then: But he's only a child. And finally: Why not act as though I didn't hear?

'My father didn't sleep for a week. When he told me about it, years later, you could still see the tension in his face.'

Chapter Fifteen

Riga

VARSHAVSKY STATION IN ST PETERSBURG CAN HARDLY BE CALLED A station at all. It is more like a vague, open lot through which one picks one's way with difficulty, a place criss-crossed with tracks and here and there a long platform. The engines roar behind their snowploughs and the carriages reek as the coal heaters are fired up for a new journey, but inside the compartments it is the very picture of conviviality. The professional busybody assigned to our carriage has settled down in the last compartment. Why would she want to be anywhere else? Her whole life is laid out in her home on wheels, with coloured cushions, flowers, her own curtains, an icon on the wall and a singing kettle on the stove. Always on the road.

Our first-class compartment is also like a salon, with two velveteen pull-out beds, red draperies, white lace curtains and plastic flowers on the table. My only fellow passenger, Andrei Morozov, deals in ship's tackle. The train pulls away, outside there is nothing but white barrenness, here and there a chimney, from the speakers the soft sound of Russian songs, and quite soon the day begins to fade.

Together we polish off two bottles of vodka. First we talk about Andrei's thirteen-year-old daughter and her favourite magazine, *Callgirl*. Then we speak of the lightness of Pushkin. Then he informs me in detail about the peculiarities of the whores who work the trains in Lithuania.

In the next carriage everyone is sitting or lying on plank bunks: farmers with red faces, shy soldiers and wizened grandmothers. My bed shakes gently, the train couplings creak, from somewhere far down the corridor comes the sound of an accordion, outside the window the endless snow slides by, the lanterns of a sleeping village, above it the stars.

I get off at Vilnius at 4.30 a.m. It is quiet as the grave. Close to the station, standing half on the tracks, four greyish-looking men are staring at the lights and the train, their faces tense from the cold, fishing equipment in hand. They do not speak a word. Then I walk down the city's main street and suddenly I see German houses, American advertising, Italian cafés and Swedish hotels, as though the city centre is cut off from the winter by an invisible glass dome.

My room is at the Hotel Neringa. I'm awakened by the groans of the man in the next room, and a few yelping cries from one of the working girls. It is quiet for a bit, and then together they sing a sweet melancholy song in an incomprehensible language. Meanwhile I lie there feeling a bit out of place in a Western bed, next to a shower that actually produces clean water. Just as my mattress springs easily back into shape, so has this entire city sprung back in a moment to European life, as though there had never been anything in between. Still, it was only ten years ago that people here first dared openly to celebrate Christmas. And ten years ago that they formed that human chain, right through three Baltic States, 650 kilometres long, with two million participants. And the bitter fighting with Soviet troops close to the television tower of Vilnius, that was only eight years ago. All the while, Lenin stood looking calmly out over Lukiškių Square.

But all that was centuries ago. On the main street of Vilnius, Western vacuity has descended with a vengeance. The yellow walls are tidily plastered, the old ornaments look like new, and Adidas, Benetton and other familiar spirits smile down on you as you walk. Halfway down the street, a new wind is blowing: six boys, two girls and one guitar, short leather jackets covered in shiny studs, above them soft, blushing faces.

The inner city here has been converted, with much European funding, into a showcase, a beacon of Western welfare. Last year, in their enthusiasm, the Lithuanians even adopted Western European time, so that now their winter evenings begin around 4 p.m. But the city's Western European image feels a bit brittle. Cross a bridge and you will find yourself in the old Užupis district, the Latin Quarter of Vilnius, full of mud, flaking walls, scenes straight out of Victor Hugo and Émile Zola, right down to the rotting hay in the courtyards. Outside the city there are wooden houses everywhere, their roofs rusty corrugated iron, a few half-rotted balconies, smoking chimneys, a horse and wagon, and crows in the bare fields, lots of crows, this is crow country. In some of the villages there are boarded-up sheds, the remains of an old wooden synagogue.

Meanwhile, the city's *jeunesse dorée* gather day after day at Café Afrika. They smoke in great earnest, drink coffee in silence, listen to French *chansons*. Lithuania has the highest suicide rate in Europe.

The spring thaw has begun. On this March day, the sunlight on the nine-teenth-century walls is merciless and clear as glass. There are not many cars on the street, the few people out walking cast sharp shadows on the pavements. I pass a mercantile house built in 1902, with striking grill-work around the roof. The house must once have had a Jewish owner. The front of the one next to it is decorated with stylised, seven-armed candlesticks. Around the corner is a centre for social work, formerly a *heder*, a Jewish school.

Vilnius – 'Wilna' in both German and Yiddish – was once a thoroughly Jewish town, a centuries-old centre of Jewish learning and culture. There was a Jewish university, and the town had six Jewish daily newspapers. After 1945, the Jewish gravestones were used as steps for the new union hall. Today there is a little Jewish museum with two Torah scrolls, the skeleton of a lectern, a couple of portraits and a handful of commemo-rative plaques. That is pretty much all that remains.

Close to my hotel is a sombre government building, a solid chunk of stone with huge doors, massive thresholds, stairs and galleries. The pillars at the front of the building remind me vaguely of a Greek temple. It could once have been a college, or a government ministry, or the offices of the district administration. It is one of those nineteenth-century govern-ment buildings of which there are hundreds all over Europe. The front is spotted with blank patches, the places where the eagles, shields, swastikas and hammers and sickles followed each other in rapid succession. Otherwise little has changed throughout the years.

In 1899 it was built as a courthouse for Vilnius, as an administrative district of the Russian Empire. That was what it remained until 1915. Then it became a German courthouse: the inhabitants of Vilnius were subject to German martial law, and the Germans enjoyed all the privileges of the new coloniser. From January to April 1919, the building housed a Bolshevik revolutionary tribunal. The Lithuanian flag flew above it for a while, then for more than fifteen years it was where justice was administered under the auspices of Poland. Between 1940–1, the courtrooms, halls and cells were used by the judges and executioners of the Soviet Union; more specifically, those of the secret police, the NKVD. In 1941 the building became the headquarters for the Gestapo, the *Sicherheitsdienst* and the notorious Lithuanian *Sonderkommandos*. After 1944 the NKVD, and later the KGB, resumed activities here. That lasted until August 1991. Today it is a museum.

The old courthouse has witnessed the entire historical drama of the Baltic States throughout the twentieth century. At this moment, Lithuania has 3.5 million inhabitants, Latvia 2.5 million (one third of whom, by the way, are Russians), Estonia only 1.5 million (also almost one-third Russians). Just like the Benelux countries, the three Baltic States are where the fault lines between a number of European cultural regions come together. Lithuania is the last remnant of a once powerful Central European empire that extended to the Black Sea. In the fifteenth century, Vilnius, Minsk and Kiev shared the same rulers. Estonia was more closely aligned with the Scandinavian world; it has been Danish, German, Swedish and Russian property, in that order.

Latvia was ruled by the *Drang nach Osten*, the Drive towards the East. From as early as the twelfth century, this pre-Christian, heathen Courland served as the hunting ground for Prussian crusaders. Into the twentieth century, the descendants of the Teutonic Order – with names like Lieven, Pahlen and Behr – ran enormous estates here. The area was officially part of the czarist empire, but unofficially it was an important German colony.

Vilnius occupied a position in the middle: forty per cent of the population was Jewish, thirty per cent Polish, two per cent Lithuanian. That was how things were at the time the old courthouse was built.

In 1918 the Bolsheviks seized power in the Baltic States. They sacked estates, murdered a few thousand civilians and established a 'people's tribunal' in the courthouse. But soon they were chased off by a joint army of German property owners and Baltic nationalists. Then the purges began on the other side: thousands of real or supposed Bolsheviks were shot without a trial. According to the French ambassador at the time, at least fifty executions took place each morning in the central prison at

Riga. And so began the rounds of slaughtering on the left and on the right that would repeat themselves again and again in the decades to come.

In 1920 the Soviet Union recognised the Baltic States' independence 'unto eternity'. The building once again became a normal courthouse. By then Latvia had lost forty per cent of its population to wars, famines and emigration. In 1926 the flow of goods through Riga harbour was only a tenth of what it had been in 1913. Entire factories had 'emigrated' to Russia. Hundreds of German estates were divided up among small farmers, and the Lievens and the Behrs left with bitterness in their hearts.

The British sent their fleet to the aid of the three little countries, but to no avail. When a youthful British diplomat stood up for Estonia and Latvia at the 1919 Paris peace conference, the British chief of staff, Sir Henry Wilson, led him to an enormous map of the Russian Empire. 'Now, my boy,' he said. 'Look at those two little plots on the map and look at that enormous country beside them. How can they hope to avoid being gobbled up?'

I wander now through the cellars of that courthouse. It is all still there: the bucket latrines of the NKVD, the Gestapo's hatches, the doors padded to muffle the screams. I see the 'little cell': officially designed for solitary confinement, but in reality often used to pack in ten or twenty prisoners; the wooden beds, dating from 1947 (before that, prisoners slept on the stone floor); the lamps that stayed on around the clock. On the wall is a photograph of a young girl with a smart cap on her head, half sitting, half lying against a wooden wall, a pair of binoculars in her lap. She is dead, her chest riddled with bullets. She belonged to the Lithuanian resistance which waged guerrilla warfare against the Soviets until 1953. These 'Brothers of the Forest' believed that, under international law, Lithuania was still an independent country. Their covert government had its own laws and its own administration. Courthouses were occupied to make sure Soviet law could not be applied. Some 20,000 Lithuanians were killed in that struggle. The life expectancy of a partisan was two or three years. Most of them were under the age of twenty-one.

A few of the cells are locked. Behind their doors lie the bones of the more than 700 Lithuanian members of parliament, priests and other prominent figures killed in a KGB massacre. The bodies were dug up in 1993 and 1994; only forty of them have been identified so far.

There is another visitor walking around down here, an old man. We strike up a conversation. Antonnis Verslawskis is back here for the first time since he was seventeen. Yes, he knows about the solitary lock-up, he stood there in cold water, forever, until he finally collapsed. His German is old and rusty. 'I had German back in my gymnasium days, but it's been half a century since I've spoken it.' He came to Vilnius today just for this, he says, and wanted to see it one more time. 'I spent three months here in Cell 19, in 1948. There were seven of us. All students. I was with the partisans.' He sighs deeply, taps his chest. 'Emotions, yes.' He points to the door of the solitary cell. 'I was in there for three days. Then they sent me to Siberia for twenty years. Digging. Chopping. I was thirty-seven by the time they let me go.' He has dark brows and sunken eyes. 'This is where it all began. I was so afraid!' He has difficulty going on, he has to dredge up the German words from deep inside, and he becomes more and more upset.

An important political barometer for the region is the *Baltic Times*. The weekly, only three years old, is put together by a dozen journalists working in a few jumbled rooms. A brief selection of this week's news: 'Female President of Latvian Association of Models Arrested for Drug Trafficking', 'Parade of Waffen-SS Veterans Divides Latvia', 'Estonian Parliament Broadens Language Demands: all Russian businessmen, civil servants, waiters and physicians must now speak Estonian'.

There is an article about anti-Semitic posters at the Lithuanian embassy in Warsaw. The text reads: 'All crimes are instigated by Jewish Freemasons, and carried out by Jews.' A demonstration by the elderly: 'My retirement pay is just enough to pay the heating bill, but the Riga City Council doesn't care. How am I supposed to buy groceries?' The mayor of Visaginas has hanged himself: an investigation had been started concerning his alleged corruption and 'pro-Moscow activities'. There is a report on the Estonian province of Polva, where the farmers have lost their Russian export market. 'Unemployment, poverty, the young people are leaving by the hundreds. The locals, worried about their future, no longer dare to have children.' The Latvian prime minister, Vilis Kristopans, is interviewed: 'If you want to see what Latvia should look like, look at the Netherlands.'

Steven Johnson, a young American, has been the weekly's editor-in-chief for the last two years. The supposed unity of the Baltic States, he feels, is only there when viewed from a distance. 'Just look at the capital cities. Vilnius was built as the capital of a huge empire, Lithuania. Tallinn is and remains an overgrown Danish village, every bit as Scandinavian as the rest of Estonia. Latvia always was more or less a remote Prussian province, and you can see that as well: Riga is a true German trading town, and always has been.'

In recent years, Johnson says, the differences are becoming marked. After 1989, Estonia immediately established an excellent image in the West, and still leads the pack. Until 1996, Lithuania was still half communist. 'The three countries may be working at the moment on a kind of economic community, but they are developing at very different rates. And that leads to a great deal of tension. You regularly hear Estonians in Riga or Vilnius shout: "What do we need these people for?"'

And what about the Russians? 'After all those years, that intertwining is more complicated than ever. I know of a city in the south-east of Lithuania where eighty-five per cent of the population speaks Russian. In that same region there's a city that is dependent on one dairy factory, which is in turn totally dependent on the dairy consumption of a number of Russian cities. That still works, but for how long?'

According to Johnson, there are also huge differences between the Baltic States in terms of their relationship with Russia. 'Latvia has always had the worst relations, Lithuania the best. Right after independence, Lithuania granted citizenship to all its Russians. In Latvia, only those Russians between the ages of fifteen and thirty were allowed to be naturalised. But if you were thirty-one and your native language happened to be Russian, then it was no go, even if you had lived there all your life. Latvian Russians are still in a tight spot: their pension rights are limited, they enjoy few or no social facilities, and they have no say in things.' Latvia would rather focus on the Baltic, and forget the rest, Johnson feels. 'The president is always talking about the Nordic Six. In his view, the Baltic must become the Mediterranean of the North.'

The young people in these countries, Johnson says, are very optimistic. The older generations simply let all the changes roll over them. 'They've become cynical, they've been through too much already, they don't trust anyone, including the West. The last time the Baltic states became independent it lasted only twenty years. Then, under the Molotov-Ribbentrop Pact, they were swallowed up by Russia again. The West never lifted a finger to help. They haven't forgotten that.'

Riga has an intimate feel to it, and at the same time the lightness of the sea. It is a true Hanseatic port, with a whiff of Denmark, and sometimes a touch of Deventer. In ten years' time, a fantastic Potemkin town has been created here as well.

Today is the first real day of spring. The centre of Riga has been transformed into a cozy place full of pleasant little streets, pretty façades, restaurants and grand cafés. On a smaller scale, the city's story is almost the same as that of St Petersburg: because the poverty allowed little construction work or demolition after 1918, Riga is a city almost perfectly intact, unchanged from the year 1900. Everyone is out strolling under the bare trees: a tall man with a moustache and a beret, a Jewish woman with a mink cap and stole, a drunken worker with torn trousers and no toecaps in his shoes. Engraved in a rusty wrought-iron balcony is the date 1879, and I think: who lived behind that date in 1918, 1920, 1940, 1941, 1944, 1989? A Jewish businessman, German officers, a Soviet civil servant and his family?

In 1939 the Baltic States were divided between Hitler and Stalin, when the two powers carefully circumscribed their future European spheres of influence. In the afternoon and evening of 17 June, 1940, while the whole world was focusing on the German occupation of Paris, a long column of Russian tanks rolled into Riga. One year later, more than 650,000 Soviet troops were garrisoned in the Baltic States. Looting was commonplace. Hundreds of 'enemies of the people' were lined up and shot. In the night of 14 June, 1941, more than 20,000 people were rounded up in Lithuania, loaded into cattle cars and deported to the remotest corners of the Soviet Union. That same night in Latvia, 15,000 people were picked up, in Estonia 11,000. Only a few thousand of them ever came back.

Riga's Museum of the Occupation contains an original *parasha*, the middlepoint of existence in all Soviet prisons. The *parasha* – also referred to as 'Red Moscow', after a popular brand of perfume – was a wide, fairly low barrel with a shelf around the edges. In the corner of each celi, each cattle car, each ship's hold and camp barrack one found these barrels full of shit, ready to slosh over the next time someone sat down on it. 'All of the barracks, all our clothes, even our food, everything was permeated with that stench,' wrote a former prisoner, Martinus Melluzi. 'That stench, that unimaginable filth, that was perhaps the worst thing they did to us.'

In the summer of 1941, the Baltic States were occupied by the advancing German Army. Nazi rule lasted for three years, until the Red Army moved back into the region in 1944. The Soviets immediately resumed their old ways: lootings, rapes, the mass execution of 'saboteurs', deportations of 'recalcitrant bourgeois'.

Again, not a single Western country came forward to support those little dots on the Soviet map. During the final days of March 1949, 40,000 men, women and children were arrested in Riga alone and deported to Siberia. In all three Baltic States, that number was 150,000. Between 1947–50, 220,000 Lithuanians were sent to other parts of the Soviet Union. Conversely, almost half a million Russians were brought into the Baltic States. By the end of the 1970s, the Latvians formed a minority in their own capital.

A replica of a camp barrack has been constructed in the Museum of the Occupation. I see a handmade spoon, a decayed violin, a letter written on bark and a book full of words of farewell, thrown in desperation out of a moving cattle car. There is also a little bookmark from 1946, woven in Riga's central prison with painstaking devotion from loose red threads: 'For Jüris, from Drosma'. But Jüris Mucenieks never saw it. He had already perished in the Siberian *taiga*, part of that number on display at the museum's exit: 'During the periods of Soviet and German occupation, Latvia lost 550,000 of its citizens, more than a third of the population. This is the number of Latvians who were murdered, killed at war, sentenced to death, deported, scattered across the world as refugees or who disappeared without a trace.'

Thank God Riga's memory is short, for otherwise it would be unbearable. It is Saturday evening. The squatters' café, called the Horseradish Sandwich, is enormously popular because of its old Soviet flotsam and cheap vodka. Restaurant Nostalgia, once the watering hole for the Soviet elite, is now full of young people. The dining room was designed in inimitable Stalinist style, with Roman pillars, heavy chandeliers, French viewing holes in the ceiling and everything else that might appeal to the party's parvenus. Ten years later the Latvian young people see this as 'cool camp'. This is the place to be, the place to be seen. I myself take to Café Amsterdama. I stare at the two Amsterdam cityscapes on the wall and the three bottles of Grolsch beer behind the bar.

This is a peculiar city, it occurs to me, a city that switches historical eras as though they were backdrops on a stage. I have brought along the fat catalogue from the Museum of the Occupation, glossy and colourful, subsidised with a grant from the *Landtag* of Mecklenburg Vorpommern. At the door I was also handed a thin, cheap brochure: *The Jews in Riga*, published by the local Jewish documentation centre. I lay them side by side. What the official catalogue – with a foreword by the Latvian president – writes about the Soviet occupation is quite striking, but striking as well are all the things it does not mention.

The catalogue correctly mentions the flowers with which the German 'liberators' were welcomed by the Latvians in 1941. I read all about the Nazis' plans to 'Germanise' the Baltic States and recolonise them. The Boulevard of Liberty in the centre of Riga was rechristened Adolf-Hitler-Strasse, the traditional holidays were banned, the economy was placed under German control, workers were sent to Germany to perform forced labour.

There is one issue, though, that the catalogue barely touches on: the zealous support the Germans received in Latvia and Lithuania for their persecution of the Jews. That morbid zeal had everything to do with the violent cycle of revolution and counter-revolution in which people had been caught up here for decades. The Jewish citizenry – some of them communists, others capitalists – were the ideal scapegoats. In essence, the pattern seen in Vienna was repeated here. 'The Jew spoke German and was on occasion more German than the German,' writes Modris Eksteins in his impressive personal history of the Baltic States. 'The Jew spoke Russian and again could be a better spokesman for Russian culture than the Russian. The Jew was a town-dweller, a cosmopolitan. The Jew was all things – but to many Latvians, caught up in the mood of growing paranoia and crude nationalism, he represented all things foreign, all things dangerous.'

As soon as the Soviets withdrew in summer 1941, therefore, the population of Latvia and Lithuania turned on the Jews. The museum catalogue, published last year, speaks only of Latvian 'Self-Defence Troops' who 'closed battle with retreating Soviet units' and with 'those who supported Soviet rule'. 'They killed approximately 6,000 Soviet party activists of various nationalities and origins: Latvians, Russians and Jews.'

But what really happened? On 29 June, 1941, even before the Gestapo and the *Einsatzkommandos* had arrived, all Jewish males between the ages of sixteen and fifty were rounded up on the market square in the Latvian town of Daugavpils. More than 1,000 of them were killed right there by the Latvians themselves. All over Riga, on the night of 2 July, Jewish property was looted and Jews were murdered. At noon on 4 July, dozens of Jewish families were driven into the Greise Hor Schul, Riga's biggest synagogue. Approximately 300 Lithuanian-Jewish refugees had also taken refuge in the cellars of the synagogue. Latvian Nazis locked the doors and set the building on fire. Hundreds of Jews were burned alive. A similar atrocity took place at Riga's Old Jewish Cemetery. The catalogue from the Museum of the Occupation mentions none of this. It shows only a photograph of the wooden steeple of St Peter's Church, which burned down during the fitful fighting around Riga in those same days, 'as did a considerable number of the old city's historic buildings'. To this it adds that the Soviet rulers ignored 'the exceptional threat to the Jewish population from the National Socialists'. Then, the authors say, the German occupiers tried to use a number of 'suggestible Latvians' to terrorise the civilian population.

But, once again: what really happened? The percentage of Latvian Jews who survived the Holocaust is lower than anywhere else in Europe: 1.9 per cent. When the German chaplain Walter S. arrived in the eastern Latvian town of Rezekne on Sunday, 6 July, 1941, the entire population was out on the street for the funeral of twenty-six victims of the Soviet reign of terror. Their communal grave had been found not long before. Walter S. was called in right away to perform the graveside service and read Revelations 21:4 ('and God shall wipe away all tears from their eyes; and there shall be no more death, neither sorrow, nor crying, neither shall there be any more pain: for the former things are passed away.')

Immediately after the service, the Latvians began the slaughter. 'The Jews, who had been pulling the strings all along, were beaten to death wherever they were found,' the pastor wrote to his wife that evening. 'They were simply cut down; with a shovel if need be, if that was all there was.' He saw Jews being driven into the mass grave and shot. He also described how some of them tried to escape into the river and were cut down there by pistol and rifle fire. Chaplain S. would have rather seen the whole thing proceed in a more orderly fashion. 'That they had to be executed, everyone was in agreement on that. But not this random slaughter.'

Was everyone like this? No. In the Gallery of the Just in a little Jewish museum in Vilnius I saw the portraits of the handful of heroes who braved all dangers to protect and hide Jewish families. The faces were ordinary ones, some pretty, others plump and friendly, but always simple: farmers, woodcutters, railway workers, caring neighbours, honest and brave people. 'It's strange, but my father never talked much about those horrible days,' one son wrote. 'Only when he was on his deathbed, wasted by disease, did he suddenly reach out and grasp my mother's hand and shout: "Take our child and run!"'

During the Second World War 70,000 Jews were murdered in Latvia, 30,000 of them by summer 1941. In Lithuania, almost all of the country's 200,000 Jews were killed. (In Estonia there were only 5,000 Jews to start with, and most of them were able to escape to the Soviet Union.) In his official report, one German officer characterised the farmers' hatred of the Jews as 'monstrous'. They had, as he wrote on 16 August, 1941, 'already done a great deal of the dirty work' before the Germans could intervene.

After mentioning these and other examples, Modris Eksteins correctly observes that the Holocaust was not exclusively a German affair. Hitler may have found 'willing executioners' among his own people, but also among the citizens of the lands he conquered. 'The Holocaust was enacted in the fevered dreamscapes of Eastern Europe where right and wrong were seldom on opposite sides, and where fear and hatred were a way of life. This was a frontier land where borders and peoples had fluctu- ated throughout history, and where the Jew and the Gypsy were symbols of transience and instability. Holocaust was a state of mind here before it was a Nazi policy.'

During these March days of 1999, the sky remains a clear blue. On the square in front of Riga's cathedral you hear only the footsteps of passers-by, and the sound of a cello. Beside the church a boy is playing Bach. Bach in an old, half-German square, on a peaceful, sunny afternoon.

I have been walking around the city all day with that thin Jewish guidebook in my hand. I try to find the place where the Greise Hor Schul once stood, that grisly spot on the corner of the *Gogola Iela*, Gogol Street. Today it is a city square. A few stones are all that remains. A monument was set up here in 1992 to commemorate all the Jews killed in Latvia. When the ruins of the synagogue were pulled down after the war, the cellars were found still to contain the charred bones and skulls of the victims of 4 July, 1941. With no further ado, the cellars were filled with debris and a little park was built over them, in honour of the 'Front Line Workers'. It was only in 1988 that a plaque was put up here.

The Old Jewish Cemetery, too, has become a park, the Park of the Communist Brigades. The cemetery wall was torn down, the old gravestones gradually removed or stolen, the graves finally cleared. At Rumbula, the place where the most Jews – approximately 30,000 – were killed in Riga, a marker has been standing since the 1960s for the 'victims of Nazi terror'. Only since 1989 has the marker clearly indicated that this is a Jewish mass grave.

Riga's little Jewish museum is full of letterheads and advertisements, all signs of Jewish enterprise from the 1930s: Adolf Levi, tailor; Leibovic, photo studio; Schenker & Co, international transport; Rabinovi, building materials; Holländer & Friedländer, art supplies. Beside them hangs an outline map taken from a report by Group A of the *Sicherheitsdienst*, neatly displaying the 'production totals' for autumn 1941. Lithuania: 136,421, with 19,500 still left in the ghetto. Latvia: 35,238, with 25,000 still in the ghetto. Estonia: 963, and the proud note '*Judenfrei*'. Beside all these figures is drawn a neat little coffin, the way civil servants in their reports might draw a house, or a tree, or a little stick figure. Everyone who saw this report in early 1942, in other words, could clearly see that the 'Jewish problem' was not being 'solved', but that the murdering was going on in the tens of thousands.

The museum also contains the famous photographs of Jewish women shivering in their underwear, four women and a girl huddled together against the cold and the shame. Pathetic bloomers. Defenceless nakedness. In the next photograph, other people are undressing. Now there is a boy among them, fourteen or fifteen years old, he's out in front, hands in his pockets. Then we see the group standing at the edge of a dune. In the last one they are tumbling down, amid all the other bodies. Beside it hangs an enlarged photograph of the boy. Now I can see the expression on his face. Great fear, his mouth wide open.

We know the names of the teenage girl who is brushing back her hair shyly with one hand, her head tilted to one side, and the woman with whom she is standing arm in arm. They are Rosa Purve and her mother, both factory workers.

All of the pictures were taken in the dunes right behind this city. On 15 December, 1941, 2,700 men, women and children were killed by the SS and Latvian guards. Long after the war was over the skulls continued to wash up on the beach: many of the Jews were first driven into the sea, and then killed. Years later a German sailor testified that a great many Latvian regulars had come to watch as well: 'Come on men, they're going to shoot some Jews!'

I strike up a conversation with the museum's director, Marger Vestermanis, a man whose face is lined and wrinkled with age. 'Here everything is always denied. If a German soldier had not happened to take a couple of pictures, the massacre in the dunes would never have taken place. That fire in the synagogue: there are still people who claim there was no one in the building. But we have the personal details of the people who were in it, we have eyewitnesses, everything.'

In 1941, Marger Vestermanis was living in Riga too. Back then he was the same age as the boy in the picture, but he does not want to talk about his own experiences. 'I'd rather talk about our research, and about the differences between Latvia and a country like the Netherlands.' He starts telling me about the continuous conflicts and the crisis in which the Baltic States were trapped from the early years of the twentieth century. Before the Second World War, he emphasises, there was no rabid anti-Semitism here. 'There was only an incredible amount of aggression in the air. That's the big difference with the Netherlands. Here there were new regimes all the time, people had to reorient themselves politically all the time. And then suddenly there was the Nazi era: time for the great internal settling of accounts. Between Latvians, too. Who had actually helped the Russians to draft their deportation lists? Who were the communists? During the first six months of the German occupation, 120,000 Latvians were arrested and often shot and killed without a trial. When it's so easy for you to mow down your own countrymen, why worry about some foreign ethnic group?'

Later I read that, at the age of fifteen, Vestermanis had become a cabinetmaker. That is how he saved himself. Every morning he and a large group of men wearing yellow stars would walk from the ghetto into town to work for the German Army. The men had to sort clothing for the *Sicherheitspolizei*, mop floors in hospitals, clean the staff offices. Vestermanis repaired furniture for the SS.

When the group came home from work one November evening in 1941, all of the elderly, the women and children, had disappeared from the ghetto. Later it turned out that the entire Jewish community of Riga, 30,000 people in all, had been taken out to the edge of town. There, most of them were shot beside enormous pits.

For the 4,000 surviving *Arbeidsjuden*, a new ghetto – the Little Ghetto – was roped off. The old ghetto was immediately put to use for new groups of Jews brought in from Berlin, Stuttgart, Vienna, Cologne, Prague and other Central European cities. For most of them, Riga was merely a stopping-off point on their way to the end. Vestermanis himself was finally sent on transport to Courland. Farmers sneaked food to him and his comrades by leaving potatoes and bread along the road. After a while he escaped, and in the woods he joined up with a wandering group of German and Latvian deserters.

But he did not want to talk about that.

Back in Vilnius I had had a strange experience. In this city approximately a third of the Jewish population, some 70,000 people in all, had been executed in a park. Paneriai is the name of the park, and it is only a few kilometres outside town. All those families are still lying there, in mass graves. In my attempts to get there I asked three different taxi drivers, but not one of them had ever heard of the place. Finally I found one who was willing to drive me in that direction.

After a lot of asking and searching, we at last found the spot. It was an echoingly quiet stretch of woods the size of a large campsite, beside some railway tracks. There were hollows and hillocks everywhere, dusted with the last covering of snow. The wind was blowing through the tree-tops. Otherwise nothing, except for a mangy horse and a little monument. Since 1991 one can read that most of the victims were Jewish – before that, the inscription spoke of 'Soviet citizens'. The taxi driver walked along with me, visibly moved. 'The things people do to each other.' About 200 metres further on were the first dachas, beyond a bungalow park.

In the plane to Berlin I flip through the glossy magazine *Baltic Outlook*. I happen upon an interview with the beautiful Ines Misan, raised in a provincial Latvian town, the child of a perpetually drunken father, today a top fashion model in New York and a welcome guest at official openings and parties thrown by the likes of Madonna, Armani and Versace. 'I have two identical Mercedes.'

Question: 'What do you find important?'

Answer: 'Money. I like being able to give myself whatever I want. That's what I love about America. There, if someone has no money, he's lazy. Or he has no education, or he's an alcoholic or a drug addict. A normal person, a man who loves a woman, knows that she needs all that. American men live with their wives for five or six years, then dump them for a younger woman. That's why I've had so many boyfriends.'

Question: 'Can you honestly say that you have never used a man?'

Answer: 'I have, I've done that, more than once. But I didn't do it to be nasty. I married an American because I knew that then I would be allowed to stay in America, but I also liked him a lot. But does the fact that you have a car, money and an apartment in New York mean that you've sold yourself? Sure, girls from the former Soviet Union go out with rich men, but in the end they marry for love and not for money?'

Question: 'What didn't you like about Europe?'

Answer: 'Whenever I go to Paris, I always end up in a bad mood. Because the people there don't wash themselves, they stink, even their so-called aristocrats stink. In America, even the workers wash themselves, they're clean. In Europe, everyone walks around with their nose in the air.'

At the pavement cafés along Kurfürstendamm, people are sitting out in the spring sun. For the first time since 1945, Germany is at war. Kosovo has tried to secede from the Yugoslav Federation, the Serb Army has rolled into the province and is crushing the rebellion with an iron fist. Albanian families are being killed or driven from their villages, hundreds of thousands of people are refugees, Europe fears a new round of genocide.

And now, since yesterday, NATO is intervening. The Germans see it as a 'humanitarian war'. On the evening news I watch aircraft decorated with the Germany military cross rolling out onto the runway, ready to bomb Belgrade and Serb targets in Kosovo. The Bild-Zeitung is selling copies faster than the news-stands can stock them. The front page is framed with the colours of the German flag. 'Our boys, at last!'

Back at my boarding house, the Jewish proprietress is sitting in front of the TV, her face white as a sheet. 'They're actually going to start the bombings,' she says shakily. 'They really are. It's madness, complete madness.' She's afraid, and keeps bursting into tears.

IV April 1918–38

FINLAND
Helsinki
Petrograd/
Leningrad
Tallinn
ESTONIA
LATVIA
Riga
LITHUANIA
Kaunas
Königsberg   Wilna
Witebsk
Moscow
RMAN
MPIRE
Minsk
SOVIET UNION
B-B
Brest-Litovsk
Warsaw
Kiev
POLAND   Rowno
Dnepr
Don
Volga
VAKIA
Chernowitz
Sea
of Azov
Krasnodar
Budapest
JNGARY
RUMANIA
Crimea
Georgian
SSR
(1921)   Tiflis
Batoum
(1921)
(Turk)
Armenian
SSR
(1920)
Black
Sea
Kars
LAVIA
Belgrade
Bucharest
Trabzon
Sarajevo
Serbia
ntenegro
BULGARIA
Sofia
Sinop
Erzurum
rana
Skopje
(1913/20)
Edirne
Istanbul
(1918-23 Allied Occup.)
Ankara
Galipoli
ALBANIA
Saloniki
TURKEY
(1923 Republic)
GREECE
Tigris
Athens
Alexandrette
Lataki
Syria
(1930 Republic)
Cyprus   Tripoli
Lebanon
Crete
Mediterranean

⟵ Geert Mak's Route

0   100   200   300 km

Chapter Sixteen

Berlin

IN THE 1920S, BERLIN CONSISTED OF THREE STREETS. FOR BERLINERS, Unter den Linden was the walking street, the boulevard where foreigners and provincials strolled back and forth to view all the cardboard grandeur of the German Empire. Leipziger Strasse was the shopping street, home to the department stores belonging to Wertheim, Israel, Tietz and Jandorf. Friedrichstrasse was the quaffing street, with bars, beer joints, grand cafés and houses of pleasure back to back. And Wilhelmstrasse was the seat of government, but that was a different story.

In those days one arrived in Berlin by train. Everyone came by train: the Russians arrived at Schlesischer Bahnhof (now Ostbahnhof), the French, English, Belgians and Dutch at Potsdamer Bahnhof. All these station districts with their eating-places, brothels and cheap hotels were like magnets around which the city revolved. 'Asia begins at Schlesischer Bahnhof,' the citizens of Berlin said, pointing to the tracks that ran all the way to Vladivostok and reminding each other of the price of a train ticket to Tokyo: 650 imperial marks. One could as well have said: 'Europe begins at Potsdamer Bahnhof', and point to the tracks running all the way to Hook of Holland. Here lay Europe's natural crossroads. Everything and everyone passed through this city.

In those days, Berlin was a city of soldiers returned home from the front. A picture taken in December 1918 shows troops marching through the Brandenburg gate: their frowning, unshaved faces lined with hunger and cold, silent crowds along the road, the soldiers step briskly to shake off the humiliation. Their comrades were broken, invalids, wreckage, they themselves had become accomplished killers. They were baffled by the defeat that had been suddenly imposed upon them. Until summer 1918, after all, Germany had won one victory after the next. Had a single enemy soldier ever set foot on German territory? And what about the capitulation, right after a new 'left wing' government had come to power, after Wilhelm's fall? 'The victorious front has been killed by a knife in the back,' the army's former commanders, Hindenburg and Ludendorff, had said – and ah, that had to be it.

Berlin was also a city of the exiled and uprooted. After 1918, more than nine million Europeans had been cast adrift. Two million Poles, an equal number of Russians, a million Germans and 250,000 Hungarians were wandering the roads between Berlin, Vienna, Paris, London and Amsterdam.

Berlin was the natural centre to which they were drawn. The signs outside the cafés and restaurants around Nollendorfplatz were written in Cyrillic letters. When bus drivers stopped at Bülowstrasse, they shouted: 'Russia!' In 1918 there were 50,000 Russians in Berlin, by 1924 there were 300,000. The city had six Russian-language dailies and twenty Russian bookshops. There were at least a dozen Russian galleries and cabarets and countless cafés, all full of failed revolutionaries, would-be Bolsheviks, drunken artists, down-at-heel nobility and armchair generals.

In his reports from Berlin, the quintessential journalist Joseph Roth described these exiles' fate. The Hungarian boy Geza, for example, who had accidentally fought on the wrong side during the revolution and now dreamed of becoming a cabin boy on a cruise ship to America. Or Mr Schwartzbach from Galicia, who poured his lonely heart into building a miniature model of Solomon's temple, complete with countless details dreamed up by Schwartzbach himself. After nine years his magnum opus was finished, and disappeared into the back room of a Jewish restaurant on Hirtenstrasse, where no one ever looked at it again. But there were also others, like General Biskupsky, the Beast of Odessa, who hoped to create a 'Russian-German alliance' with his German colleague Ludendorff, towards the day on which both gentlemen would someday return to power. Or Fyodor Vinberg, a former czarist officer and one of the first advocates of a 'final solution' to the 'Jewish problem'. Vinberg walked around all day touting The Protocols of the Elders of Zion, a fake text put together by the czar's secret police to provide 'definitive' proof of an international Jewish conspiracy.

Thousands of such confused and embittered expatriates were wandering in Berlin, running into each other everywhere: anarchists, monarchists, businessmen, everyday citizens, Poles, Hungarians, Russians. They arrived wearing their best clothes, but decline was not long in coming. The jewels were hocked, the hotel tenancy terminated, the elegant clothing became threadbare, Kurfürstendamm was given the nickname 'Nöpsky Prospekt', and the panic grew.

And in that same ragbag of a town, a miracle took place: Berlin became, for Europe, the city of the modern day. Perhaps it had to do with the way Wilhelm's Berlin had suddenly deflated like a balloon in 1918, leaving an enormous vacuum behind and the accompanying demand for new content, radically different forms and ideas. A cursory glance at the names of those who fled the city in the 1930s shows us something of the talent that had gathered in Berlin: Albert Einstein, Arnold Schönberg, Alfred Döblin, Joseph Roth, Heinrich Mann, Arthur Koestler, Marlene Dietrich, Hermann Ullstein.

In the eyes of many, Berlin was a man-eating monster of machines, factories, anonymous housing blocks and speeding trains and cars. It served as the model for *Metropolis*, the masterpiece by Viennese-born cineaste Fritz Lang. But at the same time it was the world in which Bertolt Brecht and Kurt Weill created their *Threepenny Opera*. It was there that Yehudi Menuhin gave his first concert, at the age of thirteen. Looking back on it, he found the Berlin of those days above all a neurotic place. Not an authentic society, 'but a new society based on new money, and on extravagance, brashness, show. Everything became possible. Everything became Experience with a capital "E" — and a capital "X".'

The epicentre of this movement of modernity was Café des Westens. This was where the literary magazines were passed around, hot off the presses. This is where the captains of the avant-garde granted audience to their followers, the expressionists associated with *Der Sturm*, with artists like Oskar Kokoschka, Paul Klee, Vassily Kandinksy, the young Marc Chagall and countless Futurists, constructivists and Dadaists. One of the café's focal points was the Dadaist painter George Grosz, famous for his unflattering prints of whores, beggars, paraplegic war invalids on rollers and fat-necked real-estate speculators, street scenes often not at all far removed from reality.

When the owner of Café des Westens boosted his prices in 1920, they all moved to the Romanisches Café, a huge, ugly space across from the

Kaiser-Wilhelm-Gedächtniskirche. In Paris the tone was set by the *esprit du salon*, but the Romanisches Café had the atmosphere of a popular uprising. Everyone shouted, everyone wanted to be right. Beside the revolving doors sat the old, bearded expressionist painters. Up on the balcony people played chess. There was a sculptors' table, a philosophers' table, a newspaper table, a sociologists' table. Pulling up a chair at a table to which one did not belong gave immediate cause for uproar. George Grosz would come storming in, dressed as an American cowboy, complete with boots and spurs. The Dutch poet Hendrik Marsman made 'calligrams' there ('*Gertrude*. GERTRUDE. GERTRUDE. *Slut*.'), and spoke of city life that had run amok into 'randiness, opium, madness and anarchy'. 'Berlin,' he wrote, 'hung from the sky on a silken thread, a ponderous, colossal behemoth dangling above a roiling inferno.'

Meanwhile, Joseph Roth was touring a different Germany. At the railway station in Chemnitz he saw a conductor eating bonbons out of a box someone had left behind on the train. The conductor was a serious man with hairy fists. Now he was eating this 'candy for naughty girls' as though it were a sausage sandwich. 'Six months earlier this conductor would never have eaten bonbons. Now he is overpowered by hunger.'

In Berlin he sees two prep-school boys marching down a busy street singing:

> Down, down with the Republic of Jews,
> Fucking Republic of Jews,
> Fucking Republic of Jews!

The adults stepped aside to let the boys pass. 'And no one boxed their ears.'

He sees the growth of the German 'periodical forest', its seedbed on Potsdamer Platz. 'The saplings are called the *Völkischer Ratgeber*, the *Kampfbund*, the *Deutscher Ring*, the *Deutsches Tagblatt*, and all are marked with the inevitable swastikas cut deeply these days into every bark.'

Joseph Roth also wrote a striking piece about meeting an old worker who had just been freed after fifty-one years in prison. He had skipped half a century: the final quarter of the nineteenth century and the first quarter of the twentieth. In line with his own sense of propriety, this nineteenth-century man went out onto the busy streets in search of work. He had barely noticed the First World War, he had never ridden in the U-Bahn, never seen a car – let alone a plane – and suddenly all of modern Berlin came crashing down on him. He had not been gone for half a century, no, it seemed more like three.

And now here I am, three quarters of a century further, and I feel almost as lost as that old prisoner who recognised nothing of his old home town. In 1999 one can search long and fruitlessly for the Berlin of the 1920s, for all the old cafés, restaurants, shops, department stores, boarding houses and attic apartments, for the wild city of Brecht, Lotte Lenya, Erich Kästner, Roth and all the others.

Where the Romanisches Café once stood there is now a complex of offices and middle-class residences built in the 1950s. All that is left of old Nollendorfplatz is the pump for watering horses, dating from the days of the kaiser. Along the long stretch of Bülowstrasse behind it, no more than ten pre-war houses are still standing. The busy working-class neighbour-hoods have vanished, replaced now with a great deal of greenery, they have become quiet, park-like districts. The façade of Tietz's department store is still standing, as is the lower level of the Jannowitzbrücke S-Bahn station, although the sound of the train whistles, the steam and the promise of the steel tracks is gone now. Only the old Hackescher Markt station is intact, a red-brick construction with wrought-iron archways and stonework ornaments that have survived this century as though by a miracle.

Where, then, is all the rest? Quite simple: today most of that Berlin lies in the Grunewald woods. It is covered by trees and bushes, a pile of rubble more than a hundred metres high, the Teufelsberg. Here and there a few chunks of cement stick out of the ground, a piece of marble, a rusted pipe. In the distance the new city sparkles in the afternoon sun. One hears a bird singing, a little boy's voice, the barking of a dog, the snapping of a twig. In that silence, the old Berlin lies buried.

———

The Russian embassy is a hundred-metre-long chunk of Stalin along Unter den Linden, built in the early 1950s. It is a boot heel, designed to push

Berlin as far into the ground as possible. Power, grandiosity and indomitability, that is the message shouted to the street by the hard granite, the overbearing façade and the staunch pillars. The building stands on the site of the old embassy, the elegant Courland Palace, famous for the most extravagant rococo hall in Berlin. That exquisite, light-green marble now lies beneath the rubble at Grunewald as well.

These days the embassy swimming pool is open to the public. The good people of Berlin swim laps there while the poolside statue of Lenin stares off into the distance over their heads. Russia is now in dire need of added revenue. When the first Soviet ambassador, Adolf Ioffe, arrived here in April 1918, he had with him a red flag and twelve million marks in starting capital for propaganda work. Berlin, in Lenin's view, would ultimately become the capital of the worldwide revolution. The German's subsidy for his revolution was now being turned against Germany itself. The embassy personnel hung up a huge banner right after Ioffe arrived: 'Workers of the world, unite!' Books, newspapers and pamphlets followed by the carload. Along with them there arrived new personnel, solicited and unsolicited: revolutionaries, adventurers, profiteers from the old Russia, bureaucrats from the new. Much of the antique furniture, many tapestries, chandeliers and paintings evaporated onto the black market. The use of weapons in the building became a serious problem: almost everyone carried a pistol, to 'defend the revolution'.

Despite this chaos, the Soviet embassy was one of the most important diplomatic posts for a defeated Germany. Berlin viewed with extreme interest everything that happened in and around the new revolutionary state. Here, perhaps, lay the future for German trade and industry as well. At the same time – and this double role was one the Soviet mission always retained – the embassy was a permanent jamming station for the German powers-that-be, producing a constant flow of agitprop both open and covert. In this, one man played a vitally important role: Lenin's former travelling companion, Karl Radek. He had come into the city in December 1918, disguised as a wounded German soldier, along with a group of returning prisoners of war. By then he had become a key figure in the Socialist International, and could 'stammer away' – as he himself put it – in ten languages. Yet at the same time he remained a caricature of himself, full of jokes and silly

ideas, always bearded and bespectacled, 'his pockets bulging with newspapers and magazines'.

Radek immediately established contact with the radical wing of the
German revolutionaries, the group around Karl Liebknecht and Rosa
Luxemburg. He held court almost every day in the Ukrainian restaurant
Allaverdi, where the Soviets had their own table and where Radek bantered
with the former country gentlemen and landowners who waited on tables.
All paths crossed in that restaurant, those of the old regime, the nobility,
the middle class, the monarchist officers, the local revolutionaries and the
new Soviet leaders. Radek adhered to the pure Bolshevik line, including
the use of terror against 'classes condemned to death by history'. Rosa
Luxemburg was having none of that. Others joined in the debate. All the
schisms that had arisen among the revolutionaries of Petrograd were re-
iterated in Berlin. In this way there arose German Trotskyites, Bucharinists
and Zinovyevites, and more than that. The stylistic motifs of the Soviet
Union were imitated as well: the constructivist fonts on the posters, the
russe-bolchevique fashion, everything that happened in Russia was repeated
on a smaller scale in Berlin. Except for the revolution itself. That went on
in its own, German way.

Every country and every political movement prefers to write a history
that makes it feel comfortable, a portrait in soft pastels, a story that does
no violence to the self-image. The losers are usually unable to paint any
portrait whatsoever. They simply fade away, and their story is eradicated
along with them.

Only a hair's breadth separated Germany from becoming a kind of
Soviet republic. In November of 1918, mutinies began among the sailors
in the ports of northern Germany and the revolt quickly spread to other
parts of the country. From that moment, a wave of uprisings, demonstrations and riots swept the country from north to south, from east to west
and back again. In Berlin, a full-scale war in the streets was carried on in
spring 1919. For three months, Munich was governed by a Soviet-style
republic. It was only in 1920 that relative calm returned to the country.

The German legend concerning those painful years remained in place
until 1945. After then, no one felt like thinking about that popular rebellion. It was the story with which Hindenburg and Ludendorff poisoned

public opinion after 1918. Both men, as mentioned earlier, announced that it was this social-democratic revolution that had brought defeat to Germany and twisted the knife in the back of the victorious front. That was the charge levelled against Chancellor Friedrich Ebert and his SPD party.

Thanks to letters, affidavits and sections of diaries discovered since, we now know what really happened. On that crucial day of 29 September, 1918, the day on which both army and kaiser suddenly accepted defeat, it was not the 'whining' social democrat Ebert who organised the capitulation, but courageous General Ludendorff himself.

When Ludendorff realised that defeat was inevitable, he manipulated matters in a way that would protect the army and the imperial elite. He advised Kaiser Wilhelm to 'give the government a broader foundation' by granting the social democrats ministerial responsibility. A government with such a broad popular base would then have to establish a truce, and responsibility for the capitulation could be foisted off on others. In this way the army's 'honour' could be preserved, a matter of utmost importance to its Prussian officers. 'They [the social democrats] will have to bring about the peace that must now absolutely be established,' Ludendorff told his staff. 'Those who have mixed this concoction will now have to drink it themselves.' It was a barefaced lie – he himself, the highest army commander, was the one who bore primary responsibility for 'this concoction' – but for the disgraced officers and humiliated nationalists the legend was too attractive not to believe.

On the day of capitulation, half blinded by mustard gas in a ward at the military hospital in Pasewalk, Corporal Adolf Hitler buried his burning face in the pillows and sobbed. 'So everything had been in vain. All the sacrifices and hardships had been in vain . . . Had all this taken place only so that a gang of miserable criminals could now have their way with our fatherland? Was it for this that the German soldier had borne the burning sun and snowstorms? . . . Was it for this that he had lain amid the thundering volleys and exploding shells of gas? . . . During those nights my hatred grew against those who had perpetrated this deed. In the days that followed I came to realise my own destiny . . . I decided to become a politician.'

*

The effect which winter 1918–19 had on the history of Germany and that of the whole of Europe is still underestimated. During those months the foundation was laid in Berlin, just as it had been earlier in Petrograd, for a political movement that was to have a formative effect on the continent for the rest of the century. What's more, this German civil strife would create so much bad blood between the moderate and the radical left that all further cooperation, even that needed to keep Hitler from power, was ruled out. It was a drama, and as in most dramas, the action can be divided into a number of acts.

To start with, the people of Berlin had viewed the entire war through rose-tinted spectacles. Sebastian Haffner remembers how, as a ten-year-old boy, he had stood on tiptoe each day in his attempts to decipher the army bulletins posted on walls. That lent excitement to life, and spice to the day. 'When there was a major offensive underway, with the number of prisoners taken listed in five digits and fortresses taken and an "enormous quantity of military material", then life was a party, your imagination could run on endlessly and you walked with a spring in your step, just as you did later when you fell in love.'

That mood had everything to do with the peculiar situation in which Germany found itself. Although, strategically speaking, the country had long been fighting a defensive war, it appeared the army was still on the offensive. The front lines, after all, remained fixed and far from German territory. As late as 27 September, 1918 the army bulletins were still saying that the war was all but won. Three days later, however, it had all become clear that nothing could be further from the truth. Today we know what was going on behind the scenes, but the Berliners of that day were dumbfounded. The strict imperial order, the world of the 'Hauptmann of Köpenick', all came tumbling down. In the months that followed some 1.8 million rifles, 8,452 machine guns and 4,000 mortars went 'missing' from the country's arsenals.

The new social-democrat government was still busy negotiating a truce when the first rebellion broke out on 30 October, 1918 aboard the *Schillingrede*, off Wilhelmshaven. It was a sailors' mutiny, in response to another mutiny by the country's naval leaders. Despite orders from Berlin to cease all fighting at sea immediately, the naval command had decided of its own accord to stage a major battle. The entire German fleet was

ordered to set sail for a battle that could in no way tip the balance of
the war. The only issue at hand was the honour of the *Kaiserliche Marine*:
the admiralty simply had no intention of surrendering without a fight.
That their action would foil the ceasefire negotiations and needlessly
prolong the war for months was no concern of theirs. Approximately
1,000 sailors from the battleships *Thüringen* and *Helgoland* had the courage
to stand up to this plan. They brought all activity aboard their ships to
a complete halt. This, in other words, was a pro-government mutiny.

The mutineers elected councils of their peers, disarmed their officers,
ran up the red flags, marched into the military brigs to free their comrades
and occupied public buildings. The mutiny became a revolution, and
within a few days the movement was rolling through the major cities in
western Germany. The same thing happened everywhere: soldiers and
workers joined forces, elected their own councils, officers were forced
to capitulate or flee, and civilian authorities knuckled under. On 8
November the pacifist Kurt Eisner and the poet-revolutionary Ernst Toller
proclaimed in Munich the 'Free Popular Republic of Bavaria'. That republic
of soviets would last precisely one hundred days.

The army's top command quickly dispatched the 4th Rifle Regiment
– one of its most reliable units – to Berlin, in case they were needed to
crush a revolution. By the very next day, even these soldiers had experienced a change of heart. They took up defensive positions around the
offices of the Social Democratic Party paper *Vorwärts*. On Saturday, 9
November, hundreds of thousands of badly nourished men and women
marched on the centre of town. They were solemn in their conviction
and prepared for the worst: a bloody Saturday. Those marching up in
front carried signs with texts like 'BROTHERS! DON'T SHOOT!' But the barrack
gates opened for them. In the home of Sebastian Haffner's parents, the
newspaper was suddenly no longer called the *Tägliche Rundschau*, but the
Rote Fahne.

The new, uncertain government, deathly afraid of chaos and a loss of
face, was quite unhappy with this huge and spontaneous popular movement. They feared a repetition of what had happened in Russia, where
the Mensheviks and others had been devoured by their own revolution.
At the same time they were eager to remain on good terms with their
'own' people on the popular councils. Hence their decision to 'suffocate'

the revolution, a term Chancellor Ebert actually used when discussing it with the German military commanders. The social-democratic foremen co-opted leadership of 'their' revolution, appeased the humiliated authorities, restored their power and then allowed the whole movement to fizzle out. Gustav Noske, Ebert's right-hand man, was enthusiastically welcomed by the sailors of Kiel when he arrived as the city's 'governor', and was able within a few days to call off the whole revolution, in the name of the Revolution. The councils remained, but stripped of all power. The *Rote Fahne* became the *Tägliche Rundschau* once more. Thus ended Act One.

That winter the city filled with embittered veterans. Most of them had no job, and often no roof above their head. The Allies were still blockading the German ports. Never had Berlin suffered hunger the way it did during those winter months. By the end of 1918, the city was at least as ripe for a Bolshevik revolution as Petrograd had been in 1917. Still, those events did not repeat themselves. Why?

The first reason was that the revolution's opponents had not come even close to being eliminated, as they had been in Russia. Everywhere on the outskirts of Berlin new troops were being trained, the so-called 'Volunteer Corps', composed of the most loyal and disciplined veterans. These corps, originally set up in order to have a few mobile and efficient army units available at a moment's notice, soon developed into autonomous, hardened combat groups who bowed to no one, except their own commander. Here the foundation was laid for the Waffen-SS.

Gustav Noske – who would later become minister of civil defence – did all he could to maintain order, and was willing to cooperate with anyone to that end, including the leaders of these volunteer corps. What those *Freikorps* leaders actually thought about the social-democrat government, however, is clear from their diaries. 'The day will come when I will settle accounts with this government,' wrote the commander of the *Eiserne Schar*, for example, 'and rip the masks off all this pitiful, whining riff-raff.' Or the commander of the *Werwolf*: 'We declare war on Weimar and Versailles! War – every day and by every means!' The 'Brigade', Hermann Ehrhardt's elite corps, was the first to wear the swastika on their helmets.

Meanwhile a wild bunch had gathered around the person of Karl Liebknecht. They were angry leftist veterans who roamed the city looting wealthy homes and occupying strategic buildings. Along with Karl Radek, Liebknecht hoped to disrupt the coming elections with a coup. The Russian model was to be followed, the soviets of workers and soldiers were to take power at any cost. Liebknecht remained impervious to the fact that most of the German soviets were not themselves at all interested in his plan.

The atmosphere in Berlin grew grimmer by the day, shootings became more frequent, it seemed as though everyone was carrying a pistol or a machine gun. On 28 December, 1918 the omnipresent Count Harry Kessler walked past a number of corpses lying in state. 'No one would be able to tell you what these young lives have been sacrificed for, or for what they have sacrificed themselves.' That same week was the first time Käthe Kollwitz saw young, blinded soldiers out begging in the cold with their barrel organs. 'I was reminded of a cartoon in *Simplicissimus* that appeared years ago, showing an invalid from the war of 1870 playing his barrel organ and singing: "What I am, and what I own, is thanks to you, my fatherland!"'

Around Christmas and New Year, Berlin was a ghost town. 'The stench of civil war was in the air,' George Grosz wrote. 'The plaster had fallen from the houses, windows were broken, many shops had lowered their iron shutters . . . People no longer able to bear their frightened, confined existences had climbed onto the roofs and were shooting at everything that moved, be it birds or people.'

During that same period, Karel Radek succeeded in bringing the Spartacus Movement (named after the gladiator and revolutionary leader) and a couple of other radical left-wing groups under the auspices of a new party: the Kommunistische Partei Deutschland, the KPD.

On Sunday 5 January, 1919 the second revolution broke out at last. The reason was insignificant enough: Ebert had dismissed the self-appointed chief commissioner of Berlin, a radical socialist, and the Spartacists had called for a demonstration. Radical workers took to the streets by the thousand. Then Liebknecht turned up. Harry Kessler heard him from a distance, speaking 'like an evangelist, singing the words with a soothing pathos, lento and with great feeling'. Later he ran into him amid an angry throng on Potsdamer Platz, orating again to an almost unanimously adoring audience. 'I entered into discussion with him, and within a few minutes the majority of the crowd was on my side, particularly the soldiers, because they noticed that he himself had never been in the army.'

Accounts like this would seem clearly to show that most people in the streets of Berlin did not long for a replica of the Bolshevik Revolution. The minutes of the workers' meetings held that week indicate that people were in favour rather of a replica of the German November Revolution, but that this time it should be done right. The 'traitorous' Ebert government was to be ousted. Armed groups were formed, railway stations and newspaper offices occupied. Meanwhile, Karl Liebknecht's followers drove him around the city, his convoy surrounded by trucks bearing red flags and machine guns like a Berlin variation of the triumphal progress of the great Lenin. Yet Liebknecht, as we have seen, was no Lenin. From the very start his career had been that of an activist, a militant, but not that of a political leader.

At this point the situation became very murky indeed. A general strike in which 200,000 workers took part was held on Monday, 6 January. That morning Kessler saw two processions marching through central Berlin: one of social democrats, the other of Spartacists. 'Both were made up of drab, identically dressed shopkeepers and factory maids, both waved red flags and marched in the same bourgeois cadence. The only difference was the text on their banners. They mocked each other in passing and may, perhaps, start shooting at each other before the day is done.' Suddenly he heard yelling. 'The Liebknecht boy! Liebknecht's son!' Karl Liebknecht Jr, 'a slender blond boy', was almost lynched by the social democrats, until a group of Spartacists succeeded in carrying him off to safety.

That afternoon a crowd gathered again on Alexanderplatz, ready to storm the surrounding government buildings. All was in readiness for the start of the Berlin Revolution. And nothing happened.

There was no leadership, there were no decisions made. Radek, newly arrived in Berlin, had not had enough time to impose discipline on the gung-ho Spartacists. He was utterly opposed to the idea of bringing down the government, and behind closed doors demanded that the new KPD immediately withdraw from this 'dead end' struggle.

Liebknecht was a brave, hot-headed lawyer, but no political genius. He had something quixotic about him, Kessler recorded in his diary, and simply lacked Lenin's strategic gifts. Rosa Luxemburg was an exceptional woman, brilliant and poetic, but during those weeks she devoted herself only to her newspaper and her writing. She was quite furious with Liebknecht when she heard that he had started a revolution with no preparations whatsoever: 'How could you? What about our party programme?' The soldiers' council remained neutral: they were in favour of the revolution, but also in favour of public order. By the end of the day most of the demonstrators had simply gone home. Their revolution was over.

After that, Berlin's mood took a drastic swing: the Ebert government received the support of a number of conservative army units. By dint of furious door-to-door fighting they resumed control of one occupied building after another. The building housing the offices of *Vorwärts* was taken, and when the commanding officer asked the chancellor's office what to do with the 300 people who had been occupying it, the answer was: 'Shoot them all.' Being an officer of the old school, he refused. In the end, seven of the occupiers were executed, the others severely beaten. That afternoon the first *Freikorps* marched into the city, led by the proud Gustav Noske. He was aware of the historic role he was playing: 'What do I care? Someone must play the bloodhound; I will not shirk my duty.'

This turn of events marked the start of a wild round-up of radicals and communists. Of the Spartacists who resisted, 1,200 were shot down in Berlin alone. Radek got off easily. He was sent to the Moabit, the huge Prussian prison in the centre of town, and there he remained for a year. As special representative of the new Russia, he was soon granted privileged status. His cell became a well organised distribution point for agit-prop, and he was allowed to receive whomever he chose, ranging from radical activists to prominent figures such as Walter Rathenau. Everyone in Berlin spoke of 'Radek's salon in the Moabit'. Here new ties were forged between a Germany and a Russia in transition.

Luxemburg and Liebknecht, however, did not enjoy the protective support of a major power. They were arrested on 15 January, 1919, close to the Eden Hotel, beaten almost unconscious with rifle butts and then shot through the head. Liebknecht's body was taken to the morgue. Luxemburg, still alive, was thrown into the Landwehrkanal. Their deaths united them at last in the history books, although in real life they had little to do with each other, save for their frequent differences of opinion. Käthe Kollwitz was given permission to draw a final portrait of Liebknecht: 'A garland of red flowers had been laid across the shattered forehead, his face was proud, his mouth open slightly and twisted in pain. His face bore a rather astonished expression.' Runge, the soldier who had beaten Liebknecht's brains in, was the only man in his unit to receive a (brief) jail sentence. Lieutenant Vogel, who had shot Luxemburg, was convicted only of illegally disposing of a corpse; he fled to the Netherlands and was granted amnesty there. Their commanding officer, Captain Waldemar Pabst, remained unpunished and died in his bed of natural causes in 1970.

That was the end of Act Two.

Act Three of the drama comprised the civil war which spread across Germany that winter and on into the summer, flaring up here and there like a peatland fire: in Bremen, in Munich, in the Ruhr, and then again in Berlin. It was a civil war that has been largely erased from European memory, but one fought with great cruelty and violence.

'Strangers were spat upon. Faithful dogs slaughtered. Coach horses eaten,' Joseph Roth wrote of that period. 'Teachers beat their pupils from hunger and rage. Newspapers invented atrocities by the opposition. Officers sharpened their sabres. College students fired shots. Secondary-school students fired shots. Policemen fired shots. Little boys fired shots. It was a nation of gunmen.'

The struggle was an uneven one: unorganised resistance groups from the workers' and soldiers' councils against highly trained and well-armed volunteer corps. At times it was even unclear who was fighting whom. In late January, Harry Kessler noted that the socialist movement had obviously split into two camps, 'because even the troops guarding the [administrative] centre [of Berlin] are socialists, and would probably not support any civil government whatsoever.'

In the capital the war became a normal part of daily life. One eyewitness recounted how schoolchildren excused themselves when they came home late from school by saying that they had been forced to wait in a doorway at Hallesches Tor until the shooting stopped. A westbound S-Bahn train pulling into a station might seem empty, until it stopped.

But that was an illusion: the passengers had simply sought shelter under the seats to avoid stray bullets.

Despite all this, general elections were held on 19 January, 1919 and Ebert's centre-left coalition won three quarters of the votes. The independent parties were buried beneath the landslide. In the People's Republic of Bavaria, Kurt Eisner and his people received only three per cent of the vote. Eisner was no Lenin either, and he resigned graciously. He never got the chance to hold a farewell speech, however: just as he was about to enter the Bavarian house of parliament, he was assassinated by a radical right-wing officer.

After these elections, and despite the violence in the streets, Ebert was able to rely on solid political backing: from parliament, the trade unions, the employers and the generals. And still the fighting went on. The conflict now had to do with better terms of employment, more money and greater autonomy for the councils. The Freikorps ran amok through the country in their own special fashion. One of their leaders, quite correctly, compared them to fifteenth-century mercenaries: 'The landsknechts, too, cared little what they were fighting about, or for whom. The most important thing was that they were fighting. War had become their calling.' In the end there were about seventy such corps, totalling 400,000 soldiers. Many Germans cities were the scene of widespread torture and random executions, atrocities that have survived only occasionally in individual family histories.

From May, the work of the Freikorps was more or less taken over by civil and military courts. Hundreds of death sentences were carried out. This was the Third Act.

The Fourth Act was actually an intermezzo. On 18 August, 1919 President Ebert signed the Weimar Constitution. To a certain extent, the document met the wishes of all concerned: advocates of direct conciliar democracy were given the referendum, liberal parliamentarians received the national parliament, the old-school monarchists were given a president. The new parliament met at Weimar, a city intended to become the symbol of the new German unity, the city of such great minds as Herder, Goethe and Schiller, and also of the pleasant, unsullied German countryside. Weimar was also a city that could be easily defended, if necessary, by a handful of loyal troops, but no one mentioned that in public.

Six months later, on 10 January, 1920, the Treaty of Versailles came into force. The German Army had to be reduced to a quarter of the size of the former *Kaiserliche Armee*. This meant the end of the *Freikorps*. The wild and rowdy mercenaries, however, had no intention of letting that happen; their generals, including Ludendorff, tried to seize power. The Ehrhardt Brigade mentioned earlier refused to be disbanded. On the night of Friday, 12 March, 1920, acting on orders from Wolfgang Kapp and General Walther von Lüttwitz, the *Freikorps'* 5,000 members marched in formation into the heart of Berlin to occupy the government ministries and 'crush without mercy every sliver of resistance'. The hours that followed were chaotic, the army refused to take sides, and finally – at their wit's end – the government called in the help of the former revolutionary forces. 'Fight with every means to preserve the republic! Lay aside all internal differences. There is only one effective remedy for the dictatorship of Wilhelm II: a total shutdown of all economic activity!' Then the government ministers made good their escape.

Nevertheless, the 'Kapp Putsch' was a miserable failure, the general strike called for in such desperation by the former government a resounding success. Never had Germany experienced a paralysis as complete as the one that followed. No trains or trams ran. No letters were delivered. No factory opened its gates. In Berlin there was no water, gas or electricity. Almost all government offices were closed. No newspapers appeared. The leaders behind the putsch had absolutely no grip on society. No decree made it past the minister's offices. Within a week, it was all over. It was the final, unified manifestation of a socialist Germany.

Act Five, the drama's grand finale. The violent revolution went underground. After 1920, a variety of covert groups sprang up amid the ranks of the army and the *Freikorps*. They saw Versailles as an attempt to undermine the old German values, and anyone wishing to consolidate that peace was a traitor, particularly if he happened to be Jewish and an intellectual.

'Everywhere, hatred was in the air,' George Grosz wrote, 'everyone was hated: the Jews, the capitalists, the nobles, the communists, the soldiers, the homeowners, the workers, the unemployed, the *Reichswehr* ... the control boards, the politicians, the department stores and the Jews again ... It was as though Germany had been split in two, and both halves hated each other like in the *Nibelungensage*. And we knew it, or at least we began to realise it.'

The climate was described perfectly by Joseph Roth in his novel *The Spider's Web*, a story of intrigue. The narrative thread followed two protagonists: Theodor Lohse, a frustrated young middle-class man who gradually becomes a political criminal, and Benjamin Lenz, who 'plays the pipes of the carousel' undisturbed, forges reports for foreign missions, steals documents and stamps from government offices and has himself locked up with people in custody, pumps them for information, and waits for 'his' day to arrive. At the centre of the web is Munich. Important secondary characters are Ludendorff and Adolf Hitler.

Roth spun his spider's web with such great care that something miraculous happened: his fantasy was outstripped by historical reality. Starting on 7 October, 1923, his book was published in serial form in Vienna's *Arbeiterzeitung*. The last instalment appeared on 6 November, 1923, and it was on 8–9 November that Ludendorff and Hitler attempted – unsuccessfully – to seize power. In Munich, of all places. But by then the most important switch had already been thrown.

In October 1914 Walther Rathenau wrote to his Dutch friend Frederik van Eeden: 'Who among us knows whether he will live to see peace? We will experience more difficult things than those we have seen as yet. A hard generation will arise, and may even crush our hearts underfoot.' Today a little monument stands at a bend in the shady Königsallee where Rathenau was shot and killed by members of that 'hard generation' on 24 June, 1922. By then he was Germany's minister of foreign affairs and had succeeded in reducing by almost half the reparation payments to be made under the terms of the Treaty of Versailles, and he was doing his best to restore faith in Germany. His greatest mistake was his apparent success at doing just that.

People like Rathenau were in constant danger. According to the propaganda of the extreme right, they were responsible for every disaster that had overtaken Germany since summer 1918: the stab in the back to a

victorious army, the humiliation of Versailles, and after that the collapse
of the economy in the stranglehold of the reparation payments. 'Knallt ab
den Walter Rathenau / Die gottverfluchte Judensau' was a text sung openly by
members of the Freikorps. Rathenau himself was particularly worried by
the way hatred was becoming a commonplace social phenomenon. 'When
the war was over these people were unable to find their way back to
normal life,' he told the society journalist Bella Fromm. 'Now they don't
even want to go back to normal life. The desire to kill and loot has taken
possession of them.' Two days later he was dead.

The murder was carried out by three young students, led by a young
ex-lieutenant. This officer was also part of a spider's web, the Organisation
Consul, led by the same Captain Ehrhardt who had organised the Kapp
Putsch. The schoolboys had convinced each other that Rathenau was one
of the Elders of Zion. They shot him from a moving car while he was
on his way to work.

Rathenau's corpse was at his home for viewing. Count Kessler went
there: 'He lies in an open coffin in his study, where I have spent so much
time with him, his head turned slightly to the right, a very peaceful
expression on his deeply lined face, a handkerchief of fine material draped
over the lowest, shattered part of it.'

The killers made a run for it right away: one of them was arrested
quite quickly, the other two cycled through a great part of Germany, hid
in an abandoned castle, were discovered there and killed in the gunfight
that followed. A few years later the Nazis elevated them to the status of
martyrs.

Historians are always faced with questions that cannot be asked. What
would have happened to Europe, for example, if Winston Churchill had
been killed in 1931 by the New York cab which only nicked him? Or if
Corporal Hitler had been asphyxiated during that last mustard-gas attack
in late summer 1918, instead of merely blinded? Or if the attack on
Rathenau had only . . .

But Rathenau was killed, and Churchill was not.

Rathenau's assassination was probably the most important political killing
of the twentieth century. He was every bit as exceptional a character as
Churchill or Charles de Gaulle, every bit as brilliant and charismatic. He

possessed the vision of Jean Monnet, the clarity of Alfred Einstein. 'You sensed,' Haffner wrote, 'that if he had not been a minister of foreign affairs in the year 1922, he could just as easily have been a German philosopher from 1800, an international financier from 1850, a great rabbi or a hermit.' Like Hitler, he possessed the magic power needed to move masses; the hundreds of thousands of people who took to the streets after his assassination bore witness to that. His power, though, was a positive one, a power that could have made the twentieth century turn out quite differently for Germany and for Europe.

For years, Rathenau had stood at the helm of the Allgemeine Elektrizitäts-Gesellschaft (AEG), a huge German concern his father had helped to found. He was one of the few people to recognise the imminent approach of the First World War, and did everything in his power to turn the tide. That was why he also supported the British arms-control proposal of 1912, a proposal that was immediately scuppered by the kaiser. Rathenau realised that a country's influence was based not only on military force, but every bit as much on economic power and moral authority. In late 1913 he launched a plan to arrive at an economic merger with the countries of Central and Western Europe: *Mitteleuropa*, an early forerunner of the European Union. During the First World War he was responsible for raw materials distribution, afterwards he was an extremely successful minister of reconstruction. But the most important thing was his vision, his style, his way of thinking.

Joseph Roth, too, visited Rathenau's house to pay his respects. 'Throughout the house and throughout this man's entire being, a conciliatory spirit reigned,' he wrote. Downstairs was the 'desk of the public official', upstairs 'the quiet writing table of the private man and writer,' but all of it was surrounded by books: Kant, Goethe, Plutarch, the Bible in all forms and translations. There was 'almost no name from the history of philosophy, the great, endless history of the mind, that was not represented here. And everything he read and wrote breathed that same conciliatory urge . . . 'I come past the place where he was murdered. It is not true that every murder is a single murder. This murder here was a thousandfold, incapable of being forgotten, incapable of being avenged.'

The monument on Königsallee was built a quarter of a century later. The street is narrow, the old trees have been cut down, most of the mansions have been replaced by modern villas, only the bend in the road is still recognisable. A little further along, at number 65, Rathenau's big white mansion still stands. The cars race by, the birds sing songs of spring. This is how oblivion works.

> I, Bertolt Brecht, hail from black forests old.
> My mother bore me through the streets of town
> As I lay hidden in her womb. And the chill of forests cold
> Shall gnaw within me, till death does cut me down.
> In the asphalt city I have my home.

Berlin grew cynical. In the 1920s a separate Berlin began to arise, consisting of artists and the new moneyed classes, with parties that bore no resemblance to the rough-and-tumble soirées of the Mackie Messers and Polly Peachums from right after the war. Now they were snobbish gatherings, ruled by the motto 'Love is the foolish overestimation of the minimal difference between one sexual object and the other.' After the revolution and death, the Berliners were, in their own way, reinventing sex.

Stefan Zweig, an Austrian, was flabbergasted to see how the Berliners 'practised perversion with all the systematic thoroughness in them,' and with all the pathetic eroticism that went along with that. 'Painted boys with artificial bosoms paraded up and down Kurfürstendamm, and not just the professionals: every high-school boy wanted to earn a little pocket money . . . Young girls liked to brag about being perverse: at any school in Berlin, to think that anyone might still be a virgin at the age of sixteen would have been considered ridiculous.'

The American composer Nicolas Nabokov described an evening's carousal with the exotic dancer Isadora Duncan and her brand-new husband, the brilliant and thoroughly unbalanced Russian poet Sergei Yesenin, seventeen years her junior. They ran into Count Kessler, 'accompanied by a dark-haired girl by the name of Judith or Ruth or something, wearing only a dinner jacket, a starched shirt and a top hat, leaving the extremely seductive parts below her waist covered only most imperfectly.' At the party the next evening at Kessler's home, the guests could admire a young black exotic dancer just in from Paris: Josephine Baker. Yesenin would commit suicide in 1925, Duncan was strangled two years later on the French Riviera, when her scarf became tangled in the wheels of her sports car.

'The near future has determined that I am to be ground to sausage meat,' sighed Stephen Labude, one of the main characters of Erich Kästner's novel *Fabian* (1931), during one such wild evening. 'What shall I do in the meantime? Read books? Chip away at my character? Make money? I was sitting in a huge waiting room, and it was called Europe. The train would be leaving in eight days, I knew that. But where it was going and what would become of me, no one knew. And now we are back in the waiting room again, and again it is called Europe! And again we have no idea what is going to happen. We live from day to day, the crisis knows no end.'

That was indeed the crux of it: day by day. Day by day, because every day the country's politics could change, day by day too because every vestige of economic stability was disappearing. In September 1922, Käthe Kollwitz complained for the first time in her diary about inflation and financial difficulties. 'How unbelievably expensive things are. This year Karl will earn approximately 300,000 marks, less than half of what we need. If I did not earn the other half, we would also go under, like countless others. So many are becoming impoverished.'

The figures on German hyperinflation are well known: in 1918, the rate was 4 marks to the dollar; in 1922, 400 marks; after the assassination of Rathenau that quickly became 1,000 marks; and by late November 1923 you could get 4,210,500,000,000 marks for a dollar. The Berlin daily newspaper the *Deutsche Allgemeine Zeitung* cost 30 pfennigs in May 1921; in December 1922, 50 marks; on 1 February, 1923, 100 marks; on 1 June, 300 marks; on 1 July, 1,500 marks; on 1 August, 5,000 marks; on 15 August, 20,000 marks; on 29 August, 60,000 marks; on 12 September, 300,000 marks; and on 19 September, 800,000 marks. The million-mark mark was reached on Thursday, 20 September. The next day it was 1.5 million. The Sunday edition on 28 October cost 2.5 billion marks. The paper of Friday, 9 November, bearing news of Hitler's failed Beer Hall Putsch in Munich, cost 60 billion marks.

The key effect of this inflation was the disappearance of every sense of value. Musicians and performers were paid after the show with suitcases full of banknotes. They took them to a shop right away to buy the most necessary items, for by morning the money would be worthless.

The Russian writer Ilya Ehrenburg, living in Berlin at the time, was dragged along one evening 'to an interesting place'. He arrived in a neat and tidy middle-class apartment, with paintings of family members in uniform on the walls. 'We were given lemon phosphates with a shot of alcohol in them. Then the host's two daughters came in – naked. They started dancing. One of them began talking about Dostoyevsky's novels. The mother looked hopefully at the foreign guests: perhaps they would let themselves be seduced by their daughters and pay for it, in dollars, of course.'

At the same time, many people became exceedingly rich during this same period, particularly if they were young and good at playing the money markets. Part of the city's youth lived in a world that somewhat resembles that of the New Economy bubble of the late 1990s; school parties flooded with champagne, twenty-year-old millionaires supporting their parents. While the 'old rich' had saved their money, the 'new rich' spent theirs as fast as possible. That turned the world completely upside down. The old Germany, after all, had been a culture of the frugal.

What was the economic background to these odd times, when everything – including love – was mercurial and relative? It was all because of the reparation payments demanded by that damnable Versailles, the right-wing Germans shouted. (They conveniently forgot that there actually *was* a great deal to be compensated for: in Belgium in particular, Germany had caused unbelievable damage for no good reason at all. In addition, the total sum to be paid was lower than the damage claims France had been forced to pay Germany less than fifty years earlier.) According to the terms of the treaty, Germany would have to pay 1.8 billion marks in damages annually, up to the year 1988.

In truth, however, the reparation payments had only a minimal effect on inflation. The collapse of the mark was due primarily to the enormous public debts engendered by the Germans themselves between 1914–18, for a total sum of 164 billion marks. Of that, 119 billion had been raised with the sales of patriotic war bonds – those who put their savings into such bonds never saw their money again – while the balance was funded by simply printing more money. The Germans had hoped to set everything right once they had taken Paris and could demand damages from the French and British. Germany's tight squeeze, therefore, was not caused solely by the reparation payments, but also and most importantly by the country having gambled on themselves receiving reparation payments.

The crowning blow was the damage the country had incurred in the war. For example, in the late 1920s the German government was paying benefits to 761,294 war invalids, 359,560 war widows, 73,781 fatherless children, 56,623 orphans and 147,230 parents who had lost one or more sons, for total expenditures of more than a fifth of the national budget. The final blow to the economy was dealt by the primitive way in which the government tried to deal with the problem. They printed more money. And printed it faster and faster.

Then, suddenly, the whole crisis was over. Within three months a new chancellor, Gustav Stresemann, had the Germany economy back on its feet. On 15 November, 1923 a new currency was issued: drab little banknotes on which was printed 'Rentenmark'. The value of the new currency was supposedly based on collateral consisting of Germany's total gold reserve, ground and other property. In reality, none of that was true, but the fact that the Germans believed it turned out to be enough. On Saturday, 17 November the *Deutsche Allgemeine Zeitung* cost '90 billion marks = 15 Goldpfennige'. On Friday, 22 November the paper cost '150 billion marks = 15 Goldpfennige'. Two weeks later, it was still 15 Goldpfennige. The currency held its ground. Within a month the new mark was back on a normal footing with the dollar, at an exchange rate of 4.2:1.

With the arrival of the Rentenmark, things quieted down. The pressure imposed by the reparation payments was eased by means of an ingenious plan drawn up by the American banker Charles Dawes. American money was actually being invested in the country. In 1925, Stresemann was replaced as chancellor, but continued to play an important role until 1929 as minister of foreign affairs. General Hindenburg was elected president in 1925, and even the conservatives began gaining a little confidence in Weimar under the reign of this surrogate kaiser.

International relations, too, grew less tense. For the first time, the European governments were trying to use the League of Nations to resolve a number of issues: the consequences of the collapse of the Austrian economy, the Macedonian conflict between Greece and Bulgaria, the status of the cities of Danzig and Vilnius, the issue of the Saar and the former German colonies, and the administration of the trust territories of Syria and Palestine. The French minister of foreign affairs, Aristide Briand, was tireless in his efforts on behalf of Franco-German reconciliation. He launched an early initiative for something like a European federation, aimed at creating a lasting peace within a broader context as well.

The Briand-Kellogg Pact of 1928, in which the world 'unconditionally and definitively' renounced war as a political instrument, was signed by fifteen states, including France and Germany. The League of Nations, however, never implemented the pact. That was typical of the League's role: at Versailles, the Allies had left the solving of a number of thorny and potentially dangerous issues – the status of Danzig was one of those that finally precipitated the Second World War – to the League, but failed to give this new institution the power to implement decisions. The United States withdrew from the League at the very last minute, even though President Wilson considered the organisation to be the summit of his life's work. Once the war was over, the two other initiators, France and England, focused primarily on internal affairs. On every front, the League of Nations lacked all the necessary clout.

Jean Monnet, the former cognac dealer, was only thirty when the League was established. He became its deputy secretary-general. 'We achieved results,' he wrote later. 'We overcame crises . . . we used new methods to administer territories, we stopped epidemics. We developed methods of cooperation between countries which had until then known only relations based on the advantage of power.' But at the same time, he admitted, he and his fellow diplomats severely underestimated the problem of national sovereignty. 'At every assembly the people spoke of common interests, but that was always forgotten again in the course of the discussion: everyone was obsessed with the impact a possible solution could have on them, on their country. As a result, no one really tried to solve the problems at hand: their greatest concern was to find answers that would not damage the interests of everyone seated around the table.'

The right of veto – by which any state could block any decision – was, he said 'both the symbol and the cause' of the League's inability to rise above national interests.

———

Today, one of the permanent exhibits at Berlin's Jüdische Museum is a clip from the film *Menschen am Sonntag*, a unique collage of Berlin street scenes from summer 1929. We see a calm, prosperous city with busy sidewalk cafés, with children playing in the streets and relaxed people out for a walk, with young people sunbathing on the shores of the Wannsee, and a little parade by the *Reichswehr* along Unter den Linden – with, and this is striking, many dozens of civilians marching along with the soldiers down both sides of the street.

Those summer Sundays of 1929 were Berlin's last peaceful moments. After 1924 Germany had grown calm. Politics had become an orderly affair, wages rose, food was good, and things could have stayed that way forever. 'From 1926 on, there was really nothing worth talking about,' Haffner recalls. 'The newspapers had to go looking for their headlines among events abroad.' Street life was marked by ennui, and everyone was 'most heartily invited' to be happy in his or her own fashion. The only problem – and one remarked upon as well by Rathenau before his death – was that, generally speaking, no one responded to that invitation to respectability. The young people of Germany had grown addicted to polit- ical excitation, unrest and sensation.

Later, the sociologist Norbert Elias would provide yet another explan- ation. In his view, the deep dissatisfaction with the Weimar Republic had everything to do with the abrupt transition from the semi-absolutist regime of Wilhelm II to a modern parliamentary democracy. That process usually takes a number of generations, but in Germany the change came within two to three years. 'The personality structure of the German people was focused on the absolutist tradition that had governed them for centuries without interruption,' Elias wrote. This was accompanied by the military order and obedience that had long permeated Prussian society, a way of thinking that is relatively simple in comparison with the compli- cated demands posed by life under a parliamentary democracy. What is more, the rules of a multi-party democracy emphasise precisely those values held in low esteem within military tradition. Like every parliamentary democracy, Weimar required a complicated culture of negotiation, self-restraint, mediation and compromise. The old, semi-absolutist Germany, however, abhorred the happy medium, it cried out for honour, loyalty, absolute obedience and firmness of principle. It created, in Elias' words, 'a landscape marked only by bans and rules'. And as the Weimar years wore on, many Germans felt a growing nostalgia for that old world.

This process was a slow one, and modern, intellectual, artistic Berlin had no idea what was going on at first. Dr Joseph Goebbels, Hitler's Gauleiter in Berlin from 1926, went almost unnoticed during the first Weimar years. His newspaper, Der Angriff, sold scarcely 2,000 copies a week. When Hitler's political ally Ludendorff announced his candidacy for the presidential elections in 1925, he made no headway at all. In the 1920s, no more than 20,000 copies of Mein Kampf were sold.

Nor did the results at the polls provide any indication of what was looming on the horizon. The 1925 elections were a triumph for the established order: Hindenburg, born in 1847, received 14.7 million votes, former chancellor Wilhelm Marx – the joint candidate of parties including the Catholic Centre Party and the SPD – received 13.8 million, and the communists' Ernst Thälman took 1.9 million. Hitler's National Socialists achieved no more than 280,000 votes. In the next elections, in 1928, when the social democrats won for the last time, the Nazis did not do much better: of the 500 seats in the Reichstag, they received only twelve. Two years later, when 'this rabid postman of fate' (as Ernst von Salomon once referred to Hitler) made his breakthrough, the thinking part of the nation was – with only a few exceptions – taken completely by surprise.

It was more than blindness alone. The intelligentsia, too, could summon up absolutely no enthusiasms for the established order. No one stood up for the Weimar Republic. Most of the nation's writers agreed with Thomas Mann, who openly declared war on politics as a whole 'because it makes people arrogant, doctrinaire, obstinate and inhuman'. Later, by the way, he changed his tune. In cabarets like the Tingel-Tangel the republic was constantly ridiculed, while Hitler played the part of the harmless idiot. Kurt Tucholsky called the German democracy 'a façade and a lie'.

Most of the conservative Bildungsbürger had no notion of the undercurrents in their society. The fact that no less than 50,000 Berlin students had taken to the streets during the Kapp Putsch to demonstrate in favour of that ultra-right wing coup did not register with them. And they did not even want to know what those students read: Ernst Jünger's books about the mystical *Männerbund* that arises between warriors, Alfred Rosenberg's stories about the Jewish conspiracy, Arthur Moeller van den Bruck's treatise on the new Germany, *Das Dritte Reich* (1923), which envisioned a 'spiritual volk community' led by a single führer; each of these books were sold in huge numbers. They were blind, too, to the culture of political murders, to the intimidation to which a person like Albert Einstein, for example, was exposed. 'I'm going to cut that dirty Jew's throat!' a right-wing student had shouted during one of Einstein's lectures. Nor did they have a particularly clear view of the country's economic situation, shaky despite the seeming stability.

In the cellars of Berlin police headquarters, close to Tempelhof airport, the dirty brown underworld of the 1920s is still on display for the rare visitor. Look, there we have Karl Grossmann, a fat butcher with a permanent shortage of domestic help. During a three-year period he scattered the pieces of twenty-three female corpses all over Berlin, in canals, in garbage pails, pieces of housemaid everywhere. He also had a colleague, Georg Haarmann, who specialised in young boys. After having sex with them he literally ripped their throats out. Perhaps twenty-five boys disappeared into the Leine. The police finally caught up with him after children playing in the area kept finding bones and skulls. And then there was Horst Wessel, whose name lives on in the celebrated Nazi anthem 'Die Fahne hoch', which chiselled his name in granite as a saint and a martyr of the swastika.

On 17 January, 1930, SA-Sturmführer Wessel was found badly wounded in his rented room on Grosse Frankfurterstrasse. The authorities immediately suspected a political motive, but things were more complicated than that. The rumour going around the underworld was that Wessel had run foul of the pimp 'Ali' Höhler, concerning one of the whores Höhler protected. Meanwhile, Goebbels was busy moulding him into a new hero of the movement, a victim of the Red hordes. He wrote a moving account of his visit to the hospital bed of this 'Christian and socialist', and when Wessel finally died on 23 February, Goebbels organised a funeral the likes of which Berlin had rarely seen. In the long run, it turned out that Wessel had simply failed to pay a great deal of back rent, and that the 'proletarian foreclosure' instigated by his landlady had got a little out of hand. That, at least, is what the police files say.

In 1922 a list was published of recent political killings. Since 1918, the German extreme left was responsible for 22 murders, and the radical right for 354. Of the left-wing killings, seventeen culprits were punished. Of the 354 murders committed by right-wingers, 326 remained unsolved. Only two right-wing murderers were brought to trial. Of the convicted left-wing murderers, ten were executed and the remaining seven received prison sentences averaging fifteen years. The right-wing murderers received an average sentence of four months. The thin excuse 'shot while trying to escape' had already made its appearance. Assailants were becoming increasingly deft at 'working over' their political opponents.

The great hero of Berlin's police museum is Detective Ernst Gennat. It remains a mystery why no television series has yet been based on his life, for no premise could be more perfect. Ernst Gennat weighed 135 kilos and, together with his faithful secretary Bockwurst-Trüdchen, solved almost 300 murder cases between 1918–39. His size inspired confidence and awe, and he despised all forms of physical exertion. For his work in the field he had a special car built to serve as mobile police department and forensics lab. Gennat was also the founder of 'forensic undertaking', by which mutilated and half-decayed corpses could be reconstructed. He was absolutely opposed to the use of force: 'Anyone who touches a suspect is out on his ear. Our weapons are our brains and strong nerves.' Shortly before his death he married, to make use of the police department's pension benefits for widows – but Trüdchen was not the lucky girl.

In those years, part of the Berlin underworld had organised itself under the guise of sports clubs, wrestling associations, sometimes even savings clubs. Their names reinforced the illusion of bourgeois respectability: the Ruhige Kugel, Immertreu and the Lotterie-Verein. They worked along the lines of a guild. When one of their members was arrested, his legal costs were paid. The wives of imprisoned members received a living allowance, and when one of them had to disappear from sight for a while, that was arranged as well. Reading about these *Ringvereine*, you see before you the gangs that would ultimately bring forth part of Berlin's brown-shirted

SA, the clubs of the unemployed who were given uniforms by the Nazi leaders and paid for their services in beer and sausage. Wasn't the first SA unit in Wedding, for example, called the 'Band of Robbers'? And the one in Neukölln the 'Scoundrel's Bond'? And wasn't the Horst Wessel case a typical underworld vendetta?

In the course of the 1920s, former army officers moulded some of these unoffical clans into symbols of a new order, paramilitary groups that marched through the city, emanating a hitherto unknown élan with their gleaming uniforms and rigid discipline. The original handful of sympathisers with the Band of Robbers soon became thousands, then tens of thousands. In the working-class neighbourhoods, 'SA marschiert' became a household term. The unemployed housefather who joined the SA suddenly *became* someone, a part of a 'powerful folk community' and that lofty mood was raised to even greater heights with torchlight parades and other rituals. A new jargon arose in which words such as 'pure', 'duty', 'soldierly' and 'fanatic' took on a special, laudatory meaning. And there was equality. Within the SA there were no classes; that, too, was part of its attraction. 'You had the son of the preacher, the son of the judge, the son of the doctor, the son of the lathe operator and of the unemployed man,' a former SA member recalled years later. 'We all marched side by side, all in the same uniform, all filled with the same ideals, shoulder to shoulder, without social distinction, without a sense of class conflict.'

It was on 17 August, 1924 that Harry Kessler became acquainted at first hand with this 'new order'. In Weimar he found himself in the midst of the 'German Days' organised by the National Socialists. The shopping streets were filled with pennants and flags with swastikas on them, but he detected little enthusiasm as yet on the part of the population. On the balcony of the national theatre, amid a score of swastika banners, General Ludendorff made his appearance. Someone launched into a tirade against Stresemann's 'Jewish republic'. Ludendorff gave a speech as well, but lost track of what he was saying halfway through and stopped. The general's face was saved when the band nearby struck up a fast march. This was followed by a parade of 'swastika-bearers': straight-backed older gentlemen carrying umbrellas, but very few veterans, few Iron Crosses, lots of foolish students.

The Nazis claimed that somewhere between 30–60,000 supporters had come to Weimar, but Kessler estimated that there were no more than 8,000. The reason for that, he said, was clear: a lack of money and a lack of good speakers. 'No money and no spirit, that's not how one forges a popular movement, let alone a revolution.' He was right about that. For it was precisely with regard to those two conditions that the Nazi movement was about to change beyond recognition.

On Black Thursday, 24 October, 1929, the Wall Street stock market collapsed. The crisis was felt everywhere in the world, but for Germany it came as a fatal blow. The country's cautious economic recovery, after all, was being financed largely from the United States. In effect, the Dawes Plan was little more than the forced circulation of money: Germany paid recompense to England and France, those two countries paid off their war debts to America, the United States then lent that money to Germany, and so on and on. From 1929, America suddenly kept the payments for itself, the pump broke down and the German economy collapsed once more.

In the course of January 1930, German unemployment rose from 1.5 million to 2.5 million. By April, Berlin alone had 700,000 unemployed. Shops closed by the hundred. The members of the lower-middle class, who had only just caught a whiff of prosperity, were forced back into the tenements, and the workers were put out on the street. Count Kessler lost almost his entire fortune, was forced to sell his publishing house, his Renoirs and Van Goghs, and finally even his books. In the woods around the city, thousands of the unemployed set up tent camps with collective kitchens, schools and playgrounds. In 1931, four million Germans were unemployed; by 1933 that figure had risen to six million.

Looking back on it, it is amazing to see how casually the peaceful Weimar period disintegrated. The first glimpse of decay is seen in the statistics. In summer 1929, Hitler's NSDAP had approximately 120,000 members. One year later, there were almost a million. The Nazis had expected to win a considerable number of parliamentary seats in the elections on 14 September, 1930, but even so were amazed to see their party skyrocket from twelve seats to more than a hundred. The NSDAP had suddenly become the second biggest party in Germany, after the social democrats. Financiers, particularly those from heavy industry, flocked to the party. The captains of Krupp, Klöckner and IG Farben were good for at least a million marks annually. After 1930, covert funding grew considerably.

'1932 was the year of the great contest. First came the presidential elections. Hitler – after a great deal of hesitation – entered the ring against a fatigued Hindenburg. He lost the first round, but still received 11.3 million votes, which meant his constituency had doubled again in two years. Now the Nazis gave it their best shot. The party applied the most modern campaign techniques. Hitler was flown around the country in his own private plane, allowing him to visit twenty cities a week and speak to a quarter of a million people each day. Goebbels had films made of Hitler's speeches, and 50,000 gramophone records so that even the smallest meeting rooms and cafés could hear him speak. At the height of the campaign, Goebbels had – in today's money – a budget of more than half a million euros a week at his disposal: the industrial financiers had apparently become even more enthusiastic. In the long run, Hindenburg was re-elected (with 19.4 million votes), but Hitler (with 13.4 million) had won an additional two million supporters.

The Nazi campaign went on nonstop. The focus was now on Prussia, that great social-democrat stronghold where two thirds of the German population would be going to the polls in two weeks' time. At one fell swoop, the Nazis became the biggest party there. With the support of the communists, they immediately entered a motion of no confidence against the prime minister, Otto Braun. The prudent social democrat withdrew from his post. A provisional government was set up; the SA provoked more and more disturbances; and after a few months Chancellor Franz von Papen, along with Hitler, seized the opportunity to place Prussia under political receivership. That step – in fact, an outright coup – was completely unconstitutional, but protest was to no avail. Political violence continued to mount, particularly from within the ranks of the SA. During the month of July alone, sixty-eight people were murdered and many hundreds assaulted. The victims were most often communists and socialists.

On 31 July, 1932, national elections were held for the Reichstag. The NSDAP again became the most powerful party by far: it doubled its seats, to 230 of the 604 now contested. According to constitutional procedure,

Hitler had to be appointed chancellor: more Germans had voted for his party than for any other. But this situation was unacceptable to the nation's political grandees. Hindenburg refused to appoint Hitler chancellor. He could not justify it, he said, 'to God, my conscience or my fatherland' if he were to place all power in the hands of one party, especially one party so singularly intolerant towards those with other ideas. Behind closed doors, he said that he would appoint 'that little corporal' to the position of postman, but never to that of chancellor.

The threat posed by the Nazis did not drive the social democrats and communists closer together. Their relations were still based on old grudges. In early 1932, the KPD chairman Ernst Thälmann went so far as to call the social democrats 'the moderate wing of fascism'. Ten months later, however, this did not keep the communists from joining forces with the National Socialists in a wildcat strike of Berlin trams and buses against the moderate proposals made by the 'reformist' trade unions. On Alexanderplatz, Nazis and 'Kozis' jointly stormed a tram running on line 3, fought against the police together at the Schöneberg garages and co-operated in plundering a car belonging to the SPD house organ *Vorwärts*. Tauntingly, that paper wrote: 'Yesterday one still heard cries of "Brown-Shirted Thuggery" from one side, and "Red *Untermenschen*" from the other! But today a new and solid alliance has been forged! What class-conscious worker could fail to blush at the sight!'

Papen, meanwhile, remained in office at the head of a 'national cabinet' and governed by decree. Hitler was furious. Finally, the Reichstag passed a vote of no confidence against Papen. The violence in the streets increased. New elections were scheduled. On 6 November, two days after the Berlin public transport strike, the Nazis lost two million votes, but nonetheless remained the biggest party with 196 of the 584 seats.

Interestingly enough, it was not in Berlin's working-class neighbourhoods that the NSDAP lost the most votes. Through their brief alliance with the Nazis, the communists had unintentionally given a signal that was to have far-reaching consequences: the Nazis, at least in certain workers' circles, were no longer pariahs. They belonged.

The day after the elections, the fifteenth anniversary of the October Revolution was celebrated with a flourish at the Soviet embassy on Unter den Linden. The arrival of the new order was in the air. It was to be the last major Soviet gathering – for the time being – in Berlin. Even Papen dropped in. The caviar was flown in from Moscow, the wines from the Crimea. Hundreds of guests, diplomats, army officers and journalists elbowed up to the buffet tables, while Lenin looked on.

Throughout that entire year, the success of Stalin's Five-Year Plan had been the talk of Berlin's diplomatic and financial circles: entire cities had been raised from nothing in the Soviet Union, gigantic factories for machinery and tractors built. The country was laying the foundations for lightning-fast industrialisation. In the eyes of many Europeans, the East was giving flower to an attractive and tempting alternative: it was energetic, modern, socially aware and united. Even the Nazis were fascinated by what was going on in Russia: the four-year plan launched by Göring in 1936, with which he hoped to create the most powerful military-industrial complex in Europe, was clearly inspired by the Soviet example.

In winter 1932, the German political scene was caught in a deadlock. The new chancellor, General Kurt von Schleicher, tried to forge a national coalition from all the parties represented in the Reichstag. On the right he hoped to draw the most reasonable among the Nazis into his cabinet, and on the left the most modern social democrats. He was also hoping in this way to cause a rift within the Nazi party itself. Following the electoral setback in November, Hitler was encountering major problems within his party, his support was dwindling quickly and the Nazis were faced with huge debts. Schleicher, on the other hand, was in complete control, and enjoyed the full support of the military.

In retrospect, it was this temporary setback that finally brought Hitler to power: by early 1933, a number of the country's conservative leaders considered him weak enough to cooperate with safely. On 4 January, the banker Kurt von Schröder arranged a dinner at his villa in Cologne for Franz von Papen and Adolf Hitler. Later that month they met again, at the home of the champagne dealer Joachim von Ribbentrop in the Berlin suburb of Dahlem. Within the political elite, a milieu from which he had always been carefully excluded, Hitler had become *salonfähig*.

And so it was that Papen betrayed his successor and old friend Schleicher. He told Schleicher about the meeting, and claimed that he had tried to win Hitler's support for Schleicher's government. In fact, however, Papen and Hitler had decided to form a new coalition and bring about Schleicher's downfall at the first opportunity. Hitler was to be made chancellor, and Papen would 'neutralise' this with cabinet ministers of his own persuasion. 'He is going to work for us,' is what he literally said about Hitler.

The chief remaining obstacle was the president. Papen had something of a father-son relationship with Hindenburg. For that reason, he was the perfect person to undermine the president's resistance to Hitler's chancellorship. How he did so is a mystery, even today. Papen probably convinced the old gentleman that this was the only way to prevent a putsch. In addition, the presidential family was caught up at that moment in a tax-evasion scandal, and pressure was perhaps exerted on Hindenburg's son Oskar as well.

Whatever the case, the old general became party to the conspiracy against Schleicher. When the chancellor reported to Hindenburg in January that his plans for a national coalition had failed, everyone expected the president to disband parliament and call for new elections. Instead, however, he commissioned Papen to form a new government. That was all the opportunity Hitler needed to slip into the chancellery.

The very next day, Göring was able to hang the swastika banner in front of the ministry of internal affairs. Now the Reichstag could be burned to the ground, a wild, solo attack by the Dutch Soviet-style communist Marinus van der Lubbe that was immediately put to good use by the Nazis. Now a host of decrees and emergency measures could be put into effect. Now all the critical journalists, communists, social democrats, artists, Jews and other troublemakers could be arrested and ground to a pulp.

Was Berlin, in 1933, a pro-Nazi or an anti-Nazi town? Only five days before the change of power, on 25 January, the communists organised a mass demonstration against 'the rise of fascism'. Hundreds of thousands of people took part, and even *Vorwärts* was impressed: 'In the bitter cold and lashed by the wind they walked for hours, in threadbare coats, thin jackets and worn-out shoes. Tens of thousands of pale faces which spoke of a crisis, and which spoke of the sacrifices they were willing to make for the cause they consider just.'

Five days later, on the evening of 30 January, tens of thousands of

Brownshirts bearing torches filed past the chancellery, where Hitler – in evening attire – looked on from an open window. Out on the street, Kessler noted 'a complete carnival mood'. The Nazis were ecstatic about this 'day of national exaltation' with its 'roiling, red and brightly burning sea of torches'. The other part of the city's population was stunned. 'Thinking' Berlin had never thought that Hitler could come to power. For a little while, everyone hoped against hope that it would all turn out well. And then the great exodus began. Bertolt Brecht was among the first to pack his bags, immediately after the fire at the Reichstag. Kessler went to Paris in early March and never returned: he died four years later, forgotten and penniless, in a French village inn. At Kessler's funeral, old André Gide saw none of the artists whom he 'during his life had so generously caused to be indebted to him'. The Mann family left for France, and from there for California. Joseph Roth began his melancholy wanderings across Europe, until he met his end at the Parisian Café de la Poste, felled by wine, Pernod and cognac.

The Romanisches Café emptied out. The writer Hans Sahl saw the last customers reading, playing chess, consulting maps and railway time-tables, and writing letters. 'Blessed was he with an uncle in Amsterdam, a cousin in Shanghai or a niece in Valparaíso.' In March of 1933, Sebastian Haffner was still enjoying idyllic afternoons with a Jewish girlfriend in Grunewald. 'The world was very peaceful and springy.' Every ten minutes a cheerful class of schoolchildren would pass by, led by a prim teacher wearing a lorgnette, and each class greeted him enthusiastically and in unison: '*Juda verrecke!*' In the end, he was able to escape to London in 1938.

Some had drawn their conclusions earlier, however, and had left the country after the 1932 elections. Albert Einstein left for California. George Grosz, who had already received threats, had a nightmare about the coming disaster and immediately, impulsive as he was, bought a ticket for America. Marlene Dietrich had harboured a deep hatred of the Nazis from the start. After 1932, she never set foot in Berlin again. She became a beacon to the German exiles in Hollywood and Paris, and during the war she performed on all the Allied fronts, a soldier among the soldiers. Only after her death, sixty years later, did she return to her city, to Friedhof III in Friedenau. She received flowers and many tributes, a square close to the Tiergarten was named after her, but there were also those who spat on her grave, and furious letters appeared in the papers: 'Whore!' 'Traitress!'

The last relatively normal parliamentary elections were held a month after Hitler took power: this time, the Nazis won 43.9 per cent of the vote. A new secret police force, the Gestapo, was formed. The first concentration camp was built at Dachau two weeks later. In his diary, the Jewish professor Victor Klemperer noted that the maid of one of his Jewish colleagues had already quit her job. 'She had been offered a safe position, and Herr Professor would soon probably no longer be able to afford a maid.' At a chemist's he saw a tube of toothpaste with a swastika on it. 'People have not yet started to fear for their lives, but they fear for their daily sustenance and freedom.'

A few days later, on 31 March, the Reichstag – already sorely decimated after the arrests of communists and social democrats – granted Hitler dictatorial powers. Special penal courts, the *Sondergerichte*, were now established and a new category of crimes coined, including *heimtückische Angriffe*, foul criticism of the government. The first anti-Semitic measures were announced: Jews were to be dismissed from posts at schools and in public offices, and Jewish businesses were to be boycotted. New words were heard everywhere: *Gleichschaltung, Rassenschande, Belange, Artfremd.* Käthe Kollwitz was dismissed from the Academy of Arts. For being a member of the social-democrat association of physicians, her husband Karl lost all his national health patients in one fell swoop. One month later, on Opernplatz, across from the university, the books of Walter Rathenau, Heinrich Heine, the Mann brothers, Alfred Döblin, Stefan Zweig and others were burned. Bella Fromm wrote: 'Not a day goes by without the Gestapo arresting an "unreliable" colleague.' Meanwhile, 'Heil Hitler!' had become the mandatory greeting, the Horst-Wessel song the mandatory hymn:

> Die Strasse frei den braunen Bataillonen!
> Die Strasse frei dem Sturmabteilungsmann!
> Es schaun aufs Hakenkreuz voll Hoffnung schon Millionen.
> Der Tag für Freiheit und für Brot bricht an.

That summer, the term 'total state' first began to appear in Nazi speeches. Shortly afterwards, the NSDAP was declared the only legal party in Germany. Under pressure from the Nazis, the German Evangelical Church replaced the newly chosen Reichsbischof Friedrich von Bodelschwingh with army chaplain Ludwig Müller. Shortly after his appointment, Pastor Müller had himself photographed in a toga, his arm stretched out in the Nazi salute; it was in protest against this coup that the Bekennende Kirche was established.

In July 1933, Hitler signed a concordat with the Vatican guaranteeing the autonomy of the Catholic Church in Germany, as long as they did not meddle in affairs of state. (This did not, by the way, keep the Vatican from having the anti-Nazi encyclical *Mit brennender Sorge* read aloud in all German Catholic churches in 1937.) In late November the Gestapo was officially given supra-legal status. A little over a year after the Nazis had seized power, Kurt and Elisabeth von Schleicher were murdered by six SS men in their villa on the Wannsee.

My long wait at Tempelhof airport is like slipping back sixty years in time. Tempelhof is now a little airfield and a big museum, all rolled into one. Of all the airfields I have ever seen in Europe, it is perhaps also the most deserving of the description 'field': once this was a parade ground where planes were occasionally allowed to land, and that is how it has remained, here in the middle of the city. A hypermodern terminal was built here in 1934. With its enormous semicircular awning, it is one of the few intact examples of Nazi architecture.

The circular plaza at the front fits the picture, and the former government buildings give it a fine theatrical touch. The first reaction is: keep your head down, the new order rules here, come on, raise that right arm! Then come the genteel sounds of the airport terminal, and after that the impressive semicircle of buildings, the gesture to the rest of the world that says: here comes the new Germany!

And now I am up in the waiting lounge with its 1930s Bakelite coziness. I recognise almost everything here, from newspaper photographs and newsreels: Hitler under the awning, stepping out of his Focke-Wulf Condor as the crowds cheer; Göring leaving for a working visit to the Eastern Front; Hitler's friend Albert Speer in his English-tailored tweed jacket, standing on the ladder of a plane; Field Marshal Wilhelm Keitel crossing the tarmac with firm tread on 8 May, 1945, surrounded by Allied officers; the Americans and the Berlin airlift: it all happened here.

I have never been here before, but everything in this place is etched in my memory, as though they were my own recollections.

Chapter Seventeen

Bielefeld

THE PHOTOGRAPH OF ANNE FRANK, HER MOTHER AND HER SISTER Margot has no date on it. Anne looks to be about three. It's still winter-coat weather, but the girls' knees are already bare. The place where the picture was taken has been carefully documented by the people from Frankfurt's Historisches Museum: right in front of Café Hauptwache, in the city's shopping district. The little photo-booth picture of mother and daughters, taken at the nearby Tietz department store, does have a date on it: 10 March, 1933. They are wearing exactly the same clothes, the photographs were probably made during the same shopping spree. These were the final, innocent days of Frankfurt.

Three days later the SA raised the swastika banner above the balcony of the town hall, and three weeks later a boycott was pronounced against most Jewish shops and businesses. After the Easter holidays, Margot's 'non-Aryan' teacher seemed to have disappeared into thin air. During those same weeks, Otto Frank began making plans to emigrate. Within a year the whole family was living on Merwedeplein in Amsterdam. The rest of the story we know.

Had the Franks remained in Germany, it would have been – strikingly enough – little Margot who first suffered under the deluge of measures that went into force in January 1933. I see her in another archive photo: a summery photograph of the first-form class of the Ludwig-Richter-Schule, taken during a school outing in June 1932. The girls are wearing thin summer dresses, some of them have sun hats as well. The five Jewish children are standing among the others, there is nothing different or conspicuous about them. Margot is leaning towards a little girlfriend, a typically blonde German girl.

One year later all the casualness had disappeared. Margot's 'democratic' principal was replaced in April 1933 by a Nazi. One by one, the Jewish girls in her class stopped coming to school. And she was no longer allowed to play with most of her former girlfriends, for fear of neighbours and informants.

The Frank family home at Ganghofstrasse 24 is still standing, marked by a massive stone monument dedicated by the city's young people – 'Her life and death, our duty' – and the same trees around it, now thick and old.

On my next journey through Amsterdam I was given a van to use, a little one in which you could make a cup of coffee, type a column or even sleep. That was to be it for me in the coming months, this was to be my European house.

It is clear spring weather today, and I steer my new acquisition along the back roads of the old Germany, through all those hills where our grandparents mailed their postcards in the 1930s – Pension Die Fröhlichen Wanderer, '*Gutbürgerlicher Abendtisch!*' – past half-timbered villages smelling of fresh buns and newly ironed aprons. They are still there, unchanged, the rocks upon which Germany stands. The forests have their first light-green haze, the fields are brown, farmers are out ploughing everywhere, on the village square the little soldiers in the bell tower creak the hours away.

I drive past Cologne-Klettenberg, where an Amsterdam acquaintance of mine grew up in the 1930s. In those days Truusje Roegholt lived at Lohrbergstrasse 1. On the corner across from her lived her playmates Anna and Lotte Braun, in a house hung with portraits of Nazi leaders and with a swastika banner stained with real human blood, probably from some fight on the street. 'Mr Braun was a real beast of a man, even on his deathbed he wore an armband with a swastika on it,' she told me. 'But what did we know, and what didn't we know? People simply didn't talk. The Third Reich was a dictatorship based, to a great extent, on silence. But you saw a great deal, even as a child.'

She remembered vividly, for example, the first triumphal scenes. 'Right from the start you saw everyone marching in nice, new uniforms. Heaven knows where the money came from. But the effect was stunning. All those poor people who had never owned a set of decent clothes, suddenly they were someone. They sang the greatest nonsense, but they had new shoes!'

She also told me about the great girls' secret of the Third Reich, the campaign to give the Führer a child. 'They organised solstice parties with selected blonde girls and boys, to breed children like that. A fanatical girlfriend of ours tried to get us to come, but we thought it was nauseating. These days they deny that, no one talked about it, but those campaigns really existed.'

Immediately after the great pogrom of Kristallnacht on 9–10 November, 1938 – almost 100 Jews were killed and 7,500 Jewish shops destroyed – the teachers read aloud a printed statement: the Jewish students were to leave the school. It had obviously all been arranged beforehand, down to the last detail. Ingeborg Goldstein and Edith Rosenthal packed their bags, looked around the class, then got up and walked out of the door together. 'You could hear a pin drop.' Truusje stood up and protested; after all, these were their classmates. She was told to leave the classroom as well.

On Luxemburger Strasse she saw Jewish shops being sacked. 'One Jew had hidden in his cupboard. They picked up the cupboard, with him in it, and threw it from the fourth floor, then beat him to death. It was unimaginable that something like that could happen in this peaceful city. A few people stood watching, one woman said: "Those poor Jews", another woman put her hand over that woman's mouth right away. It was like walking around in a dream.'

It snowed that winter, and she went sledging in the park with her playmate Miryam Meyer. When she walked past the Brauns' house the next day, a window opened. Lotte shouted: 'Truusje, is it true that you were sledging in the park yesterday?' 'Yes.' 'Well, then it's me or that Jewish bitch!'

Little has been said about a question that now presents itself: how could this shift in mentality take place so quickly, in both Frankfurt and Cologne, after 1933? Where, for God's sake, were all those hundreds of thousands of active communists, social democrats and Christians who had taken part in protest demonstrations not so long before this? Where were the

56.1 per cent of the public who voted against the Nazis on 5 March, 1933?

There was, of course, the atmosphere of burgeoning intimidation. Right after the National Socialists seized power, the SS and the SA were given the status of 'auxiliary' police. Atrocities took place on a daily basis. More than a hundred temporary torture chambers were set up in Berlin, scattered over all of the city's 'red' neighbourhoods. In Breslau and Munich, Jewish judges and lawyers were literally beaten out of the courthouses.

An estimated 10,000 communists and socialists were arrested in Bavaria alone in spring 1933. In Prussia, approximately 25,000 such arrests were made, and throughout the country at least another 100,000 dissidents were roughed up and terrorised.

One month after Hitler was appointed chancellor, the Reichstag burned down. Marinus van der Lubbe had, more or less by accident, set fire to the building's most vulnerable spots, the huge curtain at the back of the meeting hall and the bone dry oak panelling behind. Within minutes, the papers reported the next day, the giant hall was 'an inferno of burning benches and lecterns'.

Van der Lubbe could have done his opponents no greater favour.

Although Van der Lubbe had no ties with the German communists, the new chancellor demanded that all KPD parliamentarians be hanged immediately. In addition, Hitler had now been given an excuse to issue a whole series of decrees, to restrict civil liberties even further and to lock up countless political and journalistic heavyweights. In this way, the movements of the left were robbed of their leadership at a single blow, and that was not all. The wave of arrests also established a new norm: after that, anyone who rocked the boat could be spirited off to a concentration camp at a moment's notice. An estimated 100,000 communists or alleged communists were killed during the Third Reich. Many times that number spent shorter or longer periods in concentration camps.

Yet 'the good Nazi years of 1935–7' – a period generally ignored these days – really did exist. During that time, Hitler achieved two goals no one had ever thought possible: the six million unemployed of 1933 were all working by 1937, and Germany was once again considered a power to reckon with.

It was not the war industry, however, that served as the motor to the German economy in the early years. That change came later. At first, the country's economy was stimulated largely by huge infrastructural projects: the building of harbours and roads that did not compete with existing industry, but provided new jobs and new welfare for millions of working families. The policy was an extremely daring one in those days – somewhat comparable to the New Deal in the United States – and successful to boot. In 1938 German unemployment had fallen to three per cent, as compared with thirteen per cent in Britain and twenty-five per cent in the Netherlands.

For the first time in history, the Germans were not only farmers, workers, mothers and soldiers, but also consumers. Hitler won over the German masses with a degree of luxury they had never before experienced. The *Volksempfänger*, a household radio, was soon affordable for almost everyone. The first Volkswagens rolled off the production lines. During the 1936 Olympics, the *Reichspost* experimented with live television broadcasts: a world first. A kind of inexpensive, mass tourism – unique in those days – was developed by the Nazi organisation Kraft durch Freude (KdF) and offered weekend trips to Munich, train trips to Lake Garda and cruises to Madeira that were affordable even for factory workers. Millions of Germans took advantage of this: KdF ships such as the *Robert Ley* and the *Wilhelm Gustloff* soon became household words. The birth rate, the most reliable parameter of confidence in the future, rose by almost twenty-five per cent within a year after Hitler came to power.

This breathtaking series of successes swept away almost all of the modern Germans' reservations. Untold numbers of those who had voted liberal, social democrat, Christian or communist in 1933 were transformed from the mid-1930s into enthusiastic adepts of the führer. Even the concentration camps filled many Germans with a certain sense of well-being: the 'antisocial', the 'parasites', the 'criminals', the 'do-nothings' and 'foreign elements' were off the streets at last.

This also explains why the huge sterilisation campaign that began in summer 1933 met with no real protest to speak of. The fact that some 400,000 'recidivists' and 'degenerates' were sterilised under coercion was anything but a secret: countless newspaper articles, pamphlets, public information meetings and even films were dedicated to this 'recovery of our racial purity'. Beggars, psychiatric patients, prostitutes, homosexuals and Gypsies could be taken off the street without due process of law for 'isolation' or 're-education'. Government policy papers appeared, dealing with 'Combating the Gypsy Plague' and granting considerable attention to the positions of the *rassenreinen Zigeuner* and the *Mischlinge*. 'Lives unworthy of being lived', they suggested, were better off being terminated.

Starting in summer 1939, the Nazis introduced a special euthanasia programme for the mentally and physically handicapped. The operation had the code name T-4 (the programme's head offices were at Tiergarten Strasse 4, a stately villa that has since disappeared) and was led by a steering committee of physicians, professors and top government officials. At the start of the campaign, it was estimated that 70,000 candidates were eligible for this 'merciful death': one out of every five psychiatric patients. But, the T-4 officials realised, it would take far too much time to dispose of such a large group by means of individual injections: the use of gas chambers would be more in keeping with their planning. In the end, six institutions around the country were designated as locations for gassing, and eleven 'special hospitals' were set up to put children 'to sleep'.

Before long, the euthanasia campaign had become a poorly guarded secret. The newspapers began filling with death notices for handicapped persons, all of whom had unexpectedly died of 'heart failure'. Some families removed their relatives from the hospitals, but the general reaction to this silent mass murder was one of resignation. Typical was the request one potential victim's mother sent to the administrators of the Eckardsheim clinic at the Bethel nursing home: 'If my son is to be withheld further life, please see to it that he is put to sleep during a seizure in [his ward] Tannenwald, please give him something to that end. I know then that he will have been in the most dedicated of hands until he drew his final breath. How else can I ever be happy again for the rest of my days?'

The killing became a part of the 'great unspoken'. Doctors and nurses – hundreds, if not thousands, of medical people must have been involved in this operation – participated obediently. Protests did come, however, from the churches. Clergy presiding at the funerals of some of the victims spoke openly about how they had died. In a packed St Lambertus Church in August 1941, the Bishop of Münster, Clemens August von Galen, railed against the use of euthanasia. But the centre of resistance often named is that of the Bethel nursing home.

Today Bethel is an enormous care complex at the edge of town, a place I would never have visited if Simon Wiesenthal's big war map had not showed it as one of the few locations of German resistance to the Nazis. The reason for its inclusion was the principled refusal of its director, Pastor Friedrich von Bodelschwingh, to admit even a single euthanasiast to the grounds. When the police vans arrived to round up 'his patients', he stood in the gateway himself, spread his arms and shouted: 'You will only enter this house over my dead body.' This was what I had been told. After the war the German churches lauded him as 'a great shepherd of Christianity', 'the man with the clearest vision within the churches' and a model of 'unbending resistance, with no regard for his own person'.

I receive a warm welcome to the hospital archives. When the archivist hears my story, he smiles shyly. 'Well, I'm afraid we must be honest.' The older people probably needed a story about heroes, but the younger generation is interested only in the truth. 'It was all investigated carefully, about ten years ago. But have a look for yourself.'

He hands me a thick report, written by Stefan Kühl and published by the student association of the University of Bielefeld. The study is part of a series dealing with National Socialism in the region, and everything about it shows that Kühl left no stone unturned while researching the archives. I start reading. The story of Bethel is indeed one about courage, but also about the want of courage. It is about knowing, consciously knowing. And it is about saying nothing – above all, about saying nothing.

'An inhuman regime spreads and extends its inhumanity in all directions, also and especially downwards,' the Italian concentration camp prisoner Primo Levi wrote. And it undermines our ability to judge. 'The generally accepted realisation that one does not submit to violence, but resists it, is from now, not from then.' Resistance must be learned; in the 1930s it was a rare capacity of the few.

The Bethel dossier is a clear example of how difficult that learning process can be.

Bethel is an Evangelical Church institution. The names of the wards come from the Promised Land: Emmaus, Capernaum, Carmel. Bethany, formerly known as Patmos, consists of a complex with eight wings that today houses a neurological clinic. In the 1930s this was home to some one hundred epileptic and multiply handicapped young people. They were the direct target of the Nazis' campaign of genetic purification.

The first campaign, as we have already seen, comprised the sterilisation of 'degenerates'. Bethel's management did not protest. Everyone who fit the criteria was obediently sterilised in 1933. Six years later, when the euthanasia campaign began, the staff became more agitated. In late 1939, Bethel's auxiliary branch at Brandenburg was ordered to fill out 'registration forms' for all its patients. This, it was claimed, was merely a 'statistical measure'. When he read the questions, however, the head of the clinic, Reverend Paul Braune, became alarmed. He refused to complete the papers, and Bethel's management did likewise.

A few months later, in March 1940, Braune was asked to investigate the sudden death of thirteen epileptics. His inquiries, carried out at other institutions as well, confirmed his suspicions: in total silence, a campaign of murder had started. When he reported his findings to the authorities he was told that it would be wiser for him to investigate no further.

During the weeks that followed, Braune and Bodelschwingh warned everyone they could contact: colleagues at other institutions, government officials, ecclesiastical leaders. By summer 1940, all of the highest church authorities had been informed, including the Spiritual Advice Council of the Evangelical Church of Germany. On 9 July, 1940, Braune sent a memorandum to the church's leaders: 'We beg you to act as quickly as possible, now that the greatest danger is at hand.' The next day, the Evangelical Bishop of Würtemberg, Theophil Wurm, wrote a personal, ten-page letter to the ministry of internal affairs in which he expressed his deep concern about the rumours he was hearing.

Had the church leaders voiced a public protest at that point, the lives of tens of thousands of handicapped people would probably have been saved. Hitler was – in later years as well – very sensitive to German public opinion on this matter. Braune received a noncommital reply. One month later he was arrested by the Gestapo. Bodelschwingh was informed that a warrant had been issued for his arrest as well.

This first phase of resistance was characterised by secrecy. Everything took place behind the scenes. The most important and most obvious weapon, that of public opinion, was not wielded. Nor did Bodelschwingh ever make use of his many contacts abroad. Noteworthy was the confidence both clergymen had in the government. Both of them continued to assume that National Socialist Germany was a state under the rule of law, both saw the euthanasia programme as a mere aberration, a minor abuse in an otherwise well-run society.

The second phase began. Paul Braune was released in late October 1940, but he had to promise to no longer resist 'the measures taken by state and party'. Everyone in his surroundings knew why he had been arrested and why he was silenced. Bodelschwingh's involvement went no further than the institutions for which he himself was responsible. Unlike some of his fellow clergymen, he never again uttered a public protest.

Meanwhile, Bethel had allowed seven Jewish patients to be sent on transport. They were the Nazis' primary target, and were almost certainly gassed in the former Brandenburg house of correction. Five other Jewish patients were removed from the institution by their families in the nick of time. Soon afterwards, they too were probably killed. Bethel did not protect a single Jew.

For non-Jewish patients, the situation was very different. Bodelschwingh and his people continued in their stubborn refusal to fill out registration forms. The reason they gave was their own Christian conscience, but, as Kühl's study shows, they also sought a form of cooperation with the T-4 physicians. In the end, a compromise was reached. A committee of eighteen euthanasiasts was allowed to visit Bethel in March 1941 and submit a number of patients to further inspection. In this way Bodelschwingh hoped to win time, but the arrangement also had something ambiguous to it: we have our problems of conscience and law, you handle the dirty work. What's more, they allowed themselves to be talked into yet another concession: the patients were to be preselected by the clinic's own physicians. This was done so proficiently that the euthanasiasts went along with almost all their recommendations, and so finished their work much more quickly than they had expected.

There was, in other words, nothing like a director who almost literally threw himself before the trucks to save his patients. On the contrary. The reports show that the euthanasiasts saw the entire expedition to Bethel as a festive outing. The very first afternoon they ate 'quite sumptuously' in the city's *Ratskeller*, as Dr Mennecke wrote in a letter to his '*liebe Putteli*', and on Sunday the gentlemen took the bus together to visit the monument to the Germanic chieftain Hermann/Arminius in the Teutoburg forest. They made no attempt to disguise the real reason for their visit to Bielefeld. The personnel at the *Ratskeller* in particular overheard a great deal. 'It spread through the countryside like wildfire,' Bodeschwingh complained in a letter to Hitler's personal physician Karl Brandt, an acquaintance of his. 'Within a day after the doctors arrived there were farmers who came up to our patients working the field and asked them: "Did you know that the murder committee has arrived in Bielefeld?"' In light of the ensuing unrest, he then asked: 'Can't you ask the Führer to let matters rest, at least until after the war, when there will be a clear legal foundation for all this?'

After the euthanasiasts' visit, plans were made to warn the families of the threatened patients. And in Bethel's archives there is indeed a draft letter from Bodelschwingh in which he points out the possibility that 'in the near future, patients from Bethel may be transferred to other institutions'. In it, he emphasises that 'for many of our patients it will no longer be possible to fulfill the duties agreed upon'. Stefan Kühl suspects, however, that this warning was never sent: there are no letters to be found with questions or replies from alarmed family members. And the draft letter also shows us something else: Bodelschwingh expected to have to call off his resistance within the foreseeable future.

What am I now to conclude about the Bethel affair, after my day of research? The place of honour on Wiesenthal's map of resistance is undeserved, that much is clear. Under duress, Bodelschwingh tried to save his clinic, his conscience and his own skin. That is all quite human and understandable. It would be misleading, however, to elevate him after the fact to the status of a Protestant saint of the resistance. He was not one of those with that 'rare capacity for resistance'. The unsung Paul Braune was probably such a man, and so were a few other clergymen and physicians. Were they not fit to be made heroes of the resistance? Or was there something else? Was it the Evangelical Church's elite who were in particular need of a hero, in order to maintain their moral authority after the war?

For years Bodelschwingh's successors stymied all attempts to use the clinic's archives for research into the history of 'resistance' at Bethel. As one of them explained most frankly in 1964, such research posed the danger of making public a 'murky history of failure in many Christian circles'. He was right about that. Bodelschwingh was, as we say in the Netherlands, a typical 'wartime mayor'. He was anything but principled, he was also no hero, and at Bethel these days that heroic commemoration is simply one more burden to bear. His greatest objection to the campaign had to do with its legal basis, not with its ethics. And he was not alone in that; there were even Nazis who felt that the euthanasia campaign required special legislation.

Still, with all his weaving and dealing, this director-clergyman finally achieved his goal: he won time, and he was left alone. In Westphalia, in summer 1941, another twenty-seven hospital transports took 2,890 patients to the gas chambers at Hadamar. Bethel was spared. In late August, on Hitler's orders, the programme was stopped − for the time being. The protest from the churches, unrest such as that at Bethel, the Führer did not need that. In any case, the Nazis' original plan had already been almost completely carried out: at that point, exactly 70,273 German handicapped persons had been 'fumigated'. The T-4 civil servants calculated that the programme had saved the German people 885,439,800 marks in future medical care. The leaders of the German churches had watched it happen, with eyes wide open.

It was from that same building at Tiergartenstrasse 4, the unassuming villa in the neat Berlin neighbourhood of Tiergarten, and with the same bureaucratic calm, that the Endlösung for the Jews and Gypsies of Europe began after summer 1941. Of the 400 members of the T-4 staff, just under 100 were selected to provide leadership for 'Aktion Reinhardt', the campaign to exterminate the Polish Jews. The gas chamber at Schloss Hartheim which had been developed for the handicapped ran almost constantly from November 1941, to accommodate political prisoners from Mauthausen. The technology used there was adopted by all the other concentration and death camps. The hardened workers from the crematoria, the Brenner, became much sought-after employees.

The euthanasia project served as the experimental plot for the industrial extermination of millions that followed. It paved the way in psychological terms as well. The Nazis realised all too well that this was a sensitive issue. Their amazement was therefore all the greater when it turned out that only ten per cent of all patients' families had registered a protest. The mass majority of the German population, they could correctly conclude, would look the other way when something like this happened, even when it involved members of their own family. The road was clear.

Chapter Eighteen

Munich

MEANWHILE, AS I TRAVEL NOW THROUGH MY OWN TIMES, THERE HAS been a war going on for weeks, a real war. Europe and the United States have joined forces to free Kosovo from the Serbs. Rumours abound concerning bloody acts of ethnic cleansing in Kosovo, and at least 750,000 refugees are wandering through the region, hundreds of thousands of Albanians are appearing at the borders of Western Europe. The rest of Europe looks on in alarm, but no one is feeling particularly combative, certainly not in Germany. Only in the field of foreign policy, it seems, do we Europeans still dare to think in terms of social change being susceptible to popular opinion. The Balkans, clearly, are not susceptible. What is more, no Western soldier these days is prepared to die for an ideal. That, too, severely limits the possibilities.

In 1933, the situation was the exact opposite. The real fighting had yet to begin, but in manners and language the war had been raging for a long time. Today, in 1999, half of Europe has joined the fray, but there are no slogans, uniforms or behaviour to show that you are driving through countries at war. There are no military convoys on the autobahn, only cars pulling pleasure boats. In the air one sees only the white vapour trails leading to and from holiday destinations. No, here the war is being fought in newspaper headlines, on TV, in late-night musings, and around the tables of roadside restaurants.

Significant too is the lack of European unity, even though the war is being carried out on behalf of a united Europe. There is not an atom of team spirit, or any form of European patriotism. In Amsterdam, despite the blazing headlines, I had observed a remarkable lethargy. For the first time in half a century the Netherlands was at war, in an offensive role no less, but the prime minister did not even deem it necessary to announce that to parliament in person.

Everywhere I go here in Germany, the subject of the new war is brought up within the first fifteen minutes. The Dutch-German border suddenly turns out to be a deep chasm, a vast sea separating two worlds. According to one survey, more than half of all Germans believe that we are on the brink of a major European war. At a pavement café I begin a conversation with an older couple from Düsseldorf. They have trouble sleeping, they tell me, Kosovo stirs up old memories. 'Entire families wandered the streets at night, my father sometimes took them in,' she tells me. 'At home I still have the bicycle I used to save my own skin back then, racing along on wooden wheels just ahead of the advancing Russian Army. Everyone of my generation fled at some point, and almost everyone went through a bombardment.' Her husband, a retired contractor, says: 'The conviction that there must never be another war is etched in our souls.' His father froze to death on the Eastern Front.

A weekend in Nuremberg, city of cuckoo clocks, toys, racial laws, the NSDAP's national rallies, the war crimes tribunal and the world's biggest bratwurst hall. The city has its *Altstadt*, and fake trams for the tourists everywhere. In reality, there is almost not a single piece of cement here older than fifty-five years. The entire old city centre of Nuremburg was bombed off the face of the earth, yet most local history books grant no more than a page or two to the war. The tribunal building is now used to try everyday criminals. The Nazis' huge parade grounds have been preserved in part as a living memorial. The rest has been filled with inexpensive public housing.

That evening I sit in the grandstand at those parade grounds, one of the few elements left of the Nazi complex. It is one of those quiet, mild spring evenings full of promise. The author Gitta Sereny, who would one day write a biography of Albert Speer, ended up here by mistake in 1934, in the midst of a Nazi rally. She was ten at the time, a prim schoolgirl on her way to visit her mother in Vienna. Later she would write down her impressions; she did not understand then what it was about, but she was overwhelmed by the drama, the theatrics, 'the symmetry of the marchers, the joyful faces all around, the rhythm of the sounds, the solemnity of the silences, the colours of the flags, the magic of the lights.'

Those parts of the immense meeting hall still standing are now lifeless stone and peeling concrete. Hitler and Speer planned to make it a stadium for 400,000 spectators, twice the size of the Circus Maximus in Rome, half a kilometre long, more than 400 metres wide, the highest tier almost 100 metres from the ground. This would be the future site of all Olympic Games. In imitation of Kaiser Wilhelm, Speer said, they would 'reignite the sense of national grandeur', of which 'the monuments of the forefathers' were to be the 'most persistent tokens'. It was up to Hitler and Speer themselves, in this case, to create that 'bridge of tradition': they wanted to construct their monuments in such a way that, hundreds of years later, after the buildings had collapsed and were covered in ivy, they would still have their own unique merit as ruins. Fantasy drawings were even made of the Nuremberg grandstands after centuries of neglect.

That phantom merit is already becoming highly visible. Before me lies the unfinished 'Great Way'. The six-lane road, built for the great *Wehrmacht* victory parades that were sure to come, runs on for kilometres. Today it serves as a kind of car park. This week, all the way at the back, a fair is being held; a huge fair, in fact, complete with a six-loop roller coaster, a skyscraping light-blue Ferris wheel, two haunted houses, a dining hall for at least 300 sausage-lovers, and countless stands, gambling halls and candy kitchens.

The great tribune too, once the focal point of Leni Riefenstahl's spectacular Nazi film *Triumph of the Will* is steadily decaying. The pseudoclassical walls are covered in black and green mould, there is grass growing everywhere, some of the steps are coming loose. Up at the top a group of young people with shaved heads are drinking beer in the twilight. Blackbirds are singing. People are jogging around the old parade grounds. Beside me, four boys are practising with a skateboard, baggy pants, baseball caps turned back to front, tearing across the tribune's weathered benches, jumping from one tier to the next, dancing on this deeply charged concrete.

Stretching diagonally across Europe, from Holland through Friesland and Denmark and reaching all the way south to Austria, lies a gigantic triangle of order and cleanliness. I am driving now along its southern flank, from one Bavarian village to the other, through a landscape of green pastures and rolling hills, here and there a church with an onion-shaped steeple. The God who rules this almost heavenly piece of Europe is fond of discipline: no path is left unraked, every patch of grass is neatly mown and manicured, every house stands sprightly and foursquare. I go by way of Eichstätt and Markt Indersdorf, and then suddenly I find myself at an exit for Dachau, and there is Dachau itself: another neat little town tucked up against the sprawl of Munich.

The concentration camp, as it turns out, is just a part of the local industrial estate, no one has ever tried to disguise that, it was a part of the city's commercial life. When it was built, the *Dachaer Zeitung* spoke of new 'hope for Dachau's trade and industry', an 'economic turning point' and the 'start of happy times' for the town. Shortly afterwards, one reads, the first twelve prisoners were killed. The paper reported that the guards had acted 'in self-defence' and that the victims 'had sadistic tendencies anyway'.

Today, some sixty-six years later, the local press reports on a council meeting in Waakirchen, a village south of Munich. In early May a memorial service will be held there for the 'death marches' from Dachau, in which a great many prisoners died just before the camp was liberated. Two former inmates have been invited to the ceremony. The request to pay for their lodging has been refused by the town council. 'We have already generously allocated municipal ground for a memorial,' says Mayor Peter Finger. 'And don't forget, we'll also have to plant new flowerbeds for this memorial service.'

Dachau sees the camp's remains primarily as a public-relations project. Emphatically absent here are the names of European sister cities, something one sees everywhere else in Europe. No one wants to be friends with this town.

In the 1950s, a number of attempts were made to raze the old complex, and the first temporary exhibition there was actually removed by the police. According to the mayor of that day – who had been deputy mayor of the town in wartime – all the excitement was completely exaggerated: the camp had been occupied primarily by common criminals and 'political subversives'. Today, at the camp's exit, there are large signs drawing the visitor's attention to Dachau's true attractions: a lovely church, an old castle, pleasant restaurants.

But other voices are also heard: 'I am probably the only one of you who actually saw the death marches and the emaciated concentration camp prisoners with their linen uniforms and their wooden shoes,' Waakirchen SPD councillor Michael Mair said. And Sepp Gast of the CSU actually became emotional: his own father had been in Dachau. The two men have announced that they will pay part of the guests' expenses out of their own pockets.

Entering the camp, one finds oneself in a huge courtyard in the middle of a *carrefour* of barracks. As it is now, the entire camp is more like an education centre, a museum to be leafed through like a book, a useful, lively history lesson from which all the death and stench have been scrubbed away.

I see the wooden gallows. It stands there with all the obstinacy of a tool, its wood scratched and worn, its pedestals dented. In the exhibition halls one sees the familiar images: the starvation, the executions, the so-called 'altitude tests'. A series of photographs: a man is being placed in a little booth, a lively face, dark eyes, a Frenchman perhaps? Then the air pressure is lowered, or raised. You see his horrified look, see him raise his hands to his head. Then he collapses. The pressure is brought back to normal. A new session. At last the man is dead. The final photograph: his skull, cut open. Other tests were done to see how long a person could survive in ice-cold water. Some people were still alive after a day. Liver punctures were performed on other patients. Without an anaesthetic.

On display is a letter to the camp supervisors from Dr Sigmund Rascher, MD, Troger Strasse 56 in Munich, dated 16 April, 1942: 'After a respiratory arrest, I brought the last experimental patient, Wagner, back to life by raising the pressure. Because experimental patient W. was earmarked for a terminal experiment, because further experiments would produce no new results and because your letter had not yet reached me, I immediately began a new experiment that patient W. did not survive.' Rascher had an urgent request of his own: might he be allowed to photograph the autopsy specimens in the camp, 'in order to document the rare structure of a multiple lung embolism'?

*

Prisoner Walter Hornung provided a glimpse of camp life in Dachau in the year 1936. The SS comes stomping through the camp:

> When the knives are dripping with Jewish blood,
> Then you know we're feeling good!

Then comes the roll-call. Prisoners are selected for heavy labour. Different categories are made to step forward each time. 'Parliamentarians and secretarial personnel to the front!'; 'Editors and journalists to the front!'; and finally, 'Münchener Post to the front!' A small, crippled man steps forward from the latter group. He is the perfect target.

Why the Münchener Post? Because the journalists of this social-democrat daily had, more than anyone else, kept an eye on the Nazis from the very start, had published all their findings and had treated the National Socialists for what they were: a gang of thugs.

Hitler called the paper 'the vipers' nest'. If the Führer had allowed himself a little splurge at a luxurious hotel in Berlin, the bill was printed the next day in the Post under the headline 'How Hitler Lives'. When Hitler's niece and lover, the young Geli Raubal, committed suicide in September 1931, the Münchener Post immediately provided all the background information. The editors kept careful score on all political murders. Like some morbid syndicated column, they were published on the front page every day: 'New Victims of the Brownshirts' Bloodlust', 'Firebomb for Social-Democratic Journalist', 'Nazi Terror Against Farmhands: Six Boys Killed', 'Because Christmas is a Time of Peace: Nazis Kill Communist'. On 14 December, 1931 the paper printed a full-page list of 'Two Years of Nazi Killings'. Beneath the headline was a quote from Adolf Hitler: 'Nothing takes place within the movement that I do not know about, and of which I do not approve. Even more: nothing happens without my desiring it!' Then followed the names of sixty victims, most of them workers, who had been murdered or had died of grievous bodily harm.

A monument should be built to the Münchener Post, the American historian Ron Rosenbaum wrote in a commemorative piece, and I can only concur. The Nazis hated the Post with everything they had in them, and as soon as they were in power they tore it to the ground. On the evening of 9 March, 1933, an SA gang wrecked the editorial offices, threw the typewriters out onto the street and destroyed the printing presses. That was the end of the paper. The editors ended up in Dachau, disappeared into exile or succeeded, with a great deal of luck, in making it through the Third Reich in one piece.

I make a little pilgrimage to Altheimer Eck, a winding little street behind the big department stores in the heart of Munich. At number 13 (formerly number 19) I recognise the gateway. This was the courtyard where the *Post* was made. The printing office in the basement moved away only a year ago, but a newspaper is still being made here: the *Abendzeitung*, an airy daily featuring the occasional glimpse of a female breast. The people who work there tell me that the *Süddeutsche Zeitung* had its offices here after the war, but these days no one knows anything about the *Post*. The paper's name has been obliterated by a thick layer of plaster above the gate. There is no trace of all that heroic spirit, no plaque, not even a dot on Simon Wiesenthal's map of heroes.

The only trace that does remain of the *Münchener Post* is the Bavarian State Library. I spend an entire day there, amid conscientious and flirtatious students, rolls of microfilm and badly printed pages of the *Post*. In the 1920s the paper's tone is simply soporific, with headlines like 'The Future of Public Housing', 'Agreement on Funding Programme' and 'Employment Perspective under the Social Democrats'. The Nazis' activities are usually dealt with briefly under miscellaneous regional news.

But, from 1929, the editors awaken. The headlines are accompanied more frequently by exclamation marks: 'Voters, Think Twice!', 'Civil Servants, Wake Up!' On 20 December, 1929 the paper recommends, 'if necessitated by polling-place terror', to render one's ballot void by crossing off both 'yes' and 'no'. The Nazi murders receive full attention, and the *Post* rapidly transforms itself from a staid party organ to a hard-hitting newspaper, with revelations on an almost weekly basis. On 5 July, 1932, for example, the front page contains a careful overview of the sums paid by the Nazis to a number of soldiers for their part in the November 1923 Beer Hall Putsch. A certain Oberleutnant Kriegel received 200 Swiss francs for his participation, a common soldier received about 15 francs. A total of 1,173 francs was paid out, a capital sum in those days. The money came largely from Helene Bechstein and her husband, the famous piano manufacturer.

In its forecasts, too, the *Münchener Post* is highly revealing. As early as 9 December, 1931, the paper succeeded in getting hold of a secret plan that was circulating among the SA top brass, in which the measures actually taken later against the Jews are summed up with astonishing accuracy, up to and including vague plans for a 'definitive *Endlösung*': 'labour details' in swampy areas, whereby 'the SS in particular can play a supervisory role'.

One month later one reads of the first plans for the sterilisation campaign. On 12 January, 1932, the paper reports a speech by a Dr Stammberg from Chemnitz, 'Racial Hygiene in the Third Reich', in which he proposes a scoring system. The severely handicapped, prostitutes and professional burglars receive minus one hundred points, persons belonging to a non-European race receive minus twenty-five and the non-intelligent are given a minus six. Anyone receiving more than twenty-five minus points falls within the category of 'persons with undesirable progeny'.

On 8 April, 1932, the *Post* reveals in considerable detail the Nazis' plans for what they will do when they come to power: the local SA units will be given 'free rein for a full twenty-four hours' to round up their known opponents and 'rid themselves of them'.

The most fascinating thing about the *Post* was and is its editorial premise: the editors considered the Nazis not only a political phenomenon, but above all a subject for their crime reporting.

In his biography of Hitler, Ian Kershaw quotes top-ranking Nazi Hans Frank, who, as a twenty-year-old boy, went to hear Hitler speak in 1920. He saw a man in a threadbare blue suit and a rather loosely knotted tie, with flashing blue eyes and slicked-back hair, a plain speaker. At that point Adolf Hitler had been in politics for less than six months, but the public – the middle class shoulder to shoulder with workers, soldiers and students – lapped up every word. 'He expressed everything that concerned him and us most deeply.' His speech on 13 August, 1920 – entitled 'Why are we anti-Semites?' – was interrupted 58 times by cheers from the crowd of 2,000. The next day, the *Post*'s city page reported on 'a new attraction that has recently added lustre to the meetings of the German National Socialist Workers' Party . . . a young fellow reminiscent of Heinz Bothmer, who

has been put forward with verve and vigour . . . a humble writer, as
he calls himself', a 'zealous Mr Hitler'.

In the years that followed, the pages of the *Post* gradually revealed a
glimpse of a movement closely allied with criminal circles, and with
everything that went along with that: intimidation, mishandling, blackmail, forgery, even murder. On 12 July, 1931, under the headline 'This is
Hitler's Rank and File', the paper published a prison letter from a disappointed Nazi who said his former comrades included 'burglars, pimps,
purse snatchers, cheats, blackmailers, thugs and perjurers'. Shortly afterwards one reads about a young woman who worked in a refreshment
bar and was forced into prostitution by members of the SA. 27 December,
1932: 'Yuletide sullied by bloody SA vs SS melee in Anhalter Strasse Nazi
clubhouse'. 29 December: 'Hitler Youth is Forger'. And these are only
random selections.

Nowadays, the sinister birthplace of National Socialism is covered by
a bare car park beside the Hilton Hotel on Rosenheimer Strasse, skilfully
dynamited, demolished and smoothed over. This was the site of the famous
Bürgerbräukeller, the giant beer hall where visitors ate and drank heavily,
and where Adolf Hitler further honed his showman's talents. It was here,
too, that he and General Ludendorff held their unsuccessful coup on 8
November, 1923. When the whole thing fizzled out, the beer hall claimed
damages from this drunkards' revolution: 143 broken beer mugs, 80
broken glasses, 98 stools, 148 pieces of missing cutlery, to say nothing
of the bullet holes in the ceiling.

It was in that same year that Hitler began moving in more cultured
circles. He may have been a beer-hall orator, but he was also a fervent
lover of Wagner. That helped him to quickly make friends with the rich
young publisher Ernst 'Putzi' Hanfstaengel, who introduced him into high
society as early as 1922. One year later he met Siegfried and Winifred
Wagner at Bayreuth, and became a welcome friend of the family. Two fashionable Munich ladies entered into an ongoing rivalry to befriend the up-
and-coming young Hitler. Helene Bechstein, mentioned earlier, invited
him to all her receptions. She also bought him neat shoes and respectable
evening dress. Elsa Bruckmann, a Romanian princess by birth, taught him
not to put sugar in his wine and other useful rules of etiquette. Both of
them helped to mould him and make him ready for the bigger world.

Young Baldur von Schirach – later a prominent Nazi – saw how finally even his reserved, aristocratic father fell for Hitler's charms. Looking back on it, he could find only one explanation for this bewildering phenomenon: amid the prevailing mood of doom in the old German Empire, people from the upper reaches of society as well were desperately in search of a saviour. And Hitler, 'like a sorcerer', was able to forge together two concepts that had until then 'been as irreconcilable as fire and water: nationalism and socialism'.

The eternally nagging question about Munich remains: how in the world could this friendly southern city, this uncommonly pleasant town, this centre of the arts and good cheer, have been the birthplace of such a fanatical and destructive movement? Here, after all, was where the NSDAP was set up, it was here that Hitler discovered his own charismatic powers, here that the movement's first martyrs fell in 1923, and it was here that the 1938 peace conference was held.

In the late nineteenth century, Munich, capital of the conservative kingdom of Bavaria, developed into a baroque city of refuge with broad boulevards and glorious palaces. It was a haven for the writers, artists and theatrical people who wanted to escape the confines of Berlin. The Schwabing district was a second Montmartre. There were more painters and sculptors working in Munich than in Vienna and Berlin: traditional artists, but also people like Franz Marc, Paul Klee and other avant-gardists involved in the almanac *Der Blaue Reiter*. It was no coincidence, therefore, that the twenty-four-year-old painter Adolf Hitler decided to move from Vienna to Schwabing in 1913. 'Schwabing was a spiritual island in the great world, in Germany, mostly in Munich itself,' wrote the Russian artist Vassily Kandinsky. From 1896 it served as the home base of the celebrated *Simplicissimus*, a satirical magazine with a red dog as its symbol, a publication full of jokes about emperor and church, as well as advertising pages with 'power pills' for men and detoxification cures 'for alcohol, morphine, opium and cocaine'. After the magazine was banned, its circulation rose from 15,000 to 85,000 within a month.

Less than twenty years later Munich had become the official seat of the Nazi party, the second capital of the Third Reich. But this same Munich was also the city of the White Rose, one of the rare resistance groups in

Nazi Germany. It was in this town, in the midst of the war, that female students of the university booed the gauleiter of Bavaria when he called on them to leave school and bear children for the Führer. And in autumn 1939 it was in the Bürgerbräukeller, of all places, that the first attempt was made to assassinate Hitler, with a time bomb hidden in a cleverly hollowed-out pillar, the singular resistance of a cabinetmaker, Johann Georg Elser.

Schwabing today is a pretty posh neighbourhood of broad streets, almost Parisian-looking apartment buildings and countless restaurants, shops, bookstores and art galleries. Striking features are the massive office and school buildings from the early nineteenth century, of a size rarely seen in such surroundings. These are clarion calls from the past: here we are and here we shall remain, we kings of Bavaria.

With the exception of Amsterdam, Munich is the only major European city where even the mayor travels by bicycle. Bicycle paths have been built everywhere in recent years, and along them today a minority of the population bikes zealously, on professional-looking two-wheelers, at breathtaking speed. These Germans have embraced cycling in their own, thoroughgoing fashion. When one bicycles, then one Bicycles. Cycling here is a Deed, a Credo.

My own bike is simply tied to the back of my van. It is a straightfor-ward Amsterdam nag, an implement full of dents and rust spots, a plain fellow amid the perfect racing machines of the believers. We feel a little out of place, both my bicycle and I.

And so I thread my way carefully through Athens-on-the-Isar, as Munich was often called before the First World War, the cultural pleasure garden of Henrik Ibsen, Wagner and the Bavarian monarchs Ludwig II and Luitpold. Creaking loudly, I cycle through old archways, past graceful fountains, the pseudo-Roman national theatre and the taut, nineteenth-century Ludwigstrasse. Look, it's still there, the Bayerische Hof, the hotel where Mrs Bechstein taught Adolf Hitler how to handle oysters and artichokes. And look, that was his apartment here in Munich, on the second floor of Prinsregentenplatz 16, now home to just another genteel Munich family. And here, the street in Schwabing where he started out, filled today with the exotic odours of Chinese, Indian,

Russian, Italian and Mexican restaurants, at Schleissheimer Strasse 34. The enormous plaque that once hung here is now concealed under a thick layer of mortar.

Schwabing was an island, Kandinsky so aptly observed. Until well into the twentieth century it lent Munich a certain fame, but it remained an island. The staid citizens of Munich were disgusted by this neighbourhood full of prostitutes, students and anarchists. The residents of Schwabing, in turn, looked down on the coarse Müncheners who lived only for a plummy marriage and three litres of beer a day. According to the Bavarian historian Georg Frans, that divided Munich can be traced back to the trauma of the middle class concerning the period from 1919 up through Kurt Eisner's short-lived People's Republic of Bavaria. The rise of the Nazis in Munich, he says, was a direct result of that bloody civil war. David Large, in his account of Hitler's Munich, goes a few steps further. He feels that Munich's oft-praised urban culture has always had an anti-cosmopolitan and anti-liberal side.

In that sense, Munich resembled Vienna: beneath the harmony and good cheer lay a society deeply at odds with itself, marked by great tension between rich and poor. In the space of three decades from 1880–1910, Munich grew from a provincial town into a metropolis. The population doubled, the housing was as wretched as Vienna's, but the immigrants kept on coming. Jewish merchants, scientists and bankers set the tone in this new urban climate. It was here that Hermann Tietz, of Jewish origin, inaugurated his chain of department stores: the small shop-keepers were furious. Property prices rose: Jewish financiers were blamed. Prostitution increased: people claimed that Tietz drove his salesgirls to disrepute by underpaying them. The fashionable Staatsbürgerzeitung began complaining about 'the alarming rise in our city's Jewish element', and predicted 'the decline of the best among Munich's merchants'. Munich's first anti-Semitic party was set up in 1891. Then came the war, and after that violence crept into local politics. Finally, the tatty rabble-rouser from the Bürgerbräukeller took over the town.

Munich was built to please the eye and inspire thoughts of awe, and the Nazis knew that. From their Braunes Haus on Brienner Strasse they expanded their territory further and further. By 1940 an entire Nazi district had arisen adjacent to the centre of Munich, consisting of more than 50 buildings and providing work for more than 6,000 people. Grand plans were made for the future: the corner of Türkenstrasse was to be the site of, among other things, Hitler's monumental tomb.

The Braunes Haus was bombed, then in 1945 demolished with explosives, all except its system of secret corridors and bunkers. A fair amount of the former Nazi district is still standing, however. It was in the Führerbau, a building on Cheisstrasse that seems on the inside to consist almost entirely of an incredibly huge ceremonial staircase, that the 1938 peace conference was held with Chamberlain, Daladier and Mussolini. Today it is a house full of song and runs on the grand piano, the Academy for Theatre and Music, but history still shines through in the form of the chic stretch of pavement once laid in front of it to honour the Führer. Across the street one can also still admire the Haus der Deutschen Kunst, a gallery of overbearing pillars, hasty ornamentation, all façade architecture with no hint of eternity. Of the two Pantheons built by the Nazis at the corner of Königsplatz, only the foundations remain, now overrun by bushes. The square itself has been divested of its granite slabs. Today, covered in a great deal of pacifist lawn, it has once again become the Athenian agora the Bavarian kings dreamed of for themselves. Everything here has been ploughed under and buried.

Later on I cycle down monumental Ludwigstrasse to Professor-Huber-Platz, Geschwister-Scholl-Platz and the Ludwig-Maximilian-Universität. The names speak for themselves. Here at the university is where it all converges: the pompous stairways, the pseudo-Roman statues beside them (in reality, two Bavarian kings in costume), the stupendous dome covering the hall, but also the wispy, innocent, desperate little pamphlets that the students Hans and Sophie Scholl let flutter down from the galleries here on 18 February, 1943. 'In the name of Germany's young people we demand restitution by Adolf Hitler's state of our personal freedom, the most precious treasure that we have, out of which he has swindled us in the most miserable way.'

They had spread tracts and left behind graffiti on earlier occasions as well: 'Freedom', 'Down with Hitler'. That was all the White Rose did. This time, though, they were caught by the caretaker and turned over to the Gestapo. Four days later they were beheaded, along with their comrade Christoph Probst. The remaining activists – the students Alexander Schmorell, Willi Graf, and their professor Kurt Huber – were arrested within the year and executed. A few Munich chemistry students tried to continue the pamphleteering. They, too, were executed. After that no one dared to carry the torch.

The big university amphitheatre is further down the corridor. On this April morning, huge beams of sunlight come pouring into the building. I open a door cautiously. There is no one in sight. On the podium, a boy is playing the piano alone. Bach. He is oblivious to everything around him. His friends slip into the auditorium, remain listening breathlessly, they are young, their vision is clear. The room is full of light and sounds, images that come back, no one can escape them.

In Munich you would think that Italy was just around the corner. Here the living is easy, even a bit lazy. The city already has something un-German to it, more like Bologna than Berlin. But if you head southwards, they are suddenly there in the distance, the Alps, the guardians, the massive grey-white wall that closes this flat country off from the warm sunlight. It has been spring for some time already, but here it has started snowing again. The sky is almost black. The trees grow thicker as time ticks away, my little van groans up the slippery inclines, the roads become white and empty.

I take a room at Hotel Lederer am See, overlooking the dark Lake Tegernsee in the village of Bad Wiessee. Every now and then an avalanche puffs up on a distant mountain. The other guests are all retired couples, and the background music is perfectly attuned to their happiest years: Glenn Miller, party songs from the 1930s. I see in a commemorative book that, back then, the hotel was called Pension-Kurheim Hanselbauer. The book tells of the founders, of parties and celebrations, of the staff's hobbies; they tell of everything, in other words, that has to do with this 'wonderful world on the Tegernsee'. Interestingly enough, however, one event is left unmentioned, and it is precisely the one which gave this hotel an immortal place in European history: the Röhm Putsch.

It was from Hotel Lederer am See that Hitler, in the early hours of 30 June, 1934, had Ernst Röhm and other members of the SA elite pulled from their beds (which a few of them happened to be sharing with hand-some SA youths). They were arrested and, in the days that followed, executed one by one. Hitler also seized the opportunity to settle accounts with a whole series of other old enemies, particularly those from national conservative circles. It has been estimated that during this 'Night of the Long Knives' – which in reality lasted a weekend – some 150–200 of Hitler's political opponents were murdered. Röhm was the last. Hitler hesitated at first; Röhm was, after all, his old companion in arms. Finally, in his cell, Röhm was given a copy of the *Völkischer Beobachter* containing an account of his 'treachery', and a pistol. Not getting the hint, he sat down and started reading the paper. In the end, two SS officers had to shoot him anyway.

30 June, 1934 was almost as much a key moment in Hitler's career as 30 January, 1933 had been. It was in 1933 that he seized power, but only in 1934 did he succeed in consolidating it. That is the deeper meaning of the events at Pension Hanselbauer.

The Nazis justified the Night of the Long Knives as an act of political and moral purification. Yet the homosexual practices of Röhm and his companions had been public knowledge for a long time. As early as 22 June, 1931 the *Münchener Post*, under the cynical headline 'Brotherly Love in the Brown House', had published an exposé concerning the sexual predilections of a number of Nazi leaders, and the blackmail attempts that had resulted from them. But that, in fact, was hardly the point.

The way many of the victims were killed – in their living rooms, in their doorways, on the street – was reminiscent of a gangland war, and in some ways that is what it was. Hitler used the wave of killings to settle accounts once and for all with a whole slew of political opponents, but most of the victims came from his 'own' SA. After the Nazis seized power, Röhm's men had been allowed to do as they pleased, but before long a flood of complaints started pouring in concerning the violence and capriciousness of the SA. In her diary, Bella Fromm describes how a cocktail party she had organised, with a great number of diplomats and other top officials in attendance, had almost been ruined by a few SA men who wanted to 'smoke out' her house as a 'non-Aryan' den of spies. Only rapid intervention on the part of Hitler's personal staff prevented a diplomatic disaster. There were many such incidents – incidents Hitler the revolutionary would have applauded, but which caused Hitler the chancellor endless headaches. The SA had become a major nuisance, even for the Nazis. In 1934 the movement had four million followers, and Röhm had hopes of usurping the power of the military. Among the SA rank and file there was already talk of 'the need for a second revolution'. After all, where were the cushy jobs, the appointments, the rewards for all their efforts? Where, in gangster teminology, was their share of the loot?

In addition to all this, Hitler's position was also being threatened from within political circles. The nationalistic and conservative elites began to realise that unknown forces had been unleashed, ungovernable movements they could no longer control. They felt responsible for the fact that 'this fellow' had come to power, and wanted him to lose that power again as quickly as possible. The groups around Franz von Papen and the military top brass hoped to use the SA crisis to undermine Hitler's power. President Hindenburg was weakening with age, and they had no intention of seeing his position also fall into Hitler's hands. There was even talk of restoring the monarchy. Anything, in fact, was possible, as long as Hitler did not gain absolute power.

On 17 June, Papen gave a speech that, coming from him, was quite sensational. He railed against all the 'egoism, lack of character, insincerity, arrogance and dearth of chivalry', and even criticised the 'false cult of personality'. The same day, Hitler struck back: 'This is the clenched fist of a nation that will strike down all who dare to undertake even the slightest attempt at sabotage.' So when the Nazi leaders met with Hitler on 29 June, 1934, Goebbels thought the meeting was about a settling of accounts with the chic conservative circles around Papen. To his amazement, however, it turned out to be about the party's 'own' SA. Röhm's 'high treason' was never actually proven, and nothing points to any serious SA plans for a coup. The 'evidence' given for such plans was almost certainly trumped up.

Foreign observers saw the work of gangsters, openly now, for the first time. The reactions were outraged. Within Germany itself, however, little protest was heard. Even the churches remained silent, although Erich Klausener, chairman of Berlin's Katholische Aktion, was among those murdered. The military hierarchy forbade its officers to attend the funeral of General Kurt von Schleicher and his wife.

Ian Kershaw rightly notes that, without backing from the army – which could only profit from the dismantling of the SA – the Night of the Long Knives would have been an impossibility. The consequences were dramatic: 'Through its complicity in the events of 30 June, 1934, the army was, now more than ever, bound to Hitler.'

In this way, the generals walked into the same trap Papen had been caught in one year earlier. They believed they were using Hitler, but in fact the army itself had become a Nazi tool.

My room – the nicest corner room, between the warm oak walls of the old hotel – is on the same corridor where it all took place. Snow is coming down by the bucketful. The flakes fall on the black water, on the trees and lawns, on the pier from which Röhm's boys would dive into the lake. Did they sleep here, in this room? Did Hitler come storming in here, foaming at the mouth?

The true sense of living history will not come. That doesn't trouble me too much. The most industrious of chambermaids, after all, have been scrubbing here for the last sixty years, and scrubbing washes away the evil, snow covers everything, stillness and silence and time do the rest.

Chapter Nineteen

Vienna

THERE SEEMS NO ESCAPING THIS LONG WINTER. ON MY WAY TO AUSTRIA and Italy it starts snowing again, with a vengeance. The trucks drive slower and slower, they growl and blow great clouds of exhaust fumes into the frozen air. Blue lights flash in the distance, a snow-covered policeman waves us onto a side road, the Brenner Pass is in complete chaos, not even the snowploughs can get through.

Night falls in Innsbruck. The streets are deathly quiet, the snowflakes keep tumbling down amid the old yellow and pink houses, along the archways, against the windows of the empty *Weinstubes* – for who would send a dog out on a night like this? Some boys are playing football on the Marktgraben, a child rushes outside to catch snowflakes on his tongue, but otherwise everything is only lonely and a bit sad, this new winter in the spring.

On my way here I had come across two intractable spirits; both of them at places where, to be honest, I had never expected them.

The first one I met at the Obersalzberg, where the Alps begin and where Hitler's holiday residence, the Berghof, once stood. Four years ago the Americans opened the site to the public. From 1923, Hitler spent a great deal of time there, first in a little wooden holiday bungalow in the grounds of the Moritz *gasthaus*, later in a rented villa, and from 1933 in the Berghof. During the 1930s the area was transformed into a complete Nazi mountain, ruled and run by Hitler's secretary and right-hand man Martin Bormann. The whole party leadership moved into villas there. Pension Moritz became a *Volkshotel* for party members, Hotel Zum Türken was wrested from its owner for a pittance by Bormann himself. When there was nothing left to do above ground, he started on the construction of the enormous Alpenfestung, a system of myriad bunkers and at least five kilometres of tunnel. Most of that fort is still there.

The Kehlsteinhaus, also known as the Eagle's Nest, is there as well, high atop the rocks. The observation post, grim on the outside but decorated on the inside in 'steamboat style with a rustic touch', could be reached only by elevator. Built in 1938 through extreme hardship on the part of hundreds of workers, it was a present for Hitler's fiftieth birthday. A few hundred metres below it lies the pastureland of the Scharitzkehl and the old tourist café run by the Hölzls, a family of woodcutters. In the café's hallway I came across a framed and yellowing eviction notice, addressed to grandfather Simon Hölzl and signed M. Bormann. For security reasons, it seems, the Nazis wanted to have the café torn down, but Hölzl refused. He had no intention of giving up his lively trade in milk, coffee and beer there in that mountain pasture. The first sentence of Bormann's final reminder reads: 'The only possible reply to your correspondence of 10-2-1940 would be to send you to the concentration camp at Dachau.'

The Berghof's conversion into a kind of mountain fortress was characteristic of the change in Hitler's lifestyle. After 1936 he began to seek isolation with ever greater frequency. From a popular party leader he had turned into a moody king, creating around his person an increasingly larger court and living like a spider in that self-spun web, tolerating in his immediate surroundings only a few dozen individuals from his chosen coterie. From 1935 he suffered increasingly from hoarseness and intestinal complaints, which led him to seek assistance from the alternative therapist Dr Theodor Morell, who gave him injections of intestinal flora cultivated 'from a Bulgarian farmer's best strains'. Hitler believed he did not have long to live: 'My plans must be carried out for as long as I, with my waning health, can still achieve them.'

In his memoirs, Albert Speer describes a book of paintings of Hitler published in 1937. Each and every image showed a jovial, relaxed, normal man, rowing a boat, lying in a field, visiting artists. 'It was already obsolete by the time it came out. For even for his closest companions, this Hitler, whom I had known from the early 1930s, had changed into a withdrawn despot, barely in touch with the outside world.'

As one of the mountain's occasional residents, Speer was obliged to spend many boring afternoons and evenings with Hitler: lunch, walk, tea, nap, dinner, film. Hitler wore out his companions with his monologues, Göring with his sadistic jokes; Bormann was in the habit of molesting the secretaries during the siesta, Eva Braun was silent and miserable. Speer returned home each evening 'tired from doing nothing'; he referred to it as 'the mountain sickness'.

In spring 1999 the view of the Untersberg and Berchtesgaden is as impressive as ever, but that is the sole point of reference. The mountain is awash in a profound silence. The Berghof was bombed flat in 1945, and the ruins were demolished with explosives in 1952. The 'clear and fresh chalet' in which Hitler – 'a true raconteur' – had posed for the readers of Homes and Gardens in November 1938, the dining room with its hearth, the conference room with the famous glass wall and 'the most unsullied view in all of Europe', the terrace where Eva Braun was filmed so often: all that is left are chunks of concrete and a few bunkers, plus one window of the former garage. (That famous conference room, by the way, often reeked horribly of exhaust fumes and gasoline from the garage below, a design glitch on the part of architect Hitler.) In the woods along the road I came across a strange concrete structure that looked like a sort of patio overgrown with grass and trees. 'Yes, that was Göring's house,' says a friendly village woman. 'You won't find any of the rest of it, though. The only thing left is Speer's studio.'

The Hölzls survived it all. On that early spring day in 1999, they were still living there. A few dozen walkers were sitting outside, enjoying the sunlight on the pasture of the Scharitzkehl, the snow was melting away in babbling brooks, the birds sang, a chubby little boy was learning to walk.

The next day I drove down a narrow road into Sankt Radegund, a picturesque border village tucked away amid the Austrian hills. Two cats crossed the street. A candle was flickering in the chapel of the Virgin on the corner. An old woman wearing a brightly coloured headscarf was working in a garden. In a few days' time the fifty-second pilgrimage of Soldaten-Heimkehrer would be coming to town, but that was not the reason for my visit. This was one of those rare places where an individual had offered public resistance. I was looking for his grave.

In March 1938, all Austria stood cheering along the roads as the Nazi troops rolled into the country. For years, part of the population had been dreaming of a pan-German empire, and those sentiments had only increased after the collapse of the Habsburg Empire. As early as 1919, ninety per cent of the voters in Salzburg and the Tyrol had voted in favour of an *Anschluss*. When Hitler came to power that desire became even more intense. During the 1932 elections the Austrian Nazis won sixteen per cent of the votes; a year later they won forty per cent in Innsbruck's municipal elections. And they put their other weapons to good use as well: street violence, assaults, intimidation. On 25 July, 1943, the Catholic chancellor, Engelbert Dollfuss, was killed during a botched coup.

The Nazi revolution in Austria took place in three stages. The first was the establishment of a pro-German popular movement. In early 1934, a British correspondent wrote that an outsider driving into Graz would think he had arrived in a German town. The streets were dominated by marching Nazis and fluttering swastika banners, and their number only increased as the years went by.

Then a seemingly legal change of power was enacted at government level. A vote dealing with the issue of maintaining Austrian independence was announced for Sunday, 13 March, 1938. Hitler considered that far too great a risk. On 11 March, therefore, Göring organised the second stage of the coup from Berlin. In a series of phone calls, he placed huge pressure on the new chancellor, Kurt Schussnigg, who finally let himself be replaced by the Nazi lawyer Arthur Seyss-Inquart. Meanwhile, the Nazis had seized all central points in the major cities. The referendum was cancelled.

In stage three, the coup was completed by outside force: in the early morning of Saturday, 12 March, Germany's 8th Army rolled through the Austrian border posts, ostensibly to help the new Austrian government 'restore order'.

Despite their meticulous planning, however, there was one thing the Nazis had overlooked: the overwhelming enthusiasm of the Austrian people. To their own surprise, the advancing German troops were welcomed with flowers and cheering. German Army reports spoke of 'song and laughter' and 'an unbelievable euphoria'. American and British correspondents in Vienna described how entire crowds sang and danced in the streets, punctuated by cries of 'Down with the Jews!' and 'Sieg Heil!'.

That afternoon, to the accompaniment of chiming church bells, Hitler himself made a triumphal entry into Linz. From both Catholic and Protestant pulpits, God was thanked for this bloodless revolution. On Monday, Hitler arrived in Vienna. Hundreds of thousands of people came out. It was, according to one eyewitness, 'the biggest crowd I have ever seen in Vienna'. 'Stately trees on the pavement were literally bowed down with the weight of numbers trying to get a better view,' wrote the correspondent for the *Manchester Guardian*.

The arrests began that very weekend. Some 20,000 Austrian citizens – communists, journalists, Jewish bankers, workers, aristocrats and anti-Nazis from all walks of life – were rounded up. At the same time there began 'a medieval pogrom with a modern look'. As soon as the Nazis had seized power, on the evening of Friday, 11 March, tens of thousands of Viennese citizens marched on Leopoldstadt, the city's Jewish quarter along the Danube. Families were attacked in their homes, businessmen were pulled from taxis, hundreds of Jews committed suicide.

The American newspaper correspondent William Shirer visited the SS headquarters at the Rothschild palace. 'As we entered we almost collided with some SS officers who were carting up silver and other loot from the basement. One had a gold-framed picture under his arm. One was the commandant. His arms were loaded with silver knives and forks, but he was not embarrassed.'

Gitta Sereny, fourteen at the time, heard countless voices all over the city shouting '*Deutschland erwache! Juda verrecke!*' On the Graben, she and a girlfriend stumbled upon a few men in brown uniforms, surrounded by a crowd of laughing Viennese citizens. In the middle of the throng she saw a dozen middle-aged men and women down on their knees. They were scrubbing the paving stones with toothbrushes. She recognised one of the men as Dr Berggrün, the paediatrician who had saved her life when she had had diphtheria at the age of four. 'I had never forgotten that night; he had wrapped me again and again in cool, wet sheets, and it was his voice I had heard early that dawn saying, "*Sie wird leben.*" She will live.'

The doctor saw her walk up to the men in brown, he shook his head, but she screamed 'How dare you!' She shouted that a great doctor was being humiliated here, a man who saved lives. 'Is this what you call our liberation?' her girlfriend added, tears running down her face. Sereny: 'It was extraordinary: within two minutes the jeering crowd had dispersed, the brown guards had gone, the "street cleaners" had melted away. "Never do that again," Dr Berggrün said to us sternly, his small, round wife next to him nodding fervently, her face sagging with despair and exhaustion. "It is very dangerous!"'

The Berggrüns died in the gas chambers at Sobibor in 1943.

On Sunday, 10 April, a referendum was held to ratify the *Anschluss*. Anyone who did not openly vote 'yes' immediately became suspect. The turnout was unnaturally huge, and 99.73 per cent of the population voted 'yes'. In fact, a large majority of Austrians probably were in favour of annexation. As well as being the dream of most German-speaking Austrians, it had the support of the major ecclesiastical and political groups, and Germany was also seen as a model of miraculous economic recovery. In Hitler's birthplace, Branau, 5 of the 3,600 inhabitants voted against it.

In the little village of Sankt Radegund, thirty-five kilometres down the road, exactly one man voted 'no'. It was Franz Jägerstätter, one of village's most influential citizens. I saw a picture of him: a handsome, proud man in gleaming leathers, sitting astride a sparkling motorbike, with his parents and a little sister standing rather awkwardly beside him. Jägerstätter was a simple farmer, and at the same time a nonconformist: he read and studied, he was the first person in the village to own a motorbike, he was also the first man in Sankt Radegund to push his child's baby carriage. With his clear, sober view of the world, Jägerstätter realised right away that Nazi doctrine was incompatible with his Catholic faith. He tried to summon support from the church, but on 27 March, 1938 – to quote the pastoral letter read all around the country – that same church recognised 'with joy what the National Socialist movement has achieved.'

In 1940 he finally entered military service anyway. After six months he was sent home on special leave. He told everyone who would listen that he was not going back. He considered fighting in Hitler's army to be a personal disgrace and a grave sin. 'What Catholic could dare speak of this foray, on which Germany has already embarked and which it continues today in a number of countries, as a just and holy war?' His headstrong stance led to serious quarrels with his own family.

In early 1943, Jägerstätter, the father of three little children, was summoned to report back for duty. The local church authorities exerted pressure on him as well, but he refused, knowing full well that this meant his death. His letters from prison bear witness to a great serenity. On 9 August, 1943, Jägerstätter was beheaded in Brandenburg.

His widow went on running the farm alone with her three daughters. After the war she received no pension at first, because Jägerstätter had 'abandoned his country'. In the portal of the little white church in Sankt Radegund I saw the announcement of a reading by Martin Bormann Jr, the eldest son: 'Life in the Face of the Shadow'. In the churchyard the violets were blooming, and Franz Jägerstätter's grave was covered in them.

It behoves me here to make an aside. Jägerstätter was a Catholic, and his lonely opposition was primarily aimed against Hitler's war of aggression. The fate of the Jews, as far as I can ascertain, did not play much of a role in his stance.

In Vienna three months earlier, I had seen another monument, a commemorative monument to the Holocaust. It depicted a Jew scrubbing the street with a toothbrush. The monument's designers undoubtedly had the best of intentions, but they erred grossly. This seemed more like a monument to the people of Vienna, rather than to the Jews. It was a monument to all those who had been forced to look the other way, who were deeply ashamed, who still have nightmares about this. But what about the rest? Were there not also countless older citizens of Vienna for whom this image summoned up only cheerful memories? Viennese who loved it, those days when the Jews scrubbed the streets, who stood watching and roaring with laughter?

Unlike most German cities, in Vienna it was not merely a small group who committed violence and cheered it on. According to most eye-witnesses, the pogroms in the Austrian capital were carried out by tens of thousands of people, some estimates say even as many as 100,000. It continued night after night in the weeks that followed. It was as though all the pressure Schönerer and Lüger had built up was finally coming to a head. Department stores, shops and synagogues were plundered, apartments looted, furniture shattered, homes pillaged. Crowds cheered loudly as the beards of rabbis were shorn. After a few weeks, most Jewish firms had been 'Aryanised'. Of the city's sixty-eight Jewish banks, only eight were left. By late 1938, 34,000 of the original 70,000 homes occupied by Jews in Vienna had been appropriated by Austrians.

Scrubbing the streets with toothbrushes was one of those things people could not get enough of: women and children were dragged out onto the street and on a few occasions even doused with acid. Brownshirts herded hundreds of Jews to the Prater, where they were beaten and chased around the big carousel, some of them were even forced to eat grass. The crowd stood and watched.

The Kristallnacht held later in Germany was merely an imitation of the pogrom organised by the Austrians in Vienna nine months before. The Kristallnacht had to be carefully orchestrated, while the Viennese pogroms had largely flared up of their own accord. In *Das Schwarze Korps*, the SS correspondent in Vienna wrote admiringly: 'The Viennese have managed to do overnight what we have failed to achieve in the slow moving, ponderous past. In Austria, a boycott of the Jews does not need organising – the people themselves have initiated it.'

For the Austrian Jews, all this sudden misery had one bright side: they at least knew right away where they stood. In Germany, the occasional naïve soul could still hope that it would turn out all right, but for every Jew in Austria it was clear that he had to get out while the going was good.

Gitta Sereny's theatre school emptied out. The drama teacher, an extremely kind-hearted man, jumped to his death from a fifth-floor window. Two other teachers left for the United States. Then it was her turn. One evening in May, Gitta's mother received a warning that she and her Jewish partner were no longer safe. They packed their belongings that night, and caught a train to Geneva the following day.

The eighty-two-year-old Sigmund Freud was also harassed in his home at Berggase 19. On 4 June he was given permission to leave the city where he had lived from earliest childhood. He went to London, where he died one year later. Before being allowed to leave, the Nazis demanded that the world-famous doctor sign a document stating that he had been treated well. Freud signed without batting an eye, and added a sentence of his own: 'I can strongly recommend the Gestapo to one and all.'

By May 1939, a little more than a year after the *Anschluss*, more than half of Austria's Jews had left the country.

V May 1922–39

FINLAND
Helsinki
Leningrad
Tallinn
ESTONIA
Moscow
LATVIA
Riga
Witebsk
LITHUANIA
Königsberg
Wilna
Minsk
GERMAN
EMPIRE
SOVIET UNION
Berlin
Brest-Litovsk
Warsaw
Kiev
POLAND
Rowno
Sea
of Azov
Krasnodar
LOVAKIA
Chernowitz
Crimea
Tiflis
Budapest
HUNGARY
RUMANIA
Black
Sea
Trabzon
Belgrade
Bucharest
Erzurum
OSLAVIA
Sarajevo
BULGARIA
Sofia
Edirne
Istanbul
Ankara
Skopje
Tirana
Saloniki
TURKEY
ALBANIA
GREECE
Athens
Lataki
Syria
Dodecanese
(Ital.)
Rhodes
Cyprus
1925 Brit.
Crown Colony
Tripoli
Lebanon
Crete
Mediterranean

0   100   200   300 km

◄—— Geert Mak's Route

Chapter Twenty

Predappio

'MY NAME IS VITTORIO FOA. I WAS BORN IN 1910, SO I'M ALMOST ninety years old. Sometimes they call me the grandfather of progressive Italy, but that's nonsense of course. I did lead the union for years, that much is true. And I was an anti-Fascist, yes, that I was, from the very start.

'My grandfather was the chief rabbi of Turin. A matter of family tradition, nothing more. Like most Jewish families in northern Italy, we belonged to the city's upper classes. It was only in Rome that one had a large Jewish proletariat. No, my anti-Fascism had little to do with my Jewish background. I considered myself a son of Italy, of the Renaissance, of the Enlightenment, of freedom. It was the Germans who finally drove us Jews together.

'When did I start becoming aware of all this? I believe I was about thirteen at the time, in 1924, with the murder of Giacomo Matteotti, you know, the Socialist Party secretary who had the courage to protest openly in parliament against the Fascist terror. They abducted him right away and stabbed him to death. I was completely engrossed by that whole affair. I was only a boy, but I understood perfectly well that that murder was more than an attack on democracy, it was also an attack on the workers' movement.

'After that I saw the true face of Fascism everywhere I looked, even in my own city. I saw the violence in the streets, the arrogance of the blackshirts, the nationalism. The Fascists had burned down the union hall, I saw the workers standing silently around their burned homes.

'When I was a little older I started writing booklets and pamphlets. They were printed in France. I was part of Carlo Rosselli's underground movement, Giustizia e Libertà, along with people like the publisher Leone

Ginzburg, the writer Cesar Pavese and Alessandro Pertini, who later became president of Italy. We worked out of Turin, Rosselli was living in exile in Paris. In those days I saw Fascism as the rape of Italian history, as an excess, something that had nothing to do with Italy. I think differently these days. Fascism has deep roots in Italian history. It lasted twenty years here, while National Socialism lasted only twelve years in Germany. Liberalism, freedom, the government of law had to conquer Italy, and we're not nearly there yet.'

'In spring 1936, when I was twenty-five, a Fascist judge sentenced me to fifteen years in prison. Purely on the basis of what I had written. The secret police had informants everywhere, and one of the "champions" on our side turned out to be a Fascist. I hadn't taken part in a raid or anything like that, it was only about words and paper. I was released in 1943, just in time to join up with the resistance. It was insane: no one in prison ever asked whether I was Jewish. I was actually very safe there.

'During that whole seven-year period I heard almost no news from outside. We were totally isolated: no visitors, no newspapers, no radio. Once a week a censored letter from your parents. When I got out, I looked around in amazement. The world had changed so drastically! Germany was all over Europe, in France, in Belgium and the Netherlands, they had even occupied part of Italy. In 1936 there had been almost no anti-Fascists in Italy. We felt very much alone. But by the time I was released, all the young men were itching to fight against Germany.

'After that I started organising the political actions and the propaganda for our resistance group. Of course we knew that our struggle barely added up to anything amid that huge war, that the Russians and Americans were the ones who really made the difference. But we fought along anyway, because we wanted to be part of it too. We didn't want the new Italy to exist only by virtue of other people's sacrifices and other people's decisions. We wanted the new democracy to be stronger than the old one.

'And we felt a new unity. During my time in the resistance I made friends with people like Andreotti and Cossiga. After the war we were appointed to the assembly that was to draft the new constitution. We would argue all morning, work hard in the afternoon, and voted in unison in the evening. That sense of unity was a product of the resistance.

'Liberalism and democracy have had a hard time of it here. The Italians invented Fascism. We did that! We mustn't try to avoid that responsibility. But the anti-Fascist constitution we drew up back then is something they've never been able to take away from us.'

'Today I'm so old that I'm almost blind. When I first opened my eyes to the light, in 1915, all the countries of Europe were busy slaughtering each other. And each of those countries felt that justice was on its side. I can still remember a few things about the First World War. The whole thing is surrounded in my mind by an atmosphere of emotion and tragedy, yes, our family was quite occupied with the war. I still remember when Italy joined the war in 1915. I was four at the time, and I stayed afraid throughout the entire war.

'Now that my eyes have almost completely dimmed, I see, by that last light, that the countries of Europe are embracing each other and forgetting their borders. That whole turnaround took place within the space of my almost ninety years. I still find that unbelievable. But I also know how difficult it has been.'

———

If motorways are the cathedrals of the twentieth century, then the Brenner Pass is its St Peter's, a miracle of road building, the artery carrying the lifeblood of Europe. After days of waiting I was finally able to leave the North, across the pass, in a long, lazy convoy. Huge orange snowploughs were working everywhere, the men driving them worked in their T-shirts, they were the heroes of the mountain. Close to the top the trucks stood growling and steaming in a traffic jam without end, at least ten kilometres of washing machines from Holland, cheese from Denmark, Velux windows from Germany, a family's belongings being moved down from Venlo, Ikea furniture from Sweden, refrigerated trailers full of frozen pigs, chickens and cows, tankers full of wine and lubricant, everything Europe had on sale was being dragged back and forth across that pass.

And then the road slopes down, and suddenly the last vestiges of winter disappear, the world becomes spacious and clear, at Trento the vintners are cheerfully spraying their vines, the grasses are flowering and it's Pentecost in Verona.

At Bologna, the road is blocked. I stumble for the first time upon the new war. While Northern Europe sits quietly in front of the TV, looking at distant victims in unfamiliar towns, here the protests echo in the streets. The procession is led by a ramshackle Fiat with three loudspeakers on the roof, then the banners and red flags and behind them some 2,000 socialists, communists, anarchists, even Gypsies. In the course of a single weekend I count forty such demonstrations reported in the Italian papers: in Milan, Rome, Genoa, Naples, Cremona . . . Workers from Fiat and Alfa Romeo are rallying to the aid of their colleagues at the bombed Zastava plants. The collecting boxes rattle for Belgrade and Novi Sad.

In the old centre of Bologna the protest songs ring through the galleries, drums and trumpets are heard everywhere, a few proletarian leftist comrades have even brought along an antique air-raid siren, to make us feel as though we are in Belgrade. The group consists largely of older combatants who walk down the street conversing calmly between the shouted slogans – 'Adolf Clinton, go home!'. Their greetings are warm – 'Mio caro,' long time no see' – and amid the strains of the 'Internationale' you can hear the cheeks being kissed. In the crowd, another mobile phone rings loudly. At set intervals the progress grinds to a halt, as the boys up in front have to push-start their Fiat. The communists are singing 'Bella ciao,' the collective feminists and lesbians of Bologna form a solid bloc of floral dresses, two blind men try to cross the street between them all, groping along with their white canes, the proletarians let their siren wail, the anarchists wave their black-and-red flags, this is demonstration raised to a science, a speciality of the city.

I spend the night in my van close to the city's huge exhibition grounds. The perfume and lipstick merchants of Italy are holding a convention there. At the entrance to the car park lot stands a gigantic man with a friendly face who charges 10,000 lire for each car, and tears off vague little ticket stubs. One hour later he is arrested, but there's no hurry, he's even allowed to buy himself a sandwich before he is carted off. This is obviously a daily ritual. At night the exhibition grounds are deserted, yet a certain hecticness remains: prostitutes, shady deals, young boys, brothels on wheels. There is nothing dangerous about it, everything takes place calmly and routinely.

The next day I take the fast road to Ravenna, through the hills and the light green of spring in the direction of Predappio, the village where Mussolini was born. Driving there I almost collide with a rubbish bin along the road, stunned as I am by what I see across the street. One shop after another is selling everything that has been anathema in the rest of Europe since 1945: SS and *Wehrmacht* uniforms, Italian Fascist caps, weapons, books, swastikas. The village is one huge souvenir shop for all things from the wrong side of the fence.

The architecture of Predappio is remarkably uniform. These buildings were meant to breed model Fascists: the housing blocks with their typical square-jawed style, the warehouses of the Caproni aircraft company, the now abandoned Casa del Fascio on the village square. Mussolini pampered his birthplace. Between 1926–38 the town was converted into a Fascist *città ideale*. The order of the box of blocks rules supreme, the pillars stand rigidly to attention, the windows stare arrogantly at the sky, the barracks of the *carabinieri* greet the robust party headquarters across the square, arms raised in salute, heels clacked together.

Today the underground bunkers are used for growing mushrooms. All reference to Il Duce has been rigorously removed from the buildings, but his chunky face – complete with jutting chin – comes back a thousandfold on ashtrays, vases, lighters, buttons, posters, T-shirts and wine bottles. The house where he was born is kept in perfect condition, and one can take guided tours on request. The meter box by the front door is covered in inscriptions: 'Il Duce, I love you.'

Was Fascism an incident, a strange twist in the course of Italian history, a kind of disease that descended on the Italians around 1920 and of which they were finally cured in 1945? Or was Fascism, as the liberal Giustino Fortunato wrote in 1924, 'not a revolution, but a revelation', a movement that mercilessly exposed the weak spots in Italian society? What does Fascism tell us about Italy?

From the day the corpses of Mussolini and his mistress Claretta Petacci were left dangling upside down from a sign beside a Milanese petrol station on 29 April, 1945, almost every Italian historian has racked his brains to answer those questions.

To the outside world, Fascism was and is always seen as a single ideology, a single movement. In reality, however, the Fascists, with their many connections and backgrounds, formed a strange and motley crew. They reflected in every way the turbulent Italy of the 1920s. They included frustrated officers and industrialists, but also many frightened citizens and angry farmers. There were staunch nationalists among them, but also many who wanted little or nothing to do with the state. It was only to the outside world that Mussolini looked like the uncontested leader. In reality, he had constantly to play a game of give and take with all those different factions.

The driving force for all Italians, in all their hope and rage, was above all the inferiority factor: Italy was always missing the boat. In the second half of the nineteenth century, while all the major nations of Europe were concentrating on the expansion of their industries, the conquering of new colonies and the building of armies and fleets, the Italians were still battling for their own unity. By the time Italy had finally become a single entity on the map, it lacked the military and economic power to achieve its great aspirations. 'The Italians have such a great appetite, and such bad teeth,' Bismarck said, and so it was.

In 1914, Italy's share in the world's industrial production was 2.4 per cent, as compared to Britain with 13.6 per cent and Germany with 14.8 per cent. (Today those figures are 3.4, 4.4 and 5.9 per cent respectively.) Large landowners and speculators had bought up the estates belonging to monastic orders, and hundreds of thousands of hungry farmers had moved to the cities or emigrated. The traditional social structure had been destroyed for good. Those were years of ambition, poverty and frustration.

Was Fascism, then, simply a phase in the development of the Italian nation state, a growing pain that went away half a century ago? Predappio indicates the contrary. This same Fascism is still alive, it can be given vent to here with a form of innocent pride. Certain elements of it still resonate in Italian politics, and within Europe as well it still constitutes an important undercurrent. Fascism was, and is, more than a historical fluke.

In the 1930s the *Münchener Post* was already using the terms 'Fascists' and 'Nazis' interchangeably, and today the two movements are usually seen as one and the same. Yet, in the beginning, Mussolini had little use for Hitler. He considered him 'sexually degenerate', and his hatred of the Jews completely insane. When the Nazis tried to seize power in Austria in July 1934, following the murder of Chancellor Dollfuss, he assembled his troops threateningly at the Brenner Pass. What is more, he actually had a personal bond with Dollfuss: on the day of the murder, the Austrian chancellor's wife and children were visiting the Mussolini family, and Il Duce himself had to deliver to them the sorrowful news. One year later he decided to invade Ethiopia – earlier than planned – for he believed that within two or three years he would be at war with Germany.

The conquest of Ethiopia was the first step in Mussolini's drive to establish an empire of his own, just like the British and the French. It was to have been a fast and easy victory, and the Italians used every means – fair or foul – at their disposal: gas attacks, chemical weapons, random bombardments of the civilian population. The Ethiopians were virtually defenceless, and were slaughtered by the tens of thousands. In the end, the expedition was Mussolini's greatest diplomatic blunder. The whole world saw it as a cowardly, villainous undertaking, and to his dismay his putative ally Britain turned against him as well. After that he had no choice but to join forces with Hitler, in an unholy embrace.

Hitler, on the other hand, had been a great admirer of Mussolini from the start. The Braunes Haus in Munich contained a life-sized bust of Il Duce. To the Nazis, he was the prime example of a dynamic leader saving his divided fatherland. Less than a week after Mussolini's famous 'March on Rome', the crowd in Munich's packed Hofbräuhaus was shouting: 'Germany's Mussolini is called Adolf Hitler!' From that moment on Hitler was referred to as 'Führer', in imitation of Mussolini. And a year later in Munich, at the time of his first attempted coup, he spoke of it as the 'March on Berlin'.

But didn't they bear a striking resemblance, National Socialism and Fascism? Didn't both movements spring from the same soil? After all, Germany and Italy were both young nations in search of their own structures, and both had been formed as confederacies of small states. In both countries, stymied nationalism played a major role as well: Versailles had been a humiliating experience for the Italians too. The Germans mourned publicly for Saarland and Alsace-Lorraine, the Italians had their own 'oppressed' minorities in Austria and along the Dalmatian coast.

Another important similarity was the culture of violence. Italian has more words for 'gang' than any other language. As early as 1887 there had been a major uprising by federations of peasant farm workers, in associations known as *fasci*, against the large landowners and the state. Tax offices were plundered and large estates occupied, all under the banners of Marx, the Virgin Mary and 'good King Umberto'. Mussolini built upon those rebel traditions, upon the rural anarchism of Mikhail Bakunin, upon the struggle against the 'alien', elitist state. The *Arditi*, the 'fearless ones' – crack units formed during the First World War and operating on the fringe ever since – were the Italian counterparts of the German *Freikorper*. These commandos, some 10,000 in all, went about dressed in black, wore a skull and crossbones as their emblem and spoke only in the form of exchanges screamed back and forth between the commander and his troops. Their language, clothing and folklore was adopted by Mussolini as that of the 'typical Italian male', and later by Fascists and Nazis all over Europe.

Within a short time of Mussolini setting up the Fasci di Combattimento on Milan's Piazza San Sepolcro, on 23 March, 1919, his *fasci* could no longer be distinguished from the *Arditi*. In the first month of their existence, the Milanese *fasci* attacked and destroyed the offices of *Avanti!*, the socialist party organ that Mussolini had led with such verve in his younger years. Three years later, with the help of the large landowners, they effectively and brutally stamped out the socialist and Catholic workers' movements and purged local politics of their representatives by murder, beatings, arson and intimidation.

Terror paid off: this, too, was what Hitler learned from Mussolini. On 16 October, 1922, Mussolini and his men – under pressure from the *fasci* – decided to take Rome within the next two weeks. On 27–28 October, 1922, the legendary March on Rome was held. Some 20,000 poorly armed Fascists moved on the capital and stopped only thirty kilometres from the city; at that point, half the men turned and went home. (Mussolini himself, by the way, had simply taken the *direttissimo*, the express train, from Milan to Rome.) The government, however, was thrown into such a state of panic that it resigned. King Victor Emmanuel III refused to declare a state of emergency. Instead, the next day he asked Mussolini to form a new government. Like Franz von Papen later in Germany, the king hoped in this way to co-opt the Fascists. But Mussolini had no intention of disbanding his gang of thugs. In the April 1924 elections his government received two thirds of the vote. When the socialist Giacomo Matteotti stood up in parliament and stated that the election results were based on fraud and terror, which was nothing but the truth, it cost him his life.

By 1925, everything the Nazis could only dream of in the 1920s had already been achieved in Italy.

Then, for most Italians, began the years of indifference, of Gli Indifferenti as the title of Alberto Moravia's 1929 novel went. From 1925, the 'Roman salute' was mandatory at schools and universities, and almost everyone complied. The textbooks were placed under strict government censorship and every civil servant had to sign a declaration of loyalty to Mussolini; only a few avoided doing so. Making compromises and toeing the line, according to the American author Alexander Stille, constituted the norm in Fascist Italy; most people led their lives in a world of moral greyness, searching blindly for ways to maintain their integrity – to do their jobs well, to avoid the worst forms of obeisance, to lead a morally impeccable life – rather than follow the path of direct resistance.

All the more exceptional then were the few young men who actually did begin active resistance – those, for example, associated with Vittorio Foa's Giustizia e Libertà movement. In 1937, after giving the call to fight against Fascism in Spain – 'Today in Spain, tomorrow in Italy' – the movement's leaders, the brothers Carlo and Nello Rosselli, were murdered by French fascists operating on behalf of the Italian secret police. Foa himself spent eight years in prison, even though he could have obtained his freedom at any time by requesting a pardon from Mussolini. His friend, the brilliant Leone Ginzburg, lost his job at the University of Turin in 1933 because he refused to take the Fascist oath. In 1934 he was sentenced to two years in prison for his work for Giustizia e Libertà, and from 1940 he lived with his wife and young children in internal exile in the remote Abruzzi. He did not survive the war. Foa later asked himself why Ginzburg had waited to become an Italian citizen before taking part in 'the conspiracy'. His own answer was: 'It was precisely the Italian tradition which he considered to be the foundation for his own anti-Fascism.'

At first, however, Mussolini's experiment – unlike National Socialism – was viewed in Europe with a certain sense of appreciation. Many intellectuals found Fascism, like communism, an attractive alternative to 'weak-kneed' democracy. Terror was a price they were willing to pay. Mussolini's new society seemed to stand head and shoulders above debilitating party politics, religious feuding and the class struggle. Everywhere the dictator was lauded for his fight against 'political corruption, social anarchy and national degeneration'. The newspapers were amazed by the speed with which he carried out building projects and set up pension funds and other social services, and the comment heard wherever Europeans compared notes was that 'at least the trains in Italy are running on time again'. Winston Churchill called him a 'Roman genius', and in 1927 he assured Italian journalists that if he was Italian he would follow Mussolini 'wholeheartedly, from start to finish, in your triumphant fight against the beastly predilections and passions of Leninism'. The Indian freedom fighter Mahatma Gandhi praised him as the saviour of Italy. In October 1927, the readers of the Dutch daily *Algemeen Handelsblad* chose him as 'the greatest figure of his day', second only to Thomas Edison.

Mussolini's greatest diplomatic triumph was the concordat of 1929, which defined relations between the Vatican and Italy. When he embarked on his Ethiopian foray in 1935 – even as the Germans were expanding eastward, Mussolini wanted to build a colonial empire around the Mediterranean – the expedition was bid Godspeed by Pope Pius XI. In the cathedral at Milan, Cardinal Alfred Schuster blessed the banners which would 'bear the cross of Christ to Ethiopia'.

After that, an end came to the international appreciation for Fascism. Mussolini changed colours like a chameleon; he had always done so, but now it became obvious even to the most casual observer. In late 1937, he converted to anti-Semitism. Not only did he hope in this way to establish himself in Hitler's good graces, but he was also angry about the growing criticism of his Ethiopian adventure by the international 'Jewish' press. Criticism was something to which he was not accustomed. In imitation of Germany, marriages were forbidden between Jews and 'persons of Aryan descent', Jewish teachers and students were banned from the schools, restrictions were imposed on Jewish entrepreneurs. Leone Ginzburg, who successfully applied for Italian citizenship in 1931, despite his Jewishness, had it rescinded in 1938.

Even so, under Mussolini, neither Ginzburg nor Foa were ever persecuted for being Jewish. Italy never became a truly anti-Semitic state. The reluctance with which Italian officials and police – the Fascists among them – carried out the anti-Semitic measures stood in stark contrast to the punctuality shown, for example, by German, Austrian and Dutch officials. The deportation of Jews from Italy only began after the Germans had seized power, after September 1943. The number of Italian Jews killed was therefore significantly lower than in Germany: close to 7,000, a total of 16 per cent of the country's Jewish population. (By way of comparison, in France almost 25 per cent of all Jews were killed, in Belgium 40 per cent, in the Netherlands around 75 per cent.) In few European countries was the Holocaust sabotaged as thoroughly as in Fascist Italy.

The Fascists' racism was as void of content as many of their other slogans. It was not fanatical and principled, as it was with the Nazis, but opportunistic. From the beginning, the Fascist movement had Jewish members and Jewish financiers. Of those who took part in the March on Rome, 230 were Jews, after which Jewish party membership rose to more than 10,000. Anti-Semitic theoreticians like Giovanni Preziosi had little influence. When Il Duce and Pope Pius XI met in 1932, it was not Mussolini but the Pope who uttered overtly anti-Semitic comments. In a report unearthed by Mussolini biographer Richard Bosworth, the church's problems in the Soviet Union, Mexico and the Spanish Republic were, in the Pope's words 'reinforced by the anti-Christian spirit of Judaism'. For years, Mussolini himself had a Jewish mistress, and as late as 1932 he appointed a Jew as his minister of finance. During the first years of German persecution he granted asylum in Italy to at least 3,000 Jews. The Germany Nazi-pioneer Anton Drexler openly expressed his suspicion that Mussolini was himself a Jew.

Fascism, therefore, was an essentially Italian movement. 'Italy knows no anti-Semitism, and we believe it never will,' Mussolini wrote in 1920. Italians never cultivated any nostalgia concerning a lost 'Italian' tribe the way the Germans dreamed of a 'Germanic' tribe and an ethnically pure 'folk community'. Throughout the centuries, Italy had been populated by a shifting mixture of Etruscans, Celts, Greeks, Visigoths, Lombards, Franks, Saracens, Huns and other peoples, some of them original inhabitants, but most of them conquerors who had stayed. When Italy became a unified nation in the nineteenth century, there was no way Italians could form a 'conceptual community' by applying such terms as 'folk', 'race' and 'tribe'. The Italian symbols of unity were completely different: language, culture, the liberty of the French Revolution and virtù, that form of creative civilisation that had for centuries allowed the Italians to feel superior to the barbarians from the North.

There was yet another way in which Fascism did not resemble National Socialism: unlike the Germans, the Italians were not particularly enamoured by the phenomenon of 'the state'. From the sixteenth century, Italy had been exploited almost incessantly by Spain and Austria. In addition, the country's spirit had long been held in the iron grip of the Vatican, which had skilfully succeeded in stifling all joy in the Renaissance and the baroque. For three long centuries, in other words, the Italians had been learning to hate the state. To the average Italian, the state was an alien, an oppressor, usually corrupt, always inefficient, an institution that should best be avoided unless one could somehow profit from it. What is more, no distinct entrepreneurial class had ever developed in Italy: trade and industry had always remained closely intertwined with politics and the state, every business was part of a system of protection and preferential treatment, every businessman had some political connection, sometimes reaching even as far as the president himself. Against this background, the family was the most important place of refuge, the only alliance one could truly trust.

The Italian image of the state, based as it was on suspicion, was the polar opposite of the Prussian one, within which a central position was reserved for total surrender to 'the fatherland'. Hitler, therefore, was a very different kind of leader than Mussolini. The former had access to a finely tuned government apparatus of which the latter could only dream. Hitler led a movement of frustrated military men and merchants, while Mussolini, at least in the early years, had recourse largely to gangs of angry farmers. The roots of the National Socialist movement lay in the city. Those of Italian Fascism lay in the countryside.

In the film *Novecento*, Donald Sutherland played the definitive Fascist: big hands, nasty eyes, ugly teeth, a villain through and through. One encounters no such wonderful Fascists in Predappio. These days it is largely seventeen-year-old boys who press their noses against the shop windows and politely excuse themselves for reaching past you to pick up a copy of *Mein Kampf* or *The Fable of Auschwitz*.

For 150 euros here you can buy a Waffen-SS jacket, for 20 euros you have a brand new black shirt, but it will cost you twice that much for a cap and a Sam Browne belt to go with it.

One can also visit Il Duce himself. Mussolini's crypt is close to the church. He lies in a big sarcophagus, topped by a bust of his own massive head, handfuls of candles at his feet, two dozen fresh bouquets all around, amid a constant stream of visitors.

To his left and right lie his mother and his wife. 'He liked sturdy women,' his widow, Rachele Mussolini, announced after the war. 'Today I can tell you that Mussolini's conquests were just as numerous as those of the average Italian man who is attractive to women.' She insisted, however, that the truth be told: her husband had always slept at home, except when he was travelling. So when and where did he do it? 'Where? I think I know: at his office, where he had a sitting room, without a bed, but with a sofa on which to rest. And when? In-between times, of course.'

As individuals, Hitler and Mussolini were each other's polar opposites as well. The former was an unmarried artist, a vegetarian terrified of disease, the latter a family man with five children and any number of mistresses. The former displayed all the frustrations of the failed painter, at the age of thirty the latter was already the successful editor-in-chief of one of the biggest daily newspapers. In the eyes of the European elite, Hitler was always viewed as an erratic madman. Even before the First World War, Mussolini was seen as a promising politician. When Mussolini turned his back on socialism, Lenin sorely blamed his fellow party members in Italy for letting him go: in Moscow's view, he would have been the perfect leader for a great socialist revolution in Italy.

Today, sixty years later, the myth lives on. Four boys with shaved heads are taking pictures of each other. One of them asks me in a whisper whether I would mind taking a group snapshot, to put on Il Duce's tomb. On the prie-dieu lies the big guest book with a thousand inscriptions of 'Thank you, Il Duce!' Touring cars full of senior citizens roll up into the car park many times a day. 'Il Duce, you live on in our hearts!'

Outside I talk to the woman selling souvenirs. 'Today everyone here in the village is a communist,' she sighs, standing amid her collection of Iron Crosses. 'But in the old days they adored him.'

A little boy stands in line to pay for three postcards: one showing a woman kissing the Fascist banner, a recruitment poster for the Italian SS legion and one on which Stalin and Uncle Sam join hands across the Atlantic: '*Le Complot Juif*'. The woman cries after me as I walk away: 'That's just like the Italians! They never recognise a great leader!'

Chapter Twenty-One

Lamanère

THE NEXT EVENING I STAY AT MONEGLIA, A DESERTED TOURIST VILLAGE
on the seaside not far from Genoa. These are the days of depression. The
wind tugs at my van, the rain clatters on the roof and only Café Derna
offers warmth and safety.

The village is dominated by a highly unusual access road: a narrow
strip of asphalt along the coast, consisting almost entirely of tunnels. All
traffic, in both directions, must obey traffic lights that provide an opening
to the outside world only three times an hour, down to the minute. The
lights, therefore, determine the rhythm of village life as well: 'Hurry up
or you'll miss the green light at 3.45!'

This strange road, they told me at the café, was all that was left of a
railway line that had been built along the coast with great difficulty in
the early years of the century. A huge job, but one which would serve
for generations to come. The railway, in reality, was in use for scarcely
twenty-five years. Then came yet another rail connection a little further
along, electric, with two sets of tracks. Built, once again, for all eternity.

Elsewhere I had seen the same thing: railway trestles, escarpments,
built to last for all time, abandoned in the countryside. During the last
half-century this continent has been criss-crossed and ploughed through
with tunnels, bridges and concrete flyovers, an incredible amount of
work. The Roman aqueducts did their work for centuries. Tomorrow, the
twentieth-century tunnels and flyovers will already be antique. Never
before has progress worn so thin so quickly.

I drive on through the rain, along the coast, past Nice and the French
Riviera. At Aix-en-Provence the mistral is chasing newspapers and plastic
bags across the asphalt like little phantoms. Someone once told me that

old women sometimes faint from agitation when the mistral blows: now I can imagine it, vividly. Nothing stays put, everything whips and foments in the face of this noisy wind: branches, leaves, birds, thoughts, moods.

In the days that follow there are the comforting, colourful hills of southern France, the odours of earth and sun. At Perpignan I turn right into the Pyrenees. I drive past sleepy village squares with old men and tall plane trees, after that along a narrow road, a fifteen kilometre climb, and arrive at last in the southernmost of all French villages.

'Every valley,' an economist wrote about the Pyrenees in 1837, 'is a still little world that differs from the neighbouring world as Mercury does from Uranus. Every village is a clan, a sort of state with its own patriotism.' Villages hated each other for all perpetuity, and collectively they hated the nobility, the city and the state, for anything which came from that direction could only mean misfortune.

Lamanère was just such a village. The hamlet consists of a handful of houses scattered along the sides of the valley. About 500 people lived here in the 1950s, today there are only thirty-six. I stay with friends. We go to visit the neighbours, Michel and Isabelle, a cheerful couple in their late forties. In their warm oak kitchen they tell the unswerving story of all little European villages: a local school, lively shops, all gone within twenty years. 'There were two little espadrille factories here as well,' Michel says. 'When they closed down around 1970, the whole village just packed up and moved down into the valley, the young people leading the way.'

'But we were poor, too,' Isabelle says. 'Toadstools, blueberries, we ate anything the earth gave us. And we tried to trap any animal that moved.'

Michel: 'Everyone went hungry from time to time. We smuggled pigs across the mountains. My mother made espadrilles, too, six francs for a dozen.'

'And half of everything the land produced,' Isabelle says, 'went to the landowner. If you had two pigs, one was for M. Cassu. It was still that way in the 1960s. We worked like slaves.'

'Goats go up the hill, girls go down' was always the saying around here. To escape a life of servitude 'up the hill', thousands of nineteenth century French farm girls saw to it that they became pregnant, then left for the city to serve as wet nurses to the children of rich families. In some regions, like the Morvan, that even became a major source of local income after the first railways were built. Later, girls began working as maids, or ended up in a factory, which was better in any case than working in the stable. Masons from the Creuse, woodcutters from the Tarn, plumbers from the Livradois, all worked and lived together as fellow countrymen, in little communities, their only goal that of supporting the family farms back home. Yet, without meaning to, they fell under the city's sway. They grew accustomed to greater comfort, to better lighting, better pay and more favourable working hours. In the Creuse someone wrote: 'The workers' disobedience grows in proportion to their contact with the emigrants.' It was not that there was suddenly so much reason for discontent, Eugene Weber wrote in *Peasants into Frenchmen*, his study of rural France at the turn of the last century, 'it was that there had never before been any reason to hope for a change. What the homecoming worker taught his comrades first of all was that things were different elsewhere, and that change was not entirely impossible.'

'All the parents in Lamanère,' Isabelle says, 'pushed their children to go to work for the post office, the customs department, the police or the army. The young people were simply chased out of this village. Becoming civil servants, moving to the valley, that was the only way to escape feudal life. After that came the city folk and the hippie farmers. They enjoyed life here for a while, invested nothing, then left again. The people who were born here, they still love the land, and the old trees. But money ruins everything.'

I look out at the snowy peaks. The silence here is unbelievable: this exists only at Europe's outer reaches. At night you can hear the beat of an owl's wing. The starry sky makes you dizzy. It is as though all this has existed since time began, the endless forest, the village, the quiet breath of the land.

I talk to another neighbour, Patrick Barrière. Like all farmers, he starts off with stories about his animals. 'One of my calves died last week,' he says. 'I thought: here comes one of those hang-gliders. It was an eagle. It stood there beside that dead calf, it was the size of a big sheepdog. After that came the foxes and the lynxes: within three days, that calf was picked clean.'

Then he talks about the land, says there is nothing eternal about it. 'Oh, Monsieur, these woods never used to go on like this. In my father's day this valley was full of people, and every piece of land was put to use. It was a mixed landscape: woods, but also lots of pastureland and little fields. Not long ago there was a forest fire here. You saw all those old terraces reappear. Yes, the old folks worked their fingers to the bone. And for what? Poverty and a little food and shelter, that was all.'

Eugene Weber compared these farmers' views of the world to the look in the eyes of terrified men in desperate circumstances. In their eyes the village was 'a lifeboat struggling to stay afloat in heavy seas, its culture a combination of discipline and reassurance designed to keep its occupants alive. Insecurity was the rule, existence consistently marginal. Tradition, routine, vigorous adherence to the family and the community – and to their rules – alone made existence possible.'

The big turnaround came to Lamanère in about 1940. While the rest of Europe's farmers were turning to mechanised agriculture, in these mountains there went on working with oxen and their own bare hands. There was no way they could compete. The farm children were driven into the factories like lambs to the slaughter. The *coup de grâce* came when the government offered them an attractive price to take over their land and turn it into forest. Within ten years, half the farms, gardens and orchards had disappeared. Today, backed by piles of European cash, a monotonous layer of 'new nature' is being laid across the land. Old oaks and chestnuts are being chopped down without mercy. Varieties of trees that have never grown here before are being planted, trees that grow quickly and efficiently. Patrick Barrière has almost no neighbours these days. That, too, is something about which these families knew nothing: loneliness.

We drink another pastis, and talk turns to history. 'I've always found bullets lying around the countryside here,' Patrick says. 'There were some goings-on around here, let me tell you! In winter 1939 a couple of hundred thousand Spaniards actually came across those mountains. They had lost the civil war and now they could choose: run or die. Over in Prats-de-Mollo it was just like Kosovo: they had to pay for everything, the farmers around here took those rich Catalans for everything they could get. A loaf of bread cost one gold piece. Lodgings for the night cost a painting.'

'I'm a grandchild of one of those refugees,' Isabelle said.

Patrick's grandfather saw it all first-hand when thousands of republicans crossed these mountains into France after the fall of Barcelona. The head of their diplomatic service, José Lopez Rey, talked later about how he had pocketed the key to the last republican ministry of foreign affairs – a village school on the border – and stumbled into France dizzy with scurvy. During his last six months in Barcelona, all he had had to eat was dry rice.

Close to here, in Coustouges, at the top of an icy pass, the republican soldiers were forced to turn in their weapons. Some of the farm boys were still clutching a fistful of earth from their native villages, a handful of dirt as a souvenir. Others were singing. The French border guards upended their duffel bags on the dirt road, their last few possessions were swallowed up in the mud, photographs blew away across the slopes. A little further along were the freight wagons full of the Russian munitions, aircraft parts, artillery and other assistance the French had impounded. The republicans had made their stand alone in Europe.

Now there is a little monument beside the asphalt, placed there on the fiftieth anniversary of the Retirada of February 1939. 'Across this pass came 70,000 Spanish republicans. The hearts of one out of every two Spaniards froze.' If you drive on, you see forests of cork oak and wheat fields with poppies, and after that the earth turns dry and red.

Right-wing movements come from the countryside, left-wing movements from the cities, at least that's the idea. Farmers, and certainly large landowners, stand to profit from the preservation of property and the status quo, while workers have everything to gain from change and even, if need be, revolution. The social democrats and communists always focused on the urban proletariat, and did not know what to do with the farmer's problems – their theories did not seem to work in the countryside. The Bolsheviks solved the conflict between city and countryside by simply lumping the farmers together in a kolkhoz, by deporting or starving them. The rest of the left tended to leave this political terrain largely for what it was, and so to all intents and purposes left it to the Christian

Democrats, the conservatives, the extreme right and the many farmers' parties that arose after 1918.

There were exceptions, though. The left-wing Radical Party in France accumulated many supporters among the small farmers, because they were able to mix classic left-republican ideas with the protection of small landowners. In Italy, the communists and the socialists had a firm grip on the rural workers' unions: around 1920, a farmers' war was actually waged in Tuscany and Emilia-Romagna between the Fascists and the 'Red barons'. And in Spain one had the anarchists.

In 1935 and 1936, a young English violinist in search of the meaning of life wandered through Spain, living from his music as he went. *As I Walked Out One Midsummer Morning* is the name of the book Laurie Lee wrote later, and his story is characterised by the same nonchalance as the title. What he describes is fascinating. The Spain Lee crossed in the 1930s was not a different country, it was not even a different world, it was a different era. He describes the makeshift farmers' huts in the mountains, the houses that contained no more than was necessary for a simple life: work and the animals during the day, food and stories in the evening. 'So it was with us in this nameless village; night found us wrapped in this glowing barn, family and stranger gathered round the long bare table to a smell of woodsmoke, food, and animals.'

In the Sierra Morena he arrived, after walking for three hours 'up a rope-ladder of goat tracks', in a high, chilly 'huddle of rough-stone hovels, primitively rounded and tufted with dripping moss'. For a bottle of wine and a piece of hardened cheese he played his violin. 'I felt I could have been with some lost tribal remnant of seventeenth-century Scotland, during one of their pauses between famine and massacre – the children standing barefooted in puddles of dew, old women wrapped in their rancid sheepskins, and the short shaggy men whose squinting faces seemed stuck between a smile and a snarl.'

Spain was, in some ways, an extra-European territory. Anyone crossing the Pyrenees arrived in a country that had gone its own way, and that had skipped a number of major European developments. Karl Marx once called Spain 'that least understood of European countries'. Everything there was earlier, or later, or more extreme: the Moorish invasion in the Middle Ages, feudal relations that came too late and had to be

imposed with the use of great force, a church that repressed the
Enlightenment and intellectual progress, a powerful group of large
landowners who blocked all economic modernisation, the eternal hatred
between the regions and the central seat of power, the liberals and the
traditional Carlists, the farmers and the enormous dead weight of
nobility, church and army and the country's obsession with remaining
a world empire, even though it had long lain crippled beneath the
weight of that ambition.

'One half of Spain eats but does not work, the other half works but
does not eat.' This centuries-old saying accords well with the facts:
according to a 1788 census, almost fifty per cent of the male population
was not involved in any form of productive labour, and the nineteenth
century did little to change that. The country had once been one of
Europe's major producers of grain; now the forests had been razed, the
arable land depleted. As late as 1930, a third to a half of the population
could not read or write. Fifty per cent of the land was owned by less
than one per cent of the population. Between 1814–74 thirty-seven coups
were attempted, twelve of them successful. By the early years of the twentieth century, Spain was almost bankrupt: the army had one general for
every hundred soldiers, and a half of all the country's farmers lived on
the brink of starvation. During strikes in Barcelona between 1918–20, the
employers and the police hired *pistoleros* to kill union leaders. The unions
fought back in kind with their own snipers. Police Commissioner Miguel
Arleguí finally put an end to the uprising within two days by gunning
down twenty-one union leaders, at home or on the street.

The Spanish Civil War was not the first, but the fourth civil war within
a century. The country had been fighting itself for more than 150 years,
in a continual back-and-forth between absolute monarchists and free citizens, between bedrock conservatives and communists, between changing
nothing and changing everything.

In this polarised world, in which all of the participants in the Spanish
drama of 1936–9 grew up, anarchism played a central role. The philosophy of Mikhail Bakunin, like that of Tolstoy, harkened back to the ideal
of the *mir*, the free, autonomous Russian village community. Bakunin's
body of thought found adherents everywhere in the countryside of
Southern Europe, but in Spain 'the Idea' was generally embraced as a

new religion. In both city and countryside, the anarchists were far and away the most important revolutionary movement.

By 1873 there were some 50,000 followers of Bakunin in Spain. Anarchist teachers and students made the rounds of the villages, the way mendicant monks had for centuries before them, organising night schools and teaching farmers to read. By 1918 more than 200 anarchist news-papers and periodicals were being published in Spain. The anarchist union CNT had more than 700,000 members; the socialist UGT at that point had no more than 200,000.

Anarchism could become so popular because it was, in essence, a nostalgic rural movement. It appealed to a kind of homesickness that was felt as strongly by the farmers as it was by the workers of Barcelona, Bilbao and Madrid; most of them, after all, were the children or grand-children of farmers. Landlordism was theft. Land and factories belonged to their workers. A fair exchange of goods and services had to be achieved. Just as in Italy, the central state was alien and hostile. In its stead, a system of communities – of villages, neighbourhoods and factories that ran them-selves and made mutual agreements on a voluntary basis – was to be established. (The urban anarchists later developed a more complex model of 'syndicates', while the rural anarchists stuck to the original village model.) A general uprising was all that was needed, in Bakunin's words, to unshackle the 'spontaneous creativity of the masses'.

It seemed like a paradisal dream: the definitive answer to the rigid centralism of Madrid, the corruption of the church and the government, the oppression of the nobility and landlords. But at the same time it was a movement whose ideal lay in the past, in the days before the modernisa-tion of Europe, in the medieval urban and village communities. 'Those who would have been bandits in the 1840s became anarchists in the 1880s,' writes the historian Hugh Thomas. 'Anarchism was thus more a protest against industrialisation than a method of organising it to the public advantage.'

Sometimes I think: the left lost the civil war more than the right ever won it.

When I wake up in Barcelona, it is Sunday. My van is parked on a camping ground in a no-man's-land near the city, a place where billboards are the only thing sprouting from the soil. Hundreds of tents and mobile homes stand glistening in the sun, right in the path of the local landing patterns. Every five minutes a shiny Boeing belly comes roaring over us.

It is already hot outside. *Das rollende Hotel*, a bus containing three dozen Germans who all sleep in an enormous trailer, piled up in little berths like sausage rolls in a vending machine, has settled down in front of me. They are on a three-week tour of Spain and Portugal. 'It's not that bad,' an older man tells me. 'It's sort of like a ship's cabin.' Some of the tourists hardly leave the bus at all, they stare mutely out of the window at what the new day will bring.

Late that afternoon I wander down Las Ramblas, the city's grand prom-enade and marketplace. There are flowers and fighting cocks for sale, along the street are beggars with stumps bared and little dogs on leads, there are ventriloquists and dancing Gypsies, and through it all shuffles and drums the procession of the Virgin of Guadalupe.

A South American music group is playing in the Plaça de Catalunya. A retired couple is tripping the light fantastic; he has liver spots on his bald pate, her hair looks like lambswool, together they run through all the steps and pirouettes of half a century ago, right there in the middle of the street, and all time is forgotten.

On the quiet morning of 19 July, 1936, a young man came bicycling down Las Ramblas, his wispy red hair flopping, shouting again and again: 'The soldiers are at University Square!' Everyone began running. 'It was as if the lad had an enormous broom on the front of his bicycle which swept the people out of Las Ramblas towards the university,' an eye-witness said later. That was the start of the popular left-wing resistance to General Franco, who had set his military revolt in motion that weekend.

Spain was unlucky enough to start a civil war at the same moment that the tension between left and right had come to boiling point everywhere else in Europe. All parties saw Spain as a touchstone for good and evil, as an experimental plot for new tactics and weapons systems, as a dress rehearsal for what was about to happen.

Yet still, the civil war remained a Spanish affair above all. It was an unprecedentedly cruel and apocalyptic war, a struggle seen by both sides as a battle between good and evil. The anarchists fought with almost reli-gious abandon for their New Jerusalem, the communists, socialists and liberals fought tooth and nail for the achievements of the Enlightenment, Francisco Franco's rebels felt like crusaders defending the sacred values of old Spain. Never before had 'the enemy' been demonised as he was in the Spanish Civil War.

General Franco's coup, which triggered the conflict on 17 July, 1936, had been on its way for a long time. During the chaotic 1920s the army had already seized power once, in September 1923, when it installed General Miguel Primo de Rivera as dictator, to rule alongside the king. 'My Mussolini' was how King Alfons XIII once introduced him to a foreign guest, an accurate representation of the new situation.

The only thing was, Primo de Rivera was not a Fascist, and definitely not a Mussolini. He was an aristocrat from a prominent family, a father figure who had made a cautious start modernising the country. He dealt with anarchists and liberals with an iron fist, but was not, like Hitler and Mussolini, out to destroy them physically. His personality was both sympathetic and bizarre: a widower, he sometimes withdrew into his work for weeks on end, then lost himself for days in bouts of drinking and dancing as he drifted from one Madrid café to the next.

Primo de Rivera never succeeded in gathering around himself a major popular movement. He governed in the same way he was accustomed to live, as an old-fashioned landowner, an enlightened despot who had nothing but contempt for the law and the subtleties of the establishment. Once he had accumulated enough enemies, his fall came of its own accord: in an attempt to defend an Andalusian courtesan known as 'La Caoba' (literally, 'the Mahogany Girl'), he ordered the judge to dismiss the case against her – a narcotics charge. When the judge kicked up a fuss, Primo de Rivera had him transferred, then he sacked the supreme justice of the Spanish court for supporting the judge, and finally had two journalists who were pursuing the story sent into exile on the Canary Islands. On 28 January, 1930, the king ordered his dismissal. His final communiqué read: 'And now, now a bit of peace of quiet after 2,326 days of continuous malaise, responsibility and effort.' He left Spain. Less than seven weeks later he died, alone, at the Hotel Pont-Royal in Paris.

King Alfons decided to test the mood of his country. He saw the municipal elections of Sunday, 12 April, 1931 as a litmus test for his own popularity.

The results were ambiguous. All over the countryside his supporters maintained their majority, but in the cities the republicans won resoundingly. Rumour also had it that many villagers had been pressured by their landlords into voting for the royalists.

The next day, in a number of provincial capitals, the republic was proclaimed. The day after that the streets of Madrid filled with demonstrators. In the end, Alfons bowed to their demand that he 'leave the city before sunset'. It was the only way, he said, to prevent a civil war: 'Last Sunday's elections showed that I am no longer loved by my people.'

Power, from that moment on, lay for the first time in the hands of the reformers, in the hands of a 'young and eager Spain'. All over the country, construction began on new schools, hospitals, playgrounds, residential districts and holiday centres. But Spain soon became unmanageable. The Archbishop of Toledo refused to recognise the new republic – and was promptly forced into exile. New laws on education and divorce were not enforced. Rather than enact a single agricultural reform, the landowners preferred to chase the small farmers from their land. A general strike, and a miners' strike in Asturias, were violently crushed.

Five years later, during the parliamentary elections of February 1936, the right tried to regain power by legal means. The right-wing parties, monarchists and Carlists banded together to form the National Front. Their plan failed: the absolute majority went to the left-wing coalition of the Popular Front. Tension swiftly mounted. During the four months after the election, according to a member of the parliamentary opposition, there were 269 political murders and 1,287 reported cases of assault, 160 churches were burned, 69 political party headquarters and 10 newspapers were plundered, and 113 general and 228 smaller strikes crippled the nation. Although these figures may not be perfectly reliable, they provide an indication of the country's mood during the first half of 1936.

. It is a strange contradiction: Spain, the country that lived longest under a fascist dictatorship, actually offered no fertile ground for a fascist ideology. The country lacked the ingredients that had brought fascism to bloom elsewhere: embittered veterans, massive urban unemployment, frustrated national ambitions. And the country had traditional forces to hold it together, most particularly the church and the king. Initially, therefore, the ideas advanced by the radical right-wing Falange Española barely caught on: in the 1936 elections, the movement received only 44,000 votes (0.6 per cent). The right wing of the population felt more at home in the traditional Catholic and monarchist parties.

Unlike that in Italy, Germany, Hungary and Rumania, Spain's nascent fascism was primarily an intellectual movement. Its founder, the philosopher Ramiro Ledesma Ramos, was one of the best-read men in Madrid. The rest of the young coterie which – exhilarated by the takeover in Germany – set up the Falange Española in summer 1933 also consisted largely of nationalist writers and intellectuals. At first, their party organ FE resembled nothing so much as a literary journal; an angry Falangist wrote that 'if FE maintains such a literary and intellectual tone, there is little reason for a vendor to risk his life selling it'. This was no demagoguery: the first victim in Madrid was a student who, purely out of curiosity, bought a copy of the first issue and was promptly shot. The magazine paid little heed to militaristic Germany, but almost half of its foreign reporting dealt with Italy. The publication was hardly anti-Semitic, but it did point out that the 'Jewish problem' in Spain was not a racial problem, but a religious one.

The most important leader of the Falange was José Antonio Primo de Rivera. He too was a typical intellectual, a young and successful lawyer, a man like so many to be found in Europe in the 1930s: a reader, a thinker, a searcher. José Antonio was the son of the old Primo de Rivera, and showed it: in his nonconformity and his disgust for political parties, and in his belief in leadership and 'intuition'. As he admitted openly, his only real ambition was to continue his father's work. And love was his tragic flaw. He fell head over heels for a young duchess, a certain Pilar Azlor de Aragón. The affection was mutual, but the girl's father, a conservative monarchist, turned aside all proposals of marriage. He regarded the old Primo de Rivera as a parvenu who had cast shame on the monarchy, and wanted absolutely nothing to do with his son. Still, through various channels, José Antonio stayed in contact with the love of his life for many years.

José Antonio was the prototype of the classical Spanish hero: the man who chooses not for happiness but for his destiny, a man for whom the words 'honour' and 'pain' have special value. He was certainly not timid: when two bombs were thrown at his car in April 1934 – they failed to explode – he jumped out, chased his assailants down the street and even exchanged a few volleys with them. In the Cortes he punched a socialist parliamentarian who accused his father of 'robbery', and so precipitated a free-for-all between deputies of left and right.

However, his biographer Stanley Payne writes that José Antonio lacked 'the fascist temperament'. He was too generous, too broadminded, too liberal. He continued to associate with friends of different political persuasions, he recognised the human side of his opponents and struggled with inconsistencies in his own thinking.

During those years the major ideological discussions were held not between left and right, but within the right: between old aristocrats and technocrats, between racists and non-racists, between elitist conservatives who wanted to follow the example of the Portuguese professor-dictator António Salazar and the modern young people who favoured a popular movement along the lines of Mussolini's. And through it all ran the dividing line between radicals and non-radicals. Salazar, Franco, the Greek dictator Ioannis Metaxas and even Mussolini allowed the old existing order more or less to go on existing, and even won authority because of that. The German and Austrian Nazis were much more radical; they had absolutely no interest in making compromises, either with the church or with any other established order.

José Antonio, in fact, occupied a position somewhere between the two camps, but he was not fond of the Nazis. He considered them a 'turgid expression of German Romanticism'. Mussolini interested him much more: the Italian leader had actually been able to develop a modern, right-wing form of government without the maladies of class and democracy. Still, in his later articles and speeches, José Antonio systematically avoided the term 'fascism'. For his movement he favoured an authentic, Spanish form, and he attempted to reconcile tradition and the modern age, secularisation and religion, regional autonomy and central authority, mysticism and rationality.

From 1934, José Antonio began giving more serious consideration to an armed revolt. Late in that year he wrote a 'postcard to a Spanish soldier', addressing it to several senior army officers: in it, he said that the Spanish bourgeoisie had been poisoned by foreign ideas, that the proletarian masses were under the spell of Marxism, and that the military was the only group capable of filling the vacuum of this 'non-existent state'. The generals paid him little heed. The most important among them, Franco, paid him no heed whatsoever. In September 1935, however, the plans grew more serious. At the Parador de Gredos, close to Madrid, he and his colleagues developed a complete scenario for a coup, to be led by the Falange. (That same plan was actually carried out in part one year later, but then by the army.) And as though the Devil had a hand in it: it was at that same hotel, during those same days, that his great love Pilar Azlor de Aragón spent her wedding night with her new husband, an aristocrat and a naval officer. She had capitulated at last. For José Antonio it was, in his own words, 'the most horrific night of my life'.

Almost six months later, in February 1936, he was arrested along with a few other Falangists. The charge was clearly trumped up: the authorities said they had broken a seal the police had put on the door of their headquarters. But other charges quickly followed: illegal assembly, illegal possession of firearms and – after an emotional outburst – contempt of court. At last, on 6 June, José Antonio spat a pure declaration of war in the face of the republican government: 'There are no more peaceful solutions.' And: 'So let there be this war, this violence, in which we not only defend the existence of the Falange, but the very existence of Spain itself.' He himself, however, remained torn by inner doubt. He realised all too well that the revolt could fail, clearing the way for a long and disastrous civil war.

Meanwhile, the violence in the streets came to a head. In the night of 13 July, 1936, the monarchist parliamentarian José Calvo Sotelo was abducted by a handful of socialist militia members and, in true Soviet style, executed with a bullet to the back of his head. In some ways the attack was the mirror image of the murder of the Italian parliamentarian Giacomo Matteotti twelve years earlier. Like Matteotti, Sotelo was a prominent politician, and the reactions were equally vehement. There was a difference, however: Mussolini had been able to pilot his government safely through that crisis, but with this murder the Spanish republicans forfeited the last chance of a peaceful solution. Less than a week later, the civil war began.

Those who went to war against each other in Spain were of widely varied backgrounds. There were law-abiding Catholics who defended the republic. There were equally upstanding Catholics who fought along with Franco.

By way of the Comintern, the Soviet-controlled Communist International, some 40,000 volunteers to the International Brigade had been recruited to go to war against fascism. The young anarchists, on the other hand, wanted more: they were striving for a revolution of their own. Spanish farm boys fought against their landlords. Franco's conservative supporters fought against communism, but what they were really fighting against was progress. Their German allies, on the other hand, were quite progressive; they wanted above all to try out their new weapons. The Italians joined in for the sake of prestige. And so everyone in Spain fought their own war.

There were at least three major conflicts going on throughout the Spanish Civil War. There was the war between Franco and the republic. At the same time, there was a revolution going on within the republic, an extremely militant popular anarchist movement that was finally crushed by the communists and the middle classes. And finally, in the background, was the third conflict: between the Old Right and the New Right, between the right that only wanted to defend the old order, and the right that wanted to change and modernise that society by authoritarian, non-democratic means. In other words, between Francisco Franco and José Antonio Primo de Rivera.

Franco's coup was intended to be a straightforward revolt that would be over within a few days. But because Franco's grab for power was only partly successful, a long civil war ensued. The generals were unable to secure more than a third of the country. That gave the republicans enough time to mobilise their militias and build an army of their own. In addition, it also gave the smouldering anarchist revolution the chance to flare up and spread across the country. It was in part precisely their own coup that unleashed the 'leftist chaos' the generals had been hoping to prevent.

From his prison cell in Alicante, José Antonio foresaw the disastrous consequences of Franco's demi-coup. There are clear indications that he made a complete about-face in his thinking during the first weeks of the civil war. He wrote letters to the republican government, offered his services as a mediator – members of his family could be held as hostages – and proposed the establishment of a government of 'national reconciliation'. In other words, he did everything in his power to tether the forces he himself had summoned up.

The republican government was not oblivious to the opportunity Primo de Rivera was offering. But the situation was simply too chaotic for them to take advantage it. After September, a new and more radical government came to power. Most of the new government ministers were not interested in a compromise. Too much blood had already been spilled for that.

José Antonio's trial, which finally began on 16 November, was grim. He was accused of 'mutiny', which was not far from the truth. He was an experienced lawyer and handled his own defence. Yet the proceedings seemed to sweep right past him, 'like a man listening intently to the rain'. Only when he heard the death sentence passed against him did he lose his composure. He faced the firing squad, along with four other political prisoners, in the prison yard at Alicante in the early morning of 20 November. All that is left to say about it is this: all five of them stood against the wall with the same fatalistic dignity that thousands of Spaniards, from the left and from the right, showed in the face of death in those years.

Years later, in the Valle de los Caídos, the 'Valley of the Fallen' outside Madrid, I saw the two of them lying together in that grisly Falangist church-cum-charnel house: José Antonio on one side of the altar, Franco on the other. There were three wreaths on Franco's grave, José Antonio had one. They were watched over by thin-lipped angels with faces of stone, their hair pulled back severely, their noses pointed and wings sharp, and between their feet a sword. Visitors came and went, a Mass was held there each morning.

The grave reveals the character of the one within. The basilica that is their final resting place looks like a Russian subway station, but three times as big and ten times as oppressive, with enough space for 40,000 fallen nationalists. The hacking away of the rock alone claimed fourteen lives. 'Punitive detachments' and 'labour battalions' of former republicans worked on the basilica for sixteen years. The remains of the barracks that once housed 20,000 convicts are still tucked away in the nearby woods. No room here for reconciliation: the republicans were to remain in their unmarked graves, along the roads and in the fields, rotting in hell.

The weather that day was appropriate: a thick mist hung over the hills, the cross atop the mountain appeared only now and then from the clouds, showers clattered down on the immense forecourt. The visitors gazed in awe at the crucifixes painted in blood, the rigid faces of the Virgins, the lamps in the form of whetted swords, at the bodies stretched out on the altar of the fallen, and at the endless, empty stone expanse before this blasphemous temple where Spain still comes to pray.

It is one of history's most macabre jokes, this common resting place for two men who could not stand each other in life. This cult of martyrdom, unlike anything else in modern Europe, in no way fits the intellectual José Antonio. Franco, however, is another case: he could not have cared less, all he needed was a symbol and so, without the slightest hesitation, he annexed all those traits of José Antonio's that he did not himself possess.

José Antonio enjoyed nightlife, risks and women. Franco was a mama's boy who detested the escapades of his skirt-chasing father. José Antonio was an impassioned politician. Franco was an unscrupulous pragmatist, who placed power above all else, a brilliant opportunist, and at the same time a typical 'little man', scarred for life by the lower middle class' rancour towards the casual privileges of the aristocracy. 'Down with the intellectuals.' This was the creed on which he had been suckled in the Foreign Legion.

At the end of his life, José Antonio tried desperately but fruitlessly to close the lid on the chest of demons he had opened. Franco kept the tightest control over the story of his own life; in that regard he was an uncommonly gifted manipulator. His military career during the days of the republic, the coup, the bloodbaths after the civil war, the defeat of his political allies in the Second World War, the American plans to liberate Spain in 1945 (scotched by Churchill at the last moment) and a dictatorship covering almost forty years; Franco got away with it all.

And so too with José Antonio's legacy. Up to the moment of the coup itself, Franco was not interested in the Falange Española. That interest was only aroused when the movement began growing by leaps and bounds. Within a few weeks, more than half of Franco's volunteer troops consisted of Falangists. Ultimately, more than 170,000 Spaniards would join the Falangist militia. At the same time, after José Antonio's death, the movement went increasingly awry. The party bosses flaunted fascist symbols, donned extravagant uniforms and terrorised the cities in stolen limousines.

The party organs even began adopting the Nazis' anti-Semitic propaganda. *The Protocols of the Elders of Zion* was cited eagerly and often.

Franco had no difficulty in co-opting this runaway movement within the space of only a few months, and incorporating it into his new Falange. Suddenly the general spoke with pride of his close ties with José Antonio, suddenly an entire body of myth had been created around the Falangist pioneer and his 'natural heir' Franco. In reality, the general had not lifted a finger to free José Antonio from his cell; it had not been in his interests. In fact, when the perfect opportunity to free him with the help of the German Navy presented itself in October 1936, Franco raised so many objections that the operation was called off. And when his Falangist rival was executed, the general kept that fact under wraps. Franco's propaganda machine made skilful use of José Antonio's prolonged absence. In private, Franco even suggested that José Antonio may have been handed over to the Russians, 'and it is possible that they've castrated him'. Only in November 1938 was his death publicly confirmed.

In his cell, immediately after the outbreak of the civil war, José Antonio wrote an analysis of Spain's future, should the nationalists win that war. 'A group of generals of honourable intentions but of abysmal political mediocrity . . . And behind them: Old Carlism, intransigent, boorish, antipathetic; the conservative classes, fixed on their own interests, short-sighted, lazy; agrarian and finance capitalism, that is to say: the end for many years of any possibility of building a modern Spain; the lack of any national sense of long-range perspective.'

His Falange became the stalking horse for all this. In the end, it was also to become the longest lived right wing totalitarian movement in Europe; from the first small groups to its dismantling in 1977, forty-six years in all.

Chapter Twenty-Two

Barcelona

BARCELONA IS LIKE A SLOVENLY WOMAN WITH BEAUTIFUL EYES. AN unattractive city with lovely neighbourhoods and sometimes gorgeous buildings. A glorious city with terrible neighbourhoods. A city, too, that has trouble coming to terms with itself. When you walk through Barcelona's city centre, there are three things that strike you.

First there is the stunning uniformity, even for a tourist haven. The shoemakers, barbers, greengrocers, news-stands, cafés and haberdasheries, the endlessly varied mercantilism that once dominated Las Ramblas, have been replaced almost entirely by boutiques and souvenir shops. The news-stands all have the same assortment of papers, magazines and other printed matter, almost all the bistros serve the same brand of instant paella, the souvenir shops all offer an almost identical collection of bric-a-brac.

Secondly, there is the absence of Spain. Barcelona is French, Italian, Mediterranean, and above all itself. Graffiti, manuals, children's books, newspapers, all of them are in Catalan, even the instructions on the ticket machines. The Spanish nation? There will be none of that here, thank you.

The third, striking phenomenon is the absence of historical markers. Like the Spanish nation, the twentieth century here has simply been glossed over. During the last century a great deal of fighting has gone on in a great many European cities, and all of them deal differently with their bullet holes. In what was once East Berlin they are still to be found, especially on street corners and in doorways, though their number is dwindling fast. Ah, one realises then, back in 1945 there must have been a troublesome sniper over there. In Barcelona you must look very closely to uncover any of that. On Las Ramblas, for example, in the doorway of a clothing shop on the corner of the Carrer Deca Canula, the faint signs of a gun battle are visible behind layers of plaster. Or at the Telephone Building on the Plaça de Catalunya: today an office building with a cafeteria and a shop selling mobile phones, but back then the centre of all communication and the site of a historic battle. But only if you examine the outside of the building will you see the shadows of a few direct hits. Not a hole in sight, not a plaque to be seen. Nowhere is so much war so carefully dusted away.

In late December 1936, the English writer and adventurer Eric Blair, better known as George Orwell, had the feeling of having entered a city where the working class was truly in control for the first time. He had come to Barcelona to volunteer for militia service. By that time the city had been in the hands of the revolutionaries for five months, and under the anarchists a thousand collectives had blossomed forth. All the walls were covered with revolutionary posters. Almost every building of any size had been occupied by workers and festooned with red or black flags. Every café and every shop had been collectivised. No one said 'señor' or 'don', everyone addressed the other as 'comrade' or 'you'. Tipping was forbidden. 'Well dressed' ladies and gentlemen were no longer seen, everyone wore work clothes, blue overalls, a militia uniform. There were almost no bullfights in the city any more. 'For some reason all the best matadors were fascist.'

'All this was queer and moving,' Orwell wrote. 'There was much in it I did not understand, in some way I did not even like it, but I recognised it immediately as a state of affairs worth fighting for.' He signed up with one of the militias of the radical leftist Partido Obrero de Unificación Marxista, the POUM, a choice he barely thought about at the time but which was to have far-reaching consequences. In the POUM militia, all orders were up for discussion. The training most badly needed – how to take cover, how to handle weapons – was never provided. The youthful recruits were taught only to march. 'This mob of eager children, who were going to be thrown into the front line in a few days' time, were not even taught how to fire a rifle or pull the pin out of a bomb.' Later he would discover why: there was not a single rifle to be found in the whole training camp. Only with great difficulty was Orwell finally able to arrange a weapon for himself: a rusty German Mauser dating from 1896. But, as he wrote matter-of-factly, a modern mechanised army was not something one could organise from one day to the next, and had the republicans waited until their own troops were well trained, Franco would have encountered no resistance at all.

The front line Orwell was sent to lay within sight of Zaragoza, a narrow strip of lights 'like the portholes of a ship'. Little happened in the months that followed, except for the occasional attack by night. 'In trench warfare five things are important: firewood, food, tobacco, candles and the enemy. In the winter on the Zaragoza front they were important in that order, with the enemy at last.' In lieu of ammunition, the opposing parties exchanged volleys of words: 'Viva España! Viva Franco!' Or: 'Fascistas – maricones!' In the long run a special shouting unit was even set up, and on the republican side this catcalling was raised to a fine art. Orwell describes how, on an icy cold night, someone from a neighbouring trench shouted to his fascist neighbours across the way only what he – ostensibly – was having to eat. '"Buttered toast!" one heard his voice echo through the dark valley. "We're just sitting down to buttered toast over here! Lovely slices of buttered toast!"' No one on either side had actually seen toast or butter for weeks or even months, but mouths watered along both sides of the front.

In April 1937 Orwell returned to Barcelona: in three and a half months the city had completely changed. Now there were normal avenues along which the rich, dressed in elegant summer attire, drove their shiny cars, and along which officers in the well tailored khaki uniforms of the People's Army strolled, the automatic pistols that were almost impossible to find at the front hanging from their belt clips. It was as though there had never been a revolution. The bourgeoisie had simply put on overalls and laid low for six months.

What shocked Orwell the most was the hardening of the political climate. At the front he had never noticed any rivalry between anarchists, communists and other political factions. In faraway Barcelona, however, it seemed that a systematic campaign had been set rolling to discredit the anarchist and POUM militias, in favour of the People's Army. No more heed was paid to the muddied soldier home from the front. The radio and the communist press passed along the most malicious rumours about the 'poorly trained' and 'undisciplined' militias, while the People's Army – in accordance with the best practices of Soviet propaganda – was systematically referred to as 'heroic'. In actual fact, it was the militias which had held the front lines for more than six months, while the soldiers of the People's Army were receiving their training behind the lines.

Like so many international volunteers, Orwell had no idea at first what kind of a war it was in which he found himself. He had simply gone to Spain to fight 'against the fascists' and had ended up more or less by accident in the POUM militia. It was only there that he saw that a revolution was underway within the republic as well, that because of that war the anarchists had been forced to surrender one revolutionary 'asset' after the other; in this internal struggle, the communists were not on the side of the revolution; on the contrary, they were on the side of the extreme right. In both Madrid and Barcelona, countless battles were fought for control over certain organisations and committees. The number of killings back and forth steadily increased, and slowly the anarchist ministers lost their grip on their followers.

These internal tensions came to a head in spring 1937. Ever since the coup, the Telephone Building in Barcelona had been in anarchist hands. An anarchist collective listened in on all telephone conversations, and if a conversation did not please the listener, the connection was simply broken. At one point that became too much, even in revolutionary Barcelona. On Monday, 3 May, the communist police commissioner and his men tried to storm the building. That resulted in a gun battle, and soon barricades were thrown up. The communists moved into Hotel Colón, diagonally opposite the Telephone Building.

There was grim fighting in the streets in the days that followed, with the communists and the police on one side, the anarchists and left-wing radicals on the other. The POUM, which had a considerable following in Barcelona, was one of the first to man the barricades. In the end, in a radio broadcast, the anarchist minister Frederica Montseney ordered her people to stop fighting. The local anarchists were enraged, 'they pulled out their pistols and shot the radio to pieces,' an eyewitness said. 'They were absolutely furious, but they obeyed nonetheless.'

According to the most widely held view, this civil war in miniature was little more than the police's way of getting even with the anarchists.

Those who fought alongside the anarchists, however, said it was more than that: it was the clash between those who wanted the revolution to continue, and those who wanted to control it and slow it down. The communist press granted the affair even greater import. They claimed it had been part of a plan to bring down the government, a conspiracy cooked up by the POUM. Even worse: it was a fascist plot to sow discord and ultimately cripple the republic. The POUM was denounced as 'Franco's fifth column', a 'Trotskyite' organisation of infiltrators and turncoats in close contact with the fascists.

Eyewitnesses from the Telephone Building tell a different story. There was nothing like a planned conspiracy, they say. No backup troops were brought into the city beforehand, no supplies stockpiled. There were no preparations whatsoever, and there was no plan. It was nothing more than a street brawl, said Orwell, who had been in the thick of it, 'a very bloody riot, because both sides had firearms in their hands and were willing to use them'.

For the communists, however, this 'plot' remained a good excuse to stamp out their anti-Stalinist rivals. A few weeks later, the whole POUM leadership was arrested. The POUM itself was declared an illegal organisation, all of the POUM's offices, hospitals, assistance centres and book-shops were seized and its militias disbanded. A general manhunt began for former POUM supporters, who were often militia members just back from the front. Hundreds if not thousands of POUM members, including at least a dozen foreign volunteers, disappeared under mysterious circumstances.

Orwell escaped this witch-hunt by the skin of his teeth. His commander and comrade, the Belgian engineer George Kopp, was less fortunate. Kopp had given up everything to fight against the fascists in Spain, he had spent the whole winter at the front, during the brawl in Barcelona he had acted as a mediator and saved dozens of lives; his reward was to be thrown into prison by the Spanish and Russian communists, with no charges brought and no trial held. Orwell and his wife moved heaven and earth to have Kopp released. During the first few months they received a few letters from him, smuggled out of prison by others who had been released. Those letters always had the same refrain: dark and filthy cells, too little to eat, chronic illness, no medical care. At last, the letters stopped arriving, and the Orwells assumed that Kopp had disappeared forever into one of the secret prisons. As by miracle, however, he survived the 'international solidarity'.

At the end of his *Homage to Catalonia*, George Orwell does something unique: he issues a warning to the reader: 'Beware of my partisanship, my mistakes of fact, and the distortion inevitably caused by my having seen only one corner of events.' Such honesty is a rare thing.

No other war has ever had as many lies told about it as the Spanish Civil War. Everything, but everything, is covered in a thick layer of propaganda, and even today historians have the greatest difficulty coming close to something like the truth. We know almost nothing about how all those people like Kopp, those 130,000 victims of terror from the left and from the right, met their end, or why, or where their tormented bodies were buried.

The only concrete evidence we possess are the eyewitness reports.

The only former foreign volunteer I knew well lived in California, in Oakland. He drove around in a cream sports car, he wore an oriental shawl and he talked all the time about Betsy, Betsy, his new love. His name was Milton Wolff, he was in his late seventies, and he had been the last commander of the Abraham Lincoln Brigade of American volunteers. He was twenty-three at the time.

In two years' time his battalion had gone through eight commanders – four were killed, four were badly wounded – and Milton was number nine. In 1938, Ernest Hemingway wrote of him that he was only still alive by virtue of 'the same hazard that leaves one tall palm tree standing where a hurricane has passed.' Milton had remained standing through the fiery bloodbath at Brunete, the slaughterhouse of Fuentes and the snows of Teruel. This was the same man who drove the cream car.

The last time I saw Milton was in 1993, during a sunny meal with Californian friends. He was still a tall, handsome man, and there was a girlfriend in the background then as well, half his age, as always. He had worked for the British Secret Service during the Second World War, including a stint in Burma, and later on he had served as an American intelligence service liaison officer with the communist resistance in Yugoslavia and Italy. After the war the American government treated him, like many other former Spanish volunteers, to the fascinating title of 'premature anti-fascist'. An army career, therefore, was out of the question for him. Even in his eighties he was still out to improve the world: collecting medicine for Cuba and financing ambulances and local clinics in Nicaragua.

That afternoon in 1993, Milton was in a sombre mood. 'They're dropping like flies these days, all my old comrades.' He mumbled something about the 'bastards' who had ruined it all, then turned his attention to my girlfriend's blonde locks. The squirrels were running along the tops of the fences. From the kitchen we could hear our hostess flattening used cans with a hammer, for the collective recycling service: metal with metal, compost with compost, paper with paper.

'It was simply a temporary and local phase in an enormous game that is being played over the whole surface of the earth,' George Orwell wrote. 'But it lasted long enough to have its effect upon anyone who experienced it. However much one cursed at the time, one realised afterwards that one had been in contact with something strange and valuable. One had been in a community where hope was more normal than apathy or cynicism, where the word "comrade" stood for comradeship and not, as in most countries, for humbug. One had breathed the air of equality.'

Right after the civil war broke out, German and Italian aid to Franco began pouring in: Junkers, Heinkels and Messerschmitts, technicians and pilots, guns and munitions, thousands of volunteers. It was, in part, a purely commercial transaction: Franco sold the Germans one mining concession after another. The Americans, ostensibly neutral, provided oil and 12,000 trucks. In their eyes, a 'fascist' coup posed less of a risk than a 'communist' revolution.

The republic received support from Mexico, which immediately sent 20,000 rifles. All republican eyes were fixed on France, where the left wing Popular Front was in power at the time. French friends of the republic quickly arranged for the transport of more than seventy airplanes, but then the assistance stopped. Britain was determined not to be drawn into another unclear conflict on the continent, and France followed suit. 'Appeasement' was the key word in those years; that is to say, the containment of dictatorships by means of patience and prudence, the very opposite of the bellicosity of 1914.

And so it happened that, on 8 August, 1936, France closed the Spanish border to all military transports. This inevitably forced the republic into the arms of the only ally they had left: the communists and Stalin's Soviet Union. With that, their fate was sealed in the very first weeks of the war.

The part of the country where Milton Wolff once fought lies along today's national highway N420, about a hundred kilometres south-west of Barcelona, behind the bungalows and the filling stations. Here were his positions, amid the olive trees in the quiet hills close to Gandesa. From his memoirs: 'A lone plane appeared and circled over the hills. A lull . . . And finally the entire hill seemed to come alive with shouting and shooting and exploding grenades, and then it was over.' For him, that was a crucial moment: it was when he lost contact with his battalion. Ascó, this must be the 'poor brown village' where he hid. Behind that the Ebro, which he finally swam across to get through the lines. The water is wild and red.

Further along, Calaceite and Alcañiz lie baking in the sun, all their shutters closed. Two old women are sitting before their houses in knitted vests; the rest of the city is either asleep or dead, there's no telling which. Along the road you constantly come across flattened foxes, rabbits, badgers, weasels and partridges. Above the mountaintops hangs an endless roll of cloud, folded back on itself like a duvet. The customers at the roadside restaurant are salesmen and truck drivers, the waitress silently serves up today's special, for there is nothing else to be had: salad, stuffed aubergine, stewed rabbit.

Heading west, the countryside becomes more rugged. The hills fade into an almost treeless plain. The earth is hard and bristly, the hot wind whistles around my van. Every once in a while the road curves through a brown, silent village. This area is littered with the cadavers of abandoned farms, houses, shops, cloisters. Behind almost every ruin lies a tragedy, although there is no telling which. What, for example, is the story behind that row of fallen houses, ten kilometres or so past Gandesa? Were they burned down during the civil war, or abandoned in the 1960s when better days never arrived? And that enormous imploded house close to Alcañiz, did it simply fall down, or did soldiers blow it up? This is the old Ebro Front, where the republicans mustered all their forces in summer 1938 for a four month, last-ditch stand. Only in Belchite, an abandoned village to the East, is the war still tangible: a few piles of debris and collapsed walls, a roofless church, one and a half trees, a cross of iron. In March 1938, Milton Wolff and his Abraham Lincoln battalion were among the last group of republican soldiers in the village; his commander was killed, then they were all swept away by Franco's tanks. More than 6,000 men were killed on both sides. The ruins were recently used as a backdrop for TV commercials for the Dutch Army: 'We perform peace-keeping missions.'

All the other hard-fought hills remain unsung. The dead have been hidden away beneath the soil, without a single marker. 'Forget' is the motto here. No one wants to rake up the past.

Chapter Twenty-Three

Guernica

HALFWAY THROUGH THE EIGHTEENTH CENTURY, JEAN-JACQUES ROUSSEAU wrote: 'Guernica is the most fortunate city on earth. Its people arrange their own affairs in a meeting of representatives that is held beneath an oak tree, and the decisions they make are always of the wisest sort.' That, at least, is what all Basque sources claim. In fact the great philosopher was talking about Switzerland, but none of that matters here.

Euskadi, otherwise known as the Basque Country, has a dreamlike quality. You fall into a deep abyss, and at the bottom you suddenly find yourself in a luxuriant garden, a different world with different people and a different language. After the parched Spanish plains, here there is suddenly a green little Switzerland, inhabited by a strange and ancient people. Their language grates like cuneiform. Outsiders have no idea what these people are writing or saying. Their communication with others is largely through tastes and smells: in the kitchen, a Basque becomes a true sorcerer. The hills are dotted with white farms and cows wearing bells; you can smell the ocean. Madrid is far, far away.

The average Basque is no different from the average European. He lives in a villa or in a cruddy high-rise neighbourhood close to Donostia (San Sebastian) or Ibaizabal (Bilbao), he spends his days in an office, a shop, at school or beside the conveyor belt, he spends his weekends with friends or family, in restaurants or at the disco. Still, if you ask him what he considers the ideal life, he will start talking about a section of valley with a few cows and a farm, about the life of his grandparents and great-grandparents.

For every Basque, the Basque separatist movement has another face. You have anti-nationalists, radical nationalists, theoretical nationalists, light nationalists, violent nationalists, pacifist nationalists, nationalists who plant bombs and fight in the street and nationalists who condemn that. Never lump them all together, not the Basques, and not the Basque nationalists either. Ever since the fifteenth century, the Basque provinces – just like other regions of Spain – have been fighting for the rights of the local nobles and citizenry, and for the traditions that go along with them. That struggle was usually about practical matters: privileges, locals laws and taxes. At the end of the nineteenth century this 'feel for independence' took on a more romantic hue, as it did everywhere in Europe. The founder of this new movement, Sabino Arana, advocated a government of national character for all Basques, both Catholic and pure-bred. In his study he tinkered away at assembling a nation: from the various Basque dialects he constructed an official Basque language, he composed a national anthem and even created his own 'typically Basque' typography. His final play, *Libe*, was about a woman who chose death rather than marry a Spaniard. Arana himself married a farm girl, simply for the 'purity' of her blood. After he died, she wasted no time finding a new husband: a Spanish policeman.

Arana called his new nation Euskal Herría, meaning 'the country where Basque is spoken'. The region was to include the three Basque provinces, plus Navarra and the French Basque Country. Many Basque nationalists regard him these days as having been a bit soft in the head, but his Partido Nacionalista Vasco (PNV) is still the biggest party in the Basque Country, his bust still figures prominently in the headquarters of the PNV, the most important nationalist prize bears his name, and his racist speeches have never quite been forgotten either.

During the Spanish Civil War, Basque nationalism turned into a militant resistance movement. At first the Spanish nationalists saw the staunch Catholic Basques as their natural allies, but that changed quickly enough. Franco and his supporters wanted a strong, central government, and that was what the Basque nationalists so vehemently opposed. In exchange for their loyalty, the republican leaders gave the Basques the republic they had been dreaming of. That independent Euskadi was short-lived. After only a few months, the new republic was trampled underfoot by Franco's troops in May 1937. The nationalist leaders went into exile or were imprisoned, an end was put to all forms of autonomy, the Basque language was banned and Basque teachers were sacked. Thousands of Basques were murdered: some estimates put it at more than 25,000. In the prison at San Sebastian the executions took place every day until 1947.

The PNV survived and developed into the moderate conservative Christian party that has been in power in the Basque Country for years. For a small group of Marxist students in Bilbao, however, that was far too tame. In 1959 they took a more radical tack: they set up Euskadi Ta Askatasuna (Basque Country and Freedom), otherwise known as ETA. One of their first attacks, in 1961, was on a train full of Franco veterans on their way to San Sebastian. Franco reacted vehemently and in kind: at least a hundred people were arrested, many of them were tortured, some were executed, others received decade-long prison sentences. The most famous ETA attack came on 20 December, 1973, when Franco's crown prince, Admiral Luis Carrero Blanco, was blown up. The explosion was so powerful that the admiral, with car and all, flew fifteen metres into the air and landed in the courtyard of a neighbouring Jesuit monastery. The badly damaged Dodge, licence number PM 16416, is now on display at the Army Museum in Madrid. Blanco was Franco's last prospect of a natural successor.

According to some Basques, there never was a 'good' ETA that later went bad. 'ETA has always been bad,' writer and ETA pioneer Mikel Azurmendi said later, and that had to do with the total imbalance between ends and means. After Franco's death, and countless schisms within the movement itself, ETA gradually degenerated into a powerful terrorist organisation which financed itself by means of extorted 'taxes', which did not shrink from blowing up a Barcelona supermarket full of women and children, which would threaten anyone with death merely for voicing different views, and which, despite all this, still maintained considerable support, particularly among young Basques.

When I travelled through the Basque Country in May 1999, it was intermission time. ETA had declared a ceasefire, and people were willing to talk. I had been put in contact with Monica Angulo, a Basque sociologist who spends six months a year in America. Along with a friend, she showed me everything there was left to see in Guernica: the stump of Rousseau's legendary oak — now protected by a Grecian dome; the old hall where the free Basques once met and still meet; the museum with its paintings of priests, banners and the taking of solemn pledges; and the new oak tree that has already been in place for 140 years. 'Basque nationalism is mostly anti-Madrid,' Monica said. 'It has a very personal background. Almost everyone here has a friend, a brother or a cousin who has been in prison at some point or who has had other major run-ins with Madrid. That automatically makes people nationalistic.'

As we talked and walked, I noticed that my Basque acquaintances were driven by more than simply the pursuit of political independence. I kept sensing that something else was not being said. Monica and her friend were singularly pleasant, intelligent and committed people, but at a certain point I kept running into a brick wall. 'Why are all of you so attached to those rituals? Why is independence so important that everything else has to take second place?' I was given no answer.

Their nationalism was an amalgam of the old and new, of resistance, but also of nostalgia. On the one hand it was a belated product of the nineteenth century, an outgrowth of the fundamental conflict that divided Spain throughout a large part of the twentieth century: is Spain a land of several nations, as the republicans believed, or should it remain the unified nation held dear by Franco and his followers? On the other, it fits perfectly with those other movements that arose in Europe in the late twentieth century, peculiar and significant counterparts of modernisation and globalisation. 'The Basque movement is a typical agrarian movement,' Monica said. 'That's what makes it different from Catalan nationalism.'

Hence the movement's popularity, one supposes, in the alternative young people's circuit, here and throughout the rest of Europe. Nostalgia was – and is – an important signal: in essence it is an indictment of a modern age filled only with materialism and a blind faith in all that is new. But nostalgia can also produce monsters. From Kosovo and Ruthenia to the Basque Country, everywhere Europeans have been driven mad by the longing for a fatherland that no one ever knew, that in many ways never even existed.

All this lends the Basque Country a certain ambiguity. It is privy to the ocean's vast skies, but at the same time as impacted as an Eastern European mountain village. It is probably the most autonomous region in all Europe, it has a status of which Northern Ireland can only dream, it is modern and industrialised, it has profited greatly from Spanish and European subsidies, but none of that has brought cosmopolitanism or tolerance: in the eyes of the nationalist Basques, Madrid remains a colonial power, to be fought with all available means. What is to become of that language and that independence, I ask my acquaintances, now that a significant part of the population is non-Basque, now that almost two thirds of the Basques do not speak a word of Basque, now that almost all opinion polls show that the opponents of secession far outnumber those in favour of it? I ask them: 'Can the Basque Country you dream of ever come about democratically, when members of the opposition can only campaign when surrounded by ten bodyguards? What kind of country would that be, for heaven's sake?' Once more there is no reply.

In Guernica, the notorious German bombardment of 26 April, 1937 is commemorated with a modest monument close to the Mercury Fountain, a large stone with a hole in it, 'in honour of the victims'. That is the only text on which all parties could agree.

The bombing is viewed in as many ways as there are viewers. For most Europeans it was a characteristic Nazi atrocity against an innocent Spanish town, a rehearsal for Warsaw and Rotterdam. For the average Spaniard it was, first and foremost, one of Franco's dirty tricks. To this day, the Basque nationalists see Guernica as Madrid's violation of their 'holy city'. And the old supporters of the Franco regime take a fourth view: the whole bombardment never happened. Guernica, they say, was torched by the 'Red' Basques themselves. The Germans admitted their culpability years ago, but the Spanish government has never been willing to rescind Franco's reading. 'Let bygones be bygones' is how people deal with the past in these parts.

The issue of Guernica is typical of the relationship between Madrid and the Basques. Both parties are possessed of a brutality that keeps all wounds open, and in that they resemble each other more than they care to admit. Suspected ETA terrorists – and even the editor-in-chief of a Basque-language daily is readily counted among them – can be detained for years without due process. Amnesty International regularly accuses the Spanish police of torturing prisoners. But when a victim files a complaint, even that complaint is seen by the Spanish government as an indication of one's ETA affiliations.

Can one speak here of the classic drama of a forgotten ethnic group divided by the relative capriciousness of a national border, doomed forever within the Spanish nation to play the role of 'national minority'? Is this where the old conflict between 'national' and 'people' rears its head, marked by the same wounds as those borne by the Hungarians, the Laps, the Frisians, the Welsh, the Scots, the Irish and all those smaller European peoples who woke up one day to find that, for whatever reason, they had ended up behind the wrong dotted line on the map of Europe? In some ways, yes; in other ways, no. Historically speaking, one has never been able to speak of 'the Basque provinces' rising in unison against France or Spain. The inter-regional conflicts were at least as serious, and every bit as numerous. Almost all of the great conflicts, including the Spanish Civil War, were also internal Basque wars. Ethnically speaking, it is equally tenuous to speak of 'the Basques': due to waves of migration, particularly those of the last fifty years, the Basque Country has become an ethnic potpourri in which one can recognise the 'real' Basques at best by their Basque surnames. Basque nationalism, therefore, bears telltale signs of a last-ditch movement: too late, too weak, dreaming of a country that never existed and that probably never can or will exist.

None of this detracts from the fact that the Spanish nation is faced with a problem. During the final decades of the twentieth century, ETA – second only to the IRA – were responsible for the most victims of terror in all Europe: some 800 in all. (By way of comparison: the Italian Brigate Rosse killed approximately 400 people in the 1970s, the German Rote Armee Fraktion killed 28.) What is more, the group is not isolated, its supporters are numerous, and even the pacifist nationalists are prepared to hitch a convenient ride with ETA's 'successes'.

The result is a painful, extremely complicated situation that no government can safely ignore. The legitimacy of any democratic state is called into question when it has such a militant separatist movement operating within its territory. Any sensible government will then do all it can to negotiate longer-term solutions. That is what Charles de Gaulle did with the terrorists of the OAS, and what the British have done with the IRA. One does not seek terms of peace with the people one likes, but with one's enemies.

For years, Spain ignored that rule of thumb. It wanted to be a modern, forceful nation, with its pronouncedly autonomous regions, but deep down, the Spanish mentality still seemed to bear the mark of feudalism.

Seemed, I say, because this apparent brutality may be the product of fear, of the feeling that the country will fall apart once the final bonds are cut. The process of nation-forming, which every country in Europe has gone through at some point, has in a certain sense never been completed here. Madrid is Madrid, Catalonia is Catalonia, and the Basque Country is the Basque Country.

A similar internal confusion can also be noted within ETA. Bit by bit, one sees that there are almost more attacks carried out in the Basque Country and against Basques themselves than against Spanish targets. Some authors therefore conclude that the Basque conflict is no longer one between Spain and the Basque Country, but between the Basques themselves, based on the question: to which fatherland do we belong, anyway?

In the museum at Guernica hangs a page from the *Heraldo de Aragón*, a daily newspaper sympathetic to Franco, dated 30 April, 1937: 'After heavy fighting our troops took Guernica, where our soldiers were dismayed to find entire neighbourhoods destroyed by the Reds.' The *Diario de Burgos* of 4 May, 1937 bore the headline: 'The horror of Guernica, the work of Red arsonists'. In the late 1960s, when a German bomb was found in the mud, soldiers quickly cordoned off the area and the bomb was never heard of again. That bomb was not supposed to be there.

'Right after the bombardment, my mother ran into one of Franco's officers,' Asunción Garmendia told me. '"Who destroyed Guernica?" he growled at her. She acted as though she had not seen a thing. "The Reds did it, the Reds, you know that!"' Asunción's mother said nothing. She carried the key to their bombed-out house in the pocket of her apron until the day she died.

These days Asunción is a professional survivor of the bombardment. She belongs to the Basque nationalist group of victims, and that is a very different set from the Guernica victims of that namby-pamby Euro peace group on the square. She wants this to be clear from the start. She is a little grey-haired lady, but on 26 April, 1937 she was a pretty seventeen-year-old. 'I worked in the munitions factory,' she says. 'We made bombs, "half moons" we called them, they looked like big waffles. It was Monday, market day. There were lookouts on the mountaintops, and when they saw planes coming they would flag to the lookouts on the church steeple.

They were supposed to start ringing the bells, and the factory sirens would take over. That's how the air-raid warning worked here. But that afternoon the bells suddenly started ringing like mad, and right away a big plane came over, trawng, trawng, trawng, and dropped a bomb. Our boss said, "Get down into the shelter, fast. This is going to be bad." So we stayed down there, for four hours. You kept hearing this thud, thud, and smoke came seeping into the cellar, people were weeping and praying and all I could think was: what am I going to do when this is over, where's my family? Finally a man came in and said, "You can all go out now. But Guernica is gone, there is no Guernica any more." We went outside, and you saw a hand lying here, a foot there, a head lying over there. And the whole city was red. Everything was just silent and red, as red as this.' She points to a Coke can.

That evening I sit on the patio of Café Arrien with Monica, a Basque writer. It is warm, the trees are blossoming and over by the fountain crowds of children are playing, cavorting about and dancing in circles. Behind them lies the new centre of Guernica, reconstructed in pseudo-antique style, built by one-time civil-war prisoners in about 1950.

We talk about the 'society of silence', the way Spain tries to deal with its past. 'All my father ever talked about later was the hunger,' Monica says. 'Never about the war. Almost all the good books about Franco and the civil war have been written by foreigners. It's still taboo.

'Here you have two kinds of silence within a marriage,' the writer says. 'Partners who refuse to speak their own language, and those who refuse to talk about the war. My parents belonged to both categories. My father was a leftist political prisoner, a worker from the south who was sent here as an exile. My mother was a real Basque, a staunch Catholic. One time they had a huge fight about it, on Christmas Eve. "You communists and anarchists, you came here and murdered our priests and raped our nuns!" my mother screamed. "Not enough of them!" my father screamed back. "Not nearly enough!" That was the only time.'

Across from our café the local young people are pouring into theirs. It has pictures of Cuban, Irish and Palestinian heroes on the walls. This is the mini-world of the ultra-nationalists, the closed circuit within which approximately fifteen per cent of all Basques live, the heart of their own party, their own trade union, their own sports, language, history and cooking clubs, their own newspaper, their own celebrations. Here every Spanish official is a 'fascist', every moderate journalist a 'collaborator'. Everywhere in the city you see their slogans: 'Model A is genocide for the Basque language!' And: 'Go home!'

'Doesn't this ever end, with you people?' I ask.

'ETA has stopped for the time being,' the writer says. 'It's not a stunt, it took endless discussions to get to there. But the road of violence wasn't leading anywhere.' We talk about how the IRA has now taken a political tack, and about how ETA is trying to do the same, but with much less discipline. ETA's political grass roots consist largely of young people between eighteen and twenty-five; the issue of self-rule does not play a central role in the lives of most Basques over thirty. My companions feel that ETA has pretty much stopped thinking strategically, and is gradually using its attacks only to save its own, isolated little world. 'Take the execution of Miguel Ángel Blanco, that city councillor, in July 1997,' the writer says. 'He was just a normal guy, like everyone else. It shows you how morally poisoned the movement has become. It goes further with every attack. The one on the Guggenheim Museum, a Basque institution, killing a Basque policeman. That we could ever have come this far . . .'

The writer could say a great deal more, that is clear, but at Café Arrien there is a point at which one stops talking.

Six months later the attacks began again. A new generation had come on the scene.

Chapter Twenty-Four

Munich

EVER SINCE 29 SEPTEMBER, 1938, DISCUSSIONS ABOUT WAR AND peace in Europe have revolved around the same, fearful question: will this be a Sarajevo or a Munich? In other words: can a great deal of diplomacy achieve a shaky balance, or must evil be crushed by force? We know that, in both cases, a war was the result, we know that everything went wrong afterwards, but each time we come back to those two cities, those contrapuntal reference points for the twentieth century.

In an out-of-the-way display case in London's Imperial War Museum lies airline ticket number 18249, the British European Airlines ticket with which the British prime minister, Neville Chamberlain, left for Munich on the morning of 29 September, 1938. Hitler had been waving the banner of war on behalf of the 'oppressed' Sudeten Germans, Mussolini had organised a conference, Great Britain and France wanted Hitler to guarantee fixed borders, and the Czechoslovakian delegation sat in an anteroom waiting to hear what happened. Under pressure from the Allies, the Czech president, Edvard Beneš, finally offered up part of his country to keep the peace. The rest would soon follow. In that same display case lies the famous documents Chamberlain waved when he arrived home: 'Peace in our time!' Here, for the first time, I read the weak-kneed phrases of the agreement: 'the wish never to wage war against each other again', 'this method of consultation will be the manner in which we deal with problems from this day on'.

Germany annexed the Sudetenland, no guarantee whatsoever was given by Germany for the independence of the rest of Czechoslovakia, but Western Europe was applauding the peace. The French prime minister, Édouard Daladier, thought the crowd waiting for him at the airport upon his return had come to heckle him. He was stunned when he heard the cheering. 'These people are mad,' he told his adjutant. But that was not the case. They were merely gullible, like so many Europeans.

Munich was a classic case of winning a war that had already been fought. Almost everyone sincerely believed that a new Sarajevo had been pre-empted. In the House of Commons, Harold Nicolson was one of the very few to condemn Chamberlain openly. Chamberlain and Daladier knew their constituency to a tee. In September 1938 nothing would have driven the British or the French to war for the sake of some insignificant piece of the Sudetenland. Their fathers had all fought in the First World War, and they knew enough.

Besides, both countries were unprepared, both economically and militarily, for a new war. Chamberlain knew that too, all too well. In September 1938, therefore, he had little choice but to reach an accord with Hitler.

Munich was the greatest triumph of the 'appeasers', as Chamberlain's supporters were called. And at the same time it signalled their demise. The agreement allowed Hitler to think that the West, under the guise of peace, would do nothing to arrest his aggression. In fact, the exact opposite was true: after the fiasco of Munich, the West had no more faith in negotiations. A new tone was established. Great Britain had, in the words of Winston Churchill, been presented with the choice between 'shame or war . . . This is only the first sip, the first foretaste of a bitter cup which will be proffered to us year by year . . . We chose shame, and we will reap war.'

In the anterooms of Munich, the fate of the Spanish Republic was also discussed. The great powers were sick and tired of the war there. Mussolini actually told Chamberlain that he had had enough of Spain, that he had lost tens of thousands of men there, and that Franco had wasted too many chances. Chamberlain wanted to apply his 'Czechoslovakian solution' to Spain as well. Stalin had fewer illusions. To him, the agreement at Munich meant nothing but the old democracies' acquiescence to Hitler. And this new policy line had an immediate effect on the war in Spain. The Soviet arms deliveries dwindled, then finally stopped altogether. The International Brigades were withdrawn.

The republic allowed the foreign volunteers to leave without much ado. They had served their propagandist function, the most hardened soldiers had either died or fled, in the end three quarters of even Milton Wolff's Abraham Lincoln Battalion were Spaniards. On 15 November, 1938, the foreign volunteers held a farewell parade in Barcelona. The crowds cheered, flowers were thrown, tears were shed. Dolores Ibárruri, known everywhere as 'La Pasionaria', spoke to the women of Barcelona: 'Mothers! Women! When the years pass by and the wounds of war are staunched; when the cloudy memory of the sorrowful, bloody days returns in a present of freedom, love and well-being; when the feelings of rancour are dying away and when pride in a free country is felt equally by all Spaniards – then speak to your children. Tell them of the International Brigades.'

The years of war did not pass. By mid-January 1939, almost 5,000 volunteers from 29 countries had left Spain. The remaining 6,000 – Germans, Yugoslavians, Czechs, Hungarians – stayed. They could not return home, there was nowhere for them to go. They went down with Catalonia, and finally with the republic. Barcelona fell at the end of January, Valencia in late March. Then it was over.

Czechoslovakia is the best-known victim of the 'appeasers', Spain the least known. The Spanish Civil War was decided from the moment the democratic countries withdrew and imposed their arms embargo. The war would not have been won either if the 'Red' revolution had succeeded, as the anarchists and Trotskyites claimed later. Franco soon had access to a professional army and the most modern weapons, and those cannot be compensated for by manifestos and nationalised factories. Germany's and Italy's support for Franco was practical and immediate, support from the democratic countries for the republic was ambivalent or altogether absent, that from the Soviet Union riddled with opportunism.

In the same way that the Vietnam War would mould the mentality of young people in the 1960s, the Spanish Civil War served as a reference point for the politically aware young people of the 1930s. You could say whatever you liked about the Soviet Union, the saying went, but when it came down to it, the Soviets had fought on the right side in Spain. In hindsight, that too proved largely a matter of appearances. Stalin acted primarily out of considerations of power politics, aimed only at advancing the Soviet Union's influence in Europe. An intelligent czar, given the opportunity, would have done no different.

When the Russian military archives were opened in the 1990s, a deluge of evidence was released concerning the hidden agenda of the communists in Moscow. None of the communist 'aid' was *given*. All of the Soviet weaponry had been paid for in hard currency, the prices ratcheted up to unheard-of heights, and in the end Stalin was able in this way to get his hands on a considerable share of the republic's gold reserves. A Maksim heavy machine gun cost the republic twice what it did on the open market, and a profit of more than fifty million dollars was actually made on two types of aircraft.

In return for this aid, Stalin also increasingly forced the republic to adopt the shape of a satellite state, of a sort of DDR *avant la lettre*. This sorely undermined republican morale in the long term. Even in the first reports, the anarchists were referred to as 'the pawns of fascism', '*provocateurs*' to whom 'revolutionary justice' should be applied. After that, Comintern agents and commissars began popping up everywhere in the army, intimidating, arresting and liquidating those who did not toe the line.

Ultimately, the Comintern devoured its own children. By the end of the civil war almost none of the important advisors and commissars sent by Moscow were still alive. But not one of them had died at the front. They had been called home one by one, condemned to death by kangaroo courts or murdered in the course of one of the countless political intrigues within the international communist community.

Spain became a backwater once more. After the victory, the nationalists killed another 100,000 political opponents, and no one lifted a finger to stop them. The country is still littered with their unmarked graves. A slave army was formed of at least 400,000 forced labourers, who were put to work until far into the 1960s for the construction of roads, dams and luxurious residential areas. No fewer than 30,000 children disappeared. They were taken away from their 'Red' parents and placed in orphanages, then adopted by politically correct families. The girls usually went to a convent, were given another name and then transferred so often that they could never be found again. Europe turned its attention to other matters.

The Spanish bourgeoisie and the old feudal authorities had overturned a democratically elected government. Then they had succeeded in crushing a popular uprising. In addition, a simultaneous revolution had been blown up by the anarchists and betrayed by the Bolsheviks. A free Spain would remain an illusion for two, three generations. These were the simple facts at the end of the civil war.

The great thinkers and rhetoricians of the left and right had been killed or forced into exile: Andrés Nin, José Antonio Primo de Rivera, La Pasionaria, Gil Robles, José Calvo Sotelo. The war had cost almost half a million lives. About 200,000 Spaniards died on the battlefield, 30,000 died of starvation, the rest were murdered. Then came the long, dry years of statistics, prayers and silence.

NORWAY

Oslo

Stockholm

SWEDEN

Åland

North Sea

Edinburgh

DENMARK

Copenhagen

Baltic Sea

Danzig

Ulster
Belfast

GREAT
BRITAIN

Coventry

Hamburg

Sachsenhausen

IRELAND

Dublin

London
Chartwell
Brasted

The Hague
Amsterdam
Rotterdam

Berlin

Dunkirk

Brussels

GERMAN EMPIRE

Saint-Blimont

Sedan
Longuyon
Metz

Prague

Prot.
Bohemia and
Moravia

Atlantic
Ocean

Paris

Maginot Line

Basel

Danube

Munich

Vienna

FRANCE

Berne

SWITZERLAND

Austria

(1941)
Laibach

Vichy

Lyons

Milan

Trieste
Fiume

Bordeaux

"état français"
Vichy Goverment

CROATIA
Zara (ital)

Toulouse

Florence

Marseilles

ITALY

PORTUGAL

Madrid

Barcelona

Corsica

Rome

SPAIN

Ebro

Balearic Islands

Sardinia

Naples

Lisbon

Mediterranean

Sicily

Algiers

Er Rif

Algeria

Tunisia

VI June 1939-41

INLAND

Karelian
(1940 Soviet)

Helsinki

Leningrad

Tallinn

Moscow

Riga

Königsberg

Minsk

SOVIET UNION

Brest

Warsaw

Kiev

Dniepr

Volga

Rowno

Don

Cracow

Dniestr

Bug

LOVAKIA

Sea
of Azov

Krasnodar

HUNGARY

(Aug. 1940 Hungar.)

(June 1940
Soviet)

Odessa

Crimea

Budapest

Tiflis

RUMANIA

Danube

Black
Sea

Bucharest

(Sept. 1940 Bulg.)

Trabzon

Belgrade

SERBIA

BULGARIA

Erzurum

ONTE-
EGRO

Nish

Sofia

Edirne

Istanbul

Ankara

Tigris

tiaro
tal)

Skopje

(1941 Bulg.)

(1941 Bulg.)

(1941 under
German occup.)

Tirana

Saloniki

TURKEY

ALBANIA

GREECE

Athens

Syria

Cyprus

Euphrates

Crete

Mediterranean

Geert Mak's Route

German Troop Movements in May 1940

0   100   200   300 km

Chapter Twenty-Five

Fermont

'I AM THE SON OF ERNST VON WEIZSÄCKER. MY FATHER WAS AN official at the ministry of foreign affairs, later a state secretary and ambassador. He was the driving force behind the Munich Agreement. When Hitler came to power, I was almost thirteen.

'It's hard to draw the line between everything that was later said and written about that period, and the things you remember yourself. What I do remember clearly is my father's standpoint during those early years. The amendment of the Treaty of Versailles, by strictly peaceful means, was the political line of the entire German diplomatic corps in those years. Almost all the diplomats shuddered at the Nazis' bellicose amateurism. That was the great problem faced by my father and his colleagues. They weren't yet particularly aware of the dangers and the depraved morals of the National Socialists in general. It was unimaginable to them, it didn't fit at all into their way of thinking.

'I remember quite clearly those lovely, summery June days in 1934, that infamous weekend of "the Night of the Long Knives". It was the first time that it became crystal clear that, if necessary, the new German regime would dispense with law and order. At that moment my father was working in Bern, I must have gone with him that weekend, because I still remember how he instructed me to listen to the radio: "Richard, I want you to report to me immediately on any news from Germany!" When I think back on those days, I can still feel the deep anxiety that overcame me.

'I come from a solid, civilised German family. We were certainly not rich, at least not in those first years. Our household was sober and modest. Sunday was the only day we had butter on our bread. One time, when I broke my arm, our family could scarcely pay the doctor's bill.

'My mother was a socially engaged and very practical woman. During the First World War she had worked as a nurse and surgical assistant in the field hospitals. She played a loving, central role in our family. The ties were strong. My idealistic brother Heinrich was particularly close to me. Our house was always full of music, and at one point we even formed a trio, with my sister on piano, Heinrich on cello and I on the violin. At Christmas my parents would put on plays with an old puppet theatre. We read classic dramas aloud on Sunday afternoons, and each of us was given a role. It took a long time before we started making friends of our own outside the family circle.

'My mother began quite early on with protests against the persecution of certain clergymen, she was quite committed to that. She knew Martin Niemöller, a former submarine commander who had become a pastor and who was very outspoken in his convictions. He had written a book, *From Submarine to Pulpit*, but my father always said: "That book should be called *With the Submarine in the Pulpit!*" That's the kind of man Niemöller was. It wasn't long before he was arrested. Along with a few other people, my mother went to great lengths to obtain his release. During that period I didn't have much contact with Germany, I was usually abroad, at boarding school. Our family had a system of codes for our correspondence: a dash at the end of a sentence, for example, indicated that the opposite was meant of what had been written.

'My father kept on working for the German government. Meanwhile he had become an important negotiator. Hitler, in the same way he later showed the generals how far one could get in war by simply tossing conventional mores overboard, also based his foreign policy on a game of bluff with the diplomats. The occupation of the Rhineland and the annexation of the Sudetenland were typical political successes made possible only by Hitler's extraordinary cheek and aggression.

'Munich is always seen as the best example of that, but Hitler later stated that Munich was one of his biggest mistakes. He should have eschewed all compromises in autumn 1938, he felt afterwards, and gone to war immediately. At that point the other world powers were not nearly prepared, and he would have obtained an overwhelming head start.

'Behind the scenes in Munich, my father did everything in his power to help draft a treaty which would preserve the peace. He maintained very close contacts with the British and Italian ambassadors. In the end they were able to slip Mussolini a proposed compromise, which formed the basis for the Munich Agreement later, during the summit with Hitler, Daladier and Chamberlain. Joachim von Ribbentrop, the former champagne dealer who became minister of foreign affairs and my father's boss, was furious. It had all been done behind his back. In my father's eyes, Chamberlain's 'Peace in our time!' was a perfectly legitimate claim. Later he said: 'Munich was the last happy day in my life.'

'Then, despite the promises made in Munich, Germany invaded Czechoslovakia. That was followed by the very last series of extensive negotiations to prevent a war over Poland, but my father had the feeling he had failed even before they began. During those days he took all kinds of steps which, had they been made public, would probably have resulted in his being tried for treason. On any number of occasions he told diplomat friends of his: "You people need to act now. You have to rob Hitler of the illusion that he can go on without the rest of the world intervening. You need to send a general to Germany, and let him pound on the table to show that this has to end." As it was, when Britain declared war on Germany in early September 1939 it came as a complete surprise to Hitler and Ribbentrop.

'That's why, when they accused my father later in Nuremberg of having helped prepare a war of aggression, nothing could have been further from the truth. He and a few of his colleagues had actually done everything they could to prevent a war.

'So why did he go on working for years for the Nazi regime? Well . . . you know, one never stops widening one's awareness. So much has been written about that since. My father was a top official, and he must have been privy to a great deal. Even though his own information and his imagination could not fathom a thing like the Holocaust, when you read the documents he saw and signed back then you can only conclude that he must have known enough to draw conclusions for himself. He saved – and this has been proven – a great many people, and he must have known about the crimes against the Jews. But when the whole, terrible truth about Auschwitz became known in 1945, he was just as horrified by it as I was, as a young soldier. He wasn't really aware of the full scope of the Holocaust, I am convinced of that.

'The only reason why he stayed put, I believe, was the hope that at a certain point he could exert a positive influence on Germany's foreign policies. At first he believed he might be able to prevent the outbreak of war, later he thought he could stop the attack on the Soviet Union. Most historians agreed about that later on: one of them even wrote that my father tried 'with appropriate determination and cunning' to prevent the war.

'I've read a great deal about that period, but one never finds out everything. There is one thing, however, of which I am sure: I knew my father well, the way he really was. And I also know that an injustice was done to the essence of that man, there in Nuremberg.

'I myself went to Potsdam in 1938 to enter military service. I was eighteen at the time. Things there were run – I was assigned to a machine-gunners' company in the 9th Infantry Regiment – according to the old-fashioned Prussian model, not according to the National Socialist one. The Nazis were a very different brand of people. Just as in the diplomatic corps, great tensions arose between the *Wehrmacht* and the Nazis. Most of the officers were pleased that a strong Germany army was being created again, but they thought the Nazis were pathological parvenus.

'By then my brother Heinrich had been promoted to lieutenant in the same regiment. What he had really hoped to do was study medieval history. But the Nazis had already politicised the curriculum, so he was having none of it. For him the regiment was a kind of intellectual island, you could call it a form of internal emigration. And there were more people for whom the *Wehrmacht*, strangely enough, served as a kind of refuge.

'Did we have doubts about what we were doing? Some talking did go on within the *Wehrmacht*, but that wasn't very common. As a young soldier, I never talked to my comrades in the barracks about the things I heard at home. There was some serious criticism of the brutal actions of the SA and SS, though. Constitutional law was a part of Prussia. But you must understand: we were very young, in those years our lives were a mixture of light-heartedness and deadly earnest. It only dawned on us quite gradually that, ethically speaking as well, we now found ourselves on a battlefield, in the midst of a moral dilemma we could hardly deal with. In 1941, for example, the army leaders ordered us to advance so far in the direction of Moscow that, by mid-December, we finally broke down and froze where we were. We received orders from on high to defend positions that anyone in their right mind could see were inde-fensible. Could we actually pass along such orders to people for whom we were responsible? And even though we didn't know much about the crimes that had been committed, one thing was clear by then: by performing our duty, we ourselves had become an instrument of evil. That is the situation in which we finally found ourselves.

'Later, in October 1942, my friend Axel von dem Bussche saw with his own eyes how defenceless Jews were shot and killed, far behind the lines of battle. When he rejoined the regiment, he told me about it. He gradually arrived at the decision to make an attempt on Hitler's life, and to offer up his own life if need be. Through other friends of ours we established contact with Count Claus von Stauffenberg. It was his idea that a perfect opportunity would present itself in December 1943, during the presentation of the new *Wehrmacht* uniforms in Berlin. As a young, heavily decorated officer, Axel Bussche would present Hitler with the new uniforms, and would then blow himself up along with the Führer. I arranged the travel documents and the contact with Count Stauffenberg. But, twenty-four hours before the ceremony was to take place, the British carried out an air raid and the whole thing was cancelled. To be honest, it was a miracle that the Gestapo never got wind of that first planned assassination attempt by the Stauffenberg group.

'But, anyway, in 1939 things had not yet reached that point. Right before the war started, I was at home recovering from an operation. Suddenly I received a summons from my unit, I was to report for duty right away. Three days before it all began, Heinrich and I marched together from the barracks to the railway station. The mood was completely different from all the stories you hear about the outbreak of the First World War. There wasn't a trace of popular enthusiasm. It all went quite secretively, in low spirits, quite literally by *Nacht und Nebel*, Night and Fog. We were put off the train close to Poland, and early in the morning of 1 September, 1939, they sent us across the border.

'I knew almost nothing about the country I was entering. In the papers I had read about ethnic tensions, and that there was disagreement concerning the status of Danzig. That was it. Later on in my life, as politician and president of West Germany, my major political theme – besides continuing concern about the DDR, of course – was the restoration of good relations between Germany and Poland. But, as a soldier, it didn't mean much to me.

'I don't remember passing a border post or anything. I do remember the quiet, oppressive atmosphere. That mood only changed on the evening of the second day, when I heard the loud crack of rifle fire and we ran up against our first Polish troops. It was close to the railway embankment at Klonowo, in the woods around Tuchel Heath. Heinrich was a few hundred metres from where I stood. He was the first officer in our regiment to be killed.

'We buried him the next morning, along with the others, at the edge of those woods. That whole night I held watch beside him, beside my beloved brother.

'My mother wrote: "Can God allow one man to call down this whole catastrophe on Germany and the whole of Europe? And our sons? I am not prepared to sacrifice one of them for this war. Our family circle, the endless luxury of having children, all our pride – from the last war, I still know what that means: all gone. Then life continues and what was ours never, never comes back. New people come along who never knew the ones we were so proud of."

'She wrote that two days before he was killed.'

———————

A peaceful landscape becomes a battlefield, and after a while it is as though it never happened. I drive along the N43 from Sedan towards the sea, past gently rolling fields of yellow rape, through little villages, house after house tucked away behind deep, lush gardens. The chestnuts are in bloom, the cows are up to their bellies in buttercups. This road sprang up like a little stream somewhere close to Luxembourg, and now it meanders through fields and shy Inspector Maigret towns: an intersection, a *hôtel de ville*, a train station, three cafés, a hotel close to the station, a bakery. The houses all date from that hazy architectural period between 1880–1920. They are sooty and weathered, they have seen all of Europe passing by.

At 8 p.m. I stop at Longuyon. The streets are filled with puddles, the trees still dripping from the spring shower. Swallows buzz the rooftops, the pigeons coo between the houses, a church bell chimes clearly, once. A fisherman walks along the gravel on the riverside. The earth in the kitchen gardens smells rich, the beans are well on their way. From the café comes a roar of laughter.

Who would want to go to war on an evening like this? 'Why die for Danzig?' the French asked themselves in September 1939, and during the glorious spring days of 1940 their reluctance was even greater. They did not doubt the strength of their army, they were not resigned beforehand to defeat, but they were scared to death of seeing 1914–18 repeat itself. For more than two decades, their brothers, fathers and uncles had been talking about the trenches and the burning and thundering battlefields. Seven out of ten French soldiers had experienced Verdun first-hand.

La dernière des ders was what the French called the First World War, the last of the last. In winter 1939, when the war was already raging on paper but not yet in real life, they were hoping for *la Marne Blanche*, a diplomatic and platonic replay of the last war, but this time without passion or bloodshed. In Longuyon a war memorial of the falling-soldier-with-flag type had been erected as early as 1919, bearing 500 names – the city numbered 7,000 – and no one wanted to see a single name added to that. In the end, there would be another 150 names.

Close to Longuyon lie the chilly corridors of Fort Fermont, thirty metres below ground. The fort was a vital link in the Maginot Line, the French wall that stretched from Basle all the way past Luxembourg to protect the country from the Huns to the east. Here you can see the dream of the 1916 foot soldier: a super-trench with bedrooms, canteens, work-shops, an electric railway, secret trapdoors, sick bays, bakeries and even a cinema to help against the claustrophobia. Sealed off from the outside world, 700 men could stick it out here for months on end. On a shelf is a radio covered in mould, plastered in white flakes.

The whole structure is dominated by the thought of winning the previous war. The same could be said of France's leaders of that day: they, too, were men of yesterday and the day before. The French commander-in-chief, General Maurice Gamelin – sometimes referred to as 'General Gagamelin' – was sixty-seven. His successor, General Maxime Weygand, was well into his seventies, and Marshal Pétain, at the moment of his appointment as vice-premier, was eighty-four.

While the *Wehrmacht*'s young staff members were busy developing all kinds of new weapons systems and tactics, nothing was happening in France. Around 1937, the Luftwaffe possessed more than a thousand

Messerschmitt fighter planes, faster than anything belonging to either
France or Britain. In that same year, a report to the French senate's defence
committee said: 'The German air force is in a position to fly over France
with complete impunity.' The enormous opportunities provided by the
tank, the unparalleled possibilities for the dive bomber on the field of
battle; the French army staff could not be bothered. Tanks do not change
the tenets of war, General Pétain said reassuringly in 1939. After Major
Charles de Gaulle entered a plea for the development of a modern and
mechanised army in his book *Vers l'armée de métier*, his promotion to the
rank of colonel was postponed for three years. André Maginot's life's work
proved to be a huge, useless war monument. The wall stopped abruptly
at the Belgian border – building had been halted due to lack of funds –
and the Germans had only to march around it.

The doors, valves, lights, levers and wheels at Fermont are still fully oper-
ational. Above the fort, amid the grazing cows, an iron trapdoor opens several
times a day. The barrel of a cannon appears and revolves a few times. Everything
about this mechanism and the fort has something tragic about it, like the
clipper ship: the absolute cutting edge, yet nothing but a grave error in
judgement, because the premise had already become a thing of the past.

And then one had the Germans. For ten whole months in 1916 they had
tried fruitlessly to take Verdun. In 1940, it took them less than a day. How
could that have been?

First there was the principle of 'loser wins all'. The very fact that the
German Army had been so greatly reduced by the Treaty of Versailles
forced the generals to build up the most efficient army with the fewest
possible troops. Every invention that might be of use was tried out. In
this way, Germany, thanks to Versailles, had laid the foundation for an
ultramodern air force as early as 1931.

In December 1934, the German army launched the twentieth century's
first missile from the island of Borkum. Von Braun's A-4 rocket reached an
altitude of two kilometres.

The Germans had also learned from their diplomatic mistakes. The danger
of a new war on two fronts was, at least for the time being, skilfully ruled
out. Out of the blue, Ribbentrop and his Soviet counterpart, Vyacheslav
Molotov, signed a pact in Moscow in August of 1939. Among Stalin's staff

Ribbentrop had felt 'as thoroughly at ease as among my own party members'. The Soviets sent a few hundred Jewish and anti-fascist refugees back to Germany as a token of goodwill. In mid-November, Molotov and the members of his delegation were welcomed in turn at Berlin's Anhalter Bahnhof to the solemn strains of the 'Internationale'. Under normal circumstances, simply playing that melody was enough to obtain a one-way ticket to Dachau, but now the entire Nazi elite stood to attention. Workers waved red handkerchiefs from the windows of a neighbouring factory.

It was only in the 1990s, after the collapse of the Soviet Union, that the secret protocols of the Molotov-Ribbentrop Pact finally emerged. (As late as 1990, Mikhail Gorbachev was still denying its existence.) In those protocols, both superpowers' European spheres of influence were carefully delineated. The Soviet Union was to have its way in part of Poland, Finland, Estonia, Latvia, Lithuania and Bessarabia. Germany could go ahead in the rest of Poland, and in Denmark, Norway, the Netherlands, Belgium, Luxembourg, France, Yugoslavia and Greece. Strictly speaking, it was a non-aggression pact. In actual fact, it was a pact of pure aggression, a thoroughly worked-out scenario for the upcoming wars of conquest.

Within weeks of the invasion on 1 September, 1939, Poland had been conquered, divided, plundered and terrorised by the Germans and the Soviets. The west of the country was absorbed into the Great German Empire, the areas around Warsaw, Krakow, Radom and Lublin were transformed into SS country. This 'General Government of Poland' was to be the area to which, soon enough, all Poles, Jews and other 'non-German elements' would be deported, and which would be 'governed' by the SS.

Western Europe was still in a state of partial slumber. Belgium, the Netherlands and the Scandinavian countries cherished their neutrality. To describe winter 1939, the British later coined the term 'the phony war', a hazy state somewhere between peace and battle, the silence before what was coming. The French would have liked nothing more than to have that calm last forever. They indignantly rejected a proposal from Churchill to block supplies into the Ruhr by filling the Rhine with mines: to do that would only lead to war. At some spots along the front their soldiers had even put up signs: 'DON'T SHOOT PLEASE, WE WON'T SHOOT EITHER!' The British and the French did, however, assemble a joint force of 100,000 troops in March 1940 to help the Finns against the Soviet Union. This decision, in the analysis of the distinguished British war historian A.J.P. Taylor, defied all rational explanation. The very idea of starting a war with the Soviet Union while the Allies had already declared war on Germany, he noted, was complete and utter madness, unless, of course, there was something very different behind it: a conscious attempt, for example, to channel this nascent war in an anti-Bolshevik direction, and to forget and end as quickly as possible the conflict with Germany. Whatever the background, the campaign came too late and led to nothing. The Finns capitulated in the month the Franco-British force was raised.

In the end it was Hitler who broke the silence. On 9 April, 1940, he invaded Denmark and Norway. For the British, this came as a hideous surprise. All winter, they themselves had been working on a similar plan of attack. Neutral Norway was of vital importance to the German war industry; in winter, all major ore shipments from Sweden left from Norwegian ports. As soon as Churchill became secretary of the navy in September 1939, he proposed the idea of a surprise conquest of the Norwegian ports and the blocking of German shipping routes with mines. The British intended to carry out their plans in early April. Admiral Erich Raeder, Churchill's German counterpart, had come up with the same idea in October: an attack on Norway to secure its ports. The Germans won, only because they were faster and better organised. The British landed in wintry Norway without skis and equipped only with tourist maps of the country. 'Missed the bus!' was what enraged Members of Parliament shouted at Chamberlain. The fiasco cost him his position as prime minister, and cleared the way for Churchill.

The strategy of Hitler's great offensive was slightly reminiscent of the old Schlieffen Plan. Just as they had in 1914, the German armies swung like a scythe through north-western Europe, but this time the swathe was much wider and cut straight through the Low Countries. Hitler could easily have followed the 'platonic way' of the French, eternally prolonging the phony war of the British and ultimately ridding himself of the entire Polish question by means of negotiation. But that was not his way. His ultimate goal lay to the east: the creation of German *Lebensraum* in Poland and the Soviet Union. But to make sure that Germany would not again become caught in a war on two fronts, he first had to make short work of France and the Low Countries.

At 3.15 a.m. on 10 May, the first shots rang out: at the Dutch border station of Nieuweschans the guards were eliminated, to allow a German armoured train to roll unobstructed towards Groningen. Paratroopers landed behind the lines to seize vital positions in the Hague and Rotterdam. The Dutch government had dismissed as 'alarmist' the emphatic warnings of a resistance group within the *Abwehr*, the German intelligence service. Here and there the Germans met with stout resistance, but the Dutch – who had not experienced a war on their own territory for more than 150 years – were generally in a state of shock. They had always thought of their country as a kind of Switzerland, neutral and inviolable. By flooding strategic strips of land in the case of an emergency, they thought, this corner of the continent could be converted into an island like Britain. On that day, however, the Dutch realised that their special position in Europe – half inside, half outside – was gone for good.

Alongside that was the non-militaristic character of the Netherlands. The concept of an 'enemy' was completely new for many. The writer Anton Coolen described the great trouble to which his neighbours in North Brabant province went to give direction to a couple of German soldiers. 'They crowded hurriedly and willingly around the car, craning their necks to understand the question in German . . . A few women came out of the house carrying trays with steaming cups of coffee, they brought them to the Germans, who folded up their maps and laughed.'

I found a letter that my own grandfather sent to his daughter, my mother, shortly after the German invasion. 'The garden looks lovely at the moment, the violets are already blooming,' he wrote. 'Now I sit in my office like a king. And I'm going to practise resigning myself to the new situation. Practise being content with all that overcomes you.'

On Tuesday, 14 May, Rotterdam was bombed, the third great Luftwaffe bombardment after Guernica and Warsaw. Most of the inner city was reduced to rubble. About 900 inhabitants were killed. That afternoon – the Germans had threatened to do the same to Utrecht – General Henri Winkelman capitulated. His army had been at war for precisely five days.

King Leopold III of Belgium capitulated two weeks later. By that time at least 1.5 million Belgians were fleeing to France. The king's decision created a breach in France's northern defences, and the French 1st Army's positions around Lille were suddenly no longer tenable.

At the same time, a grave conflict arose between the king and his ministers that would continue until after the war. For the Belgian government, the country's neutrality had always been a political given, a matter of sensible opportunism imposed by the configuration of power within Europe. But now they were ready to fight to the death. For Leopold, however, neutrality was a sacred principle, a line of behaviour that corresponded to his most basic sensibilities. He was obsessed with one thing only: preventing a repetition of 1914. Every ruined street, every dead soldier was, in his view, one too many. Unlike the assertive Dutch queen, Wilhelmina (who had retreated to England) he saw no sense in continuing the European war. 'France will go down fighting, perhaps within only a few days. Britain will continue the fight in its colonies and at sea. I choose the more difficult path.' After 28 May, the Belgian king considered himself Hitler's prisoner of war.

In the afternoon of that same historic day of 10 May, 1940, Winston Churchill was appointed prime minister of the United Kingdom. Five days later, at 7.30 on Wednesday morning, he was roused from his sleep by a telephone call from the French premier, Paul Reynaud. Disaster was pending. At least seven German armoured divisions had unexpectedly broken through the Ardennes and were now rolling through the countryside close to the town of Sedan. Behind them were trucks full of infantry. It was, Reynaud feared, the beginning of the end. And that, indeed, is how France was overwhelmed by more than 1,800 tanks of General Rundstedt's *Heeresgruppe A*, backed by some 300 Stuka dive bombers, that came storming into the country through the 'impassable' Ardennes.

The next day, when Churchill – who had quickly flown to Paris after Reynaud's call – looked out the window at the French ministry of foreign affairs, he saw a remarkable sight: 'Outside in the garden of the Quai d'Orsay clouds of smoke arose from large bonfires, and I saw from the window venerable officials pushing wheelbarrows of archives onto them.' He sent the French an additional ten fighter squadrons, but reluctantly, knowing that soon he would be needing every one of them in order to survive.

Chapter Twenty-Six

Dunkirk

IN THE MIDDLE OF THE ROLLING FORESTS OF THE ARDENNES, CLOSE to the village of Brûly-de-Pesche, is a tall block of concrete amid the trees, weathered and overgrown, with two thick iron doors and a little peep-hatch. Around here people call the structure *l'abri de Hitler*, and during the first week of June 1940 this was indeed the Führer's makeshift headquarters.

The photographs in the little museum make it look like a holiday in the woods of Brûly: a relaxed Hitler consulting with his generals in front of the barracks; the group in front of the village church where they all watched newsreels every day; the same group, laughing, at the edge of the field where Göring is about to start up his plane; the entire HQ staff listening to the radio on 17 June as Pétain announces the French surrender. (Hitler afterwards slapped his thighs in pleasure, his usual way of expressing glee, but regrettably there are no pictures of that.)

Rarely has a military campaign run as smoothly as the German invasion of May 1940. Contrary to what is often assumed, the Allied forces were at least as strong as the Germans, if not stronger. Hitler was fighting with fewer than ninety divisions. The French alone had more divisions than that stationed along the eastern border, to say nothing of over forty British, Polish, Belgian and Dutch divisions. The Allies had combined access to twice as much heavy artillery and one and a half times as many tanks. To be sure, the Germans had an impressive air force with at least 4,000 planes, while the Allies had no more than 1,200. That typifies the decisive difference: the Allies thought in terms of the last war, the Germans in terms of the next.

With their Maginot Line the French had prepared themselves for an old-fashioned sitzkrieg, while the Germans came with a concept that revolved around mobility and speed: the blitzkrieg. Their army no longer advanced at the speed at which a man or a horse could walk, but at the speed of a car, thirty or forty kilometres an hour. Their airborne landings and paratrooper campaigns – in the western Netherlands, for example – were unlike anything seen before. Their ultramodern Stukas sowed panic everywhere. In the wake of the advance hung the penetrating smell of dead bodies referred to by the German officers as 'the perfume of battle'.

At 7 a.m. on 20 May, 1940, two tank divisions from General Guderian's 19th Army Corps rolled out of Péronne in a westerly direction. By 10.00 they had reached the town of Albert. A little group of British soldiers tried to stop them there, with a barricade of cardboard boxes. At 11.00 the Germans reached Hédauville, where they were confronted by a British artillery battery armed only with dummy shells. At noon the first division took Amiens, where Guderian briefly paused to view the famous cathedral. The second division thundered on. By 4 p.m. they had reached Beauquesne, where they seized the entire map archive of the British expeditionary forces. At 9.00 that evening they reached Abbeville at last, and saw the sea by the dying light of day.

On that one day in May, in a single movement, they had cut through all the Allied positions. The British, the Belgians and the French 7th Army – more than a million men in all – were caught helplessly with their backs to the North Sea. The civilians fled en masse: in June 1940, a quarter of the French population was on the run.

In Picardy I look up Lucienne Gaillard, president of the Association Nationale des Anciens Combattants de la Résistance. 'Come right away,' she said on the phone. 'We're just having a board meeting.'

At her house beside the little grey church of Saint-Blimont, three older men are sitting around the table. She introduces them to me one by one: 'He was in the Maquis, he was in the Resistance, and he's here because his father was executed.'

'And you?'

'At a certain point this whole house was full of British and American pilots. You must realise, I was only fifteen at the time, but I looked quite grown up for my age.'

The table is covered with sheets of paper, neatly typed minutes, careful calculations from the bookkeeper.

'Ah, the funding. In the 1950s we had 1,000 members,' she tells me, 'now barely 130. Every year there are fewer.'

For the men of Saint-Blimont the war began when the mobilisation notices were posted, on 2 September, 1939. 'My father worked in the sugar factory, he didn't have to go. Otherwise we didn't notice much of anything, not until 26 May, 1940, that is. I still remember it clearly, it was on a Sunday, the day of my First Communion. We were coming out of the church when we heard the cannons at Abbeville. We left a few days later, like everyone else. Everyone was fleeing south, by car, on horseback, in carts and pushing prams. The panic was truly amazing, all the fear from 1914–18 came back to the surface. My father had a car. We slept along the road in rubbish dumps, in the hay. My mother was heavily pregnant. She finally gave birth in Limoges.'

Saint-Blimont emptied out almost completely. Of the 20,000 inhabitants of Évreux, barely 200 remained at home. In Lille, nine out of every ten houses were empty. There were only 800 people left in Chartres. On Monday, 10 June, there were at least 20,000 people waiting at the Gare d'Austerlitz in Paris for one of the infrequent trains going south. The afternoon papers bore huge headlines: Italy had entered the war, Italian troops had invaded the south of France. Two days later, the Swiss journalist Edmond Dubois stumbled upon an abandoned herd of cattle in the middle of Paris, their lowing echoing in the deserted streets. By the end of that week, when the Germans rolled into Paris, almost three quarters of the three million Parisians had fled. When Albert Speer visited Reims on 26 June he found a ghost town, its shutters clattering in the wind. 'As though the lives of the townspeople had, for one mad moment, stood still; on the tables one still saw glasses, plates and cutlery, untouched meals.'

Six to ten million French people fled their homes. The American journalist Virginia Cowles drove from Paris to Chartres, and everywhere along the road she saw cars that had run out of petrol. Old people, too ill or too tired to move on, lay exhausted on the ground. Halfway up a hill, a bakery van had stalled. At the wheel was a woman. While the cars behind her began honking their horns, she climbed out of the car and, surrounded by her four children, begged for fuel. No one did a thing. Finally, three men pushed the van into the deep ditch beside the road. The van fell on its side with a loud crash, the family possessions that had been tied to the roof rolled across the field. The woman screamed. Everyone drove on. It was hard to believe, Cowles wrote, that these were the citizens of Paris, the descendants of those who had fought tooth and nail for their liberty and had stormed the Bastille with their bare hands. 'For the first time I began to understand what had happened to France. Morale was a matter of faith.'

In London, Jean Monnet – who had by now risen to be head of the Anglo-French Coordination Committee, launched a daring, last-minute emergency plan: he wanted France and Great Britain to become one. A joint pool of shipping space had already been set up, just as in the First World War, but this time Monnet wanted to go much further. In a memorandum of less than five pages he proposed that the two countries become united: their armies, their governments, their parliaments, their economies, their colonies, the whole lot. The two countries could then no longer surrender independently. In the worst case, the 250,000 French soldiers still fighting in the west of the country could be evacuated to England, and fight on under the flag of the new union. The French fleet, by the same token, could sail to British ports and begin the struggle anew from there.

Operating jointly, Monnet reasoned, France and Great Britain had so many more resources than Germany that, in the longer term, they could never lose the war. Especially not if they could count on support from the United States. Monnet's intentions were more than a mere gesture born of desperation. 'For us,' he stated later, 'the plan was not simply an opportunist appeal or a merely formal text: it was an act which, with good luck, could have changed the course of events for the good of Europe. This is still my opinion today.'

Monnet had an excellent relationship with both Churchill and Reynaud, and his idea, unusual though it may have been, was given serious consideration. 'My first reaction was unfavourable,' Churchill wrote in his war diaries. But when he introduced the proposal to the cabinet, he saw to his amazement how 'staid, solid, experienced politicians of all parties engaged themselves so passionately in an immense design whose implications and consequences were not in any way thought out.' Finally,

Churchill agreed that the plan should be explored, as did de Gaulle – who had come to England on his own authority – and Reynaud.

That June, the decision-making suddenly speeded up. Monnet drafted his proposal on Thursday, 13 June. The next evening he already had a correction to make: 'Paris might fall' became 'Paris has fallen'. On Sunday, 16 June the final communiqué was drawn up. 'At this most fateful moment in the history of the modern world . . . The two governments declare that France and Great Britain shall no longer form two nations, but one, single Franco-British union.'

Early that evening de Gaulle flew with the document from London to Bordeaux, the seat of the French government at the time. Churchill and a few members of the cabinet were to make the crossing to France that night by cruiser, to add their signatures. But while the British ministers were at Waterloo Station, already in the train for Southampton, the news came through that Reynaud had resigned. The French government had rejected the proposed union, and the war was decided. Pétain had been appointed premier. 'It's all over,' de Gaulle told Monnet on the phone. 'There is no sense in pressing further. I am coming back.' Churchill got off the train and went home. On that same night, 120 German bombers attacked England for the first time. Nine British civilians were killed, the first.

Paul Reynaud could have been the same kind of leader as Churchill. He regarded Hitler as the Genghis Khan of the modern age, he demanded total dedication and promised that his government would 'summon together and lead all the forces of France' in continuing the struggle. The problem was, most of the French loathed him. He had opposed Munich – which had cost him the support of the moderate conservatives. He was in favour of the war – which had cost him the support of the right. He was a centrist democrat, but he survived only by grace of the socialist opposition's support.

By means of all kinds of manoeuvres – one of which was to appoint Pétain to the post of vice-premier – he tried to broaden support for his cabinet. But he was inept enough to draw in more and more tired defeatists. 'You have no army,' Pétain sneered at the British minister of war, Anthony Eden. 'What could you achieve where the French army has failed?' During those weeks Churchill flew back and forth to France at least four times, desperately trying to convince the French to keep fighting. He suggested that they, with large-scale support from the British, set up a huge guerrilla organisation. 'It is possible the Nazis may dominate Europe, but it will be a Europe in revolt.' It was to no avail. Pétain felt that a guerrilla war would mean 'the destruction of the country'. General Weygand claimed that, after the French Army capitulated, Britain would open negotiations with Hitler within the week, and that it would have 'its neck wrung like a chicken'.

On Sunday, 16 June, when Reynaud presented the French cabinet with the plan drawn up by Monnet, Churchill and de Gaulle, he was laughed at. Pétain called the union with Great Britain 'a marriage to a corpse'. Other members of the cabinet feared that France would assume the status of a British colony. 'Then rather a Nazi province. We know, at least, what that involves.' Next it was proposed that the government begin negotiations with the Germans. The idea of forming a government in exile in North Africa had already been swept from the table by Pétain. He wanted, he said, always to 'remain with the people of France, to share their suffering and misery'. Imperceptibly, he had begun to twist things around: he was the true patriot, those who went into exile and continued the struggle from abroad were the traitors. Later, de Gaulle was actually sentenced − in *absentia* − to death.

Reynaud had no desire to stand by and watch it happen. On Monday morning, 17 June, the French heard Pétain's high voice on the radio stating that Reynaud had resigned, that he was his successor and that he would arrange a ceasefire with the Germans as quickly as possible. The French Army surrendered, burned its banners, buried its dead and − in so far as it was still possible − slunk off in the direction of home.

Before me lies a dishevelled, yellowed booklet, published in 1946 by the Société des Éditions Franc-tireur under the title *L'étrange défaite*. It is little more than an essay, written in summer 1940 'in a deep rage' by the French medievalist Marc Bloch. Bloch, a Jew and a Resistance fighter, died in front of the firing squad six months later. But his brilliant, unadulterated fit of rage from summer 1940 still forms the basis for almost every historical analysis of what is known as the 'May War'.

The French defeat of 1940 is generally seen these days as one of the crucial developments in the Second World War. It not only cleared the way for Hitler's occupation of Western Europe, but also for his campaigns to the east, his deportations, his slave-labour camps and his extermination industry. It is such a central event in the twentieth century that we have come to think of it as an inevitability. Nothing could be further from the truth.

Bloch's account displays, first of all, complete bafflement. For the Europe of that day, the German victory was entirely unexpected. No one, including the Germans, imagined that this campaign could succeed so easily. The *Wehrmacht*'s chief of staff, General Halder, wrote to his wife as late as 11 May that most of his colleagues considered the whole expedition 'idiotic and reckless'. Even Hitler was counting on a fairly prolonged struggle.

Among the French, on the other hand – and Bloch emphasises this forgotten aspect again and again – the mood was one of enormous self-confidence. In September 1939, a top French official reported to his superiors that 'no one, or almost no one, in the population has doubts about victory, even if they are afraid of the price to be paid.' People even wondered whether Hitler would actually dare to begin an offensive against France. In hindsight, this wilful arrogance was one of the chief reasons for the defeat.

Other reasons, Bloch says, were found in the field of military strategy: the inflexibility of the French commanders, the inferior cooperation with the British and the disregard for information from intelligence services. It was not courage that the French lacked. At Lille, in June, the French fought fiercely to provide cover for the British retreat at Dunkirk. At Saumur, the 2,500 lightly armed cadets at the military academy had succeeded for two days in halting the advance of a German armed division, albeit with heavy losses. The statistics, too, speak of a great deal of forgotten heroism. During those first six weeks of war, 124,000 Frenchmen were killed, and more than 200,000 were wounded: that is roughly twice the number of German casualties and three times those of the British.

Then Bloch points to a final cause: in May 1940, France was anything but a united and unified nation, determined to fight the aggressors down to the last man. Bloch describes the ranks of the French Army as he and his fellow officers experienced them: 'Lieutenants: friends. Captains:

comrades. Commanders: colleagues. Colonels: rivals. Generals: enemies.'
On the political scene, things were no different.

In early August, Lucienne Gaillard crossed back over the line of demarcation between Vichy France and occupied France. 'It was no joke getting
home. Our house had been looted while we were gone. Everything had
been turned upside down.' Her father couldn't bear the thought of his
country being occupied, even though he had returned to the German
part of France. He began, with minor acts of sabotage, on his own.
Later he formed a group, derailed German munitions trains, joined up
with de Gaulle and provided shelter for stranded pilots. But during
those first years he was above all lonely and bitter. 'To him, Vichy
equalled treason.'

During those six fateful weeks, one miracle took place: Dunkirk. The
German drive went so quickly as to overwhelm not only the Belgians
and the French, but also the Germans themselves. Just as General Guderian's
19th Armoured Division was about to spring the trap and drive the British
into the Channel, Hitler ordered them to halt. 'We were speechless,'
Guderian said later. There was almost no resistance. The advance posts
could already see the steeples of Dunkirk. The delay lasted three days. In
that way, Hitler gave the British precisely enough time to evacuate their
defeated army from Dunkirk.

The rescue operation had all the elements of a heroic drama. A bizarre
fleet consisting of naval vessels, rickety fishing boats, old lifeboats, pleasure
craft, brown-sailed Thames barges and a sea of private yachts was tossed
together with lightning speed. Between 28 May and 4 June, 1940, this
allowed 220,000 British soldiers and 120,000 Frenchman, plus 34,000
vehicles, to be brought back to England. As well as 170 dogs, for no
British soldier was willing to leave behind his mascot.

The historical accounts are marked by great discrepancies. 'My own feelings are rather of disgust,' a British veteran wrote years later to Walter
Lord, one of those who wrote the history of that event. 'I saw officers
throw their revolvers away . . . I saw soldiers shooting cowards as they
fought to be first in a boat.'

'Their courage made our job easy,' a naval man wrote about exactly the same situation. 'I was proud to have known them and to have been of their generation.' According to two officers of the local command, the organisation around Dunkirk was 'absolute chaos', a 'debacle', a 'disgrace'. But one liaison officer saw Dunkirk as proof that 'the British were an invincible people'.

Today, in 1999, Dunkirk is a seaside resort like any other, with a huge plastic play-castle where 'Les Colettes' perform, shrieking children, perspiring mothers, ice-cream parlours and ugly apartment buildings, all of it imbued with a routine breathlessness that goes on day after day, a life off which the past rolls like water off a duck's back.

The beach at Dunkirk is one of those spots in Europe's history where things were truly touch-and-go, where some little thing, an error of judgement on the part of a single individual, determined the course of history. For what was it that persuaded Hitler to order his troops to halt, at precisely the moment when they could have delivered their opponents the *coup de grâce*? What are we to think of this order?

First of all: Dunkirk was crucial for the British, but for the Germans it was only secondary. The eyes of the entire German staff were turned on Paris. After the debacle of 1914, it was that city which they wanted to seize as quickly as possible. Other reasons lay in the military strategy: Guderian's 19th Armoured Division simply moved too fast, there was too little to cover its flanks, provisions became a problem, a brief pause was needed. Furthermore – as shown by survey maps found later – the German high command assumed that the area around Dunkirk was extremely swampy, and that their tanks would become hopelessly bogged down there. Hitler was highly susceptible to such warnings: after all, during the First World War he had seen with his own eyes how entire divisions had become stuck in the mud in this part of Europe.

According to some historians, there was another, psychological explanation for Hitler's actions: he may have consciously wished to allow the British to escape, because in this first phase of the war he was still hoping to strike a compromise with Britain. The British were to get off the continent, no matter what that took, but they were to be allowed their own independence and their empire. He considered a destroyed, disintegrating United Kingdom to be a far greater risk. The evacuation of British troops

at Dunkirk, as Runstedt and others concluded, was therefore not Hitler's
mistake, but, deep in his heart, his desire.

What remained was the crushing French defeat, a catastrophe in every
way. Hitler's success seduced Mussolini into committing Italian troops to
the Second World War as well. (Spain and Portugal remained neutral.)
For many Germans, the victory was the definitive confirmation of Hitler's
'genius'.

For the French, the debacle meant the fall of the Third Republic and
the establishment of a collaborationist government in Vichy. For decades
this defeat would determine British and American attitudes towards France.
And ruin the French self-image, full of 'glory' and 'honour' and 'the
fatherland'.

Chapter Twenty-Seven

Chartwell

NOËL COWARD'S PLAY *PEACE IN OUR TIME* WAS FIRST STAGED IN LONDON more than half a century ago, in summer 1947. It was a kind of historical science fiction. It was set in a pub in Kensington in the period between November 1940, right after the German conquest of Great Britain, and May 1945, after the Allies had liberated the island once more. It told the story of the English resistance, the English collaboration and the role of the German occupiers in England – funny, and frighteningly close to the mark.

The play itself is long forgotten. Today, at the end of the twentieth century, we cherish the story of the ultimate happy ending, of the demonic Hitler who plunged Europe into war, of the grisly struggle between good and evil which he, of course, was doomed to lose.

There is some sense to that, but at the same time it is too easy. Hitler, in fact, was not at all doomed to lose the war. In summer 1940, peace reigned in Europe. The greatest European conflict, that between Germany and France, had already been settled, and only the British were still fighting a rearguard action against German supremacy. What is more, in 1940 Hitler was still riding on an enormous groundswell of goodwill.

'The fall of France,' wrote the American journalist Rosie Waldeck from Bucharest in 1940, 'formed a climax to twenty years of failure of the promises of democracy to handle unemployment, inflation, deflations, labour unrest, party egoism and whatnot. Europe, tired of herself and doubtful of the principles she had been living by, felt almost relieved to have everything settled – not satisfactorily, but in such a way that it absolved her of all responsibility.'

Countess Rosie Waldeck was the American equivalent of Bella Fromm.

The pen name of Rosie Goldschmidt-Graefenberg-Ullstein, she was a
Jewish banker's daughter who, after a number of divorces, ended up
writing society columns and moving effortlessly in the most select circles,
and who beneath all her charm was possessed of clear judgement and
great discernment. She committed her European experiences to paper in
1942 under the title *Athene Palace*, the name then of today's Bucharest
Hilton, where she lived and worked for seven months.

For years Rumania had had its own violent fascist movement, the Iron
Guard. From 1938 the country was ruled by strict anti-Semitic legislation. At the same time, King Carol II was trying to make himself Rumania's
dictator, as Miklós Horthy had done in Hungary in 1920 and Ioannis
Metaxas in Greece in 1936. Since spring 1940, Bucharest had been run
by a coalition of fascists and generals led by Marshal Ion Antonescu. In
September, Germany more or less took over the country, which was
crucially important for the Reich's energy supplies. Rumania ceded large
parts of its territory to Hungary, King Carol abdicated, real power was
transferred to Antonescu and the Iron Guard was given free rein and
organised one bloody pogrom after another. In June 1941, Rumania
committed itself completely by joining Germany's foray into the Soviet
Union.

In 1940, however, the country was still neutral, and in June all of
Europe was sitting side by side in the lobby of the Athene Palace, as
though nothing untoward was going on: the old Rumanian dignitaries,
the leaders of the new radical right-wing government, the American journalists and diplomats, the despondent French ambassador. The 'elegantly
bored' British – diplomats, oil men, journalists and intelligence officers
– had their own table, the young Rumanian nobility sat at the bar, there
was always a table with a delegation of whispering *Wehrmacht* officers,
industrialists, bank directors and military attachés, another German table
was reserved for Nazis, Gestapo agents and boisterous women. Later a
table was added for the German generals, all of them equally courteous.

Rosie Waldeck: 'Seeing them sit there you would never believe that
they were here to plan a war. There was nothing tense or excited about
them, nothing that would indicate they sat up all night poring over their
maps.'

Even today, Waldeck's observations are of great interest; despite her

American diffidence, she was deeply involved with everything and everyone in the hotel. Night after night she sat talking to Germans in the flush of victory, to generals, diplomats and young officers, without in any way concealing her own Jewish background. What struck her most of all during those months was the enormous élan of almost all the Germans she met, 'the dynamism of the National Socialist revolution, the dynamism which went through the entire military and bureaucratic machine of Hitler's Germany.' It was like an intoxication, she wrote. 'All said that they never felt as free in their work as they did now.'

At the same time, their diplomacy was less than brilliant. 'The Nazis were good at conquering, but deplorable at exploiting their conquests, even for their own good, not to speak of the good of the conquered.' She also knew full well that this young, intellectual generation of Germans would, sooner or later, end up in conflict with the limitations of party and state.

But for the time being, in summer 1940, she saw a continent that was genuinely impressed by this unprecedented German vitality: 'Hitler, Europe felt, was a smart guy – disagreeable, but smart. He had gone far in making his country strong. Why not try his way?'

That was how many Europeans felt, and they all expressed it in their own way. In France they spoke of the 'Pax Hitlérica'. In the upper circles of society, it quickly became fashionable to invite young SS and *Wehrmacht* officers to dinner. They represented a dynamism that had never been seen before, that could perhaps breathe new life into stuffy old France.

The leader of the Dutch Anti-Revolutionary Party (ARP), the former prime minister Hendrik Colijn, wrote in June 1940: 'Unless a true miracle takes place, the European continent will be led by Germany. It is healthy, and therefore allowable realpolitik to accept the facts as they present themselves to us.' He hoped, when things quietened down, for a new European trade system under German leadership, a sort of early predecessor of the EU. In Belgium, the socialist leader Hendrik de Man published a like-minded manifesto in which he depicted the collapse of the decaying democracies as 'a relief'. A 'realistic' alternative – the word 'realistic' was bandied about a great deal that summer – was, in his view, an authoritarian government under King Leopold III.

Similar feelings were expressed in Great Britain. On 13 May Churchill had given his legendary 'blood, sweat and tears' speech in the House of Commons: 'You ask, what is our aim? I can answer in one word: victory, victory at all costs, victory in spite of all terror, victory, however long and hard the road may be; for without victory there is no survival.' Later this speech was generally cited as a classic example of determination and courage, but the reactions at the time were not all that enthusiastic. In his diary, Harold Nicolson noted: 'When Chamberlain enters the House he gets a terrific reception, when Churchill comes in the applause is less.' Many of the British, including King George VI and most of the Conservatives, considered Churchill in those days to be a warmonger and a dangerous adventurer. There was a strong undercurrent in favour of reaching an accord with Hitler.

Five Days in London is the title of John Lukac's careful reconstruction of the British war-cabinet meetings between Friday, 24 May and Tuesday, 28 May, five days that could have changed the world. Lukac's conclusion is inescapable: never was Hitler as close to total control over Western Europe as he was during that last week of May 1940. Britain almost presented him with a peace agreement which he would probably have accepted, and only one man was finally able to stand in the way: Churchill.

Besides Churchill, the British war cabinet in those days had four other members, at least two of whom could be counted among the 'appeasers': Neville Chamberlain and Lord Halifax. The other two, Clement Atlee and Arthur Greenwood (representing Labour), had no experience in government at that time. On 25 May, as the extent of the French defeat became apparent, Lord Halifax carefully began sounding out the Italian ambassador to find out what concessions would be needed to 'bribe' Italy from entering the war. Gibraltar, perhaps, or Malta? He hoped that Italy could provide the initiative for a peace conference with Hitler, leading to a 'general European arrangement'. England was to keep the sea and its empire, while Germany could do as it pleased on the continent. Hitler would probably have agreed to such a proposal: it was roughly the same division of roles Kaiser Wilhelm II and his ministers had contemplated in 1914. As a result, the Netherlands, Belgium, Luxembourg, France, Poland, Czechoslovakia, Denmark and Norway – the lion's share of Europe – would have been transformed into a federation of Nazi countries under the unyielding rule of Berlin and the discipline of the SS and the Gestapo.

It was Churchill in particular who opposed all compromise, who talked to his fellow cabinet members for days on end and finally won over Chamberlain, who, after 1938, was also convinced of Hitler's evil intentions. 'Hitler's terms, if accepted, would put us completely at his mercy,' Churchill believed. And: 'Nations which went down fighting rose again, but those which surrendered tamely were finished.'

In May 1940 it would have been blindly optimistic to think that Great Britain could defeat the Germans without massive support from the Soviet Union and the United States. But the British were persuaded that Germany would once again encounter difficulties due to its lack of natural resources. In that same month, the British general staff came up with a war plan that anticipated a deep crisis in Germany beginning in late 1941, followed by that country's collapse. The British, therefore, did not need to prepare for a war fought in huge battles like those of 1914–18. From 1942 onwards they would be primarily engaged in terminal care for a Nazi empire disintegrating of its own accord.

In the end, Churchill succeeded in winning over all twenty-five members of his government. 'I am convinced that every man of you would rise up and tear me down from my place if I were for one moment to contemplate parley or surrender. If this long island story of ours is to end at last, let it end only when each one of us lies choking in his own blood upon the ground.'

In his war diaries he described the pandemonium that arose then among these experienced politicians from all parts of the political spectrum. 'Quite a number seemed to jump up from the table and come running to my chair, shouting and patting me on the back. There is no doubt that had I at this juncture faltered at all in the leading of the nation I should have been hurled out of office. I was sure that every minister was ready to be killed quite soon, and have all his family and possessions destroyed, rather than give in.'

In Kent, a little less than an hour south of London, lies Chartwell, the estate where Churchill's heart lay and where he spent a large part of his life from 1924–64. This is where he planned his military campaigns, lunched and met with his political allies, where he wrote his memoirs and his works of history, where he withdrew to his painter's studio when tension got the better of him, and where he spent whole summers laying bricks and roofing tiles when the political winds had abated. It is a complex of brick houses on a crest of hills, with a glorious view of the wooded landscape of Kent. The Chart Well, the estate's spring, had formed a lake there, and later Churchill would build a great many things beside, often with his own hand: a swimming pool, dams, marshy gardens and even a second lake.

He had plenty of time for that in the 1930s, when his political fate was very much up in the air. For a long time, his tirades against the abandonment of the gold standard, the politics of appeasement and against the Indian resistance leader Gandhi – 'a seditious Middle Temple lawyer, now posing as a fakir . . . striding half naked up the steps of the vice-regal palace' – made him a political outsider. 'You probably don't realise . . . that he knows nothing of the life of the ordinary people,' his wife Clementine once blurted out. 'He has never been on a bus, and only once on the Underground.'

When Churchill turned sixty in 1934, he was, in the eyes of his contemporaries, a curiosity, a romantic reactionary who had lost his grip on reality. More than one historian has noted that, had Hitler and Churchill both died before the war broke out, Hitler would probably have gone down in history as the man who, despite his peculiar anti-Semitism, had put a collapsed Germany back on the map. Churchill, on the other hand, would have been dismissed as a footnote, as just one more promising failure in British politics.

Chartwell is still the reflection of Churchill himself: the playground of an aristocrat with too much energy, the library of a gifted historian, the studio of an amateur painter not devoid of talent, the family home of a man of feeling.

The building has been restored to as it was in the 1930s, and for the sake of the museum a few rooms have been joined and objects moved. Yet Churchill is still present everywhere: in the much-used library, in a jar of brushes on the windowsill of his studio, in the brick playhouse he built for his daughter Mary, in the flowered wallpaper on the top floor, in the bizarre collection of canes in the hall, in a painting of the family at breakfast with the red cat on the table. Churchill's bedroom, behind the study, is one of the smallest in the house. Beside his bedstead hangs his reading board, a handy, pivoting table. In the morning he usually governed the country from this bed, reading, dictating, making telephone calls, dressed in an oversized 'siren' suit with big buttons, always with his watery whisky and cigar within reach. When his biographer Martin Gilbert first stepped into this room in 1970, it still smelled of Churchill's tobacco.

Domestic life at Chartwell had two centres: the low-ceilinged, intimate dining room where the festive and expansive family lunches were usually taken, and the big study on the top floor. Here was Churchill's 'factory', as he called this cozy space with its heavy beams, wooden ceiling, bright windows, bookcases and a fireplace, all dominated by a lavish painting of his birthplace, Blenheim Palace. In Churchill's day this same space was occupied as well by the secretaries and assistants who handled his correspondence, did research and converted Churchill's incessant flow of words – he even dictated letters from his bricklayer's scaffold – into more correspondence, memoranda and books. He would proudly receive visitors with the words 'Do come in and see my factory.'

Between 1929–39, the decade during which Churchill was only a Conservative MP for Epping, the factory formed the epicentre of his activities. As Martin Gilbert writes, it was there that he carried out a kind of 'unofficial opposition', including a 'cabinet' of former colleagues, friends, dissatisfied officials and political allies. During those years he was part politician, part journalist, and produced among other things the widely praised, four-volume biography *Marlborough: His Life and Times*. He did not live in isolation. His knowledge of military matters and foreign affairs was formidable, everyone wanted to hear his opinions and his countless newspaper articles appeared all over Europe. Harold Macmillan, later prime minister, happened to be in the factory on 7 April, 1939 when Churchill heard that Italy had invaded Albania. The energy that news unleashed was amazing, it was as though Chartwell were a centre of government: maps were brought in, the prime minister was called right away, an urgent message was sent to the secretary of the navy, a strategy was developed to keep Mussolini from further aggression. 'He alone seemed to be in command,' Macmillan recalled, 'while everyone else was dazed and hesitating.'

It was in his factory, too, that Churchill prepared the confrontation with Hitler, a war he felt was inevitable and should not be avoided. For deep down Churchill was, after all – and almost all his biographers point to this – a man of arms. He was not a statesman like Roosevelt, who was forced to wage a war and who understood that waging war was sometimes a part of politics. With Churchill, it was just the opposite: he was a man of arms who understood that politics was sometimes a part of waging war. All military operations had to be discussed with him minutely. He was tough and romantic, a typical wartime leader, and after the victory of 1945 the British electorate immediately voted him from his post. That was no ingratitude, but a logical reaction to Churchill's unique character.

As early as 1935, Churchill was preparing himself for the struggle. In deepest secret he received information from concerned officials and officers regarding the true state of Britain's defences. On the basis of the guestbook at Chartwell, for example, Martin Gilbert was able to reconstruct a visit by the head of the German department at the Foreign Office, Ralph Wigram, on 7 April, 1935. What did this man suddenly have to talk to Churchill about? It was made clear only decades later, when the Foreign Office released its documents from that time: the British Secret Service had suddenly received new information about the alarmingly precipitous growth of the Luftwaffe, which had almost reached the critical mass needed to go to war. According to the newest calculations, the Germans had some 850 planes at their immediate disposal, while the British had no more than 450. To the officials' dismay, their superiors did nothing whatsoever with these reports. On 2 May, 1935, Churchill used this information to bludgeon the government with a scathing speech.

Other important informants included Sir Desmond Morton and Frederick Lindemann, later Lord Cherwell. Morton, who was head of the British Industrial Information Service, lived not far from Chartwell, and at the weekend he would often walk the paths and green fields to Churchill's house, carrying under his arm a portfolio with top-secret information about German industrial production, or about the *Kriegsmarine*, the *Wehrmacht* or the Luftwaffe. Lindemann, a professor of physics at Oxford, was one of Churchill's best friends and a welcome guest in the household. He was amazingly well informed about all new technological developments with possible military consequences. He fervently advocated support for Robert Watson-Watt, the inventor of radar, who turned directly to Churchill in 1936 when the further development of his invention seemed about to become bogged down in military bureaucracy. Lindemann was also the man who pointed out to Churchill the vast possibilities offered by nuclear fission. Churchill was so impressed that he wrote an article in *Pall Mall* about a bomb of the future, no bigger than an orange, powerful enough to 'blast a township at a stroke.' He also believed in the great opportunities offered by the rocket. He imagined 'flying machines, guided automatically by wireless or other rays, without a human pilot' which would carry explosives 'in an incessant procession upon a hostile city, arsenal, camp or dockyard'.

In the field of war production, Jean Monnet was one of the key players behind the scenes. 'In 1938, Daladier had gone to Munich in the certain knowledge that the Germans can bomb Paris whenever they choose,' he wrote in his memoirs. One week after the Munich Agreement, the French government sent Monnet on a secret mission to the United States. In mid-October he had his first meeting with President Roosevelt, at Roosevelt's cluttered holiday home on the Hudson, full of guests and children. Even at that point Roosevelt considered Hitler the arch-enemy of freedom, and therefore of the United States, but he still had to convince most Americans of that.

From autumn 1940, planes began rolling off the American production lines by the thousand, as did trucks, jeeps and tanks. Without the American people realising it, a war force was being prepared. That America was able to leap immediately into battle as from late 1941 was due in large part to the production lines set up by Roosevelt, Monnet and a handful of others from 1938, at a time when most Americans were oblivious of the dangers ahead.

'I knew that we were only at the beginning of a long effort,' Monnet wrote concerning spring 1940, 'but the machinery for action was in place, and it would never stop.'

Chapter Twenty-Eight

Brasted

NEVER HAD THE BRITISH SENSE OF PECULIAR UNITY BEEN SO STRONG as it was in high summer 1940. After the fall of France, King George VI wrote to his mother about what a relief it was 'now that we have no allies to be polite to and to pamper.'

For the first time in many generations the British were once again preparing to resist an invasion from the continent. Signs and street markers were taken down. To keep gliders from landing, golf courses and cricket pitches were blockaded with carts, automobiles, beds and tree stumps. The civilians were instructed, in the event of a landing, to lay soup plates upside down in the streets: the Germans would think they were anti-tank mines. Everyone was under suspicion. When an English pilot was forced to make an emergency landing amid the hedgerows of Kent, he was immediately held at gunpoint by a 'fairly elderly nurse' who had climbed over a fence with a toy rifle and 'pointed the weapon at him in a most threatening fashion'.

At the University of Sussex a number of studies have been preserved, carried out by the British Mass Observation organisation, one of the world's first trend-watching agencies. On 16 May, 1940, the observers of 'Morale Today' noted: 'It does not occur to people that we could be defeated. The former peace and quiet has been disturbed, but is still in place. Should that suddenly fall apart, a moral explosion will follow.' 19 May: 'Outwardly calm, inwardly anxious covers the general tone of today.' 21 May: 'The fear that a Nazi invasion is possible is now beginning to appear. The bewilderment and distress is more severe today than ever before . . . The result of the speeches given in the last few days by Churchill . . . is to engender a feeling of relief, not because the situation is not serious, but because the people feel they know the worst, which is a new experience for them.'

The writer Rebecca West saw, on evenings in June, pale-faced people sitting in Regent's Park. Some of them, she wrote, walked over to the roses in great earnestness and inhaled the fragrance, as though to say: 'That is what roses are like, that is how they smell. We must remember that, down in the darkness.'

The first German bombs fell in the Greater London area on 8 June, 1940, on a stretch of open countryside close to Colney. A goat was killed. In the months that followed the English people watched as a gigantic aerial battle developed above their heads, day after day. In his diary, Harold Nicolson wrote that he was sitting with friends in the garden at Sissinghurst when he saw the German planes approaching, 'twenty little, silver fish in arrow formation'. During lunch there was a dogfight: 'There is a rattle of machine-gun fire and we see Spitfires attacking a Heinkel. The latter sways off, obviously wounded.' A Londoner, who had been talking at his club to a young man with a bandaged arm, noted in his diary: 'Life is certainly exciting when a youngster can be shot down in the sea in the morning and be in a club in Berkeley Square the same evening.'

The Battle of Britain was actually the battle for the Channel. As long as the much more powerful British fleet was still at sea, a German invasion could be ruled out. The Germans hoped to use the Luftwaffe to cripple that fleet, so that their landing troops could cross the Channel unchallenged. But before they could do that, they had first to dispense with the Royal Air Force.

Robert Watson-Watt's invention played a major role in winning that battle. In deepest secrecy, a whole chain of radar stations – the first in the world – were built along the English coast. This allowed the RAF to remain perfectly informed of the arrival of every new wave of German aircraft, without the need for constant patrolling. Surprise attacks were no longer possible, pilots and planes remained available for the fighting itself.

Despite its massive air power, however, the Luftwaffe was not prepared for a typical air war, and particularly not for an air war against Britain. The German fighter, the Messerschmitt 109, was a better plane than the

British Hurricane and at least as good as the Spitfire, but it was not suited for long-distance flights: the fuel tanks were so small that the planes could remain in British airspace for no more than half an hour.

The Blitz that came later, the series of German bombardments of London and other cities, was also an improvised affair. The Heinkel, Dornier and Junker bombers were designed to operate in unison with troops on the ground, and to attack enemy tanks and infantry from the air. In practice, they proved unsuited for carrying the enormous quantity of bombs needed truly to devastate a large industrial country.

In the end, Germany's plans for an invasion proved no more than fleeting. The *Wehrmacht* had received absolutely no training in landing operations, the country's capacity for troop transport was insufficient and Germany had almost no landing craft. Now, for the first time, the underside of the blitzkrieg coin became apparent: the *Wehrmacht*, and the German wartime economy, were attuned to brief, overwhelming explosions of energy, and not to long, exhausting struggles. By late July 1940, according to some of those in his immediate surroundings, Hitler had already turned his attention to something completely different: the march on Russia.

The White Heart pub in Brasted, close to the Kentish airfield of Biggin Hill, was the RAF pilots' local. The building itself has since been enlarged, but the area around the bar where the young airmen noted their 'hits' has remained unchanged. They were often too tired to get drunk; there were days when they made up to six flights, strafed and bombed during take-off, getting into dogfights with ME 109s, being wounded, ejecting from their planes and hitchhiking back to the base, from where they would take off again the next morning. The chalkboard with their names on it is still hanging on the wall. 'Hold my glass for me, I'll be right back,' they would say before disappearing into the sky.

During summer 1940, the life expectancy of the British pilot was four, perhaps five weeks.

Chapter Twenty-Nine

London

THE REALITY OF THE BLITZ LIVES ON TODAY ONLY IN THE NIGHTMARES of the elderly, and in a handful of war museums. It is striking to see how quickly the normal historical perspective in London has made way for the myth and the spectacle. In city museums on the continent, the key words for this particular epoch are silence and serenity. One sees photographs, a black-and-grey scale model of a badly wounded town, a handful of scorched objects, and that is usually it. In London, things are very different.

A top attraction at the moment is the Britain At War Experience, a 'realistic experience' where, after paying a few pounds, one can walk down a wartime street, hear wartime radio reports and sit in a fairy-tale air-raid shelter listening to the howl of the sirens and the thudding of the Heinkel bombers. The climax is the cleverly reconstructed ruins of a housing block, complete with flashes of anti-aircraft fire, a few limbs tossed around and the melancholy burbling of a burst water main. 'Jolly good!' the schoolboys standing beside me shout.

In summer 1940, London was the world's biggest metropolis. The city had more than eight million inhabitants (New York had almost seven million.) One out of every five Britons lived there. It was where all the lines of the British Empire converged. And after Hitler had abandoned his plans for an invasion, it was the most obvious target for the German bombardments.

The Germans started the Blitz more or less out of frustration, without any clear planning, as a sequel to the Battle of Britain. During the first half of that summer they had focused on dominating British airspace, in preparation for a possible landing. Their bombardments had been limited largely to airfields and other military installations. On 24 August, more or less by accident, a pair of Stukas dropped the first bombs on central London. Churchill seized the opportunity: in 'revenge', eighty RAF bombers pounded Berlin. Hitler was infuriated. Nearly 600 German bombers came back during the next two weeks to bomb English cities, factories and airfields. Then, at 5 p.m. on 7 September, the first major attack on London began. The docks were the primary target, but working-class neighbourhoods, the East End in particular, were also badly damaged. Some 300 men, women and children were killed. The next morning Churchill paid a visit to a bomb shelter that had been squarely hit. Forty people had been killed. Churchill burst into tears. The people shouted: 'We thought you'd come. We can take it. Give it 'em back!'

Five days later, Buckingham Palace was hit for the first time. 'I'm glad we've been bombed,' said Queen Elizabeth. 'Now I feel we can look the East End in the face.' On Sunday, 29 September, firebombs rained down on the City. The entire district, reduced to ashes in the Great Fire of 1666, was alight once again. Nineteen churches, thirty-one guild halls and all of Paternoster Row, including five million books, went up in flames. By late September almost 6,000 Londoners had been killed, and another 12,000 wounded. Harold Nicolson compared himself to a prisoner in the Conciergerie during the French Revolution: 'Every morning one is pleased to see one's friends appearing again.'

Something of the real story can be derived from the reports from Mass Observation. Some of the Londoners surrendered to their fear. Others tried, despite it all, in stubborn, angry fashion, to get on with daily life. Yet others kept their mortal fear in check with jokes and songs. Barbara Nixon, an Air Defence volunteer, saw her first victim: 'In the middle of the street lay the remains of the baby. It had been blown clean through the window and had burst on striking the roadway.' Celia Fremlin, a Mass Observation reporter, described the mood in a bomb shelter in Cable Street, at the start of the bombardments: 'They were screaming and saying, "I can't stand it, I'm going to die, I can't stand it!."' When she came back to the same shelter three nights later, the people were singing. The reason was simple enough: 'Once you've gone through three nights of bombing and come out alive, you can't help feeling safe the fourth time.' Bernard Kops, a fourteen-year-old at the time, remembered the first major attack on 7 September as 'a flaming world': the ground floor of a flat, filled with hysterical women and crying infants. The men started playing cards, the women sang songs. 'But every so often twenty women's fists shook at the ceiling, cursing the explosions, Germany, Hitler.'

In the course of October 1940, the Luftwaffe shifted its focus to cities such as Birmingham, Sheffield, Hull, Glasgow and Plymouth. On 14 November, Coventry was bombed for a full ten hours. Afterwards the cathedral lay in ruins, a third of the homes were uninhabitable, 550 inhabitants were dead and almost 900 critically wounded. The psychological effect of the bombardment was much greater than in other cities; Coventry was much smaller, and everyone had the feeling they had been personally attacked. The Mass Observation reporter noted more expressions of fear, panic and hysteria than in all the previous attacks put together. 'Women were seen to cry, to scream, to tremble all over, to faint in the street, to attack a fireman, and so on . . .'

There was little the Luftwaffe could do during the winter months, but from March 1941 the Heinkels and Junkers were back in full force. The heaviest and most prolonged attack of all took place on Saturday, 10 May, 1941. London was, as people put it, 'Coventrated'. Westminster Abbey, the Tower and the Mint were heavily damaged, a quarter of a million books went up in flames in the British Museum, the north wing of the Houses of Parliament was destroyed. About 1,500 Londoners were killed, a third of all the city's streets were impassable, all train stations, save one, were blocked, and 150,000 families were left without water, gas or electricity.

Then the bombardments stopped. The Luftwaffe sent all its planes east for the attack on the Soviet Union. There began an intermission that lasted almost three years, a sombre, dingy, frustrated period in the city's history that was later referred to as 'no light in the middle of the tunnel'.

Entire chunks of the city centre, including the busy shopping and office area between St Mary-le-Bow and St Paul's Cathedral, returned to the primal state of the old London, a wilderness of mud, rubble and tall grass, a plain where only a few footpaths bore the names of former streets. In Bread Street and Milk Street there grew wild flowers the likes of which had not raised their heads there since the days of Henry VIII: lilies of the valley, ragwort and others.

The 'little Blitz', as the exhausted Londoners of that day called this period, began in February 1944, in retaliation for the British bombing of German cities. Then, in the final summer of the war, something happened that had not been seen before. Starting in June, little, unmanned jet planes began flying into the city: the V-1s, recognisable by the loud buzzing of their motors, then a sudden silence when the machine stopped and before the bomb fell. Suddenly Londoners were stretched to their limits again: the capriciousness of these merciless, deadly 'robot bombs' generated a nervousness greater than the worst of the Blitz attacks.

A few months later, another new weapon appeared from the drawing boards of Wernher von Braun and his enthusiastic technicians: the V-2, the world's first long-distance missile. From launching pads in places like Wassenaar and the Hague in the Netherlands, the V-2 rocketed to London in only a few minutes, moving at several times the speed of sound. The V-2 was an extremely advanced weapon: the missile flew to the edge of the stratosphere and even included several ingenious guidance systems. Radar, air-raid siren, anti-aircraft fire, Spitfires – all were useless in the face of this technology. A V-2 could flatten an entire street, kill everyone who lived there. The last of approximately 1,000 V-2s struck the city in late March 1945, landing in Tottenham Court Road, on the eighteenth-century chapel of Reverend George Whitefield, at the place where the Whitefield Memorial Church now stands.

More than 100,000 homes were demolished in London, almost 30,000 men, women and children were killed. Yet the Germans were never able to hit one of the major targets: the Cabinet War Rooms. Today the secret cellar space where the British government supervised the war is in almost the same state it was at two minutes to five on 16 August, 1945, when the lights were turned out. For decades only insiders knew of its existence, today the rooms are open to all. You can even rent them for an afternoon or an evening, to throw a party.

This nexus, where all lines came together during the war, is no larger than a newspaper editorial office, and that is what it resembles most: wooden desks, maps, metal lamps, red, green and black telephones, drawing pins, lengths of twine. Churchill's office had been reduced in size to allow for the flow of visitors, Lady Churchill's has actually disappeared altogether. His private room is full of maps as well, although when important visitors showed up, a curtain was drawn discreetly across the one showing the deployment of the British coastal defences.

Even more mysterious were the sealed yellow boxes which arrived here each day, and which only Churchill was allowed to open. They contained a selection of all the intercepted German radio orders for army, navy and air force. The German high command had encrypted them ingeniously with the use of the Enigma coding machine, a device that made the secret texts completely unintelligible to outsiders. The Germans had enormous faith in their encrypting device. And they did not have the slightest clue that the Poles had laid their hands on one as early as 1928, that they had cracked the code after six years of diligent study, and that they had been sharing their knowledge with their French and British allies since summer 1939. The British perfected the decoding system with one of the first computer-like machines, the top-secret Colossus. From summer 1940 onwards, almost all of the Germans' plans and troop movements were – within days, sometimes even hours – an open book to Churchill and a few of his confidants.

It was only on 1 May, 1941, however, that the first complete Enigma machine fell into British hands, when three warships succeeded in driving a German U-boat to the surface with the use of depth charges. The German commander thought the valves of his submarine had been opened and that the vessel would sink to the bottom, rendering it unnecessary to destroy his Enigma and the code books. Two British seamen who had climbed into the U-boat discovered a machine which looked like a typewriter but exhibited some rather strange behaviour. Suspecting it to be a coding machine they took it back to their ship, not realising that their find would change the course of the war. Within a week after the ship arrived home the British had access to all kinds of information concerning the German submarine fleet: its targets, its location, even its fuel supplies.

This gave the British an enormous head start. Thanks to Operation Enigma they knew, for example, all about the German decision to cancel the planned invasion of England, about the airborne landings on Crete, about the German scenarios for the Soviet Union (and their failure) and about Germany's plans for Italy and Greece. In this way, the Allies were better able to concentrate on the real dangers, and could reserve fewer troops for 'just in case'.

One of the most bizarre spots in the Cabinet War Rooms is the little alcove behind a toilet door. This was not Churchill's personal WC, but the terminus of the top secret telephone line with which Churchill and President Roosevelt could – with the aid of incredibly advanced scramblers and more than seventy radio frequencies – consult directly. Here, from this cubicle that everyone thought was Churchill's private loo, the world was governed between 1943–5.

There was no element of the war into which Churchill put more energy than his relationship with Roosevelt, and with the United States in general. The need was mutual. In early 1941 Roosevelt had sent his friend and close advisor Harry Hopkins to England, to find out what kind of man this whisky-drinking, cigar-smoking British prime minister really was. It was an auspicious move: real fondness arose right away between the two men, a friendship that expanded to include the personal relationship between Churchill and the American president. 'I am most grateful to you for sending so remarkable an envoy who enjoys so high a measure of your intimacy and confidence,' Churchill wrote to Roosevelt. Hopkins was deeply impressed by Churchill's statesmanship, and the composure with which the British underwent the constant bombardments. Churchill, he wrote to Roosevelt, was not only the prime minister but 'the guiding force behind the strategy and course of the war in all essential points. He has an amazing grip on the British people, of all ranks and classes.'

Hopkins remained in Great Britain for more than a month, twice as long as originally planned. He and Churchill spent a great deal of time together, stayed up all night on several occasions, talking and listening to the new American dance records Hopkins had brought with him. Churchill sometimes stood up and shuffled along to the music. 'It was a turning point in Anglo-American relations,' wrote Jean Monnet, who knew both men well. 'The two countries' destinies were now linked at the highest level of responsibility.' Just before he left, at a dinner in

Glasgow, Hopkins cited a verse from the Bible: 'Whither thou goest I will go, and where though lodgest I will lodge; thy people shall be my people, and thy God my God.' And he added calmly: 'Even to the end.' Churchill was in tears.

Despite these personal ties, however, major differences remained between the British and the Americans. Churchill, in that grand, compelling way so characteristic of him, dreamed of a future union of all English-speaking democracies, unstoppable, victorious and majestic 'as the Mississippi'. Most Americans, however, were not particularly keen to come to Europe's rescue again. Until late 1941, the mood in Congress was downright isolationist. In September 1940, sixty-seven per cent of the American people believed the country was headed for war, but eighty-three per cent of them were actually against it. President Roosevelt had to manoeuvre very carefully, therefore, not to put at risk his re-election in November 1940.

The British had come out of the First World War impoverished, and could not in fact afford a long war at all. That, in part, was the background to the policy of appeasement. Chamberlain and his people feared that a second war would mean the financial ruin of the British Empire, and that fear proved justified. Roosevelt saved the situation with the Lend-Lease system, whereby American military goods could be bought on instalment. As Roosevelt put it: when your neighbour's house is on fire you don't haggle first over the price of your fire hose, you lend it to him, and later you may discuss the costs. After 1945, that discussion was explicitly carried on.

The relations between the two allies were vaguely reminiscent of those between the Soviet Union and the Spanish Republic in the 1930s. The Lend-Lease Act was Britain's salvation, but at the same time it rendered the country, in the words of A.J.P. Taylor, 'a poor relation, not an equal partner'. There was nothing like the consolidation of resources. On the contrary, the British were mercilessly robbed of their last dollars and gold reserves. Churchill's vision was based on an America that was unanimously pro-British. In fact, the Americans helped him in order to beat Hitler, and not to preserve Britain's world empire. Great Britain, Taylor wrote, 'sacrificed her post-war future for the sake of the war'.

VII July 1940–2

FINLAND
Helsinki
(1940 Soviet)
Leningrad
Narva
Novgorod
Tallinn
Estonia
Pskow
Riga
Latvia
REICH COMMISSARIAT OSTLAND
Lithuania
Witebsk
Smolensk
Kaunas
Moscow
Koltsovo
Minsk
Bialystok
Front Line
Dec. 1942
Eastern Front
SOVIET UNION
Kursk
MILITARY RULE
Warsaw
REICH COMMISSARIAT UKRAINE
Charkow
Stalingrad
Volga
Lublin
Zamość /Himmlerstadt
Kiev
Dnepr
General Government
Lember
Rostov
SLOVAKIA
Auschwitz
Don
Sea of Azov
Krasnodar
HUNGARY
(Aug. 1940 Hungary)
Odessa
Budapest
Danube
Crimea
Tiflis
RUMANIA
Black Sea
Bucharest
Trabzon
SERBIA
Belgrade
Nish
BULGARIA
Erzurum
MONTE-NEGRO
Sofia
Skopje
Istanbul
Ankara
Tigris
Tirana
ALBANIA
Saloniki
Euphrates
Syria
GREECE
TURKEY
Athens
Cyprus
Crete
Mediterranean

◁══ Geert Mak's Route
--·-- Border of Greater German Reich 1942

0   100   200   300 km

Chapter Thirty

Berlin

WHEN THE WAR BROKE OUT, HIS MOTHER SIGHED IN RELIEF: 'Fortunately, our Wolf is too young for that!' He was thirteen and had just entered gymnasium. But his father growled: 'Oh, he'll have his fill of it yet.'

I am sitting in the garden of the retired publisher Wolf Jobst Siedler (b. 1926), in Berlin's old, exclusive residential district of Dahlem. Siedler still lives in the house in which he grew up, and that is plain to see: the countless prints and paintings, the books, the warm seclusion of the rooms, the restrained luxury, the quiet garden. Dahlem was once the neighbourhood of Walter Rathenau, of the Jewish businessmen and industrialists, and of the Nazi elite, some of whom moved into abandoned Jewish mansions. Himmler, Dönitz, Ribbentrop, half the Nazi government lived here during the war, on a street where birds sang and no bomb would ever fall.

Siedler talks about how excited everyone was in May 1940. 'Lots of the boys at school thought it would be just like the First World War. Trenches, long waits, and a battle every now and again. An old friend of the family told my father: 'This Hitler, he has everyone mesmerised. The generals stare at him like rabbits at a snake.' I can still hear those words, they stopped all conversation, until dinner was served. Later that same month, reports began coming in of one victory after another. Everyone cheered. Verdun was taken, Sedan, war veterans hugged each other in the streets.'

Most people in Berlin lived through summer 1940 in a state of ecstasy. There was singing and dancing in the streets with every victory in France. When the great triumphal parade came goose-stepping by on 18 July,

the cheering crowd stood twenty deep along the streets, people climbed
into trees and on lamp posts, women ran out and hugged the soldiers,
flowers and confetti rained down. 'We, the boys of Berlin, thought the
English were fantastic as well. The Battle of Britain was, in our eyes, a
jousting match. People talked about the 'campaign against France' and
the 'campaign against Holland'. War, no, that wasn't a word we used.'

The first booty began pouring in: furs from Norway, art, tobacco and
Bols gin from Holland, wines and perfumes from France, glass from
Bohemia, vodka from Poland. In the occupied areas, *Sonderkommandos* began
combing the libraries and museums in search of the best European art
for the big Berlin museums, and for Hitler's planned Führer Museum
and Göring's Karin-Halle.

'An English bomb would fall now and then,' Siedler says, 'but that was
mostly exciting to us. We would even cycle over to a house that had been
hit, we wanted to see it with our own eyes. And at school we collected
shrapnel from the anti-aircraft guns. We traded it back and forth.'

Around Christmas 1940, the city encountered its first shortage of coffee
and chocolate. Women were no longer allowed to buy cigarettes. More
and more families began raising rabbits, 'balcony pigs', for their own
consumption. But the striptease shows went on unabated, the restaurants
served oysters, lobster and the best wines, and the citizens of Berlin lived
well. The weekly ration consisted of a pound of meat, a quarter-pound
of butter and three pounds of bread.

In the new year, talk began of another 'campaign', this time against
Russia. It was to be a matter of out and back again in a few months.
Loudspeakers were set up all over the city to broadcast marches. Music,
then a crackly voice: 'From the Führer's headquarters', followed by an
announcement of the fall of Riga, or Minsk, or Kiev, or Odessa.

It was only in autumn 1941, when the soldiers still had not returned
and winter was fast approaching, that the city grew uneasy. The loudspeakers stopped reporting victories. The shop windows were full of
empty biscuit boxes and wine bottles filled with water. The enormous
map of Russia in front of the Wertheim deparment store, where the
progress of the German troops had been charted each day, was taken
down. Gloves, wool caps and fur coats were collected for the front. By
the end, at least 100,000 German soldiers literally froze to death there.

Soviet prisoners of war were brought to Berlin to work in the factories, some 300,000 in all. Before the eyes of the townspeople, they were treated like animals. Half of them died of hunger or perished in the bombardments.

Unnoticed, the city developed into a new kind of nerve centre: Berlin became the administrative heart of the German extermination industry. At the ministry of agriculture and food supply, careful calculations were made of the number of calories to be allotted to each concentration camp, taking into account the projected 'cancellations' due to illness and the gas chambers. At the offices of the *Reichsbahn*, the state railway, civil servants wrote thousands of invoices for the Jewish rail transports, all of them at the price of a single ticket.

Wolf Siedler was sent to boarding school, first in Weimar, then to the northern coastal island of Spiekeroog. Of the group of fourteen- and fifteen-year-old boys in his class, four did not live to be eighteen. His mother had been mistaken: they were not too young for this war. Just before Siedler left for the front, in summer 1944, the family sat together in the garden of the Dahlem villa for the last time. There was home-made pie and – a rarity by then – real coffee. Suddenly it began snowing, ashes from the burning inner city floated down on the table, everyone rushed inside, poisonous yellow clouds came drifting in.

Today, on this warm July afternoon, the cafés along the shores of the Wannsee are full and the water is covered in pretty sailboats. I ask the bus driver about the monument. 'What monument?' 'For the Wannsee meeting.' 'What meeting?' He drops me off at Biergarten Sanssouci, where the Detlev Becker Trio is playing this weekend – a spectacle he says I must not miss. Am Grossen Wannsee 56/58: it was in this villa, with its civilised Prussian arches and its tranquil view of the water, that a meeting of top government officials seemingly like any other was held on 20 January, 1942; one of those informal brainstorming sessions to be followed, as the invitation has it, by a light dinner. The conference room is now a museum, and the most important documents of that meeting are displayed on its walls. Visitors file quietly by, everything is neat and tidy, no scream is heard, no tear is shed.

The topic of the meeting was the 'Jewish question'. Some historians have claimed that the mass murder of the Jews was part of Hitler's master plan from the very start, that it was part of a clear and conscious strategy. In reality, the road that ultimately led to the Holocaust was far more circuitous than that.

'The essence of Europe is not geographical,' Hitler once said, 'but racial.' In other words: the Nazis did not think in terms of nations, but of peoples, and Europe was to be reorganised according to that principle. Legal borders, international agreements concerning minorities, the equality of states, the League of Nations, none of that mattered to them: nation and people had to coincide.

While, for example, the French, English, Belgian, Dutch and Scandinavian concepts of the state were based on the will of every citizen, the German concept of state was based on blood, descent, race. 'Blood is stronger than any passport' was the core of their ideology. The German minorities in Poland, Czechoslovakia, the Ukraine and elsewhere were 'the racial friends' of the Third Reich, badly in need of 'liberation' by their 'fellow people'.

At the same time, the importance of racial doctrine among the Nazis was reinforced by a notion of 'purity' with which all European culture had been imbued since 1900. Bacteria as the source of countless ills, the importance of hygiene, freshness and purity; all these new discoveries had left their mark on the thinking of innumerable intellectuals since the turn of the century. Yet the notion of purity had an impact that went much further than medical science alone. No citizen of the eighteenth or nineteenth centuries would ever had raised 'clean' or 'dirty', 'healthy' or 'ill' to the status of creeds applicable to the whole of social life. But in many circles during the first half of the twentieth century this contradistinction became the hub around which all the rest revolved. 'Purity' evolved into a concept that dominated discussions everywhere, not only among rabid racists, but among anthroposophists, politicians and artists as well. Half of Europe suddenly seemed afflicted with a morbid dread of sickness. It is almost impossible to find a cultural essay from the 1930s in which terms such as 'pure' and 'healthy' do not appear. It was the leitmotif of the modern age.

For the Nazis, this notion of purity meant they had to make their empire 'healthy' by, among other things, 'cleansing' it of 'non-national' taints. Hence their attempts to reorganise nations, to *'entjuden'* the occupied territories, and to herd millions of *Untermenschen* into the part of Poland which became known as the General Government, and other outlying areas of their empire. These *hinausgesauberten* Jews, Poles and Gypsies could then serve as a 'reservoir' of cheap labour.

This was, in rough outline, the system the Nazis had in mind until 1940. At first they had hoped to send the Jews to Palestine. In the 1930s that was still an isolated area, economically unimportant, run by the British and far from Europe. In summer 1933, they even signed an agreement with the German Zionist Federation. Approximately 60,000 Jews took advantage of it, until the British put a stop to all Jewish immigration.

After 1939, the Nazis ran the General Government of Poland as a reserve for the Jews, until it quickly proved too small. Then the SS commander Heinrich Himmler proposed a solution to the 'Jewish question' in the form of 'mass emigration to a colony in Africa or elsewhere'. The French colony of Madagascar seemed particularly interesting to him. In his policy paper 'Some Thoughts on the Treatment of Foreign Peoples in the East' (May 1940), he touched upon the idea of 'physical extermination', only to reject it immediately.

Meanwhile the deportations continued. The General Government became overpopulated with the huge influx of Poles and Jews, the economies of the surrounding towns and villages were destroyed and huge problems arose with regard to the region's food supply, making the settlement of new German colonists almost impossible. Within the Nazi command, conflicts were soon raging between the 'ideologists' and the 'technologists'. Himmler's *Blut und Boden* (Blood and Soil) routine, after all, was turning the General Government into a kind of ethnic storehouse, while Göring and governor general Hans Frank hoped to make of it a well organised slave state.

In autumn 1941, however, it became obvious that the quick conquest of the east was not going according to plan. There are clear indications that, as early as October 1941, Hitler, Himmler and Reinhard Heydrich, head

of the *Sicherheitsdienst* and later Reich governor of Bohemia and Moravia,
had arrived at the conclusion that none of the deportation schemes were
working, and that mass extermination was the only answer. The first experiments with poison gas date from this period. Himmler, who had personally attended a mass execution by *Einsatzgruppe B* in Minsk, felt that the
shootings by roaming Eastern European commandos – in which hundreds
of thousands of Jews had already been killed in 1940 and 1941 – were
far too time-consuming. They also generated too much emotion, an undesirable side effect. He went looking for a faster and better alternative.
Equipment and personnel from the T-4 euthanasia programme were quickly
sent east. On 3 September, 1941, at Auschwitz, Zyklon B was first tried
out on 600 Soviet prisoners of war. Soon afterwards, at concentration
camp Belzec, the experimental process was speeded up on a large scale
with two mobile gas chambers – converted trucks, one for thirty persons,
the other for sixty.

The euthanasia specialists, wearing white coats and stethoscopes in
order to mislead their victims, were extremely satisfied. Their departmental
report literally read: '97,000 have been processed since December 1941,
using three trucks, with none of the machinery showing a single defect.'

The plans for forced emigration, deportation and national 'cleansing'
were transformed in this way into a single giant bureaucratic project,
aimed at a 'definitive solution to the Jewish question'.

The Wannsee meeting was held around the pivotal point in the war. The
first invitation – the conference was postponed once – dates from 29
November, 1941. One week later the German troops had ground to a halt
at the gates of Moscow, Japan had attacked Pearl Harbor and Hitler had
declared war on the United States. This lent the campaign to exterminate
the Jews of Europe a powerful political and ideological overtone. 'The
world war has arrived!' Joseph Goebbels shouted on 12 December. 'The
destruction of the Jews must be its consequence.'

The internal summit meeting, accompanied by a luncheon, was finally
held on 20 January. The participants included the state secretary of internal
affairs, Wilhelm Stuckart, the director general of the Eastern Occupied
Territories, Georg Leibbrandt, SS-Oberführer Gerhard Klopfer from the party
chancellery, Gestapo chief of operations Heinrich Müller, and SS-

Gruppenführer Otto Hofmann from the head office of race and settlement, fifteen top bureaucrats in all. The meeting was chaired by Reinhard Heydrich. Minutes were taken by SD-Obersturmbannführer Adolf Eichmann, head of the Gestapo's Jewish emigration department.

Eichmann's minutes have been preserved: fifteen neatly typed pages of euphemistic officialese. Heydrich opened the meeting and reported that he, with the Führer's permission, had been charged with streamlining the 'final solution to the European Jewish question'. The goal was to purify, in a 'legal fashion', the German Lebensraum of all Jews. The 'evacuation of the Jews to the east' had already begun, 'as a possible alternative to emigration'. Carefully compiled lists were then handed out – cognac had meanwhile been served – showing the number of Jews in each country: 131,800 in the Old Empire, 165,000 in occupied France, 160,800 in the Netherlands, 3,500 in Lithuania, o in Estonia ('Free of Jews'), 58,000 in Italy, 200 in Albania, 5 million in the Soviet Union, etc. A striking feature is the enormous ambition reflected in the count: European territories over which Germany as yet held no sway, such as Britain (330,000), Switzerland (18,000) and Spain (6,000), were included as a matter of course.

The parties agreed that Europe must be 'combed out, from west to east'. Huge columns of able-bodied Jews were to be sent east, where, as the minutes noted, 'a great number will be reduced by natural elimination'. Those remaining were to be 'treated in equal fashion'; experience had shown, after all, that failure to do so would leave 'hearths of infection' for a Jewish resurrection. A special ghetto would be formed at Theresienstadt, the old fortified city north-west of Prague, for Jewish veterans, war invalids and the aged. All complaints and questions could in this way be dealt with 'at a single blow'.

To sum all, what this flood of bureaucratic language was all about was that the function of the roaming death squads was to be replaced by enormous extermination plants, with fast and efficient lines of supply. Special death camps were designed, unlike normal concentration camps, with almost no cells or barracks. The entire system was intended to 'process' huge numbers of prisoners within several hours after they stumbled weakly from the train. Preferably without commotion.

The Berlin bureaucrats saw to it that the entire operation took place with unprecedented speed and smoothness. Operation Reinhard, the mass murder of the Polish Jews, began in May 1942. The first trains with Slovakian Jews arrived at Auschwitz. That summer the Dutch, Belgians and French followed. By late 1942, according to SS statistics, four million of Europe's eleven million Jews had already been exterminated.

The minutes of the Wannsee meeting contain no word about the fate of the some 800,000 Roma and Sinti Gypsies. After a great deal of official discussion, it was decided in November 1943 that Gypsies with a permanent place of residence would receive the same treatment as the rest of the population, while wandering Gypsies would be allocated the same status as Jews. In fact, the rounding up of the Gypsies was much less systematic: it had no major ideological motivation, Hitler and Himmler were not interested in them, and besides, most of them were as poor as church mice. They had nothing to plunder. Nevertheless, several hundred thousand Sinti and Roma were killed during the Second World War.

In Europe's most notorious meeting room, portraits of the fifteen participants now hang. Two of them committed suicide at the fall of the Third Reich, three died violent deaths, but only Eichmann was convicted for his part in the Holocaust. Nine of the fifteen received little or no punishment. Heinrich Müller was able to escape in 1945. He was recruited by the CIA and probably started a new life for himself in the United States. Wilhelm Stuckart was imprisoned for four years after the war, but by 1951 he had already become head of the Bund Heimatvertriebenen und Entrechteten. Georg Leibbrandt died in 1982 at the age of eighty-two, without ever being tried. Gerhard Klopfer led a normal life as a lawyer after the war. Otto Hofmann was granted a pardon in 1954. He became a merchant in Württemberg. These latter two died in their beds, like respectable citizens, in the 1980s.

In the garden at Dahlem, Wolf Siedler talked about his family home during the first years of the war, and about the people who visited them: his best friend at school, for example, Ernstel Jünger, son of Ernst Jünger; the Hahn family, his parents' most trusted friends and every bit as anti-Nazi as they were. 'Otto Hahn discovered the principle of nuclear reaction, but I believe he skilfully sidetracked the development of a German A-bomb.'

And then there was Else Meyer, the elderly widow of a Jewish army officer and an old friend of Siedler's grandparents. Officially, as from summer 1941, the family was not allowed to have dealings with her. 'My parents did anyway, of course, the maids were sent out of the house then, visits like that always caused quite a stir. In 1942 she told them she had received orders to report to the train station at Grunewald. For relocation (*Umsiedlung*) to the East. Before she left, she brought over a present: a teacup with a picture of the Brandenburg gate on it. She was convinced that she was only being asked to move to Lódź or something like that. "See you soon," we shouted back and forth.'

Around 1930 there were some 160,000 Jews living in Berlin. By 1945, there were only 6,000 left: most of those were partners in 'privileged mixed marriages'.

'My father did all he could, through his former diplomatic connections, to find out what had happened to Else Meyer,' Siedler says. 'It turned out that, somewhere in eastern Poland, the wagons were unhitched from the engine, which was needed more urgently for troop transports. It was winter. When they opened the wagons three weeks later, everyone was dead, of course. After experiences like that, my parents no longer had any illusions about the fate of the Jews. They were being wiped out, that was clear. From soldiers back on leave we had started hearing more and more about mass executions in Poland. There were too many soldiers present at those killings, the Nazis couldn't keep it a secret. But that they would start the production-line killing of Jews in such massive numbers, that defied our imagination. In the circles I moved in, no one could believe that a place like Auschwitz or Majdanek really existed.'

There was one isolated moment of resistance. In February 1943, the non-Jewish wives of some 2,000 Jewish workers who had been arrested attacked the improvised prison on Rosenstrasse, and the wives of other Berlin workers joined them. That unique uprising lasted several days, the SS threatened the women with machine guns, and finally the men were released. The Nazis did not want to run a risk by shooting down a few thousand German housewives in the middle of the capital.

In Berlin, however, Jews were not taken into hiding on any significant scale. Of the four million citizens of Berlin, only a few thousand at most offered any assistance to those Jews who had remained behind clandestinely, hiding in coal bins and forgotten attics. Siedler: 'Mrs Hahn was part of the organisation that collected food for them, so my family became a bit involved. We helped her acquire ration booklets, and I collected groceries. I was sixteen or seventeen at the time, it was all quite exciting really, a sort of game of Cowboys and Indians.'

In the end, about 2,000 of Berlin's 'U-boat' Jews survived the war.

Beside the former art academy, close to Wilhelmstrasse and the place where the Wall once stood, is a little, weed-covered mound. Beneath it are the remains of the former Gestapo headquarters at Prinz-Albrecht-Strasse. The building survived the war, but was finally demolished in 1949. A road was built over it, the rest remained a vacant lot. In May 1985 a team of young researchers began excavations there. They soon hit upon a network of ruins, part of the cellars and kitchens of the former Gestapo headquarters. Ever since 1987 it has served as an austere memorial, with a path along the stone foundations and what is left of the old plumbing and doors, a kind of modern archaeological site. On and beside the old walls, photographs and documents tell the story of what happened here. No more, and no less.

There are more remains of the Nazi era to be found beneath the surface of Berlin, and excursions are even organised for those who wish to visit these forms of 'historical soil pollution'. But the Topographie des Terrors is, in all its simplicity, the most terrifying by far. The stones are authentic, as are the lengths of pipe, the chunks of concrete, the wood, the documents, nothing here is a replica. The only thing one wonders is: did the Nazi regime really use that much terror against its own people?

One is struck again and again, in all the historical documents, by how small the Gestapo organisation really was, by how the Nazis repressed the entire German population with such a relatively small apparatus – particularly compared to, for example, the East German Stasi later in the same century. The Stasi employed more than 100,000 people to keep an eye on 17 million East Germans, while the Gestapo apparently needed no more than 40–60,000 for an empire of some 80 million inhabitants. While resistance groups in other parts of Europe could count on the silent acquiescence of the rest of the population, Hitler's regime maintained its generally accepted authority in Germany almost until the bitter end. In fact, large parts of the population supported that regime enthusiastically. Resistance was so uncommon that it could easily be nipped in the bud. Propaganda was readily believed, repression was a matter of loving one's country, obedience was the rule, informing on neighbours a patriotic duty.

In his reconstruction of the workings of Nazi terror, Eric Johnson – using recovered Gestapo dossiers – described the sophistication of the system of informing in a town like Krefeld, close to the Dutch border: a sixteen-year-old Jewish girl was turned in for having a relationship with an Aryan worker; a Jewish housepainter who made jokes about Hitler was informed on by his neighbour; a chauffeur sent a letter to the authorities saying his Jewish boss had smuggled illegal publications into the country from the Netherlands. Of all the Gestapo cases against Jews, Johnson's research showed that no less than 41 per cent started with an informant or a complaint. Only 19 per cent were uncovered by the activities of the Gestapo itself, and 8 per cent came from other Nazi organisations. (Similar research into dossiers in Würzburg showed that no fewer than 57 per cent of the Jews arrested had been turned in by German citizens.)

Wolf Siedler still has a cheerful group photo of his class at the boarding school on Spiekeroog, probably taken in winter 1943–4. The boys are wearing navy uniforms, one of them is having his head chopped off with an axe by Ernstel Jünger, Wolf himself is standing to the left of these two while the rest look on in amusement. Most of the boys in this picture were naval assistants, *Flakhelfer*, as people called them. 'That meant we had to do general chores around an anti-aircraft position, and that we wore uniforms. The rest of the time we spent in class, but when the air-raid siren went off we would jump up from our desks – eagerly, because of the break it provided – and race off to our positions to help with the shooting.'

In early January 1944, two men suddenly appeared and arrested Siedler and Jünger. Along with a few other comrades, they were brought before a navy tribunal.

'In those days, we talked about it openly among ourselves: about how the war had already been lost, about the horrendous crimes committed by the SS, and about how Hitler should be hanged from the yardarm.'

For weeks, it seems, one of their classmates had been reporting those conversations almost verbatim to the Gestapo. 'Whenever I would deny something, they would say: 'Oh, but at 3 p.m. on 17 November, outside the gym, didn't you say such and such?' That was typical of the situation. There's no truth in the idea that the Germans had closed ranks, or that they were terrorised by the SS and the Gestapo. Not at all: 60 per cent of the people were Nazis themselves.'

The tribunal's written verdict is still kept in a drawer at the house in Dahlem. In it one reads that Jünger, during an air battle between a few German interceptors and hundreds of British bombers, had said that the German air war looked more like a clay-pigeon contest. During an alarm in the barracks, Siedler had claimed that the 'evacuation' of the Jews amounted to nothing more than extermination. 'And Jünger added: "And if Hitler is to be hanged, then I'll tighten the noose for him! If it comes down to that, I'll walk barefoot from Berlin to Potsdam to bring him the noose!"'

Fortunately for them, the rest of the class was unanimous about the accusations: none of them had heard a word of it. Siedler: 'That saved my life. It's actually a wonder how the naval court in the field was able to keep Jünger and myself out of the hands of the Nazi courts, and let us get away with only a few months in jail.'

That miracle perhaps had something to do with the fact that Jünger's father had a legendary reputation within the *Wehrmacht*. 'Old Ernst Jünger, the writer, the First World War hero, came to visit us in the cell, wearing his uniform. When someone commented on this, he said: 'The only occasion on which one can wear one's decorations with honour these days is when one visits one's son in prison."'

In the end, the two boys were sent to the Italian Front with a so-called *Himmelfahrtkommando* in autumn 1944. Siedler was soon wounded. That saved his life. Jünger was killed the first day out, his parents heard about it only weeks later. On 11 January, 1945, Ernst Jünger wrote in his diary: 'Ernstel is dead, killed in combat, my dear child, dead ever since 29 November last year!'

Siedler would never forget those long months in the naval brig at Wilhelmshaven. During air raids, all the condemned men were put together in the same bomb shelter: it was the only time when the prisoners saw each other. Every Tuesday and Thursday, between 3 a.m. and 4 a.m., the boys would hear a couple of their companions in misfortune being taken from their cells, hear their footsteps going down the stone corridor. They heard one of them say: 'You can hang me today, but in six months' time Germany will have lost the war and then it will be your turn to be hanged.' One boy screamed: 'Let me live! I haven't done anything!' A blond sailor, a baby-faced boy with freckles, had told his fellow seamen that the 'bigwigs' had 'villas in Switzerland' they could flee to if things went wrong. That was why he was on death row, only for having said that. 'When they dragged him away, we heard him beg them in desperation whether they couldn't give him another chance: "Why don't you send me to the front, instead of hanging me?"'

Almost all these men were killed for having made a few comments. They had said that the war was lost anyway, they had talked about the crimes of the SS, or they may have simply listened to the BBC, the *Feindsender*. At the end of the war, things like that were enough to be sentenced to death for 'defeatism'. None of them had committed any act of actual resistance. And they had all been informed on by their friends or neighbours.

Siedler: 'I remember talking to this young officer whose only concern was whether he would be shot or hanged. The noose, he considered that a dishonourable death, that was something for traitors. During one of those air raids – we were sitting around in a little group – he told us that unimaginable atrocities were being carried out in the East. People there were being clubbed to death, hanged, tortured, burned alive, horrible things, for no good reason. "But," that officer said, "those stories about the death factories, that's nothing but English propaganda." That's what that officer said, with the deepest conviction, one week before he was executed.'

Chapter Thirty-One

Himmlerstadt

EARLY IN THE MORNING OF TUESDAY, 25 FEBRUARY, 1941, A WILDCAT strike broke out in Amsterdam and the towns along the River Zaan. Tram drivers occupied the garages, stevedores in Amsterdam North blocked the ports, factories along the Zaan remained closed. In the course of the morning the strike spread to the offices and businesses in the centre of Amsterdam. It was a sunny day. Ferries loaded with cheering workers crossed the River IJ from Amsterdam North to the city centre. The 'Internationale' was sung, boys picked up the factory girls and spun them around while the crowds laughed.

A large part of the city was finally closed down; even the stock exchange was shut. Rumours were flying about a strike rolling across the country, people had stopped working in Haarlem, Utrecht and the Gooi region as well. The police sympathised, and either refused to intervene or did so only much too late. Pamphlets were being spread everywhere:

> Save the Jewish children from Nazi violence, take them into your homes! Be unified, be courageous! Strike! Strike! Strike!

Amsterdam's February Strike was a unique gesture of solidarity with the Jews. And within Nazi Europe, it was a case of unheard-of rebellion. The Germans responded immediately: the *Generalkommissar zur besonderen Verwendung*, F. Schmidt, sent two regiments of the SS Death's Head Division to Amsterdam and the Zaan, there was shooting everywhere, a number of strikers were arrested, eighteen members of the resistance were executed and the leaders of the strike – most of them communists – went into hiding. Within a few days it was all over. On Saturday, 1 March, Goebbels noted in his diary: 'Calm completely restored in the Netherlands. Schmidt got his way, with the help of measures I proposed. I urgently advised him to clamp down. Which he did. We must show this gang of Jews just how big and sharp our teeth are.'

That is all the attention he devoted to the matter. We will therefore never know whether there was any truth to the stories that circulated after the war about Hitler flying into a wild rage, and about plans to deport the Dutch and Flemish populations en masse to the Polish province of Lublin. The Dutch would be replaced by 'sturdy young German farmers', and would, in turn, introduce a healthy injection of Germanic blood to Poland.

In fact, plans did exist to deport some three million Dutch people to Poland, and to relocate an equal number of Germans in Holland. Had the war turned out more favourably for the Nazis, in other words, millions of Dutchmen and Flemings would have undergone the same as count- less ethnic Germans from Lithuania, Estonia, Poland and Bessarabia. And, in a worse scenario, the Dutch and the Flemish would have met a fate little better than that of the millions of deported Poles.

From Berlin's Ostbahnhof I took the train east, and now I am travelling through rolling woodlands and fields full of poppies and cornflowers. It is a warm afternoon, the train rocks through the countryside, the girl across from me sleeps a deep and peaceful sleep. White villages slide by, the houses have big, brown wooden barns, then another half-hour of cornfields. We pass a lake, with people fishing and camping on its shores, cattle lolling beneath a clump of trees. In the fields the farmers are mowing, their chests bare, wagons piled high with hay, they are obvi- ously in a hurry, for there is thunder in the offing.

The station where I must change trains probably once played a central role in a well oiled iron machine, but today it is overgrown and rusty. A long coal train trundles by. The station restaurant sells greasy pastries. There is a computer game there that gives you three minutes to kill hundreds of Arabs with conspicuously Semitic noses. You can hear them, too: Aagh! Ooef! Gnuhuhuh! The sound of someone having his throat cut electronically.

Later that evening, past Lublin, a cool wind blows into the compart- ment. We pass a brook, a factory, kitchen gardens and orchards, the air smells of grass, hay and coal-fired stoves. In 1941, this part of the country was given the title 'General Government of Poland', and was to be the gigantic laboratory where Nazi theories about *Blut und Boden*, *Volksgemeinschaft* and *Untermenschen* would be put into practice for the first time, where the majority of death camps were concentrated and where, afterwards, the ethnic Germans were to be resettled.

The train's final stop is Zamość, the birthplace of Rosa Luxemburg, a Renaissance town in south-east Poland. It is already dark in the big market square, there are almost no street lights, but from the pavement cafés comes the murmur of dozens of beer-drinking tourists. Zamość was built by an enthusiastic Polish chancellor as a small ideal community in accordance with sixteenth century Italian norms. The pink and light-blue houses miraculously survived the war, and look today much as they did when the Italian master builders finished them in 1605. The centuries of poverty and grime that lie between have been forgotten.

Zamość was once a lively place. In 1939 the city had 28,000 inhabitants, including some 10,000 Jews. There was a preparatory school, a cathedral, a courthouse, a synagogue, an orchestra and two local papers, the *Zamojski Kurier* and the *Gazeta Zamojska*. The old synagogue, now part of the municipal library, is behind the town hall. There are no Jews in Zamość now.

That, in fact, is the most striking thing about the town: the municipal museum stops at 1939, the Rotunda – the jail complex outside the town – rightly honours and commemorates the local partisans, but nowhere is the real drama of Zamość told or remembered.

Zamość was to serve as a model for the Nazis' first ethnic resettlements, the site of the first new, pure German SS colony in Poland: Himmlerstadt.

On 16 October, 1942, all the Jews of Zamość were loaded into lorries and taken to the Belzec death camp. The original Polish inhabitants of the town died by the thousands during a wintry exodus. The cruelty towards the children was devastating. Of the younger children from Zamość and the surrounding areas, approximately 10,000 died during the deportations, and some 30,000 were taken away from their parents because of their blue eyes, blond hair and other 'pure' racial traits. They were sent to the *Lebensborn* centres that had been set up all over

Germany. There they were 'Nazified' and 'Germanised', then sent to live with SS families. A great number of those children never returned to Poland.

Zamość was a high-handed initiative on the part of the SS, the fanatical ideologists of racial purity. And the consequences of that high-handedness were not long coming. Partisan units began operating all around Zamość, mounting one raid after another. Eighteen months later, by spring 1943, the German colonists were begging to be allowed to return to the West. Their farms were under constant attack, they slept in the fields at night from fear of being killed by partisans. The *Wehrmacht* suspended its military operations against the local resistance: the divisions were sorely needed at the front. In July 1944 the Red Army finally took the city.

Very little is known outside Poland about Zamość and the surrounding villages. Yet it was here that the twentieth century's greatest liquidation of towns and villages took place.

In most cases of ethnic cleansing, a second process began after the deportations: cultural purification. A new past was invented to go along with the new future, and every memory of the original inhabitants was obliterated as carefully as possible. Monuments were taken down, signs and inscriptions removed, school curricula altered, native languages banned, and sometimes even churchyards were rearranged.

In Poland and the Baltic States, the gauleiter was ordered to make German provinces of the occupied territories within ten years. The old German names of all of the villages and towns were restored, or new ones were dreamed up. Łódź became Litzmannstadt, Poznań became Posen once more, Zamość became Himmlerstadt.

When a series of treaties between Germany, the Soviet Union and Italy forced hundreds of thousands of German-speaking nationals to leave South Tyrol, Bessarabia, Poland and the Baltic States, Himmler turned it around into a glorious story: the old blood brothers were returning at last to the ethnic fold.

Rosie Waldeck, who visited a camp for Bessarabian Germans in Rumania, described how old men sat on benches in the sunshine, how the verandas were covered in greenery, how the women chatted away as they did their laundry, how the young people sang cheerfully and marched around

under SS supervision. 'Now and then a young SS man would affection-
ately pick up a small child and carry it around on his shoulders, or dangle
it on his knee.' Meals were taken at long tables in the warm afternoon
sun. 'These typical descendants of typical colonists, who spoke the antique
German of Württemberg from Schiller's day, returned to Hitler's Germany
as to the Promised Land.' In the end, almost half a million German-
speaking Europeans took part in this mass migration, and 200,000 of
them were assigned a new home in Eastern Europe.

On Friday, 27 March, 1942, Goebbels wrote in his diary:

> Starting with Lublin, the Jews are now being pushed east out of
> the General Government. A rather barbaric method, too grisly to
> mention, is applied, and not much is left of the Jews themselves.
> Generally speaking, one can note that sixty per cent of them are to
> be liquidated, while forty per cent can be used for labour details
> . . . The Führer's prediction, made to them before this new world
> war was unleashed, is becoming horrendous reality . . . The ghettos
> vacated in the General Government are now being used to house
> those Jews deported from the Reich, and after a time the pro-
> cedure will be repeated.

In Auschwitz the elderflowers are blossoming. Oświęcim, as it is called
in Polish, is a normal town where lovers stroll by the river in the evening,
and where the rest of the local young people hang around by the bridge,
the boys bald, the girls giggling. They drink beer together from the same
glass, with a straw, 'because then you get drunk faster'. The coal cars go
pounding by behind Hotel Glob. At least a dozen tourist buses are parked
in front of the former camp. The cow parsley grows high among the
trees and the dilapidated gravestones in the old Jewish cemetery. Yes,
indeed, Auschwitz has a regular, old Jewish cemetery, with a high wall
around it and dozens of names listed on either side, the peaceful dead
who have slept through it all.

'We survivors are not only an exiguous but also an anomalous minority:
we are those who by their prevarications or abilities or good luck did

not touch bottom.' wrote Primo Levi, one of the rare survivors of Auschwitz. 'They are the "Muslims", the submerged, the complete witnesses, the ones whose deposition would have a general significance. They are the rule, we are the exception.'

Beneath wire netting on the immense parade grounds at Birkenau lie their rusty metal plates and spoons, then so precious, now apparently there for the taking. In the old barracks one can see their toothbrushes, their crutches and artificial legs, their baby clothes, their dusty locks of hair and their shoes. The suitcases bearing all those everyday names: 'Judith van Gelder-Cohen, the Hague', 'Hanna Feitsma, Holland'. Three rooms full of shoes, reflecting better than anything else the faces of those who wore them: workmen's shoes, clogs, brogues, and between them an elegant summer sandal with a high cork sole and cheerful white and red leather straps.

That, too, is part of our shame and dismay: the absolute innocence with which all those hundreds of thousands went to their death.

The prisoners knew that what was happening in the camps was too astounding to be believed. Primo Levi writes that he and his friends in the camp were almost all plagued by a recurring nightmare: that they came home and, relieved and impassioned, told a loved one about the horrors they had experienced, but that they were not listened to. In the most cruel variation on this dream, the one they told simply turned his back and walked away.

That nightmare has, in part, come to pass. For the rest of the world, Auschwitz has gradually become more a symbol than a reality. Yet it is all still there, right amid the factories in the industrial estate of modern-day Oświęcim. And standing almost casually, a little further along across the tracks, is the famous gateway of Birkenau. For a moment the mind tries to make of it a school building from the 1930s, but there it stands, unmistakable and real, the building you have seen in all those films and all those photographs, the gateway with the rails running through it and the platform beside.

The camp Auschwitz I was opened on 14 June, 1940. On that day more than 700 Poles arrived for the construction of, among other things, the crematorium. By 15 August it was ready to burn the first bodies. The oven, built by J. A. Topf & Söhne of Erfurt, had a capacity of a hundred bodies a day. At first Auschwitz served largely as a labour camp for companies including I. G. Farben and the Weichsel-Metall-Union. The larger camp, Auschwitz II, opened in 1941. Auschwitz became a labour-annexe-death camp, like Majdanek. Four dedicated extermination factories existed as well: Belzec, Sobibór, Chelmno and Treblinka. Less is known about them, however, because almost none of their prisoners survived.

The first major shipment of Jews arrived at Auschwitz on 15 February, 1942. The ruse was arranged down to the smallest detail. To this new life one was allowed to bring enough rations for two days, a mess kit, one spoon, no knives, two blankets, warm clothes, a pair of work shoes and a suitcase with personal belongings, with one's name written on it. And most people fell for it: the museum there is still full of pans, buckets, washtubs, shovels, tools and other items useful for starting an orderly new life in the East.

Dutch deportees hid letters in the cattle cars for those 'at home': it did not take the prisoners long to realise that it was always the same train that shuttled back and forth between Camp Westerbork and the East. A few of those letters have been preserved. One of them describes the pushing and squeezing in a packed freight car. 'The mood is already horrible, everyone is snappish and argumentative.' One young woman reported that the people in her freight car were in such 'excellent spirits' that they organised a cabaret performance on the first evening out. 'I will always remember one song in particular, sung by a sixteen-year-old girl by the light of a little tea-warmer on the floor of the car. It was "Nederland".' Concerning another transport we know that a barber shaved the men, and that a teacher held a 'fascinating lecture on Zionism, that quickly made everyone forget where we were headed'. And the letters always contain a final sentence, something along the lines of: 'We've stopped at Auschwitz, we have to get out. It is a big factory town, with lots of smokestacks everywhere.' Or: 'In the distance I can see a building, all lit up. So long, my dearest, we'll be coming home soon.'

The yard at Birkenau is now covered in daisies and clover. Swallows dip and soar above the few barracks that have been left standing, the bare red smokestacks, the groves of birch that grow on human ashes. A bird has built its nest amid the rubble of Crematorium III. Above the gate one can still see the soot from the hundreds of steam locomotives that pulled in here.

*

From the diary of Auschwitz camp physician SS-Hauptsturmführer Proffessor Dr Kremer:

31 August, 1942
Tropical weather here at thirty-eight degrees in the shade, dust and countless flies! Excellent service in the officers' mess. Tonight, for example, there was pickled goose liver for forty pfennigs, with stuffed tomatoes, tomato salad, etc. First inoculated against typhoid.

1 September, 1942
Sent off order to Berlin for officer's cap, belt and suspenders. In the afternoon, attended the gassing of a block, with Zyklon B against louse.

6 September, 1942
Today, Sunday, excellent lunch: tomato soup, half a chicken with potatoes and red cabbage (20g fat), sweets and lovely vanilla ice cream. After dinner welcomed the new physician, Obersturmführer Wirths, who hails from Waldbröl . . . This evening at 8.00 went to another *Sonderaktion* [special action] outside.

9 September, 1942
Early this morning received from my lawyer in Münster, Proffessor Dr Hallerman, the extremely good news that my wife and I are divorced as from the first of this month. I see colours again: a black veil has lifted from my life.
    This evening attended *Sonderaktion* (fourth time).

10 September, 1942
This morning to *Sonderaktion* (fifth time).

20 September, 1942
Today, late Sunday afternoon from 3.00 to 6.00, listened to concert by prisoners' orchestra in lovely sunlight: orchestra leader was director of the Warsaw State Opera. Eighty musicians. At lunch, braised pork. Dinner, fried tench.

*

Camp Birkenau is decaying quickly. Half a century later the rusty barbed wire crumbles in your hands, the piles of shoes are only grey and black, most of the buildings have rotted away. Only the smokestacks still rise above it all, the long rows of the remains of hundreds of barracks that once formed the camp for men and families. The inhabitants of Oświęcim themselves are already taking steps. At the edge of Birkenau, less than a hundred metres from the camp, is a brand new architectural apartment complex. The big living-room windows look out on the brownish-green yards of the camp. The complex itself is generally referred to as 'the museum', and that is what it has become for many of those who live here; a sort of park that draws a great many tourists, and nothing more than that.

I stop to talk to Adriana Warno. She is about eighteen, and has a summer job taking tickets at the gate to Birkenau. 'We've always lived here, my parents too, and we like it,' she says. 'For us the museum is what the Eiffel Tower is for Parisians. The museum is down at one end, and Oświęcim is up at the other, the two don't have much to do with each other. It's a very normal town, you know, what used to be Auschwitz. We go out and everything, no problem.'

For her there is, in fact, only one problem: the strangling boredom that has had the town in its grip the last few years. Most of the shop windows now contain only dusty book bags, macramé goods and cheap dinner settings. Oświęcim today has 50,000 inhabitants, but no form of higher education. 'We have to go to Krakow for everything.' Jobs are scarce, and tourism at the camp is declining as well. Far fewer Americans have come to Auschwitz this year, they say it's because of the war in Kosovo. The walls along the streets are full of anarchist symbols and Celtic crosses.

'Of course I think about it sometimes,' Adriana says. 'Especially when I'm in the museum. It's not taboo, you know. 'Oh well, that was back then,' that's what my parents always say. Everyone here knew what was going on in the camp, you could see it, or smell it at least. But no one thinks about that any more. If you did, you'd go crazy. And you have to live your life, and life here is hard enough as it is.'

I ask her about the people who visit the camp. She blurts out: 'You don't hear anything from the real victims and their families. But you should see the rest of the people who come here.' She tells me about women's clubs with tambourines, gurus who come to drive out the evil spirits, sobbing American ladies who come here to deal with past lives, classes of schoolchildren with Polish flags, classes of schoolchildren with Israeli flags, the French, Belgian, Dutch and Italian tour companies that offer a 'three-camp tour', starting in Krakow. 'They all claim Auschwitz for themselves. They've never suffered for a moment themselves, but my, how they'd like to hitch a ride with the real victims! It's enough to make you sick.'

Chapter Thirty-Two

Auschwitz

I HAD BEEN IN AUSCHWITZ ONCE BEFORE, AS A RADIO REPORTER IN January 1995, during the memorial services for the fiftieth anniversary of the camp's liberation. I remember getting lost at the end of one dark winter afternoon in the wooded area behind the Birkenau complex. I stumbled upon a hamlet there, like so many in Poland: chickens, geese, a dog on a chain, three old women and a farmer sitting on his wagon. To my right lay the concrete remains of Crematorium III. To the left were the ponds where the ashes were thrown: later on, ashes and bones were dumped all over these woods. A few patches of snow glistened among the trees, and a thin layer of yellowish ice floated on the quiet surface of the ponds.

Straight ahead of me were the masts of the satellite dishes, cables had been laid across the former gas chambers and bright conversation could be heard from the trailers where the television crews were sitting. When I turned and looked again, I saw a farm that must have been there all those years. The window was brightly lit, through it I saw a living room, a table, a carpet and a stove, outside the house a clothes line and a child's bike lying on its side. From there to the crematorium was no more than 300 metres.

How much did people know? What did the neighbours, the suppliers, the railway engineers and the civil servants know? And how much could they have known? And how much did they want to know?

Later, in the camp museum at Majdanek, I came across a letter from the Technisches Büro und Fabrik H. Kori GmbH, Dennewitzstrasse 35, Berlin, specialists in *Abfallverbrennungsöfen aller Art*. The letter was dated 25 October,

1941, and addressed to SS-Obersturmführer Lenzer in Lublin. The letter deals with plans to build a number of incinerators at the camp, plus an adjacent changing room and disinfection centre. 'Our drawing on page 2 CJ no. 9079 shows the solution for the problem of accommodating five crematorium ovens, with number 5 in the middle intended as back-up installation.'

It is a letter that will not stop haunting. Like the invoice beside it: addressed to the Paul Reimann firm in Breslau, 100 marks for 200 kilo of human hair at 50 pfennigs a kilo. There is no denying it: thousands of people actively took part in the Holocaust, from a distance. As noted earlier: in thousands of busy offices in Berlin alone, the administration activities went on day in and day out. At SS headquarters, at the finance ministry and the Reichsbank, huge quantities of jewellery, clothing and other personal possessions were registered and redistributed. Dozens of local people at the Prussian mint were involved in melting down gold fillings. Banks and insurance companies transferred Jewish holdings to the state treasury or Nazi accounts. Personal possessions were sent as Christmas gifts to the ethnic German colonists. The homes of Jews were plundered, in the knowledge that their inhabitants would never come back. Everyone 'knew' it in their own way.

At first the existence of the death camps was talked about only in very small circles. By autumn 1943, almost all the highly placed Nazis had been informed. That was for tactical reasons: after receiving that information, no one could bow out by pleading ignorance or innocence; now they were all part of the conspiracy. That, too, is why Himmler, at a closed meeting of Reichsleiter and gauleiter in Poznań on 6 October, 1943, spoke in relatively plain terms about the extermination of the Jews.

What he said, literally, was: 'The phrase "the Jews must be destroyed" is easy to say, but the demands it places on those who implement it are among the heaviest and most difficult in the world.'

Albert Speer's flat denial at Nuremberg saved his life. Along with Goebbels and Göring he was Hitler's closest assistant, and one of the most senior officials in the Third Reich. In his memoirs he mentioned a visit he received in summer 1944 from his mentor, Karl Hanke. The old Nazi was completely beside himself: never, never must Speer accept an invitation to visit a concentration camp in the district of Upper Silesia.

This old friend of his had seen things there he was neither allowed nor able to describe. He could only have been referring to Auschwitz. Speer: 'I didn't enquire any further. I didn't ask Himmler about it, I didn't ask Hitler about it, I did not talk about it with my friends. Nor did I have it investigated: I didn't want to know what was going on.'

Years later, in her impressive study of Speer, Gitta Sereny demonstrated that he not only *could* have known much more, but that he actually *did* know much more. Once the war was over, however, he skilfully repressed that knowledge, as did countless other Germans.

Primo Levi wrote about a German fellow chemist. Levi and his German colleague performed the same experiments, and both of them worked at the same, huge Buna site. There was one difference between them: in the evening Levi slept inside a barbed-wire enclosure, while his colleague lived on the outside. This *Oberingenieur* said later that he had known nothing about the gas chambers, and that he had never asked anyone about them. 'He did not comfort himself with lies,' Levi wrote, 'but with lacunae, with blank spots.'

How many 'blank spots' could a person live with between 1940–5?

The pamphlet distributed by the students of the White Rose in Munich spoke of 'the most beastly murder' of 300,000 Polish Jews. Tucked away in the house on Amsterdam's Prinsengracht, Anne Frank wrote on 9 October, 1942: 'We assume that most of them were murdered. The English radio speaks of gassing. Perhaps that is the fastest way to die.' One week later, in Dresden, Victor Klemperer referred to the Auschwitz camp as 'a fast-moving slaughterhouse'. On 27 February, 1943 he said that it was 'no longer probable that Jews will return alive from Poland'.

So *they* knew about it. Were they the only ones with eyes and ears?

Tens of thousands of *Wehrmacht* soldiers were involved, directly or indirectly, in the mass executions in Poland. In his classic study of the activities of a typical death squad, Reserve Police Battalion 101, Christopher Browning shows that the battalion was in a state of continual flux: respectable fathers from Hamburg reported for duty, took part in mass executions, then went home to carry on life as usual. One of the commanders, newly married, even took his young bride along: in the market square at Miedzyrzec she was a direct witness to the murder of the local Jews. The stories flew around the country: in letters that escaped the censors' attention, from soldiers on leave, in photographs sent home from the East. It was only in November 1941 that photographing such executions was forbidden.

After 1943, anyone in Germany who looked around enough – as I once heard a young German formulate it so inimitably – 'knew for sure that they didn't want to know more.' In that same year British and American bombers scattered millions of pamphlets over Germany, containing precise information about the systematic murder of the European Jews, the death camps and the gas chambers. Eric Johnson carried out a survey among older Germans in Cologne and Krefeld concerning their awareness of the Holocaust before 1945. Of those questioned, sixty-six per cent admitted to have been more or less informed.

Awareness of the Holocaust was reasonably widespread in other parts of Europe as well. Fifty years later, a group of students examined the war diaries of seventy non-Jewish Dutch people. They wanted to determine what the people in the occupied territories knew about the persecution of the Jews, and when they had found out about it. More than a third of the diarists turned out to have come rather quickly to the conclusion that the Jews were being murdered on a massive scale. The wife of a physician wrote on 9 November, 1941: 'Most of the Jews in our circles, who were taken away so quickly, are already dead – within a few weeks' time, in other words.'

On 13 December, an office clerk from Rotterdam wrote: 'In Poland, the mass murder of Jews continues. They say Himmler wants to kill all the Jews before 1943.' As from early 1943, the name 'Auschwitz' also crops up regularly in the Netherlands. One citizen of Rotterdam wrote, on 14 February, 1943: 'The execution of Jews and Poles continues: 6,000 a day, in one place; first they are undressed; then . . . (gas?).'

All these diarists were extremely indignant, and most certainly believed in the rumours about the use of gas chambers. Yet when the camps were opened after the war and it became clear that this unthinkable mass murder really had taken place, the shock was enormous, even among staunch anti-Nazis and resistance fighters. It was as though people knew and did not want to know, all at the same time; as though they knew rationally about the millions of murders, but were unable to accept it in their hearts, even after the war, because it defied imagination. The group of women with their underwear flapping in the wind in the dunes outside the Latvian town of Liepaja had a face. The 1.1 million killed at Auschwitz were merely a number.

The Allies concentrated on a 'total victory', not in retaliation for the Nazi atrocities, but to minimise the risk of individual peace treaties and to keep the mutual ties as close as possible. Only in that way could they, as one British government memorandum put it, 'solve the entire complex of human problems caused by German domination'. Anything that would distract them from that goal would also harm the Jewish cause. That was the rationale.

Telling in this regard is the story surrounding the few rare aerial photos of Auschwitz. They were taken on 31 May and 25 August, 1944, by a British reconnaissance plane that had been sent to scout out the nearby I. G. Farben complex for the production of synthetic rubber. Quite by accident, the crew left the camera on as they flew above the death camps. At the end of the roll shot on 25 August there are clear images of the platform at Birkenau, where a train had just arrived. A line of prisoners can be seen, on their way to Crematorium II. The negative was discovered by chance only thirty years later. In 1944, no one on the RAF staff noticed it.

In addition, the British and the Americans had agreed not to respond to the 'blackmail politics' of Germany and its allies. As early as February 1943, the Rumanian government under Ion Antonescu had offered to allow 70,000 Jews to leave for Palestine. The British rejected the offer. Any horse-trading with human lives would, after all, have run counter to their military strategies. Although they admitted that mass murders were taking place – the British House of Commons had even held a minute's silence for the victims on 17 December, 1942 – the restrictive refugee policy remained firmly in place.

There were instances of courage and resistance everywhere in Europe, even in the gas chambers of Auschwitz. In the grounds of Crematorium III, a series of handwritten notes in Yiddish was dug up in summer 1952. Probably left there by a Jewish member of a *Sonderkommando*, they documented a whole series of incidents. In late 1943, for example, almost

200 Polish partisans were taken to the gas chambers, along with a few hundred Dutch Jews. When they were all completely undressed, a young Polish woman held an impassioned speech, closing with the words: 'We will not die now, the history of our people will make us immortal, our will and our spirit will live on and blossom.' She also addressed the Jews of the *Sonderkommando* who were standing around: 'Tell our brothers, our people, that we are going to our death in full awareness and full of pride.' Then they sang the Polish national anthem, the Jews sang the 'Hatikva', and together they sang the 'Internationale'. 'While they were still singing, the car from the Red Cross [in which the Zyklon B was transported] arrived and the gas was tossed into the room, and they all gave up the ghost in song and ecstasy, dreaming of brotherhood and a better world.'

A little less than a year later, on 7 October, 1944, a massive uprising took place. A large group of prisoners tried to escape, but despite careful preparations, the plan failed. Four SS guards were killed, 12 were wounded, 455 prisoners were machine-gunned. As late as January 1945, four women were hanged for having smuggled explosives from the Union factory into the camp.

Today a distinction is drawn between active resistance and 'resistiveness', that is to say, the widespread resistance to deportation and other forms of Nazi terror within a normal society. Often – as in the cases, for example, of France, Denmark, the Netherlands, Belgium and Italy – the measure of resistiveness was at least as essential to the Jews' chances of survival as outright resistance.

In Germany, courageous cells of communists and Christians continued to work underground, and several pockets of resistance arose within the *Wehrmacht* as well. The scope of this covert resistance should not be underestimated: an indication of it is found in the sheer number of German political prisoners who died in the concentration camps, well over 100,000 in all. The actual number of Germans who sabotaged the regime, in one way or another, must have been many times that.

Yet in Germany there was no massive, grass roots popular resistance. Despite the success of the women's uprising on Berlin's Rosenstrasse, it remained the only demonstration of its kind there. The merciless Gestapo reprisals, especially after 1941, no doubt had something to do with it:

the students of the White Rose were beheaded for passing out a few pamphlets. On the other hand, the Berlin policeman Wilhelm Krützfeld, who courageously defended the Great Berlin Synagogue against the SA during Kristallnacht, was never touched: five years later he retired at his own request, 'with the Führer's thanks for service rendered'. Striking, too, was the attitude towards dissidents within Reserve Police Battalion 101. Approximately twenty per cent of the battalion refused to take part in the first mass murders in Poland. Those dissidents received, at most, extra sentry duty or unpleasant kitchen-police tasks, but otherwise ran no risk whatsoever. Christopher Browning has emphasised, as have others, that 'not a single case has been documented of severe punishment for Germans who refused to kill unarmed citizens'. This means that the Germans who did take part in the mass murders must, for the most part, have done so voluntarily. That compliance was probably based in part on peer pressure, partly on typical German discipline, and partly on anti-Semitism – although Battalion 101 also showed few scruples, for example, when ordered to destroy villages around Zamość populated only by Poles.

Eric Johnson interviewed forty-five Jewish survivors from Krefeld. When asked whether they had received significant assistance or support from the local population, almost ninety per cent of them said they had not. The lack of systematic resistance is also evident from Victor Klemperer's diary; he did, however, make note of individual signs of sympathy – a handshake in public, for example – when he walked down the street wearing his Star of David. In the factory where he was forced to work from 1943, Klemperer detected not the slightest trace of anti-Semitism among the German workers. According to him, every Jew who survived 'had an Aryan angel somewhere'.

In other parts of Europe, the resistiveness of civilian society was much more pronounced. Resistance was seen in many circles as something normal, often even as one's civic duty, no matter how great the risks. At Auschwitz, Witold Pilecki, a courageous officer in the Polish under-ground resistance, succeeded in infiltrating the camp as early as September 1940, and organised resistance cells for a period of two years until his escape in 1943. In Amsterdam, the communist Piet Nak openly declared the February Strike. The bankers Walraven and Gijs van Hall carried out the biggest banking fraud in Dutch history: with the proceeds, their

organisation was able to keep alive for years tens of thousands of resistance people and those in hiding.

In Marseille, the American Varian Fry helped in the escape of hundreds
of prominent European intellectuals. The 3,000 inhabitants of the
isolated French village of Le Chambon-sur-Lignon (Haute-Loire), led
by Pastor André Trocmé and his wife Magda, provided shelter throughout
the war years for more than 5,000 Jews. In Vilnius, Anton Schmidt, a
sergeant major in the *Wehrmacht*, saved thousands of Jews from the
firing squad. At Kaunas, Japanese consul Sempo Sugihara allowed at
least 1,600 Jewish refugees to escape by giving them transit visas for
Japan. In Krakow, the industrialist Oskar Schindler was able to save
most of his Jewish workers. Something similar was achieved at the
Skoda plant in the Czech town of Plzeń by Albert Göring, the brother
of Hitler's right-hand man.

In October 1943, most of Denmark's Jews were able to escape to Sweden
on a few fishing boats, aided by the police, the churches, the Danish
coastguard and countless unsung Danes. Almost all 50,000 of Bulgaria's
Jews were left in peace until the end of the war, thanks to the outspoken
public opinion against deportations expressed in the newspapers, the
pulpits and at public meetings, a popular will which the Nazis did not
dare to defy. Jews generally received protection in the areas under Italian
control as well; the Italian officers considered the anti-Semitic politics of
the Germans 'incompatible with the honour of the Italian Army'.

In Hungary, the Red Cross representative Friedrich Born, along with
the diplomats Carl Lutz (of Switzerland) and Raoul Wallenberg (of
Sweden), was able to save the lives of many tens of thousands of Jews
by means of a highly dangerous ruse involving Swedish passports and
British immigration permits for Palestine. Wallenberg came from a rich
and famous family of Swedish bankers and industrialists. During his activities in Hungary he was in constant contact with Nazis and Western
leaders. For the perpetually paranoid agents of the NKVD, that was enough
to label him a spy. Immediately after the Russians occupied the country
in January 1945, he and his chauffeur were arrested. Within the Soviet
Gulag camp system he was registered as a 'prisoner of war'; in the years
that followed, there were regular rumours of his having been seen here
or there by recently released prisoners. Those rumours were never

confirmed. In 1957, the Soviets came up with a document dated 17 July, 1947 in which it was stated that 'the prisoner Wallenberg, well known to you, died last night in his cell'. It was signed by Smoltsov, former director of the infirmary at Moscow's Lubyanka prison. Wallenberg, it was claimed, had died of 'coronary failure'. In November 2000, the chairman of a new Russian investigation committee admitted in a footnote to his report that the diplomat had probably been executed in 1947. The motive for his abduction was purely commercial: the Soviet government had hoped in this way to force the Wallenbergs to provide them with some politically sensitive supplies.

Tens of thousands of European families took Jews into hiding, hundreds of thousands of families were involved in channelling rations, countless larger and smaller resistance groups fought for and alongside runaway Jews. The risks were enormous, the sanctions were grave, yet still it went on.

In Belgium, some 35,000 of the country's 60,000 Jews were saved in this fashion: 60 per cent. In France, 270,000 of the 350,000 Jews survived: more than 75 per cent. In Norway, 1,000 of the 1,800 Jews survived: approximately 60 per cent. Of the 7,500 Danish Jews, more than 100 died: 98 per cent were saved. In other parts of the continent, the percentage of survivors was much lower: in the Netherlands, only 40,000 of the country's 140,000 Jews made it through the war: less than 30 per cent. Of the 2.7 million Polish Jews, barely 75,000 survived: 2 per cent. At the same time, for their singular courage in the war, it has been helpers from these latter two countries who have most often received the honorary title of 'Righteous among Nations' from the Israeli Yad Vashem Holocaust Museum: 5,373 and 4,289, respectively.

It would be simple enough to equate such figures, as is sometimes done, with values like 'courage' or 'humanity', or conversely with the degree of 'anti-Semitism' in a given country. Anyone providing shelter for a Jewish family in Germany ran an infinitely greater risk of being informed on than someone in Belgium. In Poland, hiding Jews was a capital offence, in Vichy France the penalty was only a short prison term. There were in Warsaw's ghetto alone more Jews than in all of France. Where were they to go? In oft-praised Denmark, the actions − without wishing to detract from the courage of the Danish resistance − involved only a very small number of Jews, who could be helped to escape with relative ease. Consider, by comparison, the problems faced by the resistance in the Netherlands, where tens of thousands of families had to be hidden in a densely populated country under strict SS and SD supervision, with no single direct route of escape to non-occupied territories.

Of the 7.5 million Jews in the parts of Europe occupied by Germany, only 20 per cent were still alive in 1945. Only one out of every five Jewish men, women and children survived the Holocaust.

Could the sole driving force behind this petty, middle-class, vindictive anti-Semitism really have been the old Jew-baiting of Paris, Vienna and Berlin, the hatred that encompassed Raphaël Viau and Karl Lueger, as well as Georg Ritter von Schönerer? There are authors who advance this claim with conviction, and who are paid particular heed in Germany. Despite the painful accusation it contains, it is also an attractive idea, because it is simple and comforting. The theory implies, after all, that mass murders of this kind will never repeat themselves once the folly of anti-Semitism has been abandoned. In other words: the Holocaust was a gruesome but one-time-only excess on the part of a generation past. Nothing like that will ever happen to us again.

The background to the Holocaust, however, was more complicated than that. Anti-Semitism played a role, of course, even a major role, but the Holocaust probably had many more causes, most of which had little or nothing to do with a hatred for Jews. The survivors of Krefeld interviewed by Eric Johnson reported almost no anti-Semitic incidents, and in only a quarter of the cases of Jews being reported to the Gestapo did motives such as 'political belief' play a role. Jews were informed against much more often because of conflicts between neighbours, love gone sour, or for financial gain.

This last factor in particular, the matter of material interests, should not be underestimated, and the Nazis put it to most effective use. The contents of the 72,000 vacant Jewish homes were distributed around the country and sold at auctions for a pittance. The historian Frank Bajohr, who studied the deportations from Hamburg, speaks of 'one of the greatest exchanges of property in modern history, a massive robbery in which an increasingly large portion of the German population took part.'

Another important factor was the total absence of a *mentality* of resistance. In Denmark, Bulgaria, Italy and on the Côte d'Azur, the persecution of Jews failed largely because the local authorities and police considered it beneath their moral dignity. Liberal and tolerant Amsterdam, on the other hand, scarcely had an anti-Semitic tradition. Yet all of the German agents and officers charged with deporting that city's 80,000 Jews could easily fit in a single group portrait. The vast majority of Jewish families were deported, almost without a hitch, by citizens of Amsterdam: Dutch policemen, tram drivers and railway engineers. The Dutch identification card was almost impossible to forge: the proud, humdrum work of a perfectionist Dutch civil servant. Amsterdam's registrar's office helped the Germans with such pinpoint accuracy that the resistance finally had to blow it up.

A similar situation applied in Paris and other French cities. In mid-1942, there were no more than 3,000 Gestapo agents in all of France. Approximately three quarters of the Jews arrested were detained by French policemen. Yet most of those policemen and civil servants were not Nazis, and in no way anti-Semitic. It is with good reason that Adam Lebor and Roger Boyes, in their study of the European resistance movements, speak of 'a massive collapse of moral and civic virtues'.

The problem was not only the mass murders themselves, it was also, as Daniel Goldhagen puts it, 'the ease, the incredible ease with which the razzias could take place, the punctuality of the trains, the efficiency with which executions were carried out, the unthinkability of the number of victims: not dozens or even hundreds, but millions. The Holocaust was a very different phenomenon from those other, all too frequent anti-Semitic atrocities in European history. It was, in addition to all the rest, a bureaucratic excess in which hundreds of thousands of Europeans calmly took part, simply because they attached greater importance to the order and regularity of their section, service, army unit or business department than to their individual conscience.

In the *Observer* of 9 April, 1944, Sebastian Haffner published a lucid, nigh-prophetic portrait of Albert Speer. According to Haffner, Speer was the 'embodiment of the revolution of managers': not corrupt, gaudy or garish like the Nazis, but intelligent and courteous. He was the prototype of the kind of man who became increasingly important in this war:

'the pure technocrat, the classless, brilliant sort with no background, whose only goal is to make a career for himself.' Precisely that lightness, that lack of reflection, allowed all young men of his ilk to continue operating 'the horrifying machinery of our age', right up until the end.

In a certain sense the Holocaust can be seen as an expression of an almost religious fanaticism, and at the same time as a wilful blindness, a deep, collective moral lapse. This is not a popular explanation. It is, after all, much more disturbing than all the theories that grasp at anti-Semitism and the evil of the German Nazi elite. It implies that a similar mass persecution, using the current technology, bureaucracies and systems of repression and manipulation, could take place again tomorrow in a different place and against a different group. The technocrats will remain. In Haffner's words: 'This is their age. We shall be rid of the Hitlers and the Himmlers, but the Speers, whatever happens to them as individuals, shall be with us for a long time.'

Chapter Thirty-Three

Warsaw

IN 1941, A VISITOR WROTE OF THE WARSAW GHETTO:

The streets are so crowded that one can barely move ahead. Everyone walks about in rags and tatters. People often possess nothing but a shirt. There is noise and shouting everywhere. High, plaintive children's voices cut through it all. From the 'Aryan' side, curiosity seekers peer at the pitiful spectacle of the tattered crowd. The children are the ghetto's true breadwinners. When a German looks the other way for only a second, they slip handily to the Aryan side. The things they buy there, bread, potatoes and such, are hidden skilfully under their rags. The challenge then is to slip back in the same fashion.

Thousands of shabby beggars elicit memories of famines in India. A half-starved mother tries to feed her child from a desiccated breast. An older child lies beside her, presumably dead. You see dying people lying spreadeagled in the middle of the street. Their legs are swollen, often frozen, their faces twisted in agony.

Sometimes the sentries will stop a group of Jews and order them to undress and roll in the muck. They are often forced to dance as well. The sentries stand and watch, bent double with laughter.

A few rather ramshackle houses, a section of tram rails, an ornament in a hallway, a potholed street a few hundred metres long is all that is left of the neighbourhood where this once happened. A grey neighbourhood of apartment buildings has been built where the old ghetto once stood. I find one section of the infamous wall with which the ghetto was sealed off: behind a stinking courtyard, along a little street where dubious men use a gentle form of extortion to horn in on the municipal parking revenues, behind Elektroland, the Holiday Inn and a branch of the Nationale Nederlanden insurance company.

Little children are playing between the apartment blocks, it is a warm day, the leaves of poplars sway above the children's heads, making dancing spots of sunlight. I ask directions from a young woman walking along with a little girl; they say they are each other's favourite niece and favourite aunt. They walk along with me for a while, then go skipping off, it looks as if they are floating with pleasure.

The young woman turns and points around her.

Yes, here was the Jewish ghetto.

On 19 April, 1943, when most of the ghetto's residents had already been taken away, a final, desperate uprising took place. The Jewish organisation – there were even kibbutzim in the ghetto – had gradually found out exactly what was happening in the camps, and no one harboured any more illusions. Starting in spring 1942, dozens of young Jewish people had started setting up a military organisation, weapons were smuggled in and, finally, about 30 combat groups were formed, comprising 750 partisans.

In the eyes of those who took part in it, the uprising was above all a confirmation of the value of human life, nothing less than that. They knew it was hopeless, but they wanted to 'die honourably'. 'Life belongs to us!' they wrote in a pamphlet. 'We, too, have a right to that! We must only understand that we must fight for it . . . Let every mother be a lioness defending her young! No father calmly watches his children die any more! The shame of the first act of our destruction must not repeat itself!'

Historians have succeeded in digging up the names and histories of 235 of those who participated in the revolt. What is remarkable is their youth: most of them were between the ages of eighteen and twenty. The oldest was the forty-three-year-old Abram Diamant. He died during the fighting in the streets of the ghetto. The youngest was Lusiek Blones. This thirteen-year-old was killed in the final hours of the uprising, while trying to escape through the ghetto's sewers. The commander of the revolt,

Mordechai Anielewicz, was twenty-four. He committed suicide along with the other leaders on 8 May, when their commando post at Milastraat 18 was surrounded and pumped full of poison gas. An impressive number of women took part: approximately a third of the membership of the resistance groups consisted of girls and young women. Almost all of them were in love.

At first, the Germans were taken by surprise. Fighting went on everywhere in the ghetto during the first few days, and both sides suffered heavy losses. But soon entire streets had been set alight by tank and artillery fire, the partisans fought back from underground bunkers, air strikes followed, and finally the resistance strongholds were taken one by one, houses and entire streets were wiped off the map.

Of the 235 Jewish partisans we know about, 72 survived the revolt and 28 died in the ghetto's sewers. Forty-four of them succeeded in escaping, but most of those died soon afterwards in fighting between Germans and partisans. Others were betrayed and sent to Majdanek or Auschwitz. Three were killed in the great uprising in August and September 1944. By 1945, only 12 of the 750 insurgents were still alive.

The ZIH-INB, Warsaw's Jewish Historical Institute, tries to document as many of the memories as possible. Local historians Jan Jagielski and Tomasz Lec have carefully located the spots from which the most famous photographs of the starving ghetto were made, and published their findings in book form. Following their lead, I now walk through the neighbourhood and see it through other eyes.

It is hard, as it turns out, to find surviving remnants of the former ghetto. Most of the locations can only be identified on the basis of kerbs, posts and other topographical details. A photograph of an emaciated corpse lying in the street, for example, turns out to have been taken from the portico of Waliców Street 6.10. The only thing marking the spot is an oval-shaped post in the foreground. The kerb against which another corpse was photographed is still there too, in front of the Church of the Holy Virgin's Birth at what is today Solidarności Boulevard 80. The set of stairs turns out to be much smaller than it looks in the photograph, the body must not have been very big either, probably a child.

Here, a photograph of a stone bench in front of the courthouse, where two Jewish men and a woman are trying to sell a few wares: the same bench, against ·the same wall, now stands vacant in sunlight, the wall behind it covered in graffiti. A picture taken in 1941: the burial of an emaciated man beside a wall. It turns out to be the wall of a cemetery, the stones are still clearly recognisable, a tiled path now runs straight over the grave.

When I stopped to take a picture of my own, in the portico on Walicόw Street, an old lady came to take a look. She spoke a little German, and I explained what I was doing. Yes, she knew the photograph, that's the way it was here, she had seen it herself. Did I happen to have two zlotys for her, she whispered. She was hungry.

I try to find the gate that once led to the ghetto, the place where Jews had once been forced to dance naked. In the background of the photograph taken in 1940, the city rolls on, big and modern. Today there is a Pizza Hut on the corner. The only surviving point of reference is an old stone wall to one side. The gate, of course, has disappeared, but the most amazing thing is what has happened to that background: where Nalewki Street once stood, a busy shopping street with cars, trams and department stores, is today a quiet park. Only the rusty tram rails, which come to a stop somewhere under the grass, show that once this really was a busy urban neighbourhood, that the whole history is not a hallucination.

I leaf through other books of photographs. The earliest pictures of Warsaw show a city of well-to-do citizens, broad streets full of pedestrians, horse-drawn trams, churches and palaces in the familiar eclectic and pseudo-styles. Around the turn of the twentieth century the city was experiencing the same rapid growth as other European metropolises: industrialisation, prosperity in the city and poverty in the countryside, farmers who came pouring in by the tens of thousands, expansion after expansion, a growth from 261,000 inhabitants in 1874 to 797,000 in 1911.

Then came the start of the Polish Republic, the panic of the Russian Revolution – the Soviets advanced to just outside the city – and then the photographs show the cheerful, elegant Warsaw of the 1920s and 1930s, with coffee houses, theatres, universities, boulevards, newspaper boys and clanging trams. Then the war.

Pictures of Warsaw in 1945 resemble pictures of Hiroshima. Only a quarter of the city was still standing. Ninety per cent of all the large buildings had been reduced to rubble. Of the 1.3 million people who lived in Warsaw in 1940, only 378,000 were still there. Almost two thirds of the city's population was either dead or missing.

Now, at the end of the twentieth century, the city has something artificial about it, as though the old city centre has been reconstructed by expert stage designers. Every crack seems to have been put there for effect, many of the houses actually look older and more authentic than they ever were. And that impression is correct: almost every stone here was first blown away, then returned to its place. In the Rynek, the central square of the Old City, a melancholy organ-grinder is turning the crank on a fake antique barrel organ, handsome men are selling ugly paintings, the beggars have crutches and infants, the American ladies are just asking to be swindled. Polish vendors lurk around the ghetto, selling souvenir dolls, funny Jewish figurines, laughing and dancing rabbis; the folklore lives on, but the dancers have died.

This is a city full of memorial plaques, probably because nothing else is left. Every street corner has its monument, every house saw the birth of a poet or the death of a hero, and new plaques are being put up all the time. Just outside the centre of town I pass a brand-new monument for an entire army corps. A little group of old ladies is standing there in the twilight, looking at the gleaming pillar. A woman in a black suit dress walks up to it, searches among the many, many names, brushes one of them lightly with a gloved finger.

Warsaw's parks are the most pleasant place to be on long summer evenings like this. They lie in a circle around the Old City, often behind the gardens of the homes themselves. Neighbours are talking across the hedges, children are running around, little boys are playing soccer, babies and prams are out on parade, the girls are the most beautiful in all Europe.

I take a walk around one of the ponds with Wladyslaw Matwin. Matwin is a historian and former politician, he was born in 1916 and has himself gradually become a living chronicle of history. 'My life was a time full of violence,' he says. 'There were always huge forces at work that kept turning it all upside down.'

He studied in Poznań, was a member of a communist youth organisation, was arrested for 'some innocent work among children', and after that no university would have him. 'In 1938, at the time of the Munich Agreement, I was studying in Czechoslovakia. I had to pick up everything and run for it. When Hitler invaded Poland I had to run again, this time to the East. In 1941 I worked in a steel mill in the Ukraine, but I had to leave there too. In Poland I was taken for a Russian agent, in Russia I was suddenly a Polish agent. The fourth time I had to run from the Germans was in the Caucasus, and after that I joined the Red Army.'

The sky is turning a hot red, the croaking of the frogs is deafening. He talks about old Warsaw. 'Today Warsaw is a monocultural city, which is some people's ideal. But before 1939 it was a typically multicultural society. Those were the city's most productive years. We lost that multicultural character during the war; along with all the rest; that was one of the greatest losses for this city, and for this country.'

By August 1944, Matwin was a lieutenant in the Red Army. He witnessed the second great uprising in Warsaw from close up; this time the revolt was led by Polish partisans and was fought out all over the city. 'We were right outside Warsaw, on the other bank of the Vistula, but we couldn't do a thing.' He still finds it hard to talk about it. 'I don't think I'm the only one. Almost every Pole here, looking back on things, has mixed emotions about it. It was a bitter tragedy. It cost us a large part of the city, and tens of thousands of lives. They fought like tigers all over town, using the strangest weapons. The girls in particular did the craziest things. Almost all of them were killed. The whole thing was very badly planned.'

But would it not have been easy for the Red Army to intervene? Wasn't that what the partisans were waiting for? So why were they left to their fate?

Matwin sighs deeply. 'There's a romantic version of the uprising, the one that's always told, the one they've made movies about. And there's also a political version. The Russians should have intervened, even if only for humanitarian reasons. But it would have been highly inconvenient for them, both politically and strategically. The uprising, in fact, was also aimed at them. There was absolutely no contact beforehand between the rebels and us, the Polish officers in the advancing Red Army. That's very strange, don't you think? When your allies are on their way, and you're planning a revolt, you try to coordinate things, don't you? But all the instructions came from the Polish government in exile, far away in London.

What they wanted, we thought, was to establish a bridgehead of their own in Warsaw, against the Russians. That's what it was about.'

In the municipal museum I had seen a few of the weapons used by the rebels: a club made from a steel spring, a long chain with a heavy bolt at one end, home-made crow's feet for puncturing tyres. There was also a transmitter dropped by the RAF. Beside it, pencilled farewell letters from partisans who knew, after two endless months, that the end was near.

'Was it really impossible for the army to do anything to help Warsaw's partisans?' I ask again. We fall silent. Then Matwin says: 'If the Soviets had really wanted to, they could have done it. Sure. Those boys and girls in Warsaw were unbelievably brave. But politics was the *schweinerei*.'

In the end, the SS and the *Wehrmacht* killed almost quarter of a million of Warsaw's inhabitants during the uprising. Only five months later, on 17 January, 1945, did the Soviets cross the river and enter the abandoned ruins of the city. Of the thirty-five million Poles, more than six million – half of them Jews – did not survive the war. Busy, cheerful Nalewki Street, along with hundreds of others, was wiped off the face of the earth. Almost nothing of the city was left, except its name.

Chapter Thirty-Four

Leningrad

ON DISPLAY IN ST PETERSBURG'S MUNICIPAL MUSEUM IS THE THIN, light-blue diary of eleven-year-old Tanya Savitsyeva. The only entries for 1941–2 are these:

> Zyenya died, 28 December, 12.00 a.m. Grandmother died, 25 January, 1942, 3 p.m. Leka died, 17 March, 5 p.m. Uncle Vasya died, 13 April, 2 p.m. Uncle Aleksei, 10 May. Mama died, 13 May, 7.30 a.m. The Savitsyeva family is dead.

> Following page: 'They are all dead.' Following page: 'I am here alone.' Tanya was evacuated and died in an orphanage, in 1944.

'I've lived in St Petersburg all my life,' says Anna Smirnova. 'I was twenty-one when it all started, on Sunday, 22 June, 1941. It was a beautiful day, and I remember how angry I was when I was awakened early that morning by the droning of whole swarms of planes. I wanted to sleep! After breakfast, we heard on the radio at noon that the war had begun. We weren't even surprised. We had talked about it a great deal, the Finnish war was already over, blackout drills had already been held. All the older people had been through a war before, and we all knew that we would experience one or more wars in the course of our lives. But this time my parents were terrified. My father said: 'This is horrible. This is disgusting. This is death.' He sensed it beforehand.

'There was a huge run on the shops that same afternoon. Whenever anything happens, of course, Russians expect a food shortage, so everyone started stockpiling matches, salt, sugar, flour, things like that. And six weeks later there really was nothing left in the shops. The war was approaching fast. In July the air-raid sirens went off all the time, we didn't have any bomb shelters, so we crawled under a couple of stone archways in the garden. We had to help dig anti-tank trenches outside the city, thousands of people were out there with shovels. Meanwhile, at the theatre school, classes went on as usual.

'On 8 September, the Germans reached the ring around our city, and the siege began. There were two million of us packed in there, closed off from everything else. You had to be in line at the bakery at 5 a.m., by 11.00 there was no bread left. It wasn't easy to walk around when you were starving, you had to drag yourself along by force of will. If possible, you kept all your clothes on in bed. You lay there like a big ball of rags, you forgot you even had a body. But, well, we were young Soviets, we had absolutely no doubt that we would be victorious. On the radio they said the whole war might last a year or two, but that the siege of Leningrad would be over soon. They kept saying that. And we believed it, what else could we do? No one told the truth. There were no news-papers, no letters arrived, all we had was the radio.

'Excuse me if I become a little emotional, I don't talk about this very often.

'The total lack of heat and water was the worst. Everyone who had a job tried to stay at work as much as possible, sometimes there was still a little heating there. The Mariinsky theatre never closed, but the ballet dancers had to wear special costumes because it was so cold. There was no more transport. And that winter was so incredibly cold, it has only rarely been that cold.

'I think that's what killed my father.

'In mid-February 1942 the theatre school closed down and I was admitted to the hospital. I was so hungry I couldn't move any more. So my mother was given a package of dry bread, a little pork and some sugar. My sister fed that to me and got me out of the hospital. I started walking again, I was able to stand in line again for food.

'That was my great stroke of luck. A few weeks later I ran into a student from my old school. "You're just the person I've been looking for!" he shouted. It seems they had set up a special theatre brigade, and their singer had fallen ill. My old schoolfriend had come back to the city from the front to look for a new one. "I'm completely worn out," I told him. "We'll fix you up," he said. And that's what they did. In April 1942 he took me to the front, and from then on I performed for the troops.

'The theatre brigade saved my life, if only because they had food to eat. I was even able to save my mother and my sister by tucking away whatever I could for them. It was too late to help my father.

'This is how it went.

'It was in late 1941, six months after that Sunday when the war started. All our money was gone. It was incredibly cold in our room. He needed warmth and medicine, but there was nothing. He just died of the cold, right there in our room. That was on 5 January, 1942. It was the worst day of my life. Most people died in January and February, those were the worst months. My sister took his body on the sled, through the snow, as far as she could. She probably just left him on the street somewhere, she had no strength left either. That happened a lot back then. But she has never talked about it.'

'It was the women who won the war, everyone knows that. Their lot was the heaviest to bear. The party bosses could leave the city and come back by plane. They had their own food flown in as well, we found out about that a few years ago. They told dramatic stories about all their heroic hardships, but meanwhile they took good care of themselves. The common people couldn't do that. We wasted away, we were being shelled all the time. On Nevsky Prospect, next to the Crédit Lyonnais, you can still the blue lettering on the wall from back then: "This side of the street is the most dangerous during a bombardment."

'Stalin could easily have had the city evacuated. But he didn't. The only route out of the city was by car, along what we called "The Life Road", across the ice of Lake Ladoga. A friend of ours was taken out of the city on that route when he was a young boy. The Germans fired on the convoys the whole time. But all he remembers is a glorious day, the sun was shining, and all around him the water sprayed up in cheerful fountains. You can imagine the kind of work those drivers did. They kept the city alive. In my memory, that gap in the siege was the start of the victory.

'We performed at the front every day. Beneath those flimsy stage costumes we always felt like we were freezing to death. The show would start with the victory song. That was very popular then. In fact, the song itself dated from the time of the czars, but the composer had been sent to Siberia so the Soviets could claim it for themselves. After that came a couple of other songs, a sketch about a stupid German, I gave a rousing speech, another girl danced, and that was it.

'The soldiers were crazy about us. For a moment, they were seeing something from the normal world, even though we lived in the same frozen trenches, under the same bombardments, with the same canisters under our head for a pillow. When we were in the city we went to plays and concerts to keep up our feeling of normalcy and self-respect. Shostakovich's Seventh Symphony had its premiere in Leningrad on 9 August, 1942, and it was dedicated to the suffering city. That was a remarkable event, none of us will ever forget it. Listen to that music again, and imagine how we listened to it, with our skinny bodies, in our tattered rags, we all stood there weeping. At the close we heard our artillery pounding along with the music. They had to keep the Nazis from shelling the concert hall.

'People were really fantastic in those times. The Muscovites did all they could to escape, but the people of Leningrad were much more loyal. They stayed put. They planted cabbages and potatoes in the parade grounds and in the Summer Gardens, and made little kitchen plots wherever they could. While they waited impatiently for their beans and lettuces to come up, they ate leaves and grass, just to have some greens.

'In early 1943 we heard about the liberation of Stalingrad. We were at the front, an officer came in with the news, it was just before a performance. We knew about the battle going on there, we were very nervous about it. Then came that report, and you should have heard the tumult it caused! All those worn-out soldiers at the front began cheering and singing, throwing their caps in the air, they almost blew the roof off the recreation hall!

'After that, everything became easier to bear. There was more food, more hope. I fell in love with a naval officer. But still, it went on for another year. It was only on 27 January, 1944, after 900 days, that the siege was broken and the first regular Russian soldiers appeared in our streets. Every year on that day, friends and family still call to congratulate each other. About 650,000 people, a third of the city's population, didn't survive the siege.'

'In May 1945 I was happy as a lark. Spring had come, I was just married, I was expecting a baby.

'My life didn't change much after that. I remember the period of transition between Stalin and Khrushchev as a difficult, scary time. In late 1953, Beria, the big boss of the intelligence service, was suddenly executed, supposedly for being a British spy. When that happened everyone began realising that real changes were on their way.

'After that, the Khrushchev era was quite pleasant. We were young, we were able to see Western films, the papers became more interesting. And after that this country simply became a huge mess. Gorbachev was a good man, but I think I'm the only one who would still say that these days. Today things are completely terrible. Everyone's a thief. The whole country has been milked dry. As a veteran, I always had a good pension. And I only had to pay half the rent for my flat. But it's become harder to make ends meet now, even for me.

'I'm still in touch with a few of those student volunteers from back then. After the war we had a kind of club: drinking, poetry, lovers, marriages, prams. When you saw them later, it was impossible to imagine how these respectable artists and intellectuals had ever survived the front. But still, they did, they even received medals for it, they still have them in a drawer somewhere.'

'We all thought another war would break out sometime during our lifetime. After all, we only went through one of them. Only in the last few years has that feeling begun to dwindle.'

Chapter Thirty-Five

Moscow

AT 3.30 A.M. ON 22 JUNE, 1941, OPERATION BARBAROSSA BEGAN. Germany rolled across the Soviet border with more than 3 million men, divided over almost 150 divisions, plus 750,000 horses, 600,000 trucks, more than 3,500 tanks, at least 7,000 pieces of heavy artillery and 1,800 aircraft.

Stalin was caught completely off guard. He hid away in his dacha, sought comfort in the bottle, and tried to seduce the Germans into a new peace treaty, in exchange for the Baltic States and other territories. When that failed, he had the four most important commanders of the western Red Army shot for taking part in 'a military conspiracy aimed against the Soviet Union'. Only two weeks later did he address the Russian people. He could not believe what was happening.

The Soviet leader had systematically ignored every signal indicating an approaching German invasion: the warnings of his ambassador Ivan Mayski in London, the reports from his own intelligence services, the secret messages from Churchill. In May 1941, Russia's top agent in Tokyo, the German correspondent Richard Sorge, had predicted Operation Barbarossa almost down to the day. At the time, Stalin had shouted: 'Tell him to stick it up his arse!'

Twenty-five years later, when asked what had got into Stalin, Ivan Mayski replied: 'Stalin was suspicious of everyone. The only person he trusted was Hitler.'

The beginning of the German advance of June 1941 was every bit as spectacular as the western attack of May 1940. At Minsk, the Soviets lost fifteen divisions within the space of a few days. About 300,000 men were taken prisoner, 2,500 tanks were destroyed or captured. Moscow was massively bombed. The Germans advanced so quickly that they reached the Russian capital five months later. It was there that they ran into trouble: their supply lines were just too long. And because there was no chance of taking the Kremlin before winter set in, their attack was stranded. It was the first time that had happened. The rains came, tanks and trucks sank into the mud, the Soviet troops began to regroup, the temperature dropped to far below zero, and the German Army was stuck.

Only then did it become clear how poorly this new German offensive had been planned. Napoleon's disastrous campaign of 1812 was described in detail in all the handbooks of military strategy, yet the Germans made precisely the same mistakes in 1941. They had only one scenario: a fast and easy victory. Their intelligence services consistently underestimated the capacities of the Red Army. The Germans were absolutely unaware of the existence of the new Soviet T-34 tank, probably the best tank in the world in 1941, until they were confronted with it on the field of battle. The path of the advance had been charted so badly that two German infantry units wandered unexpectedly into the enormous Pripyat swamps and became hopelessly bogged down. Hitler had refused to allow his soldiers to take winter equipment with them; after all, the whole expedition would be over before Christmas.

By early December 1941, three quarters of all the German tanks had become mired in the mud, ice and snow. The exhausted soldiers in the front lines could see the flash of the artillery around the Kremlin, but could not move one step closer. The Germans dealt mercilessly with Russian farmers and partisans – often youthful Komsomol members. Two photographs of eighteen-year-old Zoya Kosmodemyanskaya made their way around the world. The first one was found on the corpse of a German soldier: it had been taken just after her capture, she looked dignified and proud, aware of what was going to happen. The second photograph showed her frozen, ravaged body as it was found in the expanse of snow outside Moscow, tortured, hanged.

For Stalin, there was only one real question: what was Tokyo going to do? For him, everything depended on the situation in the Far East. Japan was clearly occupied with establishing a new empire in East Asia, and so the only question was which country they would attack next: would it be Mongolia, or the Pacific? This state of uncertainty forced the Soviet

Union to hold back a major part of the Red Army, to counter a possible attack from the east.

It was here that agent Richard Sorge's espionage network played a decisive role. On 15 October, just as it seemed that Moscow would fall, a report came in from Sorge saying that Tokyo had made a final decision to concentrate on Singapore, Indochina and the United States. This time Stalin believed him. A few days later, during the festive parade to celebrate the anniversary of the October Revolution, his troops marched almost defiantly across Red Square and straight on to the front, just outside the city.

Forty Siberian divisions were now dispatched hell for leather to Moscow, with troops specially trained and equipped for fighting under arctic conditions. They had warm white uniforms, thick fur-lined boots and fast skis. At twenty degrees below zero their T-34 tanks raced effortlessly through the snow. Atop their trucks were the strange-looking Katyusha rocket launchers that, with a gruesome howl, could fire more than a dozen 130-millimetre rockets at a time; the Germans soon began referring to them as 'Stalin Organs'. In addition, these troops were fighting under the leadership of one of the outstanding generals of the Second World War, Georgi Zhukov. They deployed unobtrusively on the other side of Moscow, and began the counterattack on 6 December.

The numbed soldiers of the *Wehrmacht* did not know what had hit them.

Not far from Sheremetyevo airport stands the most significant war memorial in Europe. Today the traffic races heedlessly past, the monument suffers from the same inflation as the medals for sale on Moscow's street markets, yet its sobriety is moving. It consists, in fact, of nothing more than a pair of tank traps, a huge cross of welded rails, highly effective obstacles against any armoured attack. In all its simplicity, however, this iron sculpture marks the divide of the Second World War, the moment at which chance took a definitive turn, the furthest spot reached by German troops in December 1941. They never got any closer to Moscow.

One week after the Germans had been routed, the Franco-American journalist Eve Curie, daughter of Pierre and Marie Curie, the famous chemists, drove out from Moscow onto the battlefield with a convoy of her colleagues. She saw tanks and armoured cars abandoned everywhere in the open field, 'stubborn, dead and cold, beneath a shroud of snow'.

Along the highway lay hundreds and hundreds of frozen Germans, amid dead horses and deserted artillery, often in strange positions, like wax figurines fallen from a display case. Beside a demolished tank she saw the bodies of three *Wehrmacht* soldiers. The first one lay on his stomach, 'his bare back looked like frozen wax', the snowflakes floating down onto his blond hair. The other two lay on their backs, their arms and legs spread wide, one of them wearing an Iron Cross. 'The uniforms were of such thin material that they would not have been warm enough even for occupied France'.

This huge turnaround in the course of the Second World War took place within the space of a few days. Everything happened at the same time. On Saturday, 6 December, 1941, the German troops were beaten back from the gates of Moscow. The next day, Japan attacked the American fleet at Pearl Harbor. On Thursday, 11 December, Hitler declared war on the United States with a lengthy tirade against President Franklin D. Roosevelt who, with the 'satanic cunning of the Jews', he said, was out to destroy Germany.

Hitler's declaration of war on America is the most baffling of all his decisions. He owed Japan nothing, their alliance in no way committed him to fight alongside Japan against the United States. But with it he gave Roosevelt the decisive argument he needed to go to war in Europe, something the majority in Congress had blocked vehemently until then.

Hitler himself was clearly itching for this war. He wanted to demonstrate that he could still take the initiative. 'A great power does not let war be declared upon it, but declares war itself,' Ribbentrop told Ernst von Weizsäcker, and that was Hitler's view as well. The attack on Pearl Harbor was exactly what he needed. After all the misery on the Eastern Front he could suddenly give a new, positive twist to his propaganda. After receiving the news about Pearl Harbor the Führer actually called for a bottle of champagne and, very much contrary to custom, drank two glasses himself.

Hitler's optimistic assault on the Soviet Union, and above all his declaration of war on the United States, belong in that row of historical errors precipitated by 'groupthink': decisions made by small groups of policymakers who see themselves as all-powerful, and who dismiss all problems by refusing to admit any undesirable information from outside. Leaders great and small – the phenomenon has been seen at all levels and in every age – can in this way create for themselves a fictitious world that will, sooner or later, but inevitably, come crashing down.

Hitler's commanders had only rarely, if ever, visited the front, Albert Speer complained after the war. 'They knew nothing about the Russian winters and the quality of the roads during that season . . . They had never witnessed the damage caused to the cities by the enemy's bombs . . . Hitler never visited a single bombed city in the entire course of the war. As a result of this ignorance, the way things were represented during the daily staff meetings became increasingly inaccurate.'

This mentality was reinforced even further by Hitler's retinue, from which almost every critical and independent spirit had been removed in the course of time. The level of Hitler's discourse at Berlin and Obersalzberg in no way approached that of Churchill's discussions at Chartwell, or the thorough reports delivered to Roosevelt day after day. In his memoirs, Speer – Hitler's closest acquaintance of long standing – hammers on and on about the all-pervasive provincialism of those with whom Hitler spent his days. Almost none of those around the Führer had ever seen anything of the world. In June 1940, Hitler had spent three hours driving through Paris in the early morning hours: that was almost the sum of what he had seen of France. Speer: 'If someone had taken a holiday in Italy, that was discussed at Hitler's table as a happening, and the person in question acquired the reputation of having foreign experience.'

For Hitler and those around him, the war in this way remained a German war, and not a world war. The Third Reich's relationship with allies like Italy, Finland, Rumania and Hungry was only fair. While the British and the Americans carefully coordinated their activities, the Germans proved incapable of any form of cooperation with their most vital ally, Japan. Hitler and the most important Japanese leaders never even met. The Germans invaded the Soviet Union without ever consulting Japan; the same applied, conversely, to the Japanese attack on Pearl Harbor. Yet both attacks served to determine the further course of the war.

It was also during winter 1941 that the first leading German figures began to realise that the Reich was on course for disaster. Germany's success depended entirely on quick victories. The country did not have the reserves to accommodate long campaigns in the field, and was utterly unprepared for a war with distant America. The German fleet could barely go to sea, the few battleships Germany had were no match for the combined British and American navies, and its air force — with all the technology available to it — could barely get further than England. Germany, in other words, was not even capable of reaching the territory of its greatest foe.

As early as 29 November, 1941, Hitler and the Nazi high command had been warned that the Soviet Union was producing more tanks than Germany, and that the military balance would be thrown even further off kilter if America entered the war. At the meeting held that day, Fritz Todt, the minister responsible for Germany's arms production, concluded that 'the war can no longer be won by military means'.

One month later, after a troop inspection, Speer found this same Todt in an exceptionally sombre mood: 'Later I would recall his words, and the extreme sadness on his face, when he said that we would probably not win the war.' Shortly afterwards, Todt was killed in a plane crash.

Brigadier General Alfred Jodl wrote from his cell in Nuremberg that, in winter 1941–2, Hitler had already grasped that victory was no longer possible. 'Before anyone else in the world, Hitler sensed and knew that the war was lost. But can a person surrender an empire and a people before matters have truly come to an end? A person like Hitler could not.'

Following the debacle outside Moscow, the Germany Army moved on in spring 1942, many hundreds of kilometres into Russia. Wolf Siedler observed that the atmosphere of triumph had disappeared completely in Berlin; even so, Hitler still enjoyed the people's confidence. His supporters were sure he would find a political and diplomatic way out. 'What the average German did not see was that not a single great battle was fought after that. The Russians simply drew back, saving their strength. In 1941 the papers were full of reports about millions of prisoners of war, in 1942 there were no more such reports.'

Only one year later, after Stalingrad, did the Germans truly begin to understand how badly, how very badly, the war was going.

———

The sound of Moscow's resurrection is that of the grinder and the exca-vator. An underground shopping mall is being built outside the gates of the Kremlin. The builders worked on day and night, using everything the

Russian Army and commerce has to offer in terms of manpower, cranes and excavators, and now the complex is finished, gleaming and glowing, the showroom for the new Russia.

Moscow is like a household after a divorce: after a period of neglect and confusion, the city is once again bursting with activity. My regular taxi driver, Viktor, calls his mafia boss: will he go along with a special rate for a regular customer? 'You pay me twelve dollars now,' he says to me, 'but don't forget: seventy per cent of that goes to him.' At the city's most chic parking spots the gates open for him free of charge: that, too, is the mafia. He shows me the wooden cudgel beside his seat: his personal protection. One of his childhood friends now owns a gym and acts as bodyguard to a big industrialist, another old friend became a sharp-shooter; he was Gorbachev's bodyguard ten years ago, and now he works for the country's biggest oil magnate.

'This is no life, this is a fire in a packed theatre!' Chekhov's poor country doctor, Sobol, shouted a hundred years ago. 'Anyone who stumbles or screams in fear and loses his head is the established order's number-one enemy. You have to remain upright, keep your eyes open and not make a sound!'

The more respectable part of Moscow's population still tries to follow those directives from 1892. Almost all the people I meet have two or three jobs and race around the city from this job to that deal. There is hammering and painting, one café after another is opened, a new merchant class is starting to take root. Everyone who visits the city is amazed by the speed with which it is changing, and meanwhile the pioneers of local trade and industry move on, further into the provinces.

In the café beside the disco on Pushkin Square, the city's *jeunesse dorée* are sipping at coffee with cognac. These are the children of the new *nomenklatura*: bankers, businessmen and odd-jobbers. The price of admission at the disco is thirty dollars, half the monthly salary of a journalist, and I am told the place is always full. 'This is the great going-out-of-business sale for savers, honest incomes and respectability,' wrote Erich Maria Remarque of the inflationary fever in the Weimar Republic in 1922, and in the Moscow of 1999 things are not very different: the vultures come flocking in from all sides, and only those with power, bad friends and a big mouth are well off.

The party now being held here signifies the end of social change from the top down. It is the great dismantling of the idea that ruled Soviet life from the 1920s to the 1980s. For let there be no mistake about this: even Stalin, with all his cruelty, was well loved in the Soviet Union during his lifetime. And his views were adhered to by a broad cross section of the population.

Stalin and Hitler were both ultra-radical, they both went to extremes in pursuit of their utopias. But Stalin was a revolutionary; in the end, Hitler, who always protected the established order, was not. And, after a certain fashion, Stalin's vision was more rational and even more optimistic. The ideal human and the ideal society were determined, in his eyes, not by birth and racial selection; no, the ideal could be *achieved*. The criminal could be rehabilitated and become a good citizen, the backward Russian masses could be remoulded into the building blocks of a new society. That was the core of Stalin's Soviet project.

For him, therefore, mass murder was not an end in itself, but a revolutionary means to build his ideal Soviet state. A 'state' indeed, for Stalin held no truck with the old revolutionary idea that the state is a 'lie'. In his view, the nation state was to assume a fully central role once more, and that was one of the most crucial points of difference with his rival Trotsky, who continued to advocate the old Marxist idea of a 'worldwide' and 'permanent' revolution.

Hitler had his Wagnerian heroes; Stalin, too, had his role models. But those models were 'heroes of the new humanity', men and women who posited human force against the forces of nature in a 'great and tragic struggle'. Their task was no longer to analyse and understand the world, as Marx and his followers did. No, in this new phase the world was to be conquered, overwhelmed and created anew. Even the concentration camps played a role in this: it was no coincidence that the camp newspaper of the slave labourers on the White Sea-Baltic Sea canal was called *Perekovka*, the 'Reforging'.

At the same time, deep in his heart, Stalin was an anti-idealist. He was referred to as the Benevolent Friend of All Children, the Wise Helmsman, the Eagle of the Mountains, the Greatest Genius of All Time, the Titan of the World Revolution and the Most Profound Theoretician of the Modern

Age, but in fact he was simply Josef Dzhugashvili, the son of a penni-less Georgian cobbler. He had been raised with a deep mistrust of people in general, and he rid himself of his last illusions after the death of his wife in 1907. After the suicide – betrayal! – of his second wife in 1932, his cynicism soured into pure misanthropy.

Everything he did or did not do was ruled by an iron logic: once you had said A, then B and C had to follow, regardless of the human cost. When his eldest son, Yakov, was captured by the Germans, he did nothing to save him. In the end, Yakov taunted his SS guards – 'So kill me, what are you waiting for?' – and they mowed him down. Stalin could not imagine others living outside these norms. According to his world view, every deviation was a source of suspicion, every ally a potential rival, every comrade a potential traitor. That, after all, was how he himself oper-ated. He had an unusually acute feeling for the weak spots of his co-workers and opponents; he could, as people say, 'open the windows to the soul', but this ability gradually became more and more clouded by his own paranoia. He saw 'spies', 'enemies' and 'counterspies' everywhere. At the end of his life, in 1951, Khrushchev even heard him say: 'I am finished. I don't trust anyone any more, not even myself.'

Stalin was also a chameleon who could fade into his surroundings, which was how he seized power after Lenin's death. The chronicler of the revo-lution, Nikolai Suchanov, described him in 1917 as a 'grey spot that became visible now and then, but never left a single trace'. The brilliant and arro-gant Trotsky called Stalin an 'excellent bit of mediocrity' and barely took him into account. That proved to be a fatal mistake.

Trotsky was an extraordinary speaker and organiser, a popular army leader and a successful revolutionary. He was one of the five members of the original Politburo, and was widely seen in 1920 as Lenin's natural successor. But he rarely or never attended a party meeting. During the same period, Stalin worked his way up through the nebulous party appa-ratus until he achieved a central position of power. Internally, he was anything but a marginal figure. Soon after the 1905 revolution he became one of Lenin's most important advisers, particularly on issues concerning national minorities. In 1917, during the events at Petrograd, Stalin played a central, behind-the-scenes role in almost all major discussions and decisions. And it was he who soon supervised the course of daily affairs within the Politburo; he was able to appoint allies to top positions and dismiss opponents, thereby further broadening his power base within the bureaucracy.

After the civil war ended in 1921, Trotsky's popularity began to wane and two thirds of 'his' Red Army was sent home. On 3 April, 1922, at Lenin's recommendation, the plenary meeting of the central committee elected Stalin general secretary of the party. Now he was holding all the cards.

One month later Lenin had the first of a series of strokes. He was forced to withdraw almost entirely from active politics, but at the same time grew ever more concerned about the behaviour of the new general secretary. During Lenin's absence, Stalin formed a troika with Grigori Zinoviev in Petrograd and Lev Kamenev in Moscow. Increasingly, decisions were made without the sick leader being consulted.

In late 1922, Lenin dictated his political will and testament. It was a bitter piece by a man badly disappointed by the course 'his' revolution had taken. He came back again and again to the problem of Russia's backwardness, and seemed in hindsight even to be in agreement with the Mensheviks: the country was, indeed, not ready for socialism. Lenin did not spare any of his old comrades, but his verdict concerning his intended successor was nothing less than damning. 'Stalin is too rude and this defect, although quite tolerable in our midst and in dealings between communists, becomes intolerable in a general secretary. For this reason I suggest that the comrades think about a way to remove Stalin from that post and replace him with someone who has only one advantage over Comrade Stalin, namely greater tolerance, greater loyalty, greater courtesy and consideration to comrades, less capriciousness, etc.'

But it was too late. Three months later Lenin lost the ability to speak. He died on 21 January, 1924. During the last ten months of his life, he was able to utter only a few syllables: *vot-vot* (here-here) and *syezd-syezd* (congress-congress).

Stalin went immediately for his former rival Trotsky. Apart from all their political differences, the two men also held each other in immense personal contempt. During the civil war, Trotsky had reprimanded his subordinate Stalin on a number of occasions, and Stalin had never forgiven

him for that. In January 1925, Trotsky was discharged as commander of
the Red Army. A campaign of slander against the 'Trotskyite schismatics'
followed. In July 1926 he was dismissed from the Politburo; Kamenev
and Zinoviev followed in October.

Eighteen months later, on 7 November, 1927, Trotsky and Zinoviev
made a final attempt to stop Stalin: they issued a public call for mass
demonstrations in Moscow and Leningrad. The secret police beat the
demonstrators back, both organisers were thrown out of the party, and
only their great fame kept Stalin from liquidating them on the spot.
Trotsky was dragged kicking and screaming from his apartment and put
on a train for Almaty. From there he was deported to Turkey in 1929, and
by way of France and Norway finally ended up in Mexico in 1936. There,
at Coyoacán, he spent his last years, a prisoner in his own house, watched
over by Mexican policemen and a handful of followers, waiting for Stalin's
death-sentence-by-default to be carried out. On 20 August, 1940, an
NKVD agent fatally wounded him with a blow of an ice-axe to the head.
He died the next day.

What effects did all these events have on daily life in an average Russian
village?

In 1997, the former editor of the *New York Times*' desk in Moscow, Serge
Schmemann, published a detailed history of daily life in Sergiyevskyo,
also known as Koltsovo. The village lay about 130 kilometres south of
Moscow, not far from the city of Kaluga, and Schmemann came there
because his mother's family had once owned an estate nearby. The Great
Revolution had reached the village in autumn 1918, when an ad hoc
committee of farmers seized the estate. Schmemann's family got up from
the breakfast table, left everything where it was, packed a few clothes
and left.

The name of the village was considered too feudal, so a few months
later it was given a new one: Koltsovo, after the writer Koltsov – who,
incidentally, had never set foot in the area. A group of Bolshevik officials
came to Koltsovo. They set up a commune on the abandoned estate,
consisting of two widows with their children and a number of outsiders.
The chairman was a veteran of the revolution from Moscow, a former
printer. The farmers saw the group primarily as a gang of thieves: they

confiscated cows, horses, pigs and machinery everywhere, in the name of the revolution.

Schmemann found the minutes of a meeting held in a neighbouring village in 1919. 'Kulaks shouted "Godless coercion!", "Down with the Communists!", "You were given 1,500 hectares, give us bread!" Some threw stones.' Ten years later the farmers were still refusing to take part in the kolkhoz, but now the chief troublemakers among them were labelled enemies of the people. Seven 'kulak families' from Koltsovo were sent into exile, their possessions went to the kolkhoz. On the heels of revolutionary enthusiasm, Stalin's revolutionary coercion crept into the village.

This growing repression had everything to do with the first five-year plan launched in October 1928. The plan was intended to make of the Soviet Union a 'second America', and before long the whole country was suffering under 'five-year hysteria'. It was decreed that the production of iron was first to increase threefold, then fivefold, and finally sevenfold. The farms were to be merged into huge, modern collectives – Stalin spoke of 'grain factories' of tens of thousands of hectares – villages were to be converted into 'socialist agro-cities', the wooden houses replaced with prim flats, the stuffy churches with airy schools and model libraries, the heavy manual labour would be taken over by hundreds of thousands of farming machines.

Joseph Roth, who toured Russia in August 1926, wrote that the young Soviet cities reminded him of the little towns of America's Wild West, 'the same atmosphere of noise and constant childbearing, the quest for happiness and the lack of roots, the courage and self-sacrifice, the suspicion and fear, the most primitive forestry beside the most complicated technology, the romantic horsemen and down-to-earth engineers'.

Between the utopia and the reality lay an obstacle: the farmers did not want it. The situation in Koltsovo was typical of that which pertained throughout the Soviet Union. In summer 1929, only three per cent of the farmers were actively taking part in collective and/or state farms. The big estates, most of the revenues from which had previously gone to the cities, had been disbanded. The small farmers produced largely to meet their own needs, and stockpiled the rest of their grain; they could earn nothing on it anyway. Grain stocks were commandeered and fixed quotas imposed, but it didn't help much. The farmers skirted the rules, hid their supplies or sold them on the black market.

For the first time since the civil war, winter 1929–30 saw lines at the greengrocers and bakeries in the cities. 'It is normal for a worker's wife to spend the whole day standing in line, her husband then comes home from work, dinner is not ready, and everyone curses the Soviet authority,' said a (secret) summary of readers' letters to *Pravda*. On 27 December, 1929, therefore, Stalin decided to collectivise at one fell swoop all agriculture in the nation's grain-producing areas. In addition, he singled out a general culprit for all the earlier failures, a new and well defined class enemy: 'We must destroy the kulaks, eliminate them as a class!'

The Politburo's resolution of 30 January, 1930 – 'On measures to eliminate kulak households in areas of mandatory collectivisation' – is not as well known as the protocol drawn up twelve years later beside the Wannsee, but for millions of farmers the results were much the same: mass deportation, followed by death. Stalin needed no gas chambers: the starvation and cold in the distant reaches of his empire turned his camps into natural death factories.

Sixty years later, Schmemann sat beside an old woman on the bench in front of her wooden hut in Koltsovo; together, they ran down a list of the nearby houses: 'The Ionovs, they were kulaks, were thrown out of that first one, over there; Uncle Borya, a simple farmhand was arrested in that red one, his only crime was cursing at the wrong moment; the next one, there, where the Lagutins live, belonged to the Chochlovs . . .' Eight of the fifteen households on her street were evicted in the early 1930s, and the families disappeared without a trace. 'The Zabotnys,' another woman said, 'there, where the telephone booth is now. They took away everything they had and sent them into exile. They'd had some stupid conflict with the leaders of the collective.' A third villager said; 'They took our neighbour too. He had flour and bread. He had a horse.'

According to the latest and most accurate estimates, Stalin's breakneck collectivisation cost the lives of seven million people: five million in the Ukraine, two million in the rest of the Soviet Union. The famine grew worse, because the enormous cost of the five-year plan was being deducted largely from the nation's food supply. Foreign material and equipment and specialised manpower were paid for mostly with the revenues from grain exports. In 1932, the Soviet Union exported two million tons of grain. In the catastrophic year 1933 that was 1.7 million tons, while the country's population starved. In 1935, domestic grain consumption in the Soviet Union was less than that of Russia in 1890.

After a tour of the Soviet Union in 1932, a gullible George Bernard Shaw wrote in *The Times*: 'I did not see a single undernourished person in Russia, young or old. Were they padded? Were their hollow cheeks distended by pieces of India rubber inside?'

In Moscow the women stand on the staircases of the metro stations, holding their scanty merchandise: a couple of sausages, a few pots of jam, a home-made vest, a little kitten. In the station corridor, Natascha Burlina sings one aria after the other, a box of change at her feet. She's a professional singer, yes, in the opera, but no one can live from that. A little further along one finds the busy shopping streets with all the major brands, Armani, Dunhill, Dior. In a side corridor I sidle past a group of young men selling anti-Semitic literature of a venomousness I recognise only from old back copies of *Der Stürmer*.

They have *Mein Kampf*, *The Protocols of the Elders of Zion*, *Hitler's Last Will and Testament*, books, cartoons and newspapers, all for sale right next to the former Lenin Museum. A Russian acquaintance translates for me a few lines of verse from the *Russian Messenger*:

> Russia stand up
> Try to free yourself from the darkness
> Don't give your life for the Jews
> So, Russia, stand up
> And destroy the Jewish Freemasons
> And wash the planet clean
> Of the Jewish plague

A few years earlier I had dined with some friends at Hotel Moskva, the huge hotel beside the Kremlin. There were a total of six guests in the dining room, a bedraggled magician was gathering roubles by going from table to table, a plate of chicken soup was almost impossible to get. I am told that the building is about to close down. I hope it remains standing, however, for Hotel Moskva is one of the most characteristic monuments of the Stalin era; because of its megalomaniacal entranceways and stair-cases that crush the visitor like an ant, because of the insanely huge dining room where thousands of cheering party members once stuffed their faces, but above all because of its bizarre appearance from the street.

Hotel Moskva is a monument to fear. Looking closely, you can see that the side of the building looks very different from the front. Soviet legend has it that this asymmetry was caused by a single twitch of one of Stalin's fingers. In 1931, when architect Alexey Shchusev presented his two altern-ative designs, the Greatest Genius of All Time accidentally approved both of them. No one dared to tell him that he had to choose one of the two. Finally, the story goes, the architect simply warped his design into one building with two different façades.

True or not, it reflects the mentality that prevailed into the furthest reaches of Soviet society: thousands of party bosses ruled their districts, cities, villages, enterprises, trade unions and collectives with ironclad chaos. The Politburo was often unable to explain precisely what it wanted, and that uncertainty was compounded even further by a sluggish bureaucracy that reacted only to simple commands like faster, slower, stop. As a result, the average Soviet citizen was constantly plagued by whimsical policy changes, impracticable directives and incomprehensible sanctions. And when anything went wrong – which was more the rule than the excep-tion – there were always 'saboteurs' and other scapegoats to take the blame.

That could take extreme forms: in 1937, for example, all the members of the Soviet census committee were arrested for having 'treacherously attempted to reduce the population of the USSR'. The number of those killed by famine was so huge that it could no longer be expunged from the population figures. The results of the 1937 census, obviously, were never published.

At Novodevitshe Cemetery, located today in a Moscow suburb, all Stalins great and small of that day lie safely buried, by the dozen, beside the likes of Gogol, Chekhov and poor Nadezhda Alliluyeva, Stalin's second wife. His right-hand man and successor Nikita Khrushchev can be visited there as well, as can his faithful foreign minister, Vyacheslav Molotov, but also the brilliant engineer Andrei Tupolev – his tomb marked, of course, with an airplane – as well as dozens of lesser gods. Khrushchev's monument is a fairly subtle one, showing his round head stuck between a lighter and a darker stone, but even on the far shore of the River Styx most of the other apparatchiks remain hard at work; a general is cleaning his pistol, a paediatrician is slapping a newborn baby on the buttocks, a minister is conferring, a staff officer even stands atop his own grave, talking to his superiors on the field telephone.

The average Soviet citizen wanted nothing more than to lead a normal life, but in this perfectly achievable society that, too, was in store for almost no one. The daily chore of shopping was 'a survival tactic'. At the end of the 1930s, the police in Leningrad reported a line of some 6,000 people before a single shoe store. The housing shortage in the cities was reminiscent of that in London, Vienna and Berlin fifty years earlier. Most Soviet citizens lived cooped up in flats with one family, and sometimes two, to each room. A third of all Moscow's flats were not connected to the public sewers.

Most forms of distribution no longer had anything to do with money, so words such as 'buy' and 'sell' soon disappeared. People spoke of 'organising' and 'getting hold of', products were not sold but 'issued'. Major and minor bosses rewarded their vassals with better housing, extra food and other favours. Everyone had a 'patron', even if it was only the accountant of the kolkhoz, the floor supervisor, the newspaper editor or the party boss of the neighbourhood committee. In this way, life in a city like Moscow was ruled by an immense barter system of services and services in return, a sort of gigantic clearing house that did not officially exist, but in which every citizen was involved.

When I first visited Leningrad in 1990 – then, too, a time of long lines and bitter poverty – that jargon still existed. You went out to buy bread, but came across a big line at the greengrocer's and came home with a giant pot of sour pickles. Because you never knew what the shops would have, you took a shopping bag (an *avozka*, meaning a 'perhaps-bag') wherever you went. The couple in whose house my colleague and I camped out lived in one and a half rooms, almost filled with a table, a bed and a dog. Both of them survived thanks to three jobs, plus a kitchen garden and aid packages from their parents in the provinces. Our hostess was able to get hold of a new pair of shoes: 'organised' for her by a friend for whom she had done some translating. Our host had his car repaired: through a friend at a travel agency, he had been able to arrange two airline tickets for the boss at the garage. The friend at the travel agency had been favoured in turn with a couple of music cassettes we had brought with us. In that way, everything fitted together.

That system was called *blat* (protection), and it was the lubricant of society. If there was no way for you to get something – from train tickets to building materials – by normal means, you went *blat*, you sought out a few contacts, you pulled a few strings. Thanks to their little gardens and to these 'leaks' in the official economy, Soviet citizens were able to survive. As one of them wrote in 1940: 'To have no *blat* is the same as having no civil rights, the same as being robbed of all your rights.'

Despite all these concerns, many people experienced the 1930s as a special period. 'We were young Soviets,' Anna Smirnova had told me in St Petersburg, still with a certain pride. The boundless optimism during the first five-year plan was not simply a matter of inflated propaganda. Most Russians truly believed that a better future lay just around the corner, and that the hardships were only a temporary phase on the road from a 'backward' past to a 'modern' future. They saw Moscow filling up with monumental buildings, they saw a fairy-tale-like metro system being built, factories rising everywhere, all harbingers of the new age. Stalin was not the only one convinced that almost everything between heaven and earth was 'achievable'; the vast majority of his subjects felt exactly the same way.

An interesting travelogue has been handed down to us from the 1930s, written by André Gide. In those years Gide was at the height of his literary fame. He was seen as the aesthetic and critical arbiter of the French people. Like many intellectuals he became enamoured of 'the experiment without precedent' taking place under Stalin's leadership, and he had defended the Soviets in numerous public debates. That was why this literary star was invited to visit the Soviet Union, along with several other authors. The trip took place in June 1936 – Gide arrived in time to attend Maxim Gorky's funeral – and his report, *Retour de l'URSS*, was published in November. During those few months, Gide's politics made a 180-degree turn.

The booklet, thin and yellow, looks like a pamphlet, and in it Gide's tone is at first flattering. He loves the Russians, he expounds time and again, and everywhere he goes he experiences 'moments of deep happiness'. The children he sees at a holiday camp are handsome, healthy, cheerful and well dressed. 'Their gaze is clear, full of confidence; their smile is naïve, innocent.' On a train he meets a group of young Komsomol members, on their way to a holiday resort in the Caucasus. They spend a hilarious evening in the luxurious compartment reserved for the writers, laughing, singing and dancing.

Despite all the wining and dining, however, Gide gradually begins to sense that all is not as it appears. In Moscow he is struck by the long lines in front of the shops, the ugly and tasteless products, the sluggish masses of humanity, the bare living rooms in the kolkhoż buildings from which all personality has been erased. In Sebastopol he remarks upon great troops of street urchins, abandoned children whose parents have disappeared or been killed during the forced collectivisations, and who now wander the country by the thousands, hungry and lonely.

After a while, *Pravda* begins to irritate him as well: every morning the paper dictates precisely what everyone should know, think and believe. 'If you wish to be happy, conform.' Gide says that 'every time you talk to a Russian, you get the feeling that you are talking to all Russians.' It's not that people speak only in slogans, but everything has its own iron logic. The cult around Stalin does not please him, either: the leader's name is on everyone's lips, and his portrait hangs even in the plainest of farm huts. 'Adoration, love or fear, I do not know; he is present, everywhere and always.'

He is struck by the Russians' complete ignorance of the rest of the world: in this way Gide's enthusiasm made way in the space of a few weeks for doubt and finally abhorrence. 'I doubt whether there is any other country at this moment, including Hitler's Germany, where the mind is less free, more bowed by coercion, more fearful and more dependent.'

A Russian joke from the 1930s.

A group of rabbits turns up at the Polish border asking for political asylum. 'Why do you want to emigrate?' the border guard asks. 'The NKVD has ordered the arrest of every camel in the Soviet Union,' the senior rabbit says. 'But you're not camels, are you?' 'No, but try telling that to the NKVD!'

The word 'Gulag' is an acronym of '*Glavnoe upravlenie ispravitel'no-trudovykh lagerei*', the Main Directorate of Corrective Labour Camps. In summer 1937, Stalin, just like Hitler, started on a 'campaign of social purification', in which 'criminals', 'riot mongers' and 'socially dangerous elements' were to be rounded up en masse. In accordance with the tradition of the planned economy, quotas were established even here: each region had to achieve a given 'production'. The objective for the entire Soviet Union, according to the resolution of 2 July, 1937, was fixed at 70,000 executions and 200,000 people sent to the Gulag. Moscow's Communist Party boss, Nikita Khrushchev, had already been presented with a quota of 35,000 'enemies' to arrest, 5,000 of whom were to be shot. Khrushchev asked whether he could also liquidate 2,000 'former kulaks' as part of this quota. By 10 July he was able to report to Stalin that he had arrested no fewer than 41,305 'kulaks and hostile elements', including some 8,500 'first-category enemies' absolutely deserving of death.

The 'production' of prisoners had to do with one of the Gulag's remarkable features: until 1937, the camps served primarily as pools of cheap labour, not as penal institutions or, as with the Nazis, extermination factories. For a large part, the prisoners served as forced colonists. As Genrich Jagoda, chief of the secret police, put it: 'We encounter a great many problems in attracting workers to the far north. If we send many thousands of prisoners there, however, we can exploit their riches.' With the help of tens of thousands of slave labourers, the Politburo said, the Soviet Union would be able to extract huge quantities of coal, gas and oil from Siberia. The construction of the 225-kilometre canal linking the Baltic Sea and the White Sea in 1932–3 – which was built by 170,000 prisoners with the most primitive equipment, and which cost 25,000 lives – was depicted by Maxim Gorky and 120 other writers as heroism on an epic scale. Yet with the Great Terror of 1937, the system became even more grim. All talk of 'rehabilitation' disappeared, and anyone daring to address a guard with the term *tovarishte*, comrade, was struck down on the spot.

We will never know exactly how many lives were ravaged and broken by the terror of the Gulag and the NKVD, to say nothing of the seven million who died of starvation in the 1930s. The Soviet regime ran on terror, on intense fear. Hitler's repression in Nazi Germany, however cruel, was clearly aimed at certain groups: Jews, socialists, communists and the 'asocial'. The German who kept his head down and his mouth shut had little to fear. Stalin's terror, on the other hand, was characterised by total haphazardness. Anyone could be its target, for the silliest of reasons, next year or tonight.

Almost 800,000 Soviet citizens were executed. During the 1930s an average of 1.5–2 million people were prisoners in the camps. By the early 1950s that number had risen to 2.5 million. Just as in Germany, however, large groups were regularly released. According to the most reliable estimates, approximately twenty-nine million Soviets spent part of their lives inside the Gulag system, or in 'special exile', between 1929–53. Four million citizens and their families had their civil rights rescinded during the 1930s, and at least a million farming families and a million others were deported. What is more, the fate of a single condemned man or deported husband had an impact on the life of the whole family; his wife was ostracised, his children expelled, after a ritual humiliation, from school or university. Women and babies were sometimes sent into exile as well. Trotsky's wife, Anna, died in exile in Siberia, as did his two sons-in-law. His own son was arrested in 1937 and died in the Gulag as well.

Stalin's terror, wave after wave of it, lasted until the end of his life, into the 1950s. Around 1930 it was largely farmers and priests who were targeted, as well as the 'bourgeois specialists'. In 1935, after the excessively popular Leningrad party chief Sergei Krov was murdered at Stalin's instigation, members of the former elite, as well as Stalin's former opponents, became the primary targets. Of the 1,225 representatives to the Seventeenth Party Congress of 1934, 1,108 were arrested within the year.

The greatest purges, however, took place in the period 1937–8. Now it was no longer about 'class enemies', but about 'enemies of the people': a subtle distinction to indicate that the 'enemies' were now to be sought within the Communist Party as well.

In St Petersburg, Anna Smirnova had told me about a girlfriend of hers at school. Her friend's father had graduated *cum laude* from the military academy, and was a leading communist. 'One day she came to school, wild-eyed. Her father had been arrested'. Everyone was in a tizzy. He had stomach problems, and her mother was terribly afraid he wouldn't be fed well in prison. But of course, in prison he wasn't fed at all. They shot him right away.' And what about her own parents? 'They didn't belong to the party. For years, they could hardly find work. But that was their salvation as well. They couldn't be found on any list.'

Karl Radek was now put on trial as well. According to an anecdote, at an international congress he once heard a comrade use the expression 'Thank God'. He corrected the man: 'These days we say: thank Stalin.' 'But what is one to say if Stalin dies?' the comrade asked. 'Oh, then we'll say: thank God.' Jokes like that were not appreciated. In January 1937 he was put on trial for having established, on Trotsky's instructions, a 'parallel anti-Soviet Trotskyite centre' to serve as a base for espionage and terror.

Like other suspects, Radek admitted to everything, in order to save his family. His irony, however, remained firmly in place. When asked whether he knew that terrorism was a capital offence, he replied that he was not familiar with that book of law. 'Then you will know it after this trial,' the people's prosecutor said. Radek: 'But then I won't know it for long.' He was sentenced to ten years in the Gulag; two years later he was dead.

Of the 394 members of the Comintern's executive committee in January 1936, only 171 were still alive in April 1938. More members of the former Politburo of the German Communist Party were murdered by Stalin than by Hitler: of the sixty-eight who fled to the Soviet Union in 1933, forty-one were killed. The executioners themselves were not spared either. On 3 April, 1937, Genrich Yagoda – head of the NKVD and the slave-labour camps until 1936 – was arrested. He was accused, among many other things, of complicity in the murder of Kirov – probably rightly so, in this exceptional case – and executed. He was succeeded by Nikolai Yezhov and, one year later, by Lavrenti Beria.

The army, too, received its comeuppance. On 10 June, 1937, the Red Army's most effective generals were all arrested, tried and executed within a day. All of the military district commanders and three of the country's four admirals ended up before a firing squad. Of the eighty-five corps commanders, fifty-seven had disappeared within the year. Half of Russia's estimated 100,000 military officers were put on trial. Once again: more Russian officers with a rank superior to colonel died at Stalin's hand than at Hitler's.

In spring 1939, the arrests stopped as suddenly as they had begun. A few months after Beria was appointed, the central committee ruled that serious mistakes had been made in the persecution of communists and others. It was time, they said, 'to draw a distinction between saboteurs and people who have done nothing wrong'.

Even after this, however, only a few exiles and prisoners were released. It was not until 1956, after Khrushchev's public admission of Stalin's terror, that the majority of the victims were rehabilitated. Public excuses were offered only to the wrongly punished communists; not a word was said about the hundreds of thousands of non-communist victims. The mass deportations continued until 1953. According to the most reliable estimates, somewhere between 2.5–3 million people died in the Gulag. Between 1928–52, some 10–12 million Soviet citizens lost their lives to purges, famine, executions and forced collectivisation.

VIII August 1942–4

INLAND

Helsinki

Leningrad

Tallinn

Novgorod

Pskow

Riga

Moscow

Smolensk

SOVIET
UNION

Minsk

Front Line
Dec. 1941

Kursk

lystok

Charkow

Stalingrad

arsaw

Kiew

Wolga

Lemberg

Odessa

Rostow

Don

OVAKIA

Sea
of Azov

Krasnodar

UNGARY

Dnepr

apest

Crimea

Tiflis

RUMANIA

Black
Sea

Belgrade

Bucharest

SERBIA

BULGARIA

Trabzon

Sofia

Istanbul

Erzurum

LBANIA

disi

Ankara

TURKEY

Saloniki

GREECE

Syria

Kefollinia

Argostoli

Athens

Cyprus

Tigris

Crete

Anogia

Mediterranean

◄— Geert Mak's Route

◄— Allied Troop Movements

Allies of the German Reich

0   100   200   300 km

Chapter Thirty-Six

Stalingrad

You needed nerves of steel to listen to the report delivered to the Führer by a young officer from Paulus' staff. He delivered his report with level-headedness and determination, without accusation or complaint, and that made it all the more shocking. I often feel like a real bastard myself, whenever I lie down on a bed in a room and, despite everything, fall asleep without a care.

GENERAL ALFRED JODL IN A LETTER TO LUISE JODL, JANUARY 1943.

'That "young officer", that was me, Winrich Hans Hubertus Behr, known to my friends as Teddy. In the 1950s I worked for the European Community for Coal and Steel, after that I was assistant secretary general of the European Community. From 1965 I served for twenty years as managing director of a telecommunications concern. We made telephones, switching systems, switchboards, alarm installations, things like that. A 12,000-man workforce. Now we live outside Düsseldorf, in a quiet area. A wonderful time.

'On a few occasions it has occurred to me that my great-grandfather, my grandfather, my father and I all have one thing in common: all four of us fought in a war against France, and all four of us were wounded. I can show you a little box containing the Iron Crosses of four generations. In those days that was seen as a great honour for a German family. But there's also something pathetic about it, don't you think?

'In 1914, my father was a battalion commander. Right at the start of the war, while leading a sabre charge on the French in a forest close to Maubeuge, he was hit by a grenade. His whole face – nose, eyes, mouth, everything – was torn apart. He lay on the battlefield for hours. Finally they collected him, sent him to Berlin and patched him up there. His face was completely mutilated. He was blind. That's how he met my mother, she was his nurse. They married in 1915. I was born three years later, on 22 January, 1918. I had a father who never saw me with his own eyes.

'My whole family originally came from the Baltic States, but at the same time my father was a typical son of the Prussian cadet academies, a real soldier of the imperial generation, just like my grandfather. He could be devastating in his criticism of Wilhelm II, but no matter how he ranted, he always spoke of "*Unser allergnädigster Kaiser*" and "*Seine Majestät*".

'He was a colonel on the general staff, and he had learned to type on a Braille machine, so he worked at home. We lived in a chic neighbourhood, close to the Tiergarten, and high-ranking officers always came to visit. We also took a lot of walks together, my father and I. I would lead him around Berlin, along the former Siegesallee with all those busts of the German rulers, and he would deliver whole history lectures. My father always said: "My boy, I certainly hope you never become a merchant." What he meant was: a non-official. He considered serving the state the finest thing a man could do, either as an officer or as a senior civil servant. All other professions, in which money was the only object, he considered second-rate.

'When I was about thirteen, there were two boys I played with all the time. One day, one of them, the son of a hospital watchman, came over wearing a brown shirt. It had an insignia on it, a setting sun. He said: "I've joined the Hitler Youth." He started talking about everything, about Hitler and about the trips they took in a truck outside the city on Sundays. He said I should come along sometime. So one Sunday morning I climbed on that truck as well. There were about fifty other boys, all of them wearing caps, broad belts and brown shirts.

'Along the way they sang songs, the truck stopped at a café where they drank schnapps and beer, people told filthy jokes and shouted: "*Juda, verrecke!*" All rude, working-class youth, in other words, all unemployed, with nothing to do. For them it was a real experience, a trip like that. It wasn't my kind of thing, though. That, in what must have been 1931, was my first contact with the Nazis.

'Meanwhile, a lot of the refined Jewish families in our surroundings began leaving the country, discreetly. Our class at the gymnasium started off in 1929 with thirty boys. I'd estimate that about half of them came from Jewish families; but to be honest, we didn't really think in such terms. When I took my final exams in 1935, there were only eight boys left in the class.

'I met a few of my old classmates half a century later, in 1988, when the school had its 300th anniversary. It was nice to see them again. But still. I had been decorated in the Second World War, I had been a member of Field Marshal Rommel's staff, and of course they all knew that. I could feel the question in the air: "How could you have been a part of that?" Fifty years of tragic history, it formed a barrier between us that we tried to bridge, but it was no use.

'I was eighteen in 1936, the year of the Berlin Olympics, and I felt grand. Such a bond between the peoples, so much common interest. That's how I felt about it. The next year I went to the *Kriegsschule* in Munich. So I became an officer, perhaps because that was the only thing that meant anything to my father.

'Because of his work for the general staff, he was very well informed about everything. "This half-baked painter, my goodness, that's going to be a lot of trouble for all of us," I heard him mumble quite often. I didn't see it that way, I was wildly enthusiastic. I took part in the invasion of the Sudetenland with our Berlin armoured division. That was no war, that was only a festive march. People were waving flags everywhere, we received an enthusiastic reception, and we thought: Hitler is slowly but surely taking Versailles apart. The march into the Rhineland went the same way. As young officers, we realised that Hitler was playing a game of high stakes, but he did it rather skilfully.

'The older officers were much more cautious. In summer 1939, when we were stationed in Pomerania and rumour had it that things would be starting in Poland soon, they were pretty sombre. "This fellow is dragging us into a new world war," they said. "This is going to go all wrong." That was the mood we were in as we advanced to within ten kilometres of the border. Then orders came to withdraw to thirty kilometres, and all the older officers started drinking in relief: "Thank God, there's not going to be a war after all. Hitler's done it again." That was the point at which Hitler had given the British another forty-eight hours to meet his final ultimatum, but of course we didn't know that then.

'In those days, please forgive me for saying this, there was only one thought that occupied me: dear God, please don't be so cruel to my father as to let his only son die at war. The idea of a messenger coming to my parents' door with the news "Your son has been killed in action", that frightened me more than the thought of my own death.

'Then we went in and the fighting started. The first person I saw die was a young fellow officer. After the war had been going for a few days, we had discovered an abandoned estate. We went into the grounds, there were a few cars parked there, there was a lovely patio, a dining room, and in it a big table set with at least twenty plates, with everything still on them, ham, butter, cheese, poultry, you name it. The occupants had obviously rushed off and left their meal behind. I casually picked up a slice of ham and, as I turned around, suddenly saw three Poles standing among the trees, their rifles aimed at me. Two young officers came up behind me right then. I was paralysed with fear. The Poles shot them, then jumped into a car and drove off. One of the officers behind me died on the spot, the other one eventually recovered. That was the first time the war really closed in on me.

'A few months later, in November 1939, we were sent to Krefeld, close to the Dutch border. I had to keep watch on a road that led into the Dutch city of Venlo, had to report on everything that happened there. We spent that whole winter on alert, ready for the invasion. In the end our division moved a little further south, to Aachen, and on 10 May, 1940 we rolled into Belgium and France, past Maubeuge. I didn't send my father a postcard.

'The campaigns against Holland, Belgium and France were quite different from what I'd heard about the First World War. I never sensed among my men the hatred for the enemy that was apparently so common in 1914. We were proud of our victories, but no one even dreamed of torching French villages. And I didn't sense much hatred among our adversaries either, at least not during those first few weeks. The French didn't cheer us along, of course, but we also never came across a waiter who refused to serve us. At least, I never encountered anything like that. We didn't have to post extra guards, we could sleep easily at night.

'There are all kinds of theories these days that say the French Army was better equipped in May 1940 than most people thought, and that the Germans would have run into great trouble if only the French had been willing to fight. I can't say anything about that. Personally, I never ran into anything like really pronounced resistance, not of the sort I ran into later in Russia, in any case. During that whole campaign only three men in my entire company were wounded, including myself: a bullet nicked the back of my neck. That was all.

'It all went so quickly and easily during those weeks in May that even my father began doubting his own judgement. "My boy," he told me one evening, "I'm too old, I don't understand the way things go any more. What Hitler's done now is truly unbelievable. In four weeks, he's done what we failed to do in four years!"

'That elation lasted less than two weeks. Right outside Dunkirk, we were suddenly ordered to halt. All our division could do was ask ourselves why, in heaven's name, we were being forced just to stand there for three days. It gave the British the chance, with the help of countless private boats, to evacuate almost their entire expeditionary force, that became clear afterwards. Why Hitler let that happen is one of the great mysteries of the Second World War. People who had been close to him told me later that he was actually hoping to sign a peace treaty with England. For him, England was something to love from afar; the British were, and remained in his eyes, a Germanic people.

'I also experienced something which shows that, in late May 1940, Hitler actually thought peace was coming soon. While I was still in training at Potsdam I helped to arrange a few parades, including one by the Condor Legion that had just come back from Spain. Because of that experience, I was suddenly assigned to the group that was preparing for a huge peace parade in Paris. It was my job, for example, to make sure that the German tanks could actually take the corners at the Place de l'Étoile and the Place de la Concorde, and to see whether certain street lamps should perhaps be moved aside, that sort of thing. Our parade group was disbanded after only a few days, though: as it turned out, there was not going to be peace after all. And my father began saying again that things were going to back-fire badly under this half-baked painter.

'In winter 1940–1 we received new orders: we were to be sent to North Africa. First by train to Naples, then by ship across the Mediterranean to Tripoli. Back in those days you could simply walk into an Italian hotel and ask the switchboard operator to put you through to any telephone number in England. That was typical of the situation. During the African campaign there was a sort of mutual code of chivalry. You see, we, the Germans and the British, formed lonely little tank groups out there in that enormous void. We raced around in the desert, we tried to outsmart the Tommies, we could intercept each other's messages, we knew each other's names. Sometimes we would leave a crate of beer behind for them, or they would leave a few bottles of whisky for us. Of course people were killed or wounded. But the war didn't have the kind of stark horror that it did later on.

'Did I have any doubts at that point about the outcome? I don't think so. We were very optimistic. Our tanks and armaments were, at first at least, much better than those of the British. Germany wanted to conquer Egypt and reach the Suez Canal from the other side as well, by way of the Caucasus and Turkey. But when we realised how dependent we were on our overseas supply lines, and when we saw how those were being cut off by the British submarines, that is actually when we started to worry.

'Rommel scavenged for his own supplies by attacking British fuel dumps. We got away with that a few times, but of course you can't run a campaign on that basis. Even that early in the proceedings we started wondering out loud among ourselves whether this would all turn out all right in the longer term. I still clearly remember crowding around a short-wave receiver in the middle of the desert at 5 a.m. and hearing that German troops had crossed the Russian border. "This is the end of our successes," I said to the soldiers around me. "This is a decisive day. Now we are getting into a war on two fronts again, and, just like Napoleon, we will get caught in it." I said that out loud, and no one contradicted me. Everyone was thinking the same thing: the Führer has gone mad. That was on 22 June, 1941.

'After that our Afrika Korps began running into trouble. The British had received reinforcements, they had a brilliant new commander, Montgomery, and they had new tanks: American Shermans. During a reconnaissance mission we were taken by surprise by the first column of Shermans we had ever seen, and we barely got out of there alive. We were hit badly. I had some shrapnel in my chest, so I was taken back to a German hospital. Once I'd been patched up again, I went back to Potsdam for further military training.

'In Berlin, I saw Jews walking around wearing stars. But I had absolutely no idea how bad the situation was for them. As young, up-and-coming officers, everyone wined and dined us, including the diplomats. But we never heard a thing about the mass murder of the Jews, which by that time was already going on in the East. I'm not trying to make excuses for myself, but, unlike many other officers, I had not personally attended mass executions on the Eastern Front. Those kinds of things were not going on in Africa. And when I got to Stalingrad later there were almost no civilians left, never mind Jews. Don't forget, staff officers like us lived in a fairly isolated world of our own. None of us belonged to the Nazi Party, we weren't even allowed to.

'I spent almost a year in Berlin. I went through training, there were lots of parties, I met my future wife. But in October 1942 that was all over. I was ordered to join the staff of General Paulus, the commander-in-chief of the 6th Army at Stalingrad. I was in charge of updating the maps that showed our positions and those of the enemy. I knew exactly how the supplies were running, how many tons had been flown in, how many tons were dropped, etc. The person who is in charge of that is one of the best-informed officers in the whole army. That's why they chose me to tell Hitler the truth.

'When I arrived at Stalingrad I was given a detailed briefing by the person in charge of enemy-troop reconnaissance, a man by the name of Niemeyer, a very pleasant fellow. He showed me his maps, they were covered with red lines. "Take a good look," he said. "We're in big trouble. That's what we tell headquarters every day, but no one up there wants to listen. Look here: 2,000 Russian vehicles, with their lights on, have been sighted over here, and over there we've spotted hundreds of tanks, all moving in the same direction. The only possible conclusion is that the Russians will be attacking soon from over here, and that they are going to grind us to a pulp." That was in early October 1942.

'Meanwhile, our superiors were assuming that the Russians were done for, that their reserves had been exhausted, and that the winter would be a quiet one for us. The good Lord himself must have struck them blind. In actual fact, the Russians had 2,000 tanks at Stalingrad, T-34s, while we had no more than 80. And even those only had enough fuel to run for a hundred kilometres. I remember thinking even then: have they all gone mad? But it was clearly a matter of keeping up appearances. No one was interested in the facts any more.

'The Russian attack started on 19 November. Our command bunker was about ten kilometres from the front, in the middle of an area that had been surrounded by the Russians. I drove all over the place, staying in contact with the troops who were doing the fighting. Paulus wanted me to keep him up to date on how his men were doing, no matter how bad the news. The cold was infamous, but the strong winds were actually what finished us off. There were about thirty centimetres of snow on the ground, with this hard crust of ice that you broke through at every step. Maybe you can imagine how that was for those infantrymen, running away from the enemy across a field of crusty snow like that, carrying a machine gun. People kept talking about how we should break through the enemy lines, but it was almost impossible – physically too – to take the offensive, let alone break through Russian positions that had been set up all around us.

'On 20 December I went to the field hospital. I'd been having problems with a wisdom tooth and the dentist was going to help me. I stepped in out of the cold and was struck by this enormous heat, mixed with a pestilential stench. I saw a big, long barrack and about thirty doctors, covered in blood like workers in a slaughterhouse, sawing off feet and fingers. That's all they did, all day long, just amputate frozen limbs.

'When I left from Pitomnik airfield on 13 January, 1943, I was one of the last ones out, they were lying . . . you know how they stack wood in the forest? Well, there were stacks of frozen bodies like that everywhere, the bodies of the sick and wounded who had been dragged to the airfield and then died anyway. Thousands of them lying there like that, the ground was too hard to bury anyone. By that time the airfield was already under constant artillery attack. It was complete chaos. You heard people crying and screaming everywhere. The *Feldgendarmerie* showed me to one of the last planes, a Heinkel III. I was the only passenger who wasn't badly wounded. Hundreds of others tried to board the plane, some of them crawling, it was their only chance of escape. They had to be held at bay with sub-machine guns. For three days after that, planes left from the airstrip at Gumrak. Then the air connection was cut off for good.

'I had some amazingly good luck. They sent me to Hitler, but first they wanted me to inform Field Marshal Manstein, at his headquarters on the Sea of Azov, of the hopelessness of the situation. He said: "Here we see it the same way you do over there. But go to the Führer yourself. It's bound to make more of an impression if he hears it from you, instead of from some overly ambitious general."

'That's how I arrived the next evening at Hitler's headquarters, the *Wolfsschanze*. When I saw all those prim officers sitting around in their tidy uniforms, my mood became grim, almost communist. Those headquarters weren't really all that posh, but when you've just come back from the bitterest misery you get angry at anyone who sleeps well at night. I was brought in right away. Hitler welcomed me, then we went to the big war room. In the middle there was this table that must have been two metres wide and ten metres long, showing the various theatres of war, all these little flags everywhere. Those were the armies and divisions. To my amazement, I saw that there were little flags all around Stalingrad as well, even though I'd seen with my own eyes that only a few units were left of all those divisions. The rest had been wiped out.

'I knew that Hitler was not fond of receiving bad news, and that he often twisted such conversations to fit one of his endless theories. That's precisely what he did this time too. He quickly began thanking me for my visit, asked me to extend his regards to General Paulus and wish him lots of luck, etc. So I mustered all my courage and told him that I couldn't leave while there was any risk of a misunderstanding, that General Paulus had given me explicit orders to inform him of the real situation at Stalingrad. And he actually let me tell my story; he listened carefully, asked a couple of good questions and didn't interrupt me.

'But the generals did: "Listen, there's an SS armoured corps headed for Stalingrad to help you break free, isn't that right?" But I knew that that SS army was not only far too small, but that it had already been torn apart by Russian T-34s close to Charkhov anyway. What Hitler and his generals were completely unwilling to see was the change the Russians had undergone. They had observed the Germans carefully, they had quickly switched to wartime industry, they had built enormous tank factories 1,000 kilometres back from the Volga, and were now beating us with our own weapons and tactics. At that moment I realised that Hitler lived only in a fantasy world of maps and little flags. It was then that I knew for certain that we would lose the war.

'So did my plain speaking, at the age of twenty-three, actually change anything? I believe it did. But the difference it made was not at all what I had been expecting. No reinforcements or other help came. But, two days later, the tone of the propaganda changed. They no longer talked about "victories", but about the "heroic battle at Stalingrad" and the "twilight of the gods in the face of Russian communism" . . . well, anyone with ears to hear knew enough then.

'After that, Goebbels began skilfully developing his theatre of heroics. General Paulus' promotion to field marshal should be seen in that light: he was to go down fighting at the head of his troops, banner in hand, the quintessential hero's death. But Paulus didn't seem to understand his role very well. He let himself be taken prisoner, appeared as a witness at the Nuremberg tribunal, then spent the rest of his days in a villa close to Moscow, playing cards and writing his memoirs. He didn't die until 1957, in the DDR, in Dresden, in bed.

'Today there are historians who say that any general but Paulus would have tried to break through the Russian lines; who claim that doing that would probably have saved 100,000 men. I wonder about that. While it was still possible, to have done that would have been in violation of all of Hitler and Manstein's orders. So it would have been outright insubordination. The rest of the Eastern Front would probably have collapsed.

'Secondly, the eighty tanks we still had were almost out of fuel. Our artillery couldn't move up or pull back, the soldiers had eaten most of the horses. And we were facing 2,000 Russian T-34 tanks.

'Thirdly, almost all our troops had to move on foot, because there was no other transport. And they had to drag their own equipment along through that icy wind. It would have been as much a debacle as Napoleon's retreat from Moscow.

'I wanted to go back to Stalingrad, to my comrades. But when I got to Taganrog three days later, the airfield commander there said I was not allowed to fly on to Stalingrad. Instead I was detached to Field Marshal Erhard Milch's staff, as special liaison officer for Stalingrad. Looking back on it, I thank the good Lord that I was kept from flying out.

'As it was, I was the one who received that famous last report, in the early morning of 31 January, 1943: "Russians at the door. We are going to break the connection." A few seconds later they sent another transmission: "We are breaking." After that, nothing more.

'By the end of the war I had served under three field marshals: Rommel, who committed suicide on Hitler's orders, Kluge, who killed himself as well, and Model, who shot himself just before Germany capitulated.

'The messenger bearing news of my death never came to my parents' door in Berlin. At the end, though, the war still dealt my father a severe blow. When the Russians entered the city, a feisty old gentleman in their neighbourhood was foolhardy enough to fire his shotgun at them, one last time. By way of retaliation, the Russian commander had all the men in the surrounding area brought out, lined up and blindfolded. My father didn't need a blindfold, of course. Then the commander chose a firing squad, counted to two, and on three he said: "Russian soldiers don't shoot old men." That left my father a broken man.

'Of my hundred classmates in Munich – I was from the class of 1937 – seventy-five did not live through the war. Of the twenty-five who did, ten were too traumatised afterwards to lead a normal existence. Fifteen of the hundred actually made it through in one piece.'

———

Only the river has remained the same. The slow river flowing endlessly past this stretch of city, this river broad as a lake in which city children bob around like corks, and across which great paddle steamers move day and night, from town to town.

In the centre of Volgograd, one of those ships is now waiting at the quay. Girls are walking along the waterfront, on the top deck a few women in bikinis are lying in the evening sun, grandmothers sit at the railings with their knitting, the final passengers drag their suitcases up the gangplank, the ship's horn blasts, everyone clambers on board and off it goes, across this endless, glistening water.

Volgograd, formerly Stalingrad, has something grim about it, and at the same time something lethargic. You can cross the street here while carrying on a conversation, for the only traffic is the occasional black car. At the airport, the worn wooden check-in desks are deserted. Sparrows fly around in the big departure hall, twittering and chirping. Luggage is piled up beside the loading platform: here, baggage handling is apparently self-service.

There is only one recreational vessel on the Volga this evening, for the rest every boat has its Rhyme and Reason. For the first time since the start of my trip, my mobile blacks out: GSM has not arrived in Volgograd. There is almost no advertising to be seen. The city is full of encouraging slogans and portraits, as though nothing has changed in the last few decades.

Volgograd is the ideological bulwark of communism, the fortress of the old order amid advancing decadence. Here the party leaders are still firmly in the saddle. The red flags wave, the parks and lawns are immaculate, black marketeers get around by bike. Every evening Comrade Lenin rises up on the Volga, in gigantic neon letters. Like cawing phantoms, hundreds of crows skim the treetops of the big memorial park.

Canned partisan anthems bray from the loudspeakers. But, a little further along, the Pepsi Cola café fights back with music of its own. A girl is being chased around by a few boys there, they catch her, drag her to the fountain, a little later I see her walk away, dripping, laughing bravely, a girlfriend in her wake. The house music throbs across the rippling water – this, too, is Volgograd.

For this city the war began one unexceptional Sunday in summer. Dozens of families were picnicking on the Mamayev Kurgan, the huge Tartar burial mound by the river, where the war memorial now stands. The air-raid sirens sounded, but almost no one paid any attention; they had sounded so often before, and for no good reason. It was only when the anti-aircraft guns began to rattle that the picnickers became startled. And once the Luftwaffe had begun its attack, there was nowhere for them to go.

The bombardment of Stalingrad on Sunday, 23 August, 1942 was one of the severest in the Second World War. The Heinkels laid a carpet of bombs across the whole city. The factories and wooden houses along the western edge went up like torches; the tanks at the oil depot exploded into huge pillars of fire; the modern white apartment complexes, the pride of the city, were blown apart. Anyone who was not in a bomb shelter did not survive. Around 40,000 men, women and children were burned alive, suffocated or buried beneath the rubble.

Meanwhile, the 16th Armoured Division of General Paulus' 6th Army moved almost unchallenged across the surrounding steppe. The photos and film clips speak for themselves: blond and tanned soldiers, laughing faces, flashy sunglasses as though on a holiday outing, commanders standing straight as ramrods in the turrets of their tanks, their troops impatiently waving their arms onward. 'As far as the eye can see, armoured cars and tracked vehicles are rolling across the steppe,' an eyewitness wrote of that summertime advance. 'Pennants wave in the dusky evening light.'

The landscape through which the German soldiers moved was of unmatched rustic charm: white houses with straw roofs, little cherry orchards, horses at pasture. In every village they could glean an armful of chickens, ducks or geese. Every kitchen garden and every house they passed was plundered. 'I have never eaten as much as I have here,' a company commander wrote. 'We eat honey by the spoonful, until we are sick of it, and in the evening we have boiled ham.'

By the end of the afternoon on 23 August the advance guard had reached Rynok, a northern suburb of Stalingrad. The soldiers could barely believe their eyes: suddenly they were standing at the Volga. They photographed each other on their armoured cars, in the background the river and Stalingrad in flames. They took out the last of the Russian anti-aircraft positions, sank a few ships on the river – not knowing they were full of fleeing civilians – and then they dug in amid the vineyards, the oleander and the fruit trees. The headquarters of the army engineers was tucked away beneath a huge pear tree, the soldiers ate of the fruit till they grew nauseous. This little paradise had become the Reich's new eastern border.

That Sunday was a historical moment for the Soviets as well: from now on, they realised, this war was going to be a life-or-death struggle. They had never imagined that Paulus' troops would be able to break through so quickly and reach the Volga so easily. Enraged, Stalin gave the order to defend 'his' city – which had been named after him back in 1925 – at any price. He forbade the undermining of factories or any other activities 'that could be seen as a sign that Stalingrad is being surrendered'.

His Ukrainian confidant Nikita Khrushchev was given command over the underground headquarters.

For Hitler, too, this battle was largely one of prestige. The original objectives of the German march on Stalingrad – to destroy the arms industry and block all traffic on the Volga – had already been achieved in late August, but Hitler suddenly decided that, despite the risk of over-extending his supply lines, the city was also to be taken and held.

Stalin's determination was shared by the people of Stalingrad. The majority of the city's population reported for duty. Schoolgirls were put to work as medics – to bring back the wounded they often had to crawl under heavy fire to the front lines. An eighteen-year-old girl medical student was put in charge of an entire hospital company. A whole female bomber-support squadron was set up, led by the young and lovely Marina Raskova.

Within two weeks the Soviets had launched their first counterattack. They landed on the German side of the Volga, drove the enemy away from the railway station there, suffered enormous losses, but held their positions in the centre of town. In the neighbouring tractor plant, which had been converted for the production of T-34s, volunteers climbed into the turrets even before the paint was dry. They drove straight off the production line into battle. The *Red Star* army gazette published a poem by Ilya Ehrenburg, written for the occasion:

> Do not count the days, do not count the metres
> Count only the Germans you have killed.
> Kill the German: that is your mother's plea.
> Kill the German: thus cries your Russian earth.
> Do not hesitate.
> Do not let up.
> Kill!

———

Stalingrad – Volgograd since 1961 – stretches out like a Dutch peat-mining village; equally boring, but many times bigger. It is a typical, elongated, riverside town, a narrow strip of buildings along the waterfront, only a few streets deep but almost a hundred kilometres long, an endless row of apartment districts, factories, power plants, dullness piled upon dullness. On all sides of that strip, stretching far into the horizon, is the steppe, a hot dusty plain reminiscent of Texas or Arizona: huge fields of grain, an occasional tree, telephone wires, a few barns, an unlatched door banging in the wind. Every once in a while a group of colossal bulldozers and excavators will loom up, working on a new road, digging a new irrigation canal. The mentality is that of Las Vegas: build it up, break it down and get out.

I take a ride on the municipal railway, examine the frown of the woman whose job it is to mark each and every ticket by hand – the stamping machine has not yet reached Volgograd – and walk around the streets and through the parks. Particularly noteworthy is the bearing of its young people: nowhere else in the former Eastern Bloc have I seen so much home-made elegance, so many women in such conspicuously beautiful apparel. Creations that would catch the eye in Paris, London or Milan pass by on the street here every couple of minutes.

Later that evening in my quiet, sedate Intourist hotel, an underground existence begins, most of which eludes me. The lobby fills with girls in their Sunday best, and the phone beside my bed rings no less than three times: 'You need girl?' When I say no for the last time – I was just dreaming of Katyushas and tank manoeuvres – the voice says in surprise 'Why not?', as though I were suffering from some disease.

An old woman is standing near the station. She is wearing sturdy boots, heavy stockings, a dark-grey skirt and knitted vest. Her grey head is a little bowed, she covers it with a brown cloth, her skin is red, her teeth almost gone. Once – in 1955 perhaps, or in 1942 – she must have been pretty, very pretty in fact, you can tell by her eyes. Now she's been standing here all afternoon. She's trying to sell five bunches of onions and two bottles of Fanta.

That winter in Stalingrad she may have been a nurse, or one of those spirited girls at the anti-aircraft guns, or one of the few thousand mothers with children who, hidden away in cellars and shafts, lived through the whole struggle from beginning to end.

The fighting in the city soon had nothing more to do with matters of strategy or the art of warfare. It was, as the Germans put it, a *Rattenkrieg*. The Soviets fought with commando groups of six to eight men, armed with sub-machine guns, but also with knives or sharpened spades, all the better to kill without a sound. At one point, in a huge brick warehouse on the Volga, there were both Russians and Germans, a different foe on each floor, piled up on top of each other like a wedding cake. The Russians stacked frozen corpses around their foxholes to serve as sandbags. Commandos from both armies fought each other in the sewers with flame-throwers. At night, Soviet soldiers in white camouflage suits crept outside to lay anti-tank mines. They were very successful at it, even though their losses were the highest among all the specialists. Their motto was: 'One mistake, and you'll never eat with your hands again!'

Without their realising it, Stalingrad had served as a gigantic piece of bait for the Germans. The most important task of the Soviet troops was defending the city and, at the same time, engaging the Germans and keeping them from moving on. Meanwhile, in deepest secrecy, a Soviet force of almost a million men was being assembled to free Stalingrad.

After almost three months, on the icy, misty morning of Thursday, 19 November, 1942, Commander Alexander Vasilevsky sprung the trap. The first bombardments and artillery salvoes were so intense that German troops forty-five kilometres away were wakened by what seemed to be an earthquake. Amid the pounding, the citizens in their shelters in Stalingrad that morning heard a new sound, a strange whining. Suddenly they knew, these were the Stalin Organs, these were their own troops' Katyushas. Their liberation had begun.

From that day on Stalingrand was surrounded by a twin siege: the Germans held the city itself in their grip, while the Soviets banded together around them. After a while the stretch of steppe between the two armies was full of dead horses and infantrymen frozen black, and when the front was quiet for a moment, tango music would come blaring across the shadowy expanse of snow: the Soviets had discovered that this music was what made the Germans most melancholy.

At first the Soviets had no idea how many Germans were at their mercy. The staff thought it was about ten divisions, a little under 90,000 men. It turned out to be almost the entire 6th Army, plus several tens of thousands of Italians and Rumanians: some 300,000 men in all. The area around the city was like Verdun all over again. With one difference: this battle would not end in a draw.

In this same flat countryside, now green and yellow with summer, a few scars of the battle can still be seen from the air: shell craters, trenches, the remains of old barricades. A taxi driver takes me across the dusty steppe to a little monument. I recognise the outlines of a trench. 'At least 10,000 men were killed here,' the driver says, pointing to the surrounding fields full of rape and cornflowers. 'They're still here, in the ground. We never had money for neat war cemeteries.'

The memorial is a plain one, it lacks the stateliness of all those parks and statues in the city, it is a monument erected by wives and mothers. In the middle of it is a scorched, dead tree that somehow remained upright amid the battle. It is hung with handkerchiefs and rags, like a spirit tree in the Orient. Every year the fields here still spew forth grenades and gun barrels, bullets and buckles, skulls and bones.

In the display cases of the Historical Museum in Volgograd one finds a small selection of the personal belongings found on German corpses: wedding rings, a fountain pen, a watch, a tiny saint's figure, a few letters. 'Yesterday again, as so often, a comrade blown to pieces by a direct hit,' Bertold D. wrote to Frau Elisabeth Sturm in Worms on 24 December, 1942. 'Now we are sitting together, celebrating Christmas Eve in Stalingrad, while the Russians outside continue to shoot wildly. We sing Christmas songs, accompanied by a comrade on the accordion. Then everyone goes to his corner and thinks of home.' Konrad Konsuk wrote: 'My darling, don't fear for me. I am doing well. This evening we were given a hundred grams of bread and a quarter-litre of marmalade.' An unknown soldier: 'I desperately wish you were with me. How badly only you, my dearest, as the only one in the world, can know.'

Very interesting is the difference in tone of the Russian letters collected by the British military historian Antony Beevor.

'Hello my dear Pavlina,' a soldier wrote to his wife, 'I am still alive and in good health . . . The war is hard. Every soldier has a simple task: to destroy as many Krauts as possible, and to drive the rest back to the West.' A lieutenant: 'Hello, Shura! I send kisses to our two little ones,

Slavik and Lidusya. I am in good health. I was wounded twice, but they are only scratches and so I can still aim my cannon well . . . In these days of heavy fighting I avenge my beloved city of Smensk, but at night I sit in the cellar with two blond children on my lap. They remind me of Slavik and Lida.' It was the last letter he wrote.

The city outside bears almost no trace of the war, except for the two ruins that have been left standing deliberately. The House of Pavlov is a plain, four-storey building where a little group of Soviet soldiers, led by Sergeant Yakov Pavlov, held up under siege for almost two months. It is now little more than a well maintained state monument. The only other real memorial is a little further on: the remains of an enormous mill, full of breaches and bullet holes, still the way it was in summer 1943, empty and desolate amid the tall grass.

'Hello, Mariya,' soldier Kolya wrote. 'I have been fighting here for three months to defend our lovely [deleted by censor] . . . Only the most stubborn SSers remain. They have withdrawn into bunkers and are shooting from there. And now I am going to blow up one of those bunkers. Greetings, Kolya.'

On the morning of Sunday, 10 January, the last great Soviet attack began: Operation Koltso (Ring). For almost a full hour the German lines were pounded by some 7,000 field cannons, mortars and Katyushas. Then the Red Army closed ranks and advanced, the red banners out in front, a T-34 tank every fifty to a hundred metres. The German divisions did not have a chance. Their ammunition and fuel were sorely depleted, the soldiers could hardly stand upright. Until the very last moment, wounded men at Pitomnik airfield were trying to fight their way on board one of the planes leaving for Germany. Overloaded Junkers, sometimes too heavy to gain enough altitude, were fired on by the Soviets and crashed. An enormous Focke-Wulf Kondor, filled to the gunnels with wounded men, took off too slowly, flipped onto its back and exploded on the ground.

Hundreds of wounded men were left to their fate in the snow. One survivor spoke later of 'an endless wailing of the wounded and dying'.

Paulus surrendered on 31 January, 1943. The agitprop newsreel cameras recorded the whole thing. The emaciated German soldiers came stumbling out of Stalingrad's cellars and bunkers. The occasional Russian shouted 'Kameraden, Krieg kaput!', but most of them only shouted 'Faschist! Komm! Komm!' Then the Germans were led off in long, tattered columns.

So came the end for all those enthusiastic soldiers who, in that warm, distant August less than five months earlier, had travelled across the steppes, eaten helmetfuls of pears and stolen honey by the spoonful. Along with Paulus, close to 90,000 Germans were taken prisoner. By the time spring came almost half of them had died of starvation and hardship. Some 180,000 German soldiers remained missing. Of the 300,000 men in the 6th Army, a little under 6,000 went home at last.

The Second World War cost the lives of 8–9 million soldiers in the Red Army, and left 18 million wounded. In addition, it has been estimated that between 16–19 million Soviet citizens lost their lives during the war. Estimates of the total number of Soviet casualties hover around 25 million, five times that of the Germans.

The Soviet Union's victory was due largely to the prowess of field marshals Zhukhov, Timoshenko and Vasilevsky, General Alexei Antonov and a number of other outstanding military leaders. Stalin had enormous charisma, he was able to whip up the entire Soviet Union to incredible achievements and sacrifices, he was intelligent and in the end he developed a good sense of military strategy. But he remained, in the words of Volkogonov, 'an armchair general: he was practical, vicious and persevering by nature', someone who had 'fathomed the secrets of war at the cost of bloody experimentation'.

In the face of adversity, and rather than revise his strategy, Stalin was sometimes unable to come up with any better plan than to mete out punishment. Infamous is Order Number 227 issued by Stalin on 28 July, 1942, under the title 'No Step Backwards'. From that moment on, anyone who surrendered was to be considered a 'traitor to the homeland'. In order 'to combat cowardice', every army was to organise three to five well-armed detachments which would move along as a second front behind the first wave of attack, and shoot down any soldier who hesitated. 'Cowards and those who sow panic are to be destroyed on the spot.'

'How many matches were burned?' some Soviet commanders would ask after a battle, when they wanted to know about their own losses. Or: 'How many pencils were broken?' For that is a forgotten element of the Russian triumphs: the huge toll in human lives paid by the Soviets for Stalin's 'brilliant strategy'.

As noted, the situation at Nazi headquarters was not so very different. Although the two leaders differed in character, Hitler too was a dilettante who had come to believe in his own mythical power. Indeed, Speer singled out dilettantism as the essence of Hitler's military leadership: 'He had never learned a profession, and had essentially always remained an outsider. Like many autodidacts, he could not judge the real significance of professional expertise. With no understanding of the complex difficulties of every great assignment, he therefore insatiably took on more and more new functions.'

During his first years in power Hitler's dilettantism worked very effectively in Germany, probably because the country and its military had always been run rigidly and bureaucratically. According to Speer, Hitler's earlier economic and military successes were attributable to his lack of knowledge of the old, fixed rules, and to the reckless energy of a layman who scarcely realises the risks he is taking.

As soon as any significant adversity arose, Hitler was in a quandary. When the German Army 'failed' before Moscow in December 1941, he could come up with nothing better than to place the entire *Wehrmacht* under his personal supervision. Like Stalin he was bound and determined to make all important decisions himself, and would on occasion suddenly meddle in the most trifling details of a military operation. But where Stalin let himself be protected by a number of excellent generals and staff officers, Hitler refused to delegate a thing.

Stalin was willing to be convinced. Hitler, due to his own war experience and his subsequent successes, was convinced that he was a second Napoleon. In Speer's words: 'The greater the failures, the more pronounced and grim his ineluctable dilettantism became. The penchant for unexpected and surprising moves had long been his strength; now it hastened his demise.'

Chapter Thirty-Seven

Odessa .

WHEN I ARRIVE IN KIEV, THE WHOLE CITY IS CELEBRATING. STARTING at the station is a long string of loudspeakers, all singing the same thing. Freely translated: 'When the chestnuts blossom in Kiev, my heart will open to you.' Everyone has the day off, there is to be a race for soldiers, and dozens of veterans, seventy-five, eighty years old, their chests hung with ribbons and medals, proud of their uniforms, are walking around with their wives, most of them with a row of medals pinned to their blouses as well.

This is the generation that won the war, that survived Stalin, that rebuilt a flattened Kiev. And these are the same people who must survive today on a pension of twenty euros a months.

Most of the older people don't understand the society in which they suddenly find themselves, and do not want to understand. They are like passengers who get off the train a few stops too late, look about in surprise, and decide that this is not where they want to be. Close to the war memorial – a hundred-metre-tall woman nicknamed 'The Bitch' – an old colonel with a megaphone spews his rage all over the crowd: 'No one pays any attention to the working people any more!' he shouts. 'This country is full of bandits and robbers! Shame on this government! We have only one mother country: the good old Soviet Union! The Ukraine is only our stepmother! We are being exploited by bandits! The Germans have invaded the country again with their money and their decadence! We have been sold out!' There are ten people standing around him.

My interpreter calmly translates the man's tirade. Her name is Irina Trantina, a brisk fifty-year-old, daughter of a Soviet general. She doesn't find it too hard to imagine the old veterans' rage. 'This is the generation that built modern Kiev up from the rubble the Germans had left behind. They worked their fingers to the bone all their lives, and now the Germans come back here, as tourists and investors, rich and powerful, while they . . .'

I had visited Kiev in 1997, and I tell Irina that I can see that the inner city has been fixed up a lot in the last two years. Many of the houses have their old colour back, soft yellow and blue pastels, and the domes of the churches and cloisters sparkle in the sun again. All thanks to the dollars, guilders and Deutschmarks.

'But that's only the centre of town. All those Western banks, all the advertising you see, it's not anything substantial, it remains on the surface of the economy. What goes on beneath – the corruption, the salaries that can't be paid for months at a time, the official ninety per cent tax on profits that makes all legitimate business activities impossible – those are the things that actually determine the way we live. What you Westerners see is a shop window. Our country is just like a family: the real problems are never aired outside the home.'

And what about freedom, the new freedom?

Irina laughs. 'We used to be afraid to talk, but we talked anyway. And things happened. Now we can talk as much as we like, but we never see any results.' She tells me about her mother, the general's widow. She died not too long ago, at the age of ninety-five. Just before she died, she asked Irina to buy her a kilo of candy, the kind she always kept in the house. 'Wouldn't it be better to start with a hundred grams?' her daughter asked. 'A kilo of candy, that costs more than half your monthly pension.' 'You're trying to trick me!' her mother had shouted. She died in total confusion.

Irina and I head out to the Women's Ravine. It lies at the foot of Kiev's broadcasting centre. I had imagined it in many different ways, but not that it would it be a pleasant, normal park in which to take a walk. Families are picnicking there, young mothers are teaching their children to walk. Beside the park is a ravine more than two kilometres long and fifty metres deep. In that ravine, which the Russians call Babi Yar, something close to 100,000 people were murdered: Jews, Gypsies, partisans, prisoners of war, up to and including the entire staff of the *Nova Ukrainski Slovo* daily. The Germans later dug up most of the bodies and burned them, but the park workers here still regularly stumble upon bones, almost every time they plant a shrub. Sometimes the skeletons are bound together with barbed wire, which is how some of the victims were forced to march to the place of execution.

On 29–30 September, 1941, just after Kiev was taken, the city's 33,771 Jews – the number was carefully noted – received orders to prepare for transport to Palestine. They were to bring money, valuables and warm clothing with them. After the Molotov-Ribbentrop Pact, Stalin had banned all criticism of Germany, and few or no reports about the persecution of the Jews had reached the Soviet Union. And so almost all the Jewish families of Kiev walked to the edge of town, a colourful crowd of people, chatting quietly, convinced they were leaving for the Promised Land. Later, the same spot was used to murder Ukrainians, Russians and Poles.

The massacre at Babi Yar was kept out of the history books for years. In 1944 Ilya Ehrenburg wrote an impressive poem about the killings, but after that all remained shrouded in silence. From 1947, Stalin's paranoia turned against the Jews and it was forbidden to mention Babi Yar. In the late 1950s – after Stalin had died – Kiev's municipal administration decided to empty the old Jewish graveyard and build a huge sporting and television complex on that spot. In 1961 the writer Viktor Nekrasov penned a stirring appeal 'not to forget Babi Yar', the poet Yevgeni Yevtushenko wrote a song of protest and Dmitri Shostakovich gave his Thirteenth Symphony (1962) the title Babi Yar. The first two were arrested and convicted. During that same period, almost all the Jewish gravestones and monuments were removed. In September 1968, when the Soviet authorities set up a memorial, the authorities who spoke at its unveiling fulminated, not against the Holocaust, but against the state of Israel. A Jewish listener who protested – he had heard someone say that 100,000 Jews were 'not enough' – was sentenced to three years' hard labour.

It was not until 1970, with the publication of the novel Babi Yar, that the story was told in full. The book described, for the first time, exactly what had happened, how the families had walked through the streets, what was said and shouted during the final moments. It wasn't until ten years after that that people first dared to gather here on 29 September.

In one corner of the park, amid the bushes and nettles, I find a few

fallen gravestones from the old Jewish cemetery, badly damaged, probably overlooked during the clearance. Only one name is still legible:
Samoeïl Richter.

One name. Eight million. Between 1941–5, a quarter of the population
of the Ukraine was murdered: eight million boys, men, girls and women.
What is one to do with a number like that?

Kiev's war memorial is, as noted, a singularly ugly thing, a towering
iron maiden dominating the city with her sword and shield. At the base
of this juggernaut lies the war museum. What one sees there is not soon
forgotten. Of course there are the ribbons, the medals, the elegantly
arranged cannons and the artistically lit wreckage of a plane. But then
one arrives at the hall of the dead and the living, a hall with drunken
dance music and a long table covered in death notices. On that table, too,
are the dented canteens, the old cups and mugs in a long row, and across
from them the modern glasses, the glasses of the living, and on the enormous wall behind the photographs of the dead, a huge collage of thousands of family pictures that speak of their lives: a young family in front
of a tent, a group portrait of a regiment, a young couple laughing before
a kettle of soup, below that three soldiers, standing rigid and upright, a
middle-class family in a garden, a sailor, two children in their Sunday
best. And the dance music plays on, that eternal dance music for all of
us, the living and the dead.

By last light I leave Kiev on the night train to Odessa, with Irina waving
from the platform and the ever-melancholy sound of the station
announcer's voice. On the outskirts of town, boys and girls are strolling
along the rails. A village: one half houses, one half freight containers. The
old straw roofs have given way to corrugated iron. Beneath the trees a
family is eating at a large table. Beside the tracks are numberless kitchen
gardens, little private fields of grain. A woman is dragging a heavy sled
loaded with potatoes along the sandy path beside the rails. Then the
endless plains.

When I climb down from the train the next morning, it is Sunday.
The bells are ringing, there are rattling sounds coming from the direction of the harbour, the air tingles with the nearness of the sea. My hotel,

situated on the loveliest boulevard in the world, is called the Londonskaya, and it is the city's most famous. In July 1941, during the bombardment, Konstantin Paustovsky stayed here for free, as the final guest, while the windows popped from their frames and the two old waiters calmly served the menu of the day: tea with nothing in it, and slimy brown vermicelli. Fifty-eight years later, fame has gone to the owners' heads. I spend one night there and pay a sum which the average Ukrainian family could live on for three months.

The view, however, is still unbeatable. Across from me, to one side, are the famous steps running down to the harbour, the steps that played such a central role in Eisenstein's *Potemkin*. The sea. Right below my window is the boulevard with its benches, lanterns and rustling chestnut trees. Beside and behind me, the city, its houses light green and ochre, its streets of a nineteenth-century allure, with only a few cars, old cobblestones, the house fronts a tableau of faded glory.

Everything a lover of Russian literature could dream of can be found in Odessa: the palace where Alexander Pushkin courted Yelizaveta Vorontsova, the wife of Governor Mikhail Vorontsov; the editorial offices of the naval gazette *Moryak* where Paustovsky carried out his own revolution in 1920; the courtyards ruled over by Isaac Babel's king rat, Benya Krik.

Along the boulevard one hears the cooing of the doves, the sound of music. Boys and girls walk back and forth here all day, because they have no money to sit in a café. There are ponies for the children. You can have your picture taken with a monkey. The swallows bob and weave between the rooftops. It is like a Sunday from long ago.

'Odessa has experienced prosperity and is now going downhill – a poetic, rather carefree and extremely helpless downhill,' Babel wrote in 1916. An old woman with grey, mussed hair is moving down the steps towards the harbour. She staggers. She shouts: 'The communists are gone! God is gone! God doesn't exist! The state doesn't exist. The only ones left are poor people, robbers and bandits. God help us! Robbers! Bandits!' And she keeps shouting that, all the way to the waterfront.

Here you can watch an empire collapse before your eyes. Ten years ago, from Riga to Volgograd, from St Petersburg to Odessa, you could pay with roubles. Now my pockets are full of the widest spectrum of banknotes, printed in meaningless denominations with the portraits of obscure gentlemen. The gigantic trading network of old Russia and the former Soviet Union has been tossed for a loop, the new nationalism has thrown up thousands of new obstacles, and the consequences are being felt everywhere: in the Lithuanian border town that lives off exports to Russia, in the vacant tourist hotels of Moscow and Kiev, in the port of Odessa where shipping revenues have gone down by two thirds since the dissolution of the Soviet Union, in the dozens of bankrupt ships lying here off the coast, waiting.

I wander into the Literature Museum. Beside Babel's lone spectacles – in a panic, he left them lying on his nightstand when he was arrested on 15 May, 1939 – I actually find a few old copies of *Moryak*. They date from 1921, they are printed on the back of packaging material used to ship tea, and they include Paustovsky's first stories. In the great hall – the museum is actually a palace – a sixtieth wedding anniversary party is underway. A women's chorus of veterans and pensioners, dressed in beautiful Ukrainian costumes, sings one rousing song after another. The bridal couple, old and fragile, stand up to receive the congratulations. The stars and ribbons of the late Soviet Union hang on their chests.

Isaac Babel wrote: 'In Odessa you have caressing and refreshing spring evenings, the penetrating aroma of acacias, and above the dark sea a moon that incessantly sheds its irresistible light.' Nothing of that has changed. I was in love with this city for a long time, before I ever set foot in it. I had first come here a few years back, travelling passenger class aboard a freighter from Istanbul that shuttled back and forth across the Black Sea, along the nether reaches of Europe. That ship, the Briz, was like an old man, its hull overgrown with crusts and tumours, and it had been carrying traders back and forth between Odessa and Istanbul for as long as anyone could remember. But the lifeboats and life jackets all said Odessa, Odessa, Odessa.

Halfway across, a cable became tangled in the propeller and we were adrift for hours. Almost none of the passengers seemed to notice. Most of them only came on deck to inspect their goods anyway. Had the fridges stayed dry? Were the Italian lawn chairs lashed down well? Were the deck-hands stealing too many tomatoes from the hundred of crates piled up there? Then they would retreat to their cabins or the ship's minuscule bar.

That was how it went, all the way to the much talked-of outer limits of Europe: an old rust bucket, a group of surly men in jogging suits, vodka, a few ship's whores, and a dozen dolphins swimming around it all.

In Istanbul, as we pushed off from the Golden Horn, we heard the call to prayer from dozens of minarets, but on the street one saw fewer women in head scarves than in a working-class neighbourhood in Rotterdam. And in Odessa everything was European again: the houses, the opera, the writers, the museums and, last but not least, the young people. For who else would one find parading here hand in hand along the boulevards but the great-great-grandchildren of Italian traders, Greek sailors, Russian civil servants, Jewish and Armenian craftsmen and Ukrainian farmers?

Europe's clearest border is the great historical divide sketched by Samuel Huntington, a Harvard professor, in his – incidentally, controversial – *The Clash of Civilisations*. It is the line that runs between the Christian peoples of the West and the Eastern Orthodox and Islamic cultures, a rift that goes back to AD 395, when the Holy Roman Empire was split in two. Both empires went their own way after that, and all those differing historical experiences caused traditions and cultures to grow asunder.

Huntington's fault line has been in more or less the same place for almost 500 years. It runs roughly north to south, from the border between Finland and Russia, along the edge of the Baltic States, straight through White Russia, the Ukraine, Rumania and Serbia, and ends in the Adriatic between Croatia and Bosnia.

On the western side of that line people drink espresso or filtered coffee, they observe Christmas on 25 December, they are influenced – usually without knowing it – by scholasticism and humanism, they have been through the Reformation, the Renaissance and the Enlightenment and they have experienced democracy and a rule of constitutional law – although in some countries this is still quite fresh and new. On the eastern side of it people drink coffee with grounds in the bottom of the cup, they celebrate Christmas by the Orthodox calendar or don't celebrate it at all, and most of them have lived for centuries under the yoke of the Byzantine Empire and other more or less absolutist regimes.

Huntington's view is shared – sometimes openly, more often tacitly – by most Western Europeans and their leaders. Yet there are also other voices to be heard. One can wonder, after all, whether there is any sense at all to the discussion concerning 'European identity', whether it is not in fact diametrically opposed to the entire history of the 'European concept'. For if anything serves as the true hallmark of European civilisation it is diversity, and not a single identity.

And if there is one city where this European variegation is in full bloom, it is Odessa. Only a few years after this half French, half-Italian city was raised up from the steppe by pioneers around 1800, Czar Alexander I wrote to Governor Vorontsov that Odessa was becoming 'too European': soldiers walked around with their uniforms unbuttoned, and Odessa was the only city in Russia where one was allowed to smoke or sing on the street. A 'native language' census held in 1897 showed that a third of the city's population spoke Yiddish, and barely half spoke Russian. Only one out of every twenty inhabitants spoke Ukrainian; almost an equal number had Polish as their native tongue. Many Russians hated Odessa. For Russian nationalists, the city served as a litmus test: anyone who liked Odessa was European. Anyone who did not like Odessa was faithful to Mother Russia. And Odessa today still has its own brand of civic pride that makes people say, not 'I come from the Ukraine' or 'I am Russian', but 'I am from Odessa.'

As Pushkin put it:

> Where all breathes Europe to the senses,
> And sparkling Southern sun dispenses
> A lively, varied atmosphere.
> Along the merry streets you'll hear
> Italian voices ringing loudly
> You'll meet the haughty Slav, the Greek,
> Armenian, Spaniard, Frenchman sleek,
> The stout Moldavian prancing proudly.
> And Egypt's son as well you'll see . . .

In the *Odyssey*, Homer relates how Odysseus, after all his wanderings, receives the order to undertake one last journey. He must go to a place where no one has ever seen the ocean, to make a peace offering to

Poseidon. The sign that he has reached his destination will be clear: he is to carry an oar over his shoulder and may only stop when he arrives in a land where the people claim that he is not carrying an oar, but a shovel. During my travels, I applied the same methodology with regard to the question of where Europe stops. I soon noticed that, in day-to-day life, the problem is not all that complicated: people decide for themselves where they belong, and they make no bones about it. Whenever there was talk of holidays 'in Europe', the quality of 'European clothing' or family members 'in Europe', I knew one thing for certain: I had crossed the shadowy outer limits of Europe.

That had happened in St Petersburg, in Moscow, in Volgograd – oh, how badly my tour guide there wanted to move 'to Europe' – as well as in Vilnius, and even one time in Warsaw. In Istanbul, too, the common parlance is as clear as can be: on the ferries across the Bosphorus, people speak of the 'European' side and the 'Asian' side. But in Greece or Bosnia, officially on the 'Byzantine' side of the line, I have never heard anyone say he was going to Europe. Huntington's line may seem convincing at a glance, but the reality is much more jagged, much more ruled by the emotions of the day, much more, too, by recent experiences.

And Odessa? My old acquaintance Natalya exclaims that she soon hopes to take another holiday 'in Europe'. Edvard, who is busy setting up a commercial radio station, complains all evening about the trouble he has getting into Europe, even for a brief business trip. 'Waiting in consulates, waiting for permits, sometimes it takes months. I'm serious: it's almost as bad as back in the days of the Iron Curtain. Only now the barriers have been thrown up in the West, instead of here.'

There can be no mistake about it: here in Odessa, people think a great deal and often about Europe, more than the Europeans themselves. The next morning I have an appointment with Charel Krol-Dobrov, a professor of European Studies at the University of Odessa. 'This is a country for advanced students only,' he feels. 'In Holland, the border of Europe is clear: it's the sea. But here? Where does it start? Where does it end? Looking at Europe from the East, you get a different perspective. Western Europe has always been content with itself, while people on the eastern borders have always been faced with the question: do we belong, or don't we? That's why there's so much talk in Eastern Europe about the nature of Europe, much more than in the West. What is Europe? What should Europe be? What should Europe become?'

He tells me about the old Russian dichotomy between Slavophiles and pro-Westerners, and about how the communists nurtured that dichotomy after their own fashion. 'Now that old debate seems to have become obsolete, because the communists have lost and, implicitly, so have the Slavophiles. But here in this city it remains a lively issue. Here people feel the Asian blood in them, but also the European blood, they must come to terms with both of them, and that has been going on for centuries.'

Outside, on the boulevard, we hear a woman singing. She is standing beneath a big black umbrella to protect herself from the sun, but it seems as though she is still on stage at the opera. In her old voice, she sings arias from *Carmen*, *Tosca*, *Aida*, *The Marriage of Figaro* and *Rigoletto*, an entirely European repertoire. Charel Krol-Dobrov cannot help but laugh: 'Who is best able to judge movement? The person on the train? Or the person standing outside, watching?'

This time I have booked a berth on the *Passat*, for the same trip I once made on the *Briz*, but now in the opposite direction. The harbour, as we move out to sea, is lit by the evening sun. Lingering, melancholy notes – a tonality they're always very good at here – drift across the quay and the decks. The smoke from the ship's funnels leaves a thick stripe across the sky, and then the city glides away, the green boulevard, the opera house triumphant on the hill. A yellow pilot boat moves along with us; the pilot, an old man, is drinking coffee on the bridge. The *Passat* threads its way through the line of ships rusting along the coast. And then we head into the Black Sea, that strange, half-dead sea, that 'wasteland of water' as Paustovsky called her, that sea where the twins 'civilisation' and 'barbarity' first met.

For a full day, there is no coastline in sight. The ship, riding high and empty, bobs across the waves like a beer can. In the restaurant, overgrown with plastic geraniums, meals are served in shifts and according to a strict timetable. Ukrainian girls in bikinis sun themselves on deck, the eyes of the Turkish traders seem about to pop out of their heads, tourists play cards and sleep. In and out of the restaurant three times a day, the rolling of the sea, dolphins before the bow, white foam behind, no-man's-land.

Chapter Thirty-Eight

Istanbul

FROM ANCIENT TIMES CONSTANTINOPLE WAS THE HINGE BETWEEN East and West, the final bulwark of the Roman Empire, the wealthiest metropolis between London and Peking, the terminus of the Chinese silk route, the advance beacon of Europe.

And today?

From the Black Sea, the first thing one sees are the green hills of Kilyos, behind them the elegant houses and gardens where Irfan Orga once spent the last, light summer of his childhood, and amid them the modern suburbs of Istanbul, lying in folds across the hillsides like cotton wool. We are sailing into the Bosphorus. The villas glide by left and right, one more extravagant than the other, with carved wooden balconies, stoops and terraces looking out on the water, brightly coloured gardens, trees, a village square, a minaret, a little wharf, a few cafés, a beach.

It is 7 a.m., but the sun is already hot. We pass a tiny fishing boat, the nets half spread in the water, three tanned and weathered men wave to the girls on the *Passat*. The great bridge between Europe and Asia lies in the distance, a flimsy thread being crossed by hundred of bugs and beetles.

We approach the heart of the city. I have said so before: here, time obviously stopped in 1948. The dozens of ferries full of fathers with brief-cases and mothers with shopping, the rusty, worldly-wise freighters from Sebastopol, Odessa and Piraeus, the bright-red tugs, the oil fumes, the glistening water: everything exudes the spirit of work and trade, no frills.

The European part of the city resembles old Barcelona, except for the occasional, echoing call to prayer. The markets are full of shouts and aromas, the stalls overflowing with milk and honey, bulging with herbs, chicken and fish, with cherries the size of plums, plums the size of apples, with vegetables of a thousand varieties. On Istiklal Caddesi, boys surf on the bumper of an old tram, their feet sliding over the rails. In the middle of the day, loudspeakers everywhere issue the call to prayer. This is Muslim country, yes, but the baroque shopping gallery where I have lunch could just as easily be Brussels, or Milan. Istanbul, like Odessa, is an amalgamated city, a city that must come to terms with all these different identities, without choosing one or the other.

I stay at the Pera Palas, an antique hotel built in 1892 as an extension of the Orient Express, a cool resting place after the exhausting train trip through the Balkans. The building breathes a nostalgic chic, an ancient lift creaks up and down all day, right through the middle of the stair-well. Gold and marble glisten in the immense halls. In the big, flaking bathrooms you can sit on the same toilet as Greta Garbo, stare out of the same window as Empress Sissi of Austria, and lie in the same bed as King Zog of Albania. The TV is turned up loudly in the room where Trotsky slept: 204.

The loveliest suite here is held eternally for Mustafa Kemal Paşa – known from 1934 as Kemal Atatürk, the 'father of all Turks'. A porter takes me by the hand, lets me peek around the door. It is a small, silent sanc-tuary: a bed, a bathroom, two easy chairs, a desk with a couple of photo-graphs and some papers. So this was the Istanbul pied-à-terre of the military dictator, this hero of the First World War who reined in the chaos of the collapsing Ottoman Empire, drove out the foreign occupiers and led the country powerfully and energetically into the modern age.

In the 1920s and 1930s, Atatürk was able to impose secularisation simply by decree, an unparalleled revolution in the Islamic world: women were no longer allowed to wear veils, men no longer the fez, polygamy was banned, women were given the vote, the Islamic lunar calendar was replaced with the Gregorian, the Arabic script with the Roman alphabet. Instead of Islamic law, Swiss law was adopted, almost word for word, Sunday became the official day of rest, all Koran schools were closed and Islam was to respect all secular legislation.

In recent decades the father of the fatherland has been honoured more than ever, despite – or perhaps because of – the country's new Islamisation.

One statue after another was raised, his portrait hung in every café and classroom. He was seen as the symbol of the great leap forward, the containment of the power of the believers, the definitive break with the 'sick man of Europe', as the Ottoman Empire was once called. Still, Atatürk was himself the product of that very same empire, an empire that was in reality less feeble than was often supposed. Like France, for example, Turkey had started a programme of modernisation as early as the mid-nineteenth century. All manner of reforms later ascribed to Atatürk actually began under the reign of Sultan Abdülhamid II: the reform of the educational system, the modernisation of the army, the reorganisation of the legislative system and government finances, the pushing back of the influence of the Muslim elite, the westernisation of clothing, the building of roads and railways.

It was under Abdülhamid that a direct overland connection was established with Western Europe: the first Orient Express steamed into the city on 12 August, 1888. The Pera Palas became the outpost for the Western elite. During those same years, eighteen new technical schools were established, as well as a university and a school of medicine. Atatürk's own youth is a shining example of the possibilities offered by modernised Ottoman education around 1900.

Atatürk's separation of church and state – Islam was to be practised only as a private faith, without legal or political influence – was also, in fact, an enactment of existing opinion. In the nineteenth century in particular, many Islamic thinkers became inspired by the modernisation of the West. They arrived at standpoints, based on the Koran, that were in many ways comparable to modern Western thought. They entertained a great many ideas about intellectual freedom, about the role of the individual and about the separation of church and state.

Alongside all this there is also Atatürk the despot, and he too, more than sixty years after his death, exerts at least equal influence on Turkish society. The country's secular character, so hated by the religious and the fundamentalist, was jealously guarded by the army. In 1961 the military did not bat an eyelid when it hanged the democratically elected prime minister, Adnan Menderes, for 'corruption' and for 'conspiring with the Islamic parties'. During a military coup in 1980, thousands of opponents were detained without due process. As late as 1998, the generals, acting

'in the name of Atatürk', brusquely shoved aside the first democratically
elected Islamic government. The Turks even have their own jargon for
this: the 'deep state' as opposed to the 'official-but-superficial state', a
'soft coup', 'pasha coups' or 'media coups'.

It is 7 p.m. on Friday, rush hour for the ferries. People come pouring up
the gangplanks carrying bags, toolboxes, baskets full of chickens, fishing
gear, bicycles, even tables and chairs. Vendors of roasted ears of corn,
sunflower seeds, peeled cucumbers and fresh fish jostle each other on
the quayside. There are people hawking dancing puppets, breathtakingly
pink children's petticoats, light-blue plastic birds with purple feathers. A
blind man plays the violin, his friend sings a sorrowful song into a badly
distorting microphone.

The toy vendors have two new dolls: an electric blonde doll that rocks
a baby, and a green commando that crawls along with his rifle, producing
regular flashes of light and deadly sounds. A little further along a man
is sitting beside old bathroom scales: for five cents you can weigh yourself. The little fishing boats moored along the quay bob on the waves,
the crew are roasting fish on grills set up in the middle of the deck,
hopping like acrobats with every wave that washes in. The beggars are
out in full force. Within a minute I am accosted by an old man, a woman
with one leg and a pitiful young girl with a baby. The fishmongers shout,
the electronic dolls quack and rattle, the ships' horns blast, the blind man
sings through it all: this is the quay by the bridge across the Golden
Horn at 7 p.m. on a Friday.

The ferry to Büyükada, one of the islands in the Sea of Marmara, is
a rusty tub full of people excited to be escaping the city, even if only
for a bit. I start talking to a young student. She tells me the same stories
about newcomers that one hears often in Amsterdam, only these immigrants are from her own country. She is frightened by the advancing
countryside, she sees tens of thousands of young people moving to the
city each year, full of illusions, only to become hopelessly bogged down
after a time, without work, without a family. Fundamentalist groups
are popping up all over. 'Istanbul is losing itself,' she says. 'There is no
more movement, no more change. Everything has become frozen by
the polarisation in the city between rich and poor, and between modern

thinking and fundamentalism. The situation is becoming more tense every day.'

Soon afterwards the city would literally quake and tear, thousands of people would die, but that was all still to come and we were able to enjoy the evening without a real care. A cheerful man is trying to sell knives, he demonstrates the quality of the blades by artfully cutting strips from a plastic bottle. Tea and fruit juice are served in huge quantities. A few boys on the afterdeck raise their voices in song. The air is balmy, the sea is dazzling. And meanwhile Istanbul runs on along the Asiatic shore, the city rolling on between the coast and the hills like a broad, greyish-white band, dozens of kilometres, hundreds of thousands of apartment blocks, ten, twelve million people who dream and want to do something with their lives, crowded together at the brim of the Asian continent.

One Sunday I wander a bit aimlessly through Fener, the old Greek neighbourhood. Some of the houses here are still wooden. In a square there is a tiny carousel, pushed by its owner. A group of children waits excitedly, a few coins clenched in their fists. According to my city guide, the names of these little streets are actually of an unparalleled poetry: Street of the Thousand Earthquakes, the Lane of the Bristly Beard, the Alley of the Chicken Which Cannot Fly, Plato's Cul-de-Sac, the Street of Nafie with the Golden Hair, the Street of Ibrahim of the Black Hell. Tantalising aromas waft over from an antique bakery. When I stop for a moment, the baker comes outside and hands me a sweet pretzel. He will not accept my money: 'This is how we make them, stranger. Taste it!'

Istanbul is still the centre of the Orthodox Church. Strictly speaking, the Greek Orthodox patriarch of Constantinople holds the same position as the Pope, but it takes me a long time to find the Orthodox Vatican tucked away in a corner of this working-class neighbourhood. The complex is surrounded by thick walls. In the church a priest is being ordained, the pews are full and in the courtyard families are standing around talking. The atmosphere is festive. The priests are all elderly men, the seminary was closed thirty years ago by the Turks, but it seems as though there's a revival in progress. The patriarchate still looks like a fort, though its perimeter walls have been daubed with graffiti: 'Long live our Islamic struggle!'

Amid this intimate gathering it seems almost unimaginable that seventy-five years ago, at the time of the 1924 census, a quarter of the population of Istanbul was still Greek Orthodox. In 1955 a veritable pogrom took place: thousands of Muslims went into the Greek neighbourhood, shattered windows, looted and destroyed. Dozens of Orthodox churches were torched. The police did nothing. In 1974, at the time of the Cyprus crisis, tens of thousands of Greeks were run out of town again. Today there are no more than 3,000 left.

It is bizarre, but true: this little group of respectable Sunday Greeks, this remote little church, these elderly priests are all that remains of the enormous Greek Orthodox power centre that was once Constantinople, of the unique amalgam of European and Eastern culture that blossomed here for at least a thousand years.

In some ways the Ottoman Empire was like the European colonial empires, but lacked one feature: the colonial disdain with which Europe looked down on other peoples. The Ottomans were not particularly interested in whether one was a Muslim or a Christian. Jews and Christians were generally left in peace. Promising young Jewish and Christian people were sometimes converted to Islam, then given influential positions in the army or the bureaucracy. For the rest, however, the religious freedom of eighteenth and nineteenth-century Istanbul was reminiscent of that in Amsterdam. While dissenters were being persecuted elsewhere in Europe, in the Ottoman Empire they were free to practise their religion. The Ottoman borders were open to Jewish refugees, and they made a welcome contribution to the economy. When the Italian travel writer Edmondo De Amicis stopped on the Galata Bridge in 1896, he saw a motley crowd passing by: Greeks, Turks, Armenians, 'a Muhammadan woman on foot, a veiled slave girl, a Greek woman with long, wavy hair topped with a little red cap, a Maltese woman hidden behind her black *faletta*, a Jewess in the ancient costume of her nation, a Negress wrapped in a multi-coloured Cairo shawl, an Armenian woman from Trebizond, all veiled in black . . .'

Almost half of that same Istanbul in which young Irfan Orga grew up consisted of non-Muslims. According to the 1893 census, almost five million Jews and Christians lived among the seventeen million Ottomans. Like the Habsburg Empire, it was a multinational. And in some ways, particularly when it became modernised, it was perhaps more European than present-day Turkey.

The question, therefore, is: where lies the greatest barrier between Turkey and the rest of Europe? Is it actually the country's traditional Muslim character? Is it not, rather, Atatürk's staunchly nationalist and dictatorial modernisation that blocks a lasting rapprochement with modern-day Europe? Or, to put it differently: does the problem really have to do with Muhammad? Does it not have just as much to do with Atatürk?

It was nineteenth-century nationalism that put an end to the tolerance of the Ottoman Empire, and by the start of the twentieth century the tension had risen to breaking point in Anatolia. But it was only under Atatürk that ethnic cleansing was adopted as government policy. His modern Turkey was to form a strong national and ethnic unit, he considered the Ottomans' multinationalism sentimental and obsolete, religious and ethnic diversity only undermined the country's identity and security. In the 1920s, after Greece had vainly tried to establish control over large parts of the crumbling Ottoman Empire, Atatürk imposed a forced exchange between Greece and Turkey, an ethnic cleansing of unheard-of proportions: more than a million Greek Orthodox inhabitants of Anatolia were sent to Greece, almost 400,000 Greek Muslims were transported to Turkey.

Their fate was mild compared to that of the Armenians. In the course of conflicts and deportations in 1915, even before Atatürk came to power, an estimated 1.5 million Ottoman Armenians were killed, a case of genocide vehemently denied to this day by the Turkish government. Merely mentioning this genocide, the first of the twentieth century, still leads to indictments and trials. The veiling of the past, the fatal forgetting of which Primo Levi wrote, is here the duty of every patriotic citizen.

All this had – and still has – an effect on Istanbul. It is a city which, despite the overwhelming beauty of the Bosphorus, despite the tenfold growth of its population in the last half of the twentieth century, despite the influx of tens of thousands of immigrants from Russia and Eastern Europe, despite the Hagia Sophia and all the other evidence of 1,500 years of culture, is losing its cosmopolitan character and is in the process of becoming, in spirit, a provincial city. The Jews have left for Israel, the

Greeks for Greece, the country's political power has moved to Ankara, the merchants have been scattered across the face of the earth.

All cities tell a story, and the story of Istanbul is above all one of shifting emphases and of vulnerability, no matter how international the metropolis might seem. In 1200, this was Europe's absolute centre of power. Today it is a remote corner, a poor, rapidly expanding Third World city, a symbol of glory past, ties forgotten, tolerance lost.

Chapter Thirty-Nine

Kefallonia

IN THE CRETAN VILLAGE OF ANOGIA, THE DAY BEGINS WITH THE crowing of roosters. A man comes by with a megaphone, trying, even at this early hour, to sell his potatoes, a whole wagonful. Then comes the clanging and bleating of a herd of goats, the shouting of a Gypsy woman with a cart full of clothing, then a car loaded with plastic buckets and basins, and then the day has truly arrived.

The old men move slowly from their houses. They carry sticks, they wear beards, black caps, stiff, heavy coats, blue jeans, every season and every age is tucked away in their appearance. The communists sit in front of their own café, where Marx, Lenin, Che Guevara and Stalin have their regular places on the wall. A busload of German tourists pulls in, they disappear into the restaurant which bears the sign 'ICH SPRECHE DEUTSCH', and everyone on the village square nods to them and greets them in a most amiable fashion. A skinned sheep is slung from the back of a truck, its head rolls over the ground. The old women are doing their errands. You can still see which one was the prettiest fifty years ago, if only from the way the old men treat this bent and bowed Calliope.

Fifty years ago: when they were still young, when Anogia was wiped off the face of the earth.

When evening comes the moon rises at the top of the main street like a monstrous disc. Anogia lies on the flanks of the Ida range. The houses are white and square, the streets slope down with the hillside, there is a square with plane trees, and everywhere there are tourist shops with colourful weaving.

Back behind the village is a museum displaying the naïve art of a talented shepherd, Chrilios Skoulas. The paintings are huge: pictures of the village with all its streets, and of the painter and his wife posing peacefully in front of their house; of the painter walking through the woods in a flurry of snow, a lamb draped around his neck; of paratroopers landing in green uniforms, the shepherds and other partisans shooting them as they descend, they fall, the green uniforms tumble, the dogs lick their blood; of the village with fire leaping from every roof, airplanes, dead people everywhere, old men being chased into houses that are burning like torches, women and children being led away and the partisans trying to rescue them. And then there is a huge tableau of peace, of the men and women who finally returned, of the church with the souls of the dead floating above it.

The present-day mayor of Anogia was ten years old at the time. All he remembers is the smoke and the smell of fire. He and a group of young boys found a cave to hide in; then they roamed through the mountains with the partisans for three weeks, living on cheese and goat's milk. 'When we finally came back to our village, there was not one stone on top of the other. There was this strange smell that we couldn't place. Then we saw the bodies everywhere, swollen bodies, soaked from the rain. No one said anything, no one wept, we stayed absolutely quiet. Talking about it now, my eyes fill with tears. But then we were petrified.' He and his younger sister decided to go to a neighbouring village, to see if their grandfather was still alive. Along the way they saw a man lying under a felled tree, a little boy in his arms. 'They looked as if they were sleeping.' Weeping, they ran on. Their grandfather was still there.

The massacre of the village of Anogia took place on 15 August, 1944. The monument to it consists of an engraved plaque bearing the text of the German order: 'Because the kidnappers of Major General Karl Kreipe passed through Anogia, we hereby order that the village be levelled to the ground and that every male inhabitant of Anogia living in the village or within a radius of one mile of the village be executed.'

The general was the German commander Kreipe, who was kidnapped by partisans and British agents and smuggled off to Egypt. More than 140 people were murdered that day, most of them women and the elderly. Most of the men had already joined up with the partisans, the others had fled into the mountains. 'But we got a lot of Germans too,' the mayor says. 'What did they know about the mountains around here?' The German reprisals were merciless: ten dead Cretans for every German killed.

The people of Anogia are obstinate, the children's expressions are open, and the women know what they want: their men, after all, spend a large part of the year wandering through the mountains with their flocks, and are often gone for months at a time. All this makes for a rather different view of the Second World War than that held by most Europeans. Here no one crawled or licked the dust, here there were no 'sensible' mayors in wartime, here there were no compromises or guilty feelings; here the people simply fought hard, and on Crete the Germans never gained much of a foothold.

Anogia was a typical partisan village, like Viannos, Kotomari and Myrtos, where the Germans committed similar atrocities. A few pictures have been preserved from Kotomari: the men of the village driven together into an olive grove; a man who tried to escape, a handsome, curly-haired young fellow talking for his life; the firing squad, the soldier out in front smiling as he aims; the corpses fallen across each other.

When he came back sixteen years later to see how things were with 'his' Kotomari, the German soldier who took these photographs was nonetheless welcomed with ouzo. And the mayor of Anogia says today: 'I saw Germans crying. I saw it when they shuffled into our ambush like sheep and didn't stand a ghost of a chance. I saw that they, too, were pawns and victims. Why should we hate them, they got killed too, didn't they?' Only in Myrtos does the retired schoolteacher refuse to admit Germans, not even German children, to his private museum. But then, the men on the square say as they shake their heads, he is suffering from a war trauma.

For the Greeks the Second World War began on 28 October, 1940, when the Italians made a vain attempt to invade their country by way of Albania. Mussolini was increasingly frustrated, for he had hardly shared in Hitler's Western European successes. His radical supporters dreamed of the return of the Roman Empire, of the conquest of Egypt, of hegemony along the eastern Mediterranean seaboard, of an empire like Napoleon's. But he also wanted to take the wind out of the Germans' sails, particularly in their attempts to seize the rich oilfields of Rumania.

That October, he decided to take the initiative. Poorly armed, without sufficient supplies or winter clothing, the Italian soldiers marched to their defeat in the mountains. They advanced no further than about eighty kilometres before they were routed.

In spring 1941, the Germans came to the Italians' assistance. The Third Reich could not allow its eastern flank in the Balkans to remain undefended, especially if it hoped to invade the Soviet Union. In late March, therefore, Hitler presented Yugoslavia with an ultimatum: it had to join the Axis. On 25 March the country entered the Tripartite Pact, along with Germany, Italy and Japan; two days later, the government of Dragiša Ćetković was brought down by a coup. Hitler's response was to launch Operation Retaliation. On 6 April, Palm Sunday, most of Belgrade was bombed flat. Some 17,000 people were burned alive or buried beneath the rubble. Then Yugoslavia and Greece were hastily occupied by German and Italian troops; the Germans, after all, still had to prepare for the great push into Russia. As a result, tens of thousands of Yugoslav and Greek soldiers were able to escape into the mountains, where they immediately began a guerrilla war.

Yugoslavia fell to pieces. The Italians moved into Slovenia, Croatia and Montenegro. The Hungarians occupied Vojvodina. Their fascist Arrow Cross corps immediately began to massacre civilians in Novi Sad: 500 Jews and Serbs were shot or bayoneted. Croatia proclaimed itself an independent republic, led by fascist dictator Ante Pavelić. To make matters even more complicated, a thinly disguised religious war began between the Catholic Croatians and Orthodox Serbs. The Croatian ustašas (rebels) commenced with large-scale ethnic purifications, including mass executions and death camps. Tens of thousand of Serbs were their victims.

The partisan army consisted of Serbs, Croatians, Slovenians, Macedonians, Montenegrins, Hungarians, Italians, Czechs and Bosnians. At the same time, however, a minor civil war was also being fought out within their ranks. After the German invasion of the Soviet Union, the royalist Chetniks began a life-and-death struggle with the communist partisans led by Josip Broz, otherwise known as Tito. The British historian Norman Davies summarised the situation thus: 'The fierce determination of the Yugoslav partisans to kill the invaders was only exceeded by their proclivity for killing each other.'

And so the Balkans and Greece went to war, pillaged, starving and poor, officially occupied by the Germans and Italians, but in actual fact dominated at least as cruelly by hundreds of competing resistance groups.

Seen from the air, Greece is mostly sea, little blue ripples with here and there an island grazed bare, a few grooves and lines in the yellowish-grey earth, at crossroads and along the coast a huddle of small white blocks, then the blue flats again, with a few fast-moving dots tying the whole thing together.

Close to Ithaca, about 300 kilometres from the Italian coast, lies the island of Kefallonia. When we land at the little airfield, a violent summer storm is underway. The sea is covered in white horses, the olive trees bend beneath each gust, the water bursts across the breakwater dividing the bay at the capital of Argostoli. The island was hit by a major earthquake in 1953, most of the streets and villages were rebuilt, and now the razing and hammering is once again going on everywhere. My hotel, the Mirabella, looks out over a market square crowded with cafés. Yet it is not the British and Italian tourists causing this huge upturn in the local construction trade. It is the homecomers.

Like large parts of the Mediterranean, this island was for decades a baby factory for Western Europe and the rest of the world. All the young people moved away, because they had no future here. I remember my first trip through Greece, in summer 1965: everywhere you came across villages inhabited only by old women. I recall a boarding house where I once ended up after a village feast: the woman of the house sadly showed me an enormous pile of beautifully embroidered blankets, made for her husband and her children. They had not been used for years.

Having made their fortunes in Western Europe, Australia and America, these prodigal sons have reached retirement age and are coming back by the hundreds. And they are all living out exactly the same dream: a two-storey house in the old village, a big balcony, a rooftop terrace, a garage with an automatic door, electric shutters and marble steps before the door. You see the men sitting in front of Hotel Mirabella, talking to their old schoolmates, toying with their worn strings of beads, gossiping about dead acquaintances. But their island has been consumed by time, there is little left of the old place, and so they stick together, the homecomers, fallen forever between two stools.

Upon arrival I announce my presence to the Grande Dame of the island, and am immediately summoned. Helena Cosmetatos (b.1910) resides in one of the few old houses that survived the 1953 earthquake and the ensuing demolition by the Greek Army. 'Only the top floor is gone.' The dark rooms are full of old paintings and antique woodwork. Her elderly husband potters about the house, occasionally singing a naughty French song from the 1930s.

During our talk in the garden, a lady friend, a grandchild and a British couple all come to pay their respects, and we move back and forth through a gamut of languages. Helena was born in Rhodesia, grew up in Athens, and now lives comfortably from her family's colonial fortune. 'I met my Waterloo in 1936,' she said. 'That's when I married a Greek. What a peaceful life I should have had if I had only gone for a British office clerk who died of a heart attack at the age of fifty-five!'

She talks about her parents, who lived next door to the former dictator Metaxas, and about the parties that were held at their house all the time. 'Ioannis Metaxas was a stern little man, he also came from these islands. But I had no idea what was going on behind all those closed doors. Back then all those men wanted to marry me, you know how it is. Metaxas was a great admirer of Mussolini, so when Italy declared war on us he felt utterly betrayed. He died not long afterwards. It was a catastrophe.'

Her husband fought against the Italians, in the Albanian mountains. 'One day he suddenly showed up at the door. At first he didn't speak a word, until finally he said: "A bath." He had come back all the way from northern Greece, on foot.'

Old Mr Cosmetatos shows me the big book of icons he has made, and whispers a racy joke in French. His wife shuts him up and starts talking about the war again.

'The Italian years were good ones. When I arrived here on the boat in 1941 – you had to come ashore in a little dinghy then – my son lost one of his sandals in the water as he was climbing out. Two Italian soldiers ran into the water right away to fish it up. That was my first encounter with our occupiers.'

She tells me how to get to the local museum, saying I should go take a look for myself. In the heat of the afternoon I flip through files containing letters and instructions written by the Italian occupiers in 1942, pictures of happy, marching soldiers, laughing men with a girl on a motorbike, and then a few clandestine photographs of the same boys sprawling on the ground, having been shot against a wall.

The garrison on Kefallonia was manned by officers and soldiers of the Acqui Division, friendly Italians who were perfectly content to have the gods of war pass them by. Occupiers and islanders lived together in remarkable harmony, they had drinks together, lay on the beach together and played football against each other. The troops attached to the little German occupational force on the island shared in that same peaceful atmosphere, they lazed in the sun, and at parties and meals let themselves be carried along by the contagious good cheer of their Italian comrades.

On 8 September, 1943, all that changed at a blow. A newly appointed Italian cabinet decided to end the fighting and sign a truce with the Allies. The Germans swiftly sent reinforcements to replace the Italians on the island. The commander of the Italian garrison, General Gandin, did not know what to do: should he lay down his weapons and surrender to the Germans, or take up arms and fight, this time on the Allied side?

Astonishingly enough, it was his soldiers who finally broke the deadlock: they held a vote, and decided to fight with the Allies against the Germans. So when two German landing craft with reinforcements approached the harbour, Captain Renzo Apollonio ordered the artillery to open fire. One of the ships sank.

More than enough opportunities presented themselves to come to the assistance of the troops on Kefallonia. The Allied navy was active everywhere in the region, and at least 300 Italian planes were standing ready at Brindisi. But nothing happened. One of the pilots later told the military historian Richard Lamb how they had urgently requested fuel and munitions, to go into action over Greece. 'Instead we were told to fly our aircraft to Tunis, out of range of the hard-pressed troops on Kefallonia.'

The Acqui Division fought till their ammunition was exhausted. On 22 September, at 11 a.m., they raised the white flag.

Then the Wehrmacht's 22nd Mountain Corps, led by General Lanz, began slaughtering the Italians. Hundreds of soldiers were machine-gunned immediately upon surrender. Those who were not were locked up in Cassetta Rosa, the little town hall at San Teodoro. The first of them to be executed was General Gandin. Then it was his officers' turn; in the end almost 5,000 Italian soldiers were killed.

In Cassetta Rosa they were administered last rites before being led outside in little groups. 'They knelt, wept, prayed, sang,' wrote chaplain Romualdo Formato, one of the few survivors. 'Many of the men called out the names of their mothers, wives, children.' Three officers embraced: 'In life we were comrades, and that is how we shall enter paradise.' Some of them clawed at the grass, as though trying to dig their way out. Meanwhile, the shooting continued.

Cassetta Rosa is still there. The house was abandoned years ago, and nature is busy devouring what is left. There are trees and bushes growing through the windows and the roof, the walls have sunken halfway into the ground; in another twenty or thirty years it will all be gone. Amid the tall grass is a plain little altar, put there only last year, bearing a statue of the Holy Virgin and a handful of artificial flowers. You can still see the bullet holes in the walls.

The bodies of the soldiers who were executed were burned, or loaded onto barges and sunk far out to sea; the *Wehrmacht* knew all too well that they had something to hide. The surviving soldiers of the Acqui Division – some 4,000 in all – were put aboard three ships bound for Piraeus, as prisoners of war. Just outside the harbour the ships ran into a minefield and exploded. The holds were padlocked and most of the prisoners were unable to escape, those who swam around were machine-gunned by the soldiers of the *Kriegsmarine*.

Any elderly person on this island can tell you about the stench and the sea full of corpses, but officially none of it ever happened. General Lanz of the *Wehrmacht* was sentenced to only twelve years at Nuremberg in 1948, because he insisted that he disobeyed Hitler's orders to kill all the Italians. His report to Army Group E, in which he confirmed that 5,000 Italians had been executed, had been meant only to mislead his superiors. According to Lanz, fewer than a dozen officers were shot, and then only because they had put up resistance. Other German officers verified his story: most of the Acqui Division had simply been shipped out to Piraeus. The American judges believed them. According to the Nuremberg tribunal, therefore, Lanz had actually *prevented* a mass murder.

At least half of the Acqui Division had apparently disappeared into thin air.

In fact, only a few dozen Italians escaped, including the legendary Captain Renzo Apollonio. 'I don't really remember how we felt in those days,' Helena Cosmetatos says. 'It was horrible, perhaps it didn't impact on us directly, but those Italians had lived with us for two years. And they were always very helpful.' While the killings were still going on, a taxi driver brought a wounded Italian soldier to her door. 'What am I supposed to do with him?' she had shouted. The driver shouted back: 'Think of something, he has a mother too!'

She nursed him back to health; today he has a restaurant on Lake Como, with fifty tables. It all worked out in the end, for him.

Chapter Forty

Cassino

WHEN THE AMERICAN WAR CORRESPONDENT MARTHA GELLHORN FIRST set foot in Italy in February 1944, she could hardly believe her eyes: no hurricane could have done more damage than the German-American front lines as they slowly rolled back. 'It is not possible that once these places stood up foursquare and people lived in them,' she noted.

She caught a lift in a French jeep, heading north from Naples, 'in a steady stream of khaki-colored traffic': trucks, jeeps, ambulances, salvage trucks, tank destroyers and munitions carriers. The windshield was folded down and the roof folded back, the icy cold hail struck her in the face. She saw endless tent encampments along both sides of the road. There was always a soldier standing alone somewhere on the flats, shaving 'with care and comic solemnity'.

When the road began to climb she saw Italian women washing clothes in an old water tank. A little further along, six-wheeled army trucks were pushing each other up a hill. Her French driver asked: 'Have you ever had an Alexander cocktail, Mademoiselle?' He himself was having a hard time of it, he was skinny and dirty, and he seemed ill. They drove past a burned-out American tank. An Alexander is a very sweet cocktail made with crème de cacao. A little further along, two army trucks had crashed into a ravine. They passed some marshes 'where nothing grows except guns'. Finally they arrived in a mountainous wilderness, with the loveliest views one could imagine, 'though everyone dislikes it, for the Germans are there'. 'I do not mean to brag,' Gellhorn's driver said, 'but I made the best Alexanders in Casablanca.'

A few kilometres further lay the monastery at Monte Cassino.

*

I had sailed from Greece to Italy aboard ships from the Strintzi and Minoan lines, a peaceful crossing that lasted a day and a night. At Patras I had spent a warm, sleepy afternoon waiting amid dozens of complaining Hungarian truckers who had been forced into this detour by the war in Yugoslavia. Then came a restless night in a shuddering hut, and then, on the sunny quay at Brindisi, my own green van. Thoughtful friends had driven the thing south, so I could head back north, along with the Allied troops.

The long, grim Italian war from July 1943 to April 1945, the five great landing operations at Sicily, Messina, Taranto, Salerno and Anzio, the enormous destruction of the country from south to north: this whole, bitter history has always remained in the shadow of the gigantic heroism of the landings at Normandy and what came afterwards. Still, more than 300,000 Allied soldiers died here, and more than 400,000 Germans. It was a slow, tough and nasty war that all parties wanted to forget as quickly as possible. It was not until April 1945 that the guns were silenced in Italy, but not because the Allies had won the fight; it was because all the other German fronts had collapsed.

The war in Italy began on 10 July, 1943 with a landing on Sicily. It was the first time – with the exception of an ill-fated 'trial invasion' at Dieppe on 19 August, 1942 – that Allied troops returned to the European continent. In early September new landings followed, at the Strait of Messina, at Taranto in the south-east and at Salerno, not far from Naples. To speed up the sluggish advance a fifth landing took place in late January 1944, at Anzio, just south of Rome. That was not a success: the Allied troops captured a bridgehead of a few square kilometres in size, but could go no further. 'You feel,' the war correspondent Ernie Pyle wrote from Anzio, 'pretty much like a clay pigeon in a shooting gallery.'

Opening this Southern European front had pretty much been Winston Churchill's idea. The Americans were in favour of a much shorter route to Berlin, by way of the Channel, Paris and Cologne, but in 1943 their armies were not yet ready for an operation of that magnitude. At first glance, moving from North Africa through Italy to Trieste, Vienna, Prague and then Berlin did indeed seem like a vast detour. But in any case, the Italian Front was needed to keep as many German troops as possible occupied in Southern Europe and provide relief for the embattled Soviets.

The British and Americans wanted at all costs to prevent a situation like that of spring 1918, when exhausted Russia had suddenly declared a cease-fire and German troops were able to swing back and reinforce the Western Front. That would have been a disaster.

Churchill also had reasons of his own for this remarkable detour. As early as 1942 he was one of the very few to take into account the shape of post-war Europe. In his view, the Soviet Union absolutely had to be kept out of Europe. Therefore, the war was ultimately to be fought in Eastern Europe, not in the West. By taking the Italian-Austrian route, the Allied armies would not only defeat the Germans but also cut off the advancing Soviet troops. Furthermore, he expected no major problems in taking Italy. He viewed it as the soft underbelly of the Third Reich, a country with an unstable regime, easily waltzed through by the Allies. As far as the regime went, Churchill was right. But the waltzing was an altogether different story.

By spring 1943, Mussolini's political movement had lost its sparkle. Committed Fascists were to be found only among young people and the middle class. The party was severely divided and sorely compromised, the country was suffering from a famine, Mussolini himself was distracted by illnesses and love affairs. The entire Italian elite – the monarchists, the clerics, the entrepreneurs, the army, the police – was sick and tired of the war. In March 1943 massive strikes had already been held in Turin, Milan and elsewhere in northern Italy; after the February Strike in Amsterdam, these were the first major workers' shutdowns in Nazi-Fascist Europe.

The success of the Allied landing on Sicily – on the 'impregnable' island of Lampedusa where, the story has it, only one Allied soldier was injured: bitten by a donkey – was the last straw. In the early hours of 25 July, 1943, in the claustrophobic Sala del Pappagallo (Hall of the Parrot) in Rome's Palazzo Venezia, Mussolini was dethroned by the Great Fascist Council. The next day King Victor Emanuel III had him arrested and replaced as prime minister by the old field marshal, Pietro Badoglio. Mussolini was sent into exile at a ski resort near Gran Sasso in Abruzzo, close to L'Aquila, to what he called 'the highest prison in the world'.

Suddenly Italy had a new, anti-Fascist government, and it all happened more quickly than even the most fervent optimists had dared to hope. The news was almost too good to believe, and the Allies were taken by surprise. They had never paid much attention to indications of a possible coup; as a result, valuable weeks were lost negotiating a ceasefire. The Italians hoped to remain neutral, the Allies insisted on Italian support as the price for the 'passage back', as Churchill put it. There are even photographs of the American general, Maxwell Taylor, during a personal visit to Rome on 7 September, 1943, where he had gone to prepare for an airborne landing. (A scene as preposterous, for example, as a photograph would be of Montgomery walking calmly through Amsterdam in 1944.) The operation was called off when the paratroopers were already in the planes. The Allies were afraid to run the risk. They considered the Italian government too divided and too hesitant. The only ones who reacted decisively were the Germans: their troops came rushing over the Brenner Pass into Italy by the tens of thousands.

On 8 September the Italian capitulation was officially announced at last, but by then the *Wehrmacht* had northern and central Italy firmly in its grasp. The next day, the king, the army chiefs of staff and the government fled in panic to Brindisi, leaving behind no instructions for their troops. They abandoned Rome, the army and the rest of the country to the enemy. The drama on Kefallonia can also be traced in part to this irresponsible flight: it took almost a month for the Italian government to officially declare war on Germany. Meanwhile the Germans treated all armed Italians as fifth columnists. The Italians never forgave their king: in 1946 they voted overwhelmingly to abolish the monarchy.

In the chaotic days of September 1943, an airborne SS commando unit performed a unique stunt: using a few small planes, they freed Mussolini from his mountain prison. The soldiers guarding Il Duce did nothing to stop them: they had not heard from Rome for days. A week later, in Munich, Mussolini had recovered sufficiently to issue a call for revenge: 'Only blood can cancel so humiliating a page from the history of the *patria*!' Hitler gave him permission to set up his own government in the northern town of Salò, but he was never more than a marionette. Alongside the war proper, a civil conflict arose among the Italians themselves that would last until the end of the war: a struggle between Fascists and anti-Fascists, between the diehard supporters of the former regime and the partisans in the mountains and working-class neighbourhoods.

In the mud with the American infantrymen, Ernie Pyle noticed little of all these political squabbles. 'It's nothing but the weather and the lay of the land and the weather,' he noted on 14 December, 1943. 'If there were no German fighting troops in Italy, if there were merely German engineers to blow the bridges in the passes, if never a shot were fired at all, our northward march would still be slow.'

The Germans had thrown up their first major line of defence, the Gustav Line, straight across the mountains between Naples and Rome, with Monte Cassino as the vital corridor. Later they withdrew to the Gothic Line, which ran between Siena and Arezzo. After that, almost until the end of the war, they held a third line, the Alpine Line, close to the Austrian border.

Cassino today is a city without a heart or a memory, one of those piles of apartment complexes one comes across all over Europe, one of those places where a catastrophe must have taken place somewhere between 1939–45. In those days, this attractive, friendly Italian city had the misfortune of forming the gateway to Rome and the north of the country. On 19 May, 1944, when the Allies had finally broken through after months of fighting, Homer Bigart of the *New York Herald Tribune* described Cassino as a ghost town full of corpses and smoking ruins, 'more grim than a Calvinist conception of Hell'.

Martha Gellhorn counted no fewer than twenty different nationalities fighting together against the Germans all over Italy, and that is reflected in the gravestones of the war cemeteries around modern-day Cassino. Beneath the neatly clipped lawns lie thousands of young men from Poland, Britain, America, India, New Zealand, Australia, Canada, Italy, Germany and France. Flags wave, visitors and family come and go, these dead boys want for nothing, save their lives.

Cassino is a bitter place, a monument to waffling politicians and timid generals, the kinds of leaders who never pay for their own mistakes. That payment was reserved for the young men who lie here. Rome was finally liberated on 5 June, 1944. It could have happened nine months earlier. But the effect of that delay, and of Monte Cassino and those confused

September days of 1943, extends much further: because of it, no iron padlock was put in place between the Soviet Union and Europe. On the contrary, an iron curtain was drawn across Europe itself. Churchill's vision did not come to fruition, but his nightmare did come true.

Until autumn 1942 the war seemed to be going well for the Axis powers. Japan had conquered Malaysia, Singapore and the Dutch East Indies, the German troops moved through Russia almost with the nonchalance of tourists. But from early 1943 the cards seemed to have been reshuffled: Japan's offensive in the Pacific ground to a halt at Guadalcanal, the German 6th Army was destroyed at Stalingrad, Rommel suffered one defeat after the other in North Africa. In July 1943, the greatest tank battle in history was waged at Kursk. For a whole week, 6,000 tanks, more than 20,000 pieces of artillery and 1.5 million soldiers fought on a muddy plain more than fifty kilometres wide. Then the Germans pulled back. Their troops were needed in the West, to head off the Allied invasion of Italy.

After that summer the Axis powers suffered only defeats. From mid-1943 the Berlin papers were filled with the death notices of fallen soldiers and officers. Starting in 1944 there were so many names to report that they were all swept together into one huge daily combined advertisement under the rubric 'a hero's death'. Life in the city was increasingly disrupted by the bombardments: by mid-1943 more than a quarter of the population of Berlin had been evacuated to the countryside. Just as in 1918, the streets were filled with war invalids, boys on crutches, men missing an arm or a leg. In autumn 1943 one even began to hear jokes about the approaching defeat: 'What are you going to do after the war?' 'I'm going to take the bike and tour the borders of Germany.' 'And what are you going to do after lunch?'

The Gestapo's relative leniency towards 'normal' Germans had evaporated. Starting in March 1942, every form of defeatism was punishable by law. In Berlin alone in the first three months of 1943, fifty-one Germans were sentenced to death for listening to enemy radio broadcasts or expressing 'hostile' opinions. In the Flossenburg penal camp in Bavaria at least 30,000 German convicts were killed, including the renowned Lutheran theologian Dietrich Bonhoeffer, Admiral Wilhelm Canaris and Hans Oster, the *Abwehr* officer who had passed along the German plans for the invasion of the Netherlands. Ninety executions a day was not an abnormal tally at Flossenburg.

That malaise spread to the army units as well. Wolf Jobst Siedler, who fought in Italy, heard soldiers shout to each other: 'Enjoy the war, peace is going to be terrible.' In the field hospital where he ended up in late 1944, the wounded soldiers listened openly to swing music on the British radio.

On several occasions, elements within the *Wehrmacht*, along with certain key figures from the German churches, the former union movement and trade and industry, seemed on the brink of open revolt. As early as May 1942 contact had been established between the British government and the resistance group surrounding Bonhoeffer and his *Bekennende Kirche*. On 20 July, 1944, an attempt was made on Hitler's life. *Wehrmacht* officer Claus von Stauffenberg concealed a time bomb in his attaché case, took it into a staff meeting at the *Wolfsschanze*, placed the case under the table and left the room. Under normal circumstances, the force of the explosion that came a few minutes later would have killed everyone in the room. But the meeting had been moved at the last moment from the command bunker to a lighter barrack, and the number of victims remained limited. Hitler himself escaped with a torn uniform, punctured eardrums and a few scrapes and burns. It dawned on him only gradually that this attack had been meant as the starting sign for a general uprising against his regime. His rage and suspicion were uncontrollable.

For the Nazis, meanwhile, the war had become a 'sacred struggle' on behalf of Europe against the Bolshevik monster. In Berlin's Sportpalast on 18 February, 1943, immediately after the fall of Stalingrad, Goebbels had declared 'total war'. His speech was interrupted hundreds of times by cheering, singing and thundering applause, and the hall went wild at his final words: 'Now, Germans, rise up – and the storm breaks loose!'

In actual fact, Goebbels' speech was a desperate move: the situation had deteriorated so far that the German people had to be prepared psychologically for hard times. As Goebbels vouchsafed to his diary, he and his old companion-in-arms Göring had a long, private discussion on 2 March, 1943. Both were worried about Hitler's mental stability, and about the chaotic situation within Nazi headquarters. The Führer, both of them felt, had 'aged fifteen years in the three and a half that the war has lasted'.

Ribbentrop had failed completely as minister of foreign affairs: he had not made a single attempt to arrive at a modus vivendi with Britain. However, at the same time, Göring said, the Nazi command could not permit itself any sign of weakness. 'With regard to the Jewish question in particular, we have gone too far ever to get out.'

Chapter Forty-One

Rome

ROME. THESE ARE THE DAYS OF THE GREAT SUMMER HEATWAVE. THE local youth stands fomenting its own discontent on Campo dei Fiori till late into the night, across Piazza Navona saunter the beanpole families of Swedish schoolteachers, between the two squares the city is white with table linen. Above the ochre houses of the old working-class neighbour-hood of Trastevere, the church bells strike their tinny strokes, year after year.

In the early 1980s I came here often. Of the dozens of grocers' shops and vegetable stalls I remember from those years, one remains. Mario with his seven stray cats and his echoing voice, the king of our little street, moved away long ago. Americans live in his house now. Of the once innumerable clothes lines flapping with laundry, only two are left; from all the surrounding streets, they have disappeared completely. Around the fountain on Piazza Santa Maria, the flirting and sighing takes place in every European language.

The Germans and Pope Pius XII declared Rome an 'open city', a city that was to be sheltered from war. Yet every day German tanks and trucks rolled through its streets on their way to the southern front lines, and every day the 3rd SS Police Battalion marched ostentatiously through the old city. On 23 March, 1944, partisans detonated a powerful bomb in the Via Rasella during that daily parade. Thirty-two SS troops were killed, many times that number were wounded.

The reprisal came the next day. Close to the catacombs, in a cave at Fosse Ardeatine, 320 political prisoners were executed: truckload after truckload, they were pulled down, made to kneel, then shot in the back of the head.

The victims now lie in 320 sarcophagi beneath a monumental slab of stone, the space of two tennis courts full of marble and artificial flowers. After they were finished, the Germans blew up the entrance to the cave, but a shepherd had heard the shooting. The local priest, who had been warned, smelled the odour of rotting corpses, prayed and gave the victims 'provisional absolution'. On 26 March, Pius XII – who wrongly believed the attack to have been the work of communists – wrote in the *Osservatore Romano*: 'On the one hand 32 victims, and on the other 320 persons sacrificed for the guilty parties who escaped arrest'; as though the partisans, not the Germans, had been responsible for this massacre.

The Vatican had been warned as soon as the bodies were found. It did nothing. Family members came to bring flowers, the Germans blocked the entrance to the cave once more, and one of the priests, Don Ferdinando Georgi, was arrested. Still, the Bishop of Rome said nothing, not even when one of his own flock was involved.

The role of the Holy See in the Second World War was later the subject of heated discussion, and that is understandable. The twenty-year reign of Eugenio Pacelli was indeed marked by major contradictions. An ascetic, he lived on little more than a piece of bread and a glass of warm milk each day, but at the same time he surrounded himself with great pomp and strict norms. His piety was beyond all doubt, but archives and other sources paint a picture of an anti-Semite, a hater of communists, and a cynical opportunist. He sent out internal directives to help Jews, he played an important role behind the scenes in stopping the deportations from Hungary and Bulgaria, but he was also a sly negotiator who, to keep from compromising his own secular power, avoided all conflicts with the Nazi regime.

In the 1960s and 1970s, Gitta Sereny spoke at length with a number of the former policymakers from the notorious Berlin villa at Tiergartenstrasse 4. They told her – and this was later confirmed by court documents – that they had begun as early as 1939 in conferring with certain church leaders concerning their 'euthanasia' campaign. Before the campaign had even begun, the Nazis wanted to know whether the Church would actively oppose it. That turned out not to be the case. Sereny: 'According to all the information currently available to us – obtained officially or non-officially, by hook or by crook, from real or defrocked priests – it can be absolutely ruled out that the Church, which according to some has the "best intelligence network in the world", was ignorant of the case at hand.'

Something similar took place in France. The occasional bishop openly opposed the persecution of the Jews, but when Marshal Pétain asked the Pope in so many words for his 'advice' – read, approval – concerning a series of anti-Semitic measures, two members of the Vatican staff – including Giovanni Batista Montini, the future Pope Paul VI – replied that there could be 'no objection' to the measures, as long as they were carried out 'avec justice et charité'.

In Italy it was later often claimed that Pius XII saved tens of thousands of Jews by ordering all cloisters to open their doors to them. And from 1943 there were indeed impressive rescue operations carried out at the local level, but no clear leadership ever came from the Vatican.

The most striking incident took place on Saturday, 16 October, 1943, when a few SS battalions drove into Rome's old ghetto and held a mass razzia for the first time. More than 1,000 Jewish men, women and children were taken to the Collegio Militare, only a few hundred metres from St Peter's. The Pope heard about the round-up right away, from an acquaintance, during his morning prayers. Any number of trucks carrying terrified Jewish children drove almost literally past his window.

That morning, pressure was put on Pius XII from all sides to issue a papal ban on deporting Jews from the 'open city' of Rome. Remarkably enough that pressure came from German circles as well, particularly from the civil authorities. Why, for heaven's sake, did the relative peace of Rome have to be disturbed by the psychotic Jew-baiters of the SS?

The Pope, however, in the words of the German ambassador Ernst von Weizsäcker, would not let himself be drawn into 'any demonstrative expression against the deportation of Jews from Rome'. Five days after their deportation, almost all those families were gassed at Birkenau. Only fifteen Roman Jews came back alive.

In 1937, his predecessor Pius XI had voiced serious criticism of the deification of the German people, in his encyclical Met brennender Sorge. The papal letter was read aloud in Catholic churches all over Germany, and the Nazis did not impose a single sanction. A new encyclical against racism and anti-Semitism, Humani Generis Unitas, was being prepared when

Pius XI died in 1939. Pius XII quickly withdrew his predecessor's draft. In his view it was not the Nazis but the Bolsheviks who formed the greater threat to the Church. In fact, in his eyes, Germany constituted the vanguard in the fight against the Red Menace.

This fervent anti-communism was also probably behind another shameful episode from the pontificate of Pius XII: the Vatican's involvement in the escape of hundreds of German and Austrian mass murderers right after the war. Dr Josef Mengele, the notorious camp physician at Auschwitz, Adolf Eichmann, the organiser of the transport of the Jews, Franz Stangl, camp commandant at Treblinka, and many others received money, shelter, false documents and an escape route to South America from Vatican prelates.

Roma, città aperta. Mussolini's imperial fantasies were charted on great stone tablets along the Via dei Fiori Imperiali. They are still there today: the Greeks, the Roman Empire, only the plaque with the little Italian Empire of 1936–43 has been removed for decency's sake. The Olympic district close to the Ponte Duca d'Aosta still glistens in all its Fascist glory, and the same goes for several bridges over the Tiber. Here, history has not been polished away.

I move with the flow of tourists down the Via Giulia. At number 23 there is a memorial plaque for Giorgio Labo and Gianfranco Mattei. This is where they were arrested by the Germans on 1 February, 1944, then tortured for days and finally executed, but they never spoke a word. In gratitude, from their comrades, a fresh wreath has been put here very recently.

This country was forced to drink the bitter post-war draught in silence. 'Of course the Allies treated us harshly,' former partisan Vittorio Foa once told me. 'But after all, hadn't we misbehaved badly?' After 1943 the Germans, in turn, viewed the Italians as traitors. Had Hitler not been so fond of Mussolini, he would probably have given Italy the 'Polish treatment'. Dozens of villages were wiped out anyway – around Marzabotto, close to Bologna, more than 1,800 civilians were massacred in October 1944. Jews – Primo Levi among them – were deported by the thousand. Some 600,000 Italians ended up as German prisoners of war, an untold number of them died. The women were left to fend for themselves.

In March 1944, Ernie Pyle described how waiting American soldiers threw crackers and chocolate from a ship's deck to a group of hungry children on the dock at Naples. One little boy, wearing a pair of huge American GI boots, drew their attention by walking around on his hands. Then a few girls came for a cautious look. The sailors whistled and threw even more crackers. A skinny old woman stood a little to one side, until a seaman threw her a whole box of crackers. It was a good throw, and the old woman made a good catch. But she barely had it in her hands before the whole crowd pounced on her. 'The poor old woman never let go. She clung to it as though it were something human. And when the last cracker was gone she walked sort of blindly away, her head back and her eyes toward the sky, weeping with a hideous face just like that of a heartbroken child, still gripping the empty box.'

Chapter Forty-Two

Vichy

AT THE ENTRANCE TO THE FRÉJUS ROAD TUNNEL STANDS A TALL
policeman with hollow cheeks. All afternoon he stands preaching in word
and gesture to the trucks and the perspiring car drivers: drive carefully,
not too fast, keep your distance. Then comes thirteen kilometres of darkness, after which I drive into another world. The fields are not brownish-
yellow but green, the houses, roads and rules are clear and well defined,
all randomness has been abolished. But here, behind the Alps, the overwhelming Italian light has also gone out too. Within Europe, I realise,
there is yet another essential dividing line: the light line.

After the tunnel the weather changes, it is raining and the evenings are
already growing longer. In the villages the doors and shutters are closed,
the only light comes from a clubhouse close to a church where a meeting
is being held, or the aerobics night for the local women's club. I spend
the night at a camping ground in a pine forest, a village of tents and
caravans that seems drab even when the sun breaks through the next
morning. The camping ground is inhabited primarily by single men. The
roofs of their caravans are weathered, the canvas of their tents has turned
grey, they appear to be gradually becoming one with this forest. 'Most
of us live here all year round,' the man across the way tells me. He crosses
the camping ground slowly, leaning on his cane, his head held stiffly at
an angle, his swollen feet in a pair of slippers. A few couples live here
as well, and a few illegal immigrants, but most of the campers are men
like him. 'I'm from Caen, that's right, a divorce. And life here is cheap,
right?' But what about the cold? 'It only freezes here a few days each
winter, most years, and I get along fine with my kerosene heater.'

The tent attached to the front of his caravan has curtains and a television with a satellite dish, and he has gladioli in his little garden.
Everyone makes the best of his own poverty, here amid these silent
trees.

I am on my way to the remarkable land of Marshal Philippe Pétain, that
unoccupied territory ruled for four years from the casino and the Hôtel
du Parc in the remote spa town of Vichy, that roped-off France which
became a 'hopeless observer of the war' after the surrender was signed.

After June 1940, France was broken into six pieces. Marshal Pétain
ruled over approximately two fifths of the country. (After November 1942
that part, too, was occupied by the Germans, leaving him little room to
manoeuvre.) The south-eastern part of the country, around Nice, was in
Italian hands. A few northern coastal *départements*, which had been more
or less annexed to Belgium, were run by the German military authorities in Brussels. North-eastern France was reserved for future German
colonisation – for the French it was the *Zone interdite*, the forbidden zone.
Lorraine and Alsace had been incorporated into Germany without further
ado. The rest fell under the authority of the *Militärbefehlshaber* in Paris. The
French themselves had to pay the costs of the German occupation: twenty
million marks a day.

Driving through the country now, one is struck by the peculiar way
those boundaries were laid out: straight through provinces, sometimes
even straight through cities and villages. It seems as though in 1940
someone simply drew a few lines on the map, with the same lack of
concern the French had once shown in dividing up Africa. That, in fact,
characterises the Vichy regime: this 'free' bit of France existed only as
long as the German had no need for it.

The choice of the bathing resort of Vichy was also made more or
less at random. With its 300 hotels, it was the only place where the
ministries that been driven out of Paris could settle down without a
problem. Pétain was immediately enthusiastic: the city had a fast train
to Paris, the climate was mild, the citizenry consisted mainly of the
prosperous and the conservative, and its remoteness made it a pleasant
place of work for every bureaucrat who did not want to be bothered
by the rest of the world.

Vichy was a town at loose ends, it was neither French nor truly cosmopolitan, it awakened in the spring and hibernated all winter. It was with Vichy that the word 'collaboration' assumed its modern connotation – but there it simply meant 'cooperation'. What we now call defeatism, it called realism. Pétain was held in adulation. Vichy was at war with Great Britain: that, at least, was how people saw it. General de Gaulle, who had fled to London with his Free French Forces, was the great turncoat. That was the attitude during the first years of the war. After 1944, half of France made a complete about-turn.

These days the French are reasonably aware of what happened in their country between 1940–4. But at first, certainly for the first two or three decades afterwards, the country lived in deep silence when it came to the war. In 1971, cineaste Marcel Ophüls was the first to produce a clear-eyed and remarkable documentary about Vichy, *Le chagrin et la pitié*. One year later the young American historian Robert Paxton got the debate rolling among his colleagues. In his study *Vichy France: Old Guard and New Order*, Paxton was the first to make use of German documents which had never been consulted by French historians. Inevitably, those documents showed that the story the French had been telling their children and themselves for years was wide of the mark. Vichy was in no way the product of an elderly president and a few hundred powerless French officials working under severe pressure from the German occupiers. On the contrary: it was a fresh new regime with great aspirations, supported and lauded by millions of French citizens. It was not merely the transitional stage, the provisional government that the official annals of French history tried to make of it. It was a regime with pronounced anti-Semitic traits, and with far-reaching plans to reorganise French society along authoritarian, corporative lines, more or less the same lines applied earlier in Portugal by the dictator Salazar.

Modern-day Vichy is not a city of lies, but definitely one of 'lacunae and blank spots'. As if by a miracle, life there has halted in summer 1939. The shaded streets behind the hotels are full of the art deco villas and pseudo-oriental castles of the once-worshipped miracle doctors and masseurs. People still converse beneath the old plane trees and chestnuts in front of the casino, the town has a long covered walkway to protect strollers from rain and sun, and every day one still runs into Chekhov's 'lady with the little dog'.

In Vichy itself, only one historical 'fact' remains visible: a high, pock-marked wall in the park along the Allier River, topped with shreds of barbed wire once put there by the Gestapo to shield its headquarters from prying eyes. That wall, along with a few coins and letters in the little municipal museum, is the only concrete reminder of 'the period', as the citizens of Vichy prefer to call the war years.

Otherwise it is only the names that continue to haunt. The Hôtel du Portugal, once the Gestapo headquarters, is still called Le Portugal, and the same applies to the Hôtel Moderne of the Milice Française, the paramil-itary organisation of Vichy whose job it was to stamp out the Resistance.

The chic Hôtel du Parc, the seat of the Vichy government and Pétain's private residence, has been christened 'Le Parc', but otherwise everything remains the same: the balcony from which the marshal received the cheers of hundreds of Frenchmen during the Sunday parades, the pave-ments along which his supporters, standing five deep, raised their voices almost every day in the Vichy anthem:

> Maréchal, nous voilà
> Devant toi, le sauveur de la France.
> Nous jurons, nous, les gars,
> De servir et de suivre tes pas.

Marshal, here we are! Saviour of France, we, your men, swear to serve and follow in your footsteps.

In those days, in the streets off the boulevards, there were scores of smaller hotels where some 100,000 civil servants found shelter. Provisional ministries were set up in the Grand Casino, with dividing walls made of archive boxes. 'In the streets of our city, the crowds of passers-by, hands in their pockets and collars turned up, scatter in every direction like nervous ants,' a journalist wrote in the Progrès de l'Allier on 27 January, 1942. To combat the worst of the cold, the officials installed simple wood stoves. 'Everywhere were the long black necks of pipes, sweating drops of sooty liquid.'

Most of the officials were young, and the atmosphere was one of excitement, often steamy and sensual. Marches were held regularly, and a concert was given each week by the *Garde Républicaine*. In 1940 Pétain was as popular with the average Frenchman as de Gaulle was at the time of the country's liberation in 1944. He signed his first laws in truly royal fashion, 'We, Philippe Pétain . . .', and the people loved it. From the very start he concentrated more power in his person than any French head of state since Napoleon. In old age he had his moments of weakness and confusion, but mostly he was clear-witted and full of vitality.

Pétain's ideal France was rural, personal, familial. It was the old, pre-revolutionary France that he hoped to resurrect in modern form, a France without individualism, liberalism, democracy and cosmopolitanism. Before me lies his credo, *La France Nouvelle*, a little booklet with a red, blue and white border that was read to tatters all over France during the war. The first lines of his manifesto: 'Man has, by nature, certain fundamental rights. These can only be guaranteed him by the communities that surround him: the Family that raises him, the Profession that nurtures him, the Nation that protects him.' I go on turning the pages, but nowhere do I find the language of Hitler or Mussolini. The book consists almost entirely of speeches and exhortations, and it is above all extremely Catholic: 'The Social Politics of Education', 'On Individualism and the Nation', 'Message concerning the Pensioning of the Elderly', 'Message to the Mothers of France', and so on.

The Vichy regime was not a National Socialist regime, it was not imposed by the Germans, it was home-grown. There were not very many French Nazis. There were, however, militant right-wing thinkers who hoped for a new, authoritarian order – a tradition present in France today. One of them, the author Robert Brasillach, wrote just before he was executed for collaboration in winter 1945: 'We were bedfellows with the Germans and we must admit that we were fond of some of them.' But above all, the regime was legitimised by respectable intellectuals and members of the upper middle class, upstanding French patriots who were none too willing to bow to their defeat, who desired no more war and were prepared to mould themselves to the Nazis' new Europe.

In practice, their 'collaboration' meant that Vichy took a great deal of work off the Germans' hands. The regime organised the country's own colonisation: the plundering of industry, agriculture and national reserves, the forced labour in Germany and, not least, the deportation of the Jews. The Vichy regime took the first anti-Jewish measures on its own initiative, without instructions from Germany, and with remarkable vigour. On 17 July, 1940, only one week after the regime came to power, it decided that public functions were to be reserved for those of French parentage: a measure with immediate repercussions for the some 200,000 Jewish refugees who had sought asylum in France. On 22 July, a committee was set up to review all acts of naturalisation. On 3 October, the Jewish Statute was implemented, the start of an avalanche of measures – professional bans, mandatory registrations, greater and lesser forms of discrimination – directed against the Jews. By late 1940, some 60,000 people, mostly non-French Jews, were already interned in around 30 concentration camps.

France's long tradition of anti-Semitism returned to full bloom after July 1940. Who else was to bear the blame but the internationalists, the decadent intellectuals, those who had 'sullied' the republic with 'modern' views, who else but the Jews? In December 1940, the Parisian anti-Semitic weekly *Au Pilori* (In the Pillory) started a contest among its 60,000 (!) readers for the best answer to how one could be rid of the Jews. First prize: a pair of silk stockings. Best entries: drop them in the jungle among the wild animals, or burn them in crematoria.

Vichy built upon this mentality, but in a different way from the Nazis. The anti-Semitism of the Vichy regime was more nationalistic than racist; for Vichy, it was about the creation of second-class citizenship for French Jews and the removal of non-French Jews, but not about the destruction of the Jewish race. Second only to Denmark, France remains the country with the highest proportion of Jewish survivors: less than a quarter of the Jewish population was deported, as opposed to more than three quarters in, for example, the Netherlands.

In that part of France occupied by the Germans, however, the mass murders continued apace. The first trains loaded with deportees left Paris for Auschwitz in early 1942. On 16–17 July, 1942, more than 12,000 Parisian Jews were arrested during *La Grande Rafle*. Thousands of French policemen were involved in that razzia. Some sources speak of 9,000 policemen in total, but what is certain is that the SS could not have acted effectively without the assistance and organisational talent of the Paris

police. At the same time, this series of raids was almost certainly sabotaged by the police as well: the SS had hoped to make 25,000 arrests.
Annette Kriegel, fifteen years old at the time, described the start of the
round-up along her own street, the rue de Turenne: 'I saw a policeman
carrying suitcases in both hands and weeping. I will never forget the tears
running down that rough, ruddy face, for you will agree with me that
one rarely sees a policeman cry in public. He walked down the street,
followed by a little group of children and old people, all carrying little
bundles.' Annette escaped, but did not know where to go. Finally she sat
down on a park bench and waited: 'It was on that bench that I left my
childhood behind.'

In Vichy and the surrounding countryside, the rounding up of Jews was
a matter for the French themselves. In an enormous razzia held between
26–8 August, 1942, at least 10,000 policemen combed the woods and
neighbouring mountains in search of runaway Polish and German Jews
who had considered themselves safe in non-occupied France. In Marseilles,
Lyons, Sète and Toulouse, too, the French police mounted large-scale raids.
    French cooperation in the deportations stood in stark contrast to the
growing resistance in the country's Italian zone. In spring 1943, the Italian
authorities in Valence, Chambéry and Annecy forbade the rounding up
of Jews, both refugees and non-refugees, by French prefects. In Megève,
the Fascist police chief blocked the arrests of 7,000 Jews. Under the
watchful eye of the Italians, Nice actually became a blossoming Jewish
centre. The refugees were issued their own identity cards, and the
commander of the *carabinieri* announced that any French policeman who
dared to touch a hair on their head would be arrested himself. In addition, on 21 March, 1943, the Italian occupation forces in France received
an urgent personal missive from Mussolini: 'The first priority is to bring
to safety those Jews living in that part of French territory occupied by
our troops, whether they be of Italian, French or any other nationality.'
The German and French authorities were enraged. As soon as the Italians
withdrew in September 1943, huge razzias were held in the area they
had occupied. Several thousand Jews were arrested, but the vast majority
were able to escape into the mountains.

Chapter Forty-Three

Saint-Blimont

'WE FIND OURSELVES IN THE EXASPERATING SITUATION IN WHICH THE fate of France no longer depends on the French themselves,' Marc Bloch wrote in summer 1940.

It was a feeling he shared with many of his countrymen. 'For my father, Vichy was synonymous with treason,' Lucienne Gaillard, president of the Veterans of the Resistance in Picardy, told me. She was the daughter of André Gaillard, better known in the Resistance by his pseudonym 'Léon', watchman at the sugar beet processing plant in Saint-Blimont. He was a true French patriot, he abhorred all forms of collaboration. As soon as the surrender was signed he began, on his own at first, with small acts of defiance against the occupier: slogans on walls, the sabotage of machinery and transports. Later he and his comrades began attacking German outposts, mostly to obtain weapons. 'They called my father and his friends terrorists and communists. But it was really a political mish-mash, they didn't belong to any political party,' Lucienne Gaillard said.

And so began the Resistance: as an ad hoc grass-roots movement of French men and women of every background, a guerrilla group comprised of enthusiastic amateurs. Soon they were receiving weapons from England and training from British undercover agents, yet they remained autonomous and self-willed. The communists hesitated at first, but after the German invasion of the Soviet Union they, too, joined the Resistance in numbers. Along with them came hundreds of thousands of refugees who often set up separate cells of their own, and quite frequently played a heroic role. In the south-western corner of the country the Spanish communists had their own 14th Corps, which had thirty-four guerrilla fighters by June 1944. The Poles ran their own intelligence service, the

R2, an important factor in the struggle. Spaniards were the first to set up a Maquis group in the Ardèche, German communists reinforced the groups in the Gard and Lozère. A British agent sent to help the Resistance at Villefranche-du-Périgord reported that his French was of no service to him there: the members of the group spoke only Spanish or Catalan.

The growing hostility – in which the clergy played an important role – towards anti-Semitic measures provided a major stimulus for the Resistance. In many other ways the Catholic Church remained loyal to the Vichy regime, but in summer 1942 a bitter conflict arose concerning the treatment of the Jews. On 23 August, the elderly Bishop of Toulouse, Jules-Gerard Saliège, had a pastoral missive read aloud from the pulpits of his diocese, in which he roundly condemned the hounding of Jews: 'Jews are men. Jews are women. They are a part of humanity. They are our brothers, like anyone else. A Christian may not forget that.'

The letter caused a chain reaction: dozens of other bishops and church leaders followed his lead. An ecclesiastical resistance group began smuggling Jewish children out of Vénissieux, one of the worst transit camps, close to Lyons. A totally new source of resistance arose in this way: Catholics who sympathised in principle with Pétain but could no longer reconcile their consciences to the burgeoning manhunt by Vichy and the Germans. They arranged countless hiding places for Jews and others on the run, they provided food and protection, and gradually many of them came to join the armed resistance. The Protestants, who enjoyed a long tradition of resistance, had gone into action much earlier. Many Jewish families were given shelter in Protestant villages in the Cevennes, often with the tacit approval of the entire community.

During that same summer of 1942, André Gaillard and eight others set up their own combat group. They destroyed German lines of communication, took in Allied pilots who had been shot down and kept watch on all German activities in 'their' zone. 'Almost everything happened in this house,' Lucienne Gaillard told me. 'Pilots, weapons, the wounded, everything.' Wasn't she ever afraid? 'Not at all. It was an ecstatic time, we all found it equally exciting.' She gave me an overview of what their group did; I cite here only those actions which took place between August and December 1943.

On 3 August, her father and his men blew up a rocket launcher.

On 23 August, they derailed a German transport train; the Germans in their zone were always busy reinforcing the coastline in connection with a possible invasion.

On the night of 23 October they blew up a troop transport headed to Russia, causing great losses of men and equipment.

On 28 October they sabotaged the Paris-Calais line, causing a train full of troops and war materials to fly off the rails at top speed.

On 11 November – using pinpoint information from French railway personnel – they derailed another military train on the same line. They were pleased with the effects of these attacks, because they blocked German reinforcements for days and produced quite a few casualties and a permanent loss of German materials.

On 16 November, a huge load of flax that had been confiscated by the Germans was burned.

On the night of 10 December, with the help of the local police sergeant, they freed two Resistance fighters from the gendarmerie in Gamaches, just before they were to be transferred to the Gestapo prison at Abbeville.

On 16 December, they blew up a munitions train; when a German backup train arrived the next day, they pulled the engineer out of the engine, set full throttle and let the unmanned train crash at full speed into the wreck of the artillery transport they had derailed the day before.

On 28 December they blockaded the rails again, causing the crash of an engine and four carriages.

By 1944, André Gaillard's little group of amateurs had developed into an experienced guerrilla company of the Forces Françaises de l'Intérieur (FFI), with 7 officers, 22 non-commissioned officers and 160 soldiers. They now formed part of one large army: the Free French Forces, who fought alongside the Allies in Africa and Italy and the various Resistance groups, of the left and of the right, within France itself.

In the end, eighteen men and women from this group in Picardy – a group likes hundreds of others in France – were killed. Two of them died before the firing squad, six others were killed in skirmishes and fifteen were sent to concentration camps. Only ten of them came back.

Meanwhile, in faraway London, General de Gaulle was trying to save the French national honour. In June 1940 he had left for England, as he said himself, empty-handed. 'My father,' Lucienne Gaillard said, 'started his resistance work after an appeal by de Gaulle. The general was very important to us, he was a symbol, but at the same time he didn't really exist. He was not closer to us than Napoleon.'

Churchill, who had a weakness for France and initially for de Gaulle as well, could help him in only two ways: he gave recognition to his French National Committee as the only legitimate French authority, and he gave him the opportunity to speak to the French regularly through the BBC.

De Gaulle made the most of both opportunities. In June 1940 almost no one in France listened to his broadcasts. By 1941, according to estimates from his Vichy opponents, there were 300,000 listeners; by 1942 there were 3 million. He always spoke of the Resistance as though it were a regular standing army, rather than a guerrilla force of beginners that consisted at first of fewer than 7,000 men and women. He saw himself as its natural commander-in-chief. That the members of the Resistance themselves, particularly the communists and socialists, had different ideas about that did not seem to concern him. From the start he worked on a new national myth, a hopeful historical tale that was to resurrect the French morale. 'In 1940, France lost a battle, but not the war,' he kept repeating.

If the notion of a 'conceptual nation' applied to anywhere, it was to de Gaulle's idea of France. A nation, after all, consists of more than shared territory and a common language, of governmental and cultural unity and everything that may flow from that, but also of a communal mentality, of the sense that that unity exists in the minds of all citizens, and that it is valuable, an honour and a joy in which to participate. In France, more than in any other European country, this sense of grandeur had traditionally been cultivated to great heights. That explains why the collapse of 1940 was so precipitous: the French had lost their conceptual nation. It was above all to this mental crisis that both Pétain and de Gaulle tried to find a solution, each in his own way.

In doing that, de Gaulle had to operate as a Baron Munchausen: only by his own hair could he pull himself and his horse out of the quagmire. He had, in reality, almost no power, even his costs were at first largely defrayed by the British government. At the same time, his conceptual nation demanded that he behave like a great and powerful statesman, self-willed and independent of the other allies. 'General de Gaulle needs constantly reminding that our primary enemy is Germany,' someone in his coterie once noted. 'For if he were to follow his natural instinct, it would be Britain.' De Gaulle's conceptual France was still a world power, and seen from that vantage both Great Britain and the United States remained his major rivals.

On 20 January, 1941, Harold Nicolson, in those years parliamentary secretary at the ministry of information, lunched with de Gaulle at London's Savoy hotel. 'I do not like him,' he wrote in his diary. 'He accuses my ministry of being *Pétainiste.* "*Mais non!*" I say, "*Monsieur le Général!*" "Well, then at least *Pétainisant.*" "We are working," I tell him, "for all of France." "All of France!" he shouts. "That is the Free France. That is ME!'" In late 1941 they dined again. 'His arrogance and fascism annoy me. But there is something like a fine retriever dog about his eyes.'

Churchill too saw in de Gaulle an impassioned and emotional spirit. Churchill knew the French, he recognised the importance of symbolic figures for an occupied France and understood the complexity of the political situation within which de Gaulle had to manoeuvre. Despite all their conflicts, there were also moments of reconciliation and friendship between the two statesmen.

Roosevelt, who barely had personal ties with de Gaulle, wrote the general off quite quickly. He considered him to be an 'almost intolerable' idiot, and seriously doubted his authority over the French. For the American president, it was unimaginable that a modern Western democracy like France could accept the authority of a strictly self-declared leader. Following a conference in Casablanca in January 1943, Roosevelt publicly joked about de Gaulle: 'One day he says he's Joan of Arc, the next day he says he's Clémenceau. I told him: you've got to decide which one you want to be!'

After two years of war, therefore, de Gaulle found himself increasingly isolated, a powerless nuisance in the eyes of the Allies, a caricature of himself in the eyes of many of his supporters. Regularly, after yet another quarrel, he would be denied access to the BBC microphone. On one occasion, in April 1942, Churchill even issued orders that he not be allowed to leave England: at that point, de Gaulle was effectively his prisoner.

Jean Monnet, acting as liaison between the three statesmen, noticed in his talks with the general 'a mixture of practical intelligence that can only command one's respect, and a disturbing tendency to go beyond the boundaries of common sense.'

De Gaulle's relationship with the Resistance in France was also a troubled one. He mistrusted the communists in particular. Many Resistance leaders suspected, on the other hand, that de Gaulle was using the guerrilla force primarily to advance his own ambitions, for after the war. Despite all his pretensions of leadership, the lines of communication between him and the Resistance only developed systematically after autumn 1941.

In March 1942, the first Resistance leader arrived in London for personal consultations. Christian Pineau, leader of the large Libération Nord organisation, described his meeting with de Gaulle as an audience with an 'authoritarian prelate' who mostly delivered monologues and had no interest at all in the daily problems encountered by the Resistance. British documents released more than fifty years later show that in May 1943 Churchill and Roosevelt were on the point of expelling de Gaulle from the Allied command. Between themselves they spoke of him as the 'prima donna' and 'the bride', and hoped to replace him with his rival General Henri Giraud. 'He hates England and has left a trail of Anglophobia behind him everywhere,' Churchill wrote in a coded telegram to his cabinet during a visit to Washington.

Yet the Allies did not dare publicly to dethrone de Gaulle. He was too important for the French, and had indeed succeeded in working his way up to the status of a kind of Joan of Arc, a living monument, a modern myth.

De Gaulle moved his headquarters from London to Algiers, where he was free to implement his own brand of politics. In June 1944, when the invasion of France was about to take place after years of preparation, he was informed about the landing with a day and a half's notice. Although the rest of the Allied command was involved with other hectic issues at that moment, de Gaulle immediately demanded their full attention. And what was his problem? The soldiers had French money with them that had been issued without his approval, and Eisenhower, in the text of his planned speech, had not said a word about de Gaulle or the Free French

Forces. Futilities and formalities in the eyes of the British and the Americans
— '*Allez, faites la guerre, avec votre fausse monnaie!*' Churchill shouted — but de
Gaulle did not see it that way. As the paratroopers of the British 6th
Airborne Division were about to seize the first strategic bridges in France,
de Gaulle decided at the last moment to recall the 200 French liaison
officers who were to accompany the invasion. He himself threatened to
go straight back to Algiers. American General George C. Marshall shouted
angrily that 'no sons of Iowa would fight to put up statues of de Gaulle'.

De Gaulle was the great nuisance again, but once more he finally took
part loyally in all the actions. But was he really wrong? In the final analysis:
no. The problem, after all, was due to the American's refusal to take him
seriously, even though — after Giraud stepped down in 1943 — all representatives of free France had emphatically recognised him as their leader.
Nor was it de Gaulle's fault that the issue of temporary authority over
France — for that, in fact, was what this was all about — was raised only
at the eleventh hour: it was the British and the Americans who had
confronted him with a fait accompli by waiting until 4 June to tell him
about the invasion.

In his heart of hearts, Churchill understood that, but his interests lay
elsewhere. During lunch that day, when an enraged de Gaulle shouted
that he had not been consulted at all, not even in regard to the provisional authority over France, Churchill sneered back at him: 'And what
about you? How do you expect us, the British, to adopt a position separated from that of the United States? We are going to liberate Europe,
but it is because the Americans are with us to do so. For get this quite
clear, every time we have to decide between Europe and the open sea, it
is always the open sea we shall choose. Every time I have to decide
between you and Roosevelt, I shall always choose Roosevelt.'

De Gaulle would never forget those words. In 1963 he used his veto
as president of France to block British admission to the European Economic
Community: by admitting them, Europe would also be admitting the
Trojan Horse of America. In 1966 he withdrew France from the military
organisation of NATO: the American troops were to leave Europe, and
certainly to leave France. About 26,000 GIs were sent home. The American
secretary of state, Dean Rusk, cynically asked de Gaulle whether 'the dead
Americans in the military cemeteries' also fell under the evacuation orders.

A cartoonist drew a GI on his way out, shouting to the president: 'If you need us again, our number is 14–18 – 39–45!' That year, de Gaulle travelled to Moscow to establish new ties with Eastern Europe.

And time after time, in intimate circles, he would recount Churchill's words from June 1944.

Finally there is the story of all those millions of French citizens in occupied France. After the confusion, the fleeing and the humiliation, they felt the impact of foreign occupation chiefly in their stomachs. On an unheard-of scale, the Germans quickly picked their part of the country to the bone, and that soon became felt. In October 1941, the Parisian authorities were warning against the use of cat meat in daube provençale.

In addition, as from 1942, millions of men from the occupied territories were transported to Germany to perform forced labour there at the factories and farms, and this new manhunt drove people all over Europe into the arms of the Resistance. Former Vichy supporters also now became convinced that, in practical terms, Hitler's European *Grossraumwirtschaft* amounted to nothing less than a European economy dedicated solely to the service of Germany.

In the Lozère, the Cevennes, the Creuze, Auvergne, the Massif Central, in all those huge, sparsely populated mountainous regions, the 'unregistered', the refugees and those dodging the *Arbeitseinsatz*, quickly formed resistance groups of their own, operating more or less independently of the official Resistance. As early as summer 1942, the word *maquis* – Corsican for rough, wooded terrain – had become a normal part of the French vocabulary. '*Prendre le maquis*' was the expression used both for going into hiding in the French interior and joining the Resistance. In autumn 1943, the southern French Resistance estimated the number of *Maquisards* at 15,000.

Unlike the official Resistance, the Maquis was and remained a spontaneous movement taken part in primarily by young people. They formed something like Robin Hood clans, each with its own subculture, its own jargon and its own leader, always on the move, always busy surviving. Each group carried out its own war against Vichy and the Germans. Most of them were hardly involved in any coordinated resistance activities, such as espionage for London, systematic sabotage or support for the Allies.

The leader of the Maquis in the Drôme, L'Hermine, wandered the countryside in a black cape decorated with his own coat of arms. When the British philosopher A. J. Ayer arrived as an undercover agent in south-west France just before the liberation, he found the region, in his own words, to be 'in the hands of a series of feudal lords whose power and influence were strangely similar to that of their fifteenth-century Gascon counterparts.'

In January 1943, the Vichy regime launched the Milice Française, a large countermovement of at least 30,000 blackshirts. Their oath of honour made no bones about the true business at hand: 'I swear to fight against democracy, against the Gaullist revolt and against the cancer of Judaism . . .' From the start to the very finish, of course, the Maquis and the Milice Française were arch-enemies, although it became increasingly unclear who was hunting whom. As it had in Italy, all this rage and desperation finally resulted in a civil war of unknown cruelty, la guerre franco-française.

A total of some 30,000 French Resistance fighters were executed between 1940–5. About 60,000 were sent to concentration camps, and 20,000 disappeared without a trace.

After more than half a century of utter silence, what remains of a real, live French village from 1944? A morning's drive from Vichy is the village of Oradour-sur-Glane. Between the charred walls lie bedsteads, rusted bicycles and the remains of a sewing machine. Grass grows on the torched boulangerie of the Bouchoule family, the wrecked cars in the garage that belonged to the family Désourteaux, the petrol station of M. Poutaraud. On summer evenings the village danced at l'Avenir Musical, while the tram peeped and squeaked down the street and Dr Désourteaux raced off in his Renault to a late house call. The overhead tram lines still hang above the street, even the doctor's Renault stands rusting beside the road, but otherwise everything here came to a dead halt on 10 June, 1944.

In the local museum you can see a brief film of the village made in 1943. It contains the following scenes: a laughing couple pushing a pram; people swimming in the River Glane, lovers kissing in the grass; a picnic – a man points jovially at the camera; a child chases a running dog, and turns for a moment to look back. That is the last movement from Oradour that has been preserved.

Zamość, Anogia, Putten, Lidice, Marzabotto – throughout the twentieth century echoes the weeping and wailing of collectively punished
villages, and since Srebrenica we know that things can get even worse.
But Oradour is about more than that. Oradour symbolises the impotence
and discord within France itself. Soldiers of the SS *Das Reich* Panzer Division
encircled the peaceful village in the afternoon of 10 June, took the children from the classrooms, herded all the villagers together and suddenly
began shooting. By midnight they had liquidated almost the entire population: 191 men, 245 women, 140 schoolchildren, 67 babies, toddlers and
young children: 643 souls. The men were shot and killed, and women
and children driven into the church and burned alive. The oldest was
Marguerite Foussat, ninety years old. The youngest Maurice Vilatte, three
months.

The reason behind the massacre remains unclear. Today people suspect
that the SS made a mistake: forty kilometres from here was the village
of Oradour-sur-Vayres, a hotbed of resistance. During the trial, held in
February 1953, the full facts of the case became painfully clear: of the
twenty-one defendants, fourteen were from France itself, from Alsace.
They had been conscripted into the German Army, they said, and had
only been following orders. After the verdict was handed down – two
were sentenced to death, the others to hard labour – so many protests
poured in from Alsace that the French government finally granted amnesty
to all the murderers.

Infuriated, the handful of survivors from Oradour-sur-Glane sent their
medals and their *Légions d'honneur* back to Paris, and refused to have anything
more to do with the French state.

A number of highly successful public relations campaigns were carried
out after the Second World War. The Austrians succeeded in transforming
themselves from enthusiastic co-culprits into fellow victims. The cautious
Dutch suddenly became robust heroes of the resistance, every one of
whom had hidden an Anne Frank in their attic. But what the French got
away with borders on the unbelievable. Whenever the war was discussed
in France, it was always in terms of glory and triumph, as though there
had been no defeat, chaos, starvation, despondency or collaboration.

That image is due to General de Gaulle and his 300,000 Free French

Forces, to the heroes of the Resistance and to courageous bands of *Maquisards*. They fought bravely all over Europe, they gave France a new dignity and a new face, and their incredible courage is justly applauded. Yet it remains astounding to see how, after 1944, all of France suddenly emerged victorious from the wings. Vichy, after all, remained the legitimate government of France till the very end: the National Assembly granted Pétain its full mandate on 10 July, 1940. At the casino in Vichy there now hangs a plaque commemorating the 80 representatives who voted against him, but nothing is said about the 569 (with 17 abstaining) who actually *did* vote for Pétain.

In Fascist Italy, the persecution of the Jews was sabotaged everywhere. From the French town of Drancy, on 17 August, 1944, eight days before Paris was liberated, a train was still able to leave for Auschwitz with 700 prisoners. A little more than a week later, de Gaulle was welcomed by at least a million cheering Parisians. What is forgotten is the hundreds of thousands who had enthusiastically welcomed Pétain only four months earlier, when he visited the city on 26 April, 1944 to commemorate the victims of war. Of 1.5 million French public officials, only around 30,000 were ever penalised in any way for their collaboration, including their assistance in the deportation of Jews. Papon, the Jew-hunter of Bordeaux, was able to build a new and glorious career in post-war France; he became the chief of police in Paris under de Gaulle, and ultimately even a cabinet minister. In 1953 almost all of the collaborators were granted amnesty. By 1958, fourteen former Vichy officials were already back in the French parliament.

After a series of complicated manoeuvres, de Gaulle was finally able to make his triumphal entry into Paris on 26 August, 1944. 'Paris, Paris abused, Paris broken, Paris martyred but Paris liberated by her own people with the help of the armies of France!' he shouted, with characteristic rhetoric. And everyone cheered, even though almost no French troops had taken part in the heroic landings on D-Day, even though de Gaulle himself had not worked on the preparations, even though only a single division of the Free French Forces had fought along with the total of 39 in Normandy, and even though only a small portion of the population of Paris – according to reliable estimates, no more than 15,000 men and women – had taken an active part in the Resistance. None of that mattered. De Gaulle's conceptual France had won, and after 1945 would even oversee one of Germany's occupied zones.

For what France needed was a grand historical account, to get back on its feet again and to redefine itself as a nation. The Resistance, the Maquis and the Free French Forces made great sacrifices. But all over the country the war cemeteries are full of 'perfidious' Englishmen and 'decadent' Americans, 'dirty' Jews and 'stinking' Spanish refugees, and countless Poles who were never given credit for a single victory.

IX September 1944–56

FINLAND

○ Helsinki   ○ Leningrad

○ Tallinn

○ Moscow

○ Riga

○ Minsk

SOVIET UNION

○ Kursk

Volga

Warsaw

POLAND

○ Kiev

Dnepr

○ Rostov

Don

VAKIA

Dnistr

Bug

Sea
of Azov

○ Krasnodar

○ Budapest

○ Odessa

Crimea

HUNGARY

○ Tiflis

RUMANIA

○ Bucharest

Danube

Black
Sea

Belgrade

OSLAVIA   BULGARIA

○ Sofia

○ Istanbul

○ Ankara

Tigris

ALBANIA   ○ Saloniki

TURKEY

GREECE

○ Athens

SYRIA

Euphrates

Mediterranean

Crete

⟸ Geert Mak's Route

⟵ Landing in Normandy, June–August 1944

0   100   200   300 km

Chapter Forty-Four

Bénouville

Cigarette Break

The skirmish was suddenly over.
We stopped to roll a smoke
and the Germans did too and
so there we stood,
insane, across from each other –
barely on our feet still.
'Cigarette break,' someone said hoarsely.
The German nodded understandingly: '*Ja, Pause. Sofort!*'
We sat down, them and us, in the grass
five paces away from each other;
we laid our rifles at our feet
and plucked
tobacco from our bags.
Yes, the things one sees in war!
Pass it along, not a soul in hell
will believe you. Then calmly, silently
– cautiously looking each other in the eye –
we ground out the final roll-ups, they their cigarettes,
and the same voice rasped, raw and bloodshot:
'End of cigarette break!'

Yuri Belash, veteran, Moscow

———

Normandy. The 84th Field Company of the British Royal Engineers at Sword Beach on the morning of 6 June, 1944. The two men in the foreground, a worried-looking soldier and a shouting corporal, are already walking on the sand. It may be the last picture ever taken of them, for the chances of survival on Sword Beach were at that point slim indeed. But it is the foreground of this first invasion photograph in particular that tells the story like a medieval painting: the landing craft in the morning mist, the men wading onto the beach – one bent double, another being helped along, a third running.

Ernie Pyle described the situation two days later: 'Men were sleeping on the sand, some of them sleeping forever. Men were floating in the water, but they didn't know they were in the water, for they were dead.' Beneath the waves lay hundreds of trucks and landing craft, often with crew and all, that hadn't made the beach. Of the thirty-two amphibious tanks, twenty-seven had sunk like bricks in the rough seas. The beach was covered in wrecked vehicles, and an entire set of office equipment had even spilled from one tracked vehicle, complete with hanging maps and crushed typewriters. 'There is nothing left but the remains: the lifeless rubbish, the sun and the flowers, and the complete silence,' Pyle wrote. 'Everything was dead – the men, the machines, the animals . . .'

Now I am walking those same beaches. All that is left to the naked eye are the concrete remains of two floating harbours, plus dozens of half-buried bunkers and turrets from the former Atlantic Wall. But beneath the cold, green water of the coast lies a complete graveyard. These days enthusiasts sometimes winch whole Sherman amphibious tanks from the water, full of crustaceans that have attached themselves through the years. In the museums the tourists crowd past the corroded soup spoons, motorbikes, telephones, amphibious jeeps, boots, rifles and punctured helmets. At a special theatre at Arromanches they can experience 'the total D-Day emotion' in only eighteen minutes. At the Pointe du Hoc – sticking up against the sky like a blade – they are amazed (and who is not?) at the mad courage of over 200 commandos of the American 116th Infantry Regiment who scaled this steep rock with ropes and ladders under heavy machine-gun fire, and conquered it on the second day. Only seventy-five of them lived to tell about it. In the countless souvenir shops the tourists rush to buy buttons, buckles and books of photographs, they search for bullet holes in the bunkers, point at the famous dummy of a paratrooper that still hangs on the steeple at Sainte-Mère-Église.

I make a little pilgrimage to the Pegasus bridge at Bénouville, along the Orne, the first patch of Western European ground taken by the Allies. In the early hours of 6 June, 1944, three Horsa gliders – enormous wooden aircraft towed from England by heavy Stirlings – landed here under cover of night. On board were ninety men of the 6th Airborne Division, linked together arm and leg to absorb the impact of the landing, singing loudly to calm their nerves. The two German sentry posts were taken entirely by surprise, within ten minutes the strategic bridgehead was in British hands.

The dance café of the Gondrée family, on the corner, was the first house to be liberated in Western Europe, and their daughter Arlette was the first liberated child. Today Arlette runs her parents' business, and does so with dignity and flair. Hanging in the bar are dozens of photographs: Arlette with General X, with Admiral Y, the crew of the British royal yacht saluting in front the door of Café Gondrée, it is all on record.

Gondrée *père* was a member of the Resistance, and spoke fluent English. Just before D-Day a British agent had urged him not to leave the house; something was brewing and he might be needed. Arlette has a few more things to tell me about that night. 'I was four at the time, and I remember the enormous shooting and thundering in the darkness. My father sent us down into the cellar. We heard the Germans pounding on the front door. We didn't react. A little later the back door opened, we heard footsteps above our head, someone tripped over a chair, and then we heard someone cursing. "Damn it, Tommies!" my father whispered. By the next day our house was already full of wounded men.'

The veterans of D-Day still come back here, and Arlette knows them all. 'This is where they meet up again. This is their home. When you've been through something like that you always stick together. But they don't talk much about the fighting itself. "He fell beside me," they'll say, but they never go into detail, not even to their families. They keep that to themselves.'

Does she still remember her liberators? 'Do I! They came down the stairs, and I started crying right away. "It's all right, chum," that was the first thing they said to my father. Their faces were blackened and they had camouflage netting on their helmets, my mother ran and hugged them, but it was still terribly frightening. They were monsters, our liberators! They picked me up, too, and then they brought out the chocolate, and everything was all right after that.'

Operation Overlord, as the Normandy invasion was officially called, was a military operation the likes of which had never been seen before. The preparations had taken two years. A total of almost three million men had been assembled in southern England, divided over thirty-nine divisions: twenty American, fourteen British, three Canadian, one Polish and one French. Among them there were also units from New Zealand, Australia, India and other parts of the British Commonwealth, as well as assorted French, Belgian, Norwegian, Polish, Czech and Dutch squads.

The invasion itself was carried out by an army of 150,000 men, with 7,000 ships, 20,000 vehicles and 11,000 planes. On the first day, 4,500 of those men were killed: approximately 2,500 Americans, 1,641 Britons, 359 Canadians, 37 Norwegians and 19 Frenchmen. Not only was the taking of the beaches a huge task, but the invasion also had to be synchronised to keep all those army units from getting in each other's way. The whole thing was planned to the minute: the military engineers were to land at zero hours plus two, supply troops at zero hours plus thirty, and the first journalists were allowed to come ashore at zero hours plus fifty-seven.

The weather remained disastrous, even after the landing. Between June 18–21 there was actually a hurricane in the Channel, the worst storm since 1900, which swallowed up 800 ships and landing craft. Four times as much military material was lost during that storm as on D-Day itself, and the Allies continued to feel the effects all summer. Still, one month after the invasion there were already a million men on the continent.

Two huge artificial harbours were towed across the Channel, one of them went down during the storm on 18 June. The third port on which the Allies had their eye, Cherbourg, was initially blocked with mines and hundreds of wrecked ships; within a few weeks, working day and night, the American 333rd Engineer Special Service Regiment succeeded in restoring the harbour installations to something like working order. Then the flood of troops and war material began rolling onto the continent.

The Belgian and French Resistance had been closely involved in the preparations for D-Day, ever since May 1942 when a French Resistance fighter was able to purloin a German map of the Atlantic Wall, an invaluable source of information for the Allied planners. At 9 a.m. on 5 June, the BBC began broadcasting lines of poetry by Verlaine, the signal that told the Resistance groups that the invasion would take place the next day, and they could begin taking their own measures. Later, Eisenhower estimated – perhaps a bit too flatteringly – that they had contributed at least fifteen divisions.

'The place of the invasion was no surprise, but the moment of the invasion was,' said Winrich Behr, Rommel's adjutant at the time. 'Those of us on the Western staff had always suspected that there would be a landing at Normandy, but Hitler and his strategists were taken completely by surprise. For a long time they believed it was a tactical feint. They refused to send reinforcements for the first three or four days, convinced as they were that the main body of the invasion would arrive at Calais.'

The meteorologists of the Kriegsmarine had predicted that, in view of the weather and the tides, an Allied landing during the first days of June could virtually be ruled out. Rommel, therefore, saw no reason not to go on holiday on 5 June. He had to return in very short order.

Behr: 'Of course, our intelligence was flawed. Remember, it had been four or five months since a German reconnaissance plane had been able to cross the Channel. We were blind. The radio broadcasters on both sides were constantly playing games with misleading information via news reports, radio plays, music programmes, all peppered with codes and messages. Later on I heard that a Scottish station had accidentally broadcast the pre-recorded announcement of the invasion, one day early. Our intelligence people picked up on that as well. But they didn't do anything with it. They thought it was just another ruse.'

Once the Allies had finally established their bridgehead, they still had to penetrate the German defence. That went much slower than expected; the German resistance was tough, experienced and effective, the Allied losses were huge, the destruction in the countryside and the cities – Caen, Bayeux, Cherbourg, Saint-Lô – enormous. The battle for Normandy lasted two and a half months, rather than the three weeks originally planned. It was not until 21 August that the road to Paris and the rest of Western Europe was clear.

From that moment on, troops and supplies were pumped from Normandy to the fronts on a massive scale along the Red Ball Express, the Allies' lifeline, an improvised, one-way road to Brussels. The fuel needed for all these army units was brought in from the Isle of Wight, a hundred kilometres from Cherbourg, through the Pluto pipeline. Pluto, built with breathtaking speed, was the world's first undersea oil pipeline, and by late 1944 it was transporting a million litres a day.

Winrich Behr spent days driving with Rommel along the Normandy fronts. 'I was twenty-six at the time, he was around fifty-five, and he was like a father to me.' According to Behr, Rommel was actually a very down-to-earth man. 'He said what was on his mind. "Hitler expects us to advance! Things can't go on like this!" he would say sometimes. But then he would come back a little later and say: "Well, Behr, we mustn't forget, Adolf Hitler is a great man." Then he would sleep on it a night, and the next morning he would say: "What a terrible person, what a windbag!" And he would pound his fists on his stomach in rage.'

Rommel, Behr believed, was not in favour of assassinating Hitler. 'He wanted the whole clique to be imprisoned, taken to trial, anything, but murder them, no. It wasn't in him to be a Brutus. But, like most of the other generals, he wanted peace to come quickly. The fatherland had to be saved. In that sense he saw himself as a second Hindenburg, who had played a conciliatory role after the First World War. After all, both friend and foe saw Rommel as a respectable German, and he knew that.'

To the east of Germany, the second great European front congealed. On 22 June, 1944, a little more than two weeks after D-Day, the Soviets began their own counteroffensive. Operation Bagration has been allocated only a tiny role in Western textbooks, but was at least as decisive as Normandy for the outcome of the war. The senior German command was once more taken unawares. They had been expecting the next great offensive to take place along the Black Sea, with the oilfields of Pripet and Ploieş as prizes. But now the fronts were suddenly moving towards the Baltic States, East Prussia, Poland, and ultimately towards Germany itself.

The size of the Soviet force came as such a shock that Hitler, like Stalin in 1941, at first refused to believe the reports: 166 divisions, 30,000 cannons, mortars and rocket launchers, 4,000 tanks, 6,000 planes. The

Soviets had twice as many soldiers as the Germans, almost three times as many cannons and mortars, and more than four times as many tanks and planes. The Russian 'steamroller', once a favourite source of speculation by paranoid military officers, had become reality.

Once Germany was caught between these two enemy armies, things went quickly. After the breakthrough of the Allied forces in Normandy, the Germans – as someone wrote later – 'started losing faster than the Allies could win'. The Allied Western offensive, however, soon 'choked on its own success': the supply lines from Normandy became overextended. Despite the Pluto pipeline and the thousands of Red Ball Express trucks driving bumper to bumper, supplies grew short. On the evening of 2 September, the advance positions bogged down. A few American Sherman tanks drove up the hill at the Belgian town of Tournai, but instead of entering the city they ground to a halt: out of fuel. A few more Shermans came up from behind and had just enough fuel to reach the centre of the town before their own engines sputtered and died.

'My men can eat their belts,' General Patton thundered, 'but my tanks gotta have gas!' The fuel crisis spread like wildfire. Only four days later were the tanks able to roll out of Tournai. At Brussels they were forced to spend another idle day. In Limburg Province they were still able to shoot, but not to advance. The Siegfried Line and the German border lay just over the horizon. In the Dutch cities, 'Crazy Tuesday' arrived on 5 September: in a panic, collaborators and German officials packed their bags and fled east. Victory seemed close at hand.

The Allied leaders were ecstatic as well, and that resulted in an understandable, but fatal, error of judgement. The British had taken Antwerp, but that did not mean they could use the port: the banks of the River Scheldt were still firmly in German hands. But after all, if the war would be over by winter anyway – and even the cautious Eisenhower was counting on that – there was no need to liberate the port of Antwerp. Commander G. P. B. Roberts of the British 11th Tank Division waited in vain for orders to deal with the German 15th Army which had fled to the Dutch island of Walcheren. Almost 80,000 Germans escaped in the meantime, and in the weeks that followed they had all the time they needed to throw up a strong line of defence. For months they were able to block all shipments along the Antwerp route.

By the time the Allies became bogged down along the Rhine a few weeks later, it was too late. Antwerp's was the only harbour suitable for the short-distance supply of munitions, supplies and fuel for an army of several million troops, but the River Scheldt had been skilfully blockaded. The mistake could only be set right by a second storming of the Atlantic Wall at Flushing and Westkapelle, in late October 1944. According to the commandos involved, that landing was more treacherous than the one at Normandy. Landing craft were shelled and burned while still at sea, the water was icy, and the troops hit the beach unprotected from the 'most concentrated barrage of fire in the world'. More than 17,000 Britons, Canadians, Norwegians, French and Poles were wounded in the battle for the Scheldt, more than 6,000 were killed.

In a display case in the Cabinet War Rooms in London hangs a dog-eared map of Europe, taped to a hinged plank with a black tarpaulin around it, covered with sheets of tracing paper full of lines and notes. It is the political map Churchill used during the war. The remarkable thing is that those scratchings already trace the fault lines which were to divide the continent for more than forty years, and which were based in part on the front lines as they were in winter 1944–5.

During the Yalta Conference in February 1945, the Soviet troops were on the Weichsel, the Allies on the Rhine. In February 1945, the American Shermans were still in almost the same positions where they had become stuck in September 1944. Meanwhile the Soviets had taken Poland, Rumania, Bulgaria, Yugoslavia, Hungary and part of Czechoslovakia, and by early 1945 they had reached the Oder. They were poised to enter Berlin. The delay in the West and those lines drawn at Yalta had much, if not everything, to do with Antwerp and Walcheren.

Normandy and Omaha Beach have been brought back to the public eye by Steven Spielberg's D-Day film *Saving Private Ryan*. Yet at Flushing and Westkapelle, the pennants of the herring boats flap in the wind as though nothing ever happened. The Allied campaign of 1944 can now be driven across in a day. After Antwerp it starts to rain, on Walcheren the water blows in waves across the road. The names of the villages I drive through in Zeeland Province remind me of the staunch radio voices of the 1950s, of my parents' worried faces as they huddled near the set, of the preachers who spoke of 'the punitive breath of God' moving over the precious, 'worldly' Netherlands, of the two Dinky toys I had to offer up to the poor, drowned children.

The years 1944 and 1953 are chiselled in stone everywhere in the cemeteries here. Flushing, along with Rotterdam and Venlo the most heavily bombed cities in the Netherlands: more than 250 graves, plus a section full of Britons, Canadians, Poles and Australians. Westkapelle: forty-four victims from just one bombed cellar beneath an old mill. Oude Tonge: about 300 graves, all bearing the date 1 February, 1953. Nieuwerkerk: 'Maria van Klinken, born 1951, missing', the rest of the family dead as well. Hundreds of family dramas lie buried here amid the clumps of clay.

First there were the May days of 1940 and the bombardment of Middelburg – after the Dutch capitulated, the French and the Belgians fought on bitterly in Zeeland Province – then, on 3 October, 1944, the Allies inundated Walcheren to drive out the Germans. Then came the battle for Walcheren, and less than ten years later, on 1 February, 1953, this piece of the Netherlands – with the exception of Walcheren, this time – was once again swallowed up by the sea with the loss of 1,836 lives.

The sea dyke at Westkapelle was bombed by the Allies in 1944 to smoke out the German positions, and the survivors always finish their accounts with the line: 'And then we found ourselves staring right into the sea.' I can see the present-day dyke down at the end of the main street, higher than the newest houses, and I can imagine how terrifying that breach must have been for those who lived there below sea level. In the churchyard lie the victims of all the bombs that went astray, ten per cent of the village population then. No one talks about it now.

Flushing, too, has girded itself against God's wrath with order and technology. A downpour races along the boulevard, a man in a bronze oilskin tries to light a cigarette in the lee of it, behind the windows of Strandveste the elderly take shelter in their apartments. Just past the city lies the tidiest beach in Europe, a row of locked bathing cubicles, a sign saying 'Surveillance', a long line of rubbish bins, and not a soul in sight.

But still, I am walking along the most important European battlefield of autumn 1944, a normal stretch of coastline that once, briefly, was what it was all about.

Chapter Forty-Five

Oosterbeek

WHAT IF D-DAY HAD FAILED? OR WHAT IF, IN 1931, A NEW YORK taxi driver had not just clipped the fat man crossing the street, but killed him? Or if the Americans had not dawdled for two years before starting the Manhattan Project, and the atom bomb had actually been available to the Allies in 1943?

And what about the Netherlands in 1944? What if Hitler had been unable to profit from the three-month respite provided him by Walcheren? Or if the Allies had won the Battle of Arnhem and been able to race across the almost defenceless German lowlands to Berlin in autumn 1944? There would have been no starvation that winter in the Netherlands, no offensive in the Ardennes, Anne Frank would have become a great writer, and at Yalta Stalin would never have been in a position to claim all of Eastern Europe. But could the British and Americans really have driven on so much further after a breakthrough at Arnhem, without sufficient fuel, without a good chain of supply from Antwerp? Wouldn't they have choked on their own success once again? What if . . .

By chance, Winrich Behr, now a major on Field Marshal Model's staff, was there at the start of the Battle of Arnhem. 'Our headquarters were at Hotel Hartenstein, in Oosterbeek. It was a lovely, quiet Sunday, we were having lunch, and suddenly we heard machine guns and the loud buzzing of planes. One of our superiors had the soup spoon shot out of his hand. I went outside and couldn't believe my eyes: floating gently down out of the sky were paratroopers. At first I thought it was a British special commando team out to liquidate a couple of generals. But the landing was so huge that I soon realised that this was something very different.'

Today there are still rumors that Operation Market Garden was betrayed to the Germans beforehand. According to Winrich Behr, no such information ever reached the German command: 'The simple fact is that we were sitting there, the whole general staff. That I was sitting there calmly, eating an egg.' The problem, Behr says, lay with the Allies: they simply had too little information. 'The British didn't know that there were a couple of SS armoured divisions at Arnhem. From what I heard later, the Dutch resistance had reported that, but Montgomery didn't trust their information; he thought we had infiltrated the resistance. Actually, our armoured divisions were there by accident. They had fought in Normandy, and then been sent to Arnhem to rest up and repair their equipment. But they were soldiers with experience at the front. And they went into action right away.'

Today, the most important landing field is covered in corn and the occasional sunflower. It was here that they came down on that lovely Sunday afternoon of 17 September, 1944, those thousands of paratroopers, those countless gliders full of infantrymen, that entire overwhelming aerial caravan some 400 kilometres long. And over there, across from the Albert Heijn supermarket in Oosterbeek, close to the patio of restaurant Schoonoord, beside the Gall & Gall off-licence and Klimop florists, is where there were mowed down.

Market Garden was one of the most daring operations of the war. After all the delays that followed the landing at Normandy, the Allies were attempting, in one great, whirlwind push from Eindhoven, by way of Veghel and Nijmegen, to cross the Rhine at Arnhem, at a place the Germans least expected it. Thousands of American, British and Polish paratroopers were to secure the many bridges along the way, to allow the British tanks to roll through virtually unchallenged. The Americans of the 82nd Airborne Division were to take the Waal Bridge at Arnhem; the British of the 1st Airborne, along with a Polish brigade, would see to the nearby Rhine Bridge. The road to Berlin would then be cleared: the Allies could be there before winter came.

This winner-take-all initiative was hatched by Montgomery, but the plan soon received the wholehearted support of Eisenhower. 'I not only approved of Market Garden, I insisted on it,' he admitted to Stephen Ambrose twenty years later. All of the Allies' precious fuel was directed northwards for the sake of Arnhem. General Patton, whose tanks were poised to break through at Nancy and Metz, had to wait. The plan was daring, and at the same time extremely complex, a chain of minor and major military actions that had to be closely coordinated and succeed without exception. If one link in the chain failed, the entire operation could fall apart. Here, more than in any supposed betrayal, lay the core of the failure of the Battle of Arnhem: in the risks the Allies took, and in the flush of optimism and nonchalance with which the plans were then carried out.

To start with, the advance of the Allied tanks from Eindhoven went much slower than expected. The Germans – and particularly those parts of the 15th Army the Allies had allowed to slip away at Antwerp – put up fierce resistance. Only with great difficulty could the Waal Bridge at Nijmegen be taken and held long enough to cross. At Arnhem, however, things went wrong. The British in their haste had taken the wrong radio transmitters with them, effectively cutting off all contact with headquarters and with each other. The consequences of this technical blunder alone were catastrophic. Furthermore, and inexplicably, the hardened American paratroopers were dropped at relatively easy positions, while the inexperienced British of the 1st Airborne Division were faced with the toughest job. Even their German foes noticed that. Winrich Behr: 'The Brits just lay there, along the lines of: what do we do now? Their radios didn't work, their plan wasn't working either, and then they proved unable to improvise. They fought bravely, no doubt about that, but they didn't seem very experienced to us.'

The 10,000-plus men of the 1st Airborne had not been counting on any serious resistance. Their commanders should have known better. On the basis of decoded Enigma reports, the British Ultra project had concluded that the Germans were planning to send their 9th and 10th armoured divisions to the surroundings of 'Venloo, Arnheim and Hertogenbusch' for 'rest and recuperation'. Yet this was put aside. When the information officer reporting to the commander of Operation Market Garden, Lieutenant General Frederick 'Boy' Browning, showed his commander aerial photos confirming the presence of the armoured divisions in the area, Browning sent the man on leave. His paratroopers received absolutely no warning. The only overt protest came from the experienced Polish airborne general, Stanislaw Sosabowski. He considered the plan outright suicide. 'These Brits had never seen a German,' was how he typified the mood within the army staff.

Fatal risks were taken as well with regard to the location of the landing. According to the original plan, most of the gliders and paratroopers would land close to the bridge. At the last moment, however, for security reasons, a landing spot was chosen on the other side of Arnhem, some fourteen kilometres from the objective. As a result, the airborne troops first had to fight their way through Oosterbeek and Arnhem before taking the bridge, while at the same time securing their landing spot for any reinforcements that might follow. Their firepower, to use the military parlance, was simply too limited for that.

In and around Arnhem the troops fought with a courage born of desperation, and sometimes with remarkable chivalry as well. For example: when the British headquarters beside the bridge, with its cellar full of wounded men, had been shelled, the medics arranged a ceasefire; the Germans, working side by side with the British, dragged the wounded men out of the burning building. Then the fighting resumed. Sosabowski's courageous Poles were deployed only after four days of fighting. They landed across the Rhine at Driel, under murderous German fire. From there, in heavy fighting, they succeeded in keeping the most important escape routes open for the trapped British troops. After the defeat, it was this same Sosabowski who served as Browning and Montgomery's scapegoat. The general ended his life as a worker in a British factory.

On this quiet Sunday I drive through Oosterbeek. Hotel Hartenstein is still there, as are many other legendary locations. Around the old parsonage lies a splendid vegetable garden, a paradise of cabbage, beans, lettuce, blackberries, currants and flowers. In 1944 this was the home of Jan and Kate ter Horst, a couple with four youngsters and a baby, but still involved up to their ears in the resistance. While Kate stayed in the cellar with the children, amid the roar of machine guns, Sten guns and field mortars, their home accommodated more than 300 wounded men. Kate was referred to respectfully as 'the Lady', she was a paragon of calm and bravery, she talked about the future of a free Holland while holes were being shot in the parsonage walls, and she comforted the boys with a

Psalm: 'Thou shall not be afraid for the terror by night; nor for the arrow that flieth by day.'

She herself wrote: 'They are all dying, and must they breathe their last amid such a hurricane? God, give us a moment's silence, give us rest – even if only for a moment, so they can die in peace . . .' When the battle was over, fifty-seven soldiers were buried in her garden. Of more than 10,000 Britons and Poles who landed at Arnhem, almost 1,500 were killed and 3,000 were wounded.

Today the river rolls slowly past the green forelands, the cows lie in the shade of trees, the occasional barge passes, then a few geese honking in flight. There is an old church amid the greenery. Every once in a while, a yellow train goes thundering across the railway bridge.

It was hard for Winrich Behr to talk about autumn 1944. He could not really remember, he said, how he had thought about it at the time. He had talked and read too much about it afterwards. Rommel was wounded during an air raid, and soon afterwards died quite unexpectedly, on 14 October, 1944. As the representative of his army unit, Behr came to the funeral with a wreath. 'I'll never forget it. General Rundstedt gave a horribly hypocritical address. An old acquaintance, an officer from the Paris parade committee, had organised the entire funeral. That evening we agreed to meet in a café. There he told me the true story: how Hitler had sent two generals to Rommel, how they had accused him of complicity in Stauffenberg's assassination attempt and said that he, because of his exemplary service record, was to be allowed to choose between being executed and having his family sent to a concentration camp, or committing suicide with a fast-working poison, a military pension for his family and a state funeral. 'It was nothing but a filthy business,' he said. So you can imagine that, after that, we of the Western staff couldn't really summon up much enthusiasm for our planned offensives.'

Behr also remembered one of his own generals, that same autumn, openly stating: 'Of course we must do our duty as soldiers. But our most important task is to allow the West to come in, to make sure the East doesn't advance too far.' Such opinions, Behr said, became increasingly common among the Wehrmacht staff. 'It sounds strange, but after the Allied catastrophe at Arnhem we became increasingly worried: what's keeping these idiots from breaking through? We all knew that the whole thing would be over soon, whatever happened, and after that autumn we didn't care about winning the war in the West. What we wanted was to defend ourselves against the Russians, that above all.'

In December, when Hitler came up with plans for the Ardennes Offensive – its target, once again, the vital supply port of Antwerp – many of Behr's colleagues in the *Wehrmacht* were furious: 'That bastard Hitler said we were going to fight the Bolsheviks, and now that the Russians are marching on Berlin he's deploying our best armoured divisions to attack the West. The idiot!' It was a mystery to Behr too how twenty-five German divisions could ever hope to assemble without anyone on the British or American staffs realising they were planning a counteroffensive. 'Sometimes their intelligence work was rather shoddy. There were even those on our side who tried to make contact with the Allies, to put a quick end to the war in the West. But the officer who did that, Lieutenant Colonel Krämer, returned empty-handed: the West was interested only in total surrender. Of course, all kinds of agreements with Stalin played a role in that. And I think the Western leaders knew well enough about the atrocities in the concentration camps. They weren't interested in doing business with a criminal regime.'

Meanwhile Martha Gellhorn was criss-crossing the fronts of Europe for *Collier's* magazine. The townspeople of Nijmegen, she wrote, were clearly God-fearing citizens who led a quiet, provincial life. But due to a bombardment – a case of mistaken identity, by the way, on the part of the Americans – 'the city now looks as though it had been abandoned years ago after an earthquake or a flood.' She gave a lift to a woman who worked for the Red Cross. Her young daughter had been seriously wounded by shrapnel, her husband had been killed, her possessions were stolen by the Germans and her house lay in ruins. 'She was a Jewess. She had returned to life as usual, in the last month.'

Gellhorn later travelled through German border towns as well: 'No one here is a Nazi, no one here ever was a Nazi . . . To see an entire people skirt responsibility is no pretty sight.' Finally, in Torgau in late April 1945, she came across the advance guards of the Russian 58th Infantry Division, which had already moved up to the Elbe. She met a nice colonel, became acquainted with Russian drinking customs, and thought they were all fantastic. 'We had been toasting "Treeman" for quite some time before I realised that we were drinking to the new American president; the way they pronounced it, I thought it was some pithy Russian expression for knocking back a drink.'

The colonel suggested they take a walk, it wasn't good to become too sombre, and it was a lovely spring evening. 'From a building came the beautiful, melancholy sound of Russian song, low and slow and mournful. In another building a young man was hanging out of the window, playing a fast and cheerful tune on his harmonica. The strangest characters were walking around: blond men and Mongols, wild-looking characters with nineteenth-century moustaches, and children not much older than sixteen. We passed a couple of burning houses that looked lovely.' The only thing was: they could go no further than the Elbe. All permission to cross to the Soviet side was denied. 'It's just that you people are capitalists, and we are communists,' the colonel explained succinctly.

Today Torgau is a provincial town like many in the former DDR: bumpy cobblestones, a half-restored centre, a hesitant pizzeria, an enormous Kaufland shopping centre at the edge of town, and around it all a ring of orchards and lush kitchen gardens. The Elbe here is not much broader than an irrigation canal; it looks as though you could wade to the other side, but in 1945 it was the divide between two continents.

In London I had happened to run into an old American solider: Phill Sinott of the 69th Infantry Division, once a machine-gunner, now retired in San Francisco. For hours he had told me about the workaday war for the average Allied soldier: brief periods of incredible fear, a few skirmishes, then months of boredom. For him the war consisted of either 'being bored to death or shitting your pants in fear'. There was no middle ground. At Torgau I was reminded of him again, because he had been there on that historic 25 April, 1945, when the Americans and the Soviets fell into each other's arms along the Elbe – in the middle of not only Germany, but also, as John Lukacs says, 'in the middle of European history'.

In reality, Torgau was quite chaotic, for both armies had been in the vicinity for a long time. 'At night in that patch of no-man's-land it was as busy as Piccadilly Circus,' Sinott told me. 'There were our patrols, and Russian patrols, there were Germans and refugees, it was one huge mess.'

Only when enough photographers and journalists had been assembled could the official fraternisation at last take place, and those photographs are familiar to us all. Phill Sinott: 'The Russians across the river had a party every day. They were always rolling these barrels around, we thought it was gasoline. Pure vodka! Every once in a while we would hear women screaming, but what could we do? That same day we liberated a prisoner-of-war camp. The American boys were skin and bones, but they didn't say a thing. All they did was touch our jeep – crazy isn't it, only our jeep. A major came out of one of the barracks, he looked terrible, but he tried to stand up straight, he saluted stiffly, then he burst into tears. So did we.'

A few days later, from a wall along the river, Martha Gellhorn watched the Soviet troops move on. 'The army came in like a flood; it had no special form, there were no orders given. It came and rolled over the stone quays and out onto the roads like water rising, like ants, like locusts. What was moving along there was not so much an army, but a whole world.' Many of the soldiers were wearing medals from the Battle of Stalingrad, and the entire group had fought its way at least 4,000 kilometres to the west in the last few years, most of it on foot. The trucks were kept rolling with impromptu repairs, the countless female soldiers looked like professional boxers, the sway-backed horses were driven along as though by Ben Hur himself, there seemed to be neither order nor plan, but according to Gellhorn it was impossible 'to describe the sense of power radiating from this chaos of soldiers and broken-down equipment'. And she thought how sorry the Germans must be that they had ever started a war with the Russians.

Chapter Forty-Six

Dresden

THE MONUMENT AT TORGAU IS COATED IN GREYISH-GREEN. IT SHOWS Soviet soldiers being welcomed by joyful German women bearing flowers, cheering men and children, and above that in big letters stand the words 'RUHM DEM SOWJETVOLK, DANK FÜR SEINE BEFREIUNGSTAT'. It is one of those DDR plaques that should immediately be put under the protective care of UNESCO, as a classic monument to the lie. Phill Sinott and his countless American comrades have been skilfully edited from the snapshot of history, and no one wants to be reminded of that screaming from across the river. For in the real Torgau of 1945, the cheerful German mothers were gang-raped by their Soviet liberators, and in the cities their children were pulverised by the thousand in the firestorms of British and American bombardments. That was the real end of the war, the retaliation, the fire and the shame, the intense humiliation about which only half a century later can cautious mention be made in Germany.

The retaliation came in all varieties. One variety came largely from the Soviet soldiers. When they entered East Prussia in January, their propaganda officers hung up huge banners: 'Soldier, you are now entering the lair of the fascist beast!' The village of Nemmersdorf (now Mayakovskoya) was taken by the 2nd Red Army Guard, a few days later German troops launched a counteroffensive and entered the town again. They found bodies everywhere: refugees crushed under tanks, children shot in their gardens, raped women nailed to barn doors. The cameras rolled, the images were shown all over Germany: this is what happens when the Russians come in.

Some two million German women were raped during that period, most of them several times. The Red Army leadership was fully aware of what was happening, but did nothing to stop it. Half a century later, in the state archives of the Russian Federation, Antony Beevor found a great many NKVD documents describing 'negative phenomena' and 'immoral acts', as rapes were called in Soviet jargon. Women who had been raped were regularly reported to have committed suicide afterwards, sometimes even entire families took their own lives. Russian girls who had been deported to Germany were referred to as 'German dolls'. A memorandum drafted on 29 March, 1945 contains a description of how Soviet officers and soldiers all along the front entered the dormitories of newly liberated Soviet women and committed 'organised mass rapes'. The report cites a woman by the name of Klavdia Malashtshenko: 'It was very bad under the Germans. But now our fortunes are worse. This is no liberation. They treat us terribly. They do terrible things to us.'

The 'Russian fury' prompted a huge, panicked migration. The roads witnessed scenes identical to those during the German campaigns of conquest into Poland and beyond, but now in the other direction: from east to west. From mid-January 1945, millions of Germans began fleeing from East Prussia, Pomerania and Silesia, on foot, with prams and horse-drawn carts, in the snow at temperatures of twenty below zero, and later by ship and train as well. By mid-February, more than eight million Germans – mostly women and children, for the men were still at the front – were on their way west. On the afternoon of 30 January, the enormous holiday cruiser *Wilhelm Gustloff*, run by Kraft durch Freude, set sail onto the Baltic, packed with somewhere between 6–10,000 refugees, including some 4,000 children. In the middle of the ice-cold night that followed, the ship was struck by a torpedo from a Soviet submarine. About 1,300 evacuees made it into lifeboats or were rescued by navy vessels that came to the scene. Thousands were trapped below deck when the water rushed in. The *Wilhelm Gustloff* went down with a 'final collective scream', a catastrophe many times greater in scope than that of the *Titanic*, which became known in wider circles due to the work of the writer Günter Grass more than half a century afterwards.

One week later, the hospital ship *Steuben* was torpedoed; 4,000 were killed. Around 150 refugee ships in all were sent to the bottom in this way, including the *Goya* – with 7,000 refugees and 175 survivors – and

the *Cap Arconda*: 5,000 passengers, mostly refugees who had been 'evacuated' on Himmler's orders from Fossenbürg and other concentration
camps, and 150 survivors.

Every day in winter 1945, 40–50,000 new refugees arrived at
Friedrichstrasse Station in Berlin. An eyewitness described the arrival of
a packed refugee train in the town of Stolp: 'Hundreds and hundreds of
bodies squeezed together, stiff from the cold, barely able to stand up and
climb off the train.' Stiff little bundles were unloaded from the freight
cars: children who had frozen to death. 'Amid the silence, the screams
of a mother who did not want to relinquish what she had already lost.'

All those refugees found themselves in the midst of a new battle, the
round-the-clock storm of death and destruction that had moved in on
Germany from the west. In May 1942 Cologne became the first target of
a *Tausenbombernacht*, as the victims called them. But Berlin was the favoured
objective, it was 'the evil capital' and the lair of 'the Huns', and also –
with its immense tank, artillery and airplane factories – the true industrial and administrative heart of the Reich. In autumn 1943 the leader of
British Bomber Command, Sir Arthur Harris, decided to focus all attention on the German capital. The actual wording of the memorandum sent
by 'Bomber' Harris to his commander-in-chief was: ' We can wreck Berlin
from end to end if the USAAF will come in on it. It will cost between
us 4–500 aircraft. It will cost Germany the war.' Churchill was impressed.

A week after Harris sent his memorandum, on the night of 18
November, 1943, the city was bombarded by an airborne fleet of almost
450 bombers. The operation was repeated a few days later, but now with
750 planes. Entire neighbourhoods were in flames, 2,000 people were
killed. And as the winter progressed the bombings became more massive;
in the end, fleets of 1,000-plus bombers were pummelling the city each
night. Berlin lay at the limit of their operating radius, and the risks were
huge. The Lancasters had to carry so much weight in bombs and fuel
that they could scarcely take off. At full throttle they would charge down
the runway, airborne only in the last few metres. Fifteen minutes later,
when they finally reached cruising altitude, the engines were glowing
hot. Countless planes went down in aerial combat or collisions, their
crews falling to their death or burned alive. One in every sixteen planes

did not come back. Until late 1944, the average crew member had a one-in-four chance of surviving the mandatory 'tour' of thirty flying missions. Of the 125,000 RAF pilots, gunners, navigators and bombardiers, more than 55,000 – almost half – were killed. Starting in spring 1944 the Americans joined in as well, with their enormous four-prop Boeing B17s, the Flying Fortresses, and Boeing B24s, the Liberators. From that moment the German capital knew no rest: the British bombed by night, the Americans by day.

On 23 November, 1943, Käthe Kollwitz's house on Weissenburger Strasse was hit squarely by a British bomb. The big parlour with the oval dining table, the enormous tiled heater, the drawings on the walls, more than half a century of family life: nothing was left. On 26 February, 1944, old Alexanderplatz went up in a sea of flames and exploding 'blockbusters'. By that point more than 1.5 million citizens of Berlin had been *ausgebombt*. In the end, seventy per cent of the city would be reduced to rubble.

Almost every city in Germany received its share of punishment from Bomber Harris. Ninety-five per cent of the glorious medieval centre of Cologne was destroyed. The city's famous Dom Cathedral was spared only because it provided such an excellent beacon for the Allied crews. In Hamburg, on 28 July, 1943, the first firestorm was created. People ran down the street like living torches; almost 40,000 people suffocated in the burning cyclone or were roasted alive in bomb shelters that quickly became as hot as ovens. Almost all the old cities along the Rhine were bombed flat: Emmerich, Rees, Xanten, Wesel, Koblenz, Mainz, Worms, twenty-three of them in a row. In Nuremberg, on 2 January, 1945, a thousand years of history were destroyed in the space of fifty-three minutes. The castle, three churches full of art treasures and at least 2,000 medieval houses went up in flames.

A sixteen-year-old medical student, summoned to help collect the bodies in Wuppertal, wrote that some of the victims looked 'very peaceful', having suffocated in the ensuing vacuum. 'Others were completely burned. The charred corpses were only about fifty centimetres long. We put them in zinc tubs and washbasins. A washbasin held three corpses, a bath seven or eight.'

Ernst Jünger had business to attend to in burning Hanover on 16 December, 1944. 'The streets were covered with piles of rubble and loose debris, and with the wrecks of cars and trams. The city was a mass of people, running wildly back and forth like a scene from some oriental disaster. I saw a woman walk past: clear tears ran from her face like rain. I also saw people lugging lovely old pieces of furniture, now covered in mortar. An elegant gentleman, grey at the temples, was pushing along a cart containing a rococo cabinet.' Jünger also wrote of a huge attack on Misburg that killed more than forty young female Luftwaffe clerks. 'The force of the blast had torn all the clothes and underwear off their bodies, leaving them completely naked. A farmer who had helped to gather their bodies was completely shaken: "All such big, lovely girls, and heavy as lead!"'

The story of the sinking of the *Wilhelm Gustloff* has since been described by Grass and others, but what happened to the survivors afterwards is almost unknown. Some 900 were put ashore at the port of Swinemünde (now Świnoujście). Many of the women – some of them girls no older than eleven – were speechless from the traumas they had suffered. They had been raped, and after that the mothers had been forced to watch their children drown. Some of them begged the German naval cadets to shoot them. Along with thousands of other refugees, they were housed in abandoned holiday resorts along the beach. The harbour and the sea before them were full of even more refugee ships.

The target the Americans might have been going for, the V-1 and V-2 installations at Peenemünde, had been moved to mountains in the Harz long before. Still, on the afternoon of 12 March, 1945, the area was bombarded by more than a thousand planes. The refugee ships in the harbour were adrift and burning, or had already disappeared under water, along with all those who thought they had found safe shelter in them.

According to official figures, this 'Swinemünde massacre' claimed 23,000 lives, but the presence of so many unregistered refugees could bring the real figure to twice that. No mention of this is made in American military annals; the bombardment is listed only as an 'attack on railway yards'.

Jünger reports that an Allied pilot was shot down close to the village where he lived. A Dutch refugee attacked the pilot with an axe, and a farmer passing with his wagon was able to save the man only by risking his own life. But many other pilots were less fortunate: during the final year of the war, some hundred Allied pilots were lynched by Germans.

During the German bombardments of England, 60,000 civilians were killed, 90,000 were badly wounded and another 150,000 were injured. The Allied raids of Germany claimed five times that number, around 300,000 victims, including 75,000 children. Almost 800,000 people were badly wounded. Seven million Germans were left homeless, and a fifth of all the country's houses were destroyed.

The effect of the bombings on the German war industry, however, was far less severe. Albert Speer estimated the total loss of production in 1943 at no more than nine per cent, a decrease for which the country could compensate. During later interrogations, he said he found the Allied tactic 'incomprehensible': why hadn't they attacked the country's basic industry (steel and oil) and transportation network? Now, despite the enormous fires, the industrial capacity of a city like Berlin remained almost intact until the final months of the war. It was only the Americans who finally began to focus systematically on oil refineries and other vital parts of the German war machine. 'The British left us with deep and bleeding wounds,' Marshal Erhard Milch said after the war. 'But the Americans stabbed us in the heart.'

This disproportion between industrial damage and civilian casualties was no accident. It was a conscious policy. Even before the war began, the British had developed the tactic of 'strategic bombardment', a method of eliminating the enemy by destroying his centres of population. The bombardments of Germany were therefore not a reaction to the German bombings of London, Coventry and other British cities, but part of a strategy that had been drafted long before that. Coventry was not an immediate cause, merely a justification.

Generals, as the old saw goes, always tend to win the war that's over, and this was no different in 1939–45. The losing strategists of the First World War, the Russians and Germans, looked back on the struggle as a missed opportunity. They had 'almost' won, and with bigger and better-equipped armies the same large-scale attacks would, in their eyes, succeed this time.

The victors, the French, British and Americans, remembered 1914–18 primarily as an unparalleled massacre of their own young people, a repetition of which was to be avoided at all costs. Hence the bold campaign in Germany in May 1940 and the similar Russian strategy in spring 1945.

And hence, too, the French Maginot Line and Eisenhower's caution. Hence too the enormous investment by the British – almost a quarter of their entire war budget – in the 'strategic bombardments'.

So arose the Allied variation on the war's 'radicalisation'. In the eyes of Harris and others, German citizens were not merely hapless souls who accidentally got in the way, but were in fact their principal target. Their strategy of 'moral bombing' assumed that the death of as many German civilians as possible would shorten the war, because it would cause morale on the home front to collapse much more quickly.

It should not be forgotten, as the British military historian John Terraine puts it, that the term 'moral' in a bombing directive means the reality of 'blowing men, women and children to bits'. In the archives, Terraine came across a memorandum from RAF Air Chief Marshal Sir Charles Portal in which he detailed the 'production possibilities' for his superiors. Within the next two years, he boasted in November 1942, he would be able to drop almost 250,000 tons of bombs on Germany, destroying 6 million houses and a corresponding number of industrial installations, killing 900,000 Germans, badly wounding a million and leaving 25 million homeless. Terraine: 'What is one to think of the calm proposal, set down in a quiet office, to kill 900,000 civilians and seriously injure a million more? One thing emerges, with absolute clarity: this was a prescription for massacre, nothing more nor less.'

This 'moral bombing' did indeed take place on a massive scale. For every ton of bombs that landed on London, Coventry and a few other places, the British and the Americans dropped more than 300 tons back on Berlin, Hamburg, Bremen, Cologne, Nuremberg and other German cities. The Allies knew what they were doing: one of the most powerful bombs, weighing over 2,000 kilos, was normally referred to as 'the Cooker', because, as people said: 'it literally brings the folks on the ground to boiling point'.

The bombardment of civilians became a special science. Although the British bombed more or less at random in 1940–1, from 1943 the targeted districts were first studied carefully on aerial photographs. A pronounced preference arose for residential neighbourhoods, as being most susceptible to 'demoralisation'. Specialists calculated which bomb could best be used to destroy which building, how a firestorm could be created by first using a blockbuster to blow out all doors and windows, how a house could quickly be set alight by adjusting a bomb to explode only after it had first crashed through three floors. To kill firemen and other helpers, time bombs were dropped that went off only 36, 72 or 144 hours after deployment.

Ironically enough, it was the Germans themselves who had done the pioneering work in these developments. They had evaluated their own bombardments of Warsaw (25 September, 1939) and Rotterdam (14 May, 1940), and applied their findings to the Luftwaffe's bombardment of Stalingrad (23 August, 1942). In the firestorm created in that city, more than 40,000 people were killed within a few days, a number equal to that in Hamburg. 'The report from *Luftflottenkommando 4* [concerning Warsaw] reads like a recommendation for Bomber Command,' writes Jörg Friedrich in *Der Brand*, his impressive account of the bombing war against Germany. He cites the Luftwaffe specialists: 'The explosive bomb paves the way for the firebomb. It forces the population into the cellar, while the houses burn down above their heads. If they are not rescued, they die of suffocation. Moral resistance is completely shattered by the impressions experienced. Destroy water supplies at the first attack! Do not drop firebombs piecemeal but in huge quantities, thereby creating ferocious "hearths" everywhere that can no longer be dealt with.'

The infamous bombardment of the open cultural city of Dresden – which many later labelled an Allied 'war crime' – was therefore no incidental excess. It was part of a well-considered strategy that had been applied for a long time . . . and which also began to meet with increasing repugnance from Britons themselves. As early as spring 1944, Vera Brittain, working under the auspices of the Bombing Restriction Committee, wrote a pamphlet calling on the RAF to resume normal military practices and cease bombing civilians. 'Owing to the RAF raids,' she said, 'thousands of helpless and innocent people in German, Italian and German-occupied cities are being subjected to agonising forms of death and injury comparable to the worst tortures of the Middle Ages.'

The protests had no effect whatsoever. That summer, Harris and Portal, with the approval of Churchill and Eisenhower, began Operation Thunderclap: a massive bombardment which would kill more than 100,000 people in a single night. It would, according to Harris, definitively destroy

German morale, despite countless indications that the bombardments had little or no such effect.

A Thunderclap attack on Berlin failed. Instead of the hundreds of thousands of victims planned, only a few thousand were killed during the great bombardment of February 1945. Five days later, the strategy was tried anew, this time over Dresden.

Today Dresden is the city of the Frauenkirche, a ruin which under the former DDR was referred to as a '*Mahnmal für die Opfer des Bombenkrieges*', but from the ashes of which a house of prayer has slowly arisen anew since the *Wende*, the turning point after which communism collapsed. The broom cupboard was the only thing that emerged unscathed from the rubble, with all the buckets and mops which had been put away there so neatly after work on the afternoon of Tuesday, 13 February, 1945. In 1999, Dresden is a city of vacant plots of land, of strange little parks full of grass, bushes and old stone foundations that wouldn't belong in any normal city. There are lovely buildings in Dresden, restored and rebuilt, lying spread out like the cards in a game of old maid, but they do not form a city. They are, at most, colourful shards in a vase reconstructed of plaster. The city, that is the vacant lots, and nothing more.

On the night of 13 Feburary, 1945, Dresden was full of refugees from the East. The city had no war industry to speak of, but that was not the point. Precisely according to plan, a firestorm raced through the streets within half an hour of the first bombs falling. To maximise the number of victims, the British and American strategists had devised a triple-whammy. They knew that, in a burning city, bomb shelters provided protection only for about three hours. After that the ground and the walls became so hot that everyone had to go back outside. It was at precisely that moment that the second attack came. The citizens of Dresden had to choose between the sea of fire outside and the oven-like bomb shelters within. Then, while everyone was busy saving themselves and others, a third attack followed.

The Stadtmuseum contains silent witnesses to that night: a few melted bottles, a half-melted bench vice, photos of bodies, some of them in a fountain that had boiled and run dry, naked, their clothes burned off.

At the start of the first attack on Dresden, just after 10 p.m., Victor

Klemperer and his wife Eva were sitting in the 'Jewish house' at Zeughausstrasse 1–3, sombre and exhausted, drinking ersatz coffee. The professor was doing forced labour in a factory, and he expected to be deported soon along with the last of the Jews. When the bombardment continued, he picked up his bag of manuscripts and walked downstairs with his wife to the special 'Jewish' bomb shelter. As they were going in, the professor was injured by a splinter of shrapnel and lost sight of Eva. Along with a few Russian prisoners of war he fled the glowing hot cellar, ended up in a huge open square that he did not recognise, climbed into a bomb crater, found an acquaintance with a young child there, lost sight of both of them, then began wandering aimlessly. The intoxication of those moments can still be felt in the entries in his diary. 'Pounding, daylight, concussions. I couldn't think, I wasn't even afraid, I felt only a great tension, I believe I thought that was the end.'

He wound up on the Brühlsche Terrasse, the 'Balcony of Europe', a high spot along the Elbe in the centre of town. 'Around me, as far as I could see, there was nothing but a sea of flames. On this side of the Elbe the extremely clear torch of the buildings on Pirnaischer Platz, across the Elbe, glowing white and clear as day, the roof of the ministry of finance.'

When it finally grew light, he took his bag and stumbled down along the lower wall of the Terrasse. Suddenly he heard someone call his name: in a row of exhausted survivors he found Eva, sitting unharmed on their suitcase, still wearing her fur coat. 'We hugged, we didn't care at all that we had lost all we owned, and that's still the way we feel about it.'

Today, local historians – who are often best informed about such matters – estimate the number of people killed in the bombardment of Dresden at 25–30,000. In the old market square in the centre of town, a funeral pyre was built that burned for five whole weeks. The cremation was supervised by SS Sturmbahnführer Karl Streibel, who had gained his experience burning bodies at the Treblinka death camp.

Chapter Forty-Seven

Berlin

ON HITLER'S FIFTY-SIXTH BIRTHDAY IT WAS, AS THE PEOPLE OF BERLIN had been wont to say in better days, *Führerwetter*. Friday, 20 April, 1945 was a glorious, sunny spring day. 'Yes, the war rolls on towards Berlin,' a woman in her early thirties wrote in her diary. 'What sounded yesterday like drumming in the distance has today become a constant pounding. You breathe in the noise of the cannons. The ear grows deaf, now you hear only the reports from the heaviest-calibre guns. It's no longer possible to tell where the sound is coming from. We live inside a ring of gun barrels that is drawing tighter by the hour.'

It was 4 p.m. when she wrote that. The Berlin radio had stopped broadcasting four days earlier. People were starving in the city. The anonymous writer called herself 'a pale blonde, always dressed in the same salvaged winter coat, employed at a publishing house', she was seriously engaged to a man by the name of Gerd who was fighting at the front, she never wanted to reveal her name, but her diary was finally published. We shall hear more from her.

It was at almost that same moment that the last images of Adolf Hitler made their way onto film: he walks stiffly along a row of Hitler Youth scouts being decorated for their suicide attacks on Soviet tanks, he caresses the cheek of the youngest of them, and tries to hide the tremor in his hand. That evening he went to bed early, while the rest of his entourage left for the chancellery. More than half a century later, Hitler's junior secretary, Traudl Junge, described that bizarre birthday party to Gitta Sereny: the dining room was deserted, there was only the huge table set for a party, everyone drank champagne, Hitler's personal physician Morell, Bormann, Ribbentrop, Speer and Goebbels danced with the secretaries to the same scratchy tear-jerker,

'Blutrote Rosen erzählen dir vom Glück'. There was a lot of hysterical laughter. 'It was horrible; I'd soon had enough of it and went to bed.'

The mood in the city, in the words of Norwegian journalist Jacob Kronika, was that of a gigantic passenger liner about to sink. Berlin was caught up in a feverish 'hunt for pleasure'. In the cellars and bunkers, in the dark bushes of the Tiergarten, between the shelves of the audio archives of the Grossdeutsche Rundfunk, everywhere it was a 'sexual wilderness'. The girls and the soldiers all said the same: 'We want everything now: the Knochenmann, the Grim Reaper may come for us tonight.'

Late that evening in her bomb shelter, our anonymous diarist noted: 'No electricity. The oil lamp flickers from the rafters above me. Outside a dark roar, growing louder.' A few minutes later the cellar walls shook from the explosions.

That same weekend, Russian war correspondent Vassily Grossman entered Brandenburg with the advancing Red Army: 'Everything is covered with flowers, tulips, lilacs, apple trees, plum trees.' He passed a column of freed prisoners of war on their way home, carrying improvised national flags, pushing carts, prams and wheelbarrows, on foot, limping along on crutches. 'The birds are singing; nature shows no sympathy with the final days of fascism.'

A total of 2.5 million men, 14,000 pieces of artillery and more than 6,000 tanks were involved in Operation Berlin. In the eyes of the Red Army, Berlin was the 'main prize' to which the Soviets had a right after all their hardships. In the West, on 7 March, the Ludendorff Bridge over the Rhine had fallen intact into American hands; the Allies could now move through the Ruhr, and the end of the war was suddenly a matter of weeks away rather than months. That gave the Soviets a sense of urgency. Stalin was convinced that the British and Americans would try to take Berlin before he could.

Churchill and Montgomery were indeed inclined to push on as quickly as possible: they saw the steady advance of the Soviet troops as a new threat to Europe. The Americans were not interested in that; they had enough problems on their hands already. Very few policymakers in Washington realised that the political boundaries of post-war Europe were being drawn up during those last weeks of the war. Eisenhower's reasoning was simple: he wanted to be done with the war in Europe as soon as possible, and with as few casualties as possible, in order to turn his attention to the war against Japan. To do that, he needed Stalin's support and he had absolutely no desire to endanger that relationship by unleashing a race for Berlin. As far as he was concerned, Stalin could do as he pleased, and he let him know that as well. Eisenhower shifted his attacks to southern Germany and Hitler's *Alpenfestung*. Churchill was furious.

Yet the race for Berlin was about more than prestige; it was also about the nuclear research being carried out there. Thanks to the communist spy Klaus Fuchs, the Kremlin had known since 1942 about the American Manhattan Project at Los Alamos, and about its German counterpart at the Kaiser-Wilhelm-Institut in Dahlem. The Soviets were keen to get their hands on as many atomic researchers and laboratories – and as much research material and uranium and other raw materials – before the British and the Americans arrived. Then the Soviet Union could finally make an atom bomb of its own within the foreseeable future. Four years later, indeed, that objective had been realised.

On Monday, 23 April, our anonymous diarist went out in search of coal. Her neighbourhood was still in German hands. The viaduct under the S-Bahn had been closed off: people said a soldier had been hanged on the other side with a sign around his neck: TRAITOR. Barricades had been thrown up on Berliner Strasse, and were being guarded by members of the *Volkssturm* in their makeshift uniforms. 'You see mere wisps of children there, baby faces under oversized helmets, you're startled to hear their high voices. These boys can be no older than fifteen, so thin and puny in their flapping uniforms.'

It was clear to everyone that the war had been lost once and for all. Victor Klemperer, who collected Nazi jargon the way others collect stamps, added a few marvellous specimens to his collection in those final days in Berlin. A propaganda paper, the *Panzerbär* (Armoured Bear), continued to appear to the end. The final edition, on 29 April, spoke of '*der Schicksalkampf des deutschen Volkes*' (the fateful struggle of the German people), and about '*neue Eingreifkräfte*' (new interventionary forces) being brought in day and night. The worse the situation became, the more strident the language: a chunk of concrete containing explosives – particularly dangerous to the one throwing it – was labelled a *Volkshandgranate 45*. A unit ordered to attack the enemy almost unarmed was a *Sturmzug*. A group of youngsters sent to fight against Soviet tanks on foot or by bicycle was a *Panzerjagdkompanie*. The panicked press-ganging of the last remaining schoolboys and old men was called the 800,000 *Mann-Plan*.

For Albert Speer, the crucial turning point had come much earlier, in late January, with the fall of Silesia: a region full of mines, foundries and steel factories. It was then that he understood that within a few weeks the German war economy would grind to an irretrievable halt. Yet he calmly continued to take part in the broadcasting of comforting reports. Arms production would 'run like clockwork', all kinds of new weapons were on their way: he hinted at things including rockets and jet fighters.

Speer did all this on purpose, as he explained later during interrogations, because the Nazi leaders had 'started becoming hysterical' in late March 1945. They were on the point of causing great destruction within Germany itself, in accordance with the 'scorched earth' tactics ordered by Hitler. Speer did everything he could to prevent the implementation of this *Nerobefehl*, and to a certain extent he succeeded. Meanwhile, on 13 March, Hitler's right-hand man Martin Bormann had ordered all prisoners to be transferred from zones along the fronts to the middle of the Reich. Gruesome death marches followed during which many tens of thousands of prisoners – some estimates speak of 250,000 – were shot or hanged. There were even plans to continue fighting underground after the defeat: the Nazi leaders had started planning Operation Werwolf in autumn 1944, and within the SS as well there were attempts to set up a partisan army through the *SS-Jagdverbände*.

Hitler issued his *Nerobefehl* on 19 March, twelve days after the Americans crossed the Rhine at Remagen. For Speer, who had protested, he had made the exception of providing a written justification of his order: 'If the war is lost, the people will be lost as well, [and] then you must not worry about what will be needed for rudimentary survival. On the contrary, the best thing is to destroy that as well. For the nation has proven itself weak, and the future belongs entirely to the strong people of the East. Those who remain after this struggle will in any event be inferior, for the good will all be dead.'

*

Speer saw Hitler for the last time on the evening of Monday, 23 April. The *Führerbunker* was shaking with the impact of the mortar shells. The day before, Hitler had thrown a fit of rage before his staff the likes of which they had never seen before. He had paced back and forth, railing against the world in general and against the cowardice and disloyalty of his political friends in particular, he had pounded his fists against his temples while the tears ran down his cheeks. Speer found a way to land a light plane in the centre of Berlin. Hitler had just turned fifty-six, but he looked like an 'exhausted octogenarian'. His complexion was ashen, he was bent and dragged his left leg behind him, probably as a result of the daily cures given him by his physician, Morell. After treating him with intestinal bacteria 'from a Bulgarian farmer's best strains', Morell had begun using increasingly stronger remedies: amphetamines, deadly nightshade, strychnine.

Speer spent a few hours talking to Hitler, constantly interrupted by adjutants who came and went, for official Berlin worked on until the very last moment. Hitler told him he could no longer fight on, he was giving up. He asked whether he should leave Berlin. Speer advised against it, saying the Führer could hardly end his life in a 'summer cottage'. Hitler's greatest fear was to be captured alive by the Russians, his corpse was also to be burned, otherwise it might be 'dishonoured' after his death. He did not, he said with a disdainful snort, mind dying: it was only a moment. 'I had the feeling I was talking to someone who was already dead,' Speer wrote later in his cell.

Then Speer visited Goebbel's wife Magda, who was lying in bed sick and pale. She and her husband had decided to let their six young children die as well. After that he went and said goodbye to Eva Braun, the only one in Hitler's entourage who spoke of death's approach in a calm and dignified fashion. Early the next morning Speer flew over the Brandenburg Gate, right past the Siegesalle, and everywhere below he saw the flash of artillery, tracer bullets flying up and the city aglow. A few hours later our anonymous diarist reported a direct hit in a line waiting in front of a butcher's: three dead, ten wounded, but the line regrouped. 'For the prospect of a few steaks and ham, even the weakest of grandmothers will stand her ground.' Everyone in her building was now more or less living together in the bomb shelter, and came out only when it was absolutely essential. On Thursday morning, 26 April, an artillery shell – a *Koffer* – crashed through the roof of the building. At first everyone screamed and panicked, but then they all ran upstairs to tidy up while the shells exploded all around. Such scenes were reported later, too: sweeping up the shrapnel as quickly as possible, dusting and then a mop over the floor. The cleaning fits of the women of Berlin were indefatigable.

Out on the street the diarist saw the last German soldiers retreating from the front aboard a truck, tired and silent. This was what remained of the Nazi myth. She wrote: 'I notice again and again these days that my feeling, the feeling of all the women towards the men, is changing. They make us feel sad, they're so pitiful and powerless. The weaker sex.'

On Friday, 27 April, hiding beside the window at 5 a.m., she sees the first Russian soldiers enter her street; two men with broad backs, wearing leather coats. A piece of heavy artillery was being pulled around the corner. A few hours later the street was full of cars, carts and carefree soldiers, a field kitchen was set up, there was even a cow walking around. That afternoon the first Russian broke into the house, that evening she was raped for the first time, on the steps, while the neighbours held the cellar door shut. More soldiers followed: 'My heart pounds like crazy. I whisper, I beg: "Only one, please, please, only one. You, if need be. But throw the others out."'

That Friday evening the first Americans reached Berlin: two journalists, Andrew Tully of the *Boston Traveler* and Virginia Irwin of the *St Louis Dispatch*, with their driver, Sergeant John Wilson. On Wednesday, 25 April, while the American-Russian feast of fraternisation at Torgau was still in full swing, the two had decided on a half-drunken whim to drive their jeep straight on to the capital. Amid all the confusion, they actually succeeded. They had taken an American flag with them from Torgau, talked their way past all the roadblocks, drove blindly down roads lined with corpses and wrecked vehicles, and finally arrived at the Berlin headquarters of Major Nikolai Kovaleski. In all innocence, Kovaleski arranged a festive banquet to welcome the three Americans – an act of hospitality for which he would later pay dearly, for Stalin was not at all fond of such 'conspiracies'.

Virginia Irwin saw Berlin as a 'maelstrom of destruction'. The Soviet artillery was pounding the city's heart without interruption. The journalists received a guided tour from a Russian soldier, 'a wild boy with a big fur cap' who jumped onto the hood of their jeep and pointed the way with an enormous rifle. 'The earth shakes. The air reeks of gunpowder and corpses. All of Berlin is in chaos. The fierce Russian infantry is pushing on towards the centre. Runaway horses which have escaped the supply wagons are roaming the streets. There are dead Germans everywhere.' After a while the soldier jumped down off the jeep, shook hands with them and joined a group of infantrymen on their way into the burning, shuddering centre of the city.

The next morning, Saturday, 28 April, it was party time again. The Soviet officers, war medals clinking on their chests, waltzed with Virginia Irwin and the female soldiers to the strains of 'Kannst Du Mir Gut Sein' and 'Love and Kisses'. Meanwhile orderlies ran in and out, asked for instructions, and went back to the fighting in the streets. Nightmarish things were taking place outside: the SS had flooded U-Bahn stations with hospital trains in them and entered houses flying the white flag of surrender near Kurfürstendamm, shooting everyone in them. There was a bloody massacre on the Charlottenbrücke, where a panicked crowd of civilians and soldiers was trying to make its final escape amid the incoming Soviet shells. An anonymous German soldier wrote in his diary: 'Through the holes in the street you can see the U-Bahn tunnels. It looks as though the dead are piled on top of each other down there.'

On the night of 29 April, Hitler married Eva Braun. A macabre party was held in the Führerbunker, while Hitler dictated his political last will and testament to Fräulein Junge in one of the antechambers.

Outside, the Battle of Berlin was raging. Upstairs, in the cellars of the Reichskanselerei, an orgy was in full swing. Junge, who had gone up to get some food, saw 'bodies in lustful embrace' everywhere, even in a dentist's chair. During those final hours, her primary task was to care for Goebbels' children. At around 3 p.m. on Monday, 30 April, she was making bread and jam for them. 'The children were cheerful, they felt completely safe with eleven metres of concrete above their heads, they were counting the explosions,' she said much later. 'Suddenly we hear a loud bang. 'A direct hit!' little Helmut Goebbels shouted. That was probably the sound of the shot with which Hitler took his own life.' Eva had already swallowed a cyanide capsule. On 1 May, Joseph and Magda Goebbels committed suicide as well; the children were each given a capsule in their sleep. Along with a colleague, Junge – disguised as a man – was able to escape from the bunker and make it past the enemy lines.

Virginia Irwin asked Major Kovaleski whether Berlin was the biggest battle he had ever fought in. 'He smiled and said sadly: 'No. We have seen bigger battles. We lost our wives and children in them.' And then the major told the story of the strange staff he had gathered around him. Each and every officer on it had lost his entire family to the Germans.'

The diary of the anonymous woman of Berlin was only published in Germany after her death, almost sixty years after the Battle of Berlin. The book was an immediate success, and rightly so, because it is recognisable, intelligent and evocative. At the same time, however, it is a document full of blind spots, and that is probably characteristic of the people of Berlin in those days. Nowhere is there a glimmer of understanding concerning the cause of all this Russian brutality. Major Kovaleski knew exactly why he was fighting in Berlin. Many of the young Soviet soldiers carried a photo of Zoya Kosmodemyanskaya, the young female partisan who had been tortured and hanged by the Germans in 1941. The words 'For Zoya' were also written on Soviet tanks and planes.

To our Berlin diarist, the war seemed merely a lightning bolt of fate. When her Gerd shows up at her door, totally unexpected, on Saturday afternoon, 16 June, they look at each other 'like two ghosts'. She is feverish with happiness, but it soon turns out that they have become complete strangers to each other in the months that have passed. When she tells him how she and the pharmacist's wife had survived, by keeping a Russian officer as their 'steady boyfriend', he becomes angry: 'You've become shameless bitches, all of you in this house.' She shows Gerd her diary, which fills three notebooks by then, all of it written for him. He grows increasingly cool, asks her what the abbreviation 'Schdg' means. 'I had to laugh: "Well, *Schändung* [rape], of course." He looks at me as though I have lost my mind, says no more. He left yesterday. He and a comrade of his are planning to wander the countryside, to go and visit his comrade's parents in Pomerania. He's going to try to find food. I don't know if he'll ever come back.'

And this is how the anonymous diary ends, on Friday, 22 June, 1945. 'No more entries. And I am not going to write any more, the time for that is over . . .'

Chapter Forty-Eight

Nuremberg

FOR MARTHA GELLHORN, THE MEETING WITH THE RUSSIANS AT Torgau meant the end of the war. That same week, on 30 April, 1945, her colleague Lee Miller took a picture of herself for *Vogue*, sitting in the bathtub of Hitler's apartment in Munich, her GI boots beside the bath; finished, over and out, the most wonderful photograph of the liberation ever.

For Anna Smirnova, who had lived through the siege of Leningrad, that spring was the loveliest of her life. 'My husband was alive, I was expecting a child, everything was going to be all right.'

The Polish communist Vladislav Matwin attended the victory parade on Red Square. 'A Russian officer was marching with a captured German flag, and he swung that thing over the street like a broom, flap, flap, at every step. And there were forty officers doing the same thing. It was the most festive day of my life.'

Victor Klemperer had liberated himself long before: early the same morning, after he had survived the bombardment of Dresden and found his wife again, he decided to take off his yellow Star of David and await the end of the war as a 'normal' German refugee. Eva removed the star from his jacket with a penknife.

Winrich Behr spent the final months of the war serving under Field Marshal Model, a typical Prussian military man who carried the adage 'generals do not involve themselves in politics' to its logical extreme. On 21 April, 1945 they found themselves in a forest, with the Americans close by. Model said: 'I'm not going to walk out of these woods with my hands up, not after thousands of my men have died following my orders.' He sent Behr away, ostensibly to scout out the surroundings.

'When I came back, he had put a bullet through his head. That same day a comrade and I escaped in civilian clothes.'

For Wolf Jobst Siedler, the war ended on 2 May alongside a road in Italy. 'We Germans stood there with a white flag, but the British tanks just rolled on by, it was one huge thundering herd. No one wanted us!'

Within only a few months, the four great leaders of the war – with the exception of Stalin – disappeared from the political arena. Roosevelt did not live to see the German capitulation: he died of a brain haemorrhage on 12 April, 1945. De Gaulle became the president of a provisional government. In that role, and with an eye to French unity in the future, he did his best to prevent retaliations against the Vichy supporters. That soon led to a conflict with the former Resistance fighters. When elections were held in October 1945, France once again proved to be deeply divided. To break the impasse, de Gaulle announced his resignation on 20 January, 1946. He was convinced that the French, shocked, would call him back and surround him with more power and glory than before. But he was mistaken: they let him retire in peace to his country home at Colombey-les-Deux-Églises. It was twelve years before France would call on the general once more.

Just as unexpectedly, the voters banished Winston Churchill to Chartwell. (But not for good: in 1951 he once again became prime minister and stayed on until 1955, when he retired for reasons of health.) During the war years, Britain had been ruled by a cabinet drawn from all the major political parties, the 'Grand Coalition', and regular elections were held again for the first time on 5 July, 1945. A landslide of opinion seemed to have taken place among the British voters: Labour, led by Clement Attlee, won 393 seats in the House of Commons, while Churchill's Conservatives made an astounding fall from 585 to 213 seats. The blow took all parties by surprise. Attlee – whom Churchill had once called 'a sheep in sheep's clothing' – was a man seemingly devoid of charisma. As second in charge within Churchill's wartime cabinet, however, he had gained great popularity: he toured the entire country, unfolding extensive plans on housing, education, health care and industry, setting the tone, in short, for reconstruction even while the war was still in progress.

Churchill, on the other hand, had seen only cheering masses during the election campaign, without realising that the British people were cheering him as a war hero, not as a politician. His own daughter, Sarah, clearly expressed the tenor of popular opinion: 'Because socialism as practised in the war did no one any harm, and quite a lot of people good. The children of this country have never been so well fed or healthy; what milk there was, was shared equally; the rich didn't die because their meat ration was no larger than the poor; and there is no doubt that this common sharing and feeling of sacrifice was one of the strongest bonds that unified us. So why, they say, cannot this common feeling of sacrifice be made to work as effectively in peace?'

The official settling of accounts took place in the hall of the war tribunal at Nuremberg. Starting in November 1945, the first trials were those of the twenty-one principal suspects – including Göring, Papen, Frank, Ribbentrop, Seyss-Inquart and Speer – followed later by other, lesser gods. Since 1960 the famous tribunal hall has become part of the regular courtroom, a place where everyday theft and divorce is weighed in the balance. The hall was closed when I came through Nuremberg in the spring, but an old porter was kind enough to allow me a glimpse. The space seemed smaller, more human than I had imagined. Sunlight streamed through the high windows and fell on the judge's bench. The clouds were all that could be seen from the witness stand. 'Nothing here is original,' the porter said. 'The Americans took everything as souvenirs, the furniture is now spread all over California, Arizona and the rest of the United States.' Only the enormous table at which the magistrates conferred is still standing in a side room, because 'it was too big to drag away'.

It is often said of Nuremberg that here the ultimate truth finally came to light. That is true in so far as it applies to the belligerence and criminality of the Nazi regime, but many important questions remained unsolved years after the tribunal was closed. This has to do with the availability of information – a treasure trove of new historical material emerged in the 1990s in particular, after the opening of the DDR and Soviet archives – but also with the strictly judicial character of the investigation: all attention was focused on the role of the defendants and of Germany in general.

Furthermore, the trials consistently suggested that the war had been a purely moral matter, that the Germans had stood only for Evil and the Allies only for Good. Yet the events between 1939–45 are impossible to explain with such a simplistic scheme. Ideology and morality played a subordinate role with the Allies as well. The 'moral bombings' instigated by Bomber Harris were emphatically aimed, in violation of all the moral conventions of war, at maximising the number of civilian casualties. Troop movements were speeded up, slowed down or rerouted for considerations of prestige, to seize an important city or sever the enemy's supply lines, but never to liberate a concentration camp more swiftly. A war leader like Churchill was driven by a fervent anti-communism and an iron determination to save the British Empire; Stalin and his generals wanted to destroy the Western enemy at all costs; Roosevelt watched over America's hegemony, and de Gaulle was less an anti-fascist than an authoritarian French patriot. States go to war primarily to serve their own national interests, and this war was no different. 'The Nuremberg trials were the source both of huge quantities of valid historical information and of manifest historical distortions' Norman Davies and other European historians rightly concluded.

In October 1946, the American *Saturday Evening Post* noted that only thirty-three out of the hundreds of top Nazi officials in the German steel industry – so vital to the war – had been arrested. The rest had simply remained at their posts. Speer, the brilliant manager of the Third Reich, succeeded in striking precisely the right tone towards his judges and prosecutors: that of the civilised technocrat, intelligent, responsible, contrite. He was sentenced to twenty years in prison, served his sentence (unlike many others), and died in 1981 like an upright citizen.

The practitioners of medicine got off particularly easily, even though doctors and nursing officers had played a central role in the Third Reich. They had helped to establish the criteria for 'racial purity', they had selected the handicapped and the malformed children for the euthanasia campaign and then 'put them to sleep', and they had carried out large-scale medical experiments in the concentration camps – often with gruesome results. Yet of these hundreds, perhaps thousands, of doctors, only twenty-three were tried at Nuremberg. They pleaded innocent without exception. Four doctors were finally condemned to death, including one of Hitler's private physicians, Karl Brandt, who had also played a role in the Bethel hospital affair. With this verdict, the case was closed for the German medical profession. Within five years, almost all of the SS physicians and euthanasiasts – including the medical inspectors who had been active at Bethel – were back at work as general practitioners, medical examiners, scientific researchers or professors.

When Ernie Pyle died on 18 April, 1945 – having meanwhile been transferred to the Pacific – he was carrying a few notes with him. They were intended for the column he had hoped to write on the day Germany capitulated. One of them read:

> Those who are gone would not wish themselves to be a millstone of gloom around our necks. But there are many of the living who have had burned into their brains forever the unnatural sight of cold dead men scattered over the hillsides and in the ditches along the high rows of hedge throughout the world.

The Second World War claimed the lives of at least forty-one million Europeans: fourteen million soldiers and twenty-seven million civilians, including six million Jews. It was a catastrophe that every day, for six long years, there were an average of 20,000 deaths. By the end of the war, one out of every five former inhabitants of Poland and the Baltic States was dead. In the Soviet Union, the casualties could only be processed by reducing the total population figures at the next census.

Chapter Forty-Nine

Prague

ALONG THE BANKS OF THE ELBE, NOT FAR FROM DRESDEN, THE AUTUMN leaves swirl down gently, every morning the grass on the campsite is streaked with brown and red. Beautiful antique paddle steamers glide past the cities on the river, every now and then you hear their mournful whistles in the cold morning mist. In the afternoon, when one of them sails by, you feel the urge to wave your cap at gentlemen in straw hats and ladies in white frocks who people the decks, as though nothing has happened for the last century.

These are lovely, late days of summer, people are gathering rose hip along the roadsides, and from the hills the landscape looks like a vast garden painted by one of the Brueghels, full of farms, fields, white houses along the rivers, here and there a village spire. In the Czech Republic, all that changes. The border crossing at Hřensko is one huge market of brass-ware, laundry detergents, alcohol, cigarettes, baskets and Third World shopping bags, there are a dozen whores standing beside the highway, and then follows one industrial monument after the other: factories, weathered smokestacks, abandoned railway yards, all of them almost antique. The surroundings must be rich in wildlife: the number of dead animals on the road increases, along the shoulders are dozens of hedge-hogs, a hare and even a crushed fox, its head still proudly raised. A shower of rain clatters on the roof, the sun leaves bright spots on the hillsides, and then I am in Prague.

It is a gorgeous Saturday afternoon. The Vitava is littered with tourist boats criss-crossing back and forth on the current, steered by big-eyed girls in sailor suits. Skaters, the heroes of Europe this year, race up and down the steps of the underground stations. On the Charles Bridge, two young men are playing Bach sonatas, the gulls cry across the water, German and Dutch tourists pass by the hundred, but right below, on the far side, there is suddenly a silent, walled orchard full of apple, pear and nut trees, a place where only a few people are sitting, reading a newspaper or a book in the warm September sun.

I'm sitting in the Hanged Coffee café, not far from the castle. Here you can order two cups of coffee and have one – empty – 'hanged' from the ceiling. When a penniless student comes in, she can ask for a 'hanged cup' and receive coffee for free. My Czech acquaintances are telling me the story of their families. Elisabeth comes from a village in the Sudetenland. Her mother and her grandfather were German, they were allowed to remain in Czechoslovakia because they were married to natives. The rest of the village fled to Germany. 'You can still see that on the houses, even after two generations. The village is dead, it has no soul.' Olga's grandfather died in the middle of the war by ridiculous chance: he was standing at the front of a line to hand in his rifle when the city hall was blown up by partisans. Her grandmother was driven almost mad with sorrow; whenever there was a bombardment she would run out onto the street in the hope of being struck down. Her mother was thirteen at the time. Later her grandmother became wealthy by reading cards for the Russian officers garrisoned in the town. Her mother married: two children, six abortions.

'If you want to know how a country is doing, you need to look at the oldest people and at the youngest,' Veronika says calmly. 'The oldest, that's my grandmother. She wouldn't be able to survive if we didn't help her. She still receives the same pension she did before 1989, and that's not enough to buy anything. She really doesn't want our help, but at Christmas we always buy her a new coat. Things like that. That whole generation is having a hard time of it now. And as far as the youngest go . . . it's almost impossible to have children here. It's simply too expensive, no one can afford it.' Suddenly she grows tearful. As it turns out, she's pregnant. 'My mother says: "It's okay, we'll be all right."'

On 26 January, 1946, The Economist described the situation in Europe as though talking about an African famine: 'The tragedy is enormous. The farmers are reasonably well off, and the rich can afford to use the black market, but the poor population of Europe, perhaps a quarter of the continent's 400 million inhabitants, is doomed to starve this winter. Some of them will die.'

The particular problem areas were Warsaw and Budapest – where tens of thousands of victims were anticipated – Austria, northern Italy and the large German cities – where an average per capita allowance of no more than 1,200 calories a day was available – as well as the western Netherlands and Greece, although the situation improved there.

Upon his return from the United States, Bertolt Brecht described Berlin as 'the pile of rubble behind Potsdam'. Amid the ruins of his old, beloved Alexanderplatz, Alfred Döblin spoke emotionally of 'the verdict of history'. The Dutch journalist Hans Nesna, who made an initial tour of Germany in an old Model-T Ford in spring 1946, lost his way in what had once been a wealthy residential neighbourhood in Hamburg. It had become a dusty flatland, not a living soul in sight. 'Most of the streets are unrecognisable and untraceable. You have to pick your way around piles of rubble and debris. All of it sunk in deathly silence.' Nesna's Swedish colleague, Stig Dagerman, made a similar journey six months later. In the Hamburg U-Bahn he saw people in rags, 'with faces white as chalk or newsprint, faces that cannot blush, faces that make you feel as though they couldn't bleed even if wounded.'

Meanwhile, in Poland and Czechoslovakia, and to a lesser extent in Hungary, Rumania and Yugoslavia, campaigns of ethnic cleansing were being carried out. Almost twelve million ethnic Germans were deported by way of retaliation. It was the largest exodus in human history. Hundreds of thousands of those deportees 'disappeared', probably having died along the way. In this way, the starving German population grew by an additional sixteen per cent.

In some villages in the Soviet Union not a single man returned from the war: of the men born in 1922, precisely three per cent survived the war. The number of kolkhoz workers sank to almost a third of the pre-war level. In Siberia, the surviving men were sometimes asked to circulate through the neighbourhood and impregnate women and girls, to ensure that at least a few babies would be born. A Russian author wrote that the first time he experienced not being hungry was in 1952, when he entered the army. Another reported that bread was back on the table again in his village only in 1954. Before that, the people had fed themselves with acorns, leaves, weeds and aquatic snails.

In August 1945, two months before committing suicide, the Nazi leader Robert Ley penned a letter to his dead wife from his Nuremberg cell about the Germany he had dreamed of: 'Kraft durch Freude, leisure time and recreation, new houses, we had planned the loveliest cities and villages, acts of service and fair pay, a fantastic, unique public health programme, social security for the elderly and invalids, new roads and streets, ports and settlements – how wonderful Germany could have been, if, if, and always if . . .'

The amazing thing is that out of the ruins of 1945 it was precisely that German dreamland which arose within the next ten years. In 1958 many German cinemas were showing the film *Wir Wunderkinder*, the story of two students who sold newspapers on Alexanderplatz in the 1930s, fell in love, married, survived the war and the bombardments and finally, in the 1950s, found respectable jobs and a certain prosperity. Their polar opposite was Bruno Tieges, an ambitious Nazi careerist who lived high off the hog during the war, sold goods on the black market afterwards, and became a respected entrepreneur in the 1950s. When Tieges is finally unmasked by the young couple, he falls in his rage into a lift shaft. And everyone lived happily ever after. That young couple was still only in their late thirties.

The *Wirtschaftswunder*, the economic upturn, was not limited to West Germany, but took place all over Western Europe. The ravaged countries recovered with astonishing speed, and during the 1950s the West actually experienced an explosion of welfare unlike any other in its history. By 1951 all the countries of Western Europe had recovered their pre-war production levels. After 1955, Austria was able to take part fully as well: the Soviets had suddenly withdrawn their occupational forces in exchange for the promise of neutrality, and hoped to solve the German issue in the same fashion.

Was this explosion of prosperity really, as is so frequently claimed, due primarily to the American Marshall Plan, that brilliant combination of aid and enlightened self-interest intended to help Europe to its feet while opening new markets for America? Clearly, generous American humanitarian assistance in the first post-war years made the difference between life and death for many Europeans. But the economic impact of the Marshall Plan was probably less decisive than is often claimed. Statistics showed a sharp revival of the Western European economies even before mid-1948, when the first dollars began pouring in. By late 1947 British and French production was already back at pre-war levels; the Netherlands, Italy and Belgium followed suit in late 1948. At that point, the Marshall aid had only just begun.

There must, therefore, have been other reasons for this unexpected boom: during the war, Europe had become acquainted with countless new – and largely American – technologies and production methods; many young people had gained a wealth of organisational experience in the army; Germany and Italy were able to replace their ruined industries with the newest of the new; the traditional and predominantly agricultural Netherlands was forced to catch up quickly, and become industrialised on an unparalleled scale. The welfare state took shape: all Dutch citizens above the age of sixty-five received a government pension after 1947, the French began their enormous HLM (affordable social housing) projects, and in Britain the National Health Service was launched in 1948. In June 1948, the Deutschmark was introduced in Germany's British and American zones, a drastic monetary reform which took an almost immediate effect: the black market vanished from one week to the next, shops became well stocked and, to their amazement, the Germans began to realise that life would go on after the demise of the Third Reich.

In 1959, the Conservative leader Harold Macmillan won the British elections with the unimaginable slogan 'You've never had it so good!'

Interestingly, along with all this, there was also a decline going on: the old, imperial Europe was being rapidly dismantled. During the war, powerful independence movements had arisen in almost all the colonies, the period saw both peaceful revolutions and violent wars of liberation, and in under two decades the sometimes centuries-old ties had been cut between Europe and the subcontinent, Indonesia, Burma, Vietnam, North Africa, the Congo and other colonies. In 1958 the British dropped the word 'Empire': from then on, 'Empire Day' became 'Commonwealth Day'. Following the Japanese occupation, the Netherlands proved unable to restore its authority over the Dutch East Indies. France, so humiliated during the war, attempted to regroup overseas: an eight-year war was fought in Indochina, until the French were decisively defeated by the nationalist rebels at Dien Bien Phu. Something similar happened in Algeria. The Belgian Empire in Africa collapsed in 1960. And in 1975, the ancient Portuguese Empire dissolved at last after a long, drawn-out war in Angola and Mozambique.

Even so, during this period, the economies of Great Britain, France, Belgium and the Netherlands blossomed as never before. Some historians explain this phenomenon by noting that the occupation of many colonies had less to do with economic gain than with rivalry between the great European powers themselves. Until 1919, Germany was present in Africa, in modern-day Namibia and Tanzania, because the British and the French had colonies there as well. The British were in South-East Asia because of the French, and in order to defend India. That is how things were everywhere. Until the start of the twentieth century, empires were profitable, or at least cost-effective. From the 1920s, however, the balance of costs and assets became increasingly unreliable: in 1921, the management of Iraq alone was costing the British an annual £21 million – more than their entire health-care budget – and they were receiving very little in return. As Great Britain reached the verge of bankruptcy, as independence movements began spreading everywhere and many of the old European rivalries lost their relevance after 1945, the European empires soon expired. By the mid-1950s the countries of Western Europe were trading more with each other than they ever had with their colonies.

Italy in particular profited in many ways from these new forms of cooperation. The country began producing for customers all over Europe: refrigerators, scooters, washing machines, cars, typewriters, spin dryers, televisions, the first luxury goods for the masses. The number of cars sold in Europe rose from just over 1.5 million in 1950 to more than 13 million by 1973. In 1947, the Italian Candy washing-machine manufacturer was producing one machine a day; by 1967 it was producing one every fifteen seconds. In 1959 the *New Statesman* published a cartoon showing an old man staring blankly at moving images on a round screen. 'No, grandpa,' a little girl is telling him, 'that's the washing machine, not the TV.'

*

In 1948 most Europeans looked a great deal alike. In the countryside especially, they lived and worked in more or less the same way their parents and grandparents had. Ten years later, Western and Eastern Europeans had grown far apart, both materially and intellectually, and another ten years later the alienation was complete.

While giant sunbeams enter his old, spacious Prague apartment, Hans Krijt (b.1927) tells me the story of a life ruled by dissent. Krijt was the son of a plumber in the city of Zaandam, a normal Dutch boy who found a job after the war in the packaging department of a factory that made flavourings for puddings. In early 1946 he decided to include a few letters along with the rum flavourings, in the hope of finding a pen pal. He received two replies: one from Berlin, from a '*sehr hübschen Verkehrspolizistin*', the other from Czechoslovakia, from a serious boy who had thought Hans was a girl. He ignored the traffic policewoman from Berlin, but became friends with the boy. And now he has been living in Prague for almost half a century, his wife Olga Krijtova is a translator, and their sideboard is covered with photographs of all his Czech children and grandchildren. That is how things go sometimes for the son of a plumber from Zaandam.

'I came here in February 1948, as a deserter,' he tells me. 'Holland was carrying out its last colonial police action in the Far East. My army comrades thought that was quite the thing, a war in the Indies, it would give them a chance to see something of the world. But the officers confiscated my copies of the left-wing weekly *De Groene*, that's the kind of guy I was, and Czechoslovakia was the only country where I knew people.'

He found work with a farmer. Less than two weeks later the Czechoslovakian communists seized power and arrested a great many non-communists. On 10 March, the popular minister of foreign affairs, Jan Masaryk, was found lying dead in the square in front of Černín Palace, which still houses the country's ministry of foreign affairs. The communists claimed that Masaryk had committed suicide 'because of the many false accusations in the Western press'. For most people, however, it was clearly a case of 'defenestration', a method used more than once in Prague to solve a political problem.

For the second time in ten years, the promising Czechoslovakian democracy had been brutally crushed. The reactions in the West bordered on panic. Now 'Ivan' had shown his true colours. New security alliances were forged, the start of NATO (1949). America stopped its withdrawal from Western Europe and would continue to watch over the security of the Western European countries for more than half a century. The Soviet Bloc reacted in 1955 by setting up the Warsaw Pact.

Hans Krijt noticed little of the communist coup. 'Only when a neighbour would come to have his cow covered, they would talk politics, always very excitedly.' But during the purges that followed, the secret police had little trouble finding him. 'They picked me up, simply because I was Dutch. In our cell there was a doctor who had just come back from a sabbatical in America, they pulled him right off the plane and put him in prison. No one knew why. I was locked up for ten days in an underground cell, with no light. We all slept on the floor. On the very first night some guy tried to molest me . . . I didn't even know things like that existed.' He was released after promising to report to the intelligence service any contact he had with foreigners. 'At first I thought: I never see any foreigners, so who cares? But it put me in their hands. I couldn't sleep at night because of it.'

In summer 1950 the first four opponents of the 'new social order', all former victims of the Nazi camps, were hanged in Prague. On a hill across the Vltava arose a huge graven image of Stalin. Today it has been replaced by a gigantic metronome, ticking away the years.

The Cold War was a forty-year battle of threats, of economic sanctions, of words and propaganda. No shot – with the exception of the popular revolts in the DDR, Hungary and Czechoslovakia – was ever fired in Europe. It was a textbook example of a long-lasting and extremely successful policy of 'containment'.

The first step leading to that war of containment was the swerve to the political left that took place all over Europe, including the West: in England, the Conservatives had been replaced by Labour, in France the Communist Party became the country's largest, with a quarter of all votes in the October 1945 elections. In Italy, by late 1945, the PCI had 1.7 million members, and in the Netherlands and Norway the social democrats were making a clear mark on government policy. Countries everywhere were rushing to establish government pension plans and other social facilities, and in France a whole series of concerns – natural gas, coal, banks, Renault – had even been nationalised. With regard to foreign policy, however, most European social democrats entertained very conventional views, and the communist cabinet ministers in France and Italy maintained a low profile as well.

Still, the Americans were becoming increasingly worried about the European 'shift to the left'. When Churchill's government was replaced by a Labour cabinet in July 1945, they reacted immediately: within a few days, the celebrated Lend-Lease agreement had been withdrawn. Strict conditions were established for receiving Marshall Plan aid. In May 1947, the communists were removed from the government of France; a month later the Italian government also took on a clearly anti-communist aspect. When the Korean War broke out in 1950 and the Netherlands did not wish to send combat troops to this 'decisive struggle' against communism, the United States immediately threatened to stop all Marshall Plan assistance to that country. Later, President Truman would admit that the Marshall Plan was intended in part to curb the popularity of the left: 'Without the Marshall Plan, it would have been difficult for Western Europe to remain free of the tyranny of communism.'

The growing tension was accompanied by an immense propaganda offensive. Harold Macmillan warned of an 'invasion of the Goths'; the Lenten pastoral letter from the Dutch bishops in 1947 dealt largely with 'Godless communism'; dockworkers' strikes in Amsterdam (1946) and London (1949), like the miners' strikes in Belgium (1948), were seen as 'communist plots' to take over the country, and books like George Orwell's *Nineteen Eighty-Four* (1949) and *The God that Failed* (1950), as well as a collection of essays by Arthur Koestler, André Gide and other former 'fellow travellers' caused great furore. Three years later, almost nothing was left of the general sympathy for the brave Red Army in 1945. *Life* magazine dedicated an entire issue to the discrepancy in the number of troops maintained by the two superpowers: 640,000 GIs were faced off against 2.6 million Red soldiers. Hollywood films like *I Married a Communist*, *I was a Communist for the FBI*, *Red Planet Mars* and *The Red Menace* played to packed cinemas.

This – at least partly spontaneous – mobilisation against communism strengthened the bonds between all non-communists. Just as during the war, a common enemy had been found, and this sense of unity became almost as important as the struggle itself. Both the left and the right began reconsidering their standpoints. In Germany, the Netherlands, Sweden and Austria, the social democrats dropped the term 'class struggle', while the Christian Democrats came up with new social policies: all across Europe, old conflicts were being abandoned or mollified. Anti-communism served in this as a kind of crystallisation point, a binding anti-ideology. Without a doubt, Stalin can be seen as one of the founders of a united Europe.

In this way, sometime in winter 1946, the Soviet Union suddenly changed from a friend into a foe. From his office in Moscow in mid-February, the American diplomat George Kennan sent his superiors in Washington a biting analysis of Soviet policies. In that historical 'long telegram', Kennan pointed out the Soviet Union's permanent urge to expand its power and entered a plea for a new 'containment doctrine'. 'At the bottom of the Kremlin's neurotic view of world affairs is a traditional and instinctive Russian sense of insecurity,' he wrote, and the main element of United States policy 'must be that of a long term, patient but firm and vigilant containment of Russian expansive tendencies'.

Three weeks later, on 5 March, 1946, the Cold War became a reality for one and all with Churchill's famous 'Iron Curtain' speech at Fulton College in Missouri: 'From Stettin in the Baltic to Trieste in the Adriatic, an iron curtain has descended across the continent. Behind that line lie all the capitals of the ancient states of Central and Eastern Europe. Warsaw, Berlin, Prague, Vienna, Budapest, Belgrade, Bucharest and Sofia . . .' Western politicians and commentators spoke of the 'great international communist conspiracy' and about 'Moscow blueprints' for taking over Western Europe. In reality, as we know now, Stalin's basic stance in the years following the war was primarily a defensive one. The Soviet Union was completely exhausted, completely incapable of turning around and starting a new war. Stalin's greatest trauma had been the German invasion of 1941, a repetition of which he hoped to avoid at all costs. He lived in deep fear of an armed conflict with the West, and particularly of the enormous preponderance of American air power, America whose bombers could make of the Soviet Union 'one huge target'. It is true that from 1949 the Russians had the atom bomb as well, but in those first years

Russian nuclear technology lagged far behind that of the West. 'Stalin trembled in fear' at the prospect of an American attack, Khrushchev wrote in his memoirs. 'Oh, how he shook! He was afraid of a war!'

There was yet another reason why there could be no such thing as a fixed 'Moscow blueprint' for a communist offensive: the political situations in the individual countries of Europe were too different. Local leaders, national characteristics and patriotic feelings played such a great role in those first post-war years that no country would have fitted an imposed Soviet scheme.

The clearest example of 'popular communism' was that of Josip Broz, otherwise known as Tito. This former Yugoslav partisan leader enjoyed enormous authority. He had led an extremely active resistance movement, and he had also succeeded in bringing together the sharply divided ethnic groups of Yugoslavia into one large, well oiled underground movement. He did not shrink from applying Stalinist methods of terror, he kept the various ethnic groups under his thumb by means of a risky policy of divide and conquer, but for the vast majority of Yugoslavs he was the natural leader. And he continued to be exactly that, for thirty-five years.

In Greece, the communist resistance of the EAM/ELAS was at least equally popular. It had a moderate socialist programme, it was a local and patriotic movement, and by the end of the war it comprised at least half a million partisans, including many non-communists. In 1944, however, Churchill and Stalin had made some clear agreements: their 'naughty documents' stipulated that Greece was to remain ninety-per cent Western. In October 1944, a sizeable British military force landed in Greece to disarm the resistance – later always referred to as 'bandit gangs' – and support a right-wing coalition government. The vicious civil war that followed ended only after the United States took over from Britain and Tito closed his borders to the guerrillas with their communist sympathies. In November 1949, after 'analysing the situation', the central committee of the Greek Communist Party decided to lay down its arms. The country had been at war for almost ten years. Half a million Greeks had died under the German occupation, and the civil war had claimed 160,000 more and left 700,000 homeless. A quarter of all the country's houses had been destroyed. All the Greeks wanted was peace and quiet.

In Poland, power was assumed by a man rather like Tito: Wladyslaw Gomulka, the leader of the communist underground. His movement too soon enjoyed a great deal of support, because it addressed those problems which all pre-war parties had ignored: widespread poverty, ethnic conflicts, the anxious relationships with Germany and the Soviet Union. In 1945 he stamped out the Farmers' Party, declaring that the communists 'will never surrender power once they have it', but at the same time he was a typical Polish patriot. He abhorred Stalin's brand of rigid coercion.

The communists in Czechoslovakia were initially in favour of a multiparty system, and there is nothing to indicate that they intended to ban other parties during those early days. They were popular enough as it was: in the May 1946 elections they won thirty-eight per cent of the vote, making them the country's largest party by far. Their movement had more than a million members. With the support of the communists, President Edvard Beneš and Jan Masaryk sought contact with both the Soviet Union and the West, and showed great interest in the Marshall Plan.

Yet no matter how firm their local and national roots were, all these communist parties were ultimately forced to submit to abrupt takeovers steered and manipulated by the Kremlin, dictatorial interventions by elite groups within the party who, once they had achieved position, refused to let go again. In the long run, the communists usually set up a general popular front in which all parties were forced to take part, as well as a broad gamut of associations and organisations, up to and including the Federation of Invalids. All dissidents were silenced by brute force. During the last free elections in August 1947, the communists in Hungary received less than twenty-five per cent of the vote; after May 1949, however, László Rajk could triumphantly announce that his Workers' Party enjoyed the support of ninety-five per cent of the population. In December 1949, the Bulgarian Fatherland Front won ninety-eight per cent of the vote, a percentage that seemed rather suspect, even to its most fervent supporters.

In 1950, Hans Krijt – 'The communist youth organisation had suddenly realised that I was a Dutch political refugee' – ended up at the Prague Film Academy. 'I was in the same class as Milós Forman, who wanted to be a screenwriter at that time. Milan Kundera was studying dramatics there. Forman was a real big mouth: he was the only one who would blurt out that the newest Russian film was completely worthless. Kundera was still a communist then, he wrote for official party organs. But we all made fun of Stalin. In Marxism class we used a linguistics textbook written by Stalin, he even stuck his nose into things like that. We made jokes about it, but everyone played along with the game, teachers and students. The lessons followed that textbook faithfully.'

'Kundera was typical of that generation of intellectuals,' Krijt's wife Olga Krijtova says. 'Right after the war they were all communists: the Soviets were, after all, our liberators. But from 1956 they began feeling more and more uneasy. Kundera started writing satires: *Ridiculous Loves* in 1963 and *The Joke* in 1967; when you read his work you could see the Prague Spring on its way. Until 1968 came and rolled right over it. Finally he went into exile.'

Olga Kritjova became a Dutch-Czech translator. She remained a member of the Communist Party until 1968. When she quit the party, she was immediately forbidden to translate or to write. 'That was a problem you solved by using a "front", someone who let you use his or her name. That did create problems, though, when a "fronted" translation won a prize. Then the person whose name you'd borrowed had to accept the prize, give readings, that sort of thing.'

In 1969 the couple tried to emigrate to the Netherlands, but their application was rejected. After that Krijt taught Dutch at a language institute. After he once explained the difference between 'I believe he's coming' and 'I believe in God', he immediately received a reprimand for spreading religious propaganda.

Olga: 'Every time a reception was held at the Dutch embassy, I had to report on it right away. What I always filled in was "Talked about the weather in Czechoslovakia and the Netherlands." The officials never put up a fuss, they had their own forms to complete anyway.'

Hans: 'My Dutch class was always packed with girls trying to escape the country by marrying a Dutchman.'

Olga: 'Those were deadly years!'

For Central and Eastern Europe, the deadly years lasted from 1948, by way of 1956 and 1968, until 1989.

*

Churchill had declared the Cold War in 1946, but the first skirmishes did not begin until a year later. In 1947 the American president decided to support the Greeks in their struggle against 'communist' rebels. In that year, too, the Marshall Plan was announced – intended in part to turn the rising tide of communism in Western Europe. In the communist world, too, the first internal conflict took place. Tito had no intention of conforming to Stalin's directives, and made no attempt to hide the fact. So in spring 1948 a public rift arose between Yugoslavia and the Soviet Union, the first crack in the façade of the Eastern Bloc. Czechoslovakia began making overtures for aid from the Marshall Plan, and Stalin's paranoia increased by the week. The Cold War escalated.

In West Germany the Americans began a new purge of the administrative system, directed this time not against Nazis, but against communists. In June 1948 the announcement was made that a parliamentary council would be set up, the start of a new and independent Germany under the leadership of the former mayor of Cologne, Konrad Adenauer, a man of unimpeachable reputation. At the same time, West Berlin and the area occupied by the Western Allies received a new currency: the Deutschmark.

The Soviet Union reacted immediately: on 24 June, 1948, all connections to West Berlin – including water, gas and electricity – were cut off. The Soviet action ended in fiasco. The Americans and British, using the enormous logistical experience gained in the war, began a bold operation: the entire city, with its 2.5 million inhabitants, received all the crucial supplies it needed – including oil and coal – by means of an airlift. For almost a year, hundreds of Dakotas, C-47s and C-54s wended their way through a narrow air corridor. Thousands of pilots and air traffic controllers took part, and in May 1949 Stalin had no choice but to back down. He had not only suffered a political and strategic defeat, but he had also handed the Americans a fantastic propaganda opportunity. The Berlin blockade convinced the West Germans that they needed the Americans. After the *Luftbrücke* the Allies were no longer an occupying army, but welcome protectors. The blockade had far-reaching consequences for the Americans as well: rather than pull out of western Europe as planned, they decided to stay.

During that same summer in 1948, Stalin decided to tighten his hold on the Soviet Union's satellite states. He may have been relatively powerless against the sovereign and popular Tito, but he still had a hold on the patriotic leader of Poland. On 3 June, 1948, in the midst of the Yugoslavia crisis, Gomulka had poured oil on the flames by announcing in a speech that his own Polish communists had not been independent or patriotic enough in the 1930s. The nod towards the present situation could not have been clearer. Within two months, Gomulka had disappeared – for the time being – from the political arena.

One year later it was Hungary's turn. On 30 May, 1949, the loyal communist and Spanish Civil War veteran László Rajk was arrested, along with seven other 'conspirators'. He was horribly tortured, and during a show trial soon confessed that, working with American intelligence chief Allan W. Dulles, he had tried to set up a 'bloodthirsty, fascist-patterned dictatorship' in Hungary. He was hanged on 15 October, 1949, and succeeded by the grim Stalinist Mátyás Rákosi. In 1951, the secretary general of the Communist Party of Czechoslovakia, Rudolf Slánský, was arrested and charged with a similar 'conspiracy'.

Slánský's trial – at the conclusion of which all the defendants were hanged – had a special twist to it: eleven of the fourteen suspects were Jewish. It was the starting sign for a new series of purges throughout the Eastern Bloc, a wave of terror with pronounced anti-Semitic characteristics. The excuse upon which it was originally based was reminiscent of the murder of Sergei Kirov in 1934. This time it had to do with Andrei Zhdanov, a member of the Politburo and a hero of the siege of Leningrad, who had died of a heart failure in a party clinic in 1948. Immediately after his death, one of the female physicians there accused her Jewish colleagues of having neglected Zhdanov's ailment, and said that they were responsible for his death. At the time, the complaint had been dismissed.

Four years later, in 1952, the dossier was retrieved from the shelves. In 1950, a man by the name of Ivan Varfolomeyer had been arrested in China; he had confessed – probably under duress – to his Russian interrogators that he worked for a group of American conspirators, led by President Truman, who were planning to blow up the Kremlin with nuclear missiles fired from one of the windows of the American embassy in Moscow. No one – except for Stalin – would ever have believed such a cock and bull story. He, however, made the Varfolomeyer affair the focal point of a new series of show trials intended to bring together all the loose ends: the American plot to destroy the Kremlin, the Zionist Jewish plot to infiltrate the party, and the Zionist physicians' plot to murder Zhdanov.

From 1950, therefore, there began a systematic persecution of predominantly Jewish doctors, military men and party leaders, and of Jews in general. In the early 1950s the camps of the Gulag were fuller than ever: at the peak, in the dark 1930s, there had been 1.8 million Soviet citizens in the camps; in 1953, there were 2.4 million. And the terror had now spread to the satellite countries as well: in Bulgaria, at least 100,000 people were detained in the infamous 'Little Siberia'; in Hungary some 200,000 political prisoners were sent to the camps. Almost 140,000 Czechs and Slovaks, 180,000 Rumanians and 80,000 Albanians were interred as well.

In familiar agitprop style, a campaign was started in January 1953 to whip up interest in the coming trials. Big articles appeared in *Pravda* and *Izvestia* telling of a 'bourgeois-Zionistic-American conspiracy' that had infiltrated the country, and the newspapers' tone grew more anti-Semitic every day. The Jews – and not only Jews – lived in fear of mass deportation.

Was it really a coincidence that, at precisely that point, on 5 March, 1953, Stalin died suddenly of a brain haemorrhage? Historians have been wondering about that ever since. The various eyewitness accounts of his death differ on essential points – a fateful sign, in itself – and it is certain that he lay dying for hours on the bedroom floor of his dacha. He had become a victim of his own terror: none of the staff dared at first to open his bedroom door, no doctor dared risk his life with an attempt to save Stalin's. In fact, for some time – whether out of fear or on purpose – no doctor was even summoned. Beria, who had been warned right away, shouted half-drunkenly at Stalin's bodyguards: 'Can't you see that Comrade Stalin is fast asleep? Get out, all of you, and don't disturb him!'

In the end, it was twelve hours after Stalin's stroke that a doctor was finally called; no good explanation has ever been given for the delay. As Stalin lay dying, his son Vasili screamed at Beria and other members of the Politburo: 'You filthy swine, you're killing my father!' And according to Molotov, Beria told him later: 'I put him away, I saved all your lives.'

Whatever the case, the fact is that Stalin's exit was a matter of life and death for many members of the Politburo in spring 1953. Most of them had come to power during the previous purges, and they remembered all too clearly how Stalin had dealt with their predecessors. Molotov's Jewish wife had already been arrested, and men like Beria, Deputy Prime Minister Georgy Malenkov and Khrushchev knew that their time had probably come as well.

When the physicians at last arrived, they hardly dared to unbutton Stalin's shirt. They asked Beria and the other leaders present for express permission for everything they did. Stalin's struggle with death lasted five days. 'At the very last moment he suddenly opened his eyes and looked at everyone in the room,' his daughter Svetlana Alliluyeva recalled. 'It was a terrible gaze, mad or perhaps furious, and full of the fear of death . . .' But Stalin had barely drawn his last breath when Beria bounded out of the room, called loudly for his chauffeur and, as Khrushchev remembered it, walked around 'beaming'. 'He knew for a certainty that the moment for which he had been waiting so long had arrived.'

The show trials were quickly called off, most of the defendants were freed, and the Gulag was slowly dismantled. Less than a month after his death, Stalin's name began not to be mentioned in *Pravda* any more. His portrait disappeared from public places. In late June, the seemingly simple and coarse Khrushchev was able to seize power. By the end of that year, in classic Stalinist fashion, his rival Beria had been arrested, condemned as a 'British spy' and an 'enemy of the people', and shot through the head. All of the older people I talked to in the former Eastern Bloc still knew exactly what they had been doing on the morning of Friday, 6 March, 1953, when the news of Stalin's death was announced.

'My father was standing in the doorway,' Yuri Klejner in St Petersburg told me. 'He wiped his eyes: they were absolutely dry. I was six at the time. I tried to cry too, because that's what everyone was doing, but I couldn't either. A little neighbour girl said: "It's not right to play now that Comrade Stalin has died."' Irina Trantina, the daughter of a general in Kiev, was eleven and heard about it on the radio: 'I started crying loudly, it was as though the world had ended. My parents were also very afraid of an atomic attack by the Americans, during those weeks everything was in a state of alarm. My father had barely escaped being convicted in an earlier purge because, as he put it, "I was wearing the wrong shoes."'

Anna Smirnova was a young mother at the time: 'I was upset, that above all. Not because of Stalin, but because of the feeling that something very bad was on its way again. What would the next regime have in store for us?' Ira Klejner, daughter of a high-ranking officer in Sebastapol: 'I was seven. I can remember eating a slice of bread with a fried egg. I realised I was supposed to weep, like everyone else, but all I could summon up was one tear. One tear. It fell on my egg.'

———

'I'm not the right person to ask. In those days I was on the wrong side. I was one of those in control. It would be like denouncing myself.

'But all right, since you insist. My name is Wladek Matwin. I was born in 1916, in a village not far from Katowice, close to the Silesian border. As boys, we were taken to school in the back of a lorry. The town in those days was inhabited almost solely by Jews, and we threw stones at them. Because the Jews were different. They wore strange clothing, they had funny hats, they didn't speak Polish, they didn't belong.

'As I said before: my lifetime was a time of great violence. In most of the things I experienced, I had no choice in the matter. There were these huge outside forces dragging me along by the hair: during the war, with the communist rebels, in the army, in the party, and finally in the factory as a mathematician. Only much, much later did I realise that we are all limited. Our points of view, our intelligence, it's all very limited. My own life was already too much for me to understand.

'I went to school in Poznan, joined the Polish communist youth organisation at eighteen and finally ended up in the Soviet Union. I fought in the Red Army, helped to reopen the Polish embassy in Moscow, and by 1946 I was back in Moscow. That's how it started.

'I became a party official. Chairman of the communist youth organisation, party overseer of Wroclaw and Warsaw, secretary of the central committee, and, in the end, more or less the right-hand man to Gomulka.

'During those first few years it was simply a matter of clearing the debris, literally as well, the way I suppose it was everywhere in Europe. All of Wroclaw had been blasted to pieces, we had to bury thousands of bodies, countless Germans were driven out, millions of Poles came in their place, it was one huge chaotic mess. Often, what we did wasn't nice, it was violence, violence against people, violence against the opposition, violence against all forms of reflection, but we thought of it as a struggle; we considered everything a struggle.

'But it would be untrue to say that everything was bad back in those days. We weren't Stalinists; for example, we kept Polish agriculture from being collectivised. We were driven by a desire to help, we did our duty, we lived and worked for a cause, and everything was subservient to that. Duty is a military thing, and also something religious. We believed in many things, the party was almost a church. These days I know that real Marxism is essentially a scientific theory, with all the associated room for doubt. The most difficult thing, of course, is to combine that sense of duty and that doubt – which is what happened after 1956 – but right after the war we were still pure believers.

'A lot of things were swept under the carpet in those years, there were things we didn't talk about, subjects we didn't touch upon. The worst year was 1948. At first Gomulka had taken part in the communist takeovers, but he refused to go on and collectivise the farms, and he was also interested in receiving aid from the Marshall Plan. But well, we knew it wouldn't be very wise to start a full-scale revolt against the Russians. That has never worked out well here, and besides, the country was full of Russian garrisons. We Polish communists were angry about that as well. As if Poland was part of Germany!

'Gomulka felt that he had made a big mistake by involving the Russians too much in the country's affairs. He was a real worker, not much of a reader, not particularly interested in the nuances, he was mercilessly frank and absolutely incorruptible. He possessed the enormous willpower that was needed in those days to say no to the Russians. In the end I couldn't work with him any more, yet he was a formidable personality. He actually ended up in prison for a few years.

'I met them all. Erich Honecker was my DDR counterpart in the youth organisation, and fanatical even then. His boss, Walter Ulbricht, was also one of those people who never laughed. He was such a nasty, drab, tale-teller of a bureaucrat! Khrushchev had something clownish about him, a smart rebel of a farm boy. He had never read much, but he had this gleam in his eye. And Stalin, yes, Stalin, I was introduced to him once, during a buffet dinner in Moscow. I was a young, ambitious Polish talent at the time, and we talked about philosophy. He was short and really quite ugly, and he spoke Russian with a horrible Georgian accent. But I'll never forget his eyes: not brown, not blue, not dark, not light; the eyes of a tiger. When we said goodbye, Stalin pointed at me and asked our minister of foreign affairs: 'That boy, does he belong to us or to Poland?' The minister said: 'To Poland.' After that I was no longer allowed to attend such functions. I had been too brash.

'Stalin, well, how I can put this? I adored the man. When he died I was party overseer of Warsaw. It was in the middle of the night, I was fast asleep. Suddenly the phone rang, it was a colleague from the central committee. All he said was: "Listen, Stalin's dead." I was crushed. Even when my father died, I wasn't as shattered as I was at that moment.

'Of course I am very well aware that Stalin was a villain, a major criminal. But to say that is to oversimplify matters. He was also a great man. History has given us a number of people like that: Robespierre, Cromwell, Napoleon, all of them villains. But when you mention those names it's not enough just to say that; then you're not speaking the truth. They were also great statesmen. They were criminals, and they were statesmen. People usually don't even want to know that such a combination is possible, I don't know why that is. But of course it's possible. That criminal Stalin, after all, also led us into battle against fascism, and that's a fact.

'The world and history are not as simple as children often imagine. It's as complicated as love. So: I loved a criminal. But if I had known in 1941 what I knew after 1956, I would never have been able to fight that way in the war. The world is complicated, my friend.

'As I said, Khrushchev was a rebel. During the three years after Stalin's death, a lot of things began changing within the party. East Berlin had revolted in June 1953, we had had an uprising in Poznan, party members were going back to Lenin, to Marx, to places where there was room for doubt. The party top brass was fearful. Our party was organised on the basis of discipline and service, not on reflection. The leaders were frightened by that.

'And then came Khrushchev's shock therapy. Despite it all, Stalin was still a person we respected rather deeply. And during Stalin's lifetime, Khrushchev had never uttered a word of criticism, he had been the most faithful vassal imaginable. Then, suddenly, there was that emotional speech at the twentieth party congress in which he explained how things really were. The entire pre-war leadership of our party turned out to have been murdered by the Soviets. Khrushchev revealed that Lenin, during the last year of his life, had tried to put a stop to Stalin. He condemned the purges, Stalin's waste of lives during the war and the collectivisation of Soviet agriculture, his paranoia and his break with Tito. Hundreds of thousands of innocent and honest communists had been tortured into making the most bizarre confessions, and Stalin had personally been behind it all. Khrushchev wanted to go back to the roots of communism, to Lenin. He flogged the aggrandisement of a man who had, in reality, never gone anywhere, who hadn't spoken to a farmer or a worker for years, and who knew the country only on the basis of newsreels in which everything had been tidied up. 'He was a coward,' Khrushchev shouted. 'He was panicky! Not once during the entire war did he dare even to come close to the front!'

'Stalin came crashing to earth, and with him our view of the world. Our Stalinist party leader, Boleslaw Bierut, had a heart attack and died a few days later. To be honest, I believe the Soviet Union never completely recovered from that speech.

'That was in February 1956. Within our very own party, a movement started that demanded greater democracy and more self-rule. It was on that wave that Gomulka made his comeback, and he stayed in power until 1970. I stood behind it four-square; rigid socialism was, in my eyes, a dead-end street. But we were all terribly concerned what the Russians would do. In October, Khrushchev and the commander of the Warsaw Pact forces suddenly arrived for a surprise visit. At the airport, the first thing he said was: 'We are ready to intervene.' Gomulka refused to talk with a loaded gun on the table. That same afternoon we chose him as our new party leader.

'The Poles are spirited fighters, we all formed a single front, and it would have been havoc for the Russians. Khrushchev knew that. In the end, despite all their differences, Gomulka was able to convince the Russians that he was an upstanding communist. Khrushchev was even touched by his words, and so the Russians agreed to allow the Poles to follow their 'own line'. That was definitely the wisest thing they could have done; Poland is quite a bit larger than Hungary, they couldn't risk an open conflict.

'It was a huge success for us. We kept up our sovereign stance towards the Russians. The DDR never achieved that level of independence, and after 1956 it became unattainable for the Hungarians as well, and it failed with the Czechoslovakians in 1968. We did it better, in silence, almost without bloodshed.

'Politicians are the people operating the machine. They hop on it, like onto a moving train, and they jump off again too. That's the way things were between Gomulka and I. I was always there for him, I advised him on a daily basis, but I was also critical. In 1956 I felt that we should launch a number of far-reaching changes, enter into a dramatic democratisation process. It wasn't enough just to change leaders. But the system remained rigid and totalitarian, an ironclad state apparatus.

'My next-door neighbour here in the street is Mieczyslaw Rakowski, he was the last leader of the Polish Communist Party. He was the one who turned off the lights when he went out of the door in 1990. When I talk to him about it now, he says: "Oh, why didn't we give them more freedom? Why didn't we let them do as they pleased, with commerce, shops, permission to travel freely? We were so stupid, we wanted to arrange everything for them, everything had to be ironed smooth and tucked in tightly." He's right about that. Socialism is only tenable as an ideal. You can't force it down people's throats, you can't steer it. It has to come from the people themselves, the pursuit of justice, freedom, equality, brotherhood. In that context, we need to keep looking for new forms all the time. Because having only market forces, only inequality, spells disaster for the world that is now on its way.

'In 1963 I asked Gomulka to release me from servitude. I went to school and studied mathematics and history, I've been a normal citizen for almost forty years now. My faith has changed to doubt. Let me tell you, my friend, politics is hard work. You must have a feeling for it, you must have a taste for it. I did it for years, but in the long run I don't really belong to that species.

'When I was party overseer in Wroclaw, I used to spend whole evenings talking to Tadeusz Mazowiecki, who became the first non-communist prime minister of Poland forty years later, the first one in an Eastern Bloc country. He was a Catholic journalist and politician at the time, but we understood each other very well. He taught me that the word "religion" comes from "religio", which means "to be attached". You are religious if you feel attached, to the world, to people, to God. "You can't always believe," he said. "But you can be bonded."

'I'm in my eighties now, and I've been an atheist all my life. But St Francis has always been very close to my heart. And he says the same thing: "That tree is my friend, that little dog is my friend."

'It's hard to understand everything that happens in your life. Sometimes my little dog understands better than I do.'

Chapter Fifty

Budapest

THE GRASS HAS BEEN MOWED. THE TREES ARE FULL OF RED APPLES. A man and a woman trudge along the road carrying pitchforks. Beside the houses lie the piles of logs, neatly stacked for the winter, heavy with the scent of resin. On a hillside two men are ploughing; one of them is sitting on a bright red tractor, the other one is guiding the plough.

At the campsite where I am staying, close to the brand-spanking-new customs house on the border between the Czech Republic and Slovakia, almost everyone has left. The last few employees sit in the canteen at night, watching television. There's a film on: a girl is seduced by a fat old man, she goes with him to bars where the patrons speak only English, a former boyfriend tries to talk sense into her, she laughs in his face, the old man cheats on her and she becomes increasingly addicted to the foreigners' lifestyle, until the ex-boyfriend . . .

Outside you hear only the crickets, the brook, an owl . . .

Budapest, after all this, is wild, footloose, careless, full of holes and dents and honking cars, not a museum or a display case but a living city. In Buda the cranes swing back and forth, in Pest one hears the chipping and chiselling of the stonemasons: like everywhere else in Central Europe, the building and the painting is going on here as though half a century must be made up for in five years.

The Monument to the Martyrs, the falling figure with which the Hungarian communists would later commemorate the 1956 uprising, has vanished from the city centre. The marble stairs lead nowhere. The former party headquarters has been taken over by the socialists, the building still hums with spirited discussions, with the sound of typing and the murmur of meetings. The monument itself has been moved to the edge of town, to the place where statues from the olden days are sent to die, a walled place of exile specially built to house the former communist memorials. And there they are, indeed: the comrades joining hands, the leaders with spectacles and briefcases, the soldiers with flags and pistols, all those popularly edifying mothers, children, tractors, flowers and flames. At least half the statues have their hands raised to the sky: in this sad compound, a muffled 'hurrah' is always present in the background. It is not all ugly, by no means, some of the monuments are absolutely lovely, it's just that they bear the wrong names, the wrong slogans and the wrong symbols.

No one in Hungary saw 1956 coming. The little square where the young upstarts first gathered lies in the space between two highways along the Danube and is dominated by a statue of the revolutionary hero of 1848, the poet Sándor Petőfi. The lawn at his feet is the perfect place for spontaneous, hit-and-run demonstrations, and that was their only intention on 23 October, 1956. Hungary, just like Poland, needed more freedom, and in the previous months a few hundred students had been meeting regularly in the university auditorium to talk. Now they had decided to organise a demonstration. But to everyone's surprise, huge crowds of young people from all over the city joined the usual group of students. They waved Polish and Hungarian flags, shouted 'Long live the young people of Poland!' and 'We believe in Imre Nagy!' The streets of Budapest were filled with a spirit of revival and adventure. Even students from the staunchly communist Lenin Institute came to the gathering, carrying red banners and a portrait of Lenin.

Rarely has a mass meeting got out of hand the way this one did. Soldiers from the barracks across the way unexpectedly joined the students. Because it was closing time at the factories, masses of workers came along as well. None of it had been planned. 'To Stalin!' someone shouted, and those who followed spent hours working with blowtorches, cables and a truck to topple the giant statue. 'To the radio station!' someone else cried, and the broadcasting centre was surrounded by thousands of people and finally occupied. The first shots rang out. In ten hours the clock advanced from 1848 to 1956, that's how fast things went in Budapest.

In European history, 1956 was a pivotal year. It was the year of Khrushchev's Stalin speech, the year of open discussion in the Eastern Bloc, of unrest in Poland.

It was the year of the Suez Crisis, the fiasco for the British and the French who had worked with the Israelis on a joint colonial expedition against Egypt to secure passage through the Suez Canal, and who withdrew with their tails between their legs when the Americans threatened to cut their funding and undermine the British currency.

1956 was the also the year in which three pretty Muslim girls carried out the first attacks on the Milk-Bar, the Caféteria and the offices of Air France in Algiers, dragging France into a humiliating war in which more than half a million Frenchmen finally took part. It was the year in which Indonesia cut final ties with the Netherlands, in which the British sent the Greek-Cypriot leader Makarios into exile, in which the brothers Fidel and Raúl Castro landed in Cuba to start a revolution. It was the year of the fairy-tale marriage between Prince Rainier of Monaco and the American film star Grace Kelly, and of Elvis Presley's breakthrough with 'Heartbreak Hotel'. And it was, above all, the year of the Hungarian uprising.

The images went all over the world, and for as long as the Cold War lasted the Hungarian rebellion was the symbol of the spirit of freedom against communist oppression. The truth was, as usual, much more complicated. After Stalin's fall from grace, the position of Hungarian leader Mátyás Rákosi, an old-school Stalinist, soon became untenable. He was replaced by an interim pope, but the man the Hungarians were really waiting for was the former president, Imre Nagy. 'Uncle Imre' was cut from the same cloth as Gomulka: a communist, a humanist and a patriot. He had actually taken part in the Russian Revolution and the civil war and had occupied a top position in the Comintern in Moscow for fifteen years. But all that work on behalf of the party had not, as his biographer Miklos Moln puts it, 'succeeded in deadening the human essence within him, party politics did not make him forget "the ideal".' Yet he was also a loner, and a doubter. He lacked Gomulka's feeling for the masses, his toughness and vigour.

The Hungarian Revolution began in the central hall of Budapest's Technical University. From 1955, it was the site of increasingly frank discussions on all manner of political issues, and the movement gained momentum after Khrushchev's speech on Stalin. Some of the students devoured the works of Western writers like Aldous Huxley and George Orwell, others experimented with modern music and painting. In spring 1956, László Rajk was posthumously rehabilitated. In September, the first issue of a new, fiercely oppositionist weekly, *Hétfői Hírlap* (Monday News) appeared, which the Hungarians fairly tore from the news-stands. On Sunday, 6 October, Rajk was solemnly reinterred. What was intended as an intimate gathering developed into a spontaneous tumult in which 200,000 Hungarians took part. As one of the early dissenters later recalled: 'That was the moment we all realised that our protest was not simply an affair for a few communist intellectuals. Everyone, it seemed, was turning against the government in the same way.'

In October, after Rajk's funeral and the successful rebellion in Poland, the students' demands grew increasingly specific: democratic reforms had to be implemented in Hungary as well. Gomulka was their hero and Imre Nagy could play the same role in Hungary, although Nagy himself was not too enthusiastic about this. A demonstration was scheduled for Tuesday, 23 October, to underscore their 'sixteen points'; the loyal party man Nagy was vehemently opposed. Later in the week, a huge conference was to be held, a kind of broad national debate about their demands. An armed rebellion was the furthest thing from their minds.

It was only on the evening of 23 October, when things truly got out of hand, that Nagy let himself be convinced by the Politburo to address the huge crowd in front of parliament. 'Comrades!' he began. 'We are no longer comrades!' the crowd roared back. The next morning he spoke of 'hostile elements' who had turned against the popular democracy. One week later he declared that the Hungarian people, by means of 'a heroic struggle', had achieved a centuries-old dream: independence and neutrality. He had become, despite himself, the leader of the Hungarian Revolution.

Later interviews showed that many students were deeply shocked by the way 'their' demonstration had degenerated into an uprising by roaming crowds 'who acted like idiots', incapable of 'putting on the brakes themselves'. Most of them realised from the start that this was bound to go wrong.

By the end of the week, fewer and fewer revolutionary students were to be found among those fighting in the streets. Most of the combatants were working youths, hoodlums and vandals, tough kids from the poorest neighbourhoods of Budapest. A Hungarian doctor, who treated many of the wounded, said later: 'There were many fighters who . . . had never even heard of Gomulka, and who, when asked why they were risking their lives, answered by saying, "Well, what good is living for 600 forints a month?"' One of the rebellious students said later: 'It's painful to admit, but it's true: they were the real heroes.'

On Wednesday morning, 24 October, long columns of rapidly assembled Soviet troops came rolling into the city. Barricades were thrown up, the tanks could go no further, and skirmishes broke out here and there. Regular discussions also arose between the tank crews and Hungarian civilians. More than once during those first days, a Russian commander announced that he had been sent to free the city from 'fascist bandits' but that he had absolutely no intention of firing on these peaceful crowds. Such declarations were greeted with loud cheers, the Russians were embraced, Hungarian flags were spread across the tanks. One Hungarian tank commander, the former communist partisan Pál Maléter, who had been ordered to use his five tanks to break through to a prison besieged by the crowd, openly took sides with the people and let the prisoners go free; he became one of the great leaders of the Hungarian revolt.

When several other such instances of fraternisation took place around the Astoria Hotel, the rumour started that the Soviet troops had taken sides with the revolution as well. But a wild shoot-out in front of parliament, probably instigated by the Hungarian secret police, soon put an end to any such illusions. Everywhere in the city after that, tanks were attacked with Molotov cocktails and the brashest among the young rioters even climbed onto them and tossed grenades straight down the turrets.

When Noel Barber, correspondent for the *Daily Mail*, drove into the city on Friday, 26 October, he saw torn-up streets and burned-out cars everywhere. 'Even before I reached the Duna Hotel, I counted the carcasses of at least forty Soviet tanks ... At the corner of Stalin Avenue ... two monster Russian T-54 tanks lumbered past, dragging bodies behind them, a warning to all Hungarians of what happened to the fighters. In another street, three bodies were strung up in a tree, the necks at ungainly angles, looking not so much like bodies, more like effigies.'

The day before, Imre Nagy had been appointed prime minister of Hungary with Moscow's approval. Khrushchev's wager was that things would then go more or less the way they had in Poland: Nagy's popularity would soon stifle the uprising, the communist regime would remain firmly in place. But there was one important difference: Hungary was not Poland. Where Gomulka stopped, Nagy continued: he let himself be carried away by the mood in the streets, in his speeches he demanded neutral status for Hungary and called for withdrawal from the Warsaw Pact. Meanwhile the rebellion spread across the country, prisons were stormed, factories were shut down by strikes, there was fighting everywhere.

On Tuesday, 30 October, after a shooting incident, an angry crowd besieged the main headquarters of the Communist Party. The army was called in, but the tank crews turned their guns and began firing on the party offices instead. When party secretary Imre Mező stepped outside waving a white flag, he was shot down. Then the building was stormed. In the crowd that day was György Konrád, twenty-three at the time and just finished at university. He told me how he saw secret police officers hung up by their feet. 'They had probably been tortured beforehand, because they were no longer wearing shirts. The people spat on them. An older man in an expensive-looking coat said: "Shame on you, the Russians have done a great deal for all of you." He was hanged as well. The scene made me very uneasy.'

Later, rumours began circulating about secret prison cells beneath the square, and people even claimed to have heard the sounds of tapping. Excavating machines were brought in and a huge hole was dug in the middle of the square. The crowd watched breathlessly. No one seemed to have the slightest idea that anything else was going on in the world around them.

In Moscow, however, as we now know, there was a strong inclination to let Hungary go. The Russians' greatest fear was that the revolt would spread to Bucharest, Prague and Berlin. 'Budapest was an enormous headache,' Khrushchev wrote later. He told the Politburo: 'There are two paths: a military path of occupation, and a path of peace; the withdrawal of troops, negotiations.' Marshal Zhukov – in his brief role as minister of defence at the time – advocated withdrawing all troops from Hungary. Central-committee member Yekaterina Furtseva said this was a lesson in military politics for the Soviet Union: 'We must look for different kinds of relationships with the popular democracies.'

Meanwhile, György Konrád – acting as bodyguard to a professor – trotted around town carrying a sub-machine gun. At the time he was also on the staff of a literary journal. 'I decided to pay a visit to the director of the state publishing house, to ask him for a bigger print run for our magazine. I asked him for 30,000 copies. "Of course, make it 50,000," he said. I didn't grasp at the time that his reaction had everything to do with my sub-machine gun hanging on the coat rack.'

A certain degree of order was restored during the final weekend of the uprising. The man who had led the lynch mob at the party headquarters was arrested. The strike ended.

In Moscow, however, the mood changed after Nagy's announcement that Hungary would leave the Warsaw Pact. Britain and France had invaded the Suez zone that week, and the Soviet leadership felt that it would be a mistake to tolerate too many 'capitalist' successes.

György Konrád: 'At night I heard the first shots. I turned on the radio, like everyone else. Very early the next morning I went to the university, with my sub-machine gun. There were Russian tanks in the streets. I knew that a number of students were armed as well, and I hoped we could defend the buildings together. But we never fired a shot. They didn't shoot at us, so we decided not to shoot at them.'

On Sunday morning, 4 November, the Russians rolled into Hungary with considerable numbers of men and material. Within a day Budapest was theirs, within a week the uprising had been crushed. A new regime was installed under the leadership of party secretary János Kádár, a former associate of Nagy who had gone over to the Russians. There was, ever so briefly, a general strike, and then winter settled in.

According to the most reliable sources, approximately 600 Soviet soldiers and 2–3,000 Hungarians were killed in the fighting; some 22,000 proven or suspected rebels were sentenced to work camps or prison, and approximately 300 – including Imre Nagy – were executed.

Konrád: 'We were cowardly or prudent, I still don't know which it was, but we surrendered the university. The next decision was whether to stay in the country, or flee. About 200,000 Hungarians left after 1956; journalists, writers, intellectuals – it was an enormous brain drain for the country. Most of my friends left, my cousins went to America. I stayed. Then there was another decision to be made: to work with the regime or not. I didn't. I accepted a marginal existence, the only goal of which was to keep the culture alive, to expand it if possible, to save what had once existed. Which brings us to the boring story of the period after 1956.'

The Hungarian summer of the final year of the twentieth century was slowly fading. There were no storms, no mists, in late September the days were still warm, the trees heavy with foliage. I had driven to the home of my friends in Vásárosbéc, across the endless plains south of Budapest. The road was full of Trabants and Warburgs, it looked as if half the rolling fleet of the former DDR had washed ashore in Hungary. Forty kilometres later the first horse and wagon appeared, close to Pécs there were dozens of them. A tanned, bent man struggled along the concrete gully beside the road, pushing a bicycle and two full canvas bags. Here and there roadside hookers in elfin skirts stood twisting a high heel in the dirt. Along the way I found myself at a little horse market, a stretch of grass beneath the trees beside a crossroads. Wagons and pairs were trotting about everywhere, showing their stuff, often with a few foals in tow. The horse traders all had bottles of beer and were knocking them back furiously. For sale a little further along were fish and sausages, cheap watches and hairpins. A drunken trader began beating two skinny horses in front of a customer, until they dragged the cart along with the brake still on. The wheels slid over the grass; blood trickled on the horses' flanks.

In the café in Vásárosbéc, Lajos (b. 1949) and Red Jósef (b. 1937) were talking about the way things used to be. Right after the war there were 1,600 people in the village, at least a hundred farmers, every patch of ground was cultivated, but they still died of poverty. Today there are fifty families and only one real farmer, the mayor. In 1956, they tell me, it did not take long for people here to hear about the revolt in Budapest, and all the farmers withdrew their cattle from the collective right away. 'But that didn't last long!' Lajos shouted. In another village the farmers had fought, but here things had remained peaceful. Communism, that was other people's business. 'Here we just tried to survive and make our own lives a little better, year by year, and that was all. There was one man in the café who was always talking politics, he had a big mouth; after 1956 he left for Germany.'

The village did have one minor source of diversion: the local cinema. Lajos: 'A man lived here, you still see him in the café now and then, he was the postman for thirty years. Every week he brought the film here from the city, on foot, summer and winter, for thirty years.'

The collective remained intact until summer 1999. 'All the ground has been given back now. But the young people have left and the older people can't start all over again. There's a big landowner who's buying everything up now. That man is going to be filthy rich. It's too late.'

And all the Dutch people and the Swedes who buy houses here? Red Jósef approved: 'They're not Gypsies, and they help to fix up the village.' Lajos said: 'Just sell the whole thing. Today is today, that's life. The cemetery is patient, it will wait for all of us.'

A Gypsy woman came in to ask if she could call the vet. Her pig was sick. We went with her to have a look. The woman stood beside the pig – her entire capital for the winter – she scratched and petted the animal, whispered in its ear, begged it to live on for just a little while. A couple of men stood off to one side. 'You mustn't feed it any more,' one of them said, and she clumsily swept the leftover feed out of the trough. She had tears in her eyes, she wiped her fingers on a dirty cloth, and then on the bristly pig itself.

Later we went to visit Maria, the church organist. Every Sunday she sat at her harmonium and played a series of notes, higgledy-piggledy, and sang along loudly. Now she was sitting on the bench beside her house, clutching two flowers, while her daughter sewed a pair of leather gloves with neat little stitches. A lot of women in the village did that, for a glove factory in Pécs, to earn a little pocket money.

Maria was, as she put it, 'forty-seven years old, but then the other way around,' and she lived in a constant state of infatuation. She caressed my friend, grabbed his hand, hinted at wild and promising events from a misty past. She served us the first wine of the year from a plastic cola bottle, it was still murky, little more than grape juice. 'Trink, trink, Brüderlein trink!' Maria sang, rocking back and forth with her glass. She was one of the last few of the elderly here who still understood a few words of Swabian, a German dialect brought here by immigrants 200 years ago and pretty much ground back into silence in the last century by Hungarian nationalists. She did not actually speak the language any more, but there were still a couple of German songs living in her head, ones she had learned on her father's lap, a long time ago. The air in the village was autumnal, smoky, sour and pungent.

Two days later I drove on, heading for the Austrian border. Along the way I picked up a hitchhiker, Iris, a little woman with lively eyes and a thin face. She spoke German and English fluently, she had once been a civil engineer, she said, but the state-owned company she worked for had shut down. After that she and her husband had started an advertising agency, then her husband died, and now she helped out at a stable. Her bicycle had been stolen a month ago, she did not have enough money to buy a new one, so now she had to walk three hours to work each day. 'They're good creatures, horses are,' she said. 'They comfort you.'

. On 19 August, 1989 she had taken part in the Pan-European Picnic, a bizarre event held on the border close to Sopronpuszta, where Hungarians, Austrians and East Germans demonstratively broke open the Iron Curtain for the first time. 'When it came right down to it, the notorious border was only a wooden gate with a sliding bolt,' she tells me. 'We had it open in no time. Fortunately the border guards understood that there was no way to stop that crowd.' Even then she had been amazed by the East Germans and the way they left everything behind: Trabants, family photos, teddy bears. 'I remember thinking: these people have brought their last, cherished possessions with them here, and now they are leaving even those things behind in order to cross the border.'

Together we went looking for the spot again, in the rolling fields behind the border town of Sopron. Today there is a small monument to the famous 1989 picnic, and an unmanned gate for bicyclists and farm vehicles; you can walk right into Austria there. It was the first time she had been back since 1989, she was a little sad about the way her life had gone. 'Capitalism was much less charitable than we ever realised,' she said. 'Back then we thought: now everything is going to be all right.'

X October 1958–80

FINLAND

○ Helsinki   ○ Leningrad

○ Tallinn

                              ○ Moscow

○ Riga

          ○ Minsk

                        ○ Kursk

        SOVIET UNION   Volgograd ○
                                         (Stalingrad)
Warsaw
                    Kiev ○
POLAND   Dnepr   Rostov ○

                    Don
·VAKIA   Dnestr

                                    Sea
                                  of Azov   ○ Krasnodar
○ Budapest
HUNGARY   ○ Odessa
                                      Crimea
      RUMANIA   ○ Tiflis

            Bucharest ○   Danube   Black
  Belgrade   Sea

OSLAVIA   BULGARIA

                ○ Sofia
                              ○ Istanbul
ALBANIA   ○ Saloniki   ○ Ankara

    GREECE   TURKEY
          ○ Athens
                                                  SYRIA
                              CYPRUS
                                       LEBANON
              Crete   Mediterranean

⟵ Geert Mak's Route   0   100 200 300 km

Chapter Fifty-One

Brussels

'I HAD RIDDEN OUT TO ZAANDAM ON A BICYCLE WITH WOODEN TYRES. When I got back, there was a car waiting in front of our house: the queen wanted to talk to me. It was May, Holland had been liberated only two weeks before, Kathleen and I were living in a little attic room for students along the Amstel in Amsterdam. We were dumbfounded, but we climbed in and were driven to the south of the Netherlands, which had been liberated for a long time already. Queen Wilhelmina had her residence there, at Breda. It was like a dream for both of us: we were put up in a hotel, in Breda the street lights came on at night as normal, you could buy strawberries in the market, the sheets were white instead of yellow. The next morning the queen asked me to be her private secretary. Which is how Queen Wilhelmina of the Netherlands became my first boss.

'The Dutch government at that time applied the following rule of thumb: if you hadn't been bad, you were good. The queen saw it precisely the other way around: if you hadn't been good, you were bad. I remember the first time she came back to her Noordeinde Palace in the Hague, hopping mad, and how the mayor and the aldermen of the city were all standing there in a row. Queen Wilhelmina walked up to the first one, and the only thing she asked him was: "Which concentration camp were you in?" And she asked the same question of everyone who was there that day. I didn't have the faintest idea what those people had actually done in the war, but it became awfully quiet in that reception hall.

'Look, this is a photograph of my father, he's the big, handsome fellow with the beard and the aristocratic air. Philip Kohnstamm, physicist, later professor. Due to all kinds of family complications, he grew up in the home of his uncle, the Amsterdam banker A. C. Wertheim, completely immersed in that atmosphere of assimilated Judaism. My father was a man of exceptionally broad interests: he was a private tutor of philosophy, he was deeply interested in theology, and later in educational theory, and of course in politics, both national and international.

'He was born in 1875, my mother in 1882. Her father was J. B. A. Kessler, director of the Koninklijke Nederlandsche Petroleum Maatschappij (KNPM), which later became the Royal Dutch/Shell Group. But when my mother was still young, the family was not at all wealthy. In those days the KNPM was only a small company with an oil concession in North Sumatra, for the production of kerosene for lanterns and things like that. My grandfather would go into the jungle and come back with a couple of barrels of oil, that's what it boiled down to. Petroleum was only a troublesome by-product, they couldn't earn anything with it, "that terrible stuff that's always bursting into flames" as he wrote in one of his letters. He brought Henri Deterding into the venture, and together they salvaged the firm. He himself was always travelling back and forth to the wells in the Indies, he was a real jungle hand, but it ruined his health. And when he would get home – you can detect that in his letters as well – it was always a bit of a disappointment. A tragic life.

'My mother was crazy about him, though. When she turned sixteen, he gave her a bicycle. She was furious with him: "You shouldn't do that, you don't have the money for it, you have to work so hard for what you have." But when he died at the age of forty-nine, he was one of the richest men in the Netherlands. The first cars had begun to appear around 1900, and "that terrible stuff" became a highly valued commodity.

'My father first met the Kesslers in summer 1899, during a holiday at Domburg on the North Sea coast. I still have a picture of them, on the hotel tennis court. My mother was seventeen then, my father seven years her senior. They married, that hundred-per-cent Jewish Kohnstamm, and that Kessler girl from the Hague's wealthier business circles. Mixed marriages like that were quite rare then. But I never heard of there being any fuss about it. My parents remained very close all their lives.

'The nineteenth century lasted in our home until 1940. Our whole neighbourhood in Amsterdam was dominated by the narrow, somewhat impoverished and entirely Jewish Weesperstraat. I remember the commotion from early in the morning till late at night, the tram edging its way through the quarter. And then the silence on Saturday, the men in their high hats and the neatly dressed boys walking to the synagogue. Did people discriminate? People told jokes sometimes, and because he was Jewish my father wasn't allowed to join one of those elitist clubs, which he wasn't interested in anyway. But there was no real sting in it yet. The tone it took on in the 1930s and 1940s, the thing we all see before us now when we think about it, that wasn't yet there.

'In winter 1939 I drove around the United States for a few months, on my own. I had received a scholarship from the American University, and I wanted to see Roosevelt's New Deal for myself. That trip had an enormous effect on the rest of my life. I came from a continent where most people seemed paralysed by Hitler and the Depression, like rabbits caught in the poacher's lights. And then suddenly you find yourself in America, where people dared to do things, where they said: "Let's give it a try anyway, who knows, maybe it will work out." During my time there I saw that politics could also be something grand. There couldn't have been a greater contrast with the Netherlands. And it drew me in, I developed a kind of determination; it awakened, as it were, the young American in me.

'This is a letter from my father, from around that time. It was just after Roosevelt's famous speech in which, for the first time, he made clear where he stood: on the side of democracy and against National Socialism. My father wrote, to paraphrase a bit: "Max, it seems to me that the worst is behind us now. The worst, by that I don't mean war, but the capitulation of the entire world – through egoism or indecision – in the face of totalitarian madness. A war does not seem to be ruled out. But that the Caesars in Berlin and Rome will actually seize control of the world seems to me, after Roosevelt's message, more or less unthinkable."

'The first time I saw Kathleen was in winter 1940, on the train to Leeuwarden. The next day a few friends and I did the Elfmerentocht, a classic skating tour. We skated the way people did in those days, all holding onto a long stick, the weather was beautiful. Suddenly I saw that girl, the same one I'd seen on the train, skating alone. I was a little shy, but the American boy in me said to her, as we passed by: "Grab hold, if you like." By the end of the day she and I were playing tag on skates on the lake close to Sneek, by the light of the full moon.

'The rest of that winter I worked on my thesis, and in early May 1940 I took my final exams in Amsterdam. So, on the night of 9 May, 1940, I went to bed as a reasonably successful young Amsterdammer. When I woke up it was war, a few days later I was a semi-Aryan, a "*Mischling ersten Grades*". Getting a job in my own professional field, Dutch and history, was out of the question. Could I really do that to her, let her marry the problematic case that I was? She wasn't even eighteen yet. That dilemma played a constant role in my growing love for her – although her parents continued to receive me very warmly in their home. In the letter in which I finally asked for her hand in marriage, written from the detention camp, you can still see that doubt. But you also see that young American, who simply dared and did.

'My life was very much characterised by the urge to build things anew, after those terrible times. After 1945, we all learned to look ahead, we never did anything else. But I also know, when I on occasion look back on those years before the war, that something was lost for all time. And that certainly applies to Amsterdam. I remember when they arrested me: I was walking through lovely, snowy Amsterdam, the city can be so beautiful at times like that, and when I got to my house on the Amstel the police were waiting for me, my landlady was weeping, and a little later I found myself walking across the bare, icy parade grounds of Camp Amersfoort, with my head shaved. I was lucky that eventually they released me again, but during those three months I still lost twenty-five kilos.

'Being in a place like that makes it clear that lawlessness is hell. Nowhere else have I ever felt so fully surrendered into God's hands. And yet, that is where the roots of my present agnosticism lie. I remember how one evening I had to drag a corpse from the mortuary, accompanied by a guard and a dog. While I was doing that, it suddenly occurred to me how ridiculous it was: a half-dead man dragging a dead man, with a German and a dog behind him. But the thought uppermost in my mind was whether, when I got back to the barracks, someone would have stolen my bread.

'In some ways Camp Amersfoort also conferred on me an accolade. There is, after all, a profound difference between being ground to pieces because of one's race and being ground to pieces because of one's political convictions. And if I had not belonged to that latter group – in autumn 1940, by way of student protest, I had read aloud a couplet from the Dutch national anthem in the university auditorium – then I don't know whether I would finally have dared to propose to Kathleen.

'Those years working for my first boss were good ones. My dealings with Queen Wilhelmina were marked, of course, by a certain distance. Her sense of duty, her grandeur, temperament and loneliness all made her a person who touched you to the quick. She hated the royal birthday celebrations on 31 August; she would never allow anyone to congratulate her, she always shrunk from that. But on 31 August, 1947 she said to me without preamble: "Next year, on this day, I will step down." When it finally came to that point, she dreaded the coronation ceremonies. She was very fatigued, and deeply disappointed by certain things.

'On the day of her abdication, a special train rode from the Hague to Amsterdam-Amstel Station. I was in her Pullman car, and I saw little more than a tired, rather difficult old lady. On the way to the palace on the Dam we were in the coach behind hers, and when we got there that old lady climbed down from the train, and suddenly she was the queen again, Queen Wilhelmina, and she strode past the honour guard and she waved to the crowd. She was grand, truly grand. And even if she hadn't been born a queen, but the daughter of a washerwoman, Wilhelmina would have been a grand woman.

'It was in summer 1947 that I first went back to Germany. It was a wasteland. Cologne, Kassel, all you saw was debris. Some of the cities were teetering on the verge of starvation. The children who came crawling out of the piles of rubble in the morning carrying their book bags, you couldn't hold them responsible for Amersfoort or Auschwitz, could you?

'It was quite a shock to set foot on German soil again, but I travelled around the whole time knowing that this country must someday come back to life again, and deal with itself in peace. I also had the feeling that we, the Dutch, were also to blame, if only for the way we hadn't wanted to know. When the first roll-call was held in Amersfoort, I heard someone behind me in our group say: "Can this really be happening?" That was in 1942!

'As a survivor, I felt guilty myself as well. The fact that you emerged alive from the camp and the occupation meant that you, too, had occasionally looked the other way when someone was in trouble. I have never been able to adopt the self-assured stance of the "pure angel" with regard to an "evil" Germany. I have often thought about the biblical story of Sodom and Gomorrah, and about Lot's wife who was allowed to flee and who, despite God's warning, stopped and looked back at the destruction and was turned into a pillar of salt. Of course we must never forget, but I had no desire to turn into a pillar of salt.

'After Queen Wilhelmina stepped down, I became an assistant to Dr H. M. Hirschfeld, the man who supervised the introduction of the Marshall Plan to the Netherlands. He also advised the government on its relations with Germany. Holland was in a tough situation in that regard. As long as the German hinterland was still in ruins, it was impossible really to reconstruct our country. We all knew that. But how could we keep history from repeating itself, how could we keep the industry of the Ruhr from once again producing bombs to destroy Rotterdam? That was our dilemma.

'Then, on 9 May, 1950, the Schuman Plan was launched. That date is now regarded, rightly, as the start of the process that ultimately led to today's European Union. For us, that plan, which was named after the French foreign minister, Robert Schuman, was truly a revolutionary breakthrough in the vicious circle we found ourselves in. It abruptly changed the whole context, it made the problem of Western European coal and steel production an issue that could and should be arranged together. Conflicting interests were suddenly transformed into a common interest that had to be dealt with jointly. Because, don't forget: in those days Germany could easily have become a plaything between East and West, any enduring subordination of Germany carried the risk of a new war. We had to safeguard that country for the West, at all costs.

'I was invited to join the Dutch delegation which was negotiating for all this, and it was there that I first heard a speech by Jean Monnet, the chairman of the French delegation and the plan's intellectual father. That was in June 1950. I was deeply impressed. It was very clear that this meant so much more to him than simply the regulation of coal and steel production. It meant putting a lasting end to the conflicts that had twice plunged Europe into war, turning national issues into common European ones. As everyone knows, a compromise is not always the best solution. And now we were truly trying to achieve the best, for all Europe.

'This way of working was ultimately to embrace the entire international community. That too was one of Monnet's premises, from the very start. "The six European countries have not launched a great enterprise intended to tear down the walls between them, in order only to build even higher walls between themselves and the world around them," he wrote in the early 1950s. "We are not connecting states, we are connecting people."

'His "Algiers memorandum" of 1943 showed that, even in the throes of the Second World War, he was toying with the first rough draft of the Schuman Plan for the European Coal and Steel Community (ECSC). That community was meant, in any event, to include Germany, France, Italy and Benelux (Belgium, the Netherlands and Luxembourg). He wanted to make sure that Germany, France and the other European countries could never fall back into their old pre-war rivalries. But his ultimate goal went further than that: he was aiming for "an organisation of the world that will allow all resources to be exploited as well as possible and to be distributed as evenly as possible among persons, so as to create peace and happiness throughout the entire world."

'The contacts at those meetings were extremely personal, there were only six small delegations present at the negotiations. The atmosphere was also very different from the rock hard bilateral negotiations we'd been accustomed to, especially in those poverty stricken post-war years. It was a liberating experience for us as negotiators: we were engaged in creating completely new structures. Everyone saw that this was about much more than just a coal and steel community involving a handful of European countries. The discussions were open, it was about the goal itself and not about all kinds of hidden agendas; it generated a dynamism we hadn't seen before.

'That wasn't easy for the Netherlands. In essence, we were not a continental country, we had always focused more on the sea and the west. When the enemy came, we relied on the water to make an island, at least of Holland. In 1940 we still had strips of land that could be flooded as lines of defence. Would the Netherlands now, for the first time in history, have to establish unequivocal ties with the European continent?

'The first European communities were therefore the product of a generation which had experienced first-hand what international insecurity and instability could mean, and how important concepts like freedom, civilisation and the rule of law could be. We knew what it meant: law as the only barrier between us and chaos. I wrote to Kathleen that this was what, in a certain sense, I had been preparing myself for in all the years that had gone before, in Amersfoort, Germany and the Hague.

'Jean Monnet was a unique individual. He was not a politician, nor was he a civil servant or a diplomat. He himself often said that all the positions he had occupied were ones that he had invented himself. But at the same time, even before the war, he had been one of France's most important strategic thinkers. And after the war, he was one of the most important in Europe. He reminded us again and again: once you start thinking that a peace treaty is something final, you're in trouble. Peace is a process that requires constant work. Otherwise everyone will do what comes naturally; the strong ones will exert force, the weak ones can only submit.

'According to Monnet, the drama of European history, that endless series of ceasefires punctuated by wars, could only be circumvented by building something that transcended national borders.

'In 1952 he became the first president of the ECSC, and I followed him there. That is how I became one of the first European officials. There were ten or twelve of us, and our offices were in the former headquarters of Luxembourg Railways. I was secretary to the High Authority of the community and had daily contact with almost all the members, as well as the top officials. In that position, I was also involved in the expansion of our little European regulatory organisation. That is how I met Winrich Behr. The first thing he said to me was: "I want you to know that I was a professional soldier throughout the war." I said: "We're not here for the past, we're here for the future." Later I heard that he was one of the last to be airlifted out of Stalingrad. At that time, in the detention camp at Gestel, we hoped that no German would make it out of Stalingrad alive. Now we were working together, and we remained friends all our lives.

'It was hard work there in Luxembourg. Monnet was extremely inspirational, but hierarchy and official structures were not, let me put this mildly, his cup of tea. One time, after a hard-fought decision, I remember him coming into the office and saying: "The high authority has to meet again to reconsider things. Last night my driver said something we should think about. And he was right."

'In 1954, the French scuppered their own plan for a European Defence
Community. That seemed like a major blow for the new European inte-
gration process. But Jean Monnet and men like the Belgian Paul Henri
Spaak and the Dutch Johan Willem Beyen were soon making new plans.
Those plans finally led to the establishment of the European Economic
Community (EEC), the forerunner of the European Union, in Rome on
25 March, 1957.

'One year before that I had resigned my job at the High Authority. I
began working with and for Monnet on his action committee for a United
States of Europe. That committee consisted of representatives of all the
major trade unions and political parties – with the exception of the
communists and the Gaullists – from the six member states.

'What did our committee achieve? It's hard to give a concrete answer.
We definitely played a role in the turnaround by the German SPD party,
which had originally opposed West Germany's integration with Western
Europe. Both before and after de Gaulle's veto, the committee worked
hard on the admission of the United Kingdom. And, of course, we also
helped to map the route which turned the original customs union into
the current EU. I still remember how Monnet came looking for me in
summer 1957, out of the blue, because we had to get the monetary union
rolling right then. The final decision to introduce the euro came forty
years later. It was a long road indeed!

'"The years of patience", as Monnet called the 1970s in his memoirs,
lasted in effect until 1985. It was then that Jacques Delors shifted the
main emphasis towards actually achieving the "common market". After
all those years it had finally become clear that a common customs union
– for the original EEC was little more than that – was completely insufficient for the creation of a real market. The treaties of Maastricht (1991)
and Amsterdam (1997), which came later, fit within that process – and
the expansion from six to fifteen member states made it all the more
urgent. In the end, the Treaty of Nice (2000) was needed to prepare the
organisation of the EU for the massive expansion with an additional ten
member states, planned for 2004. After all, the procedures developed for
the six original member states – and particularly the right of veto – could
hardly keep a community of twenty-five member states going. The negotiations in Nice failed miserably, and the Union was faced with a major

problem. To break through the impasse, a special European Convention was assigned to come up with a new European constitution, and that's where we find ourselves today.

'I have been involved with this all my life, emotionally and intellectually. Sometimes, in a pessimistic mood, I think the EU will never be more than a European free-trade zone with a golden lining. Of course I have my moments of anxiety . . . But what is the alternative?

'I remember a conversation I had with Monnet in his garden in Luxembourg, it must have been in late summer 1953. He had just returned from his holidays, and I had to report on the little that had happened during August. He listened patiently for a few minutes, then stopped me and said: "That's all very well, but how are we going to define our relations with America and the Soviet Union?"

'Today, the issue of Europe's position in the world is once again timely. After the end of the Cold War, the world – in the technical sense – became more tightly interwoven. But the political divisiveness remains, and that produces major tensions in the long run. From the very beginning we were interested in more than just coal and steel, more than just a common market, more than an economic and monetary union, more than friendship between the participating states: it was about a revolution in international relations.

'It was Thucydides who described the dealings between states as a world in which the strong do as they like, and the weak put up with what they must. Power and dominion form the basis of that system, even when a balance has been achieved within it. But neither the hegemony of a given superpower nor the attempt to prevent wars by means of a balance of power have ever led to lasting peace. The big question remains: can power be replaced as a ruling principle in international relations by justice? And how can justice, if it is not to deteriorate into mere words receive access to power? Can we, to that end, develop other forms of power, in order to establish justice between states?

'Now that modern weaponry has made the danger of war even greater, this question has become even more urgent. A European fort, a sort of Switzerland on a large scale, is an illusion in today's world. The power to destroy, once the monopoly held by the state, is now in the hands of anyone who can obtain the necessary information through the Internet.

The power of mass destruction, in other words, has become increasingly privatised in this world. In such a situation, can the international institutions with their joint responsibility provide justice that is accompanied by the power it needs?

'For our civilisation, the ability to develop a robust international rule of law is a matter of survival. Is that a utopia? No: for half a century, Europe has been proving that it is possible.

'The generation after my own, and probably later generations as well, will have to find answers to all these new questions. Peace, security and prosperity are as valuable as they are fragile. The care for their survival is something that will not let me go. Yes, of course – that has everything to do with that cold parade ground in Amersfoort.'

Brussels still smells of coffee. In Zuidstraat I see a shop window built from brown planks, containing five rolls of tape, a lectern and an old typewriter: all of it perfectly arranged. The nearby bookshop displays albums showing pictures of the lively street life of Brussels around the year 1900, the crowds on the boulevards (the city's population then was ten times what it had been a century before), the train terminuses of North and South, the carts and carriages shuttling back and forth, day in and day out, the perpetually congested streets of the old Brussels. In Spaarzaamheidstraat I duck out of the rain, into the portico of a shelter for the homeless. One of the nuns invites me in. The transients of Brussels have wonderful stories and gestures, only a few of them lean their heads on their arms and doze off on the tables. The shelter has no need of subsidies, the kitchen does wonderfully well with the crumbs from the city's table. 'In a little while we'll go to the National Bank,' one of the nuns tells me. 'They always have at least two thermoses of soup for us, and potatoes, vegetables, meat. Eurostar, the train catering department, every day: all sorts of snacks and nice things. The Atomium organises a children's party: 200 sandwiches with luncheon meat. The patisseries: leftover pastries in abundance, enough dessert for 200 people each day. All of it left over, not needed, all for us!'

When the rain stops, I climb Galgenheuvel, the old gallows hill. There, for more than a hundred years, the Palace of Justice has been sitting astride the working-class neighbourhood of the Marollenbuurt. The building is a single solid chunk of congealed power: enormous court-rooms, offices and archives, a dome the size of St Peter's, and out on the pavement a Christmas tree in memory of the five murdered children for whose lives no justice has yet been handed down. As soon as I enter the great hall I become an ant, a little ant-person in the face of the giant ambition of the young Belgian nation and of the architect, who slowly went mad during the building's construction.

Brussels is not, like other cities, a place that devours its citizens. Brussels, above all, devours itself. In every city you can take a walking tour with old photographs in hand, in every city you can shout 'Ooh' and 'Aah', but Brussels is a law unto itself. Only in heavily bombed towns does one encounter metamorphoses on such a scale. Take South Station, for example, in its decline from the exuberant neoclassical temple of 1861, via a modern Dudok-like structure in the 1930s, to the rampant complex of offices it is today. The city's main artery, Boulevard Anspach, once Vienna and Paris rolled into one, is now a bare conduit, stripped of all monumentality. Brussels has always also been adept at sophisticated self-mutilation: court-yards have been replaced by car parks, the once elegant Finistèrestraat by a concrete trough.

No one loves this city, no one cares for her, no one takes her under his wing. The way a traumatised child continually seeks the repetition of the suffering it has undergone, so this city is always busy violating itself and giving itself away. Every attempt to put an end to the disorder results only in greater chaos. The construction of the *Jonction*, a sort of tunnel between North and South stations, lasted from 1911–52, continuously delayed by wars, administrative conflicts and hundreds of other adversities. For forty long years, a deep trench through the centre of town blocked all traffic between the better neighbourhoods and the commerce of the inner city.

An entire working-class neighbourhood, Putterijwijk, was razed to build the Central Station. A huge site was excavated, then the work lay dormant for years. A highway was simply slapped down on top of the tunnel, in turn giving rise to a proliferation of office towers. The well-to-do citizenry, for whom all those boulevards were built, had long since fled to suburbia. Then NATO and the EU tore Brussels even further apart, totally uninterested in the nature or appearance of their capital, demanding only more and more office space and altitude.

In the course of my walk I end up on Luxemburgplein, the square where the city once presented itself to travellers from Etterbeek, Charleroi and points further afield. For decades it was dominated by Leopoldswijk Station, a friendly, white, nineteenth-century building, flanked left and right by rows of cafés and little hotels with a Southern European air. But walking into the square today one sees, glistening in the afternoon sun, a vast wall of glass rising up behind the station. A few scaffolds are still standing, here and there a final cement mixer churns, but the metal detectors and security cameras are already hard at work, and suddenly one sees how dismal and small the station is in contrast to this enormity of steel and glass.

This is Europe's brand new house of parliament. I go looking for an entrance amid the chaos. Again I am overwhelmed by the sense of my ant-ness. At the door I stop and turn around, and then I know it for sure: the forecourt of this building is clearly designed to roll on to Luxemburgplein and on into the city. And roll on it will, there can be no doubt about that. In half a year, or in five years, the little station – like cheese made from unpasteurised milk, like French bread kneaded at home, like real chocolate, untagged cows' ears and the thousands of other things an ant-person values – will have been erased by Europe. The dark brown panelling of the passengers' waiting room, the friendly, one-toothed woman at the sweet shop, all will be steamrollered away for good.

Brussels is the capital of Europe, the city is officially bilingual, but anyone who thinks this creates a cosmopolitan climate is sadly mistaken. At my hotel, the only person who speaks a word of English is the African chambermaid. More than three decades after the end of the Belgian language struggle, the lingua franca in the great majority of shops is French, and most of the city's inhabitants – with the arrogance of provincial dignitaries – will speak nothing else.

An experiment for the visitor: try, in this officially bilingual city, to speak your own language. You will be looked at like a madman. During my travels I had carried out some fieldwork-by-the-square-inch into the extent to which Europeans understand each other, a not unimportant factor for those who hope one day to form a single continental community. How many passers-by did I have to approach before finding someone who spoke a language other than their own? Lisbon, Amsterdam, Stockholm and Helsinki received excellent scores: one or two at most. Rome and Berlin: three. Paris: four (an increasing number of young French people like to speak English). Madrid and St Petersburg: six to eight. London: the same (although German is on the rise in business circles).

The bilingual capital of Europe had an interestingly low score: three to four. And between Brussels and the rest there was another essential difference: everywhere else, despite the difficulties, there is a strong will to understand each other. But not in Brussels. This city is still dominated by a considerable reticence with regard to the phenomenon of language.

Belgium is a special country. In the 1950s it survived a language dispute that would have plunged almost any other European country into civil war. Afterwards, Belgium was divided *de jure*. For the outside world the country has remained unified, a tiny nation that manoeuvres skilfully around the great fault lines between Northern and Southern Europe. And, as far as that goes, Brussels resembles Odessa: precisely because of their problematic position, the Belgians have thought harder and longer about the national and cultural borders that still separate Europeans. But this has done nothing to heal old wounds; on the contrary, they have, if anything, become deeper. Despite outward appearances, Belgium is caught up in a never-ending process of disintegration.

In *Poor Brussels*, his wonderful book about the city, urban chronicler Geert van Istendael describes the true tolerance of Brussels on the basis of the daily greeting he receives from his neighbour: 'He raises his hand, smiles politely and says: "Hello! How are you?" But in fact that's not quite how he says it. It sounds more like: "Allo! Awa you?", because my neighbour is not only polite, he is also French-speaking. The Dutch-speaking van Istendael always returns his greeting with equal politeness: "Bonjour! Ça va?" '

That is how Europeans from different cultural regions everywhere should deal with each other, but that is not how it goes. I take a little side trip to Sint-Joris-Weert, a red-brick village close to Leuven with a drowsy café, an agency for *Het Nieuws* and a set of railway tracks running right down the main street. 'If you want to see the real language border, go and look there,' van Istendael had said. Or, as the local baker's wife explained: here it's Flemish, on the other side of the railway bridge, in Nethen, it's French. Communication in her own shop, at least for the Walloons, is by means of mumbling and sign language. On Roodsestraat, the border actually runs down the middle of the street. I go to take a look: that means the red villa on the left speaks Flemish, the white cottage across the street speaks French, the curly kale in the garden on the right is Flemish, the willows across the way weep in French.

There is, to the naked eye, nothing remarkable about Roodsestraat. Yet it is part of the most important line of demarcation between North-Western and Southern Europe. 'The language border here is centuries old, razor sharp and absolute,' van Istendael said. On the Flemish side there are Dutch books on the shelves, the people watch the Dutch comedians Van Kooten en De Bie on television and the Flemish and Dutch news, films and political discussions. Their neighbours, eleven paces across the way, watch *Mezzo*, *TV5* and *Arte*, they read *Le Soir* and discuss French politics and literature. They live the same lives, eat the same bread, but their world of thought is attached to a completely different cultural system.

Every language stands for a world of its own; those worlds shift and groan, and merge only with the greatest of difficulty. The Roodsestraat in Nethen is something Eurocrats prefer not to think about.

Chapter Fifty-Two

Amsterdam

'ALL THOSE PROUD WOMEN ON THEIR BICYCLES.' 'THE ORDERLINESS, with that thin layer of anarchism.' 'Not a single paving stone out of place.' 'The variety, the languages.' 'They are all so tall, especially the young people!' 'Those enormous, prosperous bodies one sees everywhere.' 'And their teeth, their teeth, so lovely and strong!'

In the Hotel Astoria in Budapest, György Konrád had mused endlessly about faraway Amsterdam and everything that strikes a foreigner about it. He had just written an ode to that city, and he read part of it to me out loud. His Hungarian eyes saw bicycling female derrières, husky blonde mothers and children, 'sturdy and compact, like mature cheeses'. They saw a city that stood out by virtue of its ability to be 'an ant by day, a cricket by night'. And they saw, above all, a calm, uninhibited people. 'The concept of the "national curse" is unknown to them. In front of them the sea, behind them dubious Europe. Germans? Russians? In whom ought they to have confidence, except in themselves?'

Now, for the moment, I am back in my own town. I am at the cheese shop, and I hear one of Konrád's pretty girls beside me saying: 'I want to try something wild with pastrami and pine nuts.' Nowhere else do you see so many people eating out of rubbish bins as you do in Amsterdam, which has to do not only with the uninhibited nature of Dutch junkies, but also with the outstanding quality of Dutch rubbish.

I read in the daily *De Volkskrant* that, in 1999, fifty-three per cent of all Dutch fifteen-year-olds have a television in their own room, twenty-four per cent have their own computer, thirteen per cent have a mobile phone, five per cent own a weapon. The newspaper runs a special feature about the 'hippest couple' in Holland, a computer artist and his girlfriend. They spend most of their time on Ibiza. He describes his life as 'the total integration of life, events, art and parties'. She says: 'For me, just being liberating comes first, no matter what I'm doing.' An amazing country, the Netherlands, especially when you have been anywhere else in Europe for a while.

In September 1965, as an eighteen-year-old student, I moved from the provinces to wild and woolly Amsterdam. The canals lay dreamily in the autumn sunlight, thousands of new experiences awaited, I was free and happy, and everything was possible. With a small group of friends, I explored this new world. We went to strange and unfamiliar cafés, bought our first foreign newspapers, met up at the municipal museum, watched the newest French films with mouths agape.

We also noticed that something unusual was going on in the city. Cigarette advertisements were everywhere being defaced with slogans like 'Gnot!' and 'Hack, hack!' A deathly silence settled over the student cafés when images of the war in Vietnam appeared on TV. There was a herb going around, marijuana, that produced the strangest visions. In the square at the Spui, around the statue of the street urchin called the Lieverdje – a gift to the city from the Hunter tobacco company in 1961 – so-called Provos were holding demonstrations.

In my attic I still have a few cardboard boxes full of newspapers and pamphlets from those astonishing years. I wriggle them out from beneath layers of dust and, sneezing as I go, begin to leaf through them. It is as though I am holding newspapers from 1910 or 1938, or some other long-gone era.

I pick up the narrow, rectangular magazine Provo, compiled by the anarchistic student Roel van Duijn, the working-class boy Rob Stolk from Zaandam and a group of writers and theatrical artists; a golden combination in hindsight. 'Provo is aware that it will, in the long run, be the loser,' they wrote at the start, and they bravely pasted one little red exploding cap into every copy of the first edition.

They also produced Hitweek, the 'Professional journal for teenagers, 38 cents.' The circulation was, for those days, enormous: somewhere between 30–50,000. The scantily-clad girls on the cover are seen nowadays in every underwear advertisement, but created a huge uproar at the time.

One reader, Arthur de Groot, reported on 30 December, 1966 that he had been kicked off an Amsterdam bus, number 19, simply for reading his favourite magazine: 'The whole bus got involved: "scandalous", "everywhere you look" and "young people these days"'. The editor, André van der Louw, later mayor of Rotterdam and minister of culture, recreation and social work: 'The greasers are out of the picture. Their place has been taken by a new youth.' I find only one ad in the whole publication: 'Clearasil dries up acne.'

The initial phase of the young people's rebellion of the 1960s, the cultural upheaval, was at first a largely British affair. The Beatles made their breakthrough in 1963, followed by the Rolling Stones a year later, and in 1965. the skinny London model Twiggy was gracing covers all over Europe. In that same year, the Italian *Epoca* described the youth of Britain as 'five million young people under the age of twenty-one who have undermined all the customs and conventions of British society; they have broken through the borders of language and class; they pay a great deal of attention to what they wear, they make noise and rebel against the prescribed restraint and modesty concerning sex. What do they want? Nothing, save to live in this fashion.'

Two years later, the pivotal point had shifted to Amsterdam. In the Summer of Love in 1967, the city filled with exotically dressed young tourists who slept in the Vondelpark and spent hours lounging around the National Monument on the Dam. Music that summer centred around the new Beatles album *Sgt Pepper's Lonely Hearts Club Band*, 2.5 million copies of which were sold within three months. *Hitweek* wrote: 'Playing in parks and on squares, just because we're all beautiful and need each other.'

The mid-1960s was an exceptionally romantic period, perhaps the most romantic since the start of the nineteenth century. But just as there had been worlds of difference between the countless splinter groups of the right and ultra-right in the 1930s, thirty years later the progressive revival also split off into many movements which ultimately had little to do with each other. In Holland, the groups surrounding *Hitweek* and *Provo*, for example, lived in different worlds. *Hitweek* was concerned with music, parties and lifestyle. *Provo* was a typical urban movement which brashly addressed social issues: pollution, traffic jams, the housing shortage, the decay of the old neighbourhoods.

The students in Paris, in their turn, primarily sought contact with workers and trade unions; their movement was bigger and much more political. German activists, on the other hand, adopted slogans that the French and Dutch students would never have used: 'Be high, be free! A little terror is the place to be!' The hippies foraged wherever they could: they mostly shut themselves off from the political and urban world, they chose emphatically for a rather drugged, relaxed and sometimes even sluggish way of life – a clear reaction to the hustle and bustle of the 1950s – and they were often enamoured above all with each other and themselves.

Were the young people the only ones who, in the words of the Dutch 1960s specialist Hans Righart, granted themselves the luxury of 'placing the creation of the earthly paradise on the agenda'? Was the 'teen boom' the only cause of all this unrest?

That would be too simple. The 1960s constituted a mentality crisis for both the older and younger generations. Starting from their own pasts and backgrounds, everyone suddenly had to respond to an overwhelming series of changes. And this time the crisis was caused not by an economic depression, as it had been in the 1930s, but by its opposite: unparalleled economic growth throughout Western Europe; a striking increase in leisure time and mobility; an endless series of technological innovations; the mass availability – for the first time – of cars, motorbikes and other luxury articles; a contraceptive pill that 'liberated' sexuality from the burden of reproduction after 1962; a decline in the ideal image of America as a result of the war in Vietnam, and the enormous rise of the television and the transistor radio, making young people from San Francisco to Amsterdam feel united in the same rhythm of life.

Provo Rob Stolk told me how the new era started for him: it was on the day a white car entered his street, full of young girls who passed out a new kind of soup to everyone there: Royco soup from a package. 'That was unheard of. People were simply given soup to try out, something they'd had to stand in line for only a few years before. Suddenly they were being taken seriously as consumers. A new era started for me that day.'

It was not only Rob Stolk and my little group of friends who had to find a way to deal with that, it was our parents as well. We, young Western people, had never known anything but prosperity, a prosperity that also kept growing. Older people, on the other hand, were being confronted with a society that was changing so quickly it took their breath away. They still attached great value to a materialist value system, which had proven its worth in times of poverty and war. Their children, who had grown up in safety and luxury, dared to go a step further. For them, bare existence was no longer the issue.

In this way, the young people's rebellion around the 1960s formed, after the Second World War, a new dividing line in Western European history. One can hardly speak of 'the' movement of 'the 1960s': in actual fact, the period covered more than a decade and a half, between the release of the movie *Rock around the Clock* in 1956 and the start of the international oil crisis in 1973, with the years 1966–8 as its zenith. What our little group of friends was experiencing – we were, in fact, hardly aware of it – was a high-speed change in mentality, a pounding surf full of currents and counter-currents, a revolt with a character all its own. It was, as meteorologists say, a 'perfect storm', a temporary conflux of four or five elements that unleashed hitherto unknown forces.

First there was the factor of youth. The letters to the editors of *Hitweek* remarked upon it time and again: everyone older than thirty was suspect, everyone older than forty was the enemy. The editors wrote: 'In November 1966, fifty-two per cent of the Dutch population was under thirty. High time to start running things for ourselves.' The feeling of 'us against the rest' was continually underlined in music, clothing, hairstyles, symbols and rituals.

This generation gap was widened, however, by the cultivation of the phenomenon of 'youth' itself: 'youth' was no longer seen as a preparatory phase for adulthood, but as the 'definitive and most perfect stage of human development'. In comparison with our parents and grandparents, we children of the middle class in the 1960s were able to leave home earlier. But, at the same time, all manner of new facilities – student grants, social benefits – shielded us for much longer from a tough, adult life. Many young people, in other words, were able to remain for years suspended in a state of perpetually postponed adulthood. In this way, the universities in particular developed into 'islands of young people'.

The second impetus behind this 'perfect storm' was the exceptionally international, even intercontinental, nature of the revolt. In every student town from Barcelona to Berlin, one saw the same books in shop windows: Herbert Marcuse (the individual is merely a means of production, divorced from all joy and pleasure), Marshall McLuhan ('the medium is the message' and the omnipotence of the modern media) and the new proclamation as gospel of the works of Karl Marx. The London fashion – boots, brightly coloured stockings, jeans and miniskirts – designed by the youthful Mary Quant in her boutique in Chelsea, was to determine the look of young people all over Europe and North America. The same went, from 1962, for the long hair and the music of the Beatles.

This sense of particular identity was further boosted by a newly won sexual freedom. The very first issue of *Provo* magazine contained a plea for a 'completely amoral promiscuity'. On 30 June, 1967, *Hitweek* published an extensive dissertation on the question: 'Where can you make love peacefully, uninterruptedly and with full concentration?' The author advocated the organisation of festive 'sex-ins' and the creation of public 'copulation zones' to be used by all those who felt the urge. The Pill became the ultimate free ticket, abortion could be no crime, jealousy was an anachronism. At the same time, also thanks to the Pill, baby boomers could keep postponing marriage and parenthood and thereby extend their adolescence even further.

The 'sexual revolution' took some countries by storm: in 1965 almost half the Dutch population still felt that a woman should remain a virgin until her wedding day; by 1970 that had become only one in six. In the 1950s, fewer than one per cent of all British brides had lived with their future spouse before marriage; by 1980 that had become almost twenty-five per cent. In Belgium, France and the Netherlands in 1985, the number of divorces was approximately three times what it had been in 1970.

Crucial to the storm of the 1960s was the fourth ingredient: the unique growth – and, above all, the mass character – of Western prosperity. In summer 1967, French sociologist Edgar Morin began work on a portrait of the little Breton village of Plodémet. In it, he described the two new means of communication that allowed young people to feel independent from the adult world: motorised transport in the form of the moped, or even a small second-hand car, and telecommunication in the form of their own transistor radio, which was never turned off. 'These days, there-fore, the young people of Plodémet have the same facilities, the same passwords (*vachement*, fantastic, *terrible*, horrible), the same antenna, the same culture as the young people of the city. They feel the same wind of change.'

At the same time, the young rebels also felt a great ambivalence towards the wave of prosperity. The real hippies were those who chose to drop out of society altogether. They attached great importance to the natural-ness of clothing, food and lifestyle: unbleached cotton, bare feet, macro-biotic diets, meditation, rest. Cities were artificial, and therefore wrong. The ideal was a peaceful, communal existence in the countryside – where, by the way, most of these urban children lasted no more than six months. 'In Holland as well, more and more right-thinking young people are getting out,' *Hitweek* wrote in 1969. 'They're starting a new, radiant life that the world they come from doesn't understand at all.'

There was also a fifth force, deeply hidden, which propelled this storm to great heights: fear. Much of the thinking of that day exudes an intense nineteenth-century optimism, the conviction that one could make one's own 'radiant' life. Yet it is also impossible to understand the 1960s without understanding the existential fear that held many Europeans in its grip. The whole generation of the 1960s had been raised under the perma-nent threat of a new war, many saw the atom bomb as an immediate threat, many young people wanted to ban war and oppression from the world at any cost.

Early in October 1967, newspapers all over the world ran the famous melancholy portrait of rebel leader Ernesto 'Che' Guevara. He had been killed in the jungles of Bolivia, and that was the moment his myth came to life. His image was carried in demonstrations, it hung everywhere in cafés and students' rooms, it symbolised a new solidarity with the Third World. With increasing frequency, publications like *Provo*, *Salut les Copains*, *ABC*, *Konkret*, the British *Oz* and the Italian *Mondo Beat* dealt with the burning questions of the day: the relations between rich and poor, the ethical aspects of technology, the exploitation of the planet, the limits to growth.

Just as the Spanish Civil War had set the tone in the 1930s, the American intervention in Vietnam was the touchstone for the 1960s. In early 1968, more than half a million American soldiers were involved in that dirty and unwinnable conflict, a war which could also be seen on TV every day. One demonstration after another rolled through the capitals of Western Europe and America. Tens of thousands of young American men refused the draft.

Within the 'islands of young people', Marxism and Maoism often served as anti-ideologies, radical ways to distance oneself from the charged past of older generations. Both constituted attractive methods to press modern society into a mould that was easy to grasp, and also the ideal weapon to provoke and oppose the anti-communist establishment. 'Real' workers – as long as they fitted within that theoretical framework – were cherished by the young rebels. Parisian students embraced the Renault workers from Flins. My acquaintances in Amsterdam adopted working-class accents. Joschka Fischer, who would become Germany's foreign minister, went to work on the production line at Opel in 1970 in order to 'live alongside the workers'. No one wanted anything more to do with the bourgeoisie.

In hindsight, the statistics show where the real rebellion took place: in 1965, more than half of all Dutch people felt that children should not call their parents by their first name, and more than eighty per cent felt that mothers should not work outside the home. In less than five years, these percentages had been halved. The real revolution of the 1960s took place indoors, at hundreds of thousands of kitchen tables.

Chapter Fifty-Three

Berlin

THE DIVIDING LINE BETWEEN FLOWER POWER AND THE SOBERING 1970s lay somewhere around 1968. With increasing frequency, the troubadours interspersed their cheerful songs with grim, bitter lyrics. The Rolling Stones sang the praises of the 'Street Fighting Man', Jefferson Airplane openly summoned 'Volunteers' to join the revolution: 'One generation got old,/One generation got soul,/This generation got no destination to hold,/Pick up the cry!' Both songs were banned by numerous radio stations.

The cultural movements may have been international, but the concrete and often inevitable conflicts that resulted from them were – with the exception of the opposition to the war in Vietnam – largely national by nature. Provo was typically Dutch, Mary Quant was English, Rudi Dutschke was German to a tee, and May 1968 was eminently French.

The British, who had not been occupied by a hostile army and had experienced less of a crisis and fewer jolts to their prosperity than other Europeans, were those least affected by the generation gap. Young people particularly had a bone to pick with the 'British' way of life, which had ground to a halt somewhere in the 1920s: the fashion, the music, the censorship and the laws governing morality.

In Poland – for there too a small student rebellion was underway in 1968 – the major issue was freedom: when the staging of a nineteenth-century drama at Warsaw's national theatre was banned, a group of angry students marched into the censor's office. Fifty of them were arrested, and their leaders, Adam Michnik and Henryk Szlaifer, were expelled from university. In the disturbances which followed, some 50,000 students took part. A number of sympathisers on the faculty were sacked, including Zygmunt Bauman, who was later to achieve fame across Europe. The official reason for his dismissal was that he had been 'influenced by American sociology'.

In France, the oppression exercised by the old bourgeois society was felt most keenly in regard to the educational system and police violence. 'We are fighting because we do not want to make a career as scientists whose research work will serve only a profit-based economy,' read a student brochure handed out at Nanterre. 'We decline the examinations and the honorary titles used to reward those [few] who are willing to accept the system.'

In Italy the focus was on corruption and public scandals, as well as education and police violence. Between 1960–8 the Italian student population had doubled, while the universities had seen little in the way of change since the nineteenth century. 'Never have I met an Italian student who felt he had received a good education,' George Armstrong wrote in the *New Statesman* in 1968. 'The universities are the rigid feudal domain of the older professors. They are the haven of the sons and daughters of the middle classes, who usually have no intention of working in the field for which they have been trained.' In Rome, 300 professors were charged with teaching more than 60,000 students.

In the Netherlands, as in Britain, the revolution of the 1960s was a largely playful one. The student movement was a serious affair, but Provo and its adherents never stopped playing: with public opinion, with the medium of television, with the 'public image'. It was an artistic form of protest linked to anti-monarchist and anti-German sentiments (made manifest during the wedding of Crown Princess Beatrix and Claus von Amsberg in March 1966), anti-bourgeois ideals (expressed in the happenings around the *Lieverdje* and elsewhere) and a kind of anti-fascism-in-hindsight (with the storming of the daily newspaper *De Telegraaf* in June 1966).

In Germany, that playfulness was nowhere to be found. There things revolved, in essence, around the legacy of the Second World War.

In 1968, the American philosopher Joseph Berke visited Commune 1 at Stephanstrasse 60 in Berlin. Arriving at 6 p.m., he found the entire community still fast asleep. The two televisions in the building were on all the time, albeit with the volume turned down. When the communards finally left their beds, they sat staring at the screens in silence. In his report, Berke said they were all high, despite their initial rejection of drugs as a 'bourgeois distraction from the political revolution'.

Commune 1 had been set up in March 1967 by Fritz Teufel. Teufel's notoriety began after he broke into the dean's office at the Freie Universität, took his cigars, toga and chain of office, then rode a bicycle through the corridors to the auditorium, where he allowed the cheering student body to appoint him the school's new dean. His first official act was to sack all of the unpopular professors. Teufel spent more time in jail than outside it. In imitation of the Dutch Provos, his Commune 1 used constant provocations to lure 'the system' into betraying its 'true nature' as aggressive, repressive and capitalistic.

A former Amsterdam activist once told me how shocked he had been by the violent character of the Berlin demonstrations. Provo toted cap guns, carried banners with nothing written on them, but the members of Commune 1 had no such sense of humour. 'In Holland, a nod was sufficient, as long as you observed a few rules. But in Berlin, that disciplined marching back and forth and then standing to attention . . . We thought it was scary, it wasn't our kind of thing.'

When Rudi Dutschke, who lived in the commune for a time, refused to abandon the 'bourgeois private relationship' with 'his' Gretchen, the group took a vote and decided to go into collective psychoanalysis. Klaus Röhl, husband of the journalist Ulrike Meinhof and editor-in-chief of *Konkret*, said the commune seemed to him to be a group of neglected, over-privileged adolescents who had been given 'too much pocket money and too little human affection'.

'They lived,' he said, 'like Russian revolutionaries in the winter of 1917–18, wearing leather jackets and grubby trousers which they didn't bother to remove when they lay down to sleep somewhere. They ate and slept irregularly, sent their children to school irregularly, and only attended the university in order to hand out pamphlets and shout manifestos through their megaphones. When – despite this detailed replication of decor and lifestyle – the revolution failed to materialise, when it turned out (as Dutschke had predicted long before) that there was no way to avoid the long, grinding and rather unromantic march through the halls of the established order, they became disillusioned.'

In spring 1967, 300 people were killed in a fire in a Brussels department store. Soon afterwards, Fritz Teufel and his fellow communards Andreas Baader and Gudrun Ensslin began handing out pamphlets in which responsibility for the fire was attributed to Belgian 'cells' who actively opposed the war in Vietnam, and suggesting that their example might very well be followed in Germany. '300 fattened citizens and their exciting lives were snuffed out, and Brussels became Hanoi.'

Teufel and an accomplice were arrested for inciting arson. That summer, during a violent demonstration against a visit to Germany by the Shah of Persia – 'The new Hitler!' – a student, Benno Ohnesorg, was killed by a police bullet. A few months later Dutschke was gunned down by a neo-Nazi. Students all over the country took to the streets by the hundreds of thousands.

In April 1968, Baader and Ensslin made their first real attempt at burning down the Schneider department store in Munich. During their trial that October, rioting broke out. About 400 sympathisers were arrested. The demonstrators chanted: 'What is civilisation? Is it a Mercedes? A nice house? Is it a soothed conscience? I ask you again, comrades, what is civilisation?'

In late 1968, Ralph Blumenthal of the *New York Times* visited Commune 1 and found only one female member and a couple of men still living there. Ulrich Enzensberger, brother of the writer Hans Magnus Enzensberger, sat there 'stoned, examining his painted fingernails'. The last communards lived largely from giving interviews on the subject of revolution and capitalism, and they demanded hefty sums for doing so.

From the early 1970s, Baader, Ensslin, Horst Mahler and others banded together to form the Baader-Meinhof Gang, also known as the Red Army Faction (RAF). The allusion to the Royal Air Force (RAF) was no accident: just as the British had bombed Germany from above, they now planned to raze the 'new fascism' from within. In 1970, Baader and Ensslin were helped to escape from prison by a group of friends led by Ulrike Meinhof. According to those involved, it was a purely impulsive action: there was no well-organised network of safe houses or hiding places, no longer-term 'urban guerrilla' action had been prepared, the group was almost completely unarmed. Very soon, however, they began receiving support from the Middle East and the DDR – even though the intensely conventional East German communists had little use for the RAF's tactics. After Baader and Ensslin's escape, the group robbed a number of banks. Bombings of the American army headquarters in Frankfurt, the head offices of the Springer publishing concern (whose newspapers included Bild-Zeitung and Die Welt) and government buildings in Munich and Karlsruhe followed. Then began a chaotic game of cat and mouse with the authorities. When the presence of Ulrike Meinhof's twin seven-year-old daughters began forming a hindrance to this 'people's war', the group decided they should be sent to a camp for Palestinian orphans. 'Ulrike clung to her children, more than a mother, more like a mother hen,' her ex-husband wrote. That, in fact, was precisely why Baader and Ensslin demanded that she free herself of this 'remnant of her bourgeois past'. But El Fatah refused to cooperate: even their Palestinian contact person felt that this was taking things too far. In the end, probably at the insistence of Meinhof herself, the children were handed over to their father.

In early June 1972, Baader and Ensslin were reapprehended. This time, Meinhof was arrested as well. Their followers fought on, increasingly obsessed with the idea of freeing the three ringleaders. On one occasion they met with limited success: in 1975, Peter Lorenz, chairman of the Berlin branch of the CDU, was abducted and exchanged for three RAF prisoners.

In 1976 Meinhof committed suicide in her cell. Violent demonstrations broke out again; in Frankfurt, Joschka Fischer – at the time a fervent street-fighter – was arrested for 'attempting to take the life' of a policeman. Within the next year the group's sympathisers singled out and attacked more than 150 targets, killed German Attorney General Siegfried Buback and bank director Jürgen Ponto, and, in September, kidnapped the foreman of the German employers' collective, Hanns Martin Schleyer.

That autumn, all of West Germany lived in a shifting state of fear, rage, bitterness and paranoia. The RAF, which had gradually come to represent only itself, demanded the release of Baader, Ensslin and nine other prisoners. Despite desperate pleas from Schleyer himself, the German government refused to budge. To further underscore the demands, three

Palestinian RAF supporters then hijacked a Lufthansa Boeing; a lightning raid by German commandos at Mogadishu airport on 18 October, however, put a speedy end to the hijack. Schleyer's body was recovered the same day, and that night Baader, Ensslin and Jan-Carl Raspe were found dead in their cells – apparently having committed suicide as well.

The films made later about the autumn months of 1977 bear titles like *Die bleierne Zeit* (The Days of Lead) and *Deutschland im Herbst* (Germany in Autumn). The young German democracy did, indeed, seem on the verge of backsliding to a situation very like that of the 1920s and 1930s; precisely what the left-wing radicals hoped to 'prove'. Roadblocks were set up everywhere, police helicopters patrolled above the roads, 'conspiratorial locations' were permanently wiretapped and watched, emergency measures were tightened and all outspoken support for 'terrorists' was made punishable. On the basis of the Radicals Law, dissidents were faced with a vocational ban: they were excluded from all public functions, including teaching. RAF prisoners were put into isolation and submitted to a special regime. Their lawyers, including future minister of home affairs Otto Schily, received constant threats.

The Baader-Meinhof Gang's supporters remained active for another fifteen years. In total, the RAF carried out almost 250 attacks, robbed 69 banks, kidnapped a few dozen politicians, businessmen and journalists, and murdered 28 people.

The vast majority of the German student movement and the radical left had long since turned their back on these violent tactics. In Berlin alone, in 1980, an estimated 100,000 people were living within a subculture of alternative cafés, communes, action groups, political hippiedoms, squats, *Spontis* and *Wohngemeinschaften*, but almost none of them would have anything to do with the RAF.

In Italy, however, things were different. There the left actually granted a certain degree of support to extremists, and even to the RAF's Italian counterpart, the Red Brigades, which began its activities in 1969. In the late 1960s, the old civil conflict between Fascists and anti-Fascists had been reignited with an escalation of attacks by more or less covert neo-Fascist terror groups and the Red Brigades. These Italian 'days of lead' were far more violent than those in Germany, and ultimately claimed more than 400 victims.

The first bomb exploded on 12 December, 1969 in a bank on Piazza Fontana in Milan: sixteen people were killed, eighty-four were injured. The anarchist Giusseppe Pinelli was arrested and, during interrogations on 15 December, 'accidentally' fell to his death from a high window. The killers were never located, but most evidence pointed to neo-Fascists and right-wing elements within the Italian intelligence service. The funerals of the victims of the bombing turned into a demonstration in which 300,000 people took part. Attack after attack, demonstration after demonstration followed.

The Italian people were frightened, and rightly so. The Red Brigades, which its members claimed was a continuation of the resistance movement from 1944–5, went on terrorising the country for years. Meanwhile, speculating on the country's ongoing disintegration, neo-Fascist groups set to work on a right-wing coup by the Italian Army. It had worked in Greece, so why not in Italy? By the late 1970s, each year saw an average of more than 2,000 terrorist attacks. Even today it is not certain who was responsible for a number of them – including, for example, the infamous bombing which killed eighty-five people at Bologna's central railway station on 2 August, 1980. There are indications that foreign intelligence services were involved in other as yet unexplained attacks, and that during this same period a covert campaign was underway to halt the brand of Euro-communism so popular in Italy. There is, however, still no clear evidence for this. On 16 March, 1978, the prime minister, Aldo Moro, was kidnapped by the Red Brigades. His fellow party members and friends refused to enter into negotiations. Twenty-five days later, Moro's body was found in a Roman shopping street, crammed in the boot of a Renault 4.

Is it merely a coincidence that the 1960s culminated in so much violence in Germany and Italy – the former Axis powers – while radical-left terrorist movements gained little or no foothold in, for example, France, Britain, Belgium and the Netherlands? Probably not. All over Europe, the 1960s constituted the delayed repercussion of the war experiences of generations past. Public officials and policemen were systematically referred to as 'fascists'; the Provos of Amsterdam even shouted that epithet at their mayor, Gijs van Hall, who had been one of the country's most coura- geous resistance fighters during the war. Countless texts referred to the legacy of the Second World War, to 'collaboration' and 'resistance'.

But in Spain (ETA), in Italy, and in Germany above all, these senti- ments were taken to much greater extremes, leading some to demonise the state as a whole. The sociologist Norbert Elias described the young people's rebellion as a 'purification ritual for the sins of the fathers'. The great empires had crumbled, national ties had to be redefined and confirmed, and young people viewed the ideals and actions of older generations with a new, more critical eye. In Germany in particular, the younger generation had many questions to ask of the men and women who had been in power at that time, who had participated actively in public life throughout the war. Yet no answers were forthcoming.

In 1969, the Bavarian Christian Democrat Franz Josef Strauss voiced openly what many older Germans had been thinking for a long time: 'A people who have delivered such economic achievements have the right not to hear about Auschwitz any longer.'

For this war generation, Elias writes, the reconciliation with the Nazi past was completed with the Nuremberg trials and the rehabilitation of real or alleged party members. 'Officially, they had nothing to fear and nothing to regret. Their consciences may have bothered them now and then, but in the public life of Germans in positions of leadership, it seemed, the nightmare of the Hitler years could be buried.' However, their own sons and daughters, in voices which grew louder and louder, were demanding a retrial.

At home, I found an interview I had once made with Christiane Ensslin, Gudrun's sister. Christiane was the real protagonist of Margarethe von Trotta's film *Die bleierne Zeit* (1981), the woman who had taken in Gudrun's son after the child had been badly wounded by a right-wing fanatic, and who sympathised with her sister but refused to choose the path of violence. When I visited her at her Cologne apartment in 1984, she was unem- ployed, precisely because her surname was Ensslin. Her boyfriend was not allowed to hold a job in his own professional field, simply because he was her boyfriend. Her father had encountered great difficulty finding a graveyard where her sister could be buried: even in death, Gudrun Ensslin was not to be allowed to repose amid 'normal' people.

Together we looked back briefly at the 'days of lead' in the 1970s, but ultimately the discussion focused on her generation and that of her parents. 'Most older Germans see the war as, well, tough luck,' she felt. Her own generation refused to see things that way, and was therefore, in her eyes, more frustrated than its contemporaries in other countries. 'We were the country that applied fascism to the highest degree of perfection. Our most recent history, that of our parents, is so unimaginable for us, their children . . . And that means something. The greater the wrong you have behind you, the more you must watch out for what you do in the future. To that extent, the historical debt we have to pay is much heavier than that of other European countries.'

She talked about a scene in *Die bleierne Zeit* which was true to life. When her father, a brave and critical pastor, showed his congregation a film about the concentration camps, she and her sister Gudrun left the room, sick to their stomachs. 'As a child of course, when you see something like that, you think: What? Did my father know about that? And he just sat at home and ate his dinner? That can't be true, can it? And then you promise yourself: I'm going to pay very close attention, if people start disappearing again or being mistreated or murdered, I'll take up the fight!'

Christiäne Ensslin talked about feelings and frustrations: 'Our German perfectionism, the concept of power that's behind it, the frustrations it has created and still creates among young people . . . If you ignore feelings like that you can never understand history. No action ever takes place without a feeling!' Old Norbert Elias saw it, above all, as a drama: 'The tragedy was that some members of this young generation, in their attempts to create a better, warmer, more meaningful kind of human life as counterpoint to the National Socialist regime, arrived in turn at increasingly inhumane actions. And perhaps it was not their tragedy alone, but also that of the state, of the society they were trying to transform, and even of the older generation that had all the power firmly in hand.'

Chapter Fifty-Four

Paris

GO TO THE CAFÉ IN COLOMBEY-LES-DEUX-ÉGLISES AND ASK ABOUT the general, and they all launch into stories right away. About how he sat in church, straight as a ramrod, the seats beside him always empty, 'it was as if there were a glass cage around him'. How he lowered all his defences for his handicapped daughter Anne, how he danced around and slapped his thighs. How his wife Yvonne, during his period as an unemployed civilian between 1946–58, did her shopping in the village and counted every centime. How he left in summer 1958 to save France once again: this time from the Algerian ultras and the threat of civil war. How he, even as president, always came back to the village, 'my home and my mistress'.

Colombey is a simple rural hamlet with one huge eighteenth-century house, La Boisserie. De Gaulle bought it in 1937, especially for Anne. With the many elections and referenda, the term of his presidency was a perpetual propaganda campaign, and gradually de Gaulle came to believe all those stories himself. Over time his already considerable ego took on absolutely mythic proportions. He was, in his own eyes, the body and soul of France, he thought what la France thought, and eventually he began referring to himself in the third person, as though he had entered history during his own lifetime. But in the village he was simply himself.

Now he lies amid the families of Colombey, his grave marked by a simple marble cross, beside Anne and his wife Yvonne. During his funeral on 12 November, 1970, the myth became fused with the village, once and for all. The men in the café show me a photograph: it shows them with rusty wheelbarrows, preparing the big grave. The places at the funeral were reserved for the family, the old companions in arms and the town council of Colombey. 'But still, 40,000 people came to our village that day. And the boys here turned a pretty penny! They sold little bags of earth, supposedly from the cemetery, for five francs apiece! What a day!'

Pilgrims are allowed to leave their own tribute against the wall of the graveyard. It is full of crosses of Lorraine and marble plaques reading 'Regrets'. And there is always a sentry standing guard. 'Always?' I ask the gendarme on duty. 'Yes, day and night.' 'Even after almost thirty years?' 'Yes, but of course, it's the general!'

If de Gaulle had not been de Gaulle, if he had not been that theatrical, brilliant, stubborn spirit, would France be a different place? The trust placed in him by the French of which he spoke so proudly in 1940 was only so much hot air; he imagined it, and only received it once the war was almost won. But as a role model, as father of the fatherland, he restored the self-respect of the French as no one else. That process repeated itself when the French Empire fell apart, when the nation's pride was deeply hurt by the humiliations in Indochina – where 20,000 French soldiers were killed – the Suez conflict, and when the Algerian question cut the nation to the quick.

In Algiers in October 1954, the Front de Libération Nationale (FLN) began a national uprising that led to countless attacks on French targets; gradually the French – its army under the command of General Jacques Massu – became entangled in a violent, urban guerrilla war.

In 1958, under the title La Question, the European-Jewish Algerian Henri Alleq, editor of the Alger Républicain, published a detailed report of his arrest and interrogation by French police: the continuous hitting and kicking, the electrodes attached to ears and mouth, the partial drownings, the barbed wire in the mattress, the salt water to quench his thirst, the drugs to make him talk.

This dealt yet another blow to the national self-image: many French people felt deeply ashamed. Their own soldiers were applying methods associated with the Gestapo.

In spring 1958 the already divided Fourth Republic was shaken to its foundations; under Massu's leadership, an ultra-right-wing coup was in the offing. French paratroopers based in Algeria were made ready to be dropped in Paris, de Gaulle was called in to restore order, and what finally happened was reminiscent of the Second World War: the French rebels in Algeria called on de Gaulle to save their cause, de Gaulle used them to consolidate his own power, and in the end there was little or no heed paid to their demands.

On 1 June, 1958, de Gaulle was appointed prime minister. Within three months the country had a new constitution which placed the most important executive powers in the hands of the president. De Gaulle's Fifth Republic was born. Four years later, Algeria gained independence.

In essence, de Gaulle's utopia was a nineteenth-century one: a regal France within a Europe of self-aware 'fatherlands' from the Atlantic to the Urals, led by the French-German axis and excluding Britain and America, and with a gradual thawing of relationships with the East. But when Warsaw Pact troops put a brutal end to the Prague Spring in August 1968, the general was forced to abandon his dream.

But even more dramatic were the events that had taken place three months earlier, when it turned out that France possessed neither the internal equilibrium nor the economic power needed for European leadership. In fact, in May 1968 it seemed that de Gaulle's political role had been played out. One last time he brought all his theatrical talents to bear, one last time he succeeded in restoring calm to the country; at the same time, however, he realised better than anyone else that 1968 had sounded the death knell for the rule of classic French father figures, and certainly for that of this self-appointed father of the fatherland.

The French May Revolution of 1968 was more than a student revolt, it was also the most massive wave of industrial action in French history, a rebellion by ten million French men and women against the bosses, against the state, against the constraints of ordinary life. It was a popular movement, and no one had seen it coming. On 29 April, 1968, the weekly *L'Express* ran a cover story under the title 'France's Number One Crisis: Housing'. In an article bearing the headline 'Students: The New Hussars Don't Have Much Luck', a journalist wrote: 'Perhaps, here in France, we are all growing a little bored.'

Two weeks later, on Saturday, 11 May, the official tally drawn up after a single night of fighting in the streets was: 367 wounded, 460 arrests, 188 damaged or burned-out cars, dozens of barricades. That day *L'Express* spoke of 'a storm over Paris' and the appearance of 'more rioters than the Fifth Republic has ever seen.'

Just as generals are fond of winning the war that is over, governments always have a way of dealing definitively with revolutions past. On place Jussieu, one finds their memorial: a graceful university complex with, remarkably enough, its principal administration building constructed on poles. The entire complex has only one entrance, and the whole thing can be sealed off with an impenetrable barrier at the push of a button. It is a true masterpiece from the drafting tables of architectural agency Paranoia, Inc; here a Maginot Line has been thrown up for all time against the imagination that once, briefly, ruled these streets.

Nine months after 1967's Summer of Love, the European and American young people who – with the exception of the Germans – had preached peace and freedom took to the barricades with stones in their hands. During winter 1967–8, everything happened at once. In January, Vietnamese guerrillas penetrated Saigon during the Tet Offensive. America turned out to be anything but invincible. With each passing month, the demonstrations in Europe and the United States grew in size and number. On 1 March, 200 people were injured in battles on Rome's Spanish Steps, including almost 150 policemen. Spain followed: on 28 March, General Franco closed Madrid University indefinitely in response to illegal demonstrations against the regime, and a month later the country witnessed four days of heavy rioting. In Nanterre, the student administration building was occupied on 22 March under the leadership of Daniel Cohn-Bendit, signalling the start of the 22 March Movement. On 4 April, Martin Luther King was murdered in Memphis, Tennessee. One week later, Rudi Dutschke was shot in the head and barely survived. In Berlin, thousands of students marched down Kurfürstendamm carrying pictures of the Spartacist martyrs of 1919, Rosa Luxemburg and Karl Liebknecht. Two people were killed in the streets of Munich. On 6 June, American presidential candidate Robert Kennedy was assassinated. On 30 June, after fierce rioting, a state of emergency was declared in the Californian university town of Berkeley.

Meanwhile, the spring which had come to Prague that year was a historic one. In January, orthodox Communist Party leader Antonín Novotný was replaced by the amiable Alexander Dubček, who immediately loosened the reins: press, radio and television were allowed to criticise the regime freely, persecuted writers and intellectuals were granted amnesty, and plans were made to reform the economy along Western lines. The impending thaw became visible in the streets of Prague, in the length of men's hair, the cautious miniskirts, the home-made pop music, the screening of Western movies such as *Cleopatra* (featuring Elizabeth Taylorová) and *Viva Mária!* (with Brigitte Bardotová). The opposition paper *Literární Noviny*, which reappeared under the name *Literární Listy*, published an essay by playwright Václav Havel about true democracy: 'Democracy is not a matter of faith, but of guarantees' which allow 'a public and legal competition for power'. All 250,000 copies of the magazine sold out within a few hours.

The demonstrations in Berlin and Paris elicited, at most, a vague sympathy among the students of Prague. They had other things on their minds: their 'socialism with a human face' was under increasing pressure from a ranting and raving Leonid Brezhnev, the Soviet leader who had succeeded Khrushchev in 1964. On the night of 21 August, 1968, he drummed up half a million soldiers from five 'socialist brother states' to invade Czechoslovakia. When Soviet spokesman Gennadi Gerasimov was asked in 1987 to explain the difference between the Prague Spring and his boss Mikhail Gorbachev's perestroika, his reply was: 'Nineteen years.'

A Parisian friend of mine once told me that, right before another storm blew in, he had walked past the cordons of riot police in the streets of the capital and saw behind their visors, to his amazement, not the faces of robots but of tired, middle-aged men, probably with teenage children at home. We were sitting in the evening sun in front of Café Flore, one of the revolutionary road houses of that day. 'Ah,' he said, 'the people here haven't really changed. They're just acting in a different play.'

> Run, comrade, the old world's on your heels.
> Forbidden to forbid.
> Power to the imagination.
> Count your hard feelings and be ashamed.
> Be realistic, demand the impossible.
> Beneath the paving stones lies the beach.

*

The memory of May 1968 may be preserved in such lovely one-liners, but the actual daily practice of the celebrated Parisian revolution was a fairly chaotic one. During those May evenings in the Latin Quarter, one former student demonstrator said he had felt more or less like Stendhal's protagonist Fabrice del Dongo during the Battle of Waterloo: events were happening all around, but he barely understood what was going on. At first the revolt had been little more than a prolonged and massive series of street skirmishes, prompted largely by the violence displayed by the police. That had begun as early as 22 March at Nanterre, where demonstrators had been badly beaten, and on 3 May, when students still committed to non-violence were thrashed out of the Sorbonne. After that, day by day, the fighting in the streets of Paris escalated, until finally the boulevards were filled with hundreds of thousands of demonstrators.

At the same time, there was the imagination, the dream that briefly ruled the streets. The Dutch writer Cees Nooteboom has described how, sitting at the feet of a lady who launched into the 'Internationale' every ten minutes, he watched a demonstration pass by: 'A never-ending procession, filling both sides of the boulevard, students, Spanish workers, hospital personnel in white, setters, printers, drivers, hotel employees, teachers, all groups with their own songs, of all ages, often arm in arm, an incredible number of women and girls among them, everything that fills the pavements of Paris, a happy crowd that finally merges into itself like a river.' Later he went to the Odéon, where a packed auditorium was in the midst of self-examination. 'A young man in the centre aisle of the theatre is leading the talk. It remains glorious: someone speaks from one of the golden theatre boxes, the lovely and serious, the faces – no longer bored – at last turn in that direction, the arguments flow back and forth in the longest conversation in the world which has been going on for days, around the clock.'

As a young reporter for a student paper, I went with a colleague to Paris to report on the revolt. I remember a truck full of students tearing down the Champs-Élysées waving red flags, a classroom at the Sorbonne where girls passed out bread and sausage donated by sympathetic Parisians, the plush and the gold leaf of the packed Odéon, and a Spanish Gypsy family that put on shows in front of the theatre with a dancing monkey and a goat in culottes. Red flags, trucks, free food: if this wasn't a revolution, we didn't know what was. I found a few of my old notes from the weekend of 18 May.

Concerning the atmosphere in the occupied Sorbonne: 'The lack of sleep begins to assume major forms. 'In view of the rising number of nervous crises and depressions, the auxiliary services organisation asks you to sleep at least five hours a night. Comrades, people can only contribute to a revolution when they sleep and eat regularly.' Beethoven, Chopin and jazz that sounds like Erroll Garner is playing in the hall. A boy with a clarinet tries to play along, everyone claps, a drunken clochard dances in circles.'

Concerning the uneasy contacts between students and workers: 'After the fifteen-kilometre walk, the reception at Renault-Billancourt was a disappointment: the students were not allowed onto the grounds. Great excitement when a number of workers finally came to the Sorbonne. A whole series of rooms was set aside for the commission ouvriers-étudiants, volunteers were summoned to enter into discussions with the workers, collections were held for the strikers, yet relations remained strained. At midday, there were a total of five people on the above-mentioned committee. These differences are, of course, not hard to explain: judging from the wall posters, the workers' demands are largely material; those of the students are increasingly immaterial, or even anti-material.'

Concerning the night: 'In the nursery, a boy with a harmonica is trying to play the children to sleep. The press centre is packed. Exhausted girls type new mimeographs and manifestos all the time. In a bottle, in the midst of all the mess, is a red rose.'

On Sunday, 19 May, the Committee for the Defence of the Republic distributed the first pamphlets calling for resistance to the 'rabble-rousers in the factories, workshops, offices and faculties'. Gaullist assault groups were being formed everywhere. One of my notes mentions a counter-demonstration by the extreme right, a group of about 750 people marching by with banners reading 'Á bas l'anarchie' and 'Pas de communisme'. At the time, we considered it a meaningless incident. Yet this was the start of the counter-revolution, and the end of the revolt.

On Wednesday, 22 May, the French parliament rejected a motion calling for the government to step down. De Gaulle promised a referendum. François Mitterand came forward as an alternative candidate for 'the new left'. Negotiations between the trade unions, employers and the government began at the end of that week. The only problem was that the unions and the student organisation had little or no control over their own members. In the Latin Quarter, the fighting between police and demonstrators was grimmer than ever. During the entire May Revolution, 8 people were killed and almost 1,800 injured – including a considerable number of policemen.

On Wednesday, 29 May, after weeks of studied silence and absence, de Gaulle finally took the initiative. His countermove began with a brilliant bit of theatre. First he suddenly 'disappeared', and that mysterious manoeuvre drew attention away from the events in Paris. In fact, he had gone in deepest secrecy to Baden-Baden, to assure himself of the support of his old rival, Massu, and the rest of the French Army staff in Germany. At 4.30 p.m. the next day he held the most important radio speech of his career. In it, de Gaulle succeeded once more in enchanting the French. Within the space of four and a half minutes he was able to fill the power vacuum everyone had been talking about, to resuscitate the danger of 'totalitarian communism' and to move his Gaullists out onto the streets.

On place de la Concorde, an estimated million French citizens demonstrated with flags and portraits of the president; one day later the first strikers went back to work. In early June, the French revolt dwindled as suddenly as it had arisen. The front of ten million striking workers diminished within two weeks to a million. On 16 June the Sorbonne was cleared, four days later the last barricade was removed from the Latin Quarter. The elections brought a landslide victory for the Gaullists: they received 358 of the 458 seats in the assembly. It was insane: the most massive and inspirational revolution of the 1960s had ultimately resulted in a parliament more conservative than the general's old order.

'You know,' one of the leaders of May 1968 told me later, 'there was a moment when [we] could have seized power. Everyone was in a panic, and de Gaulle was about to step down. The fact that we never seriously thought about that, not even for an instant, says a great deal. People weren't really out for power. They wanted the power to criticise, the power to prove themselves right, but not the power to run things on a daily basis, to get their hands dirty. And that pattern kept repeating itself.'

He himself had become an adviser on social facilities for disadvantaged neighbourhoods, all over Europe. 'I still come across ordinary students from 1968 all the time, they work as aldermen, as project leaders, and they're always on the move. But their leaders were actually quite arrogant. The real work, normal power, they thought that was beneath them.'

Yet France would never be the same after 1968. The May Revolution had knocked de Gaulle's paternalistic regime off its pedestal. The general's power had always resided in his ability to mobilise all Frenchman against a common enemy: the Germans in 1940, the Algerian ultras in 1958. But, in the unclear situation of 1968, that no longer worked. There was no common enemy; the people in question were often the children of de Gaulle's own constituency. One had to apply tact and compromise, and that is where he failed. The criticism from the farmers and the merchants, his traditional supporters, grew rapidly throughout that summer and beyond. Finally de Gaulle tried to save his own skin one last time with an 'all or nothing' bid. He linked his political future to an insignificant referendum about regional relationships. On 27 April, 1969, his proposals were defeated by a tiny majority, and he drew his own conclusions. Under his successor Georges Pompidou, who was elected president in June, various reforms in the spirit of May 1968 were introduced anyway, now without furor.

General de Gaulle was finally at liberty to meet with a political leader who he had always held in great – if unspoken – admiration: Francisco Franco. The two men dined together on several occasions, but it did not result in a lasting friendship. When push came to shove, the theatrical de Gaulle remained a democrat, albeit a formal and primitive one. He was not, like Churchill, a man of the substantive democracy, of the heated democratic debate, of the democratic compromise. He sought the people's mandate, then went on to regard that as a licence to act as he saw fit. In that way he prefigured later Southern European leaders like Silvio Berlusconi and José María Aznar. But whatever else he was, he was not a dictator who tried to bend the press and the courts to his own will.

'The country could accept him on his own terms, in other, words unconditionally, and without demanding from him a programme,' his biographer Brian Crozier wrote. 'Or else it could stew in its own juice. If it chose the latter he would, as he said on several occasions, return to his sorrow and his loneliness.'

Chapter Fifty-Five

Lourdes

MY BUS IS PARKED ALONG THE CREUSE, AND I EAT MY APPLE BESIDE the old building where the villagers of Chitray once did their laundry. The stones are warm in the October sun, a squirrel is knocking nuts from the trees, the river churns. The spring water continues to run into the basin, day after day, but the women who laughed and gossiped here for centuries are gone, they are forgotten and lie now in the churchyard, just like the women from the wash houses in all the other villages of France.

One of my brothers lives close to here, in a dot on the map with about a hundred inhabitants. In 1900 there were 1,400 people living in that village, most of them in dire poverty. In the summer the men earned a little money working as masons in Paris, and when concrete was introduced and they could also work there throughout the winter, they took their wives and children with them. This was the first wave of rural families to move away. After the war, when the big factories in the cities began taking on thousands of workers, the second wave came. Today there are only retired people living in the village. 'Every once in a while someone from Paris buys a house here,' my brother says, 'but after a couple of years most of them throw in the towel.'

All over Europe I had seen the remains of that farming culture, the infrastructure that was still shaping the entire world at the start of the last century, and that had been wiped away a hundred years later: ruined farmhouses in Spain and Italy, abandoned wash houses in France, overgrown fields on the slopes of the Pyrenees, empty village hovels in Poland and Portugal and forgotten kitchen gardens in Vásárosbéc. In cities everywhere I had met former farmers and their children, adrift in the huge grey blocks of flats in Bilbao, in the churches of Warsaw, in the refugee centres of Holland.

In 1951, more than forty per cent of Italy's population lived from agriculture and fishing. By 1972 it was seventeen per cent. In Holland, one out of every five families lived on a farm in 1950; fifty years later it was one out of every fifty. In France in 1999, some 15,000 villages were in danger of vanishing completely. The British were moaning about the creation of a 'brave new countryside', where no one had dirt under their fingernails.

My brother shows me the stump of a tree that once stood in the middle of an overgrown path, between what used to be the pastureland and gardens of his village. 'I counted the rings,' he says. 'This tree began growing around 1950. In other words, by that time there was no longer any real reason to keep this path cleared. It was a turning point, apparently most of the villagers had left by then.'

Here, after the great dying out, came the great flourishing. Everything became covered in forest. 'All the woods you see here are new, all those terraces have become overgrown, this whole view didn't exist back then,' my brother says, waving his arm. 'Only a few old people still remember what the old landscape looked like. I know them, but it won't last very long. Then even the memory will be gone.'

A few days later I drive into the Pyrenees. The days are warm and clear, the nights cold, the houses low and grey. A girl is herding her sheep, a cigarette between her lips. The road becomes narrower all the time. A lone bird of prey is circling high above. A barn, '*Vive de Gaulle!*' written on it in faded blue. My newspaper, which I read on my laptop, welcomes the six billionth earthling. When my father was born in 1899, we reached a billion. Now it's six times that. We're living in strict accordance with the disaster scenario sketched for us by the Club of Rome in 1972, which, along with the oil crisis, rang in the end of the golden years of 1945–73.

At the time, the club's calculations brought the world down with a bump. It appeared that less than a third of the human race consumed four fifths of the most important raw materials, and those were quickly becoming depleted. At the same time, the world population continued to grow by leaps and bounds. 'Under these circumstances,' the report

said, 'people everywhere are increasingly confronted with a series of
intractable problems, almost impossible to deal with: environmental distur-
bance, a crisis in norms and customs, bureaucratisation, the uncontrollable expansion of the cities, uncertainty concerning employment,
alienation on the part of young people, economic disruptions and the
rejection by a growing number of people of our society's value system.'
These seemingly divergent issues were extremely complicated, showed
up all over the world and had a pronounced mutual interaction 'in a way
we cannot as yet comprehend'.

Within the next twenty-five years, the report said, countermeasures
could still be taken, but after the year 2000 it would be impossible to
turn the tide. 'The world system simply no longer has the space and the
abundance to tolerate such egocentric behaviour on the part of its inhabitants,' and if the world did not impose 'limits on growth', it predicted
scarcity, catastrophe and wealthy states which would increasingly withdraw into themselves.

A quarter of a century later, what everyone talks about most is climate
change: in a pub in Kent, people wonder aloud about why it has not
snowed there since they were teenagers. 'The average English garden
moves 200 metres south each day,' a British magazine reports; my friends
in central Italy note the arrival of strange, multicoloured birds, apparently from the tropics; my newspaper in the Netherlands reports regularly on unprecedented flooding; Wladek Matwin in Warsaw sees the
spring growing shorter, the winters growing longer, and by late May it
is already as hot as in the middle of summer, all very unusual.

I pick up a hitchhiker, a man from around here. He spends his Saturdays
as follows: he climbs a mountain, turns the contents of his bag into a
giant bird, jumps off the mountain and then flies around like an eagle
amid the summits and valleys. 'That must be fantastic,' I say. 'Yes,' he
says, 'but there isn't much more I can say about it.' A silence. 'Yes, it's
fantastic.' Again he falls silent. 'It's totally peaceful up there, only the
wind. Unless the weather starts acting up, then you get a rollicking too,
my God, yes . . .'

In late afternoon the first billboards begin popping up – Hôtel Sainte-
Bernadette, Hôtel de la Grotte, Hôtel Virginia – and then the Las Vegas
of Sorrows looms up before me. I pull into Lourdes just in time for

dinner at the Hôtel Majestic. There is a lot of cheerful laughter at the tables. One of the groups is discussing prayer. How frequently does one pray? 'I pray for an hour each day,' an older gentleman says. 'That's enough for me and my children.' The women at the table do it more quickly, and besides, praying for an hour, how many requests can one have for Jesus anyway? 'Jesus?' the man says sternly. 'Yes, we always pray to Jesus.' 'And what about the Virgin?' 'Well, not as often.' This raises a new question: to whom does one pray? Or rather: to whom does one pray for certain problems? And we still have the whole evening in front of us.

At the spring, hundreds of people are waiting in line to fill their plastic bottles with holy water. The crowd in front of the cave is completely silent, there are thousands of people standing or sitting or lying there in prayer, here and there a deformed child is held up: all the better for Mother Mary to see them. A determined man trudges around with a gigantic banner for the Virgin, the huge pennant flaps all evening above his head.

The shops of Lourdes are full of plastic Mary bottles to hold the spring water – the Virgin's head serves as a screw-on top. They also sell huge framed colour photos of Jesus on the cross – when looked at from a certain angle, he open his eyes or closes them again – and ashtrays, vases, Padre Pio and the Pope in a thousand different shapes and sizes. And, at the same time, Lourdes is a place where every franc is pinched till it bleeds. You have souvenirs starting at around five francs, less than a euro. There are cheap hotels, the food is simple and filling, the men tote groceries around in big plastic bags, the women wear cheap coats, the faces are lined, the eyes glance shyly at all this strange opulence.

Two pilgrim trains are about to leave the station: one for Boulogne, the other for Perpignan. A few dozen young spastic people have been lined up on the platform, beside them four wooden trolleys full of worn suitcases, crutches and jerry cans of spring water. Many of the passengers are carrying fluorescent plastic Virgins and marble grave decorations, for there is no reason why the dead cannot receive gifts as well.

Today, in 1999, the pilgrim trains are no longer the stinking, miserable carriages that Émile Zola described in his novel Lourdes (1894); they are mostly silver high-speed trains in which the suffering is neatly covered up. Except, that is, in the Train Vert; the hospital cars for the lame and terminally ill who are headed for Perpignan still exude the old-fashioned smell of illness and Lysol. Unlike in Zola's day, today there are antibiotics, TB has been eliminated, the patients are mostly well nourished and all illness and suffering has been skilfully excised from public life. Except in Lourdes. Lourdes is the clearance sale for all the suffering our society normally hides from sight, and for a few days it leaves its isolation. Is that the comfort this pilgrimage brings? I enter into a conversation with an old woman in a wheelchair, she has scarves wrapped around her head, a pair of what look like motorcycle goggles protects her eyes. She saved for this trip for eighteen months; she enjoyed herself. 'Oh, sonny,' she says, grabbing my hand. 'When you're here you're close to heaven's gate for a while.' The locomotive blows its whistle, the train begins to move. Patients wave, some of them lie on their mattresses and pray.

The next evening there is a huge procession. First, thousands of pilgrims swarm around the enormous square before the basilica, men in their Sunday best, women in crisp dresses, old people cough, children hobble along on crutches, an incredible swarm without system or goal. But then darkness falls, the procession begins to take shape, and there they go: hundreds of men and women in wheelchairs, candles held high, moving their lips along with the 'Ave Maria' blasting from the loudspeakers, some of them slouching under their blankets, some with bandaged faces, a few with faces blemished from AIDS. A husband and wife try to support the head of their paralysed son: look, look at the Virgin. All the despair from all the back rooms of Europe bursts out here.

Everyone is old, everyone is poor. The pace is overwhelming, the helpers are almost sprinting, sometimes whole human chains are formed to keep the rushing wheelchairs on course. Then come the beds, at the same pace, the patients lying beneath a red sheet, handbags resting on their stomachs, a boy races by with an intravenous drip dangling from his hand, father and mother praying on both sides, a little runaway pietà.

The next day I cross the Spanish border again, and a few hours further along I see what I call the Lake of Dried-Up Expectations. On the mountainside are a few villas, a hotel and a boarded-up village bar, but the eye is drawn only to the gravel bottom of what was supposed to be a large mountain lake, with cheerful beaches and vivacious young people.

Lying here and there in the mud are a few lost boats, all that is left of all this promise. It is an absurd place, this bare valley and this drained water basin, with its brave hotelier and a few homeowners holding out in the face of it all: someday this will turn out all right, someday we will have cheerful beaches again, discos and pretty girls.

After Franco had been in power for about ten years, right after the end of the Second World War, a visitor described Spain as a 'washed-away chunk of South America': parched earth, constantly circling vultures and the introspection of a dream castle. The great wars more or less passed it by, the democratisation was in no hurry. It is only in the last two decades that things have started rolling again. Franco's economic policies were based on pure autocracy, and for the Spanish this resulted in a level of starvation and disease unknown since the Middle Ages. On 31 December, 1939 he announced that all the country's problems were over: 'Huge amounts of gold have been found in Spain!' It was one big swindle. Not long afterwards, the Austrian Albert von Filek convinced the dictator that he could make petrol from water and a secret plant extract. He was allowed to build a factory on the River Jarama, and for a long time Franco believed that his own car was the first to run on this new fuel. Between 1940–4 alone, some 200,000 Spaniards died of starvation.

In Madrid I take a little city tour of Franco's sanctuaries. For this general who liked nothing more than playing king, El Pardo was the perfect palace: just outside the city, nothing in the surroundings to provoke unrest, yet positively dripping with aristocracy. For fifteen years the Francos lived here in complete isolation, interrupted only by brief trips to other parts of Spain and no more than three foreign visits: to Hitler, Mussolini and Salazar. Greece is the only missing name in that line-up of kindred spirits; it was not until 1967 that Georgios Papadopoulos imposed his shaky nationalist dictatorship, and by then Franco was too old to travel far.

Some thirty years after the war, three of the four big Southern European countries were still living under taciturn, oppressive, fascist dictatorships. Strikingly enough, all those regimes came to an end almost simultaneously: in April 1974, during the Carnation Revolution, a group of Portuguese officers seized power from Salazar's successor Marcelo Caetano;

three months later the Greek regime collapsed, isolated and exhausted after a student revolt and a Turkish invasion of Cyprus, and in November 1975 Franco breathed his last, after having held Spain in a stranglehold for almost forty years.

The palace guide leads us from one room to the next full of gold leaf, tapestries and pompous furniture. Look, there is the dining room where no table companion ever dared bring up the country's problems: they spoke only in terms of 'traitors' and 'ingrates'. On the wall is a still life of hams, lobsters and slaughtered stags. The little cinema is still there, with Franco's seat right in the middle. The table where the council of ministers met. The enormous television, almost the only window on the world the dictator had in his final years.

In her memoirs, published in 1980, his sister Pilar wrote: 'Of course he paid no rent for El Pardo, and his expenses were paid by the national treasury. But I know for a fact that he never let the state pay for his clothing. He paid for his own underwear himself.'

And, oh, there is his bedroom, light green in neo-imperial style, with two cute little brown reading lamps, one for him and one for his doña Carmen. The room still has the same carpet, the one that was drenched in blood on those November nights in 1975 as the life slowly flowed out of him. Next to it is his red marble bathroom; of course, we are free to view everything, even the bathtub, even the little white toilet. The only thing it brings to mind is: so this is where it began, that unparalleled theatre of medical technology, that deathbed of the old Spain.

Franco addressed a crowd for the last time on 1 October, 1975. It was hard for him to speak, because he had trouble breathing. Two weeks later he had his first heart attack, and more followed. On 24 October, the gastric haemorrhages began. The Spanish radio began playing mournful music. Franco developed pneumonia, followed by more internal bleeding. An emergency operation was carried out in the palace. Kidney problems. Some Spanish papers began running daily maps of Franco's body, as though it were a war zone, with arrows pointing to vital organs and other positions under siege. On 5 November, two thirds of his stomach was removed. In the days that followed he was hooked up to all manner of life-support equipment, probably only for the sake of winning enough time for the reappointment of his vassal Rodriguez Valcaral to a few important government posts. The press offered capital sums for photographs of the dying dictator; his thirty-two physicians refused categorically, but his son-in-law took one snapshot after the other. 'How difficult it is to die,' was the only thing Franco himself could whisper. Another haemorrhage, another operation. It was only on 20 November, after thirty-five days of struggling against death, that the dictator's coterie allowed him to depart in peace. In Barcelona, 'the champagne corks flew through the autumn air,' Manuel Vázquez Montalbán wrote, 'but no one heard a thing. Barcelona, after all, was a city that had learned good manners. Silent in both joy and sadness.'

After Franco's death, the prognoses for Spain were exceptionally pessimistic: the experts were almost unanimous in their predictions of old hatreds and new violence flaring up. Yet they had been deceived by the regime's outward appearance. Most countries pretend to be more modern than they are, but here it was precisely the opposite. Alongside and despite Spain's primitive system of government – Franco himself, for example, knew nothing at all about economic politics – the country had also witnessed the gradual rise of a modern trade and industry, backed by a great deal of foreign funding and led by technocrats with little affinity with the regime. In 1959 they convinced Franco of the need to abandon his old tenets. A sizeable package of reform measures was launched, including the Stabilisation and Liberalisation Act to free up trade and investments. Industrialisation was stimulated and the influx of foreign companies was encouraged. During the 1960s alone, Spanish industrial production tripled, and the economy grew faster than anywhere else in Europe.

In the course of this change to a more or less democratic Spain, leading roles were played by two unlikely figures: the new prime minister, Adolfo Suárez, and the young King Juan Carlos, who Franco had already appointed as his successor in 1969. In a carefully planned coup, Suárez succeeded in ridding himself of the last members of the regime and forcing through a democratic constitution. It was an exceedingly delicate and dangerous operation, for the threat of a new civil war dangled continually over the country. The German writer Hans Magnus Enzensberger therefore rightly picked Suárez as one of his 'heroes of the retreat'.

Behind the scenes, King Juan Carlos, grandson of King Alfons XIII, had been carefully manoeuvred into place to play a modest role within the dictatorship; when it came down to it, however, and at precisely the right moment, he stood his ground. When pistol-toting Colonel Antonio Tejero tried to take the Spanish parliament hostage in 1981, Juan Carlos blocked his moves with a few fast manoeuvres of his own. In the appointments he made, he consistently chose innovators and democrats. And then, after this bloodless royal revolution, he withdrew into the lee of the parliamentary monarchy.

Even while Franco was still alive, Franco's Spain had ceased to exist. His popular support was extremely limited: in the country's first free elections he received barely two per cent of the vote. Suárez was quickly forgotten. After all, as Enzensberger wrote, he remained a turncoat in the eyes of his former comrades. And, for the democrats he had helped into power, he would always remain one of Franco's lackeys. 'The hero of the retreat can be sure of only one thing: the ingratitude of the fatherland.'

Chapter Fifty-Six

Lisbon

'I'M TELLING YOU MY STORY AT A STRANGE MOMENT. MY FATHER-in-law recently took a bad fall, in a shop, one of those silly accidents that can finish off the elderly, and now he's in hospital. He may recover, but it could also go badly, I don't know. We're standing vigil by his bed, the phone is always within arm's reach, you probably know how it is, those strange days full of memories.

'I was born in Mafra, in central Portugal. My father was a clerk, my mother worked as a switchboard operator at the post office. Like all red-blooded Portuguese boys, I ended up in the army after secondary school and spent six years in our former colony of Mozambique. That was in the 1960s. I worked at the commander's office, and that's where I met my wife. She was Governor Almeida's daughter, and also his private secretary. I often helped out as an interpreter, and that's how we got to know each other.

'When the colonial wars began I was sent to Angola as an infantry captain: ambushes, skirmishes, hopeless. In Mozambique I had simply done my job as a professional military man, I hadn't thought about it much. But in Angola that all changed. My comrades and I ended up in the filthiest situations, and we realised more and more that this was not going to solve the problem of the Angolan rebellion. We, the young officers, had endless conversations, and we always arrived at the same conclusion: colonialism was a misguided system, and also completely outdated. We were being asked to buck the tide of history. Portugal would never, ever win this war.

'It's no coincidence that the Carnation Revolution was largely started by officers of that same generation. We had all attended the same classes, gone to the same boarding schools, carried on the same discussions. The conspiracy itself was put together within a few months, but only after ten years of thinking and talking.

'In 1970 I was sent back to Portugal, as a major on the general staff. Salazar died that same year, but he had appointed his protégé and ally Marcel Caetano as prime minister in 1968. Our country was as poor as could be. Child mortality was four times as high as in France, a third of all Portuguese people couldn't read or write. Some villages were inhabited only by children and old people: millions of people had emigrated to Brazil or the United States. So, if only for economic reasons, the burden of the colonial war was too much for the country to bear. I saw it happening right before my eyes. I was involved in the logistics, I had to draw up the budgets for the purchase of arms and munitions. I did it precisely according to the norms, but I noticed that it was becoming more difficult all the time. For example, we had to order eleven million units of meat for the troops. The government could only come up with two million. We needed so many rifles, and so much ammunition. We received only a tenth of it. It was as though the leaders in Lisbon were telling the soldiers: "Go throw stones, try saving yourself that way!"

'So the army was the seedbed for the Portuguese revolution, from the moment when the military top brass was forced to admit boys from the lower and middle classes to officer rank. I went through that process myself; it started with my dissatisfaction as a commissioned officer, and I ended up as a revolutionary. We were, after all, confronted each day with the mistakes and stupidities of the regime in Lisbon and with the cruelty of that senseless war in Angola. That was the background of our Captains' Movement. It was the only way we could save our lives, and save our country as well.

'In February 1974, General António de Spínola , the army's real rising star, published a book in which he called for an end to be put to the war as quickly as possible. One month later the Caetano government stripped him of all his functions. It just so happened that we were all in Portugal around that time. That was an exceptionally favourable coincidence, and it established the moment for our revolution. In March 1974 we drafted our political programme. Then we decided to carry out the coup, Otelo de Carvalho, Vasco Lourenço and myself. The date we chose was 25 April, in the same week that the red carnations began blooming in the fields. That is how the Carnation Revolution was born.

'Organising a military coup is extremely complicated. We started by setting up the Armed Forces Movement, the MFA. We held big meetings, and all the army units sent representatives. My job was to maintain contacts with the air force and the navy. The most I could get out of them was their promise not to intervene. We were quite skilled at the art of maintaining secrecy, but the government must have noticed something, it had to, there were too many people involved. But then, what could they do? If they had arrested all of us, they would have had no one left to send to war.

'Alongside that, I had a major personal problem: my father-in-law. At that same moment, as chance would have it, Almeida was chief of the general staff. And I, Vítor Alves, had to start a revolution against him. It was an extremely painful situation. My father-in-law was crazy about me, he only had daughters and from the moment I showed up in the family I was an unexpected joy for him, his favourite, a son. Our relationship had always been intense. But back then, in 1974, Almeida was the last person I could talk to about what I was doing. His daughter, my wife, also took part in the rebellion, she knew that something was on its way, all the major meetings were held at our house . . . Yes, indeed . . . Brutus . . .

'Finally, the moment arrived. On 23 April a man was sitting on a park bench behind the statue of the Marquis de Pombal, discreetly handing out envelopes to a few passers-by. All the instructions for the next day were in there, the entire scenario: troop movements, positions, everything down to the minute. That night, of course, I didn't sleep a wink. At precisely 12.25 a.m., Radio Renaissance played the forbidden song 'Grandola'. That was the signal we had agreed on for the rebellion. All over Portugal, MFA units came into action. By 3 a.m. they had occupied the radio and television stations, the airports and the centre of Lisbon. My job was to neutralise the army top brass, and that all went very well, exactly according to plan. Prime Minister Caetano fled to the police barracks in the Largo do Carmo, that evening he surrendered, and by the end of the day it was all over.

'My father-in-law was treated well, I saw to that, no one harmed a hair on his head. But still, that coup – I must be frank – placed a great burden on our relationship. He kept saying: why didn't you tell me? But if I had told him I would have placed him in an impossible position. He would either have had to turn us all in, have his daughter's husband arrested, or be a traitor to his own government.

'Spínola became the head of our provisional government, we officers stayed in the background, we wanted the international community to see that respectable people had seized power here. The only unexpected thing was the reaction in the streets: we had never expected our coup to generate such a massive explosion of joy and sympathy. And, at the same time, that was a problem for us. It was a bottle of champagne that was suddenly uncorked, and drops flew everywhere; hundreds of political groups began popping up. Within two months our own MFA was deeply divided. One group ganged together around Spínola. That was the most conservative movement, they attempted a couple of coups and then disappeared from the scene. Then you had the Otelists, left-wing radicals around security chief General Otelo de Carvalho. That was the group we belonged to, socialists and social democrats. And there was a big communist group around Vasco Gonçalves.

'A number of things turned out well. Peace came to Africa: Guinea-Bissau, Mozambique and Angola became independent. But Portugal itself looked like it was gradually disintegrating. That first year – I had been appointed deputy prime minister – we put most of our effort into breathing new life into the country's locked economic and social life. And the army had to be reorganised and agricultural reforms carried out. At the same time, all kinds of people were coming back from Africa, some of them relieved, others angry and disappointed, and that didn't make the political situation any easier.

'In March 1975 the right-wing elements made a final attempt to get back into power, under Spínola. When that failed, he fled to Spain. The next month, on the first anniversary of the revolution, elections were held. The communists didn't do too well, Mário Soares' social democrats won, but the group of officers around Otelo de Carvalho didn't want to abide by that. Finally, in November 1975, we carried out a second coup under General Antonio Eanes, threw the radicals out of the government and organized new elections. After that, the political situation gradually calmed down. But it wasn't easy, organising a coup against your old comrades . . .

'Now we're a quarter of a century further along. We lost Africa, and now we belong to an expanded Europe. In 1986 Portugal suddenly became a full member of the European Community, and all the other European countries thought that was wonderful. But still, it was a big mistake. We should have arranged things here at home first. Our country was too far behind, it had no chance against the other member states. What did we have to offer? Only the beaches and the sun, only a growing tourist industry. Why would anyone set up operations here when they can have the most modern of everything in North-Western Europe or northern Italy? Why grow oranges here when inexpensive fruit from Spain is already flooding our local markets? We can't deal with that economic onslaught, and it's only getting worse.

'We should have created a transitional phase to allow Portugal to reach a more or less equal level with the rest of Europe, before becoming a full member of the EEC. And, what's more, the government should have held a referendum, before making that decision. But Mário Soares had a political reason for having us join up so quickly: the democracy had to be safeguarded, and he felt that could only happen under the EEC. I think he was wrong. That democracy was something we had already appropriated for ourselves, during the Carnation Revolution of 1974 and the November Movement of 1975.

'For the members of the European club, Portugal is totally uninteresting. All they want, following their political logic, is hegemony over the entire Iberian Peninsula. They don't see any blank spots or cracks in that picture. For centuries, the Spanish tried to conquer our poor little plot of land, and now they are easily succeeding through the European Union, with the money they use to buy up everything, with the meat and vegetables that are flooding our villages. Things will get better for us, I don't doubt that. But we will lose our identity. That was at the core of the Carnation Revolution: our democracy and our identity. Now we're handing that back to Europe.

'And what about my father-in-law? It was inevitable, our clash, sometimes you have to make choices, it was about democracy, about freedom for everyone. He also realised that there was no sense in staying angry with me, but he suffered. In 1974 he was Caetano's crown prince; if there hadn't been a revolution he would have been Portugal's next strongman. And suddenly there we were in the spotlights, standing on his stage, playing a role that was meant for him . . .

'It was always our custom for the whole family to eat together every Sunday afternoon. Meanwhile I became a cabinet minister, deputy prime minister, ambassador, presidential adviser, and he remained bitter. Those remarks at the table all the time, I couldn't take it any more and I stopped going. For twenty years I ate alone on Sunday afternoon. My wife and my daughter went, I wanted them to, family ties are important.

'And now here I am, sitting beside his bed, holding his hand.'

Some people claim that Portugal is an island, that you can't get there without getting your feet wet, that all those stories about dusty border roads to Spain are simply fables. The weather map on Spanish TV shows Portugal in blue, almost all sea, barely any land. And indeed: I find myself cruising down the quietest four-lane motorway I have ever seen, not a car in sight between me and the horizon, I sail across the mountains. The two Iberian countries live back to back. In Lisbon, for the first time since Odessa, I hear people talking about going 'to Europe'.

On the ferry across the Tagus, the evening rush hour floats to the far shore. For twenty minutes, commuters sit on the top deck: civil servants, office girls, workers, nurses, poor, wealthy, young, old, white, brown, all with bags on their laps and their eyes on the horizon. The sky above the river is red from the evening sun. I see the contours of the impressive suspension bridge, ships in the haze, the ocean in the distance. The passengers are silent, but everywhere the electronics twitter like an aviary. A black businessman is playing tunes on his telephone, a young boy wearing a baseball hat is fighting space invaders in the palm of his hand, the black girl across from me is playing with a discman, her beautiful mother stares dreamily at the water.

The Lisbon of this top deck seems almost American. Nowhere else in Europe have I seen the Third World so naturally present as it is here. The *retornados*, the flood of emigrants from the former colonies, have been taken in by the Portuguese with the fatigued tolerance of a family that already had so many mouths to feed. And most of them have got by, even the non-whites. Today, over two decades later, they are so much a part of Lisbon that it seems as though they have lived here for ten generations, proud and self-aware, for if there is anything that stimulates integration it is the solidarity of the poor. Once at quayside the crowd scatters away, rushing for buses and cars. In the twilight, great clouds of smoke hang around the little stands that sell roasted chestnuts.

That evening I have dinner with a friend from Lisbon, in a crowded and aromatic establishment. 'We still walk around with the inheritance of our isolation,' he feels. 'To a certain extent, Spain actually participated in the European adventure, it accepted American aid and modernised in the 1950s. But Portugal under Salazar turned its back on all that. Agriculture here was almost medieval, everything revolved around the colonies. When they revolted, that also meant the end of the Portuguese economy.'

He cites statistics: fifteen per cent of all Portuguese citizens are still illiterate; in some villages it's as high as forty per cent; since the opening of the borders with the EU, the country's agriculture has almost collapsed; in rural areas, the standard of living is half that of the European average; the villages continue to empty out; almost one out of every three families lives beneath the poverty level. There are nearly as many Portuguese people living in and around Paris as there are in all of Porto.

Later that evening we stroll through the narrow streets. The rain patters down; this is a place that makes you melancholy. Every once in a while a staggering black man appears from the darkness, reeling from the alcohol, drugs or misery. The sea is everywhere.

I dedicate a large part of the next day to Lisbon's loveliest tourist attraction: tram line 28. The driver picks his way like a jockey through the old town, rattles his throttle, clenches the silver brake handle as we descend steeply, then kicks in the groaning electric motor again, back uphill. We creak around a corner into an alleyway, stamp like an elephant past cobblers and tailors, the bells ring, the manometers tremble, the pumps rattle, but we make it through every era.

Lisbon is possessed of a great, dilapidated beauty, the same beauty as some Eastern European capitals, but without the intense buffing-up that has taken place there in the last decade. 'An entire country, embalmed like a mummy for forty years! That was Salazar's achievement!' Hans Magnus Enzensberger wrote twelve years ago, during a visit to this city. 'Salazar was, in his own way, a utopian. His ideal was a world where nothing moved, a state of total hypnosis.'

During that visit, Enzensberger also took a ride on line 28. Back in 1987 he saw the trams still in their original condition, with little folding gates at the entrance, plush on the seats and all the patents from 1889–1916 stamped on plates in a nickel frame. Today I see buttons, electric sliding doors and leatherette. Along line 15 the supertram glides through the streets like a black and red snake; the old trams have been sold to American amusement parks. Line 28, too, is undergoing a metamorphosis, from a means of transport to a tourist attraction. In the local papers, the panic is rising. There is talk of the danger of landslides in this already hard-struck city, due to the construction of a new subway line, right under the old town. 'Dozens of old buildings may collapse any moment into a pile of rubble and dust!' O *Independente* writes. The mummy is finally beginning to stir.

In Lisbon there are almost no traces of the turbulent 1970s, of those days when Portugal seized and held the attention of all Europe. Democratic deeds of heroism are not commemorated with pompous blocks of stone. At Largo do Carmo, a lovely old square, a simple round paving stone is the only thing commemorating the historic scene that took place here in 1974: Caetano's surrender to the rebel tanks and the cheering crowd.

I try to meet with a few of the protagonists. The left-wing revolutionary hero Otelo de Carvalho cannot be reached. He runs a trading office these days, acquaintances tell me, and is probably in Angola at the moment. I'm able, however, to make an appointment with Fernando Rosas, currently professor of modern history, in those days a student and a favourite prey for the secret police. 'I was fairly active in a Maoist cell, the MAPP,' he tells me. 'On two occasions I spent more than a year in jail, in 1971 they tortured me three times by making me go a week without sleep, and after that I went into hiding.' I mention the fact that Western Europe's last three dictatorships all collapsed around 1975. He has an explanation for this: 'Besides all their differences, the Spanish, Greek and Portuguese dictatorships had one thing in common: they were all pronouncedly autocratic, they tried to survive without foreign "infection", either economic or political. By the mid-1970s that had simply become impossible. The world became too intertwined.'

On 25 April, 1974, friends woke him in the middle of the night: come listen to the radio, there's something going on. 'Everyone knew the army was up to something. But no one knew when it was going to happen, or how, or by whom. So, for us, those first few hours were very tense: was this going to be an extreme right-wing coup, or a more progressive one? It was only around 11 a.m. that we started to realise who was who, the crowds began cheering for the rebel soldiers, the government troops stopped taking orders from their officers, after years of waiting it was no longer a matter of thinking, but of doing. And so, finally, we all ended up at Largo do Carmo.' Was Rosas actually there, at that historic moment when the defeated Caetano handed over the reins? 'No, of course not,' he says, 'I had to go, there were resolutions to write, standpoints to establish, meetings to attend!'

To the north-east of Lisbon lies the province of Ribatejo. First you take the highway along the Tagus, then the traffic squeezes across an old bridge, and after that the road runs through endless forests of cork oak before coming to a huge plain with low sheds, the old walled haciendas of the former landowners, villages spread out around a petrol station, fields full of tomato plants. Beside the road lies a crumpled truck, atop the TV aerials the storks have built their nests, crop-dusters roar across the horizon.

I am on my way to Couço, a two-hour drive from Lisbon, one of the many villages where farmers seized the estates in summer 1975 and began their own cooperatives. Many of those little local revolutions were never recorded, but the course of events in Couço was excellently documented by the Italian photographer Fausto Giaconne. His pictorial report begins in spring 1975, after Spínola's aborted coup, when the four local landowners fled to Brazil. On Saturday, 30 August, 1975, the general council of Couço met in the village cinema to start the actual expropriation. The next day, hundreds of poor farming families headed for the abandoned estates on tractors and gaily decorated hay wagons. They took with them hampers of wine, bread and home-made cheese, and banners waved along the dusty roads with slogans like 'Only when the land belongs to those who work it will we have true socialism!' and 'Down with the exploitation of people by people!' Giaconne's photographs show carts full of men and women singing, glowing faces and dancing children. Between 8 a.m. and midnight, 8,000 hectares of land were seized by one huge rolling people's celebration. Sol Posto, the home of one of the local landowners, was broken into: in the photos we see farmers' wives admiring in amazement the softness of the beds, the pillows and the tablecloth. Nothing was to be taken, the army sealed off the house. It was, if Giaconne's pictures are anything to go by, the village feast of the century.

'Look, that's me,' says Joaquim Canejo, pointing to a photo that shows him talking to two women wearing traditional high hats. Now he is a quarter of a century older, he is missing one of his little fingers, and he and his son are sitting down to a huge plate of sausages and chops. Later he will go back to work behind the bar run by his son at the coopera- tive. Politically speaking, the red Portuguese revolution ended with the defeat of the left-wing radicals in November 1975, but most of the farming cooperatives were only dismantled in the course of the early 1980s. Today, father and son are the only ones left from the feast of 1975. Together they run the big hall at the edge of the village which bears the sign 'Conquista do Povo – Cooperativa de Consumo dos Trabalhadores do Couço' (The People's Conquest – Consumption Cooperative of the Workers of Couço). Inside are long shelves full of Becel margarine, Fitness grain breakfast cereal, Servitas cheese, Huggies Nappies, Seven-Up Light, Nuts bars, Mars bars, Heineken beer and everything else that capitalism has to offer.

A part of the People's Conquest has been sectioned off with wooden panels. This is the village café where fifteen time-worn men sit in silence, watching a football match on television. On the wall are three clocks, a football poster, a picture showing thirty different species of fish, and a printed notice: 'Due to the proposal to eliminate section 3 of article 42, a general meeting of the Collective of the Consumption Cooperative will be held by appeal on the 30th of this month at three o'clock . . .'

I go in search of Sol Posto, the house with the soft beds. Amid the stinging nettles, only the walls are still standing. In the restaurant a little further along, the proprietor comes and sits at my table. 'Things are going well in this part of Portugal, yes,' he says. The rest of Portugal, that's a different story, but here a lot of European money has flowed in and is starting to produce results. 'Do you know how many tomatoes we get from a hectare of land these days?' He writes it down for me: 100,000 kilos. 'When they're ripe, the whole plain here is bright red, it all goes to the paste factory and we sell it all the way to Russia.' He says that's why he came back to Couço. He carried out his own private revolution by leaving the village, worked as a painter in a French body shop for twenty years, came back and now he has a restaurant and a twenty-year-old son who does nothing but work with horses, and absolutely nothing else.

The next morning, all Portugal is dripping with rain. I drive on, a little closer to the coast. There are decaying haciendas everywhere and old factory buildings where the harvests were once dried or canned long ago. Now they are overgrown ruins with birds flying in and out. In the village of Vimeiro the houses are drab and sagging, the rotting doors almost falling apart. Beside the old abandoned factory is a wood where the crows nest, and if you climb the dark path there, past the autumnal kitchen gardens and a neglected orchard, you suddenly find yourself standing before the humble birthplace of António Salazar, tall and stern, like an overly-tended Dracula castle.

For years Portugal was dominated by academic hubris, by the overweening pride of this professor who thought he could squeeze a whole country into his theories. But whatever else you can say about him, he was not a man given to appearances. In the village cemetery the better families have stacked their loved ones' coffins in neat little houses, some of them with venetian blinds at the windows, like railway carriages to eternity. There are no less than nineteen children's graves, all but three of them covered in flowers. But the Salazars rest beneath bare, grey stones, nameless, and the only thing lying on António's grave is a brown, mouldy rose.

Chapter Fifty-Seven

Dublin

'GOLD,' THE MAN IN THE SCARLET SWEATER SAYS. 'MARK MY WORDS, get into gold!' The man he's talking to has bulging eyes and a red face. He starts talking about his house in Spain, the bathroom fittings, the guest house, the swimming pool. 'But unfortunately, it's ripe for selling,' his wife says. 'At first the village was so cute and simple, but now the villagers have smelled money and then it all goes downhill quite quickly.' 'That's right, then the property loses its charm,' the sweater man says. 'Then it's time to divest.' 'Money ruins so much,' the woman says. 'Fortunately it's not too late, it hasn't lost its value.'

The car deck of the overnight ferry from Santander to Plymouth is full of dusty Land Rovers, the mood in the ship's restaurant remains animated all night. The news-stand on board sells the *Daily Mail*. War has broken out again, this time between England and France, over meat imports and whatnot, and feelings are running high. The newspaper systematically refers to the French as the 'Huns', an epithet once reserved for the troops of Kaiser Wilhelm and Hitler. An English footballer reveals how he was spat on by a French player: 'I could smell the garlic.' The editors: 'England calls on all British consumers to do their duty: don't buy French meat.'

Upon arrival at Plymouth, a storm is brewing. The wind whistles at the windows of the Winston boarding house, and in the communal living room a robust English girl is warming her backside before the glowing electric coal-effect fire. The BBC reports that several islands are experiencing electrical blackouts.

The next morning the wind is still blowing hard. My van shudders in the gusts, leaves chase across the fields. Completely illegible signs begin appearing along the road, as though a cat has been walking across a type-writer. The rain washes across the asphalt. It is Saturday afternoon and the hours pass slowly, village after village, cement-grey, deserted streets, satellite dishes. All the hotels are fully booked; in one of them, a wedding reception is being held, the women dressed in bright silk, the brides-maids draped across the steps like white napkins, exhausted even before the big dinner begins.

In the village of Llangynog I wash ashore at the Wern Inn. I collapse into a deep sleep, but a few hours later I am wide awake again. Blasting from the pub downstairs are the strains of 'The House of the Rising Sun' and 'Mrs Robinson', followed by 'Oh, Boy', and everyone's singing along. I get dressed. Downstairs, in the bar, the whole village is rinsing away defeat: Wales has lost to England at rugby. The regulars are singing karaoke; 'Oh here's to you, Mrs Robinson . . .'

This is South Wales, the backyard of England, the site of desperate strikes in the 1980s. In March 1984, almost 200,000 British miners, led by Arthur Scargill, walked out in protest against the government's plans to reorganise the state mines and 'destroy the mining communities'. It was a last-ditch attempt to breathe new life into old-fashioned workers' solidarity. Scargill succeeded through intimidation and social pressure in keeping his miners in line, but his National Union of Mineworkers (NUM) did not dare to have things brought to a vote. The Conservative govern-ment of the time stressed that fact again and again. As the mining fami-lies' financial situation became more acute, the panic and violence increased, effectively putting an end to the public's sympathy for the strikers. And when it was revealed that the NUM had accepted money from the Libyan dictator Colonel Gaddafi, it was all over. By February 1985 half the miners were back at work, and a month later the strike ended. It was a trauma: for a year, tens of thousands of miners' families had lived in dire poverty to save a world that was long-since obsolete.

I notice soon enough that my pub is filled with those same miners and their wives, couples who went through the whole thing. The men stopped working in the mines long ago, they have become older and stouter, but most of them still live close to their mine. Some of them have started little farming businesses, others are still unemployed. I strike up a conversation with Thomas Frigger, a big man in a bright red jacket.

After the mines closed he went to work on a drilling platform, nine months on, three months off. 'The only thing I knew was mining, and oil is the closest thing to that. What else can you do?' I ask whether his life has improved in the long run? He has to think about that. 'I earn the same as I used to, but now it's tax free, so that makes a good difference. But nine months a year away from home is not something you do for fun.' An old comrade comes over to bid Thomas farewell: he works on a platform too. 'See you in six months, you old bastard!' Then the music blasts out again, new lyrics appear on the screen, and everyone sings along. The men get drunk, one of them jumps up onto a table and starts stripping, the women screech, the men hang on each other's shoulders. 'Oh, Boy! Oh, Boy!'

And then there is the other side of the story. In the mid-1980s, the only thing these same men and women talked about was politics and the workers' struggle. Their great foe was the Iron Lady, the nickname given to the cocksure prime minister, Margaret Thatcher. Born in 1925, the daughter of a shopkeeper in the provincial town of Grantham, Thatcher brilliantly succeeded in combining classic English conservatism with the ideology of the New Right, and an unshakeable faith in the power of market mechanisms. She used the past failures of her Labour opponents to great advantage – 'Labour Isn't Working' was her party's election slogan – and she offered a clear alternative, not only to Labour but also to the old-school Conservatives and those floating in the middle of the road.

When Thatcher entered office on 4 May, 1979, the country was in disrepair. Great Britain, at the start of the century the most powerful empire on earth, the victor in two world wars, had been reduced in the 1970s to an economic disaster area. The statistics resembled those of a Third World country: economic growth lagged far behind other Western European countries, inflation fluctuated between fifteen and twenty-five per cent, the country was regularly crippled by strikes, Rolls-Royce was bankrupt and, in 1976, Britain became the first Western power to appeal for aid from the International Monetary Fund.

What Great Britain saw as its decline was, in fact, the result of the rapid modernisation of the rest of Europe. The country's traditional heavy industry – textiles, coal, iron – could not keep up with the changes, and so, on the heels of the British Empire, the British 'Workshop of the World' collapsed as well. The crisis applied to Europe as a whole, it was only that the abrupt end of the golden years was felt first and most painfully by the British. Three years later, for example, when the new Dutch prime minister Ruud Lubbers began on his 'chore' in 1982, the economy of the Netherlands had been stagnating for years as well: it had a budget deficit of ten per cent, annual inflation of more than six per cent, and half a million unemployed.

Margaret Thatcher got to work hard and fast. She announced a strict regimen of cuts, she raised VAT, and lowered income tax – particularly for the highest incomes. Many utility companies – rail, water, gas and electricity – were privatised, the system of inexpensive public housing was dismantled, and public rental properties were sold.

Thatcher's tough-minded reorganisation seemed successful. Great Britain climbed – at least statistically – out of its dip. Traditional industries were quickly and rigorously taken apart and new high-tech firms were given fresh opportunities, albeit with a change of personnel and in other parts of the country. British production was brought back into line with the European average, the country's enormous rate of inflation was tamed, and from 1983 the average household income rose by an annual three per cent.

Still, the Iron Lady never completely lived up to what she proclaimed from the mountaintop. Public spending, which she had promised to cut as never before, had barely decreased by the end of her time in office: from 42.5 per cent (in 1977–8) to 41.7 per cent (in 1987–8), to be precise. Her neoliberalism was combined with a strikingly authoritarian system of government: local bodies, universities and other institutions lost much of their autonomy, centralised power was consolidated everywhere and – thanks to the Official Secrets Act – her intelligence services were granted unparalleled power. Within Thatcher's neoliberalism, in other words, civil liberties were limited.

After ten years under Thatcher, Great Britain was 'the most right-wing country in Europe'. In no other member state were there such great disparities between ranks, classes and regions. A small portion of the population had profited greatly from the privatisations and tax cuts. At the same time – according to Eurostat figures – almost a quarter of British families were living below the poverty line (a figure exceeded only in Greece and Portugal). London was thriving, but Liverpool, Scotland and Wales were in dire straits. The privatised railway and postal systems had degenerated into prohibitively expensive chaos. (All the talk at the Wern Inn that evening in 1999 was of the big train crash at Paddington, which had almost certainly been caused by negligence.) A quarter of the male working population was jobless. The celebrated National Health Service was falling apart: those who could afford to do so were turning to private clinics. The same thing was happening in education. It was the vulnerable parts of the population – the poorly educated, the elderly, the chronically ill and single mothers – who particularly suffered.

Thatcher's way of doing things clashed loudly with the German 'organic harmony', the French, Belgian and Italian patronage system, and the Dutch polder model. Yet it would be a mistake to view the significance of Thatcherism only in terms of her economic policies. The essence of Thatcher's message went much further than that. Her historical importance, as Mark Mazower has noted, had to do with the 'reassessment of what the modern state can and cannot do'.

The British problem, after all, was not limited to Great Britain. Ever since the 1960s, more and more European countries had been confronted with unparalleled price rises, and the sense of economic vulnerability was heightened even further by the 1973 oil crisis. During the October War between Israel and the Egyptian-Syrian alliance in that year, the Arab countries used oil as a weapon for the very first time: they raised their prices across the board and confronted some countries with an embargo. In less than three months, the price of oil had quadrupled. It was an historic turning point: Saudi Arabia, Kuwait and other vassal states of the West had suddenly begun flexing their muscles. It was a frontal attack on the international status quo which had been firmly in place throughout most of the post-war years, the end of almost a quarter of a century of optimism and confidence. A lengthy recession followed, marked by a combination of rising unemployment and inflation; average unemployment in the EEC rose during this period from 1.5 to more than 10 per cent. Reason enough, therefore, for the British historian Eric Hobsbawm to speak of the period following the oil crisis as 'the Earthquake': 'The history of the twenty years after 1973 was that of a world that had slipped its anchors and drifted away into instability and crisis.'

Meanwhile, wealthy Europe continued to attract immigrants, both legal and illegal, from all over the world: workers and asylum seekers, pioneers and reunited families, new talents and rose peddlers, rivals and marriage partners.

In 1968, British ultra-conservative Enoch Powell made a fiery, now almost classic speech against this immigration. 'Those whom the gods wish to destroy, they first make mad,' he shouted to a stunned crowd in Birmingham. 'We must be mad, literally mad, as a nation to be permitting the annual inflow of some 50,000 dependants, who are for the most part the material of the future growth of the immigrant-descended population. It is like watching a nation busily engaged in heaping up its own funeral pyre.' Thirty years later, his train of thought had become commonplace among large groups of Europeans.

As early as 1956, during a visit to Rome, Chancellor Adenauer had promised free train tickets to all Italians willing to work in distant Germany. In 1964, the millionth *gastarbeiter* was welcomed to loud applause. The fortunate individual, a Portuguese man, received a Zündapp moped from the employers' collective. At that time, approximately seven per cent of the country's workforce consisted of foreign workers, a percentage similar to that in England and France. The Netherlands was still actively recruiting abroad: the country signed recruitment contracts with Italy (1960), Spain (1961), Portugal (1963), Turkey (1964), Greece (1966), Morocco (1969) and Yugoslavia and Tunisia (1970). In addition, some four million Algerians had emigrated to France after their country received independence, and Great Britain, Belgium and the Netherlands took in huge numbers of immigrants from their former colonies as well. The percentage of foreigners was rising all over Europe: from 3.7 million (1.3 per cent of the total European population) in 1950, to 10.7 million (3.8 per cent) in 1970, to 16 million (4.5 per cent) in 1990.

Added to this were many hundreds of thousands of immigrants – estimates from 1998 put their number at around 3 million – who lived and worked in Europe illegally: in restaurants and cleaning firms, in nursing and health care, in agriculture and construction. Their contribution to the

European economy should not be underestimated. In 1990, the *Financial Times* claimed that it was to a large extent the work of illegal immigrants that 'kept the wheels turning'. 'The construction sector depends on it, including the construction of the Channel Tunnel; the clothing industry would collapse without its illegal worker; and all household help would evaporate.'

Europe, which had been faced in the early 1950s with the phenomenon of emigration – hundreds of thousands of Irish, Portuguese, Spaniards and southern Italians in particular had left each year for the United States and South America – was now suddenly the destination of millions of immigrants. The number of Muslims in France rose to seven per cent of the population, in the Netherlands to more than four per cent, in England and Germany to over three per cent. Problems arose primarily in those neighbourhoods where the newcomers huddled together – immigrant concentrations of seventy per cent were noted here and there – and where a competitive struggle arose for such scarce resources as jobs, housing and educational facilities.

In 1981, violence and rioting broke out in working-class neighbourhoods in London, Liverpool and Manchester. They had to do with the dearth of opportunities – at least for Britain's poorest inhabitants – during the Thatcher era, but racial conflicts also played a role. Starting in the early 1990s, that dissatisfaction began to play a role in European politics as well: in France, the vehement nationalist Jean-Marie Le Pen won some fifteen per cent of the votes; in Germany, the *Republikaner* party of former SS man Franz Schönhuber – whose memoirs about his great role model Adolf Hitler sold around 180,000 copies – took between five and ten per cent of the vote; in Austria, the FPÖ of the young right-radical Jörgen Haider became – with a quarter of the votes cast – the country's second largest party in October 1999; in the Netherlands, the Centre Democrats – including a number of splinter parties – came on the scene, and in Belgium the Flemish Bloc of Filip Dewinter created a furor with slogans like 'A Flemish Flanders in a White Europe'.

Without exception, opinion polls reflected the same pattern: the majority of Europeans remained reasonably tolerant, but the group opposing a multicultural Europe had grown since the 1980s. In a survey held in 1997 among a thousand citizens from each of the EU member states, forty-one per cent stated that there were too many foreigners living in their country. One in ten felt sympathy for racist and ultra-right-wing organisations. In 2000, more than half the Western Europeans surveyed felt that their lives had worsened with the arrival of immigrants, and that their social system had been undermined.

Halfway through the 1990s, the journalist Will Hutton sensed a clear shift in mentality in Britain, a waning tendency to bear collective responsibility, a 'dissipation' of values such as 'an honest day's work for honest pay' and 'the idea that success and hard work go together'. 'Businessmen are mesmerised by their personal salaries. Politicians are no longer able to step outside their tribal circuits. Jobs are easily lost and never found again. A lifetime's savings can easily be stolen . . . The prevailing mood is one of general fear and apprehension.'

For ten years Thatcher damned equality and extolled the virtues of inequality. Inequality was the key to her ideology, the driving force behind her success. In this way, following the post-war consensus ideology, she set a new tone. And, despite her dubious achievements, this tone was adopted by an increasing number of European countries in the 1990s. Four decades after the war, the sense of togetherness, the solidarity after all the shared hardships, had run its course.

It is the morning after in Llangynog. The empty pub still smells of beer and sweat. On the car radio a church service in Welsh, indecipherable yet highly familiar. The trees have already lost most of their leaves, the countryside is a greenish-brown, the sky an unbroken grey, the light watery. Then comes the quiet little port of Fishguard and the wait for a ferry. A few dozen wooden ships are listing on the muddy flats, a little further along emergency repairs are being carried out on the Queen Beatrix, three sandpipers are grubbing after a worm, a little girl runs in circles on the pier, a hardy family is having a picnic in the wind. The entire scene is immersed in the sound of waves, gulls, the clang of metal.

Late that afternoon, after the crossing, the road leads through little Irish villages, past low houses, a factory with bars at the windows. There are betting shops – the bank branches of the poor – everywhere. A hunched farmer is holding a red flag: his wife drives a herd of cattle across the road. The countryside is full of crows. At dusk I arrive at the home of my Irish acquaintances, Declan and Jackie Mortimer. Declan has just come back from the hunt, beside the mower and the compressor in the barn hangs a good-sized deer, a tub of blood on the ground beneath it. Declan works for a contractor. 'Everything is expensive, and you don't earn much around here,' he says. 'But you can always go hunting, and the river is full of trout. And now it's time to dig peat and bring it in, we all have our own little section of peat bog, it's been in the family for centuries.'

They take me along to the pub. Jackie goes into one of the side rooms for her weekly folk-dance lesson: step up, step back, turn, and turn. Meanwhile I sit by the fire and hear the local gossip: about Crazy Mary who sells lottery tickets and always lets her family win; about the local judge who drives all the single ladies mad; about the Dutchman, Willem, who never stops building and whose head, if you sawed it open, would reveal one huge do-it-yourself catalogue with all the Dutch and Irish prices listed side by side, down to the final decimal point. A song is sung, then another, outside the rain rattles, the judge tosses another chunk of turf on the fire.

Dublin is the capital of all these soggy heaths. Keeping up appearances is a concept completely foreign to Dubliners. They gave up the fight long ago, everyone trundles down the street here in equal disarray. According to Brussels' statistics, Ireland is one of the fastest-growing economies in the European Union, but I do not notice a bit of it. Quilted vests are the pinnacle of fashion here, the women push rusty prams. Even in the Czech Republic, the roads and houses look better cared for than they do here.

Concentrations of wealth do exist, of course, and they are doubtlessly on the increase. Successive Irish governments have made massive invest-ments in education and training, a third of all Europe's computers are built in Ireland, and for the first time in modern memory there are Irish emigrants coming home in huge numbers. A sheen of luxury has settled over Dublin's shabby city centre, 'simple' restaurants charging ridiculous prices are popping up all over, and so a new product is gradually being created: a nostalgic, dirty, drunken and poetic Dublin for the new rich and the weekend tourist. But is this really Dublin? The television shows reports of a fire in a working-class neighbourhood on the edge of town, a complete shambles, two children killed. The camera zooms in on a burned roof, a few cheap pieces of furniture and curtains, toys, a wet street, skinny ladies. No matter what the statistics and the folders say, my eyes see a nation of farmers still marked by the poverty of generations.

Life here has always required poetic, dreamy, romantic and nostalgic spectacles, in order to put up with this life and give it meaning. Without such spectacles Dublin is little more than a great nineteenth-century working neighbourhood, a sea of squat brick blocks of flats with here and there the grey columns of a large historical building. At almost all these buildings, a hero once died.

Listen to the Irish Proclamation of the Republic, read aloud by poet Patrick Pearse outside the General Post Office on Easter Monday, 1916: 'Irishmen and Irishwomen: in the name of God and of the dead generations . . .' The wings of the angels in the statuary along the street are still riddled with bullet holes, but that particular revolution did not succeed. Pearse and fifteen others died in front of British firing squads. The popular fury this provoked resulted at last in modern-day Ireland.

The Troubles, as the British call any problem in Ireland, are the aftermath of a centuries-old colonial conflict that is not yet over. From the sixteenth century, Protestant England was lord and master over poor, Catholic Ireland, and in 1800, after the ratification of the Act of Union, the country was even formally annexed by the United Kingdom. Ireland itself was sorely neglected. Only the north of the country kept up with the times. Protestant colonists from Scotland built estates – where the native Irish worked in virtual serfdom – and heavy industry grew rapidly. By 1900, Belfast resembled a second Manchester.

After the 1916 Easter Uprising, a bloody war broke out between the Irish Republican Army (IRA) and the British Army, and a compromise was reached only in 1921: the largely Catholic south was to become independent, while little Northern Ireland would remain a part of Great Britain. In the north, the Protestants were in complete control.

'The dead generations . . .' I take a tour of 200-year-old Kilmainham Prison, the Bastille of Ireland and now a favourite location for gloomy costume dramas. The courtyards have high grey walls; between them, hundreds of little children, often nothing but petty shoplifters, took their exercise in the nineteenth century. Their forgotten bodies are still buried here beneath the paving stones. A few doors down is the prison chapel where poet Joseph Plunkett married his beloved Grace Gifford at 1.30 a.m. on 4 May, 1916. They were given exactly ten minutes together. Two hours later he faced the firing squad.

And then: the same grey walls against which the Irish executed each other later, during the brief civil war between the IRA and the Free State Army, until the IRA literally buried its weapons in 1923. What was that bloody fratricide all about? Strictly speaking, about whether to accept a peace with Britain, with a divided Ireland as part of the bargain. But, above all, the war had to do with the two eternal questions posed again and again by the dead in every war: hasn't it been enough? Haven't too many of us fallen already? Or: was that all, is this what we died for, why don't the rest of you push on?

That is how the dead generations have always ruled over this land.

Empty beer barrels rattle through the narrow streets of early morning Dublin. In Henry Street the Christmas decorations are already being strung up. At St Mary's Pro-Cathedral, near O'Connell Street, at least a hundred people are attending morning Mass on this normal working day: office workers, housewives, a striking number of young people. The church itself is sober and square, white and grey, no statues, no gold. The people pray intensely for peace, everyone is holding hands. The cry of gulls can be heard above the dome.

Later I drive through the pleasant hills of Armagh. The border between the republic and Ulster slips by unnoticed, but soon you see them popping up: villages encircled by British and Ulster flags, flapping islands of Protestantism. Tractors come by pulling beets and manure, I see trailers full of family-owned turf, along the road are dead foxes, badgers and weasels, enough meat to feed an orphanage, just lying on the road here every night.

'The Killing Fields' is what they call this part of the country. More victims have fallen among these prosperous hills than in all the poor neighbourhoods of Belfast put together. For years the IRA did its best to terrorise the Protestant farmers into moving away, so they could have the land for themselves. Farmers' sons were the primary targets. For more than thirty years, Western Europe's last religious war raged between the villages here, but today it has little to do with faith. Religion here seems to be in a state of suspended animation: ever since the seventeenth century it has been raining heaven and hell here, without pause.

Omagh looks like a provincial Dutch steel town: a post office, a Boots chemist. At the top of the shopping street, a redevelopment project is in progress; huge holes have been excavated left and right. One of the houses beside the construction site is blackened. On a lawn lie three bouquets, still in the florist's wrapping.

The bomb that exploded here on the busy Saturday afternoon of 15 August, 1998 was made from Semtex, artificial fertiliser and motor oil. It took the lives of Brenda Devine, twenty months old, Oran Doherty, a boy of eight, Samantha McFarland and Lorraine Wilson, two seventeen-year-old girlfriends, and twenty-four others. It was a last-ditch attempt by the Real IRA, a radical splinter group, to block the peace process. It had the very opposite effect, and united all Ireland in abhorrence.

Omagh was the worst outrage of the war: two whole housing blocks were blown up. It was also one of the most cruel: a warning had been telephoned in beforehand for another location, so that many people had crowded together at precisely the spot where the bomb actually exploded. Everywhere that afternoon parents were out shopping with their children, to buy new uniforms for the start of the school year. 'I saw people with protruding abdominal wounds,' one policeman said. 'We used Pampers Nappies from Boots to staunch the bleeding.'

The infirmary looked like a field hospital at the front lines. Thirty children lost their mothers. The toddler Brenda Devine was buried in a little white coffin, carried by her father. Her mother had burns over two thirds of her body, and knew nothing about her daughter's funeral. Brenda had been asked to be a bridesmaid; her mother had taken her into town to buy new shoes for the wedding.

Belfast is the city of fences: barbed wire around schools and neighbourhoods, armoured barriers around police stations, metre-high constructions around every clubhouse. Even the traffic lights are protected by iron screens. On Dublin Road, all niceties have been burned away by thirty years of war. Crumlin Road consists largely of burned-out shops and Protestant flags: the smaller the bay window, the bigger the flag. Only Wilton Funeral Directors is still in tip-top condition. The Good Friday Agreement, a historic ceasefire according to all concerned, has been in place since April 1998. It was then, for the first time, that David Trimble's Unionists agreed to share power with Gerry Adams' Sinn Féin. For the first time too, the IRA announced that the force of arms was to play no role in this new situation, in which 'Irish republicans and Unionists will pursue our different political objectives as equals'.

On Shankill Road, a group of about twenty men are marching through the quiet Sunday afternoon with their sashes, cockades and bowler hats. They parade along behind a British and an Irish flag, with two drummers and an accordionist out in front, behind them about a hundred grey, worn-out men. There is not a single young person to be seen.

The evening news according to ITV Ulster on 30 October, 1999:

Gerry Adams says that the peace process is in trouble again.

Gerard Moyna of Belfast has been sentenced to seven years in prison after a Semtex bomb he was transporting through the city went off prematurely.

Victor Barker, the father of a twelve-year-old boy killed in the Omagh bombing, wants the damages committee to pay back his son's tuition, all £30,000 of it. 'After all, it's done us no good,' Barker says.

Preparations for Halloween have begun in Londonderry, ghosts look out of the windows, children run screaming down the darkened streets.

The Reverend Clifford Peebles has been arrested; he believes that the Protestants of Northern Ireland are one of the last, lost tribes of Israel. He has been charged with possession of a home-made pipe bomb.

The very first victim of the new Irish civil war was John Patrick Scullion, aged twenty-eight, a warehouse worker. On the evening of 27 May, 1966, as he was stumbling drunkenly down Falls Road in Belfast, he shouted at a passing car: 'Up the republic, up the rebels!' A little later he was shot and killed outside his door. His Protestant killers said later: 'We had nothing against him. It was because he shouted "Up the rebels!"'

The choice of Scullion as victim was typical of this civil war: he was not a militant, not a member of the IRA, he was simply an ordinary citizen who made the wrong gesture at the wrong place. The war has often been characterised as an explosion of sectarian violence, a seventeenth-century religious feud with a new look, in which many Northern

Irish took part passionately. In reality, it was the very opposite, right from the start.

In 1968, when the new civil war broke out, the traditional Catholic and Protestant neighbourhoods of Belfast intermingled, mixed marriages were becoming common, religious fanatics and sectarians were regarded as loonies. Sociological research between 1989–95 showed little prejudice among the older generations, in contrast with those who grew up after 1968. A good forty per cent of the Northern Irish surveyed said they wished to be associated with neither the Catholics nor the Protestants.

What suddenly turned Northern Ireland into a war zone was therefore not latent, widespread religious tension, but the disastrous spiral of violence in which the IRA, the Protestant Unionists, the Royal Ulster Constabulary and the British troops became entangled.

The revolt had begun in the 1960s as a moderate reaction to Protestant intimidation and discrimination. In 1967, a number of Catholics, inspired by the student protests elsewhere in Europe, set up the Northern Ireland Civil Rights Associaton (NICRA). Taking American civil rights activists as their model, they applied peaceful means at first: demonstrations, meetings, sit-ins. For those in power in Ulster, however, this was taking things too far. On 5 October, 1968, a NICRA march in Londonderry was broken up heavy-handedly by police; the demonstrators fought back with stones and Molotov cocktails. The maniacal Pope-hater, Reverend Ian Paisley, fueled the fires even further, his Ulster Protestant Volunteers began terrorising the Catholic neighbourhoods, and the IRA came back to life.

On the surface at least, the conflict in Northern Ireland resembled the one in the Basque Country. The movements in both places fought for their own rights. But whereas the issue for the Basques has been the preservation of a vanishing people, for Northern Irish Catholics it was about the ascendancy of a majority that was not yet recognised as such. The Catholics produced more children than the Protestants, they were the winners in a demographic sense, but they remained oppressed. The routes taken by the traditional Orange marches are telling in this regard. Until far into the twentieth century, the Protestants marched only through Protestant neighbourhoods. Gradually, however, those same neighbourhoods became populated by Catholic families; the routes, though, remained identical to what they had been thirty years before. Detours from the ritual path, after all, would have amounted to a recognition of the fact that those neighbourhoods were no longer predominantly Protestant.

The Catholics increasingly came to regard the marches as an annual provocation, the supreme symbol of discrimination and humiliation. And so, in summer 1969, things erupted: the Protestant marchers in Catholic districts were pelted with stones and bottles. The neighbourhood riots grew into small-scale popular uprisings. British troops were called in, and within a few months the violence had escalated into a civil war that would last for more than three decades.

At first most of those killed were Catholics: the retired farmer Francis McCloskey, who wandered into a riot on 14 July, 1969, had his skull bashed in by the police; contractor Samuel Devenney, father of nine, died three days later from injuries sustained in an attack by the RUC in April; bus conductor Samuel McLarnon was struck down in his own living room by a police bullet.

The British government decided to knuckle down in Northern Ireland. Catholics briefly hoped that the British would rescue them from the harassment of the Protestant militias. But soon the situation deteriorated even further; in 1972, 467 people were killed in bombings and shooting incidents; in 1973 that figure was 250; in 1974, 216 people were killed; in 1975 it was 247, and in 1976 the death toll was 297. Belfast became a war zone, neighbourhoods were cordoned off with barbed wire, sentry posts and armoured cars. Successive British governments proved unable to mediate. During their terms of office (1974–9), Labour prime ministers Harold Wilson and his successor James Callaghan allowed the situation to get completely out of hand. Countless IRA suspects were imprisoned without due process. Margaret Thatcher wrote in her memoirs that her 'own instincts were deeply Unionist'. With only a tiny majority to keep him in power, her successor, John Major, was entirely dependent on the Unionist MPs. In 1984, more than a third of all adult Catholic males in Ulster were unemployed. For years, the annual death toll hovered around eighty. Only after Tony Blair's Labour government came to power in May 1997 was there room for a breakthrough.

Compared with many other twentieth-century conflicts, the civil war in Northern Ireland was relatively limited and isolated. The extent of the drama only becomes clear when one sees how small Ulster really is: not much larger than Friesland province in the Netherlands. The conflict there nevertheless has claimed more than 3,500 lives, and left at least 30,000 people injured. Around 1995, one out of every twenty inhabitants of Northern Ireland had been the victim of a bombing or a shooting, one in five had witnessed a bombing, and the same number knew someone in their immediate surroundings who had been killed or badly wounded.

The lives, long and short, of the 3,637 victims to date have been detailed in the encyclopaedic *Lost Lives*, including the circumstances leading up to their deaths: militancy, camaraderie, loyalty, revenge, brotherly love, the luck of the draw. The book had just come out when I was travelling around Ulster, and everyone was talking about it. With its 1,630 pages, it was the result of eight years of research by a little group of independent journalists. Its impact was shattering.

Take lost life number seven, the first child to be murdered: Patrick Rooney, nine years old, schoolboy, killed on 15 August, 1969 by police bullets while lying in his bed. His mother would later lose a whole series of friends and relatives; because of this book, all those connections have suddenly become clear as well. The chain reactions of revenge, back and forth: in January 1976, three Protestants were murdered in a bar by IRA supporters; in revenge, six Catholic men were shot and killed in a living room during a 'post-New Year sing-song' around the piano; in response, the IRA machine-gunned a van carrying ten Protestant workers close to Kingsmills. Nineteen lives lost within a week. The grisliest details: limbs that flew over rooftops, decapitated victims. The weapons: baseball bats, butcher's knives, pistols, fire bombs, fertiliser bombs, machine guns, Semtex bombs. The nightwatchman Thomas Madden, tortured by Unionists, screamed: 'Kill me, kill me now!' The heroic deaths: the woman who threw herself in front of her husband, a soldier, during an IRA attack. The deaths from sorrow: Anne Maguire, whose three children had been killed in 1976 and who cut her own wrists four years later – there was no life for her without her babies. Those who were simply in the wrong place at the wrong moment: the old woman in a pub who was struck by a gas bomb. The brutal errors: the IRA gunman who burst through a door, shot the father of the family and then cried: 'Damn it, wrong address!'

The IRA and other republican groups accounted for most of the casualties: 2,139. The Protestant Unionists were responsible for 1,050 killings.

The British Army and the Royal Ulster Constabulary killed 367 people. The majority of the victims were, as noted, not activists. An increasing share of the violence, in fact, served only to maintain the groups' internal authority. The tables drawn up in *Lost Lives* speak for themselves: 115 IRA members were killed by the police and the British Army, 149 by the IRA itself, 138 Catholic citizens were killed by actions taken by the British Army, 198 by the IRA.

Worth noting in this regard is the story of Jean McConville from West Belfast, a young widow with ten children, born Protestant but married to a Catholic contractor. The couple lived in a Protestant neighbourhood at first, but were harassed there so badly after 1969 that they moved to a Catholic section of town. In early 1972, her husband died of cancer. Soon afterwards, during a skirmish outside her house, she provided assistance to a young British soldier who had been wounded in front of her door. For the IRA, that deed of compassion was reason enough to put her on its blacklist. On 6 December, 1972 she was abducted and beaten for several hours. She escaped, but the next evening, while she was taking a bath, four young women entered her home and dragged her outside. Her eldest daughter – fifteen at the time – had gone to the chip shop, the youngest children clung to their mother and begged the women to let her go, the older children were hysterical with fear.

They never saw Jean again. The children kept quiet about the kidnapping for several weeks, and tried to survive on their own. Finally, welfare bodies pulled the family apart. For the children, that was the start of a year-long odyssey from one orphanage to the next.

Lost lives. Just outside Belfast, at the foot of a road embankment, lies a wilderness of tall grass, crooked stones, rusty iron and grey Celtic crosses: Milltown cemetery. To the left lie the republicans, finally in possession of their full names and ranks, as in a real war cemetery. 'Capt Joseph Fitzsimmons, killed in action, 28 May, 1972, IRA'; 'Officer Danny Loughran, People's Liberation Army, murdered 5 April, 1975 by NLF'; 'Joseph and Pete McGouch, "One day I will walk with you . . ."'

On 16 March, 1988, the Unionist Michael Stone disrupted an IRA funeral here with shots and hand grenades: three dead, sixty wounded. He had thrown his hand grenades too soon. 'If they had exploded in the air, he would have killed a great many more republicans,' his sympathisers complained later. Stone is still their hero.

Lost lives. 'We have good hope,' says Teresa Pickering. 'But there isn't a family in Northern Ireland that hasn't been damaged.' Teresa is a mother of three, one of countless women who have had to pilot their families through this war. 'Whole groups of boys were always on the run, including my own seventeen-year-old brother. There were always people hiding out, police raids, arson.' She tells me about how one night three British soldiers forced their way into her home one night and pulled her out of bed. 'I was puking with fear.' She had to hold down two jobs, because the men of the family were no longer bringing in money. Her sister and her baby were caught in the crossfire, her brother was sentenced to life imprisonment. She got married, her husband was sent to prison, a life of arrests, searches and caring for prisoners. 'The strange thing was: at the same time, we just lived on as normally as possible, like everyone else. That was pure survival instinct.'

I had been introduced to Teresa by a mutual acquaintance; now she sits a bit uneasily in the hotel lobby, it's still hard for her to talk about it. Her first husband was tortured: British soldiers blindfolded him and put him in a helicopter, flew around and then threw him out, two metres above the ground. A joke. It led to a ruling against Great Britain by the European Court of Human Rights. Teresa herself was detained for a week, in total darkness, interrogated at the strangest hours, without any charges pressed. 'When I came out, I was completely disoriented.' That was only two years ago.

In 1976, a spontaneous peace movement arose among the women of Belfast; the two initiators, Betty Williams and Mairead Corrigan, actually won the Nobel Prize. 'I knew both of them well. I sympathised with their idea completely, but of course all those wonderful meetings didn't work. After all, it wasn't about a personal conflict between Catholics and Protestants. It was about a Northern Irish government that treated us like trash, simply because we were Catholic.' According to her, that is what finally put an end to the women's peace movement as well.

Now the thaw has truly begun. The police stations are still electronic fortresses, but the armoured cars are off the streets and the men of the

IRA are gradually coming out of prison and out of hiding. Teresa knows quite a few of them, they are all thirty-five or forty years old by now. 'Some of them were always on the run, had all kinds of girlfriends, marriages fell apart. Most of them have spent a good part of their lives in prison. They were already falling behind when the civil war started, and now it's even worse. What's more, today we have a completely different Northern Ireland from when they went into prison. That whole generation has to find its way back to a normal life.'

Teresa was divorced, and recently remarried. 'When I go out these days, I'm still afraid. But then, so many women have led a life like mine.'

Lost lives. Jean McConville's children never stopped looking for her. This spring, the IRA finally admitted that she had been murdered. In June 1999, a search began of the beach at Templetown to recover her remains. The McConville children, adults by then, gathered in the dunes and watched as policemen dug a huge L-shaped hole behind flapping plastic curtains, then systematically dug up the rest of the beach. 'Finding her body would bring us back together again as a family,' Helen McConville, the eldest daughter, says. 'This is destroying us.' A reporter from the Independent wrote: 'One of Jean McConville's daughters walked across the car park, her eyes fixed on the ground, full of sleeplessness and worry, an attitude of pain and despair. She walked to a car in which other members of the family were sitting. The digging was over for the day, and there was little reason to stay any longer, but the family remained, maintaining their endless wake for reasons deeper than any logic . . .'

Jean McConville's remains were finally found in summer 2003. For the IRA, her death had been merely a working accident: she had been interrogated with a plastic bag over her head, and had suffocated.

XI November 1980–9

FINLAND

Helsinki

Tallinn

Leningrad

Riga

Moscow

Minsk

Kursk

Volgograd
(Stalingrad)

Brest

Chernobyl

Warsaw

Kiev

SOVIET UNION

Rostov

OVAKIA

Odessa

Sea
of Azov

Krasnodar

Budapest

Crimea

HUNGARY

RUMANIA

Black
Sea

Tiflis

Belgrade

Bucharest

GOSLAVIA

BULGARIA

Sofia

Istanbul

Ankara

ALBANIA

Saloniki

TURKEY

SYRIA

GREECE

Athens

CYPRUS

LEBANON

Crete

Mediterranean

0   100   200   300 km

Geert Mak's Route

Chapter Fifty-Eight

Berlin

'FAMILY,' MY GERMAN FRIENDS TELL ME, 'FOR US IT WAS ALWAYS family ties that determined the choices we made in life.'

There are eight of us at the table, it's a chance get-together, and I cannot remember how we hit on the subject. 'I was born and raised in Wuppertal,' the woman across the table from me says. 'But only because my mother was bombed out of her house in Berlin while she was still pregnant, and the only thing she could think of was that she had family there somewhere. That's how I became a real *Wessi*.'

'With my mother, it was completely the other way around,' says the woman next to her, who comes from the former DDR. 'She was pregnant too, my father was in the army, and he had family in Rostock. That's how I ended up there.'

Her husband: 'Almost all of us have a story like that.'

The woman beside me starts talking about the building of the Berlin Wall. 'I'll never forget it. 13 August, 1961. I was eighteen. I was standing there in Oranienburger Strasse when workers began rolling out the barbed wire and throwing up a wall. Meanwhile, the most amazing things were happening. It's been described so many times, but I saw it with my own eyes: how two friends were standing on the east side, they said goodbye, one of them took a running jump over the wall into the West, the other one started a life in the East. A *Wessi* and an *Ossi*, and no doubt it was years before they saw each other again.'

She herself had felt absolutely no urge to jump over the low wall; there was no way she would have left her mother behind. 'Everyone around me had been thinking about it for a long time, most of them had already decided what they would do even before they started building the wall. My older brother chose to go to the West, he was seventeen, and he left as soon as he'd finished his final exams. My closest girlfriend went too, suddenly she was gone, without a word. That was terrible. Now she lives in Nancy, she married a Frenchman.' She herself met a Pole, and these days she lives in Warsaw.

Everyone at the table starts talking at the same time. 'Yes, that's exactly the way it was at first, in the East: as far as you knew, you were making a decision for the rest of your life, for ever.'

'There was hardly a German family that didn't have brothers or sisters, grandfathers and grandmothers, nieces and nephews on the other side.'

'You weren't even allowed to cross the border for your parent's funeral.'

'It was only in the 1970s that *Wessis* were first allowed to travel to the East, every now and then. Finally you saw the brothers, uncles, nieces and nephews who you'd been talking about and writing to so much.'

'And then it turned out that you really didn't have anything to say to each other.'

Berlin, 9 November, 1999. In the dilapidated head offices of the former national bank of the DDR, just off Unter den Linden, the tenth anniversary of the fall of the wall is being commemorated by an unusual concert: the favourite music of both former chancellor Helmut Kohl and former DDR leader Erich Honecker. We listen to the Hennigdorf brass ensemble ('My Way'), the Berliner Schalmeienexpress (stalwart DDR marches) and the Generation Berlin Orchestra with a special piece composed for the opening of a lignite mine. Between the pieces of music, someone reads out texts written by Kohl and letters from Honecker. The arches of the great hall of the old bank have been patched with bare brick, there are huge holes where the proletarian art once hung, the rain rattles on the roof and drips through the ceiling. The audience, mostly young people and artists, listens intently.

A record player starts up with the song 'Ein Augenblick der Ewigkeit', a hit from the old DDR radio programme *Stunde der Melodie*. The evening's host reads a letter, written to Honecker when he was in prison. 'Dear Mr Honecker, thank you very much for the lovely music we were able to listen to for thirty years, thanks to you.' Outside, the great celebration is being skilfully stage-managed by the new Germany: the Brandenburg

Gate glistens in a firmament of television camera lamps, there are three police cars on every corner, and through it all the Berliners walk in the rain, drinking beer and being mostly silent.

Later, for no real reason, I stroll over to the playground close to Hotel Adlon. There is no one there. I sit down on a bench. Pop music is blasting in the distance, to the left are the bright lights of the new Potsdamer Platz, to the right the fireworks. Beneath the grass and the climbing frame lies the bunker, forgotten now. Four mentally handicapped people are taking the S-Bahn home, accompanied by their supervisor. They cheer at every illuminated glass palace they pass, sing along with every electronic peep, admire the new glass dome of the Reichstag as though it were a firework display. They are the only ones who view the new Berlin with unadulterated pleasure, ten years after the collapse of the wall.

The next morning Alexanderplatz reeks of old-fashioned DDR coal. The smoke is coming from the chimney of a wooden caravan. On the door is a sign: 'SIND IM WESTEN'. In front of it are racks of cards on which all passers-by are invited to write down their thoughts and wishes concerning the 9 November celebrations. Dozens of people stop to read. 'It went too fast,' someone has written. 'And the thinking is still going too fast.' Someone else writes: 'I wish for better education and less violence. Oh, if only we were back in the DDR!' 'I certainly wish YOU were!' someone else has written angrily beside it.

Big words like 'freedom', 'democracy' and 'heroism' are used at all the commemorative meetings, and famous names are dropped: Helmut Kohl, George Bush, Mikhail Gorbachev. But the ones who actually razed the wall were the people of Berlin themselves, and ten years later their feelings are a good deal more complicated. Their thoughts hang in the rain on Alexanderplatz, on all those cards: 'We must learn from each other, really learn. Not accuse, not exaggerate.' And: 'From the terror of the Stasi to the terror of consumption. Congratulations, Ossis!' And: 'The DDR took my youth, and it took other people's lives. Only after turning fifty am I allowed to see the world.' And: 'I want a dog and a house, and I want my parents to get back together, and a bicycle and an electric toothbrush, and I can't say much about when the wall fell, because I was only three then.'

What is left of the barrier that once divided this town? Along Bernauer Strasse, the last remains of the wall have been elevated to the status of monument. Aficionados can still hear the linguistic differences between West and East Berlin: forty years is apparently enough time to develop a separate dialect. The last *Goldene Hausnummern* – the DDR insignias for model tenants – are being unscrewed from the shabby doors. But the cheerful little DDR man on the traffic lights is allowed to stay, he walks straight ahead through red and green, nobody pays him any attention.

I spend an afternoon with Walter Nowojski, retired DDR journalist, radio and television programme maker, editor-in-chief of the Writers' Union journal and editor of the diaries of Victor Klemperer. He got to know the old professor back in 1952, as a student in Berlin. Klemperer, he tells me, was a cult figure even then, the only one in the entire DDR who had something to say. 'His lectures were real happenings. He was old and sick, he talked mostly about eighteenth century French literature, but the auditorium was always packed. His book about the language of the Nazis, LTI: Lingua Tertii Imperii (1947), made a deep impression in the DDR. Everything in our minds was contaminated, we knew that, it was all old Nazi garbage. What he carried in his mind, though, was an almost forgotten treasure: the German-Jewish intellectual tradition, of which he was one of the last great representatives. When he began talking we would cling to every word, in complete silence, for an hour and a half.'

It was not until 1978 that Nowojski first heard about the existence of Klemperer's diaries. Rumour had it that they were being kept in the municipal archives in Dresden. He took the train the very next day, and from that moment he spent almost all his free time on the project, in total fascination. It proved to be a Herculean task: the war diaries in particular turned out to be full of errata, misspelled names, all kinds of things. 'Klemperer was in a special house for Jews, he barely went outside at all, he heard everything at second hand. But at the same time, in that closed house, he was often better informed than the general population. And he knew what to write down, which is another thing that makes his diaries so fascinating. He made notes about how people in the street greeted him, as a Jew, about what people ate, the rumours about the camps, everything. As a historian he had an unerring sense for the details that could be important later on. Some of the bathing resorts on the Baltic had signs saying 'JUDENFREI'. Was that in 1938? No, it was in 1924! Everyone has forgotten that, we only know about it thanks to Klemperer. He did the same thing with the language, with all those buzzwords he documented: *Weltjuden, volksnah, volksfremd, Staatsakt*. For me, as a thirteen-year-old in 1938, the word *fanatisch* had a very positive connotation. Klemperer documented that. And the diaries show that he continued his collection during the DDR period. *Kämpferisch, gigantisch*, he was able to put together a whole dictionary again, just like that.'

How could an old man like Klemperer have such a productive life in claustrophobic East Germany? 'It's very simple, really: he had a great sense of urgency. Between 1933–46, for thirteen of the most fertile years of his life, he had been unable to do a thing. In the West he would have been put out to pasture. In the DDR, though, they regarded him as a celebrity, they made him a professor at Humboldt University, just what he had always dreamed of.'

That feeling is one that Nowojski, a celebrated literary critic in the DDR, experienced for years himself. 'I was at the centre of the system, but from 1978 I still worked each and every evening on Klemperer's diaries. I knew exactly how the DDR censors worked. I led a schizophrenic existence: propagating the official literature by day, working by night on Klemperer, a set of volumes which I knew would never be published here, for a host of political reasons. But I couldn't leave it alone, I couldn't stop, I was too enthusiastic.'

In essence, the choice he made was the same as Klemperer's. 'I owed the DDR a great deal as well. My father was a miner, the DDR system was the only thing that made it possible for me to study. That ambiguity clouded my view of the regime for years. I could see the dark sides, but my gratitude kept me from drawing conclusions. That's the problem with our whole generation, especially the intellectuals. Many Westerners will never understand how we had to live in the DDR. The nagging, the red tape you had to go through just to get your bosses to do something, the fussing about, the waste of talent. Lots of political questions, therefore, were essentially matters of character: how do you keep going, how do you deal with your principles without destroying yourself? That same inner conflict also applied to Klemperer.

I recognise myself in his diaries, including that feeling of urgency and wasted time.'

And now everyone had become a Stasi-hunter: 'The last few years here have been dedicated to one huge parlour game: who was spying on whom? I came across my own name in Stasi reports, I was evaluated as a "revisionist" who was trying to achieve a central position in order to "further advance revisionism by means of legal machinations of power". And, couched in their own terminology, that was a pretty accurate description of what I was in fact trying to do. Who was spying on us? No one I wouldn't have suspected of doing so, with the exception of one person: my best friend, my chosen substitute in our literature programme. We're still good friends. He came to me one evening to tell me about it, in 1994. He had a weak character, I knew that, and there must have been a blemish somewhere they could blackmail him with. But I remained the head of the programming department for eleven years, so he couldn't have said too many bad things about me. He also covered up for me a great deal, I'm sure of that. And that's what I told him: it's better to be spied on by a friend than by an enemy.

'I've known two Klemperers in my life; the cheerful, inspiring Professor Klemperer with his openness and his remarkable sense of humour, and the Klemperer of the diaries, who was bitter and angry about everything the DDR dictatorship brought with it. The two Klemperers were one and the same: the outgoing Klemperer needed the Klemperer of the diaries in order to stand up the next morning in front of his students and be cheery. "We vomit out our souls to our friends," he wrote at various points. All those nights working on his diaries had the same effect on me: I vomited out my soul with Klemperer.'

There is a remarkable anecdote about Joseph Roth, or rather about Berlin. Around 1970, when an American historian was researching Roth's Berlin years, he found himself constantly amazed by the distances between the places where Roth had lived, where he worked and where he frequented his favourite cafés. 'Roth must have spent hours in the S-Bahn every day!' Until finally a Berlin acquaintance showed him a detailed map of the city: in fact, all those places were quite close together. The difference with Roth's day was that a wall had since been built between them.

The story says something about the way the wall was taken for granted, timeless and ineluctable as a river running through the city. But it also shows how the wall threaded its way through the very warp and woof of Berlin. On the East Berlin side alone, more than 120,000 people had lived close to where it was built. Most of them were finally forced to move. This allowed the DDR authorities to create a bare strip of land several hundred metres wide between the Hinterlandmauer, the actual barrier for the East Germans, and the wall itself. On the other side of that, in turn, lay a closely monitored border zone 2.5 kilometres wide.

Meanwhile, however, the S-Bahn remained the official property of the DDR until 1984, and during all those years the personnel trains shuttled blithely back and forth between East and West. Three West Berlin lines of the U-Bahn ran, in turn, beneath East Berlin, past fifteen bricked-up ghost stations. For years, telephone calls between the two parts of the city had to be routed by way of Sweden, or via the internal lines of the S-and U-Bahns. Mourning became a subject of deep mistrust: a special 'grave card' was needed to visit the Invalidenfriedhof and the Sophien-Friedhof, the two cemeteries along the border. At the same time, however, Werner Fricke, an employee of the East German Potsdammer water company, calmly walked past the guard posts each day, to tend to the pipes and valves that happened to lie on the western side of the wall.

Only once had I seen the wall from the wrong side. It was during a student-exchange visit, and our DDR guide invited us to come and take a look. We climbed onto a platform and suddenly found ourselves standing eye to eye with all those Westerners on the platform on the other side. We stared at each other and saw ourselves, it was insane.

Of the 19 million East Germans, 2.5 million left for the West, the great majority of them in the 1950s. Approximately a thousand people were killed while attempting to escape the country, most of them along the Berlin Wall. One particularly spectacular and successful escape was organised by Reichsbahn engineer Harry Deterling, who rammed his locomotive number 78079 (and a few carriages full of family members in the know) past the stunned border guards and into the West. The conductor, an East German policeman and five unwitting passengers walked back to the East in a huff, along the rails.

Very unusually, the East German songwriter Wolf Biermann – later '*ausgebürgert*' – was allowed to give a concert in the West in 1965. For the occasion, he wrote 'A Winter's Fairy Tale':

> In German December then flows the Spree
> From East to West Berlin,
> And there I swam with the railroad,
> High over the wall again,
> I threaded my way across a wire of steel,
> High over the bloodhounds again . . .

The barrier over which crowds climbed in 1989 was the fourth-generation wall. Seized DDR documents showed that the technical staff of the border police were by then already working on plans for a fifth generation. This High-Tech-Mauer-2000 would be able to resist all attempts at escape, without a shot being fired. In the DDR policy paper, dated 8 May, 1988 and entitled *Zur Entwicklung von Grenzsicherungstechnik für 1990–2000*, the policymakers enthused about 'micro-electronic sensor technology', 'microwave modules' and 'seismic alarm systems' designed to detect intruders immediately. There was only one problem: the sensors could not distinguish between people and stray dogs. Such documents are clear proof that the wall, in one form or another, was intended to outlive us all.

On 26 May, 1987, nineteen-year-old amateur pilot Mathias Rust landed his little Cessna in Red Square, right in front of the Kremlin. Taking off from Helsinki and flying just above the trees, he had passed the Soviet lines of defence unchallenged. It was meant as a joke, but the Soviet leaders were thoroughly shocked. This was impossible, but it had happened anyway.

Looking back on it, Rust's escapade was historic. His landing in Red Square was an unignorable symbol, the writing on the wall, a sign that the all-powerful Soviet Union was no longer fully in control. At the time, however, no one recognised its significance.

Starting in the mid-1970s, Western intelligence services had begun to wonder about the Soviet Union's defence spending, especially after a political refugee reported that the Soviets were spending as much as twelve per cent of their gross national product on defence, double what the CIA had thought. One of the agency's Soviet experts, William Lee, then calculated that the actual figure was probably twice that, around twenty-five per cent. The only possible conclusion was that the Soviet economy was on the verge of collapse. His bosses, however, drew exactly the opposite conclusion: this level of defence spending was a clear indication that Moscow was still aiming for world domination. As late as October 1988, three months after Mikhail Gorbachev came to power and announced his moderate revolution of glasnost (openness) and perestroika (reconstruction), CIA Soviet specialist Robert Gates warned: 'The dictatorship of the Communist Party remains unchallenged and unassailable . . . A long period of rivalry with the Soviet Union still lies before us.'

At that point, the military and nuclear spending of the Soviet Union was no less than five times higher than officially admitted, around thirty per cent of GNP. At the same time, almost no modernisation was taking place: while the digital revolution of the 1980s was in full swing in the West, the communist world had almost no computers. The heavy industry set up by Stalin continued to belch forth vast quantities of chemicals, steel, tanks, trucks and aircraft, while the country's production of common consumer goods lagged far behind. A considerable share of Russia's agricultural production came from the kitchen gardens of farmers and workers: half the country's food was being grown on three per cent of its arable soil.

In 1989, the spending deficit of the joint Eastern European states was four times what it had been in 1975. The Soviet Union was governed by the elderly: the average age of the members of the Politburo was seventy.

At first these problems were camouflaged by successes in foreign policy (new Soviet-oriented regimes in Vietnam and Angola) and an economic crisis in the West. In addition, the ailing Soviet economy was propped up for years by the billions it received in revenues from oil exports. But after 1979 oil prices began to drop and the Soviet Union entered into a hopeless war in Afghanistan. Almost all of the Russians I spoke to remembered a given moment, usually around 1983, when they realised that something was very wrong indeed with the Soviet economy: there were inexplicable problems with the electricity supply; butter suddenly became unavailable; queues for bread appeared one week and were still there the next, and one month later no one knew any better. The birth rate decreased drastically, as did the general health of the population: in 1988, the number of healthy conscripts was down twenty-five per cent from what it had been in the 1970s. Child mortality had risen by a third. Alcohol consumption was around twice the European average.

To make things worse, a new arms race began, this time at technologically advanced levels. In the late 1970s the Soviets had deployed seventy SS-20 missiles, medium-range nuclear weapons that suddenly posed a threat for all of Western Europe. NATO responded in 1979 with what was referred to as the 'double decision': if the Soviet Union was unwilling to dismantle its SS-20s, NATO would deploy nuclear weapons – the Pershing II and the cruise missile – all over Western Europe. The short distances involved meant that only minimal warnings would be given of an attack. In Western Europe, the fear of a nuclear war, and above all of an accidental nuclear war, was greater than it had been since the 1950s. Hundreds of thousands of demonstrators took to the streets. In the end, the INF (Intermediate-range Nuclear Forces) Agreement between Gorbachev and Reagan in December 1987 put an end to this potentially fatal competition. Two months later, under the watchful eye of the Americans, the first SS-20s were dismantled in Kazakhstan.

As the British historian Richard Vinen has observed, the Soviet Empire as a superpower was weaker and poorer than many of its colonies. Satellite countries such as Poland and Hungary still had a strong tradition of small private companies capable of working with relative efficiency.

The DDR was seen as the showpiece of the Eastern Bloc. In reality, however, that country lived largely from the loans, at an estimated total of three billion Deutschmarks, that had been flowing eastward since 1973 as part of Willy Brandt's Ostverträge. With those loans, Chancellor Brandt and his successors were able to 'purchase' all kinds of concessions from the DDR regime: the relaxation of travel restrictions, the release of political prisoners, the reunification of families. These were, in effect, the first breaches in the wall.

In 1983 the DDR's debts had risen so far that the federal government of the West was forced to cough up an additional billion Deutschmarks. In

1988, Politburo member Günter Mittag warned his colleagues that the DDR's finances were on the point of 'capsizing'.

This financial crisis was kept a deep secret, but the outside world was not blind to major problems facing the country. 'There were too many things happening all around us that were quite simply impossible economically,' said my old acquaintance Inge Winkler, who worked as a paediatrician in the east of the DDR at the time. 'People who did nothing all day, factories that stopped working because there were no more raw materials. It was perfectly clear to all of us that things could not go on the way they had in the past.'

Wolf Jobst Siedler travelled regularly from West Berlin through the Eastern Bloc, and its problems were clear to him as well: 'There were gigantic fleets being built, but the government was unable to repair the potholes in the streets. Helmut Schmidt once referred to the Soviet Union as "a developing country with a hydrogen bomb", and of course he was right.'

His friend Richard von Weizsäcker: 'Obviously, none of us knew that the wall would open up on Thursday, 9 November, 1989 at 9 p.m., no one knew that.' Weizsäcker was president of West Germany at the time, and even at the highest levels of government there was no indication that matters would accelerate so quickly. As late as July 1987, Gorbachev had personally told Weizsäcker that German reunification could very well take another hundred years or more, and definitely no less than fifty. Weizsäcker himself was convinced that the wall was, by definition, a temporary matter. 'My only doubt was whether I would be around to see it fall.'

Hans Krijt in Prague: 'You could see the old system crumbling, in that last year, but we were simply expecting it to transform itself into capitalism with a human face. In early October 1989 the West German embassy in Prague was suddenly stormed by thousands of East Germans seeking asylum in its grounds. The Iron Curtain there was no higher than a garden wall with a fence on top, and rumour had it that you could reach the West via that escape route. In the end, it turned out to be true. We lived quite close to the embassy, and when we went for a walk in the evening we would see the streets full of abandoned Wartburgs and Trabants, prams, even suitcases that had turned out to be too big to drag along. I looked into one of those abandoned cars: there was a teddy bear on the back seat, forgotten in the rush. I thought about the panic that child must have felt.'

Richard von Weizsäcker: 'And then, in autumn 1989, things started going very fast. On 9 October, after a church service, 300,000 people took part in a silent demonstration in Leipzig. The Russian soldiers remained in their barracks. One month later, on 4 November, at least 600,000 demonstrators gathered on Alexanderplatz. It was an incredible mix of political and other figures, from the writer Christa Wolf to the top officials of the SED. But even at that point I still had absolutely no idea that the wall would fall within five days, and without bloodshed.

'The day after it collapsed, on Friday, 10 November, the mayor of Berlin and I were the first to make a ritual crossing of the Glienicke Bridge. But after that I couldn't stop, I walked all over town, everyone was flabbergasted. Finally I ended up at Potsdamer Platz. Today it's been completely built up, but back then it was still a vacant lot with the border running through it. There was a little group of people standing on the western side, they were wondering whether you could cross, and I said: "I want to see for myself!" So I walked across the open ground until I got to the barracks of the DDR border guards. A lieutenant from the *Volkspolizei* came out, recognised me, saluted and said calmly: "Mr President, I would like to report that there is nothing special to report."'

1989 was one of those moments when everything seems to happen at once, an *annus mirabilis*. Within two years, nine communist dictatorships collapsed, including that of the Soviet Union itself. In January 1989 the Polish independent trade union Solidarity was granted official status: for the first time, legal opposition became possible in the Eastern Bloc. Lech Walęsa, the great trade union leader, signed the agreement with a pen bearing the portrait of Karol Wojtyla, a tribute to the Polish Pope John Paul II who played a seminal role in dismantling communism in Central and Eastern Europe.

Elections were held in Hungary in March, with non-communists candidates permitted to stand for the first time in forty years. The regime received a solid trouncing. In May, Czechoslovakian dissidents demanded free elections as well. Václav Havel was released from prison. On 27 June, in a symbolic ceremony at Sopron, the new Hungarian foreign minister and his Austrian counterpart jointly cut the cords of the Iron Curtain. The guard towers and barricades blocking the border were swiftly taken down.

In the same month, Mikhail Gorbachev and Helmut Kohl signed an agreement in Bonn, ratifying the right of all European states to determine 'their own political system'. It came as no surprise to the leaders of the communist countries: as far back as November 1986, Gorbachev had stressed at a closed meeting of the Comecon that the Soviet Union could no longer fend for them. In the years to come they would have to learn to stand on their own feet. And in summer 1988 he repeated that message in Moscow: as far as he was concerned, the era of Soviet interventions was past.

In August, a chain of two million people joined hands to link together the three Baltic States of Estonia, Latvia and Lithuania; a little later, hundreds of demonstrators broke through the Austro-Hungarian border at Sopronpuszta. Before long, at least 120,000 East Germans had crossed Hungary to the West. A few thousand more refugees escaped via the West German embassy in Prague: they were finally allowed to travel in sealed trains to the West by way of Dresden.

Meanwhile, Rumanian leader Nicolae Ceauşescu was feverishly calling his communist colleagues: wasn't it about time the Warsaw Pact intervened in Poland? Erich Honecker in particular liked the idea, but Gorbachev vetoed the plan right away. In September a non-communist government was installed in Poland, the first in Eastern Europe since 1945. A moderate manifesto, calling for open dialogue on political reforms and signed by thirty church leaders and intellectuals, was published in the DDR by a group calling itself the New Forum. Later in September, the Slovenian parliament decided to change the constitution to allow for the country's secession: that was the start of the disintegration of the Yugoslav federation.

On 7 October, the fortieth anniversary of the creation of East Germany was celebrated solemnly in Berlin. For the last time, the army goose-stepped past the ailing, seventy-year-old Honecker. That evening a huge torchlight parade moved down Unter den Linden. The honorary guest, Gorbachev, described the scene in his memoirs: 'Bands played, drums rattled, searchlights. When the torches were lit one saw – probably the most impressive thing of all — thousands and thousands of young faces. The participants in the march, I heard later, had been carefully selected.' That latter fact made it all the more amazing when, from within the ranks of this party youth marching past the leaders in time-honoured fashion with portraits and red flags, slogans and chants were suddenly heard: 'Perestroika! Gorbachev! Help us!' Polish party secretary Mieczyslaw Rakowski turned to Gorbachev in excitement: 'Mikhail Sergeyevich, do you hear what they are shouting? "Gorbachev, save us!" And these are the activists of the party itself! This is the end!' The same thing happened later at the Soviet memorial in Treptower Park, where thousands of young people had gathered to see the Soviet leader: 'Gorbachev, help us!' When the demonstrations were over, he warned his DDR colleagues that their rigid stance could prove fatal: 'In politics, he who arrives too late will be punished by life itself.'

In the same week, the Hungarian Socialist Workers' Party voted to disband itself: the new leaders had no desire to be associated with the 'crimes, mistakes and incorrect ideas and messages' of the last forty years. The party organ Népszabadság (People's Freedom) appeared for the first time without the slogan 'Workers of the world, unite'. Meanwhile, Poland opened its borders to East German refugees in transit. In Moscow a government spokesman told foreign journalists that the Brezhnev doctrine of military interventions had been replaced by 'the Sinatra doctrine: "My Way".'

Honecker stepped down on 18 October, eleven days after the celebration of East Germany's fortieth anniversary. His successor, Egon Krenz, was horrified when he encountered the financial shambles of the DDR. According to a report from the central planning agency, the country subsisted almost entirely on loans from the West. Stopping them would mean 'the immediate lowering of the standard of living by twenty-five to thirty per cent, and would make the DDR ungovernable'.

In his public appearances, Krenz used an entirely new jargon, peppered with terms such as 'openness', 'dialogue' and 'change'. But the popular movement could no longer be stopped. Citizens' forums were being set up all over the country. The demonstrations grew with each passing week, from 120,000 demonstrators in Leipzig on 16 October to half a million Berliners on 4 November. 'Gorby!' they shouted, and 'Wir sind das Volk!'

and sometimes even '*Deutschland, einig Vaterland!*' The demonstration in Berlin was broadcast live on East German television. The writer Stefan Heym said: 'It is as though a window has been thrown open!'

On 7 November, the East German government was trying desperately to contact Moscow: the pressure at the borders had become too great, the relaxation of travel restrictions to West Germany could no longer be avoided. But the Soviet leaders were unreachable; they were too busy with the festivities surrounding the anniversary of the October Revolution. That day the East German council of ministers stepped down, followed the next day by the Politburo of the SED.

On Thursday evening, 9 November, the DDR regime decided to expand the possibilities for its citizens to go abroad, although border documents were still required and travellers had to meet certain criteria. Afterwards, the general secretary of the central committee of the SED, Günter Schabowski, held a chaotic press conference that was broadcast live. Without having thoroughly read the minutes of the meeting, he announced that East German citizens were now allowed to travel abroad without prior permission. 'Starting when?' a journalist asked. Schabowski: 'Starting immediately, I think.' It took a moment to register, but then everyone realised what this meant: the wall had fallen.

East Berlin clergyman and opposition leader Werner Krätschell, along with his twenty-year-old daughter Konstanze and her girlfriend Astrid, were among the first to drive across the border at Bornholmer Strasse. The notes he made that day read: 'Dream and reality become confused. The border guards let us through. The girls cry. They huddle together on the back seat, as though expecting an air raid. We drive across the strip which, for the last twenty-eight years, has been a death zone. And suddenly we see West Berliners. They wave, cheer, shout. I drive down Osloer Strasse to my old school, where I received my diploma in 1960. Out of the blue, Astrid asks me to stop the car at the next junction. All she wants is to put her foot down on the street. To touch the ground. Armstrong stepping onto the moon. She had never been in the West before.'

The dramatic images of that night were seen around the world. But the next day, if only for a moment, the Kremlin seriously considered restoring the old situation by force. Four of Gorbachev's closest advisers urged him to have the Soviet army intervene. In their eyes, an open border posed an unallowable risk. But Gorbachev understood that any attempt to turn back the hands of time would lead only to a head-on conflict with the United States and West Germany. That was a conflict he dearly wished to avoid. He was still optimistic about the inner resiliency of the system: the transition to greater freedom and openness, he believed, would strengthen communism rather than weaken it.

And the communist regimes fell like dominoes. The dissident movement in Prague grew each day; in late November Václav Havel and Alexander Dubček stood before a cheering crowd of a quarter of a million people. Stasi offices all over East Germany were attacked and rifled. In Sofia, 50,000 Bulgarians demonstrated against the Communist Party's hegemony. In Bucharest, Ceauşescu and his wife Elena were booed by the crowd, riots broke out, and the Rumanian Army stopped following orders.

Meanwhile, an unknown KGB agent in Dresden, Vladimir Putin, had tried to pile so many documents into a burning stove that the thing exploded.

Chapter Fifty-Nine

Niesky

IN THE FAR EASTERN CORNER OF THE FORMER DDR, CLOSE TO THE Polish border, lies the town of Niesky. Everything here looks brand new: the houses are freshly plastered, the streets have a new layer of asphalt, the big town square is dotted with hanging baskets. I'm here to visit my old friends, Eckart and Inge Winkler, good acquaintances from the turbulent years after the *Wende* of 1989. They still live in the same flat on the edge of town, on Plittstrasse, and from their living room you can see the edge of the forest that stretches out for more than fifty kilometres, far into Poland. '*Das Tal der Ahnungslosen*', the valley of the unsuspecting, is what East German intellectuals called this corner of the country where no Western television station could penetrate.

Eckart is a construction engineer. He has his own design agency these days, his youngest employees barely remember the DDR. In his free time he is the pastor of the local New Apostolic Congregation. The members of his church are as active and lively as ever, but the number of young people is decreasing: they are all leaving for the West. This year he even lost his organist, a wonderful boy; he found a job in the West and he was gone.

During the last decade, Eckart and Inge's flat has been completely revamped. Today, in 1999, Inge no longer does the laundry by hand. Central heating has been installed, a dishwasher is humming away in the kitchen and Eckart no longer has to get up at 5.30 to stoke the boiler with lignite. But they still don't have a television: they don't like trash coming into their home.

This was the same attitude that kept them going throughout the DDR era: sitting in their flat with a good book, they could shut out the rest of the world. Now the big yellow tile stove has disappeared, but I can still see that corner of the living room in my mind's eye: the stove radiating its gentle heat, their daughter Gudrun – home from school for a brief vacation – sitting against it and studying, their granddaughter Elisabeth playing on the floor, their son Burckhard tinkering in his room, their other daughter Alund making a doll from an old handkerchief and a tennis ball. Alund's husband, Jens, was a conscript in the army.

Ingrid worked in a paediatrics clinic, Eckart worked for the Christoph Unmack construction firm. They did not have a lot of money, but the rent was low, the company saw to a warm meal every day, and the state guaranteed a secure existence.

It was late February 1990 when I first stayed with them. The border with the West had been thrown open barely three months earlier, the DDR was still intact; it was right before the first free elections for the *Volkskammer*, and a colleague and I were putting together a radio portrait of the *Wende* in this forgotten corner of Germany. Around 5.30 a.m., at first light, the streets were blue with the smoke from hundreds of stoves and furnaces. A little procession of greyish-green Trabants put-putted across the big Zinzendorfplatz, the same square where the SA had marched in the 1930s, where the Soviet soldiers were buried after 1945, and whence – long, long ago, people said – the aroma of lime blossom could be smelled 'all the way to Berlin'.

The city had about 12,000 inhabitants in those days, and most things revolved around the big Christoph Unmack works, which manufactured railway cars, prefab wooden houses and more. The few shops in the square sold carrots, cabbage and grey writing paper.

The town itself was founded in 1724 by Moravian Brothers, led by Ludwig von Zinzendorf. Those pious refugees from Bohemia and Moravia also gave it its name: Niesky, meaning 'humble' – and that is how life there remained; quiet, sober, modest. Yet the collapse of the wall precipitated a great many changes: enthusiasts set up a branch of the New Forum opposition movement, a few hundred people held a candlelight march on Zinzendorfplatz, and in early December the fifty local Stasi agents were almost literally chased out of town by an angry crowd.

After that, things happened quite quickly. The price of a new Trabant dropped by fifty per cent in three months. The neighbours purchased a satellite dish and began watching only West German television. Eckart, who had been required until recently to ask permission from his bosses for every international telephone call he made, could suddenly cross the border whenever he pleased. Gudrun already had plans to visit family in Canada that summer. 'It was as though we'd been living in a scary fairy tale all that time,' she said later. 'We were as happy as rabbits that had been let out of their cage for the first time in years. But after we had danced in the field for a day, something else suddenly occurred to us: what happens if a fox shows up?'

They were exciting times, and our unexpected arrival was yet another sign that major changes were on their way. We had brought wine with us, and coffee and tea, and fresh fruit and Dutch chocolate, and Eckart talked about days gone by and his countless skirmishes with the Apparatus. Before the *Wende*, he had been required to report every rehearsal of the church choir. The second-hand plastic paint buckets from Christoph Unmack, extremely popular among the locals for use in their kitchen gardens, first had to be dipped in grey paint to cover up the gaudy Western labels. When Eckart heard about that, he stormed into the office of his technical manager – a well known Stasi agent – and shouted: 'You people are no longer a party of workers, you're a party of bucket-dippers!'

He never heard anything more about it, but Gudrun – who was one of the best pupils at her school – ran into difficulties when she wanted to go to university. Eckart: 'As long as you don't forget that: it wasn't Erich Honecker who did that, it was the work of thousands of little people together, all making each other's lives miserable.'

The revolution in Niesky in spring 1990 was subtly visible in the masthead of the *Sächsische Zeitung*. For as long as anyone could remember, the local paper had been falling on the Winkler's mat under the title *Organ der Berzirksleitung Dresden der Sozialistischen Einheitspartei Deutschland*, but from early December 1989 it was simply a *Sozialistische Tageszeitung*, and from January 1990 the paper called itself the *Tageszeitung für Politik, Wirtschaft und Kultur*. In that same month appeared the first advertisements for trips to Paris: 'No need to eat at expensive restaurants. Simple meals will be served on the bus, and can even be paid for with DDR marks.'

Niesky lived breathlessly, as though a fairy godmother had promised all the town's inhabitants three wishes: free travel, a solid Opel, and all

party nabobs thrown overboard. In the final weeks before the first free
elections, however, a certain bitterness crept into the flat on Plittstrasse.
Eckart had a good memory, and it was now working to his disadvantage.
His managers, who had begun calling themselves 'entrepreneurs', were
the same men who had recently insisted that all colourful plastic buckets
be painted grey. For years many of the neophyte CDU candidates had
toed Honecker's party line, enthusiastically and without question. They
were *Wendehälse*, weathervanes. Eckart considered this the 'selling out' of
everything for which they had all worked so hard. Inge: 'During the
demonstrations in November there was a pride in our own country unlike
anything we had felt for years. We dreamed of something between capitalism and socialism, the best of both worlds. But when the West German
politicians began interfering in our elections, it was all over. They're much
better talkers, those *Wessis*.'

On election Sunday, 18 March, 1990, the whole family stayed glued to
the radio. That morning in church they had been able to laugh about it,
but the mood soured as the results trickled in. The 'Western' Christian
Democratic Allianz für Deutschland received almost half the votes, the
coalition of ninety opposition groups surrounding the New Forum barely
three per cent. What it boiled down to was carte blanche for a merger
with the West.

Friends from all over began calling. 'What's it like over there?' 'Is this
what we risked our necks for all those years?' 'We did all the dirty work
for these new party bosses, we took the risks. They're just swimming
along with the new tide.' 'Now they're all snapping to attention in front
of Kohl.' 'They did it for a car, for the money, to fill their stomachs!'

Gudrun and Inge sat in their living room, weeping.

When my colleague and I returned to Niesky two years later, in 1992, the
fairy godmother had actually come by. The houses and side streets still
looked a little dilapidated, but the main roads had been repaved, the air
was twice as clean – new cars and stoves work wonders – and the shops
were overflowing with kiwis and video recorders. All the Karl-Marx-
Strassen and Friedrich-Engels-Strassen had been transformed into Goethe-
and Schiller-Strassen. At the edge of town, a consortium of Western companies had within a few months thrown up an ultramodern shopping mall,

and the people of Niesky were packing their cars as though they'd been doing it all their lives: washing machines, colour TVs, it was one huge catch-up operation. Most people could afford it as well. Life in the DDR had in many ways been so inexpensive, with so little to be had, that almost everyone had saved up a considerable nest egg.

Niesky made a sprint through time; in one fell swoop it seemed to have swung from the 1950s to the 1990s. Everything it had taken a comparable Western European town forty years to achieve happened here in less than forty months. The grimy café on Görlitzer Strasse, where two years earlier the drunken and crippled comrades had spent their evenings arguing with the five local punks – 'Do you snots have any idea who did the work around here for all those years?' they shouted – had been turned into a kind of French tearoom: white tiles with light-blue trim, ornamental chairs, quiet music and neat tables covered in damask. Only the bicycle repairman had kept something of the flavour of the old days: he sold two varieties of bells: the shiny West German ones for five marks, and the old, indestructible East German bells for one mark.

Niesky in 1992 was one great paean to capitalism. The aerials on the old party headquarters were rusting, still aimed at Berlin. The building now housed an employment agency, and in its hall sat dozens of the unemployed, waiting with number in hand. One man there told us he had worked for a storage firm where, back in the days of the DDR, sixty employees had once whiled away their days, even though there was barely work for ten. Today that firm employed five people. Unemployment in Niesky was hovering around thirteen per cent, and rising all the time, especially among women. The fairy godmother had seen to that as well.

A modern bathroom had been installed in the Winklers' little flat, the old DDR radio had been replaced by a brand new CD player, a computer screen flickered in one corner, and Eckart's ten-year-old Wartburg had made way for an almost new Opel.

In a way, Niesky during that second visit seemed like a German variation on Twin Peaks: it was a town with a past, with a secret everyone shared and which constantly threatened to disturb the peace and quiet of the present. Beneath the town's friendliness and Gemütlichkeit lay a morass of confusion, of right and wrong, of loyalty and betrayal. Almost every week, another, even deeper layer was revealed: betrayal after betrayal, disloyalty beneath the old disloyalty, evil that went on and on.

Among the advertisements for 'introductory visits to the Costa Brava', the *Sächsische Zeitung* ran almost daily articles revealing local Stasi activities. It turned out, for example, that a doctor from a nearby psychiatric institution, acting on orders from the Stasi, had poisoned a dissident clergyman with psychoactive drugs. The clergyman – now a cabinet minister in the state government – had appeared on television after seeing his dossiers. He looked like a broken man.

Eckart and Inge wanted nothing to do with any of it, although they were sure that both of them had hefty dossiers as well. 'Don't let the future be ruled by the past,' they said.

On 6 October, 1991, Gudrun married her *Wessi* fiancé, a young doctor; at the wedding, all of the contradictions between the two Germanys seemed to meet. Eckart and Inge felt there were far too many guests, the West German family found the party much too sedate. The West felt that Gudrun's East German girlfriends were too docile and subservient, the East was amazed that the West German women depended on their husbands for their status. West felt that East was badly dressed, East found the West German women silly and lazy, and Gudrun found herself caught between the two extremes. It made her feel, she said later, 'almost like a traitor'.

1993 was an important year for the family. Eckart had shaken off the yoke of his former DDR managers and, together with Jens, had started his own company in a little attic room. They earned a mere pittance in those days – even the purchase of a new drafting lamp was reason for intense consultation. But their enthusiasm was boundless, and gradually the jobs began trickling in. The bucket-dipping comrade was still managing director of the old plant. But he had done his best for all his employees, and Eckart had gradually – to his own surprise – come to appreciate his old enemy. He was optimistic about competing with the West, at least in his own field. 'They're a little complacent, those *Wessis*, a little bit spoiled. They're going to have to deal with us.'

Meanwhile the *Sächsische Zeitung* was writing about attacks on foreigners, about the 26,000 illegal immigrants who had been rounded up on the Saxon border in 1993, and the classified ads offered work in a 'famous nightclub' for ladies between the ages of eighteen and thirty-three, including housing and excellent amenities. Almost everything on the supermarket shelves came from the West. As part of the local drive to 'Buy Saxon Wares', Inge had done her best for a time to purchase milk, vegetables and other groceries exclusively from local suppliers. But those suppliers had proved almost impossible to find. The West saw to everything, the East barely seemed to exist any more.

In September 1994 I went to visit Gudrun. The last time I had spoken to her, she had read aloud to me from one of her old textbooks:

> We are the class of a million millionaires
> Being our own dictators makes us free
> For us, good work is a duty and an honour
> And each of us is a part of the party . . .

Four years later she was living on the other side of Germany, in a Dortmund suburb. 'Sometimes I wish I hadn't been born in the DDR,' she said. 'Sometimes I feel ashamed. And sometimes I sit in the car here, I see how everyone here eats and argues, and then I hate the West.'

For years, as though seeing something of herself in a mirror, she had been able to pick out other women from East Germany whenever she saw them on the street: by their rather subservient posture, their uncertainty, their clothing. 'For one whole year I wore the same thing to church each Sunday: a white dress with a pullover. Out of protest, but also out of insecurity.'

They still go back to Niesky on occasion, and last time there was one thing in particular that had struck her: there were no children being born. Almost all the young people had gone west. From Gudrun's class alone, nearly half the people had left. Since 1989 the town's birth rate had decreased by a third. 'The women have become unsure of themselves,' Gudrun says. 'They are the first to be laid off, the company meals and other facilities that once allowed mothers to keep working are being dismantled. The women are being sent right back to the kitchen sink.'

Today, in autumn 1999, Niesky looks like a town where nothing has ever happened. The houses are painted in cheerful pastel tints, the new library

is the pride of the surroundings, on Zinzendorfplatz the final chrysan-
themums are blossoming in festive hues. The *Sächsische Zeitung* talks about
the local high school's recent field trip to Prague: the bus was searched
at the border and no less than seven children turned out to have hashish
with them. Hashish! In Niesky!

This Sunday a wedding service is being held in the church. Eckart is
wearing his black cleric's garb. I sit beside little Elisabeth, she's eleven
now, pretty and soft as a fawn. Two little girls in crisp starched dresses
play a violin duet. The choir sings. My friend preaches – off the cuff,
without much ado or outward display – on a text from the Gospel of St
John about peace, meekness and acceptance. The choir sings again. Eckart
addresses the bride and groom, he speaks of 'a humble life before the
eyes of God'. The bride keeps her own eyes on the floor, while the groom,
a chunky blond boy in an ill-fitting black suit, wipes away his tears. They
say 'I do', and kiss shyly.

Now the whole congregation files past to congratulate them: Inge,
Jens, Alund, Elisabeth, the catechism teacher with her purple hair, the
little group of hunched widows, a pair of burly workmen from Christoph
Unmack, the choirgirl with the naughty piercing in her nose. Then
everyone goes outside. They throw rice, the children step forward for a
song, a curtsey and flowers, the groom tosses a few coins, there's a bit
of singing again, then everyone shouts: '*Hoch!*' The bride and groom climb
into an antique car and drive off. We all standing waving at the curb. 'A
1934 Opel!' says Eckart, always the impassioned technician, even when
in his clergyman's suit. 'If only that car could talk!'

———————

'As a student, I went to Berlin once with a few friends on one of those
inexpensive junkets. It was 30 April, the queen's birthday in Holland, so
we decided to go on a spree in East Berlin. Which explains how I ended
up the next morning in that huge, deathly quiet Stalin-Allee, walking
along there on my own, not another soul in sight. Then suddenly, still
half asleep, I heard a rumbling and saw something moving in the distance,
and there they were: Russian tanks! Having grown up in Holland, you
think: the war has broken out! Until I realised that it was only the start

of the 1 May parades. But that's how violent our reactions were back then, still moulded by that constant tension between East and West.

'I was born in 1939; in the 1950s Europe to me was the Marshall Plan, cities, travelling, culture. In the 1960s I suppose I didn't have much to do with Europe. There were Catholic young people's conferences of course, international seminars, I even stayed in Lisbon for six weeks once. But, unlike my future colleagues Helmut Kohl or Jean-Luc Dehaene, I was not caught up in the "European adventure" from an early age. Europe was alive for me, very much so, but not as a political idea.

'In 1973 I was appointed finance minister in the Netherlands. That was when I first started hearing talk of Europe, the jokes about de Gaulle, Luns and Adenauer. But to me, Europe in those days was more of a technical matter: massive dossiers, endless meetings, the old boneshaker in which you were driven to Brussels all the time. That's where the committees met, and it was only natural for a finance or foreign minister to play an important role. In those days, the meetings were hard-nosed, they had nothing to do with European idealism. You were there as a cabinet minister with administrative responsibilities. And, of course, a lot of issues were still being dealt with entirely outside the EEC. The Netherlands, for example, had a head-on trade conflict with Japan, and as a Dutch cabinet minister in those days you went to Japan to negotiate directly. It was only gradually that things like that became European issues. The 1973 oil crisis wasn't seen as a European affair either: we still saw that as a Dutch problem. The OPEC boycott, after all, directly impacted only the Netherlands and the US.

'Four years later, as parliamentary leader for the Dutch Christian Democratic Alliance, I first became acquainted with the European Christian Democrats. That was the first time that I met men like Kohl, Martens and Andreotti as fellow politicians. And gradually I began to form a new perception of Europe, a political perception, very different from the bureaucratic Europe I had known before.

'In 1982 I was appointed prime minister of the Netherlands. In Copenhagen, at the European Council of Ministers, I met my European colleagues for the first time. I already knew Wilfried Martens, Helmut Kohl and Margaret Thatcher, of course, but there in Copenhagen I saw the whole club together for the first time. Right from the start of that meeting, there was this incredible tension between Thatcher and Mitterrand. The crux of Mitterrand's arguments was that investing in Europe meant turning our back on America, discovering our own strengths, protecting ourselves. After that, and on that basis, one could start initiating dialogues outside Europe. His story, in short, was an anti-American one. Our own strengths first. Thatcher said: "Rubbish. Rot. Open the doors. Free trade."

'The bureaucracy of the 1970s seemed to have vanished, and I found myself taking part in a political debate, all afternoon. Ten years before that, as far as I know, such open discussions between European heads of government simply did not take place. In those days Europe was still seen as a matter for intergovernmental officials, plus a few cabinet members, usually the ministers of finance, agriculture and foreign affairs. That was it, that was Europe. Very concrete, based on a limited number of institutions, dealing with practical problems.

'That evening in Copenhagen, after dinner, the discussion continued informally about what Europe really meant, about European culture, even about the role of the Reformation. At that point, looking back on it now, we were already working on an entirely new concept of Europe – not a technical Europe, but a political one. And despite all our differences, we formed a kind of club.

'Which is not to say that the practical cooperation between our countries went without a hitch. There was a lot of talk, wonderful plans were made, but it all went rather awkwardly. Bit by bit, though, between 1982–9, we succeeded in conquering that "Eurosclerosis". At Schengen in 1985 we decided to do away with internal border controls between the Benelux countries, France and Germany. Later on, more and more countries joined. In that way, a single policy could be formed with regard to border controls, security and asylum issues. In 1989 the internal market was ready to go and then finally in 1991 you had the Treaty of Maastricht which made way for, among other things, the arrival of the euro in 1999 and 2001.

'In the 1980s, though, we had to deal not only with a European policy line, but also with a NATO line and everything that brought with it. The EEC and NATO were two distinct cooperative structures, separate worlds, each going their own way. Helmut Kohl and I, for example, were very opposed to the stationing of cruise missiles, while Mitterrand was much more accommodating on that score. Not because he was pro-American, but because he felt that a clear reply to the Soviets was needed.

'Naturally, we were very interested in what was happening in the Soviet Bloc, and we talked about it among ourselves, along the lines of, "What do you think of this Gorbachev fellow?", but we didn't see it as a common issue. Until the wall came down. Then, suddenly, we had to deal with it. Kohl foresaw the consequences right away: this was the historical opportunity for which Germany had been waiting so long. He put everything he had into effecting the merger of the DDR and the Federal Republic in 1990, and he succeeded. But for us, well, how does one deal with that? Were we to grant unconditional support to a reunified Germany? And what would happen after that? Wouldn't that new Germany go on to lay claims to what had once been East Prussia? Historians are wrong when they say that, around 1989, no one was worried any more about the sanctity of the Oder-Neisse border with Poland. Because there were powerful political forces at play within Germany, people who would have loved to see the old situation restored. Major potential conflicts still lay between Germany and the rest of Europe.

'So Mitterrand and Kohl made a deal: you, with your strong Deutschmark, will support the European Monetary Union (EMU) and the new European currency – and, along with it, the French franc. In return, we will support German unification – on condition that you leave no room for doubt concerning the definitive status of the Oder-Neisse border. I was worried about Poland as well, but Kohl gave me his word that maintaining the Oder-Neisse border would be the *sine qua non* of the debate. He was convinced of that, but I still had my doubts. Had a decision to correct the border in an easterly direction been put to the vote in Germany – and all kinds of groups were trying to get things to that point – we would have had a major problem on our hands. And Kohl was enough of a politician to know that the slightest thing could have moved it all beyond his control. Those millions of old *Heimatvertriebene*, such powerful forces, there were such strong emotions involved . . .

'Later, Kohl wrote to Gorbachev and said: I've made the German parliament abide by the Oder-Neisse border, and now I'd like you to do something for me . . . I don't think that was merely bluffing on his part. He really saw it as his own personal achievement that, by acting calmly and wisely, he had reconciled the Germans to the immutability of the Oder-Neisse border. But if that was truly an achievement, logic says there must also have been a chance that things could turn out differently. Kohl was always reassuring the people around him, including me, telling us there was no need to worry. But to say it wasn't an issue, oh no. Of course it was an issue.

'Ruud Lubbers and Helmut Kohl, two old European friends who split up over German reunification, that's the way publicists wrote about it later. But that's not what it was about. We were on very good terms, true enough, we often carried on long conversations. And until Maastricht, one year after German reunification, everything was still fine. Right before the Maastricht summit, in fact, Kohl and I had lunch together. We had a good talk, both of us were in favour of the creation of the EMU, that was our common line of approach. Kohl accepted the fact that I would chair the meeting, not only on technical matters, but also in terms of its content. At that point I was probably the only one who could keep the British from exercising their veto. The treaty was hammered out with a great deal of difficulty, but the old feeling was still there: excellent, so now we've done that. Europe was on the move again, we were actually headed towards a single currency, that had all been taken care of.

'But at the same time, Maastricht was also the start of a new era. Thatcher was gone. Mitterrand wasn't getting any younger. And within that same general atmosphere, Kohl began distancing himself from me as well. Maastricht was behind us and relations within Europe were being reshuffled. More and more, the Bonn-Paris axis began ruling the agenda.

'Yet I believe that the essence of our parting of the ways was largely personal. Following the enormous success of reunification, Kohl became a different man. He had steamrollered his way over a few opponents before then, of course, but he had always been quite a good colleague, quite amiable. After 1990, however, he began towering above himself, he became the first chancellor of a reunited Germany, he excelled at that, he revelled in it, but he was no longer able to see the other leaders as his colleagues, unless they happened to be the president of the United States. He began treating Mitterrand the way Yeltsin later treated Gorbachev, condescendingly, humiliatingly. And when I wanted to do things differently, that irritated him no end.

'At Maastricht, most of the member states had been in favour of having the new European Central Bank in Amsterdam. He was the only one who favoured Frankfurt; he had to go out of his way to force that one through. Not long afterwards, the Croatians announced their secession from the Yugoslav federation. We considered that extremely dangerous, we believed it could mean the start of Yugoslavia's disintegration, and we were right: it finally resulted in a long, violent civil war. But Kohl supported the Croatians openly, he saw their right to self-determination as an extension of that of the German people themselves. Our fearless foreign minister, Hans van den Broek, protested vehemently against that standpoint, again and again. And Kohl's attitude changed to one of: those damned Dutch again! At the drop of a hat, Ruud Lubbers was no longer a partner but a troublemaker.

'In 1994, Jacques Delors asked me to succeed him as chairman of the European Commission. The Spanish prime minister, Felipe Gonzalez, publicly announced my candidacy. I went to Mitterrand. "No," Mitterrand said, "Kohl and I have agreed to support your Belgian colleague, Jean-Luc Dehaene. You're *trop marin*, too Atlantic, you focus too much on England and America."

'At that point you could already see the contours of the new Europe taking shape: Kohl and Mitterrand simply put their heads together at Mulhouse and decided things like that, just the two of them, then announced it and expected everyone to go along with them. Kohl, the colossus of Europe, choosing his own man, his aide in Brussels, Dehaene. And he was *so* angry when the Netherlands didn't accept that decision.

'The shortest talk I ever had with him was also the last one we ever had. It was about that chairmanship. Kohl had terrorised the little countries, one after another they had bowed to his pressure, but four countries were still standing: England, the Netherlands, Spain and Italy. Kohl said: "But this is undemocratic. Eight of the twelve are for Dehaene. Why won't you accept that?" I said: "I see things differently. Together, the four countries who oppose Dehaene's candidacy account for half the population of the EU. Fifty per cent of the European population is saying no to this, no matter what you and Mitterand say. Dehaene and I should both withdraw our candidacy." Kohl was furious. But that's the way it was, and that's the way it went.

'In late August 1994, I stepped down as prime minister of the Netherlands. Do you know how that goes here in Holland? My wife was in the hospital, I had my chauffeur drop me off there, then he drove on to our house. My daughter let him in. He had three of those huge satchels full of my personal documents. He upended them here, on this table, he said "Bye, Heleen," and he left.

'That was the end of twenty-one-years in Dutch politics.'

Chapter Sixty

Gdansk

IN THE TRAIN ON THE WAY TO GDANSK, WINTER ARRIVED. THAT MORNING the air had still been cold and clear, but around noon the sky suddenly disappeared behind a curtain of grey, and autumn was over. The wind came up, it started hailing, then the fields turned calm and white. The farms were asleep, the village chimneys were smoking, snow drifted beside the tracks.

Gdansk is smaller and more intimate than you would expect. It is the perfect city for strikes, uprisings and revolutions. The cranes at the ship-yards, the church steeples, the hotel apartment for the foreign press, the inner city with its Dutch Renaissance houses, all are within fifteen minutes' walk of each other. How many revolutions have failed because the move-ment was too diffused, too fragmented? Here it is the very opposite, here you can literally shout freedom from the housetops and everyone will hear.

It was in this forest of churches and cranes that it all started, the tiny fissures that ultimately brought about the earthquake of 1989. An enor-mous strike in 1970, bloodily beaten down, put an end to Gomulka's old brand of communism. In 1976, an assistance committee for the families of those who had been arrested formed the basis for Solidarity, an oppo-sition movement – openly supported by the Polish-born Pope – which soon had approximately ten million members. A strike in 1980 at more than 300 locations led to freedom for the trade unions, and to Mass being read on the radio each Sunday.

The December 1981 coup by General Wojciech Jaruzelski turned back the clock for a time, a state of emergency was declared, but it was too late: the influence of the church and trade unions on broad sections of the population could no longer be undone. In addition, the country's economic problems had become more than the regime could handle. A round-table conference in January 1989 – by which time the country's annual inflation had risen to 600 per cent – finally brought free elections and freedom of speech. Gdansk was the place where it all began, and that was no coincidence, for it was here that all of communism's weak spots overlapped: religion, nationalism, rebellious industrial workers, the obstinacy of an old German Hanseatic port, a clear organisation and a wind that always came blowing in from overseas.

Former dockworker Kazimierz Rozkwitalski drives me around the town. That is where the synagogue used to be. Burned down on the Kristallnacht in 1938, it is now a car park. This seaside bunker still bears the bullet holes from September 1939, the first shots fired in the Second World War. Look, the Gestapo used to have its headquarters over there, they started murdering intellectuals here right after the occupation began. Here we have the town hall, bombed to rubble in 1945, but can you really tell it wasn't built in the Middle Ages?

Kazimierz is a wonderful storyteller, and his German is excellent. Where did he learn it? He lets the name roll from his tongue. '*Inge Zimmermann, hundertachtzig Procent Nazi!*' Between 1939–45 she hammered the German language into his youthful skull, and there it remains. He shows me the former Lenin dockyard, now Stocznia Gdańska SA. An enormous monument of stainless steel, anchors and crosses makes sure no one overlooks the fact that this is historic ground. Here was where the electrician Wałęsa delivered his first speeches, here began the decline of an empire. One tattered banner is still hanging.

Why, after all the other failures, was it in Poland that the revolt against the communist nomenklatura finally succeeded? 'After the Soviet Union, Poland was by far the biggest communist country in Europe,' Kazimierz reminds me. 'It had two or three times as many inhabitants as the other Eastern European countries.' In addition, there was the all-powerful church. And the outspoken Polish patriotism. Plus a weak communist tradition. 'The regime always left loopholes. For us, the common workers, the 1970s under Edward Gierek were perhaps the best years of all, it was never as good again after that. We always had work and food, we were allowed to go on holiday, some of us already owned cars, the schools and hospitals were well organised. That's more than you can say these days.'

January 1990: the Polish Communist Party disbands itself. September 1993: the last Soviet troops leave Poland. August 1996: Gdansk's Lenin dockyard goes bankrupt. And now? We walk through the slush, the dockyard is a city in itself. 'Tot,' Kazimierz murmers, 'tot', just the way he learned it from Fraulein Zimmermann. 'Fifteen years ago this place was full of ships and stevedores. There were still 30,000 people working in the harbour then. Today there are only 3,000. Of the 17,000 people who used to work at the Lenin dockyard, there are maybe 2,000 left.' The grass grows tall between the paving stones, the brick warehouses are empty, rusty railings run from one bush to the other, in the silence you can hear the melting snow gurgle through the zinc gutters. But the yards are not completely dead. A huge crane comes clanging past, a railway engine appears from around a corner, workers are welding and sandblasting. This is not bygone glory, more like a slowly dissolving past.

I am reminded of the story a lady friend, a photographer, once told me about an encounter in a small Portuguese village, not long after the Carnation Revolution. An old man she met there had pulled a crumpled piece of paper from his pocket. 'Look,' he said. 'A member, for forty years.' It was his certificate of membership in the Communist Party, the symbol of dozens of years of silent resistance, of hope of a better life – if not for him, then at least for his children. The collapse of the communist experiment was inevitable. For many it came as a liberation, but it was also a trauma, and this fact is systemically ignored in a triumphant Western Europe. It brought democracy and intellectual freedom, but only a small portion of the population was better off materially. In Poland, you can clearly see both sides of the story. The figures are amazing: inflation went down from 600 per cent in 1990 to 5.5 per cent in 2001. Foreign investments rose in that same period from several million to almost $5 billion, the country's per capita national production more than doubled from $1,500 in 1990 to almost $4,000 in 1998.

At the same time, the average Polish citizen experienced something very different. Many of the social facilities that were once free or very inexpensive – medicine, hospitals, day-care centres, schools, care for the elderly – today cost a great deal. Millions of Poles lost their jobs, and the pensions for the elderly and invalids lost much of their buying power. As a fellow passenger told me in the train to Gdansk: 'We used to have plenty of money, but there was nothing to buy. Now there's plenty to buy, but we have no money. In the final analysis, we're no better off. We've been fooled.'

The collapse of the wall did not bring prosperity to huge numbers of Eastern European families, but rather shortage: at home, in the schools and hospitals, in every area. Figures from the World Bank clearly show the scope of the drama: in 1990, seven per cent of all Central and Eastern Europeans lived below the poverty line. In 1999 that had risen to twenty per cent. In that regard, Eastern Europe was worse off than East Asia (fifteen per cent) or Latin America (eleven per cent). The United Nations signalled the same trend: in 1999 there were ninety-seven million people living below the poverty level in the former Eastern Bloc, as compared to thirty-one million in 1990.

The situation has to do in part with the legacy of years of stagnation and Soviet exploitation, with hopelessly obsolete industries, with maintenance that lagged behind by decades. In Poland, the small farmers are in big trouble. They cannot keep up with the competition from Western Europe and the rest of the world. In Berlin, fountains of water regularly burst through the asphalt: yet another broken water main from the DDR years. The Prague metro still used the leaden Soviet train carriages which the Russians had once foisted on the Czechs; in 1998, one of the capital's subway bridges nearly buckled under their weight.

After the collapse of the wall, communism may be viewed as a failed and twisted experiment in social modernisation. 'But,' the writer, politician and acadamic George Schöpflin observes, 'at a deeper level it was much more than that. It tried to create a new civilisation, and to base that on a fundamentally different way of arranging the world.' The fall of communism also meant the fall of an entire system of morality, and it is within this vacuum that Eastern Europeans must struggle towards the development of new forms of citizenship. 'Huge numbers of people have essentially no idea what politics is about, what can be reached through it and what cannot. They expect immediate results, and are filled with bitterness when those results do not come . . . Slowly, very slowly, the myth of the West is being replaced by the reality of the West.'

*

Gazeta Wyborcza is Poland's biggest media company. The daily newspaper of the same name has a circulation of more than 500,000, spread over 20 local editions, and the group has 2,000 employees. In Warsaw I met cultural editor Anna Bikont, one of the paper's founders in 1989. 'Gazeta Wyborcza means "Election Paper", and that is literally what it was,' she explains. 'Because of the elections, Solidarity was allowed to publish its own newspaper for two months, the first free newspaper in the Eastern Bloc. Adam Michnik came up with the idea – he always thought ahead – while the rest of us were still living entirely in that little, underground world of Solidarity. So we started the *Gazeta*, with four women at a kitchen table.'

For the Poles, the paper's appearance was a major event. 'The most important thing was the language in which the paper was written. We were complete amateurs, we didn't write in the officialese of the Polish press agency PAP, we wrote in normal Polish. We used news from foreign press agencies, and we called our friends to verify things, we took our news straight from the source.' The *Gazeta* was characteristic of Solidarity's tactics: its founders and readers did not fight head-on against communism, they simply organised themselves outside the apparatus, and on a massive scale. After the communists were voted out of office, the newspaper continued to be published.

Anna Bikont: 'A whole world opened up for us, we got to know more and more people, correspondents began working in all the cities. At first the newspaper and Solidarity were one and the same, we were activists who were making a newspaper, not much more than that. But gradually we became more professional. We found out that there were different kinds of responsibilities: one old comrade became a cabinet minister, the other became a parliamentarian, and we became journalists. It was hard to be critical, because ministers were often personal friends as well. I remember the first time it really became messy. The Solidarity ministers had been given expensive apartments, just as under communism, and we wrote that this was completely inappropriate. They were furious.'

Within their own ranks as well the editors engaged in heated discussions. 'Solidarity was a myth,' Bikont continues. 'It was, after all, a coalition of three totally diverse groups: trade union people, democratic dissidents and nationalists. In Gdansk, the trade unionists set the tone. In Łódź it was the nationalists; the discussion there was all about changing the names of the streets. In Warsaw, people were concerned with democratic reforms, with procedures, with maintaining the rule of law. We had had a common enemy to keep us together, but as soon as the enemy disappeared the movement burst like a bubble. For the rise of a democratic Poland, however, our myth proved invaluable.'

In the end, Lech Walesa himself helped the editors of the *Gazeta* to break out of the dilemma. 'The masthead of our paper included the Solidarity motto "Nothing divides us". One day, Walęsa forbade us to use the union logo any longer. I remember how sad we were about that, it had always been a kind of spiritual anchor. But after a few months we started feeling relieved, it was as though the umbilical cord had been severed, as though we had finally grown up.'

Today, ten years later, Bikont looks back on it all with mixed emotions. 'It was a huge success, both Solidarity and our paper, but in the end there were no real winners. The nationalists lost, because instead of their ideal Poland we got a democracy and a European Union. The church lost, because the priests didn't gain a foothold in the world of national politics. The democratic opposition lost too, because they didn't anticipate the traumas that a tough new brand of capitalism would bring to a country that had lived so long under a planned economy.

'But there may be one group that won: the young people. They're in favour of Europe, they speak languages, they've travelled, they're open to the world. Great opportunities lie in wait for them. But for the generations that spent most of their lives under communism, hope was the only thing they had, and that hope has never borne fruit.'

That evening I dine with Jaroslaw Krawczyk, historian and editor-in-chief of *Centuries Speak* magazine. His hangover from the night before needs dealing with, and he does so with large quantities of beer. Outside the snow is falling by the bucketful, the grey flats are almost hidden by the flurries. Krawczyk strides through the neighbourhood, steps down to a cellar door, and we find ourselves in his favourite bar, an underground cavern where couples are kissing and a hefty blonde girl keeps putting brimming glasses down on our table.

We talk about Solidarity. 'That was our 1968, the struggle of our generation. Many of our fathers were generals, party bosses. My father, for example, still can't revise his opinions, he's still a communist. And as you know, we all hate our fathers.' About the church in Poland: 'A new religious movement is on the rise here: Radio Maryja. For the ill, the lonely, the pensioners. Nationalistic, almost fascistic. The poor people's hatred has a way of growing very quickly.' About Europe: 'As a Western journalist, you can travel all over the place, you do as you please. But look at my coat. It looks fine, but I bought it second-hand. That's the way we intellectuals have always lived here. You people in the West can talk all you want about Europe, but we *are* Europe, just like the Czechs, the Hungarians and the Rumanians.

'The new Czech ambassador once told me that he had had to deal with complete idiots, but we Poles had very intelligent communists. I tried to refute it, but I finally had to admit he was right. The repression here actually *was* much milder than in the rest of Eastern Europe. The Communist Party was never really big here, it never had more than half a million members. Gomulka was never anything but a dim-witted tyrant. And Gierek always kept the door ajar to you people in the West.'

We talk about what came afterwards, about the differences between Poles and the rest, about how the misleading symbol of the Berlin Wall made it seem as though an abrupt end had come to communism everywhere at the same time. In reality, the old communist elites in Rumania, Serbia and Bulgaria remained in power for years, although they operated under a new, nationalistic flag. The Hungarians and the Poles, on the other hand, had done away with the old communism long before the wall fell. Hungary joined the IMF and the World Bank in 1982, the country had been living for years with a mixed socialist-capitalist economy. The Polish leader, General Jaruzelski, had been following the same line since 1981: first heavy oppression to put an end to the strikes and uprisings, then a gradual thaw and economic liberalisation. The state of emergency and the censorship were relaxed from July 1983; in 1986 Poland joined the IMF. After that the country became increasingly free. Krawczyk: 'When I was twenty, I had no problem hitchhiking to Italy. And that was a real shock, let me tell you. Our reality was so drab. And suddenly there you were in that gleaming, colourful Venice. Horrible.'

His girlfriend comes in – a beautiful, friendly woman – and for a little while our table seems aglow. She works for the Soros Foundation, the Eastern European network that uses the Hungarian-American billionaire's money to help stimulate democratic processes. 'Because of her, I'm getting a divorce,' Krawczyk says, and falls silent for a moment. Then: 'We're all Soros' whores. At least, that's what Radio Maryja says. The church, Poland, that's the only real Europe. But Soros superimposes his own Europe on top of that, the Europe of the liberals, intellectuals, Jews. Yes, I'm sorry, but that's the way those people talk.' His girlfriend agrees, yes, that's the way they talk, but she cannot stay any longer. Her son has announced that he's going to try out vodka with Tabasco sauce, and she wants to be there when he does it.

As the evening goes by, Krawczyk and I sink into a pleasant kind of melancholy. 'You people with your money. We're expected to accept whatever you people in the West say about us, but don't you ever wonder what we might have to offer? The assertiveness of the Poles, the circumspection of the Czechs, the perseverance of the Hungarian dissidents, the dilemmas the East Germans have been faced with? Isn't that exactly what the West needs? Things like that? Courage, principles, experience?'

Eastern Poland is a frozen white plain of thickets, birch forests, little villages and the occasional smokestack giving off a courageous white plume. This is the land of Radio Maryja, of all those millions – a quarter of the population, according to Anna Bikont – who feel no affinity whatsoever with the new Polish society. The countless small farmers, for example, who operate on the same postage-stamp scale as their grandparents. The workers from the bankrupt agricultural collectives, for whom there is no work anywhere. Listen to Radio Maryja: prayers, Ave Marias, calls from listeners, stories about poverty, old age, illness, misfortune, a priest who promises to help, and then a speech: do you have any idea how many Jews there are in the Polish parliament and cabinet? Then another prayer, everything is sinful, the world is sullied, only Radio Maryja and Poland can save us.

The Warsaw-Moscow Express is packed with merchants who drag their own wares along with them. The overhead baggage racks are full of packages and bundles, the men fill the corridors and compartments with their goods before starting in on some serious drinking. A big, bare-chested fellow is smoking in the corridor, a half-naked woman in a pink bra is pressing up against him. Every stop lasts forever: along this transit route the loading and unloading never ends, textiles, cheap radios, nondescript electronics.

At the dusky station in Brest, on the border with Belarus, the carriages are stormed by women. For a few measly cents they will sell you milk, bread, cheese, vodka and themselves. A pretty, curvaceous woman throws open the door of my compartment: would I be interested in buying a friendly little half-litre? And might it not be a good idea for us to knock it back together, just to ward off the chill? During all this, the carriages are being rolled into a huge shed for a nineteenth century workers' ballet: the wheels are loosened at lightning speed, the cars jacked up, broader wheels are installed and then the whole thing is lowered onto the rails again, wrenches clatter, the women hop off the train, and within the hour we are off speeding through the cold once more.

In the restaurant car, two carriages down, the passengers have made themselves at home. They've taken off their shoes, cheerful music is playing, and the bottle goes from hand to hand. I sit down at the table with Pyotr Nikonov and Anatoli Grigoryev, two officials from the Russian Border and Excise Service, animated and cheerful after a party with their Belorussian comrades. 'We've just celebrated the sixtieth anniversary of the Russian customs office in Brest!' I make a quick calculation: that was in autumn 1939. Both of them have sons, life is not particularly easy for them, but they remain loyal to President Yeltsin. 'Why?' I ask. 'Things haven't really become much better for you, have they?'

'No, you're right, but he's our president. When Gorbachev was our president, I thought he was okay. Because he was our president.'

The restaurant car is furnished like a village café; in the little kitchen a woman with greasy, stringy hair is frying lumps of dough, a tired, skinny man is leaning behind the bar, an old woman is working her way down the aisles with vodka and pretzels. A Pole begins playing the harmonica, the carriage rocks like a ship at sea, the old woman shows us a few lively dance steps. She speaks a few words of German, and asks me where I'm from, how old I am, what my name is. She goes into the kitchen, then comes back. 'Olga,' she says, pointing to the exhausted woman frying dumplings, 'finds you very attractive. Wouldn't you like to keep her company for a while?' I tell her that I'm already well taken care of in Amsterdam. She laughs, passes the message along, comes back again. 'Olga says Amsterdam is far away, and she's here, right now . . .'

Chapter Sixty-One

Moscow

'SO THERE WE WERE, ANGRY AND INSPIRED, AT THE HEART OF THE EMPIRE of the Lie, and somehow we had to find a way to survive,' the pop journalist Artemi Troitski wrote of Moscow in the 1980s. One Russian rock singer spoke of his contemporaries as the generation of 'concierges and night-watchmen', which was nothing less than the truth. Young Russian people took the lowliest, worst-paid jobs in order to remain independent of the state system, and to spend as much time as possible on what really mattered to them: *tusovka*, which may be freely translated as 'the mood' or 'the big mess'. Troitski: 'No other generation has ever produced so many musicians, painters, photographers and otherwise artistically oriented young people. And, at the same time, we had more young alcoholics, drug addicts and prostitutes than ever before. For them, it was not about protest – not about saying "to hell with the entire system" – no, life itself was simply so dull and shitty that there was nothing left for them to do. That same generation, by the way, also provided the country with a horde of unbelievable bureaucrats.'

During the final years of the Soviet Empire, rock musicians and their followers were the real dissidents, more so than the country's writers. Their concerts were attended by thousands of young people, and their lyrics spoke of things not openly addressed anywhere else: the defeat in Afghanistan, corruption, the abuse of power. Viktor Tsoi, a kind of cross between James Dean and Bruce Lee, wrote:

> Changes.
> In our laughter, in our tears and in our veins.
> Changes.
> We're waiting for changes . . .

The singer Boris Grebenshtshikov filled one stadium after another with lyrics that just made it past the censor:

> Sons of the days of silence
> Look at other people's films
> Play other people's roles
> Knock on other people's doors.
> Please, won't you give a sip of water
> To the sons of the days of silence?

A text by the rocker and poet Misha Borzykin:

> Throw off the yoke,
> Sing what you feel inside,
> We have a right to roar,
> Break loose, we were born to be free,
> Break loose, get away from here!

The band received standing ovations, the communist officials went pale, and Borzykin succeeded in getting himself banned in Moscow even at the height of perestroika.

Children of Glasnost is the much-acclaimed book that Artemi Troitski wrote about them afterwards. After the Soviet Union fell apart in 1994, a Dutch colleague and I went to visit him. He told us about how he had recently come across a wedding photograph, taken in 1984. 'There are about thirty people in that picture, all of them friends from the music and art scenes. When I picked it up and looked at it I suddenly realised that, even though it was only ten years ago, I was seeing a completely different world.'

That picture was taken right after the Brezhnev era, a period Troitski says was marked by complete paralysis, by a comatose atmosphere in which no one believed in anything any more, and in which no one had any interest in the rest of the world. 'At the time that picture was taken we talked about music, about friends, about sex and drugs and alcohol, but we never talked about the future. We weren't interested in the future. We thought nothing would ever change. The only thing left to salvage was our inner freedom.'

Ten years later, in 1994, the idols of Soviet illegality were wildly popular everywhere. Troitski could name all of the thirty men and women in that picture, he counted off their lives on his fingers, that old club of friends, that band of dissidents. A number of them were not available for comment: they were dead. They had been killed in accidents or had fallen ill, with alcohol usually playing a key role in the story. Some of them had passionately yearned for a turnaround, but when that arrived they were unable to cope with the new, risky life it brought. Of the dozen girls in that photograph, almost half had left the country. One of the boys had become a movie star. A few others, active at the time in the Komsomol, had become successful businessmen. Others were bus drivers or teachers. But the one thing that applied to all of them was that, after 1984, none of them were ever the same. They had all experienced major rifts in their lives, for better or for worse. And none of them had an inkling of that at the moment the shutter clicked.

Ten years later, Troitski was a famous journalist, he owned his own record label and had a regular talk show on TV. He was faced with only one major problem: there were no more good pop groups to write about. 'The Russian underground was always fed by its resistance to the party, to the bosses and the KGB. It was us against them, and that was our main source of inspiration. The same went for the underground writers, poets, film-makers and artists. After perestroika, that game was suddenly over, and all the arts had to go looking for new forms.'

After leaving Troitski, we went looking for a few of those old pop heroes. My colleague knew them all from the early days. We found Misha Borzykin and his former guitarist Sasha Belyayev in the cellar of an old theatre in St Petersburg which was now a squat. In 1987, their band Televizor had thrown half the Soviet Union into a panic with the lyric: 'The fish is rotting around the head, they're all liars, the fish is rotting around the head.' Now they were sitting at a darkened table, drinking vodka and eating sausage. They were doing their best to bury an old grudge. Sasha had set up a travel agency, and Misha had revived Televizor. The band was going well, but all his old fans had disappeared. 'Half of them have turned to drink,' Misha said, 'and the other half went into business for themselves. Within two years they forgot what music was about.'

Later that evening we went to Sasha's flat to celebrate a friendship restored. There was plenty of food and drink, but soon Misha nodded off with his head on the table. We went on drinking and singing, and he lay on the sofa and could not be roused. The next day we met him at a crowded metro station; he'd said he wanted to show us some lyrics, some of his newest work. He pushed a crumpled sheet of paper into our hands, turned on his heels and was off. We read:

> I don't like having guests in my head
> they don't give a fuck about me
> they come to gobble up my secrets
> to drink my soul
> to breathe my air
> they wear friends' faces
> and I, hospitable lackey that I am,
> I smile.

Today, on 24 November, 1999, it's eighteen degrees below zero, the cars in Moscow sport icy moustaches, but the Volgas and Ladas steam along as though nothing has changed. The newspaper runs a picture of pensioner Nikolai Skasylov, bundled up warmly, fishing in a hole in the frozen Moskva. 'One fish lasts us three days,' he says. 'Not bad!'

Russia is doing well these days. The flirtation with the West is over, the price of oil is back to thirty-five dollars a barrel, the IMF has nothing more to complain about. In Moscow, for reasons unknown, an apartment building with a hundred people in it has been bombed, President Yeltsin has fingered his successor (fresh-faced former KGB agent Vladimir Putin), investigations into corruption within the presidential entourage have been suspended, the reports from the Chechen front are bringing patriotic Russian blood to a boil. No one in the cafés has any desire to speak English any more: go learn Russian, stranger. Doors are being closed, borders drawn, just like that, without the help of a single politician.

The McDonald's in Pushkin Square is packed all day with schoolgirls, businessmen, old ladies, housewives and children celebrating their birthdays. No one here is extremely rich or extremely poor, this is the new Moscow middle class par excellence. For a hamburger and a soft drink they calmly count out half a week's wage. The department stores are full of television sets, video cameras, refrigerators and washing machines. The vacuum cleaners are just as expensive as they are in the Netherlands, and they are going fast. At the delicatessens, the gilded pillars and richly decorated ceilings give the impression that nothing has really changed since the days of Czar Nicholas II. The tone of the language spoken here has made a drastic shift. 'Democrat' has become a swear word, 'privatisation' is synonymous with 'robbery', 'free market' with 'chaos', 'businessman' with 'mafioso', 'the West' with 'humiliation'.

In the Revolution Square metro station, a young violinist is playing something which I believe is by Scarlatti. He is barely twenty, he has a wispy beard and obviously a great deal of talent. His nose is red from the cold, and on a morning like this, he says, he earns one dollar. A little further along, a group of older people, most of them women, have queued up. They have their money in one hand and an application form of some kind in the other. In a heated cubbyhole between two swinging doors, a man and woman have set up a little office: they are trading in impressively printed and stamped bonds, reminiscent of the old Russian Railways coupons, documents laden with hope and security.

But I am on my way to see Anatoli Artsybarski, former commander of the Mir space station. Cosmonauts in the Soviet Union once enjoyed a much greater status than even war heroes or movie stars, and in 1991 Artsybarski was a demigod. He receives me in a suffocatingly warm little office behind a church; his three secretaries are busy filing their nails, Artsybarksi has a Delft-blue astronaut on his desk. These days the former cosmonaut's mission is to save the crippled Mir which is still hanging in orbit, for the greater honour and glory of the Russian fatherland.

While Artsybarski was circling the earth, the Soviet Union was crumbling into the abyss. Gorbachev was fighting with all his might to keep his Communist Party – in his own words 'this colossus of conservatism . . . this dirty, mean dog' – under control. According to his closest aides, Gorbachev clearly realised that the system he had inherited was an obstruction to the country's modernisation. But he underestimated the extent to which that same communism, despite its rigidity, was holding the country together. And he had only a few, vague theories concerning the free, market-oriented system with which he hoped to replace it. To paraphrase the words of the conservative writer Yuri Bondarev: perestroika was a plane that had been ordered to take off, with absolutely no instructions about how or where to land.

The consequences soon became apparent. In some of the republics, only a quarter of the recruits conscripted into the Soviet Army around 1990 actually reported for duty. In January 1991, a revolt broke out in the three Baltic States. In Vilnius, Soviet troops fought with demonstrators for control of the television-broadcasting tower. Fourteen people were killed. In Riga, the Black Berets, a special unit of the Soviet ministry of internal affairs, stormed the Latvian ministry of internal affairs. Five people were killed. Popular as Mikhail Gorbachev was abroad, his position within the country was growing more feeble all the time.

On 18 August, 1991, while he was on holiday in the Crimea, the Soviet leader received an unexpected visit from a few of his cabinet ministers. They had come to tell him that an emergency committee had been set up in Moscow to save the Soviet Union, that his dacha was surrounded by mutinous troops, and that he would have to hand over the reins to the vice-president, Gennadi Yanayev. Gorbachev refused, but when he tried to call Moscow he discovered that all lines to the outside world had been cut. The next day the conspirators – including members of Gorbachev's own government – held a press conference and declared a state of emergency. For the time being, Yanayev would serve as acting president.

It was an old-fashioned communist takeover, with all the attendant conniving behind the scenes. In the old days it would probably have succeeded, but this was the age of television, a fact the apparatchiks had overlooked: one of their leaders, Prime Minister Valentin Pavlov, partook of too much liquid courage before his first TV appearance, and once on the air Yanayev was unable to disguise the way his hands were trembling. Meanwhile, millions and millions of Soviet citizens watched as thousands of demonstrators gathered before the parliament building in Moscow to defend the young democracy, as the newly elected Russian president, Boris Yeltsin, climbed onto a tank to demand the immediate release of his Soviet colleague, as army units refused their orders to support the coup and attack the parliament building. Within two days, the palace revolution was over. Yeltsin was more popular than ever, but Gorbachev had been so grievously humiliated – not least by his 'saviour' Yeltsin – that his position became untenable. Shortly afterwards, the Communist Party ceased its activities.

While all this was going on, the Soviet cosmonauts continued in their orbits around the eternally blue planet. On 17 September, 1991, Estonia, Latvia and Lithuania were admitted to the United Nations as independent states. The crew aboard Mir heard the report, looked down and joked among themselves that the three countries had clearly changed colour. On 7 December, the leaders of Russia, Belarus and Ukraine held an impromptu summit in a remote hunting lodge by the Polish border. According to one of the participants, the host, Yeltsin, was so drunk at the moment the other delegates arrived that he fell from his chair. The first thing they saw upon entering was a scene straight out of Gogol: Yeltsin's enormous bulk being slung onto a divan by his two fellow presidents. Several members of the Russian delegation then carried him to a side room, where he slept throughout most of the historic meeting. At 2.17, however, the three presidents signed a joint communiqué: 'The Soviet Union has ceased to exist.' In the days that followed, the remaining republics ratified that agreement. On 25 December, 1991, Gorbachev stepped down. He was given a dacha, an office in Moscow, and a pension of around 140 euros a month. The red flag above the Kremlin was lowered that day.

Anatoli Artsybarski made it back to earth just before the Soviet Union fell apart, but his colleague, Sergei Krikalev, remained suspended in space for five months longer than planned. Later some people claimed that he had stayed in space so long because there was no money to bring him back, that his prolonged orbit was due to the fact that the country that had sent him into it no longer existed. 'Nonsense. Journalistic claptrap,' Artsybarski growls. 'There were simply a few technical problems.' The only thing he really wants to talk about, however, is his 'people's collection' to save the Mir space station, about the 'revitalisation of the prestige of the Russian cosmonauts', about the 'stimulation of prizes, diplomas and medals', about pride lost.

In early 1998, The Economist published the results of an opinion poll held among a significant cross-section of the Russian population: under which leader, in their view, had life in Russia been at its best? The president at the time, Yeltsin, received fourteen per cent; Stalin and Czar Nicholas II both received six per cent; Gorbachev took three per cent; Lenin – the great leader and model for more than seventy years – received one per cent. A massive preference was expressed for one of the last, dyed in the wool communist leaders, Brezhnev, with forty-two per cent.

I ask the beggars around St Basil's Cathedral in Red Square about their pasts. A young man in uniform tells me he lost his leg in Afghanistan, most of the women once worked in factories, one had been widowed at a young age – her pension had been melted away by inflation – and the last one I spoke to had worked all her life in a clothing store. No, they had never thought they would end up here, in this shivering line-up, clutching a plastic cup.

Russia was living in the final weeks of the Yeltsin era, the post-communist period that had started so propitiously just seven years before. A liberal democracy! A market economy! A constitutional state! Local self-government! Individual freedom! Western prosperity! In late 1991, all of that was still to arrive.

In practice, though, democratisation and the introduction of a market economy in the former Soviet Union was a spectacular failure. From the ranks of the former communist nomenklatura there arose a new elite that absconded with the key national industries and resources, including the banks, the energy sector and the media. These oligarchs elaborated on the time-worn mechanisms of the old Soviet hierarchy: a combination of brute force and extreme servility, patronage between senior and junior managers, a system of nepotism, blat and bribery.

In 1992, Yeltsin began with the head-over-heels introduction of the market economy. Shares in the state-owned companies were distributed among the population in the form of coupons. Most of those coupons were then bought up for a pittance by a handful of businessmen. Car dealer Boris Berezovski, for example, secured a major interest in Siberian Oil (Sibneft), Aeroflot, the state broadcasting company and several newspapers. Viktor Chernomyrdin, Yeltsin's prime minister between 1992–8, used his status as former managing director of the Soviet gas company to set up a firm of his own, Gazprom. It was the world's largest energy company, with a market value of hundreds of billions of dollars.

During that same period, as part of the 'shock therapy' propagated by Western economists, Yeltsin's reformers lifted all government price control. The results were disastrous. In the howling inflation which followed, most of the pensions held by the elderly and the disabled became almost worthless within the month. Thanks to the influx of foreign investments, Moscow, St Petersburg and several other large cities witnessed a new prosperity, but in the rest of the country the shock therapy resulted in a national tragedy.

This was clearly not the 'transitional period' spoken of so widely in the West, but a decline in almost everything essential to daily life: salaries, benefits, food supplies, health care, education, government services and public safety. Between January 1993 and January 1996, Russia's industrial production decreased by a third. More than half of all Russian families ended up below the poverty level. Symptomatic of the malaise was the collapse of the country's air traffic: the number of passengers tumbled from 135 million in 1989 to 20 million in 1999, and more than half the country's airports were closed during this same period.

Statistics on Russia's population following this shock therapy showed trends similar to those in a country struck by war or famine: between 1989–99, the average life expectancy of Russian men decreased by five years, to fifty-nine: fourteen years less than the average Western European male. The total population dwindled at the rate of one million annually – a phenomenon unique in modern history. Russian mortality statistics were reminiscent of those in Zimbabwe, Afghanistan or Cambodia; tuberculosis, AIDS and alcoholism became major causes of death. The birth rate, that perpetual indicator for the 'mood of the nation', fell by fifty per cent.

A second selling-out of the former Soviet Union took place in 1995. Three years after Yeltsin took office, his government could barely pay the salaries of its officials. With elections on their way, the president and his men found themselves in dire straits. In deepest secrecy, therefore, a deal was struck with the country's principal oligarchs: in return for loans to the government, they would receive temporary receivership over the shares in the remaining state-owned companies, including several gigantic oil and mining complexes. Because the loans were never repaid, the oligarchs were ultimately able to take over those shares for next to nothing. By this and other manoeuvres, Yeltsin was able to raise half a billion dollars for his 1996 election campaign. He won, thanks to an overwhelming media offensive.

In the McDonald's in Pushkin Square, I talk to two teenaged girls. Tautly made-up little faces, somewhere around seventeen. Could they remember anything about the communist era? 'The queues. I remember my mother standing in line for a pair of boots.' 'Me too, I was five, I stood in line with my grandmother to buy soap, she had numbers written on her hand, I don't know why.' 'But I also remember the May Day parade, they used to give us sweets.'

Do they ever buy *Cosmo*? The younger of the two does on occasion, she likes to leaf through it and daydream. She earns enough money to buy the magazine with a part-time job, but it costs her a day's pay. But the older one thinks the magazine is stupid. 'It's about dumb men, but it's written for dumb women.'

The striking success in Russia of the glossy women's magazine *Cosmopolitan* is a phenomenon in itself. Everyone I spoke to about it had an opinion on the subject. 'The people have an enormous need for new symbols and icons, for new ways of interacting,' one person tells me. 'Most of the bosses here are either ex-communists or criminals or corrupt. What's more, they're usually dirty old men, they can't keep their hands off women. *Cosmopolitan* shows a completely different lifestyle, with modern and open relationships between men and women, bosses and employees.' Someone else says: '*Cosmopolitan* provides new role models for Russian women: unattached women, well educated, working women who are able to take advantage to the fullest of the joys of postmodern society. Women who are in control over men.'

Dutch media magnate Derk Sauer, founder and owner of the company that publishes *Cosmopolitan* in Russia, can himself only partly explain the magazine's success. 'The first issue of the Russian edition appeared in 1994. It was Russia's first women's glossy, and it was one of those cases of being in the right place at the right time. A magazine is the ultimate medium for expressing a lifestyle. In the Soviet days, everyone was

expected to be equal. This magazine taught people to express their indi-
viduality again. It became their guide to the new life.'

The 40,000 copies of that first issue were sold within an hour.
Circulation peaked at around 500,000, now it stands at around 350,000,
and Sauer is currently working on concepts for new magazines. 'Soviet
propaganda was quite effective: at first, the Russians had a very naïve
view of capitalism and the West. Everyone expected huge profits right
away, trips to Spain, a Volvo parked at the door. Now they're starting to
discover themselves again. Nestlé sells more and more of its products
under Russian names. So do we. That's why the title of our new financial daily newspaper is classically Russian: *Vedomsti*, Reports.'

Derk Sauer arrived in Moscow ten years ago. At that time, the market
was bare. Today he is the head of Russia's biggest independent media
concern, with 550 employees, two daily newspapers – the *Moscow Times*
and the Russian *Financial Times* – and sixteen magazines, including *Cosmo* and
the Russian *Playboy*. He is cheerful, enthusiastic and optimistic. After all the
misery, he says, the Russians have an incredible talent for dealing with
setbacks and overcoming them. That's how they have been able to form
an entire economy, uniquely their own.

His own company's results are an eloquent example of that: officially
speaking, the figures are impossible. The total circulation of his
Independent Media Group is over a million, but according to government figures there is no way so many Russians could buy his publications. Supposedly, only a very small group can afford them. 'If the statistics
were right, this publishing house would have gone down the tubes long
ago. Our turnover definitely does not depend on those couple of thousand exceedingly wealthy families. I have only one explanation for it:
there is a sizeable, relatively solid middle class on the rise in the cities,
people who get up early, work hard and actually have money to spend.
The only thing is, they don't exist in the official statistics. And that's only
logical: after all, who wants to pay eighty per cent taxes?'

He tells me about an acquaintance who imports washing machines.
'He's a clever fellow, he bribes the border guards and sells his machines
on the black market. Officially, he doesn't exist. But he has quite a few
people working for him, it's a real company. His employees don't declare
their earnings either. And they still live in their old Soviet apartments,

which cost next to nothing. Almost everything they earn is disposable income. We estimate that approximately a fifth of the Russian population, about thirty million people, profit from this new economy in one way or another. Of course, that still leaves you with 120 million others.'

Chapter Sixty-Two

Chernobyl

THE COLD HOLDS NO SECRETS FOR THE RUSSIAN RAILWAYS. UPSY-DAISY, scoop a little more coal into the furnace and the train compartments turn into cozy living rooms, the corridors into warm loggias, the passengers eat and drink, someone sings a tune, and meanwhile the Moscow-Kiev Express barrels on through the moonlit night. In the bar, as they say here, 'we let our souls fly'.

The next morning, Irina Trantina is waiting for me at the station in Kiev. Through her many contacts, she has arranged a special tour for me, and it's all she can talk about. As soon as we are in the car she says: 'Do you know where I was that day, 26 April, 1986? Right here, at this station. I worked in the ticket office, I had night duty, and the first thing that struck me in those early morning hours was the total silence. There were no police, no one. We thought that was very strange, but no one could explain it. The next day a friend of mine picked up a report on Voice of America, they said something about an explosion near Kiev. That was all. When I got to work that day, the whole station was full of panicked people. Someone said: "They're from Chernobyl. The nuclear power plant there blew up." More and more rumours like that started going around. On 30 April I saw a special train from Chernobyl come through here, full of top officials and their families. Then everyone in Kiev knew that something had gone very wrong. But the radio still didn't say a thing.'

Kiev celebrated May Day in the normal fashion, with the usual shows and parades. 'The whole charade had been going on for five days, and I'd had enough of it. A friend of the family was quite high in the military, and I called him. He was extremely candid: "Irina, we have an enormous problem. A nuclear power plant has blown up. No one knows what to do, that's the reality of it." The next day all of Kiev was in total panic, everyone was trying to get away, it was like a war. We simply devoured iodine, we thought that could keep the problems at bay.'

The official announcement came on 5 May: 'There are a few problems, but absolutely no risk.' Four days later the order came for all children to be evacuated. The newspapers in the West talked about nothing else. But most of the people of Kiev still knew nothing at all.

The disaster at the Chernobyl plant, along with the war in Afghanistan and the cruise-missile question, is generally seen today as the start of the decline of the Soviet Union. Just as the great famine of 1891 had mercilessly laid bare the failure of czarism, almost a century later Chernobyl clearly showed how divided, rigid and rotten the Soviet regime had become. The principal policy instruments, secrecy and repression, no longer worked in a modern world with its accompanying means of communication. The credibility of the party leadership sank to the point at which it could sink no further.

In the early hours of 26 April, 1986, two explosions took place in one of the four reactors at the giant nuclear complex. It was an accident of the kind scientists and environmental activists had been warning about for years, particularly because of its effects: a monstrous emission of iodine-131 and caesium-137. Huge radioactive clouds drifted across half of Europe: first in the direction of Sweden and Finland, then across Poland, Czechoslovakia, Germany and Austria, by way of Switzerland, northern Italy and France, all the way to Great Britain and Norway. Some residue also reached the Netherlands, Greece, Spain, Portugal, Turkey and Rumania. Twenty countries were contaminated. Years afterwards, British sheep were still failing inspection on the grounds of being a threat to public health.

Around 200 people died during and immediately after the explosions, but in the years that followed thousands more died from radioactive contamination and resulting illnesses. According to the most conservative estimates, the disaster claimed a few thousand lives; other reports speak of many times that number.

These days Chernobyl is inhabited again. It is an inconspicuous town, only an hour from Kiev, full of people whose job it is to make sure that no one else comes to town: forest rangers, security people, soldiers, firemen, maintenance personnel, office workers, cafeteria help. Cars drive in and out of town, laundry flaps cheerfully on the line, three babies have been born here recently. At least 10,000 people work at Chernobyl these days – more or less at their own risk, only time will tell. But then, with two weeks on and two weeks off, an early-retirement plan and double overtime, what Ukrainian could resist?

Thanks to Irina's efforts, I am today the guest of Nikolai Dmytruk, assistant director of the Chernobyl InterInform agency of the ministry of emergency affairs. He shows me his collection of maps, full of faded ink spots, red, yellow and green. The official 'zone', as the most hazardous area is called, is shown on the map by means of concentric circles tightening in around the exploded plant, several kilometres apart, each one indicating greater danger, each one accompanied by increasingly strict security controls, as though the good Lord himself had gone to the drafting table during the explosion with compass and ruler. The truly radioactive areas look much more jagged on the map, big red smears, blown along by the wind. Some sections of the zone were upwind during the disaster itself, and are now quite safe. But on the other hand, in the densely populated town of Narodichi, in real terms outside the zone, the radioactivity is just as strong as in Chernobyl itself.

Some 100,000 people have since moved from the most heavily contaminated areas, but around 200,000 remain. Ukraine simply lacks the funds to evacuate them. Meanwhile, strange things continue to happen. Osteoporosis, cancer of the larynx and immune diseases, the statistics tell it all. Almost all of the young people here have health problems. In the same way Belgian or Dutch physicians deliver the diagnosis 'stress' when they don't know what else to say, the doctors in Kiev say 'radiation' and go on about their business.

Dmytruk has me put on a kind of prison suit, then we climb into an old Volkswagen van and drive to the reactor. 'Everyone expects to see something unusual here,' he says. 'Ruined forests, rabbits with six legs, death and destruction. But that's exactly it: you don't feel anything, you don't see anything, you don't smell anything, not a single human sense sounds the alarm.' The scene of the disaster itself, popularly referred to as 'the sarcophagus', looks like a huge concrete coffin built around the ruins of the reactor. The Geiger counter reads 1.05 microroentgens. 'Not bad,' Dmytruk says. 'When the wind is blowing hard we sometimes get up to 1.5. Then you can hear the sarcophagus creaking and groaning in the distance.'

Fifteen minutes further along lies the Pompeii of the twentieth century.

In the 1980s, Pripyat – specially built for the workers at the power plant – was a modern town of about 50,000 inhabitants, mostly young families. It was, by Soviet standards, a model town: lots of greenery, good schools, excellent facilities. Then, on 26 April, 1986, everything suddenly stopped. Hundreds of cars and buses were driven to the central square; all of the city's inhabitants had to leave within the hour and none of them moved back. Only very few among them have ever set foot here again.

In the city we enter, the Soviet era is still in full bloom: the central square with its hammers and sickles, the square buildings, the mottos inscribed above the entrances: 'Lenin's Party Leads us to the Triumph of Communism'. Between the blocks of flats it is deathly quiet, the snow on all the streets and squares lies untouched, as if in a remote forest. A little fancy fair, ready for the May Day celebrations, is still standing: a rusty Ferris wheel, weathered bumper cars, sheets of canvas on the ground. A little tree is growing out of the floor of the hall of the hotel.

In the cupboards at the day-care centre, the little shoes still stand neatly in a row, the way they were left behind thirteen years ago. On the floor are two red canisters of toy cars, a box of building blocks, a toy shop, two dolls with plaster in their hair, a shelf of honour bearing the best clay figures of the week. The next room is full of baby beds, with half-decayed sheets and mattresses.

'This must have been an excellent day-care centre,' Dmytruk says as we walk through the abandoned rooms. 'Look at all the things they had here. It's almost hard to believe: in those days, every child in this country still went to school, they got a warm meal every afternoon, later they could fall in love with whomever they pleased, Russian, Ukrainian, it didn't matter, we were all brothers and sisters.' The snow has drifted into the corridors. On the wall is a drawing of the May Day celebration, half finished.

Night is coming and the air is icy cold. We drive on, through Kopachi, a village buried beneath a layer of soil, past rows of long mounds, a graveyard of houses and barns. Then a medieval darkness falls, the sky is full of stars, here and there we see the blinking of a candle or a kerosene lantern.

Dmytruk and my interpreter think I should meet old Nikolai Czikolovitch. Nikolai and his wife Anastasia Ivanovna live deep in the woods, in the middle of the restricted zone, in the lee of the plant. They are deeply attached to their smallholding, their chickens, pigs and cows, and after the catastrophe they stubbornly went on living there. Today they are among the 600 or so people who live illegally in the zone.

Anastasia, wrinkled and bowed, climbs down hastily from the tile stove when we come in; she had already gone to bed. Amid the groves of Chernobyl, it appears, Philemon and Baucis still reside, no radiation seems to touch them, they live on and on like two trees sharing one trunk. They have been together for more than half a century; he was once a tractor driver, she worked all her life at the agricultural collective. After that they received their pension, which these days they use to buy a little soap and tobacco every month, then it's gone. In their poverty, they produce everything themselves. The fireplace is poked up, the cupboards are plundered, home-made vodka, eggs, sausage, pickles and jars of cherries appear on the table, all for the guests.

We talk back and forth in sign language, take pictures of each other, laugh, sing a song, have another drink, Dmytruk from the ministry of emergency affairs, the interpreter, Nikolai, Anastasia and I, the ikons bless us all, day and night.

XII December 1989–99

FINLAND
Helsinki
St Petersburg
Tallinn
ESTONIA
Moscow
LATVIA
Riga
RUSSIA
LITHUANIA
Vilnius
Minsk
Kursk
BELARUS
Volga
Chernobyl
Warsaw
Kiev
Dnieper
Don
Rostov
UKRAINE
Sea
of Azov
Krasnodar
SLOVAKIA
Dniester
MOLDAVIA
Bug
HUNGARY
Chișinău
Odessa
Crimea
Tiflis
Budapest
Novi Sad
RUMANIA
Black
Sea
Bijeljina
Belgrade
Bucharest
Danube
Tuzla
Srebrenica
Sarajevo
BULGARIA
Mostar
SERBIA
Sofia
Pristina
Istanbul
Ankara
Tigris
Kosovo
Skopje
MACEDONIA
Euphrates
Tirana
Saloniki
TURKEY
ALBANIA
SYRIA
GREECE
Athens
CYPRUS
LEBANON
Crete
Mediterranean

0   100   200   300 km

← Geert Mak's Route

Chapter Sixty-Three

Bucharest

'DO YOU WANT TO KNOW WHY THIS COUNTRY IS SO MELANCHOLY? I'll tell you: the Rumanians have always seen history in terms of a single person. When you look at old Dutch paintings, usually you see groups: the city militia, people partying, street and village scenes. The Rumanians in their paintings are always quite alone, they are kings or dictators: Prince Michael, King Carol II, Nicolae Ceaușescu. That dependence on a single person, it's deeply embedded in us. It also provides us with a sense of certainty, even if it's only the certainty of life close to the minimum.

'For us, the academics at the University of Bucharest, the problems started in 1971, after Nicolae and Elena Ceaușescu visited China. The two of them came back wildly enthusiastic: our country too needed a cultural revolution. Agriculture was to be fundamentally reorganised, old villages had to be torn down, flats had to be built for the farmers, the birth rate was to be raised artificially.

'Back then we didn't have all that many material worries, it was more the moral pressure we lived under. For example: I once quoted Marx during a meeting. That was a real blunder: we were allowed to quote only from the collected works of Ceaușescu. When I walked out of the room, a colleague came up to me. He shouted loudly, so everyone could hear: "Cezar Tabarcea, why were you drinking again before you came here?" That man saved me. Because, after doing that, he could write in his report to the Securitate: "Cezar Tabarcea came to the meeting drunk, and did not realise the inappropriateness of his comments." That, in the situation of the day, was a very great favour.

'Yes, we all went through a great deal together at the institute. Of course we always taught the mandatory subjects, but we were able to insert our own irony in the margins, and the students never failed to pick up on that.

'The revolution of December 1989 was not unexpected. Why do I say that? Purely on the basis of my own feelings. That autumn, I suddenly sensed a great excitement among my students. And then came the Christmas holidays. They always start here in the middle of the week, and the students usually begin going home the weekend before. So I was used to presiding over almost empty classrooms during those last few days. That last Wednesday, I was actually hoping I wouldn't have to give a lecture. But to my utter amazement the auditorium was packed to the brim. Between passages of my lecture on grammar, I wondered aloud what was going on. After the lecture a student came up to me and said: "Are you with us?" I said: "You all know that my existence revolves exclusively around every one of you, so I'm afraid I don't understand your question." Then they all came up and stood around me and sang to me. That was on 20 December, three days after the massacre at Timişoara. There was a Hungarian preacher there, László Tökés, who had stood up for the rights of the Hungarian minority. When the Securitate tried to close down his church by force, a revolt broke out. The Securitate shot and killed dozens of demonstrators. Everyone was furious – and maybe that was the idea. It is not beyond the bounds of possibility that certain elements within the Securitate were deliberately trying to bring about Ceauşescu's fall.

'That same afternoon I was to give my final lecture of the term, and again I was hoping no one would turn up. But once more, the auditorium was full. Outside, it had begun to snow. The students came with tea and sweets, they started singing Christmas songs, which is the tradition here. After that we all listened to Radio Free Europe, and we all wept over Timişoara. When my students left I made them go out in small groups, there was a ban on public gatherings, we had to be very careful.

'Then, the next morning, something interesting happened: the heating in our flat, which had been shut down for weeks because of an energy shortage, was suddenly working again. There was even hot water, and my wife began washing clothes right away. I sat there watching TV, the Bulgarian channel, because all kinds of things were going on there as well. I remember complaining: "The rest of Eastern Europe is up in arms, but there's nothing going on here!"

'A little later, though, it started happening here too: a big crowd had been assembled at the central-committee building for the traditional cheering of Ceaușescu, and all of a sudden thousands of voices began chanting "Ti-mi-șoa-ra". I couldn't believe my ears, it was all being broadcast live on our own Rumanian television. Nothing of the kind had ever been seen before. People shouted: "Ceaușescu, we are the people!" and "Down with the murderers!" We saw Ceaușescu looking around in disbelief, he was speechless, and finally a security man pulled him in from the balcony. Then the screen went blank. Total chaos had broken out in the square.

'We went down there. My wife got into an argument with a policeman, and he began to cry, saying: "Madam, my daughter is out there in that crowd!" Later we all went to the state television complex, the tanks had their guns aimed at the crowd. I still remember clearly how, at a certain point, a soldier took off his helmet and threw it on the ground. The tanks turned their guns away from the crowd. The people started climbing onto the tanks, giving the soldiers tea and bread. It was all very emotional. The next day, on Friday, it was announced that the Ceaușescus had fled. They were captured the next morning, and executed on 25 December. For years I had dreamed of being able to shoot that man, I hated him so much, but when it finally came down to it . . . On TV they looked like two homeless people who had been put up against the wall. You almost felt sorry for them, part of the videotape was edited out as well. It was very intense, they were in a huge panic, you could see that, they were also very much together in those last hours, they talked to each other very personally.

'In hindsight, it was all a big mistake. That trial, those accusations, "genocide" – legally speaking, it was complete nonsense. No, I would have condemned them without wasting a bullet. I would have forced them to listen endlessly to classical music, to look at wonderful paintings, to drive around in today's colourful Bucharest. They would never have survived that.

'What this country needs to do is to start believing in its own possibilities. After 1990, I was able to do a great many things that had been impossible for most of my life. I am fifty-eight now, and I'm still making up for lost time. I believe that one is obliged to do the things one is able to do. I worked with students for thirty-five years, and they kept me young. Without my students, I am nothing. I love them, they support me, they stand around me like a fortress, and someday they will take my place. They are my life.'

———

I dream of complete disaster. Passing through a railway bridge, a big dredging machine has collided with a high-tension electricity pylon. A train is coming, a blue train with an old-fashioned electric 1100 engine. It thunders right past the red signal, it just keeps barrelling along, I see it happening right in front of me. The train is falling off the bridge. 'There we go, another carriage bites the dust!' the people around me are cheering. The brakes shriek, everything goes skidding down the rails.

The train from Kiev to Bucharest has stopped for a signal. It is 3 a.m., the carriage sighs and breathes, a snowplough approaches, then the engine starts up again. Outside I see a huge white figure on a pedestal, probably an overlooked Lenin. Then we creep on through a landscape lit by stars. The electricity is out almost everywhere at this time of day. Every once in a while a flickering yellowish light appears from behind a window, a sleeping village, almost unchanged since 1880, 1917, 1989.

When I wake up later, it has begun to get light. We have stopped again. Barbed wire, watchtowers to the left and right, beside the train shivering soldiers with Kalashnikovs. Ukraine and Rumania are among the poorest countries in Europe, but their borders are guarded like gold. A female guard dutifully copies every syllable from my passport, up to and including the mysterious 'Burg. van Amsterdam'. And there it comes: I am not in possession of the appropriate visa. She looks at me archly, but in her mind the proper order of things has been disturbed. She makes me unpack my bag. 'Aha, computer, export!' 'Aha, antique, export!' (this in respect of an old Russian banknote). 'Aha, hundred dollar!' The train is standing still, the delay is increasing. The day before yesterday I read in the *Kyjiv Post* that the flight of capital out of Russia currently totals $2.9 billion a month. It was from Ukraine that the former prime minister, Pavlo Lazarenko, supposedly siphoned away $700 million. 'Aha, again hundred dollar!'

Later we roll along the border with Subcarpathia, otherwise known as

Ruthenia, the latest addition to a whole row of countries in the making. The snow eases up. I see wooden houses, women in bright headscarves at a market, two horses wearing plumes and pulling a festively decorated cart. In a brown field beside a tin warehouse, twenty-two little boys are running after a soccer ball. Damn, that's right, this is just a normal Saturday afternoon.

Bucharest is a city of more than 2 million inhabitants, with an estimated 300,000 stray dogs. You see dogs everywhere, alone or in packs: along the roads and in the back streets, around the few antique churches, in front of the former dictator Ceauşescu's mad-hatter's palace and between the shrubs in Ghencea cemetery, where everyone arrives in the end. In the houses of prayer the incense wafts, the singing rises up, this Sunday is the day the food is blessed, with candles, loaves of bread and bottles of Coca-Cola.

There are dozens of coffins on sale beside the cemetery gate. Every fifteen minutes another family comes in by cart or by car, the bell-ringer leans into the ropes, priests, gravediggers and beggars come rushing up.

I watch as Grigore Pragomir (b. 1909) is buried, as his open coffin is slid from a dented blue van, as one of his grandsons walks around paying everyone from a big bundle of banknotes, as Grigore is pulled along on a squeaky cart by two boys with cigarettes between their lips, as the cross with his name on it slowly disappears among the headstones.

At the grave of Nicolae Ceauşescu – a mound of earth, a small head-stone with his portrait, five withered bouquets – three visitors are standing around. 'You see that? They buried him crossways!' one man says. 'His feet aren't pointing east, they buried him like a witch. Until he's put back straight, things will keep going badly with this country.' 'No, no,' a wizened female beggar cackles. 'His grave is full of stones. He's not dead at all. At his execution, all they did was drug him, he flew off to be with his friend Gaddafi. He lives in a lovely palace there, I saw a picture of it in the paper.' 'Nonsense,' a prim lady in black mumbles. 'He had to die, it couldn't be any other way in a country like ours, with such a history of murder and bloodshed!' 'That's right,' the man says, 'but it wasn't a pretty sight.' 'Go to the devil!' the dwarf-woman shouts. 'And Nicu, his son, isn't dead either. He lives with his father. But *she* is dead!'

She escorts us to the grave of the former First Lady, another mound of earth marked with nothing but a dirty little wooden cross. Two dogs come staggering by, still stuck together after mating. At the gate the bell is tolling for Floarea Ene (b. 1947), who is being brought in on the bed of a little red truck. The dogs and beggars come rushing up again. Her four daughters are sitting beside the coffin, caressing her face, one of them weeps inconsolably: 'Mama, mama!' While she is being lifted down, the mobile phone belonging to one of her sons starts ringing. Then Floarea is lifted onto the cart as well, it is time for her to go with the boys with the cigarettes, there is nothing else for it.

People in this country are wild about magical events, preferably accompanied by lots of death and doom, because after that, reality always comes as something of a relief. This morning a Sunday paper opened with the headline: 'Professor Virgil Hincu predicts major earthquake in Bucharest on 15 January!' A magician in the city claims to have found a remedy for cancer. People have lined up in front of his door, holding bottles, because the elixir must be 'refreshed' every week. Stories still circulate about the Securitate, rumours full of secret prisons and tunnel complexes where the Ceauşescus still reign supreme.

Above ground, however, little remains of their intellectual heritage. In the national library, for example, I searched fruitlessly for *Omagiu* (Homages), a quaint volume consisting only of foreign accolades addressed to Ceauşescu and distributed around the country in hundreds of thousands of copies in honour of his sixtieth birthday. But like the dozens of works by the great leader himself and his spouse, it is nowhere to be found.

What did Europe think of this dictator, who let dissidents waste away in their cells by the hundreds? Much later, in the unsurpassed library of the University of Amsterdam, I stumble upon a copy of *Omagiu*. It contains a succession of phrases like 'appreciation for the enormous contributions of Nicolae Ceauşescu', 'the welfare of country and people', 'unflagging efforts' and 'peace and cooperation among the peoples'. Signed by, among others, President Jimmy Carter, King Juan Carlos, King Carl Gustav and Holland's Prince Bernhard – 'With the fondest of memories'. The compilation contains cheerful photos with Tito (1969), Emperor Bokassa (1972),

King Baudouin and Queen Fabiola (1972), President and Mrs Pat Nixon (1970), Queen Juliana and Prince Bernhard of the Netherlands (1973), and many other heads of state. Nixon is quoted: 'Because of his profound understanding of the most important world issues, President Ceauşescu can make a major contribution to solving the most urgent problems facing humanity.' As a professor at the University of Bucharest, Elena received honorary doctorates and other commendations from institutions including the New York Academy of Sciences and the Royal Society of Chemistry in London.

The son of a farmer, Ceauşescu was one of Europe's most popular leaders in the late 1970s. Like Gomulka in Poland he was seen as a left-wing nationalist, and always maintained a certain distance from the Soviet Union. Within the Warsaw Pact he regularly caused commotion by doing things like recognising the state of Israel and condemning the intervention in Czechoslovakia. But unlike Dubček in Czechoslovakia, he never really challenged the system. This allowed him to maintain a skilful balance between Moscow, Peking and the West.

Within Rumania itself he ruled like a European Mao Tse-tung. In the 1970s, the economy began encountering the same problems faced by other communist states. The nation's industry was pronouncedly obsolete, the enormous oil refineries worked at only ten per cent of their capacity, and as a result of its collectivisation the agricultural production of Rumania – once a breadbasket of Central Europe – was waning fast. In 1981 the country even began to ration bread.

Ceauşescu dealt with these problems in his own peculiar way. The only problem, he claimed, was that Rumanians ate too much, and so in 1985 he introduced a 'scientific diet' for the whole country. Energy consumption was subjected to rigorous restrictions: while chandeliers with more than 7,000 bulbs were being hung in the Palace of the People, the only thing the shops sold were 40-watt bulbs. Two thirds of the lamp posts in Bucharest were disconnected.

The country's female population was sorely tried. Ceauşescu was worried about the sharp decrease in the birth rate: abortion and contraception were banned. Working women had to report to a gynaecologist every month. From 1983, all women were expected to bear at least five children; childless and sterile women were punished with higher taxes. These population policies had dramatic results: crowded orphanages full of abandoned children, countless women who died or were maimed at the hands of illegal abortionists.

Rumania was the most extreme example of Stalinism-without-Stalin and of the leader-worship and megalomania such a system brings with it, and in the regime's final years the situation only became worse. Work was resumed on the notorious Danube-Caspian Sea canal; in the 1950s, rumour had it, the regime had already worked to death some 60,000 of its opponents on that project. The old plans to 'systematise' the rural areas and incorporate the farmers into 'agro-industrial communities' were revived. In the end, though, only two villages – both of them close to Bucharest – were actually wiped off the map. But traditional houses were razed to the ground everywhere: their inhabitants were given twenty-four hours to pack their belongings and move out.

Meanwhile, the Ceaușescus lived in a wholly different world. Today one can rent their villa in Bucharest for $650 a night, and my interpreter had arranged for a guided tour. I go in and I find myself in the house of a cowherd who has just won the lottery. The mind boggles: the gold toilet-roll holder belonging to son Nicu, the hot pink bathroom belonging to daughter Zoë (the drainpipe under the washbasin is gilded too), the dining room of carved oak, the sentimental paintings of a Gypsy girl and a pine forest, the bedroom wallpaper with 2,000 hand-painted roses, Ceaușescu's personal bath with 12 taps and 10 pressure gauges, the home cinema with a system of bell signals for the projectionist: Wait a minute! More volume! Stop! Lights! Change the film!

The cellars are still full of the remains of their blithe existence, with hundreds of the duo's coats, suits, dresses and shoes, now on sale for anyone who wants them. 'I don't understand,' my guide says, picking up one of Elena's light-blue mules. 'Lovely, expensive, excellent quality. But we can't get rid of them. The young people don't want this model any more. And look here, aren't these fantastic pyjamas?'

He tells me that, in the course of their hurried departure on 22 December, 1989, the couple left this house carrying only two blue bags filled with blankets and large loaves of bread. In their final hours, Nicolae and Elena had again become what they truly were, deep down: two farmers' children on the run.

*

My interpreter takes me on a tour of the city's ring road. We zigzag carefully around one pothole after the other, below us lie the metal rooftops of an old prison complex, a herd of sheep blocks the way, a Gypsy family has set up camp along the road with two wooden caravans, a child comes trotting by with a horse and wagon. Finally we reach Bucharest's rubbish dump. The tip covers an immense plot, an endless series of grey, smoking mounds marked by the occasional orange fire, an inferno of soot, rotting food, bottles, cans, car tyres and old plastic. Through the clouds of smoke you can see figures poking around everywhere, rummaging, bent over, every day.

Rumania is probably the poorest country in Europe, according to the Human Development Index (2000). It is even worse off than, say, Cuba. Average annual inflation hovers around sixty per cent. The population is decreasing, less than half have access to good drinking water, only one in every five households has a telephone. Thirty to forty per cent of the voters choose ultra-right wing, nationalistic parties.

At this moment, some 4,000 homeless children wander the streets of Bucharest. You see them everywhere: they beg, sell cigarettes and matches, wash windscreens at traffic lights. I even saw one diminutive beggar, with big, pleading eyes, kissing the front of a car. They have run away from home, or have simply been sent out to live in the street. At the House of the Smart Boys, Tonio, his balaclava pulled down to just above his eyes, is acting as doorman. He lived in the city's tunnels for more than five years. He looks seven, but he is twelve. Nicu is smoking a cigarette. He looks eight, but he is fourteen. Alexandru welcomes me and shows me his new white jacket, and beneath it his little dog. He looks nine, but he is thirteen. All of them, however, radiate an extraordinary energy and self-sufficiency.

'Living on the street ensures that two things become well developed: your ability to fend for yourself, and your social skills,' says Adriana Constantinescu, supervisor of this children's home. 'Some of them can't give you the time of day, they sniff glue, but if for any reason they get into trouble they know immediately how to react. The only thing is, they've never known any form of human affection. This leaves them completely disoriented in life. We're a kind of substitute family for them, a stopping-off place between the street and a new family, or a life on their own. We give them a bed, food and they go back to school. And that works well.'

This project reaches about 300 children a year. The clothes worn by newcomers are burned behind the house. The pile of rags smokes and stinks. Sometimes a foreign television crew will show up at the door: where are the children of Ceaușescu? Adriana: 'Those journalists want to show the television images from the 1980s all over again, with emaciated, sick children. They don't realise that those children have already grown up, they're in the army, or in prison, or they're working as body-guards for the new rich.'

She knows all about the crowded orphanages of the Ceaușescu era, because she worked in them herself. But today's street children are of a different ilk. 'Under Ceaușescu there was a shortage of everything, but in that time many families still lived just above the subsistence level. It wasn't until after the 1989 revolution that they sank beneath the absolute poverty line. Then there was no way for them to get by. These days you sometimes find entire families living on the street, sometimes you also have very young children who grow up as transients.' These are, as she repeats again and again, the children of 1989, of the post-communist era, of the West's shock therapy, of the promised land that never arrived.

Chapter Sixty-Four

Novi Sad

FIRST YOU FLY TO BUDAPEST, THEN YOU SPEND FIVE HOURS BOUNCING
along in a minibus; that is how you finally arrive in the world of Slobodan
Milošević. Serbia has been boycotted by the West since 1991, the airport
at Belgrade has been closed for years, and this is one of the few means
of getting there. Many of the passengers wear tracksuits – the standard
former Soviet Bloc outfit of the 1990s – or black leather jackets. Behind
me, a man's voice drones away like a dentist's drill. Occasionally I am
able to make out a word: Davidoff, Volkswagen, America, Ben-Gurion
airport.

This part of the country is called Pannonia. The wooden derricks above
the wells stand out like gallows on the marshes. 'Welcome to the black
hole of Europe,' the man beside me says. He works as a football coach in
Oldenburg, and he is a product of the old Yugoslavia. 'I was born in Belgrade.
My mother came from Montenegro, my father was born in Bosnia. My
sister lives in Croatia, and I live in Germany. Work that one out!' At the
border, the Serb militiamen yank open the doors of the bus.

For centuries, rich and fertile Vojvodina was a part of the Habsburg
Empire. Today it is Serbian, but the area is still inhabited by Croatians,
Germans, Bosnians, Jews and Hungarians. It is the land where 'the
Hungarian celebrates in tears' and where, according to the author Aleksandr
Tisma, the people hang themselves from the rafters 'the way other people
say goodnight'. The broad skies above this land will never offer anyone
peace and safety.

It was in the early 1990s that I first visited Novi Sad, the hub of Tisma's
world. There was no writing going on then in this Serbian provincial
capital: the Yugoslav wars were in full swing and everyone was too busy

arranging for petrol, cigarettes and bread. The Western boycott had resulted in a devastating shortage of everything. New banknotes were being issued almost every week, in new denominations with eight zeroes or more, all bearing the portraits of serious-looking professors, generals and national poets.

The streets were lined with cars with flat tyres. The petrol smuggled with great difficulty past the embargo was sold in two-litre soft-drink bottles. The road in from the border was dotted with burned-out wrecks, in which something had apparently gone wrong with the plastic jerry cans stuffed under the back seat. At a street market I saw an elderly woman trying to sell her best coat. She lowered her eyes in shame. It was a dark blue cloth coat with a light fur collar and elegant buttons, once purchased in a festive mood and proudly cherished, now worth no more than the price of a piece of bread and a few potatoes.

In December 1999, however, Novi Sad comes as a relief after Bucharest. That is, at least at a first glance. My newspaper reports that the West still considers the economic boycott one of the most effective means of putting pressure on Milošević's regime. Those government ministers should walk these streets. Everywhere in the city – officially almost devoid of energy – the lights are on, the traffic is heavy, the markets and shops are full of Western European goods. Heaven knows where it all comes from. The black market, it seems, has found thousands of leaks and loopholes, and some people are making a bundle off of all those Western European principles.

I am welcomed to town in Novi Sad's newest restaurant, run by a former fashion model and opened only last Sunday. French wines, Dutch beer, fresh fish brought in daily from Greece. The restaurant is cheery and full.

My table companion is an old acquaintance, Sarita Matijević, a one-time television journalist who now works for George Soros. As the evening proceeds she becomes increasingly melancholy, she talks about how once, long ago, she visited Amsterdam on the queen's birthday. 'We travelled around the canals by boat, everyone was dancing and singing. But then it was as though all the sound had been switched off. Suddenly I realised, for the first time, that my life would never be normal again. I thought: from now on, we no longer belong, we're no longer a part of Europe.'

I had met Sarita during that first visit to Novi Sad, in 1993. It took place during a few completely normal weeks in February: the children with their backpacks slipped and slid over the frozen piles of snow on their way to school, the shopkeepers opened their shutters, the girls applied their make-up, the teachers started their lessons with a grumpy cough, the trains blew their whistles, the factories churned out goods and the hissing of the espresso machine in Café Sax sounded like a promising start to the day.

One might almost have thought that there was nothing wrong, back then in Novi Sad, had it not been for the blackouts at the strangest times of day, if only the hospital behind the dark red walls had not been full of wounded soldiers, of amputees, and if only the radio had not broadcast reports from the front all day. The city's favourite cafés and restaurants had fallen quiet, and it was that sudden dearth of laughter and conversation that frightened the people of Novi Sad more than all the fighting and inflation put together. Everyone was working and the muddy buses were still running on time. But as the few students still left in Café Sax told me, the mood was one of 'make believe'; they lived, as they put it themselves, 'in the twilight zone'.

Just imagine: for a cup of coffee that cost 15 dinars only last summer, you now paid 3,000 dinars. So then, what difference did it make? In 1990, a doctor's monthly salary had been around a thousand euros at today's rates. After three years of war, that same pile of dinars was worth no more than twenty-seven euros. One of Sarita's colleagues says: 'As intellectuals here, we live as though we're in Berlin in 1933: are we going to leave, or will we stick around and see what happens? No one here talks about anything else.'

I went with Sarita to visit her parents. After dinner the Serbian news came on, a programme that sometimes lasted for up to ninety minutes. Handy electronic maps showed the shifting front lines as though it were a weather report, the analyses made constant reference to blood, soil and the Serbian knights of the Middle Ages, the atrocities committed by the Croatians and Bosnians were exhibited in grim detail; those on the Serbian side remained unmentioned.

Often enough, the propaganda did not even consist of lies, but of half-truths, which made it all the more convincing. 'If you listen to Radio

Zagreb you hear exactly the same stories, but with the roles reversed,'
Sarita said. She provided a simultaneous translation of everything that
was said, including her father's comments; before long, however, she lost
her professional discipline and began peppering her translations with
comments like 'at least, that's what my father says,' and 'at least, that's
what my father's generation thinks' and 'which is, of course, utter
nonsense'. In the end, all attempts at translation ground to a halt, and
father and daughter spent the next hour shouting at each other.

In the 1990s, four wars broke out within what had once been Yugoslavia.
The first was a brief armed conflict that arose when Slovenia declared its
independence in 1991. The second was an all-out war in 1991–2, and had
to do with Croatia's secession. The third and most complicated conflict
was fought out in Bosnia-Herzegovina from 1992–6. And the fourth war,
in Kosovo, broke out in 1998 after years of tension, and ended with NATO
intervention in 1999.

The Yugoslav wars formed a bitter finale to the twentieth century. They
belonged to that century, and were in many ways a product of it: the
collapse of the Habsburg and Ottoman empires, the crude carving-up –
'like a cake' – of Central Europe and the Balkans in the conference rooms
at Versailles and Trianon, the massacres of the Serb population by Croatian
Nazis, and countless other unsettled accounts from the first half of the
twentieth century. The regimes of Slobodan Milošević, Franjo Tudjman
and other nationalistic leaders reflected tendencies that had been seen for
decades in Eastern Europe and the Balkans. They were anti-democratic
and anti-liberal (the heritage of almost half a century of communism),
they focused on ethnic purity (a legacy of National Socialism) and they
were pronouncedly nationalistic and anti-Western (a leftover from the
pan-Slavic movements that preceded the First World War).

The unexpected dynamism of their nationalism, the vent they gave to
the huge pressure on millions of humiliated farmers and town dwellers
in an impoverished Eastern Europe was new, yet at the same time all too
familiar. It was a primal force that leapt out of the darkness, like the
monster everyone thinks is dead at the end of a scary movie. But this
monster had not been defeated yet.

NATO waited a long time before intervening, and clear rifts were regularly seen between the United States and its European partners. That, too, was new. When the West finally took decisive action in 1999, the attack was of a strikingly technical nature: the operations took place at high altitudes and from great distances, with as few risks as possible for the Western soldiers involved. It was a war of bombardment, aimed particularly at Belgrade, Novi Sad and a small number of other cities. And so, for the West, the war in Kosovo, the final war of the century, served as a counterpoint to the First World War. The national governments in 1914 had willingly sacrificed hundreds of thousands of troops. In 1999, for NATO, that was unthinkable. The fighting was limited to the use of missiles and bombers. In Kosovo, the West never engaged in a ground war.

In the final account, the Yugoslav wars were also typical publicity wars. There was a constant manipulation of death counts. NATO smugly televised direct hits on Belgrade, as though the city was a pinball machine. For Milošević, the national television stations comprised his most important asset, more important even than the army, politics or party. The wars ran on fear, particularly among the Serbs: the fear of decimation, the fear of a repetition of the cruelties of the Second World War. And nothing whipped up those fears more effectively than television.

The history of the Yugoslav wars is complicated. From the fifteenth until far into the nineteenth century, Yugoslavia – like the rest of the Balkans – had acted as a highly prized buffer zone between the three great religious traditions: Roman Catholicism, Eastern Orthodoxy and Islam. Many mountain people lived almost exclusively within their clans and isolated village communities, and it was to them that their loyalty was given. Boys and men were regularly press-ganged into the armies of the warring powers; most of their contact with differing convictions took place on the battlefield. The key virtues were bravery, a sense of honour and loyalty to the clan.

At first there were no major ethnic tensions. The Ottoman Empire was relatively tolerant, its population divided only along religious lines and not by ethnic origin. Western Europeans travelling through Thrace around 1900 noted to their amazement that the people in a mixed Greek/Bulgarian village had absolutely no idea whether their ancestors were Greek or

Bulgarian. That played no role whatsoever. All they knew was that they were Christians.

The First Yugoslavia, also known as the Kingdom of Yugoslavia, was created at the Versailles peace conferences, as part of the dismantling of the Habsburg Empire. The new nation was dominated by the Serbs; partly because they formed the largest local minority, and partly because they had fought on the side of the victorious Allies. Croatia, Slovenia, Bosnia and Herzegovina had sided with the Habsburgs and were seen rather as the spoils of war and treated accordingly. Meanwhile, the central government remained weak and the villages fought out their own disagreements: Serbs against Croatians, Croatians and Serbs against Muslims, Croatians and Muslims against Serbs, 'my brother and I against my nephew, my nephew and I against the foreigner'.

During the Second World War this traditional local violence began escalating like never before. The National Socialist Croatians set up an independent state, and their Ustaše movement, along with certain Muslim groups, set out to cleanse all of Croatia and Bosnia-Herzegovina of Serbs. On 9 April, 1942, thousands of Serb families from the region surrounding Srebrenica were driven into the River Drina and massacred by the Ustaše, a bloodbath that horrified even the German occupiers and left a deep mark in the Serb collective memory. The Serbs' Chetniks, by the way, struck back just as mercilessly, storming Ustaše strongholds and descending with their supporters on dozens of Muslim villages. During this ethnic fighting many hundreds of thousands of people were killed, particularly on the Serbian side, including several tens of thousands of Jews and Gypsies.

The Second Yugoslavia was formed after the war, under Tito, who succeeded in combining an effective central authority with a large degree of autonomy for the six Yugoslav federal republics. The national constitution drafted in 1974 further decentralised the country's administration: each of the federal republics was to have its own central bank, its own police force, its own system of courts and schools. The country rapidly began modernising, and new schools, roads, factories and housing estates were built everywhere. Until the 1980s, in fact, Yugoslavia was seen as far and away the most advanced communist country. Tito declared that the old complex conflicts had been forgotten and forgiven, and the Yugoslavs were able to live with that for more than thirty-five years.

It was only after the old leader's death in 1980 that things went wrong. Tito, it turned out, had left behind enormous foreign debt, and inflation quickly escalated. Savings and pensions melted away, huge shortages of food and fuel arose, the old certainties were proving worthless. As had happened earlier in other Eastern Bloc countries, this resulted in a huge protest movement. But here, however, the anti-communist rebellion also led to new conflicts along old ethnic divides. Under Tito the expression of nationalist sentiments had been strictly taboo, but some Serbian, Croatian and Slovenian intellectuals continued to foster such ideas on the sly. To remain in power, therefore, the former communist apparatchiks once again conjured up the ideals of nationalism, and with considerable success.

During summer 1988, Yugoslav news reported day after day on mass demonstrations calling for Serbia to re-establish its authority over the 'autonomous province' of Kosovo. That, it was claimed, was the Serbian people's historic right: after all, Kosovo had been sacred ground to them ever since they had lost the battle against the Ottomans at the Field of the Blackbirds (*Kosovo Polje*) on St Vitus' Day in 1389. The Serbs had, in their own view, been more or less harassed out of Kosovo: ninety per cent of the population there was now Albanian. The demonstrators turned that same rage effortlessly on the former communist 'office hogs', speaking of an 'anti-bureaucratic revolution' and 'the people's movement'. The communist leader Slobodan Milošević had suddenly undergone a complete metamorphosis: he now promoted himself as the 'national' alternative, and showed great verve in trading in his communist rhetoric for new views and new enemies.

The communist leaders from the other federal republics, particularly Croatia and Slovenia, kept a watchful eye on the developments in Belgrade. Not Kosovo but Milošević himself was their worry. They saw, and not without reason, the Serb complaints as a pretext for their re-establishing power over the Yugoslav federation. With the help of the army, consisting largely of Serbs, this would amount to the reinstatement of a centralist, authoritarian Yugoslavia dominated by Belgrade.

The Serbs were disappointed by their Slovenian and Croatian brothers' lack of solidarity concerning Kosovo. Things came to a head in 1990. The Slovenian and Croatian leaders withdrew from the Communist League of Yugoslavia, both republics stopped paying taxes to the federal government in Belgrade, and in spring 1991 the federation fell apart.

The American anthropologist Bette Denich has described how, during her visits to Yugoslavia in the 1960s and 1970s, Tito's policy of integration and modernisation was setting the tone throughout the country, and how the pan-Yugoslav identity continued to gain strength. No one would have dreamed of bringing that process to a halt. Even after Tito's death, in May 1980, Yugoslavs to a man sang along with the pop song 'After Tito – Tito!':

> So now what, my southern land?
> If anyone asks
> we'll tell them: Tito again,
> After Tito – Tito!

Denich was all the more amazed, therefore, when she returned in the late 1980s. 'Belgrade, as I knew it in the 1960s, was emphatically the capital of Yugoslavia, an administrative and intellectual centre that drew in people from the other republics to assume governmental and other functions. Now, instead of that, I found a Belgrade that emphatically presented itself as the capital of Serbia.' The fronts of buildings and houses had been cleaned and repainted with Old Serbian motifs, bookshop windows were filled with new works dealing with Serb history, literature and other national legacies.

Looking back on this time, Bette Denich saw an almost psychopathological process taking place in Yugoslavia, a rampant spiral of projections between 'us' and 'them', full of 'self-fulfilling prophecies': each participant in the conflict represented himself as a victim or a potential victim, and the other side as a threat or a potential threat. 'And by reacting, mutually, to the other side solely as a threat, both parties of course became truly more threatening.'

In Café Sax in early 1993, I had been introduced to the writer László Végel, an amiable, square-built man. He had just returned from Budapest and was sitting at a table, mulling over the future. He was wearing a new grey jacket, and his friends teased him a bit about it. Earlier that week, as part of the political purges being rushed through by the new government, he had been dismissed as director of Novi Sad's television broadcasting organisation. Before he went home, the writer György Konrád had advised him to begin by buying a new coat, to keep up his spirits and show those people in Novi Sad that he was still a man to be reckoned with.

In spring 1991, Konrád had written about the insecurity of his fellow Eastern Europeans in the face of a capitalism they had not grown up with, about their aggrieved sense of self-importance, and about the 'suspect talents' they were beginning to apply. 'Before long, anyone who isn't angry at one of our neighbouring countries will be suspected of treason. Hate is standing in the wings, waiting only to be told who to pounce upon.'

Konrád sensed that tension quite acutely. On 25 June, 1991, Slovenia and Croatia declared their independence. Tito's Yugoslavia had ceased to exist. Milošević placed all his bets on the formation of a new and powerful Balkan state, an ethnically pure Greater Serbia into which large sections of Croatia and Bosnia were also to be incorporated in due course. That spring, extremist Serbs in Croatia seceded and formed their own ministate, the Serb Republic of Krajina. From the start, they displayed two traits that would prove formative for all conflicts to come in former Yugoslavia: an extreme predilection for local autonomy, and great enthusiasm for the use of violence. It was in Krajina that the first of those militias were set up – by people including the Rambo-esque Željko Ražnatović, also known as Arkan – which would later play such a deadly role in Bosnia.

Meanwhile, the protagonists of the drama, Milošević and the Croatian president, Franjo Tudjman, started in on a series of secret consultations at Karadjordjevo, one of Tito's favourite holiday villas. Later, at Split, they even included Bosnian-Muslim leader Alija Izetbegović in their talks. They were trying to circumvent a war, and at the same time Milošević proposed to Tudjman that they more or less divide Bosnia between them along ethnic lines. Izetbegović expressed interest in that proposal as well; he was hoping to work together with Tudjman against the Serbs, and did not wish to offend him. Whatever agreement they finally reached – the arrangements between Milošević and Tudjman in particular are still shrouded in mist – within a few days their accord was overtaken by the facts. A Serb paramilitary force attacked a Croatian police post, the first casualties fell, and the war had begun. In July 1991, the Yugoslav Army openly sided with the Serb rebels in Krajina.

For the first time since the Second World War, campaigns of ethnic cleansing were once again taking place within Europe: approximately 500,000 Croatians were driven out of Krajina, around 250,000 Serbs in Croatia lost their jobs and were forced to flee for their lives. The Gypsy population was persecuted as well: more than 50,000 eventually left the country.

In autumn 1991, the war came close to Novi Sad. The picturesque town of Vukovar on the Danube, an hour away, was besieged for months. Panic broke out among the young people of Novi Sad. Schools, university canteens, Café Sax: they all emptied out. Many of the boys fled to the stands of willow along the river, and the girls went there in the evening to bolster their spirits with food and blankets and other comforts. These days people still whisper about the orgies that went on there; no one gave a damn any more, they were all going to die anyway, they thought.

The EU, full of optimism and self-confidence, now adopted the role of mediator. The Common Market, after all, was proceeding as planned, the Treaty of Maastricht was on its way, there were far-reaching plans for a common currency and a common security policy. This would be the first test case for the community's new joint foreign policy. Three representatives – the Luxembourger Jacques Poos, the Dutchman Hans van den Broek and the Italian Gianni De Michelis – travelled to Zagreb and Belgrade to meet with the warring factions and, as the negotiators were still frequently saying, to 'bang their heads together'.

Little attention was paid at that point to the structural and historical contexts of the conflict. For years, as the closely involved BBC journalists Laura Silber and Allan Little wrote, the European negotiators acted as though the conflict had been caused only by the vaguely delineated 'temperament' of the Balkans, 'an irresistible southern Slavic tendency –

be that cultural, be that genetic – towards fratricide.' The warring groups had only to be convinced of the foolishness of war, nothing else was needed to bring about peace. What they overlooked, however, was that the background to these wars was often not as irrational as all that. For the Yugoslav leaders, Silber and Little wrote, war was quite often 'a completely rational affair, and indeed the only way for them to achieve their objectives'.

The Serbs almost completely flattened Vukovar. After the city surrendered on 18 November, a large number of wounded men were carried off and never seen again. They probably still lie in a mass grave in the surrounding countryside.

In January 1992, Milošević and Tudjman agreed to a ceasefire. Whatever role the European negotiators played, that was a rational decision: the battle of prestige for Vukovar had been won, a quarter of all Croatian territory was now occupied by the Serbs, an international peacekeeping force was on its way to guard the new borders, and Milošević's Greater Serbia had come another step closer. As far as Tudjman was concerned, Croatia's recognition by the international community granted him enough time to revamp the Croatian Army thoroughly. What is more, both men were planning to breathe new life into the 'gentlemen's agreement' formerly reached at Karadjordjevo, and to move on together towards the next prize: Bosnia.

Milošević more or less left the Serbs in Krajina to their own fate. In August 1995, the tables were turned at last and a modernised Croatian Army rolled into Krajina and chased out almost the whole Serb population. Belgrade, Novi Sad and other cities filled with refugees.

In 1993, just before I left Novi Sad, I found a long letter waiting at the front desk of my hotel. It was from an acquaintance, a Croatian woman. She urged me to be careful, and finally she wrote: 'I had a dream in which there was no war. I breathed the fresh air of Slovenian snow, I ate the bread of Croatia, I drank Bosnian wine, I sang songs from Serbia and I lay in the beautiful fields of Vojvodina. It was my country, it was my home. For twenty-eight years I lived in a beautiful country and now, after only two years, they're trying to tell me it was all my imagination, nonsense, illusions. Except: twenty-eight years is not an illusion to me.

My father was born in that imaginary land, and so was my grandfather. How can that be a fantasy?'

She had translated the letter into English with great difficulty, having to look up almost every word in the dictionary. I went to where she lived to say goodbye. She and her husband lived in a lovely house on the Danube, no one in those parts had ever cared whether you were a Serb or a Croatian. Then the war came. The rumbling of the battle at Vukovar carried across the river and into their home, like the sound of distant thunder, every night.

One morning, down by their neighbour's orchard, the body of a woman had floated up, her eyes wide open, staring at the sky. And when they tried to whitewash the gate of the fortress of Novi Sad – this all happened around the same time – snakes came crawling out of every nook and cranny, hundreds of snakes of a kind they had never seen before. 'We want to leave here,' she had written, 'but we don't know how, with a four-year-old child, where can you find a new job and a house?' She had no intention of going to Croatia. 'If I must be a foreigner, then I'd rather be a foreigner in China.'

It is a clear December morning in 1999. The film director Želimir Žilnić and I are taking a long walk beside the river. The words of György Konrád in Budapest still echo in my mind: 'The sooner Milošević and his gang are gone, the better. But no Hungarian, no Czech, no Bulgarian, no Rumanian would ever come up with the idea of bombing the bridges of Novi Sad to accomplish that. To think up something like that you have to be far, very far removed from our reality.'

And so there they lie. No attempt has been made to clear the rubble. The oldest bridge in particular is a dearly departed one. Atop the lanterns, partly under water now, a row of gulls is sitting in the sun. 'The next morning, there were a lot of people standing on the banks, weeping,' Želimir told me. 'On the far shore, the nationalists began singing their songs, that was horrible too.' The traffic now hobbles across a makeshift pontoon bridge.

A friend of his had seen the last of the bridges collapse before his eyes. 'It was 3 p.m., lovely weather, you could see the cruise missile come sailing in across the river.' A few other acquaintances had fought in Kosovo, they had told him how to deflect cruise missiles from their course: a big sheet of cardboard or chipboard painted green, in the shape of a tank, with a hole in it. Behind the hole you lit an alcohol burner for the infrared, and even the smartest of warheads thought it was homing in on a tank. 'It costs ten marks, and it will take out a missile that costs a million.'

We walk past the big gleaming headquarters of the NIS, Milošević's state oil company, close to the bridge. It had not been scratched. In Shanga, however, a Gypsy neighbourhood, we end up by the ruins of a hovel that did take a direct hit. The woman next door is willing to talk to us, and invites us in. Her name is Dragica Dimić, she's twenty-three, she has two children and her world consists of a leaky roof, a dark room that measures three metres by four, two brown, lice-ridden beds, a wood stove and a little flickering TV. She has nothing in the world but herself, her intelligence and her unconditional love for her children and her husband. The only bright things in the room are a loaf of white bread and her eyes.

'It was last June,' she says. 'Late in the evening, we were standing outside talking to the neighbours across the fence. They'll probably come after the refinery again, we told each other. We heard the planes coming, there was a bright light. We went inside. Suddenly there was this sound: sssss. We were thrown against the wall, everything shuddered and burst. More explosions. We threw ourselves on top of the children, covered them with our bodies. Then we raced out of the house, it was all dust and smoke. Our youngest son was covered in blood. Water was spraying out of the pipes, power lines were hissing and popping. We ran out into the field. I could hear my neighbour screaming in the distance. Their house had been hit, her husband was bleeding to death. I was so frightened, I thought: they're going to start shooting at us with machine guns, from the air. Our house was in ruins. That week, it rained the whole time. We built it back up more or less by ourselves.'

We talk a little about her life, while the children nuzzle up to her. 'Do you ever go out these days? To a wedding, or a name day, or something?' Želimir asks. 'Sometimes I go out with my friends, to gather wood in the forest. Then we're gone for half the day. That's always a lot of fun.' Her husband works on building sites, he earns just enough to buy a few potatoes, a couple of kilos of fat and a carton of cigarettes. 'I'll tell you the truth: I like this life, as long as the war stops. I'm happy that my children and I can sleep together again, the way we used to, please write that down.'

Ever since the early 1990s, a bus full of young people has left each night for Budapest: you save your hard-earned money for a ticket, you pack your bags and you go. After receiving their diplomas, students pick up their suitcases and walk straight to the bus. In a gallery along the street, beneath the words 'We have left', the wall is covered with passport pictures, thousands of them; politicians, journalists, professors, young people. All the stories of flight come down to the same thing: gather your wits, take a good look at the situation, save your money, buy a ticket, get out and then see what happens.

In a survey taken in those years, the Serbs were asked what they would prefer: a secure job and a fixed salary for the next twenty years, or four times the salary with a fifty-fifty chance of losing their jobs. Ninety-five per cent of them chose job security. 'Every family here has gone through terrible things,' someone tells me. 'At this point there's only one thing the people want: stability. They have learned from bitter experience that every change brings with it huge risks. I'll tell you this much: poor people don't want a revolution, all they want is security. That's the first law of poverty, but they don't know anything about that in the West.'

Sarita's parents welcome me warmly to their home again. Father Matijević still believes whatever the Serbian television tells him. Our conversation always returns to talk of plots and spies. The Serbian war crimes never took place, and within an hour father and daughter are fighting like cats again. During the bombardments, Sarita's parents had worked together to build a new brick shed in the garden, they went on working no matter what, it was their way of making a stand.

After dinner, Sarita takes me to the beauty parlour down on the corner. It is already dark, almost closing time. Two girls are still sitting under the hairdryers. I ask all the women in the place what has been on their minds most this week. Marita, thirty-five, has a fifteen-year-old son who wants to go out tomorrow night, but she doesn't have a cent to give him.

Gordana, the thirty-three-year-old beautician, wants a new lover. 'How else can I find the inspiration to go on?' Mirjana simply wants to go away, far away. 'I was seventeen when this misery started, now I'm twenty-three. I've lost the best years of my life to this stupid war.'

Mirjana is dazzlingly beautiful, beside her I suddenly feel old and fat. She has an office job at the state oil company; it's Serbia in miniature, she says. 'The idiots, the brown-noses, they take everything. The people who think about things and do their work well are the ones who get left behind.' Gordana says: 'Almost all my old friends have left. The ones who stayed are all crazy.' She laughs, but she means it.

Her brother Goran, twenty-two, comes in and eagerly joins the discussion: 'There were five of us, friends. Three of us have already left, and that's all we talk about now.' Ten buses now leave Belgrade each night for Budapest, he tells me. 'That's 500 people a day! If things keep on like this, the whole opposition will be living outside the country before long. And all our girls want is a husband with a mobile phone!'

Mirjana stares dreamily into space: 'Canada, that might be nice, don't you think? Or Holland, maybe?'

'They asked a colleague of mine, a playwright, whether what was happening to this country was a drama. He said: "No, this isn't material for a drama, it's material for a comedy." And he was right. All the big countries of the world going to war against this weird little Yugoslavia. All the evil of the world suddenly gathered together in this poor country. The 100,000 Albanians the Western papers say were murdered by the Yugoslav Army . . . but now, suddenly, they can't find the graves. Of course, horrible, terrible things have happened. But in essence it's a comedy, not a tragedy.

'Every poor man is a fool, you know. Simply because he's poor. His clothes don't fit, his hair isn't styled, he's dirty, foolish. And in that way we're fools as well. We are the village idiots of the world. We live in a ghetto, we don't have any contacts with anyone any more. We used to have excellent ties with France and Holland, for example. But the NATO planes which bombarded us came from those countries too. They're on the other side now as well. Everyone's on the other side, except for us. That's not sad, that is, above all, foolish.

'This can't be serious. You can't believe this is really happening. I still have the feeling that these things are not really going on, that it will be over tomorrow, like a head cold. But I'm afraid it's going to last a long time. Because there's no way out. We lost the war in Kosovo, we signed for our defeat, but everything has stayed the way it was. No politician can pull us out of this quagmire.

'The bombardments were sort of like a comedy too. They bombed day and night, you got up with it and you went to bed with it, but you knew they didn't want to kill civilians, you could tell that from the targets they chose. So I wasn't afraid of a bomb falling on my house. Everything in the city kept on going, the cafés, the shops, even when the air-raid sirens were blasting. The farmers simply came into town to the market, the way they always had, and their prices weren't any higher. The run of the mill Yugoslavs weren't thinking about their role in history, mostly they were just flabbergasted.

'When I was young, Novi Sad was more or less the same city it is now. Of course bits have been added, but life was the same, the mentality too. People here aren't interested in things that happen outside their own street. They're cool, and they're also a little dumb. The people who have put together these policies and caused all this trouble, they don't come from here. Radovan Karadžić, Milošević, Ratko Mladić, they're all mountain people. Those of us from the flatlands suffer under the things that happen, but we're not active in them.

'This is a tolerant place, though: during this war there wasn't a single Albanian, Muslim, German or Dutchman harassed. But we're not cosmopolitan. We'd like to be, but no one is interested in us. We don't produce anything that's worth their while, no clothes, wine or meat. We don't have anything others want but don't have. We write books, okay, but that's for a tiny little group. Besides, as you know, people who read books don't make politics. They stay at home, they read and think about things.

'Sure, a lot of intellectuals supported Milošević. And now they support him even more; with his defeats, he has now become the symbol of this tormented nation. He has become a fool, they have become fools. He's no longer allowed to travel in Europe, they're no longer allowed to travel in Europe. More and more, they're becoming just like Milošević. We share the same fate now, because of this war, and because of our isolation.

'Under Tito, the legends were forgotten. Tito wasn't a Serb, even though he was pro-Serbian. After he died, everything went wrong. The Serbs panicked and started fantasising about their past. Suddenly they remembered that there had once been this big empire, and that they'd had kings, things like that. The poverty, the country's disintegration, all those uncertainties created a reality in which it was almost impossible to live. And from that myths were born, the one more fantastic than the other. So that's an answer to a situation, but that's not how it begins. What else can we do but tell each other stories?

'And that foolish poor man? He still believes in it, after all these years, and at the same time he doesn't believe in it any more. He needs those stories to comfort his soul, but he doesn't believe that they will save him. A resurrection of Serbia, dreams like that, no one believes in them any more. That poor man is in a state of shock.

'I once had a dog named Jackie. One winter's day that dog ran away, along the Danube, and somehow he got out onto an ice floe. Some children from the neighbourhood came and got me. "Mr Tišma, your dog is going to drown!" I ran down there, called to it, all the dog had to do was take one little step, but it just sat there as if it were paralysed. The animal was in a complete state of shock. Finally the children were able to get a hold of him, and everything turned out all right.

'That's the way this country is too: it's sitting paralysed on an ice floe, doesn't know what to do, and meanwhile the ice is floating away on the current.'

Chapter Sixty-Five

Srebrenica

WHAT WOULD HAPPEN IF MARSHAL TITO ROSE FROM THE GRAVE? ON my last evening in Novi Sad, Želimir showed me one of his short documentaries, a fascinating experiment. He'd had an actor made up to look exactly like Tito, he put Tito's sunglasses on him, and then he walked around all day with this fake Tito through the shopping streets of Belgrade.

The film went like this: 'So tell us what has been going on in our beautiful country,' Tito asks his old driver – the real one – after he has risen from his mausoleum and got into the back of his Mercedes – the original one. 'It fell apart, sir,' the man sighs. 'They destroyed the federation, they took down all the red stars, and then the war started.'

As soon as Tito gets out of the car in the middle of Belgrade, a crowd gathers. For the first few minutes the crowd plays along, but soon they become bitter. 'Traitor!' a few angry passers-by shout. 'But I left a lot of reliable people behind, didn't I?' Tito murmurs. 'Forget it. It's your fault. You were the leader of a bunch of bandits, those are your successors. When you go back to the hereafter, please take them all with you. I'm not even allowed to build a pigsty nowadays!'

Tito walks past a bookstall: 'What are these weird symbols? And why are we using German money?' A young man, overwrought: 'The young people loved you. We learned poems about you, you were the sun shining down on us. We formed an honour guard in front of your portrait when you died!' A woman: 'I wept, too. You took wonderful trips to foreign countries, you lived in villas, meanwhile I worked shelling peanuts in a factory, but I still wept. God, do I ever regret that now.'

A man, beaming with joy, pushes his way to the front of the crowd.

'So you're back again. We used to have one Tito. Now we have a dozen of them. Great to see you back again!' Tito: 'There certainly are a lot of people just hanging around. Don't any of you have to work? Do you all have the day off?'

Želimir: 'Then the police came and arrested us for disturbing the peace. Me, Tito, the whole crew. We were lucky. The police officer at the station had a sense of humour, he snapped to attention right away: "Mr President. What an honour to meet you again. Of course, this is all a misunderstanding, we'll take care of it right away." A few minutes later we were back out on the street.'

Nothing can create new order out of poverty and chaos, nothing but the story, and the belief in that story. As though it were a royal wedding, Serbian television has devoted a whole day to the marriage of the arch-criminal Arkan, leader of the notorious Arkan Tigers paramilitary organisation, to the singer Svetlana, also known as Ceca. Ceca's newest hit – she sings what they call 'ethnofolk' – has been echoing in the cafés for weeks now.

A few headlines from the popular weekly Twilight Zone: 'Jacques Chirac, whose support played a definitive role in the war against the Serbian nation, will die on Christmas Day'; 'Creatures from outer space kidnapped a man for 300 years'; 'America to fall apart on 17 January, 2000!'; 'During the solar eclipse on 8 August, a new Hitler was born'; 'The young wife of Václav Havel, the man who supported the war against the Serbian nation, does not have long to live'; 'Will China conquer America in 2008?'

It is Sunday afternoon, and I have been invited to tea by a little group of female intellectuals. I find about a dozen women sitting around in a spacious nineteenth-century apartment; most of them are over sixty, they are writers, journalists and professors. The walls are covered with paintings. The group holds its salon here every second Sunday of the month and has been doing so for years, right through all the revolutions and bombardments, with home-made cakes. Today there is even Ukrainian champagne. The curtains have been drawn, the street is far away for the moment.

The women's group is worried about the hundreds of thousands of homeless people wandering the country after the war, and about all the young people who are leaving. 'We're not talking about semi-mafiosi or frustrated soldiers; these are doctors, engineers, lawyers; the professional people this country needs to build itself up again.' 'There are even young writers leaving the country, we've never seen this before!'

'I'm so tired of these never-ending complaints from Western Europe,' a lady growls. She has just returned from an international conference on Kosovo; the French representative had stated her concern about all the inexpensive Yugoslav streetwalkers upsetting the neatly organised prostitution in Paris. '"Well, what are they supposed to do?" I asked her. "Being a prostitute in the West is an excellent way to earn a living these days for a poor, intelligent Yugoslav girl!"'

The next morning at breakfast, I see a boy walk past the window of the hotel, his head shaved. Suddenly two men in leather coats come running up, they jump on him, a fight ensues, two policemen arrive and the four of them force him onto the ground. The boy lies face down on the pavement, motionless as a cornered cat. Now the policemen are on the phone. Two unmarked cars appear. They boy is kicked a few times, then carried away by two plainclothes gorillas, God only knows why. The whole arrest has taken two minutes at most.

'You caught a glimpse of Milošević's Praetorian Guard,' my guide, Duško Tubić, tells me later. 'A large portion of the population of this city has just come back from the war: refugees selling matches, former soldiers from the front lines, policemen . . . those may have been the men in leather coats. They were probably catching a thief, but it could also be something else, you never know.' Nothing surprises Duško any more, for years he's been working as a fixer for Western journalists and camera crews, guiding them along fronts of every hue. We drive past the burned-out television tower and the partial ruins of the city's police headquarters, past offices and government buildings with huge holes blown in them. The main road to Zagreb is more or less abandoned; after a while we turn off towards the south, and by nightfall we're in Bijeljina, Duško's birthplace, not far from the Serb-Bosnian border.

That night I sleep in an ethnically cleansed town. Of the 17,000 Muslims who lived here in 1991, there are no more than 1,000 left. All of the mosques have been wiped away. The spot where the biggest mosque stood is now a gravelled lot with a few cars and rubbish containers. On the site of the second mosque, a church is now being built. In the third, Jamia Pero – the tricky snake – has opened a shop selling pots and pans. And mosque number four is now a market square with rusty stalls. The youngest children in Bijeljina don't know that the town ever had four mosques. The commercials shown by the local TV station crow and cheer as though none of it ever took place: women whisk away stains, cheerful families gather around a tasty meal, little elves polish kitchen floors.

After 1992 the local graveyard tripled in size, today it is an expanse the size of eight football pitches, full of shiny new marble. Most of those who lie here died between the ages of twenty and twenty-five, almost all of them between 1992–5. The portraits of the dead have been painstakingly etched in the marble. Faces stare at you, serious, laughing, some of the men are sitting in jeeps on their way to the hereafter, others are raising a glass in camaraderie, a young paramilitary soldier stands life-sized atop his gravestone, his machine gun clenched in both hands, squeezing off rounds all the way to heaven.

The next morning we make our way into Holbrookeland, a curious collection of mini-states stitched together at an airforce base in Dayton, Ohio in late 1995 by American negotiator Richard Holbrooke. To the south lies the federation of Bosnia-Herzegovina, which is in turn an amalgam of the former Croatian and Muslim republics. Lying somewhat curled around it, to the north and east, is the Serb Republic. This separate little republic leans on Serbia, but the Serbs themselves want little to do with it these days; it has become something of an estranged little brother.

Until 1991, Bosnia was seen as the most ethnically balanced part of Yugoslavia: of over four million inhabitants, forty-four per cent were Muslim, thirty-one per cent Serbian and seventeen per cent Croatian. The capital, Sarajevo, had developed into a cheerful, cosmopolitan city. More than forty per cent of all marriages were mixed. Given a few more years, little would have been little left of that multi-ethnic community.

The Bosnian war lasted three and a half years and claimed more than 200,000 lives. Two million people were left homeless. The war was more or less a continuation of the Croatian conflict, when Serb paramilitary organisations began using certain parts of Bosnia as their base of operations. In autumn 1991 the Serbs announced that 'their' areas were now five separate autonomous regions, and not long afterwards the Croatians

did the same with that part of Bosnia in which they formed the majority.
The Yugoslav Army, a Serb Army for quite some time already, began digging
in heavy artillery at strategic spots, including the hills around Sarajevo.
In a referendum held in late February 1992, an overwhelming majority
of Bosnians voted for independence. That, after all, would keep their
country unified. Two thirds of registered voters went to the polls, most
of them Muslims and Croatians. The Serbs boycotted the referendum:
their leaders propagated a Greater Serbia, and the idea of an independent
Bosnia was at loggerheads with that. They decided to set up their own
Serb Republic in the Serbian sections of Bosnia. At Pale, a ski resort close
to Sarajevo, they formed their own government and their own parliament. Then they went on to seize some seventy per cent of Bosnia by
force, and in late April 1992 laid siege to Sarajevo from the surrounding
hills. After all, it was to be their own capital one day.

That summer the Croatians established their own little republic as well,
with Mostar as its capital. The praesidium of the Bosnian republic had
little choice but to set up its own army then, which was in effect the
army of the Muslims.

The first major fighting took place around Sarajevo, but the stand-off
soon resulted in a siege which lasted forty-four months. The Serb/Yugoslav
Army did not have enough manpower or munitions to take the city, and
the Bosnian Army was not strong enough to break through their blockade.

In the areas they occupied, the Serbs immediately began the process
of ethnic purification. All over north-western Bosnia, non-Serbian villages
were attacked and plundered, and thousands of Muslims and Croatians
were interred. The most notorious camps were Trnopolje and Omarska,
an abandoned mining complex not far from Banya Luka. The women
were held at Trnopolje under barbaric conditions, and were systematically beaten and raped. The men of the police and militia jeered that this
way they would at least bear 'Serbian babies'. Omarska was discovered
in summer 1992 by Ed Vulliamy of the *Guardian*. He visited the camp
'canteen' and watched in horror as thirty emaciated men were given three
minutes to gulp down a sort of piping-hot gruel. 'The bones of their
elbows and wrists protrude like pieces of jagged stone from the pencil-
thin stalks to which their arms have been reduced,' he wrote. 'They are
alive but decomposed, debased, degraded, and utterly subservient, and

yet they fix their huge hollow eyes on us with looks like blades of knives.'

All these camps were part of a strategy of terror and intimidation that soon began having the desired effect: within six months, most Muslims and Croatians had left the Serb territories. Europe experienced the biggest refugee crisis since the one right after the Second World War. By late 1992, almost two million Bosnians had fled, with more than half a million of them seeking asylum in Western Europe. The Serbs were almost satisfied: they now had their hands on most of the country, and almost all of the Croatians and Muslims had disappeared from their territories. The only problem they had left had to do with Sarajevo, the capital of their dreams, and with the handful of remaining Muslim enclaves, towns filled with refugees that had until then been able to repulse the Serbian attacks. Towns like Goražde, Žepa and, most famous of all, Srebrenica.

The old village of Srebrenica was once an idyllic place which had grown up around a silver mine and was, from the nineteenth century, a fashionable spa. In fact, it was nothing more than a single long street at the end of a deep valley. There was a boulevard where the young people strolled, a café with a terrace where you were served by waiters in bow ties, the 'Bosnia' cinema, an excellent hospital and, at Hotel Guber, a world-famous spring 'for healthy blood'. Around 1990 there were 6,000 people living there, a quarter of them Serbs, the rest Muslims.

Srebrenica, however, lay in the middle of the area which the Serbs had claimed for themselves. And when they also began their campaign of ethnic cleansing here, a well organised local movement began offering strong resistance.

One of the most important Muslim leaders was Naser Orić, a former bodyguard to Milošević. Orić and his gang, in turn, began terrorising the surrounding Serbian villages. At first these Muslim militias did their best to conquer entire sections of countryside, and even to link up with the Muslim area around the city of Tuzla. But that did not work out. Around Srebrenica itself, however, a huge Muslim enclave soon arose in the middle of Serb territory. Orić became the local hero. In summer and autumn 1992 he attacked a large number of villages and farmhouses in the surroundings, murdering Serb families who had stayed behind and plundering their stores.

In the course of time, these forays became vitally important. The Serbs had blocked all roads into the enclave, and as winter approached the food supply became a major problem. The inhabitants of Srebrenica were forced to live on feed corn, oats and dandelion salad. At night the town was plunged into total darkness: the only electricity was generated by a series of primitive waterwheels in the nearby stream. At a certain point the Muslims even proposed an exchange of prisoners: one live Serb for two fifty-kilo sacks of flour. During winter 1992–3, dozens of men, women and children in the enclave died of starvation.

The Muslims, by the same token, had burned down at least thirty villages and seventy hamlets. Estimates are that somewhere around a thousand victims fell among the local Serb farming population, and the Serbs were furious. At the Yugoslavia Tribunal in the Hague, British negotiator David Owen later stated that Milošević had warned him in early 1993 that if the Bosnian Serbs took the enclave, there would be a 'bloodbath' or a 'massacre'. And, starting that winter, the Serbs actually began gaining ground in the area around Srebrenica. At last, all that remained was Srebrenica itself and a little fringe of land, a tiny island in Serbian Bosnia packed with Muslim refugees.

The immediate threat to the enclave was countered thanks to the mediation of the United Nations. In March 1993, the French commander of the UN troops, General Philippe Morillon, appeared in Srebrenica. He addressed the townspeople: 'Do not be afraid. As from now, you are protected by the troops of the United Nations. We will not abandon you.' The UN flag was raised in the city with a great deal of ceremony. The elated municipal government made Morillon an honorary citizen.

In early May, the UN announced that Srebrenica was now a demilitarised safe haven. Women and children were allowed to leave for Tuzla aboard UN trucks. All able-bodied men between the ages of sixteen and fifty-five were to remain behind. Once an estimated 23,000 women, children and elderly people had left Srebrenica, however, the Muslim leader, Orić, ordered a halt to the evacuation. Any greater exodus would leave his enclave too weak. Approximately 40,000 Muslims remained behind in the claustrophobic safe haven, held more or less prisoner in this Bosnian/UN ghetto.

Later it became clear that, by that point, all parties involved had actually given up on the enclave. The half-heartedness of the Americans and

Western Europeans can, in hindsight, be seen simply from the number of UN troops they allotted for peacekeeping forces throughout Bosnia: a total of 7,000 soldiers and officers, only a fifth of what was considered necessary. Dutchbat, the Dutch UN battalion which succeeded the Canadians as the protectors of Srebrenica in February 1994, consisted of some 3–400 lightly armed soldiers, with only 150 trained combat troops.

The Bosnian government, too, ultimately withdrew its support from the enclave. In late April 1995, Naser Orić and his officers were transferred to Tuzla, supposedly to receive instructions in connection with the expected Serb attack. For whatever reason, Orić and his men never set foot in Srebrenica after that. From that moment, his paramilitary supporters were forced to do without his leadership.

On 11 July, 1995, therefore, the Serbian troops led by General Ratko Mladić were able to enter the city virtually unchallenged. Under the circumstances, and after these events, their advance was entirely predictable. What no one had foreseen, however, was the drama that followed: the Muslim men were separated from the women and children, a number of them were able to escape through the mountains, and the rest were never seen alive again. In a cold-storage warehouse near Tuzla, in more than 4,000 white bags, many of those murdered are still waiting to be identified.

Holbrookeland is a charming, mountainous area, with panoramas reminiscent of Switzerland or Austria. The higher parts of it are forested with pine, still higher up the greenery disappears beneath a heavy layer of snow. Then the first ruin looms up along the side of the road. The farmhouse looks as though God had stuck his thumb through the roof, all the way down to the cellar. A hundred metres further along is the second, half-incinerated ruin. Then a wrecked bus. Another two kilometres and there are only the skeletons of houses, scattered across the hillsides. Duško Tubić stops the car beside a muddy field. 'This is where the first mass graves were found, in summer 1996. But don't hang around too long, this area can still be rather bad for your health.' We drive past a dilapidated Dutch sentry post, then another wrecked car and a few hollow-eyed villas.

The former health resort of Srebrenica looks desolate. The department store has been boarded up, roofs have collapsed, the town square has buckled and is covered in weeds. In the stream you can still see the remains of the home-made electrical turbines from the starvation winter of 1993. On a wall beside the entrance to the former battery plant, in faded letters, 'Dutchba'. This is where the Dutch soldiers were quartered. Inside, on the walls, there is still some graffiti: 'A mustache? Smel like shit? Bosnian girl!'

At the moment, the building is inhabited chiefly by Serbs who have fled Sarajevo. These urban families have a hard time surviving amid these mountains. The café has been renamed 071, the area code for Sarajevo. The hospital received electricity again only two days ago. It had been without lights for three weeks, until the doctors and nurses finally paid the bill themselves. The medical supervisor: 'The economic situation in this city is disastrous. There are almost no jobs, everyone on my staff is underfed.' The manager of Hotel Guber – he saved the lives of a few Muslims – pleads for outside investments. 'Our image, that's what it's all about, and that will never be fixed.'

In the café, a few rowdy men are drinking slivovitz. I end up next to the owner of the battery factory. His father was buried recently, the plant is bankrupt, none of the machines are working. His words roll out slowly, drunkenly. 'Holland, ah, Holland, yes. They weren't bad, those Dutch. But so young. Just girls. Supposed to protect us. Made no difference. Waved goodbye to them. Thank you, all of you. So young . . .'

Meanwhile, enough books have been written about the Srebrenica debacle to fill three bookshelves. About the taking hostage of the almost 400 UN soldiers, even before the attack, including the 70 or so Dutchbatters who were very publicly shackled to bridges and other objects; a Serb media show that actually did not last much longer than the time the TV producers needed, but which had far-reaching consequences. About the extreme caution exercised by the UN after that, so as not to endanger these men any further. About the ensuing lack of air support, even after Srebrenica had been rolled over and Dutchbat found itself in an extremely precarious position. About the so-called 'blocking positions' that the Dutch soldiers had to assume on orders from the Hague, a thin cordon of 50 soldiers and 6 lightly armed armoured vehicles against 1,500 Serb infantrymen backed by tanks. About the inept Dutchbat commander Ton Karremans, who embarrassedly raised a glass with Ratko Mladić for Serbian television and, ten days later, still referred to the Serb general as 'a professional who knows his stuff'. About the party the Dutch Army top brass threw afterwards for the Dutchbatters.

When it was all over, the Dutch were accused of laziness and a lack of courage. French president Jacques Chirac felt that '*l'honneur de la nation*' of the Netherlands had been besmirched, and UN commander Bernard Janvier later told a French parliamentary investigative committee that things probably would have gone quite differently had French soldiers, rather than Dutch, been stationed at Srebrenica: 'In all honesty I can say that French soldiers would have fought, with all the risks that might have brought with it.'

But Janvier knew, better than anyone else, that his Dutch blue helmets had been in a hopeless position right from the start. That, after all, was precisely why there were no French troops in Srebrenica: no other country was willing to burn its fingers on the problem. Only the Dutch government was naïve enough for that.

Before me lie the Dutch newspapers of Monday, 24 July, 1995. 'A toast to freedom,' says the headline of the *Telegraaf*, above a photograph of twelve cheerful Dutch soldiers in Novi Sad, enjoying a post-hostageship meal with the compliments of the Serb government. Most of the other Dutchbatters were welcomed back to Zagreb by Crown Prince Willem-Alexander and Prime Minister Wim Kok. In its commentary, the paper writes: 'Their dedication shows once again how well equipped for its tasks the Dutch military is, when it comes right down to it.' 'For Dutchbatter, Serbs are now "the good guys"', reports NRC *Handelsblad*. Commander Karremans speaks of an 'excellently planned offensive' by the Serbs, who had 'outmanoeuvred' the Dutch battalion in 'spectacular' fashion.

In late 1995 — the courageous Catalan war correspondent Miguel Gil Moreno had meanwhile filmed dozens of corpses and mass graves, and Duško Tubić had already travelled with David Rhode of the *Christian Science Monitor* into the killing fields — Ton Karremans was promoted to the rank of colonel. A roll of film shot by a Dutch soldier, with photographs of the events in Srebrenica, had – uniquely in the history of military photography – been destroyed while it was being developed.

Anyone studying the role of the Netherlands in the Srebrenica affair cannot help but be struck by its unworldliness. Not only during the final events, but even from the start, when parliament and cabinet – with the overweening pride of an all-knowing Western country – light-heartedly plunged the nation into this Eastern European debacle. The Netherlands is not accustomed to power politics, and also has a long non-militarist tradition. No one seems to have thought beforehand about the possibility of some very ferocious fighting around Srebrenica, no one seems to have anticipated that the whole thing could end up in a spree of rape and murder. Here too one finds traces of the compromising spirit of the polder: Dutch blue helmets are known around the world as excellent peacekeepers, better than anyone else at bringing calm to a population – but they are not fighters. The documents released afterwards show that the Dutch gave the highest priority to getting their own troops out safely. In the directives from the Hague given to Commander Karremans on 13 July for his negotiations with Mladić, there is absolutely no mention of protecting refugees: the demands had only to do with Dutch personnel and Dutch material, and with the evacuation of the few locals who worked for the UN.

On 9 July, just before the fall of the enclave, when an American representative at NATO headquarters in Brussels proposed sending in air support for Srebrenica, the Dutch ambassador refused straightaway: to do that, he said, would be 'counterproductive' and 'dangerous'. In his memoirs, Richard Holbrooke remarks: 'The first line of opposition [to air strikes] was formed by the Dutch government, which refused even to consider air strikes until all its soldiers had been withdrawn from Bosnia . . . The Serbs knew that, and held hostage a considerable portion of the Dutch troops . . . until they had completed their dirty work in Srebrenica.'

On the morning of 11 July, when the definitive attack on Srebrenica began, NATO planes finally dropped a few bombs on Serb troops around Srebrenica: one tank was probably hit. On behalf of the Serbs, one of the Dutch officers being held hostage immediately phoned his commander: if the air strikes were not stopped immediately, the Serbs would not only shell the refugees and the Dutch compound, but would also kill their

Dutch hostages. Without any consultation with NATO or the high command of the UN peacekeeping forces, the Dutch defence minister, Joris Voorhoeve, then called the NATO base in Italy: 'Stop, stop, stop!'

The Dutch – with a few exceptions – therefore played a fairly uncourageous role at Srebrenica. The only question is whether, by that point, they could have done otherwise. After all, looked at in the cold, clear light of day, it would have been madness to send only 150 troops into a battle which 4–5,000 motivated and seasoned Muslim fighters no longer dared to enter. The Dutch government found itself trapped – partly by its own doing – in an almost unsolveable deadlock. The Dutch soldiers on the spot were desperate. Some of what happened was not pretty – the mentality was pronouncedly anti-Muslim, the Serbian troops were seen as fellow soldiers – but there is little else for which they can be blamed. During those last few days they helped hundreds of wounded people, and did their best to save what could still be saved.

Furthermore, at the moment itself no one knew what it would all lead to: a massacre the likes of which Europe had not seen since 1945. The testimony of Serb officers present at Srebrenica, given later at the Yugoslavia Tribunal, showed that it was only after the enclave was taken that they hit upon the idea of killing all the men, in order to avoid the bother of guarding prisoners or dealing with guerrilla fighters. The orders for the massacre were given by Ratko Mladić himself.

Many of the Muslims killed were not buried. When Dutch journalists Bart Rijs and Frank Westerman visited the area almost a year later, in May 1996, they found at least fifty skeletons, 'like monstrous marionettes', still wearing the clothes they had on, on a hillside close to the ruined Muslim village of Islamovici. The possessions of the murdered boys and men were still strewn out across the fields: 'a rucksack made of flour bags sewn together, a plastic water bottle, an empty wallet, a school ledger full of notes on home economics, a pile of stuck-together colour photos . . . an identity card with the number BH04439001, registered to Nermin Husejnovic, born 9 June, 1971, in Srebrenica'.

The three bookshelves full of reconstructions make one thing crystal clear: in summer 1995, all parties – with the exception of the local population – wanted to be shot of Srebrenica. No one was prepared to lift a finger to help. For the Serbs, it was a matter of prestige, an account to be settled, no matter the cost. The Dutch blue helmets wanted only one thing: to get home safely. The UN high command wanted nothing more than to put an end to the chaos surrounding the enclaves in eastern Bosnia. After the fall of Srebrenica – and, a little later, that of Žepa as well – their negotiators were finally able to draw up maps with clear and practicable lines of demarcation.

The average Bosnian saw Srebrenica as a stronghold of brave resistance, but the Bosnian army command saw things quite differently. Srebrenica had absolutely no strategic value, it was merely a fly in the ointment, it kept troops out of action that were sorely needed elsewhere and it interfered with the formation of clearly defensible front lines. That was almost certainly the background to the 'kidnapping' of Naser Orić and the other paramilitary leaders, and to the withdrawal of a great part of the Bosnian troops, leaving the town virtually undefended in summer 1995.

The fall of Srebrenica, in other words, came as a great relief even to the Bosnian strategists. But no one will ever hear about that.

Chapter Sixty-Six

Sarajevo

IT IS SNOWING ON THE HILLS OF BOSNIA. IT SNOWS ON THE OLD trenches around Sarajevo, the blasted trees, the SFOR cars patrolling Pale, the little road up to the newly built villa of Radovan Karadžić. I suggest that we drive past it. 'No,' Duško says grimly. 'That would really be very unwise.' At the entrance to the market sits the picturesque old woman who has appeared on every television screen in the world. 'So there you are again,' she shouts to Duško. 'You haven't forgotten what I say, have you? Radovan Karadžić is and will always remain our president!' She makes no bones about it: he is her hero, her liberator from the Muslims of today and the fascists of the past; for her all wars have melted into one, and she is willing to protect him with her life.

We wind our way carefully down the hill. The windscreen wipers sweep the snowflakes aside. On both sides of the border, taxis are huddling against the cold, thirty metres away from each other, strictly divided by descent and religion. No Serb taxi driver dares show his face in Sarajevo, no Muslim in Pale. Anyone who wants to go to the other side has to switch rides. In the middle of the pine forests, a desperate businessman from Belgrade asks us for directions to Sarajevo. The Serbs will only tell him the way to their Sarajevo, and that is Pale. The real city no longer exists for them.

The snow covers everything: the shiny, rebuilt shopping streets, the ruins of the newspaper building and the antique library, the packed apartments on the outskirts, the street corner along Apple Quay where Gavrilo Princip fired his shots in 1914, the dome and the flashing illuminated minaret of the new mosque, the rusting trams, the fields with their thousands of graves, the shell-blackened flats along the big road – nicknamed

Sniper Alley – to the airport. 'I always had to drive like mad along this road,' Duško says. 'If you stopped to take a picture, you were safe for three seconds. A sniper needs one to two seconds to spot you, and another three seconds to get you in his sights. With three seconds, you were always okay.'

The snow keeps falling. We have settled in at Pension 101 on Kasima Efendije Dobrace. The street was renamed recently, like others all over the city, this time after a Muslim cleric. The Gavrilo Princip Bridge no longer exists either, it has become the Latin Bridge again, just like before 1918. The other guests at the boarding house include two representatives of a German pump manufacturer, someone from the ING bank, a French camera crew and an Italian diplomat.

The next morning, the city is deathly quiet. The only sound that carries in the freezing air is the clatter of shovels, and now and then a voice. All of Sarajevo lies beneath a white layer at least a metre deep. Cars become stuck, some roads are blocked by fallen branches. Halfway through the morning the electricity goes out, an hour later it suddenly pops back on again. The airport is shut down tight. Everyone is jammed together in the little departure hall: aid workers, businessmen, journalists, tired Bosnians off to visit family in the West, American GIs with big duffel bags full of Christmas presents. I kill some time with Captain Gawlista and Sergeant Niebauer of the *Bundeswehr*; they've been down here for six months in the service of peace, and now they have precisely ten days' vacation, their wives and children are waiting for them in Frankfurt. A tour in these parts is no picnic, every snow cloud in the Balkans drops its load in this miserable valley. Then the electricity goes out again, but everyone remains in good spirits: Christmas will be here in three days, surely then this will all be over.

We are living in the aftermath of the fourth Yugoslav war. The television at the hotel shows endless relief convoys that have been stranded for days at the border, in the mountains of Macedonia. For reasons of some bureaucratic harassment or other, they are not being allowed to enter Kosovo. That was to have been my final destination as well. I still have people to meet in Skopje and Priština, but this snowstorm is making a complete mess of things. Instead I end up spending a melancholy afternoon at Café To Be or Not to Be, with Hrvoje Batinić, journalist, Sarajevo expert and professional pessimist. 'For me, pessimism is a way of life,' he claims. 'So whenever my expectations turn out wrong, I'm always pleased. During the siege, I felt great. Friends who came by would always say: "Batinić is a complete mystery. He's lost all his gloominess. It's as though he likes it!" But to feel free, all I had to do was look at the clouds. These days my depressions are back.'

He talks about the first year of the siege, and about the army unit in which he served: 'Serbs, Croatians, Muslims, there was no difference. We all saw ourselves as citizens of Sarajevo, normal people being attacked by madmen in the hills. But then, in September 1992, all the Serbs were kicked out of the Bosnian Army. That's when it started, that thinking along ethnic lines, even among us Muslims. And now we're right in the middle of it. Today there is only one thing to which no financial limitations apply: the building of mosques.'

According to Batinić, these are the days of the great game of peek-aboo. Bosnians of every party hide themselves in the crowd, behind a stronger and wealthier leader. 'During the election campaigns, no one talks about the normal issues any more, only about vague things like the "universal question" and the "nation". That keeps you from being account-able for anything. That way it's always the other guy.' Many of his fellow citizens still have no idea what has happened to them. 'Everyone's confused. At first, people blamed the war for all their problems. Now they're noticing that they've also lost all the economic security that socialism brought with it: jobs, health care, housing, education. Right now, unemployment here is at around seventy per cent.'

A legion of Western relief workers has descended on Sarajevo and the rest of Bosnia. They drive around pontifically in their expensive Land Cruisers, make calls to all over the world on their mobile phones, stay at the Holiday Inn to the tune of 350 marks a night. They are the heralds of wealthy Europe and America, the humanitarian activists and flashy 'nation builders', the media heroes hopping from one cause to the next. Batinić leans over and looks me straight in the eye. 'Tell me, Geert, honestly: what kind of people are you sending us anyway? The ones at the top are usually fine. But otherwise, with only a few excep-tions, the people I have to deal with are third-class adventurers who would probably have trouble finding a job in their own country.' It makes him furious. 'To them, we're some kind of aboriginals. They think they have to explain to us what a toilet is, what a television is, and how we should organise a school. The arrogance! They say Bosnians are lazy people, but it takes them a week to do a day's work. And you should hear them chattering away about it! At the same time, everyone sees how much money they spend on themselves and their position. They put three quarters of all their energy into that.'

We order another drink, and Batinić starts complaining about the corruption in Bosnia, the rise of religious leaders in the city, the enthusiastic discussions at the university about 'the Iranian model'. 'Sarajevo isn't Sarajevo any more. The city has filled with runaway farmers. Of the people who were here during the siege, maybe twenty per cent are left.'

Batinić's pessimism has had the upper hand again for some time now. 'When our children grow up,' he predicts, 'there's a great chance they'll be even more fanatical than the people who started this war. That thought is more than normal people can bear. We still remember how it was, the Yugoslavia of ten years ago, a normal European country. And look at it now. We lost everything we were good at, and we kept everything that was bad. Is it easy for you to look at yourself in the mirror? Do you dare to admit that you've ruined everything, even for your children and grandchildren? That kind of courage, that's what's missing here. But let me tell you: we've had the wars, and now nothing is moving any more, nothing changes, it's all just standing still!'

It's been snowing for days, and now a cold, heavy fog has blown in as well. No planes are leaving. At a certain point, though, you notice that it is something after all, just to quietly watch the snowflakes fall outside the window of the To Be or Not to Be.

Then suddenly, that same evening, I have the chance to get away. I catch a ride with Esad Mavrić through the winter night, to Split; don't ask me how he does it, but he does it. We go slipping into the mountains, weave around an avalanche, wait behind a bogged-down SFOR convoy. 'Now we're thirty-five kilometres from Sarajevo,' Esad says after three hours. It has stopped snowing.

Esad was once a civil engineer and championship sharpshooter, but that was in a past too distant to measure. He has two families to support. We talk about the siege, about what you could do with one plastic bottle full of water – make tea, brush your teeth, wash your shirt, even take your Sunday bath – and about the never-ending cold, about the thick pile of blankets under which you spent your days. 'I had the loveliest dreams back in those days, I've never had dreams like that since,' Esad sighs as he manoeuvres around a stranded bus. The moon is shining over the mountains. The villages are asleep beneath the thick layer of Balkan snow.

He talks about the secret tunnel, the lifeline to the free zone, and the smuggling that went on. Water was extremely precious. 'One time I saw an older man who had tapped too much water at the spring beside the brewery, two ten-litre jerry cans. They were so heavy that he couldn't move quickly any more. He was crossing a field and they got him right away. Two boys saw him go down. They took a gamble: one of them drew the sniper's fire, the other one risked his life by running to where the man lay, grabbing the jerry cans and then racing off. They left the man lying there.'

Esad reminds me of the statistics: of the 400,000 inhabitants of Sarajevo, 11,000 were killed during the siege, including more than 1,100 children.

Then suddenly we are out of the snow and approaching Mostar. Ruin after ruin looms up in the silvery night, one scorched and blasted housing block after the other. The river thunders past the world-famous remains of the sixteenth-century bridge. How lovely it must have been once, how impressive, how powerfully built. Those who blew that ancient span to rubble – and that must have been quite a chore – knew what they were doing: they were breaking down what had been built up. It is the same mentality which lay behind the destruction of Dubrovnik and the famous library at Sarajevo. 'It was the farmers getting back at the city,' Esad mumbles. 'That's what happened everywhere during these wars. It was maybe even the heart of the matter.'

The next morning there is the warm sun on the quayside in Split, the sparkling sea, the hissing of the waves rolling in from Italy. And that evening, as though it were the most normal thing in the world, I find myself wandering around the Christmas market in Strasbourg again. African men are selling socks with little coloured lights on them. A busker is singing Yiddish songs. Turkish boys are sweeping the streets. For a handful of francs, a travel agency is offering a weekend in New York. The Alsatian gingerbread smells of Christmas, 1900.

Epilogue

'THE RHINE IS A MAN', HEINRICH BÖLL WROTE. THE NAME IS CELTIC, the cities along its banks are Roman, the voices are French, German, Dutch, the bridges are American, the castles are Germanic and dead. The Rhine is also Europe.

If you wish to do justice to Mr. Rhine, Böll said, you must imagine that he has dried up, that he no longer exists. Cologne would be a dull market town for cattle and produce. A few historical remains would be found in the dry river bed: a great many medals and insignias, a bust of Hitler that people would mistake for some strange river deity, a tank that ran off the bridge at Remagen in 1945. The Rhine has swallowed it all graciously.

Now I am cruising along that man, through Europe and through history, out of the twentieth century. The ship is called the *Marla*, the pride of the Danser Container Line, 110 metres long, built in 1999. One hundred and fourteen containers are piled high on the deck in front of us. They contain car parts and electronics, and the belongings of a Swiss man who is being transferred to Japan. The pilothouse seems like a cross between an office and a cockpit. The ship's helm has withered into a simple metal knob. The radio crackles and sings all day.

The newspaper and I had come up with the idea of a boat trip down the Rhine, as a fitting final chord to those three hundred daily travel cameos on the front page. Arrangements had been made, therefore, for me to cover the last few hundred kilometres of my journey aboard the *Marla* from Strasbourg.

A deckful of containers first had to be unloaded and loaded, but now we are sailing calmly downstream. In the twilight, the illuminated living room of a Rhine barge from the town of Thoolen goes gliding by; in its pilothouse the captain's wife is busy decorating a Christmas tree. 'Oh, those are the Kortes!' We ourselves have a few Nativity stars and an electric Christmas tree, always good for a little holiday ambience. A cigarette between his lips, Captain Dinus Jasper maneuvers his way into the locks, one eye on the monitors at his feet. Later the moon appears, and the river glistens.

Captain Jasper sails by the dots and lines on the colour radar screen. In the darkened pilothouse we begin to talk about our families, what became of them, my grandfather as sailmaker, his as peat-barge captain. 'My grandfather was born in 1893, my father in 1928', Jasper says. 'A deckhouse full of children, all wooden ships, everything still went by sail.

'Waking up at one in the morning, hey, the wind has come up, we're off! My father even worked towing the barges for a while, with a huge Belgian workhorse, pulling sailboats along. I was born in 1958 aboard the *Risico*, a motorized barge, one hundred and sixteen tons. Around 1961 my father bought a hundred-and-fifty-ton boat. That was really gigantic at the time'.

Close to Karlsruhe, Heini, a grey-haired river pilot, clambers on board. He speaks a mixture of German and Dutch, the old language of the itinerant merchants and field hands, the language of the river as well. Heini is an old friend, and because it's Christmas he has a big pie with him; his wife baked it herself. We're moving along on what they call the 'Advent flood', a high surge of river water that usually starts in Basel in December and rolls its way down to the North Sea. The men of the *Marla* are busy calculating whether they'll clear the bridges; meanwhile Heini pilots the ship calmly through the red dots on the radar. A cluster of rocks pops up on one side, the current pushes us sideways, we avoid it all by inches. But Heini and Dinus know exactly what they're doing, long generations of captain's blood run through their veins.

'My father couldn't stand sailing in the fog like this', Dinus says. 'My goodness, he hated that. In 1983 we bought a big, modern ship, with radar and everything, so we could sail night and day. My brother and I didn't mind, but my father would pace around the pilothouse. Sailing a ship without being able to see a thing, that went against his nature.'

'We had captains like that, too', Heini murmurs.

'It didn't take him long to retire', Dinus says.

He lowers the pilothouse for the bridge, we can barely see above the containers. 'And what about your grandfather?' I ask.

'I think he'd be lost these days'. The current in the Rhine is so powerful that the *Marla* rolls seaward almost of its own accord, we go gliding through the darkness like a Batavian canoe. The next morning the crew breakfasts at six. Junior seaman Jeroen introduces me to unheard-of combinations: bologna sandwiches smothered in tomato ketchup, vanilla pudding with a thick layer of chocolate sprinkles. Close to the Lorelei daylight arrives, misty and grey as lead. The hotels, hills and caverns of the old Heimat cult pass by on the right, at the Deutsches Ecke in Koblenz, where the Moselle meets the Rhine, Kaiser Wilhelm I sits on his steed, looking out over the river. At Leutesdorf the quays are flooded, outside Remagen, you can still see the ruins of the Ludendorff Bridge.

There isn't a lot to do, the pilothouse feels homey. The boys seem excited as puppies. Jeroen is trying to earn his Rhine diploma and wants to learn the names of all the villages and towns along the river by heart. Ton, the visiting captain, teaches cabin boy Anthony a new knot. The river dispatch on Channel 18 reports that a red buoy is floating loose in the channel. 'Be careful, and happy holidays!'

In the wee hours of morning, we approach Dordrecht. It's busy on the old Maas, the radar screen is filled with moving inkspots, all *Eben Haëzers*, *Marias* and *Op Hoop van Zegens* trying to get home for New Year's. The lights in the darkness no longer come from the moon and stars, but from buildings, roads, refineries. We go sailing into a slumbering land of cities. Dinus takes a look at the unloading plan on his computer monitors, passes it along to the terminal. The rain clatters against the windows. At seven o'clock the Dutch radio awakens. There is something about tax cuts for doctors and a rebellious broadcasting organization, an MP is angry, an old man has died. Then the retrospection cuts loose, a look back at the year gone by, the century: every commonplace is weighed anew, every stone is turned. This would be impossible anywhere else in Europe. There, repression of the past is a necessity if you don't want to go mad with guilt, rage or misery. A blessed country this, to have such current-affairs programs.

When the *Marla* finally reaches a remote quay in the Botlek, an unbelievable scene unfolds: huge virtual claws pick out containers, hook them to cranes, send cargo carriers scuttling around, pile, sort. There is not a single soul in sight on the gigantic loading dock.

In the pilothouse, the boys are talking about the New Year's lottery and what they'll do when they become millionaires in the next century. They'll buy houses and cars and treat their family to every conceivable luxury, you bet. On shore, the processing continues, it's a wonder, and we, this lonely little clump of human flesh, can only look on.

I wrote the final lines of this book in the autumn of 2003, and ran through it all again in the summer of 2007. It was only six and a half years ago that *De Telegraaf*, the Netherlands' highest-circulation newspaper, crowed: 'We're rolling in it! Party-going Holland smothered in luxury'. The champagne was no longer sold by the bottle but by the crate, the Dutch were dressing 'chicly and eccentrically" for the party, and the traditional New Year's Eve beignet was steadily losing ground to 'exclusive delicatessen products'. When I came home from my travels, everyone was talking about a television series in which one could follow, around the clock, the activities of a group of young people who had been locked up together in a house for three months, with no contact with the outside world. What the viewers saw was, above all, themselves: people hanging around in boredom on the couch, in the kitchen or the bedroom. No other television series had ever been received with such enthusiasm. A young man by the name of Bart, from the town of Roelofarendsveen, won the contest and became the nation's sweetheart.

And a great deal has happened since. Kosovo has once again become a forgotten corner of the globe, and these days we can hardly find Bosnia on the map. Slobodan Milošević died in a prison cell in the Hague during his trial before the International Court of Justice. What we talk about now is 9/11, about the terrorists and the European Constitution, and about Iraq, America and the international rule of law.

The climate kept changing. In 2007 alone, most European countries experienced the warmest month of April ever, England and Wales had the wettest May in human memory and south-eastern Europe saw a record-breaking heat wave in June and July. Meanwhile, the euro has grown up, become a currency more sought-after than the dollar, even among oil sheikhs and Colombian cocaine barons.

With the success of the Union, Europe's attractiveness continued to increase as well. One quarter of the population of Amsterdam's city centre now consists of 'expats'. In London, English is no longer the mother tongue of one in three children. Immigration and integration – necessary in themselves for the vitality of the continent – are increasingly coming to be seen as hindrances. The problems surrounding certain groups of newcomers have in this way become a European issue – although the symptoms are different from one country to the next. With this, the chances increase that a permanent underclass will arise which, for whatever reason, will be unable to take advantage of the upward social mobility offered by European prosperity. In this way, the global divide between rich and poor can slowly grow into fault lines that will tear apart European cities and regions. The attacks on New York and Washington in September 2001, Bali in October 2002, the bombings in Madrid in March 2004, the murder of controversial filmmaker Theo van Gogh in Amsterdam in November 2004, the bloodbath in London in July 2005: all these expressions of religious extremism have had their effect on the political climate. In some countries, politicians and others have wondered aloud about the extent to which Muslim immigrants in particular have been integrated into society, and in some circles, the phenomenon of immigration itself has become a bone of contention: 'Own People First!'

At the same time, unrest has grown among Europe's seventeen million Muslims. Are we still welcome? Do we truly belong? In this way, Europe has in recent years become the unwilling front line in a conflict that must ultimately be fought out within Islam itself, a conflict concerning how such a traditional world religion must deal with secularisation, globalisation, individual liberties, women's rights and all the rest that goes with a modern society.

The concept of the unilateral 'humanitarian intervention', so popular at the time of the Kosovo conflict, was short-lived. After the American debacle in Iraq, it seemed to fade away completely. In the Balkans the circus of international aid workers is largely gone. The biggest war criminals, Ratko Mladić and Radovan Karadžić, are still free men. The bombed bridges of Novi Sad were pulled carefully out of the river by the Dutch titans of the Mammoet salvage concern. Summer 2000 was a hot one. Little Gypsy boys, dangling their feet in the water, watch from the broken blocks of concrete, dreaming of far away lands. Meanwhile, the city has filled with the new homeless: the tens of thousands of refugees who, after years in the West, have been sent back to Serbia. The youngest among them do not even speak the language, the older children have experienced an orderly life as pupils at schools in Germany or the Netherlands. There is no work or housing for any of them. In Sarajevo, the sixteenth-century Begova Dzamija mosque has meanwhile been 'renovated' with piles of Saudi cash: antique decorative tiles have been removed, ornaments have disappeared, the walls have – in true Arab fashion – been covered in white plaster. Serbia is back in the picture as well: in May 2007 the country won the Eurovision Song Contest, due in no little part to votes from Bosnia, Croatia, Macedonia, Montenegro and Slovenia. Bosnia has counted its dead: 97,207. China, these days, rules over the exchange rate of the dollar. And Russia, contrary to expectations, has not thrown itself into the arms of the family of European democratic countries. Yeltsin's successor, Vladimir Putin, invested the office of president with unparalleled privileges. With the help of massive energy revenues, he was able to give the country a new pride and self-confidence. At the same time, the parliament there has been hobbled, Russian television is under state control, the press has been muzzled and the Kremlin keeps the captains of trade and industry on a short leash. It would seem that Russia has abandoned its former imperial ambitions, yet it remains a powerful factor in European politics. By almost turning off the energy tap a few times, it made clear to all Europeans exactly where the power and the dependency lie: with oil and natural gas. With that same renewed self-awareness, Russia has also obstructed Kosovo's autonomy, and does its best to make Poland and the Baltic States toe the line.

No, Europe is no longer the friend it was ten years ago. A submarine has planted the Russian flag on the seabottom beneath the North Pole: a new territorial claim has been staked out. According to the Russian edition of *Forbes*, there are now more billionaires living in Moscow than in New York. Aeroflot has tried to take over Alitalia. Which does nothing, by the way, to detract from the fact that the Russian airlines are still considered among the most dangerous in the world, that half of all

Russian pensioners must still live on starvation-level benefits and that the country's death surplus is so high that within the next fifty years the Russian population will shrink from 145 to 110 million.

On 1 May, 2004, the European Union was expanded by no fewer than ten new members: Poland, Estonia, Latvia, Lithuania, the Czech Republic, Slovakia, Hungary, Malta and Cyprus. In one enormous leap the population of the EU suddenly rose to more than 450 million. On 1 January, 2007, Bulgaria and Rumania were added as well. Amid all the haste, however – the 'political gesture' played an overwhelming role in this mass accession – an enormous faux pas was made: the island of Cyprus was admitted even though, contrary to all commitments made, the perennial conflict between the Greek and Turkish Cypriots had not yet been solved. In this way, the Union inadvertently became a partner in that conflict, thereby further muddying the already murky negotiations with Turkey. The talks that had started in October 2005 had already come to a halt in 2006, following fundamental differences of opinion concerning the island. Yet unity was nowhere to be found. The leaders of some member states still saw the EU as a source of peace and stability, particularly in the long term. Others were attracted primarily by the market. Others still were drawn by the huge funding distributed by Brussels. For the new members from the former Eastern Bloc, the EU was above all the best way to escape the former Soviet Union's sphere of influence, and to make the definitive step to the West. They were not at all interested in the kind of European super-state that inhabited the dreams of the French, the Germans and the Italians in particular, with the euro and a new constitution as its most important symbols. They, after all, had only recently recovered their freedom as nations. For them, the British, Polish and Scandinavian model – one in which the EU was seen more as a free economic zone, managed by arrangement between the various member states – was more attractive than a distinct, cohesive political identity. On 17 June of the same year, 2004, the first summit meeting of that new Union immediately ran aground: the twenty-five members could barely agree on a new leader. In an atmosphere grimmer than any experienced before, the Portuguese José Manuel Barroso was chosen at last.

Barroso immediately took the opportunity to state that he was not allied with any of those 'naïve federalists'. With that, the feud between the 'federalists' and the 'intergovernmentalists' had, in fact, been settled. Outside, as usual, demonstrations were held by tens of thousands of people to whom no one listened.

One year later, the slumbering unrest erupted. In a referendum held on 29 May, 2005, a majority of French voters rejected the proposed European 'constitution' – which was, in fact, more a package of existing treaties, supplemented by a number of hardly controversial improvements in the fields of administration and democratic procedure. Two days later, on 1 June, the Netherlands followed suit with a resounding 'no'. To add insult to injury, the European summit held barely two weeks later was also a fiasco. Even when it came to budgetary matters, the differences proved almost irreconcilable.

Now it was no longer the small, new or somewhat marginal member states that were causing the problems. No, the core of this profound constitutional and financial crisis lay with the traditional member states, the founding members themselves. Two years later, at the Euro summit held on 21–24 June, 2007, a new treaty served to contain the damage somewhat, but the old solidarity seemed to have run its course. The prime minister of Luxembourg and temporary president of the European Commission, Jean-Claude Juncker, warned that – now that the memories of the Second World War were fading – there was not much time left for the current generation of political leaders to develop a sound structure for the EU. 'I don't think the generation after us will be able to put together all those national biographies in such a way that the EU will not be split back into its national components – with all the dangers that entails'. The cover of The Economist showed the corpse of the French revolutionary Marat in his bath, murdered by citoyenne Charlotte Corday: 'The Europe that died. And the one to save'.

I leaf again through the 1906 edition of Bellamy's Christmas in the Year 2000: 'Workers' issues. Solved in the year 2000 . . . Bankers no longer necessary under new arrangement . . . Dickens, the most popular author of the year 2000 . . . Prisons now obsolete . . . Music, public concerts transmitted by telephone . . . War, done away with in the year 2000'. And, concerning Europe: 'The major European countries, along with

Australia, Mexico and parts of South America, have an industrial structure based on the model established by the United States. Peaceful relations between these peoples is assured by means of an ad hoc league of states stretching out all over the world'.

What really *has* happened in and around that once so auspicious year 2000? Some elements of Bellamy's utopia have actually been realised and more. European unification was – and is – above all a unique peace process. From Charlemagne to Adolf Hitler, leaders have tried to create a Europe unified as one people under one ruler. This time, however, the United Europe was a joint construct, and that changed everything. It brought to the heart of the continent – particularly to the two, eternal antipoles of France and Germany – a stability that had been lacking for centuries. In the last sixty years there have been no more wars throughout most of Europe, a situation unparalleled in history.

It was, at the same time, an unparalleled movement with regard to democratisation and human rights. During the last half-century, the Council of Europe, set up in 1949, developed into a pan-European organisation in this regard. The greatest success is the European Court of Human Rights in Strasbourg. There, citizens can file actions directly against their state – unique in the annals of international law – for violations of human rights. And often enough, their claims are honoured. The Court's authority is enormous: its verdicts are legally binding, resonate throughout the legal systems of all affiliated states, and no one would dream of ignoring them.

In addition, the unification was also the most important European process of modernisation since the Napoleonic regime in the early nineteenth century. At this moment, the EU comprises the largest economy in the world. Europeans feel the advantages of that, if only in their pocketbooks: the average European citizen earns on the average about ten per cent more than he would without the unification. (According to the Social and Cultural Planning Agency and the Central Planning Agency in the Netherlands, the average working Dutchman benefits to the tune of about 3,000 euros yearly.) With the introduction of the euro, member states have finally been forced to put their own economic households in order. Thanks in part to the European markets, Italy has grown in the course of fifty years from an impoverished land into a prosperous nation.

Something similar is taking place in Ireland: employment there has doubled in the last fifteen years, unemployment has almost disappeared, and for the first time in human memory the Irish are not emigrating to the United States, but are returning from there to their mother country. Within a single generation, Spain, with the help of a great many European facilities, has been transformed from an infirm dictatorship into a reasonably modern country. In this regard, the latest expansion of the Union's membership has also been extremely successful: the economies of most of the new member states are growing faster than expected.

The European experiment is being watched carefully from other parts of the world. Although, in comparison with the EU, organizations such as ASEAN (Association of Southeast Asian Nations), the South American Mercosur (Mercado Común del Sur) and the African Union are only taking their first steps, their programmes follow the same lead. The same applies to the North American Free Trade Agreement (NAFTA). Europe still cannot hold a candle to the dynamism, flexibility and energy of American society, but when it comes to quality of life the average citizen of the Old World – particularly its western regions – has quietly left his American cousin in the dust. Average life expectancy in Europe is longer, there is less poverty, daily life is safer, there is considerably more leisure and holiday time for all, one can – at least for the time being – retire much earlier, social security facilities are often more generous and, even in Slovenia, the infant mortality rate is lower. And with regard to modernisation of the infrastructure: today, in 2007, a high-speed train begins its trip between Paris and Lyon – lasting a little less than two hours – almost every thirty minutes, and nobody finds that remarkable. The one daily Amtrak service between San Francisco and Los Angeles, a comparable distance between comparable population concentrations, takes almost a full day, and plans for a high-speed line are no more than doodles on the drawing board.

America is, in short, no longer Europe's shining example, not by any means. Almost unnoticed, we on this continent have taken a road completely our own. 'Europe', writes the American social-economic publicist Jeremy Rifkin, 'had become a huge laboratory for rethinking humanity's future. In many respects, the European Dream is the mirror opposite of the American Dream. While the American Dream emphasises unrestrained economic growth, personal wealth and the pursuit of individual self-interest, the European Dream focuses more on sustainable development, quality of life and the nurturing of community'.

No one foresaw the current EU. Who would have dared to predict in 1953 – the year in which Stalin died, in which George Marshall and Albert Schweitzer received the Nobel Prize for Peace, in which Princess Elizabeth became Queen Elizabeth II, the year in which the East Germans rebelled and the Dutch-Belgian border was the scene of a fierce manhunt for butter smugglers – who would have dared to predict that half a century later there would be an EU of twenty-seven members, with its own currency and its own parliament, a free space with largely open internal borders, that would stretch from Ireland by way of a united Germany to the very borders of chaotic Russia? And, by the same token: who would have dared to predict in 1953 that diverse feelings of national pride and unity would play such an important role in European politics at the start of the twenty-first century?

After their introduction, French writer Régis Debray referred to the new euro banknotes as 'play money', printed for a virtual community known as 'Euroland'. It is, indeed, anything but the coinage of a political union with a sense of what it is and where it wants to go. For too long, European unification was a technocratic project set up by idealistic pioneers and soon taken over by businessmen, bureaucrats and government leaders, with only the occasional starry-eyed statesman to shake things up again. The new European cooperative venture was, in that way, largely a top-down affair. From the very start, the common market was a major goal. And in the long term, of course, many European entrepreneurs would be lost if Europe did not develop into a single, huge, common domestic market. But the creation of a free European market has increasingly edged out the original objective, which is to provide a structure for peace.

The European project was and is closely interwoven with the phenomenon of globalisation. As early as 1919, the economist John Maynard Keynes described how a person in London, drinking his morning cup of tea in bed, could order almost any product in the world, in the certainty that it would be delivered to his doorstep as quickly as possible. That international interweaving has since developed to what a person of that day would have considered unbelievable proportions. According to some, the EU played – and continues to play – a major role in curbing and controlling these chaotic international networks and concentrations of power. In the eyes of others, however, the EU is very much an expression of the kind of globalisation against which increasing protest has arisen since the turn of this latest century; a globalisation driven by the nigh-religious belief that 'the market' is a panacea, that burgeoning international trade will ultimately work for the good of all, that poverty and tyranny will duly vanish of their own accord, that economic figures determine everything, that privatisation always has a beneficial effect, that competition is always best, that within these global systems the nation states will ultimately become obsolete. It is the philosophy of most political elites, but many citizens – even the majority in any number of European countries – don't believe in it at all.

It is precisely this credibility gap which, as opinion polls showed, played such an important role in the rejection of the European Constitution by the French and the Dutch. It is not European unification itself which they rejected, but the way in which the project has been given form and continually expanded, until it has become so vague that they can no longer identify with it. For them, Europe meant the lifting of the bell jars under which each European nation had lived for centuries. It meant the dissipation of sources of conflict, the opening of markets and cultures, the freedom to go where you wish. But it also meant the abandonment of the national context within which the culture, economy, legal system and democracy had developed for centuries. For these voters-in-protest, borders did, sometimes, have a positive function: as the delimitation of their familiar, predictable, influenceable, safe world.

Those same European pioneers, therefore, underestimated just how important such feelings of national cohesion can be, particularly in times of great change and turbulence. Or, better said, the way in which the rise of guarantor states after the war would provide a completely new basis for national sentiment. For, in addition to the old national ties of language, culture, economic and military power, the 1950s saw burgeoning welfare arrangements that elicited a new brand of nationalism. Each land developed its own 'legacies', valuable claims that no one wanted to surrender – and preferably not share with foreigners: ample pension facilities, good health care, generous disability benefits.

In this way, a complicated situation arose. Max Kohnstamm, one of the last living pioneers, put it this way during one of our conversations: 'The market is a merciless god. Its counterpoint, compassion, cannot be based entirely on charity; if it hopes to remain durable, it must be based on rules of law. The market these days is regulated on a European scale, but the compassion is organised largely at the national level. And it is apparently very difficult indeed to raise that compassion to a European level, because, traditionally, it differs so widely from one country to the next'. When it comes to communal social regulations, therefore, that single Europe still seems far away – and it may never arrive at all.

Much more complicated was the political manoeuvring surrounding the expansion of the Union. For the Germans, whose country has more neighbours than any other European nation, the expansion was vital. Only in that way, after all, could peace and stability in that corner of Europe be guaranteed for future generations. The British saw in the newcomers, above all, a group of new allies. The Central and Eastern Europeans were never in favour of a strong federal Union and, after long years under communism, were dead opposed to excessive market regulation. The French had no choice: they realised that their 'baby', the European Union, was very much taking on a life of its own, but at the same time they could not, morally, permit themselves to use their veto against expansion. In desperation, therefore, they voted for 'le beau geste'.

'The community we have created is not a goal in itself', Jean Monnet wrote at the end of his memoirs in 1978. 'The community is merely a step towards the organised world of tomorrow'. That prediction has, in part, come true: the European experiment has indeed proven to be an inspiring example to other parts of the world. Yet in many ways, exactly the opposite has happened: the European Community often acts as a fortress, as a hermetic trading bloc with which to obstruct and frustrate the emergence of poorer countries.

In the course of this half century, the political mood within the EU has greatly changed. The democratic clarity of the first years has disappeared. The mediating power of the political parties has been weakened.

With the rejection of the constitution, the ideal of the European federation could be stowed away. Potential new members are received without
much enthusiasm. The tone is no longer set by the community itself, but
by divergent national interests, and by a million and one intergovernmental issues. The chance that a 'two-speed Europe' will arise, a wealthy
Euro-bloc with a series of poorer satellite states, is clear and present. At
the same time, the EU remains the most successful experiment in the
field of international political institutions since the Second World War.
The Union constitutes the largest market on earth. It is the largest exporter
and the largest foreign investor. It is home to many of the world's largest
and most successful concerns. The introduction of the euro went swimmingly, the expansion of the Union was a textbook example of successful
'soft power': never had so few means been required to so greatly promote
democracy, prosperity and stability throughout such a large part of Europe.
The pioneers present at the outset of the European Community were
brought together by a common fate. All six countries had, in one way
or another, made it through the war, all those who participated in the
negotiations had experienced enormous chaos and destruction. The solutions they came up with in the space of those fifty years were designed
for that little group of six countries, small and surveyable. But with
twenty-five countries now taking part, the EU can no longer be run in
that fashion. The right to veto of five hundred thousand Greek Cypriots,
for example, can forever frustrate the negotiations for the admission to
the Union of sixty-five million Turks. If only for that reason, a new organisational foundation – be it in the form of a new kind of constitution
or a new Treaty of Rome – is sorely needed.

The foundations upon which the EU is built are now increasingly a
part of the daily reality of each citizen. It is no longer the pioneers, the
statesmen and the nations that shore up the Union, it is above all that
immense warp and weft of businesses, cities and people, that slowly
developed, self-evident European existence, that will have to weather the
storm. Everything has changed and the organisation has grown too slowly
to accommodate it, that is the major problem at this point. And the feeling
of solidarity that existed in those early days, that is gone as well. During
my travels I saw, by chance, a remarkable TV commercial for the British
Conservative Party. As far as I remember, it went like this. Two prosperous

thirty-somethings appeared on the screen. It was morning, she was sitting on the edge of the bed, he in the bathroom, shaving. Talk between the two gradually turned to Europe. He saw no problem in it, to him Europe meant the Tuscan sun, a Mercedes, Dutch cheese. His wife protested: but what about the euro, and all that bureaucracy in Brussels? He began having doubts of his own, and finally she was able to convince him. At the end, the couple tumbled back into their cosy bed. The punch line was: 'In Europe, not run by Europe'.

Just as European leaders and bureaucrats have sometimes neglected the reasonable need for national cohesion, this commercial showed how many Europeans go to the other extreme: the almost fearful brush-off given to all the international and European ties that have slowly come to form the basis of our daily lives.

Telling in this regard is the marginal interest shown in the European parliament: the average turnout fell from sixty-three per cent during the first elections in 1979 to forty-four per cent at the most recent polls. The rejection of the constitution, on the other hand, was strikingly clear and powerful. During the last European parliamentary elections, only thirty-nine per cent of the Dutch voting public went to the polls, while the referendum drew sixty-three per cent. In France, the discrepancy was even more striking: forty-three as opposed to seventy per cent. Surveys in Germany, Denmark, Britain and other countries indicated a similar mood. This was no longer a crisis of confidence amongst national governments, but a fundamental rift between European citizens and their political leaders. The European project is faced, in other words, with a gigantic legitimacy crisis. That hiatus is due in large part to the vagueness and limitlessness of the European project. Limitlessness in the most literal sense: where, after all, does Europe end? It is no coincidence that the physical limits of the current European Union – with the exception of Switzerland, Norway and Greece – largely coincide with the scope of Catholic Christianity in the Middle Ages. To a monk in the year 1006, the map of the European empire of 2006 would look rather familiar. But what if the expansion of the EU were to simply continue, what if expansion were to become an independent trait of the European project, like a bicycle that must keep rolling if it is not to fall over? Would it not eventually become something completely unrecognisable to the citizens of the original member states? And, besides that: would the Union not be running the risk of a European variation on 'imperial overstretch?' Might not an all-too-rapid modernisation and democratisation in certain regions – the Balkans, Turkey – unleash uncontrollable forces? And might not the Union itself in that way become too unstable?

In addition, there is, for the average citizen, that other form of limit-lessness: the 'Brussels bureaucracy'. Despite what is often claimed, it is not the size of the apparatus that is the problem: the Union is run by fewer than 17,000 civil servants, half of whom are engaged only in trans-lation work. In a city like Amsterdam, for example, the body of civil servants is one and a half times that size. The quality of the Union's appa-ratus is generally quite high. The problem is found in the enormous quantity of regulations spread by the EU – due often enough, by the way, to the fact that all manner of national 'fixers' are pleased to take cover under the wings of 'Europe'. The total of some 80,000 pages of Union directives could fill a bookcase, their limitlessness extends from the prescribed thickness of bicycle tires and the length of window washers' ladders to the composition of chocolate bars and the methods for making goats' cheese. I strolled about the Saturday street market in Dieppe, one huge celebration of fruit, vegetables, farmhouse cheeses, homemade sausages and other local delicacies. Still, a large proportion of the wares on that market were – and are – illegal: stringent EU directives would ban the sales of many of these farm products. At the moment that poses a problem for the farmers and market-goers around Dieppe. But in the long run, this unreal situation is mostly a problem for the European Union itself, for its workability, its legitimacy and its ability to inspire confidence: even for its survival.

Europe is no longer a network of separate nations but is gradually becoming one huge interwoven body of companies, cities and people, a new super-country beside and above the traditional nation states. This situation definitely does not always work to our advantage, it sometimes creates huge problems, more than half of all Europeans are unhappy with it, but it is not something we can simply choose to ignore. Soon every European country will be able to arrest the subjects of all other European countries, the new pan-European arrest warrant will abolish national forms of legal protection, and meanwhile the values have been turned upside down: it will, after all, not be the best national systems of law that establish the European norm, but the weakest among them. The same thing is happening to democracy. For no matter how you look at it, in a country where hundreds of thousands of demonstrators take to the streets every time their leaders meet, there is something fundamentally wrong with the democratic system. The same applies to the EU.

The new constitution drafted so laboriously in recent years may be an improvement for the EU itself; in comparison with the constitutions and democratic systems of many of its member states, however, it often amounts to nothing more than a return to the way things were before 1848, when the national parliaments still had to fight for most of their powers. Furthermore, there is no guarantee that this cautious, formal democracy will assume sufficient critical mass within Europe. The demo-cratic tradition has been limited largely to the continent's north-western corner: Scandinavia, Belgium and the Netherlands, England and France. Right after the collapse of the great monarchies in 1917 and 1918, the rest of Europe also embraced the loveliest democratic constitutions with the most liberal basic rights, but that honeymoon did not last long. Political conflicts had a way of degenerating into civil wars, and the elite in many countries chose anti-communism first, and only afterwards democracy and the rule of law. In Hungary, Italy, Spain, Portugal, Poland, Greece and Rumania, power was quickly seized by generals and populist dictators, and this finally happened in powerful Germany as well. After the war, the communist parties imposed their authoritarian policies all over Central and Eastern Europe, while Southern Europe, with the excep-tion of Italy, was run until the 1970s by ultra-right-wing dictatorships.

In large parts of Europe, unlike in the United States, democracy is therefore a fairly recent phenomenon and hardly to be taken for granted. There is also the bureaucracy. In the United States, most of the obvious federal tasks – defence, foreign policy – rest immediately and clearly with the federal government, while the states have far-reaching autonomy on all other matters. California's environmental policy is very different from that in Texas, and there is no reason why the bread in Vermont should taste the same as that in Arkansas.

In Europe, the exact opposite is the case. Here, in recent decades, a dangerously skewed development has taken place: a plethora of regulations has arisen regarding precisely such matters of detail, while cooperation on obviously communal issues – common defence policies, a unified foreign policy – is still, after all these years, in a pristine state at best. It is precisely the groundwork of a federal government – budgetary legislation, foreign policy and military organisation – that is still in the hands of the national states within the EU. Although the Union has access to a reasonably large budget, it pales by comparison with the combined budgets of the national states. There is work in progress on a quickly deployable European army corps, the old plan for a European Defence Community is being revived under the auspices of the European Security and Defence Policy (ESDP), but the forging of national armies into a single military force with global aspirations is still, for the time being, unthinkable. This imbalance as well, clear for all to see, permanently chips away at the authority of the Union. The tragic thing about Europe, as other observers have noted, has to do with the fact that those very measures needed to survive in the long term – the influx of young immigrants to reverse the demographic trend towards ageing, reorganization of the welfare states to strengthen Europe's competitive position with regard to other continents, open dealings with the Muslim World, good stewardship with regard to raw materials and the environment, the further strengthening and de-nationalisation of Europe's military forces – are, at the same time, often grist to the mill of paranoid populist movements. The times, at least at the moment, are in their favour. 'You people have no idea how many people are waiting in the wings until all those European promises fail to pan out', said film director Želimir Zilnić in 1999. 'Things seem to be going well, but there are also disillusioned people falling by the wayside everywhere, humiliated men, frightened women, angry farmers'. His predictions came true.

Nationalism has made a major comeback on the stage of European political fashion. In Portugal, former dictator António Salazar was voted the greatest Portuguese of all time. In the Netherlands in 2002, the same honour was given to the assassinated right-wing politician Pim Fortuyn – Baruch de Spinoza never made it past twenty-first place. The prime minister of the Czech Republic spoke of the collective campaign promises of his opponents as an 'Auschwitz myth'. The ruling coalition in Poland today includes the ultra-right wing, homophobic and anti-Semitic 'League of Polish Families'. That party's foreman, currently minister of education, would like to see the works of Kafka, Dostoyevsky and Goethe removed from school curricula. There are also purges in the offing: this same government wants to look into the antecedents of more than 700,000 Poles, to see whether they had connections with the secret police before 1989. In the words of former dissident Bronislaw Geremek, this amounts to the creation of 'a new Ministry of Truth and a new brain police'. The European project is a unique one in history. It is not an empire, it is not a federation, it is something all its own, just as new and unprecedented as the Republic of the Seven United Netherlands was in the seventeenth century. And it will require a great deal of time: such integration processes are not to be thought of in terms of years, but of generations. History, however, also shows us that such projects are not doomed.

In the nineteenth century, a large part of the French population spoke no French at all, and the fact that they were Frenchmen and Frenchwomen did not interest them one whit. The only identity they recognised was that of their village, their city and sometimes their region. On occasion, that identity was defended by force of arms, as in the Pyrenees, the Ariège and, even today, in Corsica. Yet France still entered the First World War as a nation. Not due to speeches and clever PR techniques, but above all thanks to the building of countless railways and roads, the construction of thousands of schools and, last but not least, thanks to its system of military conscription. When the Dutch students Jacob van Lennep and Dirk van Hogendorp went walking through their newly formed fatherland in 1823, different currencies were still circulating everywhere. In the midst of what is today Zeeland Province they encountered passport problems, the country's political life usually came no further than the local men's club, and the two were often unable to make themselves understood amid all the strange local dialects. By that time the Netherlands had already been a constitutional federation for some 250 years, but it was only in the course of the nineteenth century that something like a 'conceptual community' arose at the national level.

From 1831 to 1832, the French aristocrat Alexis de Tocqueville travelled through the United States. Upon his return, he published a collection of journal entries and notes on this new nation under the title *De la démocratie en Amérique*. It was to become a seminal historical document about rights, democracy, nation-building and, above all, about the common mentality of the Americans. But, even today, it also shows the enormous differences between that nascent United States and today's European project. Everything de Tocqueville took note of almost 200 years ago in that young America – the single language, the public's great interest in the new forms of government, a clear consensus on the roles of the various parts of government, a strong sense of democratic legitimacy, a system of simple but solid rules of play between the various powers – everything that unified the United States then can hardly be found in the Europe currently under construction. If only for that reason, the use of the word 'constitution' during the 2005 referendums was misleading: the complicated system of treaties with which the old European states bind themselves together in no way resembles the clear lines which the Founding Fathers were able to impose on their new world in the Philadelphia of 1787.

It has been noted often enough before: the view Europeans have of Europe is a – usually unconscious – projection of the idea they have of their own society. For the Germans, Europe will become one big Germany, for the Poles one great Poland, and the Dutch bravely continue to see Europe as being just as orderly and compromise-oriented as themselves. The problem is that all this leads to an endless flow of conflicts and misunderstandings.

For there is no European people. There is no single, all-embracing community of culture and tradition that binds together Jorwerd, Vásárosbéc and Kefallonia; there are at least four of them: the Northern-Protestant, the Latin-Catholic, the Greek-Orthodox and Muslim-Ottoman. There is not a single language, but dozens of them. The Italians feel very differently about the word 'state' than do the Swedes. There are still no truly European political parties, and pan-European newspapers and television stations still lead a marginal existence. And, above all: in Europe there is very little in the way of a shared historical experience.

Almost every country I travelled through, for example, had come up with its own account of the unimaginable explosion of violence between 1939–45, its own myth to explain all that unbelievable madness, to justify wrongdoings, to bury humiliations and create new heroes. The British compensated for the loss of empire with the myth of the Blitz.

From the shame of Vichy, the French constructed the glorious story of General de Gaulle and the Resistance. The Soviets came to terms with Stalin's unnameable waste of human lives through the story of the Great Patriotic War. The Germans explained their dearth of morality during the Nazi era – the Nazis were always 'the other people' – with the legend of Hitler as 'the evil demon'.

All these mollifying, explanatory, comforting myths cannot exist without a national context. People need stories in order to grasp the inexplicable, to cope with their fate. The individual nation, with its common language and shared imagery, can always forge those personal experiences into one great, cohesive history. But Europe cannot do that. Unlike the United States, it still has no common story.

The Amsterdam sociologist Abram de Swaan speaks in this regard of Europe's 'pedagogical deficit': the lack of political fire at the European level, of that spirit so indispensable to a vital democracy. The absence of a common European language almost certainly has something to do with that, although it is estimated that eighty per cent of the conversations held within the EU bureaucracy are now in English. Much more serious, however, is the total lack of so much as a forum for mutual discussion: there is still no European coffee house, no place where Europeans can together mould their opinions, where ideas can be born, viewpoints examined. Without such an agora all further political processes remain hanging in thin air, without such a permanent debate Europe remains a cascade of phrases, a democracy for the sake of appearances, and nothing more.

The British chronicler of Europe Timothy Garton Ash speaks in this regard of the *grand ennui*, the risk that the entire European project will collapse under its own inertia. 'If I wish to reach the broadest intellectual European audience', he writes, 'then I can best write an essay for the *New York Review of Books*, or a shorter editorial in the *International Herald Tribune* or the *Financial Times*'. That is funny and absurd, but it illustrates above all how deep the problem lies: what seems to be missing here is a common attitude to life, an attitude like the one that existed, for example, within the chaotic Danube monarchy. The coffee houses of Vienna, the barracks, the theatres and clubs in all those far-flung provinces, that entire monarchy on the Danube was dominated by a carefully cultivated mixture of lightness and great earnest, a German musical full of Italian drama and Slavic melancholy, a common culture that, more than all the rest, bound together the national elites. For years, it was this culture which propped up that strange, dégagé empire.

Have you ever heard Europeans shouting 'We the People?' Yes, perhaps at the mass demonstrations against the American intervention in Iraq, in spring 2003. And certainly one year later, during the mass demonstrations in almost every capital on the continent against the bombings in Madrid. But those were the very first times.

In 1924, Joseph Roth's *Hotel Savoy* was published, a novel about a hotel full of disenfranchised guests stranded on the edge of Europe. Hotel Savoy was crawling with the victims of war, refugee families, whores, speculators, lottery-ticket touts and the unforgettable Croatian veteran Zwonimir Pansin. Zwonimir is always dreaming of a better world, and he loves America so much that he underscores all things commendable with the cry: 'America!'. 'If the food in the mess hall was good, he said: "America!" If a scaffolding was built well, he said: "America!" Concerning an "outstanding" first lieutenant he said: "America". And because I was a good shot, he called my bull's-eyes: "America".'

The main character in *Hotel Savoy* is a black hole, an eternally missing person, someone for whom everyone else waits and waits. His name is Bloomfield, a Pole who has garnered a massive fortune in America and is now coming back to visit his father's grave. Everyone in the hotel has put their hopes in Bloomfield. 'All over town, people were waiting for Bloomfield. In the Jewish quarter, people were waiting for him, everyone was holding onto their money, trade was slow. . . At the soup kitchen, everyone was talking about Bloomfield as well. Whenever he showed up, he met their every wish and the earth took on a new appearance'. The people go down to the railway station every day to wait for Bloomfield, until one day he actually shows up, fleeting and ephemeral as always. Bloomfield has passed through Europe twice: in 1917, and again in 1941 (not counting the Marshall Plan, the Berlin airlift and the American intervention in the Yugoslav wars, when Europe proved unable to deal with that problem as well). On two occasions, America – not without interests of its own – has pulled Europe out of the mire. America set the tone of post-war European history. It was the pacesetter behind the European Community, it provided the atomic umbrella beneath which Western Europe could grow and blossom in the 1950s and 1960s and, by the same token, it forced the national politics of the European countries into a tight anti-communist straitjacket: if you're not for us, you're against us.

During the first post-war decades, the United States and Europe travelled almost identical paths. Around the mid-1980s, however, both partners began going their own ways. While the phenomenon of immigration was regarded with increasing fearfulness within the EU, the United States continued to keep its own borders slightly ajar: between 1980–2000, that country took in about twenty million immigrants. In the short term, America's policy in this regard resulted in the problems regularly associated with integration. In the longer term, however, it will – as demographic projections from the University of Michigan show – ensure that America remains young, ambitious and energetic for some time to come. Unless policies change, the average age in the United States in the year 2050 will be thirty-five. In Europe, that will be somewhere around fifty-two. A prognosis from the Institut Français de Relations Internationales points in the same direction: Europe will gradually exhibit less vitality and participate less and less in the global economy. Around 1950, a quarter of the world's population was European; around the year 2000 it was twelve per cent. By 2050, it will be seven per cent. Unless policy changes, the active population of Europe will decrease in the next half-century from 331 million to 243 million. (Meanwhile, the active population in Canada and the United States will grow from 269 million to 355 million.) Yet the position of the United States is not unassailable either. In economic terms, the situation in which America finds itself is actually reminiscent of Great Britain after 1918: still the most important empire in the world, still in possession of the mightiest army and the greatest fleet, but at the same time locked in a fundamental struggle with growing economic, financial and social problems. Many longer-term prognosticators expect that China, where a quarter of the world's economy will be concentrated halfway through this present century, will ultimately surpass the United States as a superpower. China, after all, not only possesses a staggeringly huge reservoir of diligent workers, but its economy is also open to an unprecedented extent to trade and innovation. China is therefore generally considered the new driving force in the world economy, a motor which will also exercise a great influence on economies in other parts of the world. (It remains entirely possible, of course, that factors such as climate change or major epidemics will once again overturn all these economic prognoses.)

The proud American national self-image is still very much alive. But it does not necessarily imply that the old family ties with Europe will remain a part of that image. Around the year 2055, the majority of American voters will be former immigrants from Africa, Asia and Central and South America or their descendants, people who no longer have any affinity with Europe, with European problems or the Europeans themselves. In the coming decades, the descendants of immigrants from Ireland, Germany, Friesland and Holland will enter the minority once and for all. Europe, in other words, must set a course of its own: politically, economically and militarily. Within a ninety-minute flight from Berlin, the Kremlin reigns over the unstable remnants of the former Soviet Empire – including a doomsday struggle in and around Chechnya. Two hours from Rome begins one of the world's major hotbeds of unrest, the Arab world. Five hours from London lies the centre of power of the old Atlantic alliance, now fallen into deep crisis, whose leader, the United States, is increasingly less interested in the international order to which it once gave shape. We shall not catch Bloomfield coming to the rescue of Hotel Savoy for a third time.

I have often had the feeling that, despite our common heritage and our present-day contacts, Europe as it was in spring 1914 exhibited a greater cultural unity than it does today, more than ninety years later. Then, a worker in Warsaw led more or less the same life as a worker in Brussels, and the same went for a teacher in Berlin or in Prague, a shopkeeper in Budapest or in Amsterdam.

Our common disaster can be summarised briefly. Around 1900 there was a tree and an apple, and everyone ate of it. At the heart of Europe lay a young, unstable nation that did not recognise its own destructive potential. Two hellish wars followed, and we all experienced them in our own way. After that, for the East, began four deadly decades, while for Western Europe the gates opened onto a paradise of mopeds, electric mixers, cars and televisions. Close to the end of the century, the Wall fell, but for millions of Eastern Europeans hard times arrived again, the years of humiliated men, frightened women and broken families. At the same time, the West was celebrating the boom of the 1990s, without realising what their Central and Eastern European kin were suffering. Immigrants from other cultures came and went, closed societies were broken open, there arose a new set of dynamics with new tensions. In short, we still have a great deal to tell each other and a great deal to explain, and all that has yet to begin.

This winter I was back in Vásárosbéc. In the café, people were whispering that the owner planned to close the place in May: EU regulations demanded the installation of strictly divided men's and women's toilets, and there was no way she could afford that. Lajos and Red József had passed away: sixty is a respectable age for men here. They lay in the churchyard beside the veteran, who had been found dead one summer morning, flat on his face in the road.

The post office had closed down and the school was about to close. There were houses for sale everywhere. 'People want to leave', our friend had written. 'Others are dying or already dead'. The German grocery chain Lidl – long live the EU! – had invaded Hungary with dozens of supermarkets, all of them brand-spanking new, all of them opening at once. By selling vegetables and other products at barely cost price, they were now grinding the small shopkeepers to a pulp. The greengrocer and the little shops in neighbouring Szigetvár were going under. But there was good news as well. The mayor had found a source of European funding: a new cultural centre was rising up in the middle of the village, a big building with shiny roof tiles. Almost all the men had work now, the wages were going up, even the toothless man had a steady job. Everyone had become a little more prosperous, except for the postman's wife. Her cow had died. One of the Dutch people had already offered to buy her house, just to have a little extra space.

The last stretch of sandy road had been paved. The council had purchased a mowing machine, the Gypsies with their scythes had disappeared, the moments of quiet had become rare. Apples fell from the trees into the grass, no one came to pick them any more, no children even came to gather them; they had never seen anything like it around here. I would have liked to finish this story, this story of Walter Rathenau, Harry Kessler, Winston Churchill, Franklin D. Roosevelt and Jean Monnet, of Yuri Klejner, Hans Krijt, Anna Bikont, Viktor Alves, Želimir, of the Winkler family and all those others, with a happy ending. But that ending is still a long way off.

Europe's weakness, its diversity, is also its greatest strength. Europe as a peace process was a resounding success. Europe as an economic union is also well on its way. But the European project will surely fail unless a common cultural, political and, above all, democratic space is soon created alongside the rest. For let us not forget: Europe has only one chance to succeed.

Acknowledgements

THIS BOOK HAS TAKEN THE FORM OF A TRAVELOGUE THROUGH TIME AND across the continent. Except for the background literature, almost all of the material – interview and articles – was collected during a journey through Europe that lasted throughout nearly all of 1999. In a few cases, I have also fallen back on older material, such as the descriptions of Niesky, Novi Sad and the Russian pop scene. For practical reasons as well, it was impossible to hold all of the interviews in 1999. In 2001 and 2002, therefore, I carried out several interviews and retraced my steps along a few of my routes. But those remain the exceptions. The year around which everything revolves is 1999.

In Europe reflects the work of a great number of historians, journalists and other chroniclers, a long row of the living and the dead who continued to inspire me with their books and their journalistic work. In addition, I also made regular use of first-hand, eyewitness accounts and observations. That offers advantages: it brings history closer to people, it reveals certain moods, it sometimes uncovers important details and makes inexplicable matters suddenly understandable. At the same time, everyone knows that such observations are not always reliable. Memories serve to process the past, and to impose a certain sense on our personal histories – and every person has the tendency to focus on certain matters and let others lie. That goes for individuals, but also for whole nations. The stories in this book therefore speak for themselves, with their weak and their strong points.

The form this book has taken has resulted in certain limitations too. Being on the road put me in contact with unexpected eyewitnesses, it opened up new sources of information – newspaper archives, many local museums – and it confronted me again and again with the remarkable atmosphere surrounding the phenomenon of the 'historic location'.

But it also made for certain constraints. For practical reasons, there were countries I could not include in my itinerary, certain subjects I could not cover, others on which I placed more than the usual emphasis. Such choices, as every journalist and every historian knows, are not to be avoided. All of Europe cannot fit in a single book.

A project of this scope, covering more than twenty countries, could only succeed thanks to the help of a great many friends and colleagues. They gave me advice, made contacts, acted as interpreters and guides, and supported me wherever they could.

With regard to the European Union, I could have wished no better mentor than Max Kohnstamm. The evenings I spent with him and Kathleen were unforgettable. And there are many others to whom I am extremely grateful as well. In Amsterdam: Laura Starink, Hubert Smeets, Martin van Amerongen, Rudy Kousbroek, Sasz Malko, Gisela and Dik Linthout. In Belfast: Pauline Kersten. In Belgrade: Saša Mirković. In Berlin: Isabelle de Keghel, Wolf and Imke Siedler, Gisela Nicklaus, Rüdiger Safranski. In Bucharest: Cornelis van der Jagt. In Bosnia: Duško Tubić. In Brussels: Geert van Istendael and Pierre Plateau. In Guernica: Monica Ibañez-Angulo. In Kiev: Irina Trantina. In Lamanère: Martine Groen and Paul Kuypers. In Lisbon: Rui Mota. In London: Frans van Klaveren and Hieke Jippes. In Madrid: Steven Adolf. In Moscow: Frank and Suzanna Westerman, Adriënne van Heteren, Tony Crombie. In Normandy: Max and Els van Haasen. In Novi Sad: Želimir Zilnić – a prominent authority on the Russian *Cosmopolitan* – and Sarita Matijević. In Odessa: Natalya Syevkoplas and Charel Krol-Dobrov. In Prague: Veronika Havlíková. In Rome: Gianni Principe and Anne Branbergen. In St Petersburg: Nadya Voznenko and Yuri Klejner. In Stockholm: Lars-Olof Franzén. In Chernobyl: Nikolai Dmytruk and Rita Rindenko. In Vásárosbéc: Peter Flik and Edith van der Poel. In Warsaw: Wladek and Rosita Matwin. In Bussum: the boys and girls of Gerco Travel (ATP).

During the writing of this book, there were also a few people who remained at my side: my publishers Emile Brugman and Ellen Schalker, who supervised the project from beginning to end with great calm, friendship and professionalism; Charlotte Schrameijer, who helped me with the research; René van Stipriaan, who, in sometimes exuberant night-long sessions, carefully ran through the text with me; Koen Koch, who critically read through the whole thing again – I myself, of course, bear full responsibility for all blunders that remain; Sjoerd de Jong who, keen as always, saved me the embarrassment of dozens of misspelled names, incorrect dates and other assorted mishaps. All this work took place behind the scenes, but without their knowledge and expertise this project could never have come to a good end.

The same goes for my very closest surroundings. For five long years I terrorised my friends and family with Europe. I spent months in a permanent state of transit, then lived for ages with blinkers on. Yet my life-partner remained with me, everywhere and always. She travelled with me when she could, she was constantly enthusiastic, stimulating, supportive and, at difficult moments, incredibly loyal.

It is therefore only natural that this book be dedicated to her.

Glossary

Italics indicate a separate entry

Adenauer, Konrad (1876–1967): German statesman. As the first Chancellor of the Federal Republic of Germany (West Germany) 1949–63, he presided over its political and economic reconstruction after the *Second World War*.

Atatürk, Kemal, 'father of all Turks', also known as Mustafa Kemal Paşa (1881–1938): Founder and first President of the Republic of Turkey 1923–38. Military dictator who imposed far-reaching reforms to make Turkey a modern, secular state.

Attlee, Clement Richard, 1st Earl Atlee (1883–1967): British statesman, Prime Minister 1945–51. The Labour Party, led by Atlee, won a landslide victory over *Winston Churchill*'s Conservatives immediately after the *Second World War*. His government created the National Health Service in Great Britain.

Baader-Meinhof Gang, also known as the Red Army Faction: left-wing, West German terrorist group formed in early 1970s and named after two of its leaders, Andreas Baader and Ulrike Meinhof.

Blackshirts: paramilitary group in Italy who belonged to *Mussolini*'s Fascist movement in the 1920s and took their name from the colour of their uniforms. The term was later copied by *Hitler* in *Nazi* Germany, who issued black uniforms to his elite *SS* corps.

Bormann, Martin (1900–45?): prominent party leader in *Nazi* Germany. As *Hitler*'s private secretary, he gained his trust and was believed to be his closest collaborator. A staunch advocate of the extermination of the Jews.

Brandt, Willy, born Karl Herbert Frahm (1913–92): German statesman and Chancellor of West Germany 1969–74. Recognised internationally for his policy to improve relations with East Germany and other communist nations. These efforts won him the Nobel Peace Prize in 1971.

Braun, Eva (1912–45): mistress of *Adolf Hitler* for many years. They married while the Battle of Berlin was raging, shortly before taking their own lives.

Brezhnev, Leonid Ilych (1906–82): Soviet statesman. As General Secretary of the Communist Party of the Soviet Union, he was, in effect, the leader of the Soviet Union for eighteen years, from 1966–82. Largely responsible for the Russian invasion of Czechoslovakia in 1968.

Brownshirts: members of the SA (*Sturmabteilung*), a *Nazi* militia founded by *Hitler* in 1921 who wore brown uniforms similar to those of *Mussolini's Blackshirts*. Instrumental in *Hitler's* rise to power, but ceased to play a major political role following the *Night of the Long Knives* in 1934.

Ceauşescu, Nicolae (1918–89): Rumanian statesman and leader of Communist Rumania from 1965 until shortly before his death. In 1974 he was elected the first President of the Socialist Republic of Rumania and ran an increasingly totalitarian and corrupt regime. Executed in December 1989 following a popular uprising.

Chamberlain, Arthur Neville (1869–1940): British statesman and Prime Minister 1937–40. Pursued a policy of appeasement with *Nazi* Germany and in 1938 signed the *Munich Agreement*, which granted almost all of *Hitler's* demands. Forced to abandon this policy following *Hitler's* invasion of Czechoslovakia in 1939.

Churchill, Sir Winston (Leonard Spencer) (1874–1965): British statesman, Prime Minister 1940–5 and 1951–5. Opposed all compromise with *Nazi* Germany and led the British people through the *Second World War*.

Cold War: a period of conflict and rivalry between the United States and the Soviet Union and their respective allies from the end of the *Second World War* until the early 1990s.

Davison, Emily Wilding (1872–1913): entered history as the woman who, in support of female suffrage, threw herself in front of King George V's horse on 4 June, 1913 at the Epsom Derby, dying four days later.

de Gaulle, Charles (André Joseph Marie) (1890–1970): French general and statesman, head of the provisional government 1944–6, after the liberation of France from German occupation, and President of the Fifth Republic 1959–69. An organiser of the Free French Forces during the *Second World War* and remembered for restoring calm to the country after the student uprisings and strikes of May 1968.

DDR (*Deutsche Demokratische Republik*, 'German Democratic Republic'): official name for the former East Germany.

Dreyfus, Alfred (1859–1935): French army officer of Jewish descent, falsely accused of supplying military secrets to the Germans, whose trial and imprisonment caused a political scandal in France at the turn of the century which became known as the 'Dreyfus Affair'. The army finally rehabilitated him in 1906.

Dubček, Alexander (1921–92): Slovak statesman and First Secretary of the Communist Party of Czechoslovakia 1968–9. Driving force behind the political reforms of 1968, which prompted the Soviet invasion of Czechoslovakia and his removal from office in 1969.

Eisenhower, Dwight David 'Ike' (1890–1969): President of the United States 1953–61. As supreme commander of the Allied forces in Western Europe during the *Second World War* he supervised the successful invasion of France and Germany in 1944–5.

ETA (*Euzkadi ta Askatasuna*, 'Basque homeland and liberty'): A separatist movement in Spain still conducting a terrorist campaign for an independent Basque state.

Euro: the single currency adopted by a number of European states, launched in 2002. The following are presently members of the so-called Eurozone: Austria, Belgium, Finland, France, Germany, Greece, Ireland, Italy, Luxembourg, Netherlands, Portugal, Slovenia and Spain.

European Economic Community (EEC), also known as the Common Market: forerunner of the European Union, an economic association of Western European countries set up by the *Treaty of Rome* in 1957.

European Union (EU): economic and political association now comprising twenty-seven member states, with its own currency and parliament. Created on 1 November, 1993 when the *Maastricht Treaty* came into force. The following 27 countries are now members: Austria, Belgium, Bulgaria, Cyprus, Czech Republic, Denmark, Estonia, Finland, France, Germany, Hungary, Ireland, Italy, Latvia, Lithuania, Luxembourg, Malta, Netherlands, Poland, Portugal, Rumania, Slovakia, Slovenia, Spain, Sweden, United Kingdom.

First World War (1914–18), also referred to as the Great War: fought primarily in Europe where the German Empire, Austria-Hungary, Bulgaria and the Ottoman Empire were defeated by the Allied forces of Britain, France and

Russia, later joined by Italy and the United States. An estimated ten million people – soldiers and civilians – were killed. Resulted in the disintegration of the German, Austro-Hungarian, Russian and Ottoman Empires.

Franco, Francisco (1892–1975): Spanish general and leader of the Nationalist forces that overthrew the Spanish Republic in the Spanish Civil War (1936–9). Proclaimed himself leader of Spain and presided over a government that was essentially a military dictatorship until his death in 1975.

Franz Ferdinand (1863–1914): Austrian archduke next in the line of succession to the Austro-Hungarian throne. His assassination in Sarajevo on 28 June, 1914 by Gavrilo Princip precipitated the Austrian declaration of war which, in turn, triggered the beginning of the First World War in Europe.

Franz Josef (1830–1916): Emperor of Austria 1848–1916 and King of Hungary 1867–1916. Aroused many European political tensions when he annexed Bosnia-Herzegovina in 1908. The assassination of his heir apparent, Archduke Franz Ferdinand, led Austria and Germany into the First World War.

Gellhorn, Martha (1908–98): American novelist, travel writer and journalist. Particularly known for her work as a war correspondent, reporting on the Spanish Civil War, the rise of Hitler and the Second World War. The first journalist to report from the Dachau concentration camp after it was liberated.

Gestapo (Geheime Staatspolizei, 'secret state police'): political police force of Nazi Germany which ruthlessly suppressed any opposition to the Nazis in Germany and its occupied territories. Jews and others disappeared into concentration camps after being arrested by the Gestapo, who also arranged the deportation of Jews to extermination camps in Poland.

Goebbels, Joseph (1897–1945): German Nazi politician and Hitler's Minister for Public Enlightenment and Propaganda from 1933 onwards. With control over the press, radio and all aspects of culture, he was responsible for presenting a favourable image of the Nazi regime to the German people.

Gomulka, Wladyslaw (1905–82): Polish communist leader who served as First Secretary of the Central Committee of the Polish Communist Party 1956–70. His attempts to implement reforms were viewed with alarm by the Soviet leadership but made him a popular figure among Poles.

Göring, Hermann Wilhelm (1893–1946): German military commander and politician, leading member of the Nazi Party and Hitler's most loyal supporter.

Founded the *Gestapo* and established concentration camps for the 'corrective treatment' of opponents to the regime.

Gorbachev, Mikhail Sergeyevich (b. 1931): Soviet statesman, elected General Secretary of the Communist Party in 1985 and President of the Soviet Union 1990–1. He introduced the major reforms known as *glasnost* (openness) and *perestroika* (reconstruction) which helped bring an end to the *Cold War*. An attempted coup in 1991 led to his resignation. Awarded the Nobel Peace Prize in 1990.

Gulag: system of forced-labour camps established in the Soviet Union between 1930 and 1955. These detention camps imprisoned millions of people, including criminals, peasants arrested during collectivisation and political prisoners.

Havel, Václav (b. 1936): Czech dramatist and statesman, President of Czechoslovakia 1989–92 and first President of the Czech Republic 1993–2003. A passionate supporter of non-violent resistance, he became a leading figure in the Velvet Revolution of 1989, which ended communism in Czechoslovakia.

Himmler, Heinrich (1900–45): German military commander who became the second most powerful man in *Nazi* Germany. As head of the *SS* and *Gestapo* he proposed a definitive solution to the 'Jewish question', overseeing the mass extermination of Jews and other groups in the death camps of Eastern Europe.

Hitler, Adolf (1889–45): Leader of the National Socialist (*Nazi*) Party, Chancellor of Germany from 1933 and Führer (leader) from 1934 until his death. Pursued an aggressive policy of territorial expansion which precipitated the *Second World War*. His fanatical racial policies called for the indiscriminate extermination of the Jews of Europe.

Honecker, Erich (1912–94): German communist statesman and head of state of the *DDR* 1976–89. In 1961 he was in charge of building the Berlin Wall which closed the border between East and West Berlin for twenty-eight years. After reunification, he was tried for crimes committed during the *Cold War* but was released from prison due to failing health.

International Monetary Fund (IMF): an organisation which emerged at the end of the *Second World War* to promote international trade and monetary cooperation and stabilise exchange rates.

IRA (Irish Republican Army): militant organisation based in the Republic of Ireland, created with the intention of rendering British rule in Northern Ireland ineffective.

Kessler, Count Harry (1868–1937): German diplomat, publisher and art collector. After the First World War he became a committed internationalist and pacifist which led to his exile from Germany upon the Nazi seizure of power. His extensive and detailed diaries, from 1918–37, give an extraordinary insight into events of the time.

Khrushchev, Nikita Sergeyevich (1894–1971): Soviet statesman who succeeded Stalin as First Secretary of the Communist Party of the Soviet Union 1953–64 and was Premier of the Soviet Union 1958–64. In 1956 he delivered an historic speech denouncing Stalin, which marked the beginning of more open discussion in the Eastern Bloc.

Klemperer, Victor (1881–1960): decorated veteran of the First World War and Professor of Literature. Of Jewish descent, he kept a diary which provides a day-to-day account of life under the Nazi regime and the struggle for survival among Jews from 1933 to the end of the Second World War. Became a post-war cult figure in the DDR.

Kohl, Helmut (b. 1930): German politician, Chancellor of Germany 1982–98 and Chancellor of West Germany 1982–90. Played a significant role in effecting the union of the DDR and the Federal Republic in 1990.

Kristallnacht: the name given to the organised and coordinated pogroms, carried out by Nazis throughout Germany and Austria on the night of 9–10 November, 1938, in which Jews were beaten to death and their properties destroyed.

Lenin, Vladimir Ilych (1870–1924): Founder of the Russian Communist Party, prime mover behind the October Revolution (1917), and first head of the Soviet Union 1917–24. Formulated a body of political principles known as Leninism.

Lloyd George, David, 1st Earl Lloyd George of Dwyfor (1863–1945): British Liberal statesman and Prime Minister 1916–22, who guided Britain through the latter part of the First World War. Introduced health and unemployment insurance in Britain, laying the foundations of the modern welfare state.

Lubbers, Dr. Rudolphus Franciscus Marie or **Ruud Lubbers** (b. 1939): Dutch politician who led three successive governments as Prime Minister of the Netherlands 1982–94. Has held many positions in both public and private sectors and was the United Nations High Commissioner for Refugees 2001–5.

Maastricht Treaty: a treaty on European economic and monetary union negotiated by the heads of government of the member states of the European

Community in December 1991, which came into force in November 1993. It removed the word 'Economic' from the name of the community and led to the creation of the EU.

Matwin, Wladek (b. 1916): Polish historian and former politician. A communist since his student days, he became the First Secretary of the Wrocław Voivodship Party Committee immediately after the *Second World War*. In August 1944, Matwin was a lieutenant in the Red Army and witnessed the Warsaw Uprising first hand.

Milošević, Slobodan (1941–2006): Serbian politician, President of Serbia 1989–97 and President of Yugoslavia 1997–2000. In promoting Serbian nationalism he was a key figure in the Yugoslav Wars in the 1990s and the Kosovo War in 1999. Indicted by the United Nations for war crimes in 1999 and found dead in his cell in 2006.

Mitterand, François (Maurice Marie) (1916–96): French statesman and member of the Socialist Party, President of France 1981–95. As President, he nationalised financial institutions and key industries, raised the minimum wage and decentralised government.

Monnet, Jean (1888–1979): French political economist, inspirational and strategic thinker. In 1940 he proposed a daring plan to *Winston Churchill* that France and Great Britain become one. Architect of the Schuman Plan to create the European Coal and Steel Community and its first president in 1952.

Montgomery, Bernard Law, 1ˢᵗ Viscount Montgomery of Alamein, also known as Monty (1887–1976): British Field Marshal and prominent commander of the Allied forces in the *Second World War*. His victory at El Alamein in 1942 against Rommel was a significant Allied success. In 1944, his daring initiative to cross the Rhine at Arnhem, Operation Market Garden, ended in failure.

Munich Agreement: agreement between Britain, France, Germany and Italy, signed in Munich on 29 September, 1938, under which the Sudetenland in western Czechoslovakia was ceded to Germany. *Hitler* subsequently annexed the remainder of Czechoslovakia and invaded Poland, precipitating the *Second World War*.

Mussolini, Benito, also known as Il Duce (the leader) (1883–1945): Italian Prime Minister 1922–43 and Fascist dictator. Entered the *Second World War* on the side of *Nazi Germany* in 1940. When the Allies invaded Italy he tried to escape but was captured and executed by Italian communist partisans.

NATO (North Atlantic Treaty Organisation): international organisation established in 1949 to counter the Soviet military presence in post-war Europe. The strongest military alliance in the world.

Nazi: Belonging to the Nazi Party (National Socialist German Workers' Party) which, under the leadership of *Adolf Hitler*, governed Germany 1933–45. Nazi ideology called for the expansion of Germany and its policies were based on nationalism, racism, anti-communism, anti-Semitism and the belief in the superiority of 'Aryan' Germans.

Nicholas II, Czar (1868–1918): last Russian emperor who reigned 1894–1917. Forced to abdicate after the February Revolution in 1917 and shot with his family the following year.

Nicolson, Sir Harold George (1886–1968): British diplomat, author and politician. Parliamentary Private Secretary to the Minister of Information in *Churchill's* 1940 wartime government. Supported British rearmament and was one of the few to condemn *Chamberlain* and oppose the *Munich Agreement*.

Night of the Long Knives: the night of Saturday, 30 June, 1934 – and the following day – when the *Gestapo* murdered between one hundred and fifty and two hundred of *Hitler's* political opponents, including almost the entire *SA* leadership.

October Revolution: in a coup led by *Lenin* in October, 1917, the Russian Bolsheviks seized power from the provisional government established after the February Revolution of the same year. Civil war and the creation of the Soviet Union followed.

Orwell, George, pen name of Eric Arthur Blair (1903–50): English novelist and adventurer. Best known for his novels *Animal Farm*, a satire on communism under *Stalin*, and *1984*, which describes a totalitarian future state. *Homage to Catalonia* draws on his experiences in Spain when he volunteered for militia service to fight against the fascists.

Ossi: colloquial term for a person from the former East Germany.

Paisley, The Reverend Ian Richard Kyle (b. 1926): militant Protestant leader in Northern Ireland, MP for North Antrim since 1970 and leader and co-founder in 1971 of the Democratic Unionist Party. Outspoken critic of the Roman Catholic Church and a vociferous defender of the Protestant Unionist position in Northern Ireland.

Pétain, Henri Philippe (1856–1951): French general, head of state of the French government of Vichy 1940–4. Viewed as a war hero in France for his leadership in the First World War but discredited for cooperating with the Germans in the Second World War. Sentenced to death for treason but this was commuted to life imprisonment by de Gaulle.

Pogrom: organised and extensive violence against the persons or property of ethnic, religious or minority groups. The term can be particularly applied to attacks on Jews in Russia in the late nineteenth and early twentieth centuries, and in Germany and Poland during the Nazi rise to power.

Radek, Karl Berngardovich (1885–1939): communist propagandist and key figure in the Communist International. Played an important role in the First World War in secret negotiations with Germany regarding funding of the Bolsheviks and acted as a mediator between Lenin and the Germans.

Rathenau, Walther (1867–1922): German statesman and industrialist who organised distribution of raw materials during the First World War. Helped form the German Democratic Party and was appointed Minister of Reconstruction in 1921 and Foreign Minister in 1922. His political policies and Jewish origins led to his assassination that year.

Reagan, Ronald Wilson (1911–2004): Republican statesman and President of the United States 1981–9. His talks with the Soviet leader Mikhail Gorbachev in Geneva and Reykjavík, where the two sides pledged to make the world a safer place, contributed to the ending of the Cold War.

Ribbentrop, Joachim von (1893–1946): German politician and Foreign Minister under the Nazi regime 1938–45. The negotiation of the non-aggression pact with the Soviet Union, also known as the Molotov-Ribbentrop Pact, was his greatest diplomatic coup and cleared the way for Hitler to invade Poland in 1939. Tried at Nuremberg and hanged for war crimes.

Roosevelt, Franklin Delano (1882–1945): Democratic statesman and President of the United States 1933–45. Played an important role during the Second World War, providing Britain with financial support and supplying the Allies with arms to defeat Nazi Germany.

Roth, Joseph (1894–1939): Austrian novelist and journalist, best known for his novels The Radetzky March, which portrays the latter days of the Habsburg monarchy, and Job, a novel of Jewish life. In his books he draws upon his own experiences of war, revolution and social upheaval. On Hitler's rise to power he was forced to flee Germany and spent most of his final years in Paris.

Rust, Mathias (b. 1968): German amateur pilot who, at the age of nineteen, on 26 May, 1987, landed his Cessna aeroplane in Red Square, in front of the Kremlin, without being challenged by Soviet air defences. Shortly afterwards, *Mikhail Gorbachev* replaced the ministers responsible, who were opposed to *glasnost* and *perestroika*, with men who supported his policies.

SA (*Sturmabteilung*, 'assault division'): also known as *Sturmabteilung* or Brownshirts. Until the *Night of the Long Knives* this was the *Nazis'* leading paramilitary organisation.

Second World War (1939–45): a worldwide war in which *Nazi* Germany, Fascist Italy and Japan were defeated by an alliance including Great Britain, France, the Soviet Union and the United States. In Europe the war ended with the German surrender in May 1945. An estimated fifty-five million people were killed.

Siedler, Wolf Jobst (b. 1926): German journalist and writer who lives in Berlin. For nearly twenty years he was head of Ullstein & Propyläen publishers and, from 1980 to 1998, of his own publishing house. Keen critic and commentator on political and historical events in Germany.

Solidarity: Polish independent trade union movement, founded in 1980 and led by *Lech Walesa*. An anti-communist coalition of diverse groups, it advocated non-violence in its campaign for political change. Banned in 1981 with the imposition of martial law in Poland, legalised again in 1989, and won a majority in the elections of that year.

Speer, Albert (1905–81): German architect and high-ranking *Nazi* official. A highly efficient organiser, he became Hitler's Minister for Armaments. At *Nuremberg* he was sentenced to twenty years' imprisonment for his role in the Third Reich. Released in 1966, he wrote two bestselling autobiographical works and died of natural causes in 1981.

SS (*Schutzstaffel*, 'protective squadron'): *Nazi* special police force, founded as Hitler's personal bodyguard in 1925. Under the leadership of *Heinrich Himmler* from 1929 until its dissolution in 1945, the SS provided powerful security forces including the *Gestapo* and operated the concentration camps and the extermination camps.

Stabilisation Force (SFOR): multinational force deployed by NATO in Bosnia and Herzegovina whose key task was to uphold the Dayton Agreement, a peace agreement reached in 1995 to end the war in Bosnia.

Stalin, Joseph (1879–1953): Soviet statesman and General Secretary of the Russian Communist Party 1922–53. Dictator of the Soviet Union for a quarter of a century, his Five-Year Plans for economic development, rapid industrialisation and enforced collective farming made his country into a major world power. In the 1930s he initiated the ruthless purges of the Communist Party ranks.

Stasi (*Staatssicherheitsdienst*, 'state security service'): security force and intelligence organisation of the former East Germany. Disbanded in 1989.

Thatcher, Margaret Hilda, Baroness Thatcher of Kesteven (b. 1925): British Conservative politician and first woman Prime Minister 1979–90. Nicknamed the 'Iron Lady', she had unshakeable faith in the power of market mechanisms, entrepreneurialism, privatisation and trade union legislation.

Tito, born Josip Broz (1892–1980): Yugoslav statesman, effective head of Yugoslavia from 1943 and President 1953–80. Successfully combined central authority with a large degree of autonomy for the six federal republics, providing Yugoslavia with more than three decades of stable leadership.

Treaty of Rome: treaty which established the European Union, signed on 25 March, 1957 by France, West Germany, Italy, Belgium, the Netherlands and Luxembourg.

Treaty of Versailles: peace treaty, signed in 1919, which officially ended the First World War. It re-divided the territories of the defeated nations, included a 'war guilt' clause and reparation terms which Germany considered severe, and created the League of Nations.

Trotsky, Leon, born Lev Davidovich Bronstein (1879–1940): communist revolutionary and politician. A leader in the October Revolution and founder of the Red Army, he lost to Stalin in a power struggle to succeed Lenin. Was exiled from the Soviet Union and settled in Mexico where he was assassinated.

Truman, Harry S. (1884–1972): Democratic statesman and President of the United States 1945–53. In 1948 he introduced the Marshall Plan which provided financial, economic and technical assistance to rebuild the war-shattered allied countries of Europe. Also established the NATO mililtary alliance in 1949.

Wałęsa, Lech (b.1943): Polish politician, President of Poland (1990–5). Chairman of Communist Poland's first independent trade union, Solidarity, he was a key figure in establishing the first non-communist government in the Soviet Bloc. Awarded the Nobel Peace Prize in 1983.

Warsaw Pact: treaty signed in 1955 which established a mutual defence organisation composed of the communist states of Central and Eastern Europe. Created following the integration of West Germany into NATO in the same year and lasted throughout the Cold War.

Wehrmacht ('defence force'): name given to the armed forces of Nazi Germany. The Wehrmacht was abolished in 1945 at the end of the Second World War.

Weizsäcker, Carl Friedrich von (b. 1912): German physicist and philosopher, son of the German diplomat Ernst von Weizsäcker, and brother of former German President Richard von Weizsäcker. During the Second World War, he was a member of the team that worked on the development of an atom bomb for Nazi Germany.

Wende ('change' or 'turning point'): term used to refer to the collapse of the communist system, signified by the breach in the Berlin Wall by the East Germans in November 1989.

Wessi: used in a similar way to Ossi as a colloquial term for a person from the former West Germany.

Wilhelm II, known as Kaizer Wilhelm (1859–1941): last German Emperor and King of Prussia 1888–1918. Supported Austria-Hungary following the assassination of his close friend Franz Ferdinand in a conflict which developed into the First World War. Abdicated in 1918 and went into exile in the Netherlands.

Yeltsin, Boris Nikolayevich, (b. 1931): Russian statesman and first President of the Russian Federation 1991–99. Employed 'shock therapy' reforms with the massive privatisation of state-run enterprises to introduce democracy and a market-based economy. Resigned in 1999 and was succeeded by Vladimir Putin.

Index